Employment and Vulnerabilities in the World of Orchestral Musicians: Symphonic Metamorphoses

List of Abbreviations

ACM	Autoriteit Consument & Markt, Netherlands Authority for Consumers and Markets
BIS	Culturele basisinfrastructuur; Dutch government cultural basic subsidy
BSO	Boston Symphony Orchestra
DCC	Burgerlijk Wetboek, Dutch Civil Code
CAO	Collectieve arbeidsovereenkomst, collective bargaining agreement
CBA	Collective Bargaining Agreement (CLA: Collective Labor Agreement UK)
CSO	Chicago Symphony Orchestra
ECJ	European Court of Justice
EEOC	Equal Employment Opportunity Commission
HBO	Het Ballet Orkest, Dutch Ballet Orchestra
HR	Hoge Raad (HR) Dutch Supreme Court
HRM	Human Resource Manager
ICSOM	International Conference of Symphony and Opera Musicians
ILO	International Labour Organization
MCO	Muziekcentrum van de Omroep, Dutch Broadcasting Music Center
NMa	Nederlands Mededingingsauthoriteit, Netherlands Competition Authority
NLRA	National Labor Relations Act
NLRB	National Labor Relations Board
RSO	Netherlands Radio Symphony Orchestra
OCW	Onderwijs, Cultuur, Wetenschap, Ministry of Education, Culture and Science
OR	Ondernemingsraad, Works Council
PvFM	Platform voor Freelance Musici

RCO	Royal Concertgebouw Orchestra, pre-1988, Concertgebouw Orchestra
RFO	Netherlands Radio Philharmonic Orchestra
RKF	Radio Kamer Orkest, Netherlands Radio Chamber Orchestra until 2005; post-RSO merger, Netherlands Radio Chamber Philharmonic until 2012
RvC	Raad voor Culture, Dutch Culture Council
SCOTUS	Supreme Court of the United States
SOM	Stichting Omroep Muziek, Broadcasting Music Foundation
TFEU	Treaty on the Functioning of the European Union
VSR	Stichting Remplaçanten Nederlands Orkesten, Dutch Orchestral Substitute Players Foundation
VvNO	Vereniging van Nederlandse Orkesten, Association of Dutch Orchestras
WAB	Wet Arbeidsmarkt in Balans, the Labor Market in Balance Act
WOR	Wet op de ondernemingsraden, Works Council Act
ZZP	Zelfstandig Zonder Personnel; literally, self-employed without staff, self-employed persons

Foreword

To have a prestigious career is, unfortunately, all too rare. To have two such careers is very rare indeed. To have two such careers simultaneously is so remarkable that it would be almost incredible – if one did not know Dr Kurzbauer. A professional orchestral musician at a very high level internationally and a renowned academic lawyer on a world stage. In this book, based on her Ph.D. thesis, she has combined both music and law.

In it, she examines the plight of orchestral musicians in their post-2008 financial crisis, post-COVID-19, workplace. Her powerful description of the difficulties posed by cuts in funding both State (in Europe) and private (in the USA), with the precarity of employment consequential on loss of orchestras and reductions in the size of orchestras, is deeply disturbing. Insecurity of job is matched by insecurity of income as orchestras seek to utilise more casualised forms of engagement of their musicians with lesser rights (*see* below). The short length of the career progression in orchestras and the paucity of jobs at each successive level, accentuated by the nerve-wracking process of audition to (join and) climb the stages of an orchestral career, aggravates the precarity of the musician's working life. Collective bargaining should be a vital tool to balance the asymmetry of workplace power, but Dr Kurzbauer's researches show an uneven and diverse pattern of negotiating machinery (and, indeed, worker/union organisation), particularly as between the USA and the Netherlands. Problems are exacerbated by the tension between hierarchy and democracy inherent in any orchestrated activity of a large number of people, a tension which regrettably tends to the authoritarian in some orchestras and to significant differentials in pay in most. In addition, there is a striking lack of homogeneity in corporate governance and culture.

And, of course, there is racism and sexism which is by no means confined to ethnic and gender pay gaps.

The picture she paints (to mix metaphors) is disturbing but is surely one of the manifestations of the ending of the social-democratic post-Second World War consensus which brought an uneasy stability to (among other things) arts funding, employment, collective bargaining and industrial relations in Western Europe and the USA until the Reagan-Thatcher neoliberal revolution which affected first the USA and UK and then metastasised into Europe.

The book itself is arranged like a classical symphony. That is not merely deferential to its subject matter, but it is also a logical and helpful methodology for Dr Kurzbauer's brilliant exegesis.

One of the areas on which she focuses is of particular interest to me as author of a private members' Bill in the House of Lords, the Single Status of Workers Bill (which successfully passed the Lords but fell on the prorogation of Parliament in 2021). The Bill was intended to address the fraught issue of the status in law of workers (including musicians) by creating a single class of 'worker' excluding only those in self-employment in business on their own account with their own clients or customers.

The problem Dr Kurzbauer addresses in relation to orchestral musicians is one common to national legal systems all over the world. Workers (including musicians) are categorised by law in different ways; each category has a different suite of employment rights. The most obvious demarcation in most, if not all, legal systems is that between the 'employee', on the one hand, and the 'self-employed', on the other. Some systems (like the UK) have an intermediate category between these two. Some have 'special' categories. There are yet other categorisations with differential entitlements. Among employees, the permanent employee has more rights than the employee on a fixed-term contract, a zero-hour contract, or the worker employed or engaged for a session or a shift. Then there is the fake self-employed, her status dressed up by the employer as self-employment but, under the forensic gaze of a judge, found to be, in reality an employee with all the rights that go with it. There is the worker who (usually unwillingly) agrees to be the employee of a company of which she is the director and principal shareholder, thus ensuring that the real employer avoids all its employment obligations since her rights may only be claimed from her nominal employer, her company. To this jumble of categories must be added the agency worker supplied to the real employer by an agency but whose employment rights are only exercisable against the agency. Not all these forms of legal status figure in the orchestral world, but Dr Kurzbauer demonstrates the pressure to exploit these categorisations and place musicians on successively lower rungs of the ladder of legal status.

Another issue with which she deals is that courts have held that collective bargaining by unions representing aggregated workers necessarily breach the free market principle of competition. The illegality bestowed on collective bargaining in consequence was resolved in the UK and Ireland by legislation in 1871 but reared its head again in the European Court of Justice (ECJ) which exempted collective bargaining on behalf of employees but not those who were self-employed. Dr Kurzbauer analyses the pathetic compromise judgment of the ECJ in the *FNV* case.[1] The argument was roundly rejected by the European Committee on Social Rights in *Irish Congress of Trade Unions v. Ireland* No. 123/2016, 12 September 2018 (competition law is not a legitimate bar to collective bargaining by self-employed workers), a proposition with which the EU Commission is now grappling.

1. *FNV Kunsten Informatie en Media* C-413/13 [2014].

This is a brilliant book and provides an extraordinary insight into the world of work (but not the music) of the orchestral musicians and the factors which have caused them so much stress and insecurity in recent years. The legal and factual analysis is available nowhere else. Dr Kurzbauer deserves the congratulations of both her fellow orchestral musicians and her fellow labour lawyers.

Lord John Hendy KC
Bedford Row, London
3rd October 2023

Prologue

This book began as an attempt to mitigate desperation. Twenty-six years of orchestral bliss, thanks to a professional chamber orchestra that was as much of a family as it was an internationally acclaimed ensemble, crumbled to an end following colossal culture cuts in the Netherlands in 2012-2013. Living through that process raised uncertainties and questions. Beyond culture cuts and bureaucratic banalities, a Pandora's box of employment-related vulnerabilities presented themselves. While Dutch-based employed musicians were protected along the highways and byways of strong national labor laws and a finely tuned social plan, there was an uneasy feeling that much was amiss during the long reorganization process.

The voices of the many freelance musicians who had made their musical mark on concerts, recordings and tours were silenced, as if they had never existed. This research is dedicated to the many orchestral musicians who raised their voices and shared their stories; it is hoped that mitigation will give way to empowerment.

Acknowledgments

With Gratitude:

John Varga and Dr. Jean Carriere, pathfinders
PhD supervisors and visionaries: Professor Evert Verhulp and Professor Beryl ter Haar
Guardians of language: Andrew Faughnan and Ruth Kurzbauer
Countless colleagues and students at the University of Amsterdam Law Faculty; union stalwarts; confrères at the Federation International Musicians (FIM); Platform voor Freelance Musici (PvFM); and orchestral colleagues the world over
Dr. Robert Kurzbauer, Lisa Rates Kurzbauer, Ben Bonouvrier and Yaël Kurzbauer whose love abides

Prelude: A Prologue on Orchestras at the Brink

> "What's past is prologue."[2]

> "But in the thousand combinations that are possible with the monumental orchestra there would reside a harmonic richness, a variety of sounds, a succession of contrasts, which cannot be compared with anything ... . When in a state of agitation, it would recall tropical storms. Its silence would strike awe through its solemnity."[3]

> "An anachronistic picture of the arts begins to emerge. Uncertainties turn out to be typical for the arts."[4]

> "One does not begin with a theory and prove it. Rather, one begins with an area of study and what is relevant to that area is allowed to emerge."[5]

The first decade of the 21st century wrought bitter changes for orchestral musicians the world over. From prestigious US symphonies to Europe's finest, orchestras were silenced in the wake of the 2007-2008 financial crisis. Disquieting reports from the US on the state of the orchestral arts proliferated as the mighty Philadelphia Orchestra announced bankruptcy in 2011 and several regional orchestras toppled. Across the Atlantic, such misfortunes even reached Germany, where a long-standing reverence for symphonic culture encouraged generous state support since the late 1800s. Trouble in

2. William Shakespeare. *The Tempest* Act two scene 1.
3. Hector Berlioz. *Mémoires De Hector Berlioz: Comprenant Ses Voyages En Italie, En Allemagne, En Russie Et En Angleterre*, 1803-1865 162.
4. Hans Abbing. "The Artistic Conscience and the Production of Value" *The Value of Culture* 1996, 145.
5. Anselm L. Strauss and Juliet M. Corbin. *Basics of Qualitative Research: Grounded Theory Procedures and Techniques* 2014, 23.

German paradise was signaled following the announcement of a reorganization and merger between two famed German orchestras.[6]

Akin to Germany, state and municipal subsidies form the basis of financial support for cultural institutions in the Netherlands. Drastic budget cuts led to an unprecedented number of consolidations, closures, and dismissals in the Dutch orchestral sector following the 2007-2008 financial crisis. At the outset of the 21st century's third decade, stage lights all but dimmed completely, and musical life was jettisoned as the international community grappled with the COVID-19 pandemic. As the sector moves forward post-pandemic, the world of work for orchestral musicians, from those employed in major orchestras to the ever-precarious freelancers, is in more flux than ever before.

From the outset, this was to be an inquiry into employment-related predicaments that impacted orchestral musicians when a sacrosanct Dutch orchestra was dismantled in 2012-2013. The realization that even musicians who were fully employed under solid collectively bargained agreements could be vulnerable was something of an epiphany as accepted definitions of precarious employment customarily exclude the fully employed. The strikingly vulnerable position of musicians who assumed that they would be protected from job loss is the point of departure for a study that grew in scope to extend its reach to examine a diversity of vulnerabilities in the orchestral microcosm within the context of the larger cultural sector. As we soon shall discover, orchestras depend on a significant cadre of freelance substitute players who work side-by-side with fully contracted colleagues and share performance responsibilities. Their vulnerable employment position calls attention to vexed questions at the center of the freelance dilemma in which the freedom to choose employment has diminished as a result of increased financial vulnerability and reduced employment opportunities within the sector.

In a tale of two countries where musicians face increased ongoing employment challenges, musician narratives place the musicians at the heart of the research and support the hypothesis that the concerns iterated anecdotally resonate with orchestral musicians regardless of their positions or locations. To bring the research home to those who are most deserving of support calls for cognizance of musician articulations expressed through the myriad anecdotes that unfold here. This book plumbs the depths to explain the particular vulnerabilities of orchestral musicians in a series of *movements* and *intermezzi* that uncover aspects of vulnerability in a profession increasingly challenged by labor market insecurity and financial instability.

The reactions of orchestral musicians to complex interactions between culture, finance, and legal processes are a reflection of this musical vulnerability. The not-so-hidden prescriptive aim of these pages is to fortify the call for equality at the workplace and add to the discourse on how to change institutional and legal norms that perpetuate disadvantage. Grounded in the experience of musicians-as-workers and triggered by anecdotal leads, the book turns the spotlight on external as well as internal

6. Proposed merger between the Stuttgart Radio Symphony and the SWF Orchestra Freiburg 2016.

factors within the orchestral organization that have increased musician vulnerability. The predispositions inherent to the relationship between a musician and his/her métier compound the difficulties in "getting to yes" with regard to employment protection as the *movements* and *intermezzi* that follow will soon reveal.

The choice of two countries is certainly not intended to lead the reader down a comparative research path. Decades of performance opportunities as a professional orchestral violinist in the Netherlands and the US have afforded me a sizeable network of contacts in both countries. The access to stakeholders who share similar professional concerns yet operate within orchestral organizations differentiated from one another in terms of external factors and advanced the opportunity to consider diverse vantage points. Ideally, the experiences of musicians from two musically important countries will reverberate with great intensity to musicians worldwide.

A music-related subject calls for musical structure: the sounds of music have not only motivated but also moved the research along its course. The choice for *movements* and *intermezzi* to replace traditional chapters is intentional, placing content and context on a similar wavelength, and reflecting the desire to lend musical structure to a music-related subject. *Movements* can be compared to chapters in a traditional inquiry, whereas *intermezzi* are interludes that true to their musical form convey information to enhance the *movements*.

The challenges faced by orchestras and their musicians, including the growing number of increasingly vulnerable freelancers, have met with renewed interest from nonmusicians post-2007-2008 financial crisis. As the original gig workers who inspired that term, musicians' trials and tribulations in the employment market have piqued the curiosity of those concerned with various aspects of atypical work. "Until recently, the music sector was mainly ignored as the problems faced by musicians seemed to be peanuts, ancillary to the problems of 'big labor,' or care, food industry and/or delivery workers. Nowadays, everyone in labor and employment circles is trying to get a grip on the rapid recent variations at the workplace. Musicians have always survived, always found creative ways to move through different varieties of employment. Now more than ever, they can inspire us."[7]

The eminent sociologist and public policy commentator Pierre Bourdieu questioned "the ability [of academics] to raise speculative problems for the sole pleasure of resolving them not because they are posed ... by the necessities of life."[8] My research has been prompted by the other side of the coin as it addresses the true necessities of life for traditionally employed and freelance orchestral musicians in a sector plagued by financial instability and employment crises. Protective employment regulations that took decades to put in place were flouted by employers in the wake of financial crises. This was further exacerbated as a consequence of the devastating impact of the COVID-19 pandemic on the cultural sector. Bourdieu's necessity factor surpasses the

7. Conversations with Tino Gagliardi, President Local 802, American Federation of Musicians (AFM) 2010-2018.
8. Pierre Bourdieu. "The Scholastic Point of View" 1984, 380.

delights of academic consideration, as musicians worldwide face challenges of diminished employment opportunities and unrequited promises of fair pay for fair play.

Initially motivated by direct involvement as a musician-employee who had experienced several Dutch orchestral reorganizations firsthand, I was fascinated by the process that unfolded as musicians approached the firing line. Even though a commendable system of legal protection, from EU and national labor legislation to the orchestra's Social Plan, was in place, musicians perceived and reported irregularities concerning positions lost and positions gained. Of all the elephants lurking in rooms and corridors, the largest of them all was the fact that orchestras became a particular target of massive subsidy reductions in the Netherlands post-2007-2008 financial crisis. News from the orchestral front in my native United States was even more dismal as bankruptcy bailouts, lockouts, and strikes became commonplace as a 21st-century orchestral state of affairs. Voices from both sides of the Atlantic clamored for more information in an attempt to share best practices and possible solutions to the increased vulnerabilities within the sector.

Keeping the Atlantic in mind, a poignant anecdote that illuminates musician vulnerability comes to mind. On a fateful afternoon on the deep seas in April 1912, a band of five musicians played on as the great ship Titanic sank. A distressing footnote sheds light on an inconceivable concept: posthumous vulnerability. Two weeks following the tragedy, the musicians' family members received late payment bills for uniforms lost at sea. Booked as performers by a noted Liverpool impresario, the Titanic musicians were under contract to perform services for White Star Line. The latter chose not to include musicians as crew members, listing the five as second-class passengers. This conscious exemption on the part of the employer left family members bereft of any recourse to insurance benefits, and, adding insult to injury, led to late payment charges. Over a century later, musicians and media reporters alike allude to the orchestral sector as a sinking ship: "Music industry heads warn of a devastating landscape for British orchestras, as the live music sector struggles to stay afloat."[9]

My objective throughout this symphonic metamorphosis has been to weave an analysis of orchestral employment in two countries that goes beyond statistics and economic reports. Field research based on interviews with the people who perform, direct, manage, and bear the responsibility to finance orchestras garnered unexpected answers to standard questions. These in turn opened the doors to new questions, new perceptions, and new paths within the research process. Weaving through the myriad questions and answers is the theme of vulnerability: orchestral musicians are not only subject to the vicissitudes of external vulnerabilities related to organizational financing but also affected by a wide swath of internal predispositions or vulnerabilities related to workplace hierarchies and modus operandi.

Inherent predispositions:

- Musicians refer to their profession as "a calling"—their work is their passion, and vice versa.

9. Maddy Shaw Roberts reporting for ClassicFM August 6, 2020, 12:53. Available at https://www.classicfm.com/music-news/coronavirus/british-orchestras-losing-six-million-month/.

- Like athletes, musicians' paths to success start at an early age and involve years of focused preparation. Singularity of purpose to attain success in a highly competitive field influences musicians' interpretations of and reactions to employment situations.

The employment experiences of regularly employed orchestral musicians as well as the experiences of the even more vulnerable freelance substitute players are given equal voice. Within the professional orchestral world, the demarcation between the designation freelance substitute and freelancers is blurred. First, freelance musicians do not refer to themselves as freelance substitutes, even if this term is the most accurate description of their employment. Second, there is no formal definition that separates freelance substitutes from freelancers in general.

Selected external factors:

- changes in the perception of the value of classical culture leading to decreased financial support;
- lack of clarity in the legal frameworks covering workers who are seen by the law as employees and those who are seen as self-employed;
- general economic crises and the COVID-19 pandemic's effects on workers in a sector plagued by labor market insecurity.

Selected internal factors:

- traditional hierarchical structures within the orchestra foster individual musician's passivity;
- long-established discriminatory practices in orchestral organizations with regard to gender, race, and age;
- increased market strain as supply (top-class musicians) far exceeds demand;
- musicians eager to perform often have limited access to disability payments, pensions and other related employment rights;
- orchestral hiring relies on a stratum of substitute players who work under temporary contracts and perform alongside regulars. Conventionally categorized as self-employed, these musicians report unequal access to benefits.

An inquiry linked to the impact of crisis on a specific category of workers in two countries crosses a multiplicity of fields. Legal considerations have sometimes taken a back seat to economic, historical, and social factors in the orchestral sphere, and this foray into uncharted territory called for broad-based reading across multiple music-related disciplines and revealed a marked lack of literature specifically focused on orchestral musicians' work lives.

A description of **movements** *and* **intermezzi**

Prelude: a prologue on orchestras at the brink

Introduces the subject matter, the motivations for the study, its scope and novel methods.

I. Background to Orchestral Journeys

(1) **Background to orchestral journeys** opens with **FAQs: Answers to Questions Regarding the Orchestral Workplace** to answer a wide range of questions posed by nonmusicians, many of whom vociferously expressed strong opinions that music-making was more of a pleasant diversion than a real profession, insinuating that musicians are not suitable subjects for serious inquiry. The *movement* intends to fill general knowledge deficits with regard to orchestral organizations and their musicians.

(2) **Haydn rewrites history** sheds light on important historical processes and employment-related problems relevant to modern orchestral narratives. Haydn's inventive leadership style and his interactions with an extraordinary band of musicians in the late 18th century paved the way for a deeper understanding of links between past and present orchestral employment vulnerabilities.

II. Symphonic Variations: Orchestral Employment, Freelancers and the Law

(3) ***Intermezzo*: Follow the money, economics at the orchestra** studies aspects of orchestral financing with special emphasis on the seminal works of William Baumol and William Bowen, pioneers in the field of cultural economics, and Robert Flanagan's follow-ups. The impact of their theories on contemporary cultural decision-making has provided justification for orchestral downscaling and massive subsidy cuts.

(4) **Requiem for an orchestra:** The story that provided the original impetus for the book exposes the inner workings of reorganization at a premiere Dutch orchestra in 2012-2013. Historical background, insider documents provided to orchestra members, and conflicting reports from politicians and cultural subsidy stakeholders are assessed to expose the trials and tribulations of orchestral musicians faced by dismissal.

(5) **En Route to *FNV KIEM:* Of musicians and Labor Law** takes a doctrinal focus to examine leading ECJ cases that tackled social protection in light of competition law. The *FNV KIEM* case with its introduction of the concept of the false self-employed contributed to changes in the status of orchestral freelancers.

(6) **A long and winding road: freelancers in a tale of two countries** focuses on freelancers. Litigation in both countries studied opens the space of deliberation to examine the role courts have played in the classification of workers.

III. Dissonance: Orchestral Workplace Discrimination

Gender, race and age are the focus of this pair of movements and *intermezzo*.

(7) **Of *Rowe* and race** exposes gender stereotypes that have plagued the profession for centuries to set the stage for a pay-disparity case that rocked the music world in 2018. Issues related to race raise awareness of implicit bias in the orchestral sphere.
(8) ***Intermezzo: Singing the #metoo classical blues*** gives pride of place to two #metoo narratives to uncover how two major orchestras (true to form, a US and a Dutch orchestra) responded to harassment allegations.
(9) **Greener Pastures: coming of age** presents case-based materials on another group of vulnerable giving voice to older musicians. Attention is paid to specific procedural restrictions that have had a deterrent effect on US discrimination cases.

IV. Closing Chords

(10) **Orchestral employment in times of pandemic** describes the increased sectoral vulnerabilities during two turbulent years of crisis and leads to the **Coda** conclusion.
(11) **Coda: new vistas on orchestral employment post-COVID-19** presents updates on current failures and successes in the quest for greater employment security for vulnerable musicians post-pandemic.

Movements and *intermezzi* can be read as parts of a whole symphonic metamorphosis or can be extracted individually to engage readers with specific interests. For example, those familiar with the orchestra and its distinctive characteristics could skip the **FAQs: Answers to Questions Regarding the Orchestral Workplace** and proceed to **Symphonic Variations: Orchestral Employment, Freelancers and the Law** or peruse **Dissonance: Orchestral Workplace Discrimination**. The curtain rises.

I Background to Orchestral Journeys

1

FAQs: Answers to Questions Regarding the Orchestral Workplace

> One may think of the orchestra as a large instrument that is capable to produce simultaneously or in succession a multitude of sounds of different kinds. The performers who together make up the orchestra are quite simply the strings, tubes, boxes, flat surfaces, of wood or metal, they are like machines endowed with intelligence activated by a vast keyboard played by the conductor under the direction of the composer.[10]

> An orchestra is not a pottery course but a performance-oriented society.[11]

> In the wild, an orchestra would more closely resemble an antebellum cotton plantation or a feudal estate than it would a modern workplace.[12]

Coming to grips with the vulnerabilities within the orchestral profession calls for an understanding of the orchestral musician in the largest sense of the term, embracing both the fully employed and the freelance substitute players who augment orchestral ranks with regularity. The history of this profession, its similarities to other performance fields including sports, and a deeper look into what defines the profession in the 21st century (stimulated by comments and questions posed by hundreds of musicians on both sides of the Atlantic) not only expose embedded assumptions and vulnerabilities but also stimulate a call for legislative and in some cases enforcement action. Value of culture debates and the #metoo *intermezzo* might seem to be, pun written blushingly, strange bedfellows: however, orchestral musicians in the here and now as employees find themselves drawn into the vortex of these present-day vulnerability-related concerns.

---

10. Hector Berlioz. *Grand Traité d'Instrumentation et d'Orchestration Modernes* (author's translation) 1855, 406.
11. Munich-based conductor and producer Christian Gansch, https://www.bsi-software.com/en/magazine/article/what-companies-can-learn-from-orchestras-1.html.
12. Robert Levine, Chair Emeritus International Conference of Symphony and Opera Musician (ICSOM).

As research shows, the contrast between support for the arts in the last decades of the 20th century and the massive cutbacks post-2007-2008 financial crisis in the Netherlands and the US is striking. Cultural funding in the US was encouraged by the National Endowment for the Arts, which has all but closed its doors in recent years. Post-crisis, endowments have drastically diminished. Philanthropists have turned to other forms of giving far beyond the orchestral sector, and subscription sales have lagged. In the US, the precarious situation is marked by acrimonious collective bargaining negotiations, bankruptcies, and a marked increase in industrial actions. In the Netherlands, post-crisis subsidy cuts have decimated the field of funded orchestras, "leaving the rest of us to wonder not if but when we will be the next orchestra to go."[13] Freelancers in the orchestral world face deep doubts as to the financial viability of their chosen musical occupation, yet despite this pessimistic portrayal, the music does play on. "It has always played on, especially in times of adversity, when all else fails, music communicates the promise of triumph."[14]

Lawyers confronted with complex fact patterns pre-litigation often set the scene with the facts and attempt to find answers to basic questions before delving further into the subject matter at suit. This *movement* marks an attempt to answer essential questions to lay the groundwork for the *movements* to follow. Questions were gleaned from inquiries posed by outsiders, including colleagues and music-lovers from all walks of life as to the what, why, and who of the orchestral profession. The *FAQs* roam a wide territory, from questions regarding the size of an orchestra to an attempt to explain collective bargaining culture in the sector. Other essential questions focus on the hierarchy that is part and parcel of orchestral organization; the movement closes with crisis chronicles from orchestral frontlines.

1.1 WHAT IS IN A NAME: AN ORCHESTRA, A SYMPHONY, A SYMPHONY ORCHESTRA, A PHILHARMONIC, OR ALL OF THE ABOVE?

An examination of the oft-confusing nomenclature associated with musical organizations creates its own level of questions. Currently, the terms "symphony," "orchestra," and "philharmonic" are used interchangeably. Combing through conventional English language dictionaries, the reader learns that the term "symphony" derives from ancient Greek roots, "sýn" meaning together and "phone" meaning sound. To the ancient Greeks, the term "orchestra" indicated a circular space in front of the stage in which the chorus would act out words through dance or "*orchesis*." The humanist revival of Greek and Roman cultural ethos foregrounds new meanings. By the early 17th century, the orchestra designated the area in a theater where instrumentalists performed.[15]

13. Conversation with Roland Kieft, former Artistic Director Hague Philharmonic.
14. Conversations with Gian-Carlo Menotti noted composer, founder Spoleto Festival dei Due Mondi.
15. Martin Staehelin. "Orchester" in *Handwörterbuch der musikalischen Terminologie* H.H. Eggebrecht (ed.) 1972.

European medieval texts point to various functions of the term "symphonia" in relation to specific instruments (dulcimer, hurdy-gurdy) as well as a generic term referring to a pleasing, harmonious sound made by a group of instruments. By the early 17th century, symfonia (various spellings, sinfonia or symphonie) was used to denote the compositions written for musical ensembles. As orchestras were established throughout Europe, the meaning of the term changed to reflect not only the placement of instrumentalists but also their collective. Jean-Jacques Rousseau's entry for Diderot's *Encyclopédie* shows a sensitivity to the dual nature of the term "orchestra":

> (Orchestra) means sometimes the place where those sit who play on the instruments, as the orchestra of the opera-house; and Sometimes the place where the whole band in general are fixed, As the orchestra of the spiritual concert at the Château des Tuilleries; and again, the collection of all the symphonists[16]

To add a bit of confusion to this brief etymological inquiry, English speakers might call their orchestras symphonies or double up by referring to these performing groups as symphony orchestras. To provide US examples, the top-10 orchestral ensembles include the Chicago Symphony Orchestra, the Cleveland Orchestra, and the New York Philharmonic—all large orchestras with over hundred musicians employed. The term "philharmonia" from which philharmonic is derived stems from the ancient Greek "love of harmony" and is primarily used to refer to an orchestra or the society that sponsors the orchestra. This brief description of the complexities of the nomenclature associated with the orchestra is only a prelude to the chaos in terminology when reference is made to an orchestra's manager, sometimes titled as director, manager, CEO, president or in the case of several major US orchestras, a combination of two of the above (as in, CEO and President of New York Philharmonic Orchestra).[17]

1.2 OF COMPETITIONS, HORSE RACES AND ORCHESTRAL AUDITIONS

The great Hungarian 20th-century composer Béla Bartók reputedly quipped, "competitions are for horses, not musicians."[18] His wisdom notwithstanding, the competitive arena is part and parcel of classical musicians' experiences en route to orchestral positions. For prospective orchestral musicians, replace the term "competition" with the word "audition" to gain an understanding of the competitive selection process that opens the door for the select few who secure a place in an orchestra. In the early and mid-20th century, auditions were often solitary exercises in which an aspiring performer would come face to face with the orchestra's music director. The great maestros of the 20th century handpicked their musicians, often trading or even poaching solo

16. Jean-Jacques Rousseau. *A Complete Dictionary of Music* (William Waring translation) 1779, 301.
17. For example, Deborah Borda serves as President and CEO of New York Philharmonic Orchestra https://nyphil.org/about-us/artists/deborah-borda.
18. Joseph Szigeti. *Szigeti on the Violin* 1970, 14, https://archive.org/details/szigetionviolin0000szig_h2g4.

players from other fine orchestras.[19] Cronyism and protectionism often played a role in determining who would be given a chance to play: members of musical dynasties and the favored students of pedagogues who played in the orchestra were commonly chosen above unknown talents.[20] "Old time maestros maintained total control of the hiring and firing processes and we musicians had to fight a real uphill battle to change the entrance requirements in our orchestras. The artistic and audition committees who hold great power in orchestras nowadays were unthinkable a few decades ago."[21]

Present-day orchestras show some variance in audition procedures with regard to the composition and voting procedures of audition committees. In many major orchestras, an audition committee holds the majority of the votes. Variance as to the composition of the committee is marked: some orchestras require all members to cast a vote,[22] some orchestras require a smaller number of members including principal players, and yet others require an entire orchestral section to vote. How an orchestra goes about selecting a new member speaks volumes as it discloses information on how the orchestra operates and reveals aspects of its internal culture and traditions. The selection process also is telling with regard to the extent of the music director's (MD) power. "After all, unless the conductor has encountered the player at work in another orchestra or at an earlier point in their career, the audition is often the first meeting point, the first hearing point to listen to a future member of the club."[23] In some orchestras, the MD holds veto power, and in others, the MD has only one vote.

Turning to the two countries researched in this study, an increasing number of orchestras in both the US and the Netherlands require applicants to submit a pre-recorded sample of specific orchestral excerpts to gain admission to the first round as a matter of efficiency, given the volume of musicians who apply for openings. Live auditions usually consist of a minimum of two official rounds in which candidates play selections from the orchestral repertoire and solo pieces behind a screen. Aside from the famed Berlin Philharmonic,[24] the majority of 21st-century orchestras apply a blind audition procedure for preliminary rounds: the term "blind audition" refers to an audition where the player is behind a physical screen, thus masking the candidate's gender and identity from the jury members. "The stress level is almost inconceivable; audition execution takes you into a sort of lion's den. Usually, before you walk out for your screened ordeal, you are assigned to warm up in a communal room full of peers who intimidate with flashy playing. You know you are going to run a gauntlet, so anything you can do to make yourself mentally comfortable is a plus."[25]

19. The New York Philharmonic's archives are replete with reports on player poaching, http://archives.nyphil.org/index.php/search?.
20. Conversations with Szymon Goldberg, former concertmaster Berlin Philharmonic, famed pedagogue.
21. Conversations with former Cleveland Orchestra members Maurice Wolfson and Gino Raffaelli.
22. Vienna Philharmonic and Berlin Philharmonic voting model, orchestras members are entitled to one vote http://www.instantencore.com/buzz/item.aspx?FeedEntryId = 143393.
23. Conversations with Maestro Michael Schønwandt.
24. *Polyphonic*, https://www.hornmatters.com/2010/06/auditioning-berlin-philharmonic/.
25. Author's interview with a wind player who auditioned for 17 orchestras before winning a position.

According to audition conventions dating back to the last three decades of the 20th century, the screen that blocks visual contact between the candidate and the committee is removed for the final round. What does an orchestra look/listen for? Aside from an impeccable technical performance level, sound quality, rhythmical integrity, and the notion that the player will fit in with the orchestra's "sound" are a few of the ingredients that make for a successful audition.

Orchestral musicians speak of certain traditions specific to their orchestra, customs that might not translate to other orchestras. Fairness of course is the best policy; however, should an orchestra that counts the music directors' vote double set the standard for an orchestra? From inside, the Los Angeles Philharmonic, another variation on the blind audition resounds:

> The fairest way would be to have all rounds played behind a screen, and all voting done via electronic counter, where no committee member is allowed to visually or orally indicate which candidate they prefer. We do this, except for the screening of ALL rounds. Each committee member holds a "clicker" that is tied into a central monitoring device. Two members of the standing audition and reviews committee watch that counter, and when a pre-determined number is hit, the candidate is excused. We are not allowed to discuss any candidate prior to voting (which is done via secret ballot) until the very final round.[26]

Most orchestras reserve the right to dismiss candidates who do not make the mark of high expectations, and warnings appear in disclaimers in posted vacancy announcements.[27] "At the New York Philharmonic, we have been known to dismiss candidates after one line of music. This is not a reflection of arrogance, but simply a matter of self-protection. How long should you let a candidate play if you know that they are in no way suitable? One phrase speaks volumes, an insider in the orchestra can hear immediately if the candidate is on the level of the section. The audition system is not inherently pleasant, nonetheless, it should be fair, and it should be effective."[28]

1.3 THE EMPTY CHAIR PHENOMENON: HIGH STANDARDS OR ANOTHER ECONOMIC REPERCUSSION POST-CRISIS?

Another audition-related issue that contributes to increased vulnerability within the orchestral profession is the empty chair phenomenon. To avoid taking a decision that might be disappointing down the line, many orchestras simply do not fill positions by offering regular employment to a candidate but instead hire qualified freelance substitute players. While British orchestras lead the way with a tradition of offering trial positions to several players in seriatim without offering any single player a

26. James Wilt, associate principal trumpet, Los Angeles Philharmonic https://www.trumpetherald.com/forum/viewtopic.php?p=1321795.
27. For example: "The Audition Committee reserves the right to dismiss immediately any candidate not meeting the highest professional standards of The Cleveland Orchestra," https://www.clevelandorchestra.com/About/Auditions-and-Careers/Musician-Auditions/.
28. Conversations with Judy Nelson, New York Philharmonic Orchestra violist, 1983-2019.

full-time position, the trend is increasingly popular in the US and the Netherlands. "Do the math, you will discover that it costs the orchestra less money to hire a freelancer than fill a position. This situation can go on for months, sometimes even years ... and once one orchestra sets a precedent, others follow suit."[29] Interestingly, in EU countries, orchestras are only permitted to organize an international audition where participants can compete regardless of nationality following two unsuccessful auditions open to hopefuls with EU residence/permits. Thus, in Europe, the empty chair repeated audition phenomenon could contribute to breaking through nationality barriers. Musicians vying for orchestral positions in the US do not face the same nationality barriers: orchestral auditions are open to all applicants who pass a preliminary screening round.

1.4 THE IDEAL CANDIDATE

The Amsterdam-based Netherlands Philharmonic Orchestra has added a new dimension to its audition procedure that takes factors above and beyond candidates' musical abilities as a factor for acceptance:

> NedPhO/NKO musicians have a driven and flexible work ethic ... Members of the orchestra sometimes perform in unusual locations ... and make an active contribution to further enhancing social support ... NedPhO seeks new colleagues who ... do not object to receiving visitors during rehearsals at times.
>
> Selection: The artistic selection takes place through the audition. Then, an interview takes place regarding the candidate's affinity with the orchestra to establish whether knowledge, skills and personality match the demands of the job.[30]

From recent conservatory graduates to established freelancers, concern has been expressed regarding this additional requirement. In their minds, it veils an excuse to exclude foreign players who might not have a good command of Dutch. As all orchestras set strict requirements for trial periods, the purpose of a pre-trial interview is questionable: the candidate should be judged on specific performance on the job, not on interview skills. A former artistic director of the Hague Philharmonic observed that this requirement was created out of necessity after seasoned orchestra members resisted nonstandard orchestral activities including school and outdoor concerts added to their work portfolios post-crisis.[31] The jury is still out as to how a fair audition should be conducted, an important question when dealing with musicians' vulnerabilities. Audition outcomes have found their way to court proceedings on both sides of the ocean, in both countries. An analysis of this jurisprudence in later *movements* reveals some of the lacunae in judicial cognizance of this essential orchestral process.

29. Conversations with ICSOM representative and National Symphony Orchestra violist, Jennifer Mondie.
30. https://www.orkest.nl/english-summary/orchestral-musicians---profile.
31. Conversations with Roland Kieft.

1.5 OF ORCHESTRAL MUSICIANS AND SPORTS TEAM PLAYERS

> The athlete to orchestral musician comparison is really quite apt. In many ways, assembling an orchestra is similar to a pro ball franchise fielding a team. And just like a top sports team...you have to pay for quality if you're going to play at the big-league level.[32]

> Sports—although they do not qualify as art in the narrow sense—offer a commonly observed stage to a world of many diverse and specialized performances.[33]

> This collaboration is like the football field, a coach and the players, we do not have an opponent, but we grapple with ourselves if we do not get the spirit of the composer.[34]

On the path to culling and organizing scores of inquiries concerning the orchestral profession, an important comparative question emerged: can one possibly compare the orchestral collective to any other sort of ensemble or team? Historians, sociologists, and economists who have turned their attention to orchestras argue as to whether orchestral musicians operate in a unique collective or whether musicians should be taken off an exceptional pedestal and placed on par with other members of a labor force required to exchange specific services for remuneration.[35] Most musicians balk at the generic classification and are quick to point out that the career trajectory of a professional orchestral player is analogous to a member of a sports team, a parallel that deserves more than peripheral scrutiny. Top team players and orchestral musicians are recruited, undergo complex audition/acceptance procedures, and are compensated for public performance. Whether kicking a football or wielding a cello bow, athletes and musicians endure long hours of individual practice as professional training starts from early childhood.

Cross-referencing sports and music is not anathema to academic circles as cultural economists have delved into comparative studies in terms of behavior and earnings. David Throsby and Ruth Towse selected the two areas of endeavor as examples of controlled and single-minded environments in their quest to expand the boundaries of cultural economics. A comparative examination of a leading sports team, a prize-winning restaurant and the Royal Concertgebouw Orchestra (RCO) published in 2006 offered a heady mix of components that link seemingly disparate teamwork professions.[36] Subsequent studies on achievement in diverse professions have concentrated on the distinctiveness of talent and skill-driven activity in music and sports.[37]

32. Manny Laureano, principal trumpet, Minnesota Orchestra https://maskoftheflowerprince.wordpress.com/2016/09/30/what-does-it-take-to-be-a-professional-orchestra-musician/.
33. Tyler Cowan. *In Praise of Commercial Culture* 2000.
34. Emmanuel Pahud, principal flute, Berlin Philharmonic https://www.youtube.com/watch?v=jnKhE5ij1GI.
35. Jutta, J. Allmendinger, Richard Hackman and Erin V. Lehman. "Life and Work in Symphony Orchestras." *Musical Quarterly* 1986. Paul Judy supports special classification, "The Uniqueness and Commonality of American Symphony Orchestra Organizations." *Harmony* October 1995.
36. Xavier Bekaert et al., *Toonaangevend: wat bedrijven kunnen leren van Het Concertgebouworkest, een toprestaurant en een rugbyploeg* 2013.
37. For a populist approach, see Daniel Coyle. *The Talent Code: Unlocking the Secret of Skill in Maths, Art, Music, Sport, and Just about Everything Else.* Arrow Press 2010.

Like many arts-related vocations, the orchestral profession is shrouded in mystery and apt either to be overly romanticized or conversely dumbed down: "you musicians play, while real, hard-working citizens work." A comparison to professional team sports provides a thought-provoking point of departure as it brings the orchestral musician into a perspective understood by a wider public.

1.6 PARALLELS

The parallels between team sports practitioners and orchestral musicians are, pardon the football pun, striking. To perform music with highly trained colleagues in an orchestra requires high levels of individual skill and group coordination: each musician contributes to a collectively created artistic result. The legendary American football coach, Vince Lombardi, was revered particularly for his ability to take a losing team and turn it around to create a winning team. His firm conviction in the power of individual practice as an indispensable ingredient in team success echoes the words of leading music instructors. Compare his famous adage "[p]ractice does not make perfect. Only perfect practice makes perfect," to the Juilliard School's legendary violin pedagogue Dorothy Delay's observation, "[y]our practice is so much a part of your life as a performer that it has to be perfect. And enjoyable, that's the trick."[38] The mention of two greats from the past, Vince Lombardi and Dorothy Delay, highlights another similarity in music and sports training: the lineage, a reverence for the greats who preceded present-day players, is central to practitioners in both professions.

Entry into an orchestra is highly selective and driven by an extremely competitive audition process followed by rigorous review preceding tenure. Like sports practitioners, musicians spend hours each day using the same muscles repetitively to perform the physical tasks necessary to play an instrument at a high level. And, like sports practitioners, musicians play because they love the tactile act of playing their chosen instrument just as athletes are addicted to certain motions. "To play the recorder, you must love the feeling of pushing air through a tube to create sound, it's that simple. Wasn't it the wizard footballer Johan Cruyff who said:

> 'I really dislike a player who moves but doesn't know where he is going?' Any musician should be able to relate to that as if we become obsessed with what we do on the instrument, or for that matter as a conductor on the podium. Knowledge and obsession lead to knowing where you are going."[39]

Another analogous point is the importance of the coach or pedagogue in shaping the individual athlete/musician. Both sports and music performance provide fascination and fixation for the wider public as consumers, passionate hobbyists, and armchair experts.

38. Green Bay Packer legendary coach Vince Lombardi's quotes, https://everydaypower.com/vince-lombardi-quotes/ Dorothy Delay quote, courtesy of the author.
39. Conversations with Frans Brüggen, musician extraordinaire. Johan Cruyff's quote: "Ik heb een vreselijke hekel aan iemand die beweegt, maar niet weet waar naartoe."

Success in the orchestral profession, akin to success at the pitch, calls for special abilities. Almost all of the orchestral musicians interviewed make mention of a combination of skills that easily translate to the sports world. Focused, professional training from a young age, the ability to perform at peak level under stress, and the wherewithal to block out stress are commonalities shared by musicians and athletes, indispensable to longevity in their professions. However, there is a difference between the two disciplines in the legal realm: although sports law is a recognized field of inquiry, the law pertaining to musicians' collectives is not significant within legal research, with the notable exception of the law applicable to performance rights and royalties.

1.7 A CAVEAT: THERE IS A PAUCITY OF RELIABLE STATISTICS AND DATA-BASED EMPIRICAL RESEARCH

Like sports teams, orchestras have provided scholars from a wide array of disciplines with food for thought: economists, historians, musicologists, public policy analysts, psychologists, and sociologists have scrutinized the orchestra. In recent years, researchers and commentators have conducted many interesting studies on orchestra financing, with a special focus on the nonprofit sector and the changing nature of state subsidies in Europe. Yet, despite the wealth of research, comparatively little research has been undertaken with a focus on labor relations and the institutional dynamics at play within orchestras.

There are several reasons why there is a paucity of research concerning musicians' employment/labor situations. First, unlike sports professionals or rock stars, orchestral musicians are not high-profile wage earners or media celebrities. Their orchestral team might well garner some modicum of fame; however, much of that status is based on the maestro's drawing power or the appearance of a superstar soloist supported by the orchestra. Even orchestras that have gained star status, such as the RCO, are praised for their so-called collective output, not for the star players that are members of the ensemble as a whole. Second, culture generally occupies a small percentage of public expenditures with lower percentages for orchestras as a component within the larger culture category.[40] This relatively small percentage matches a "general lack of concern for the orchestra unless of course we indulge in cultural economics or look at ensembles from the point of view of collective behavior."[41] One might argue that an insignificant public expenditure would provide some form of shelter/immunity from financial cuts. The Dutch and US examples central to this research show, however, that even when arts spending amounts to a fraction of other public expenditures, cutting arts budgets is just as easily said as done, with little general outcry on the part of the public. "Orchestras are not perceived to have much

40. *Eurostat* groups cultural expenditure (country-by-country) together with expenditure on recreation and culture, *see* http://ec.europa.eu/eurostat/web/culture/public-expenditure-on-culture-recreation-and-religion, whereas the US federal funding for the National Endowment of the Arts is roughly 1/40 of German funding, Europe's leader in terms of arts spending.
41. Conversation with cultural economist, Ruth Towse.

importance whatsoever: the loss of an orchestra passes almost unnoticed while any movement within the sports world receives pages of print media attention, tv and radio coverage and social media commentary."[42]

Third, for all the broad similarities between sports and music, there are enough differences between the professions to cloud comparison. Economic conditions always influence employment terms and working parameters set forth in collective bargaining agreements. There are no million-dollar trading fees for orchestral musicians, and certainly no bonuses for musicians who perform at the level of a football club like Ajax or Chelsea (pay scales at Amsterdam, and for that matter London orchestras) fall far short of the six-figure range: average professional footballers' *weekly* salaries are often higher than the *annual* salaries for orchestral musicians, with the exception of a few US-based top-tier orchestral principals[43] whose salaries fall within the $100,00-500,00 range.[44]

As mentioned above, generally, the salaries of top athletes are considerably higher than those of top orchestral musicians. Nevertheless, there are comparable factors between the two professions in remuneration: top club athletes earn considerably more than minor league players.[45] Similarly, orchestral musicians in the top eight US orchestras earn as much as four times more than orchestral professionals in regional symphonies.[46] Taking a closer look at the underbelly of professional sports, the high percentage of players in every sport who do not take home six-figure salaries share similarities with musicians. FIFPro reported that almost 50% of professional football players worldwide earned less than $1,000 a month.[47] "It is much like any other talent-based career: actors, too, have extremely poor job security, and their careers can be cut short by injury or illness. Talented individuals are treated like pawns and are constantly competing with other talented people. The path of a professional footballer is one of high reward, but also high risk."[48]

There are no winners in the champions league of orchestras, just survivors who hope that the upcoming season will lead to solvency and a solid future without the threat of a "dark theater." Although some media attention has been paid to lists of the

42. Conversations with Hein Glaubitz, former Managing Director RFO and RKF, 2006-2008.
43. According to *Football Today*, Ajax average year salaries €400,000 per annum in 2020, https://www.ajaxshowtime.com/tag/ajax-spelers-salarissen#; Chelsea's lowest paid player earns 25,000 pounds per week, one tenth of most of his colleagues, https://www.sportsindus.com/football/chelsea-players-salaries/. As facts and figures brought to the fore in *Of Rowe and Race* show, many top-tier US orchestra principals earn over $300,000 per annum.
44. Compare the salaries of Royal Concertgebouw Orchestra (RCO) members with an average pre-tax monthly income of €5.040 to Chelsea players' salaries, https://sillyseason.com/salary/chelsea-players-salaries-67985/.
45. For insights into earnings at top (eredivisie) Dutch football clubs, Voetbalzone's report, *Gemiddelde jaarsalaris van Eredivisie-voetballer stijgt met tweeduizend euro*), https://www.voetbalzone.nl/doc.asp?uid=332101.
46. Top-Tier Orchestral Compensation, https://adaptistration.com/2018/05/25/top-tier-musician-compensation-2018/.
47. Fifpro Global Employment Report 2016 https://fifpro.org/news/2016-global-employment-report-top-findings/en.
48. Ben Cisneros. *Keep Calm and Talk Law* http://www.keepcalmtalklaw.co.uk/fixed-term-contracts-in-football-foul-play-or-fair-game/.

world's top 10 orchestras,[49] and most of the orchestras on that list are among the best-paid orchestras worldwide, there is no direct connection between orchestral fame and high remuneration for several of the top groups. For example, members of the RCO ranked #2 on the *Gramophone* magazine list but are paid almost 50% less than the #9 ranked Boston Symphony Orchestra (BSO).[50]

1.8 JUSTIFICATION FOR HIGH COMPENSATION PACKAGES FOR ATHLETES AND MUSICIANS

While high salaries in professional sports are rarely questioned, those who are directly concerned with nonprofit financing (in the US) have questioned how to justify compensation packages for orchestral musicians. Several answers spring to mind: sports events attract larger audiences, and sports teams function on a star system kept in place and encouraged by the media. Sports teams are extraordinary businesses that earn their keep through multiple spinoffs such as multimedia and marketing package deals. Orchestras cater to a smaller audience and are too often typecast as elitist. Musicians' salaries at top-tier orchestras are earned by a select few top performers who work with the same intensity as athletes and not only have spent hours to prove themselves but also often have spent small fortunes to purchase the priceless tools of their trade.

1.9 GLOBAL BUSINESS IN SPORTS AND MUSIC

The Dutch economist Hans Abbing pointed to parallels between the role of sports agents and music impresarios as gatekeepers who exercise control over their respective fields.[51] Not only it is impossible to test the veracity of the comparison but also it is important to point out that the role of impresarios is negligible when the discussion centers on orchestral musicians. An area of comparison that does deserve further research is the sizable difference between payments and bonuses for the highest-paid members of the "team" and the rank-and-file players who perform on the same team. This issue is central in the analysis of the *Rowe* (2018) case which informs the *movement Of Rowe and Race.*

Sports leagues have developed into mass-market businesses holding substantial market monopolies and lucrative links to media/internet dissemination akin to the US top orchestras with multimillion budgets and substantial media contracts. As one of the world's most influential art collectors commented concerning global tendencies in the cultural arena, "art in today's society has risen to become a new dominant culture,

49. A 2015 selection chosen by a small list of music journalists excluding North American critics offered a not-so-surprising Eurocentric list of the "toppers," whereas *Gramophone* magazine chose the Hong Kong Philharmonic as the best of all orchestras in 2019. *See* https://bachtrack.com/worlds-best-orchestra-best-conductor-critics-choice-september-2015.
50. *See* Dr. Gerald Mertens for additional information on German orchestras, http://www.miz.org/musical-life-in.../06_Symphony_and_Chamber_Orchestras.pdf.
51. Hans Abbing. "The Autonomous Artist Still Rules the World of Culture" 2004, 55-66.

anchored like sport and showbiz in the system of international companies and the mass media."[52] By extension, if orchestras can become "players" in the field and compete with multimedia offerings, they have a heightened chance for survival. Endeavors by the Los Angeles Philharmonic that embrace multimedia, as well as the orchestra's considerable social justice projects,[53] and the Berlin Philharmonic's Digital Concert Hall prove that some orchestras are investing in global coverage.[54]

In terms of replacing individual players: while the market in both competitive sports and orchestral music is glutted with players eager to join the "big leagues," the highly competitive nature of the top teams and orchestras and the selection systems that lead to a coveted position make it difficult to gain entry. The specificity of a career in sports entails short-term careers based on the physical demands of the sport; careers of short duration mean that athletes need to maximize their earning potential over a relatively short time. Orchestral careers for the most part span longer periods depending on the instrument played and a performer's general condition and proclivity to certain performance-related ailments.

By and large, team employment arrangements and the legal status of athletes is somewhat similar to that of orchestral musicians. Athletes most often provide their services to a team, while orchestral musicians provide their services to the orchestra. Yet, beyond this simple statement lies the different employment status accorded to many of the freelance substitutes in both fields. Interestingly, the UK courts characterized a professional athlete's occupation in a comparative association with an actor's/actress' work as "peculiar," and, by and large, within a field in which "success entirely depends on pleasing the public and constantly being before the public."[55] There are differences between collective bargaining that regulates the terms and conditions of contracted sports and orchestral musicians' contracts, taking into consideration the fact that a musician will more often than not become a lifer in the orchestral workplace in contrast to the short-lived careers of professional sports practitioners. Matters related to injury prevention are becoming commonplace issues for contractual consideration at the orchestra, just as they are with athletes.

1.10 SPECIAL EMPLOYMENT RELATIONSHIPS?

Special employment relationships, a major theme in fixed-term sports contracts in the decades following the enactment of the "fixed-term directive" Directive 1999/70/EC,[56] lead to speculation concerning the parallels between the professional sports application and orchestral "fixed-term" contracts discussed with regard to the *Pintus* case in a subsequent *movement*. In Heinz *Müller v. 1*, FSV Mainz 05, the labor court at first instance examined the employment relationship between a top-tier (Bundesliga) club

52. Harald Falckenberg. "The Art World We Deserve?" *Financial Times* April 11, 2014.
53. https://www.laphil.com/about-2/gustavo-dudamel-2/.
54. https://www.digitalconcerthall.com/en/home?utm_source=www.berliner-philharmoniker.de&utm_medium=website&utm_campaign=dropnav&a=bph_webseite&c=true.
55. *Herbert Clayton and Jack Waller Ltd v. Oliver* [1930] AC 209.
56. Council Directive 1999/70/EC concerning the framework agreement on fixed-term work UNICE and CEEP [1999] OJ L 175/43.

and a professional football player finding that there are many specific features that lead to a characterization of special status.

The 36-year-old goalie Heinz Müller was employed by the Bundesliga team Mainz 05 on a fixed-term contract from July 2009 to June 2012. His contract was extended by two years with an option to renew for an additional one-year contract on the condition that he played 23 times with the club's first-level team in 2013-2014. Demoted to the reserve bench in December 2013, Müller never played a single game. He sued the team for loss of salary and extra nonaccrued benefits, monies that he could have earned had he remained on the A-list at Mainz 05's top team. The crux of the dispute was whether his fixed-term employment contracts, agreements that are the rule rather than the exception in professional football, breached protective German legislation under the aforementioned EU directive as he was never provided with the obligatory objective justification for demotion.[57]

At first instance at the Mainz Labor Court, Müller was granted an indefinite contract.[58] The court clarified that although all employment relationships could be construed as "special," professional sport transcended the level of normal employment. "It therefore must be a specificity, the nature of which transcends in an exceptional way the particularities inherent to every (normal) employment relationship, wherein also industry specific features have to be considered."[59] One of the specific features applicable to *Müller* was the high degree of uncertainty concerning the amount of time a player could pursue his career successfully at the club. Uncertainty with regard to an individual player's performance has always been an inseparable element of not only football but sports in general, and for the sake of comparison, for orchestral musicians. To digress for a moment down the musical track, it is entirely possible for a superlative musician to win an audition and gain a coveted seat in an orchestra only to be dismissed within the probationary period, customarily between one and three years:

> That's why orchestras will only offer tenure after a trial period and strict regulations to vet a player before the permanent contract is signed. It is really in everyone's best interest to find a match not only in terms of virtuosity but more importantly, to find a real team player to lend and also to inspire.[60]

An important missing consideration that ultimately swayed *Müller* in another direction on appeal lay within a discussion of the expectations of the club and its fans. If a player cannot meet the high-level demands both mentally and physically on the pitch, this shortcoming could lead to discontent on the part of financial stakeholders and the public at large. The German Labor Court overturned the initial ruling confirming that the special nature of performance-related work in professional sports mandated fixed-term contracts, with age-related physical decline construed as a

57. *Ibid.*
58. *Müller v. 1, FSV Mainz* 05 3 Ca 1197/14.
59. *Ibid.*
60. Conversations with Valerie Heywood, Buffalo Philharmonic principal viola, 1991-2017.

disproportionately important factor for top sports professionals.[61] Age-related factors on the orchestral pitch will lead the discussion in *Greener Pastures*.

Is there competition between orchestral teams?

Aside from media rankings of world orchestras that lead to enhanced revenue in the form of tours and marketing deals for the top-ranked orchestras, there is no such thing as direct confrontational competition between musical entities.[62] An exception to this situation can be found in Europe, where state subsidies still dominate the financing for orchestras. "Orchestras compete for funds from the same subsidy pool as other orchestras. Especially at times of economic crisis we become competitors, this does not create a healthy situation in terms of solidarity."[63] Perhaps relevant to a comparison of sports and music at the professional level would be a consideration of cooperation between different clubs aka orchestras:

> In a professional sports league, a club competes against other clubs in some areas—for example, in the labour market for players' service—but must collude with those competitors within the structure of a league on other commercial aspects of the competition such as the negotiation and sale of media rights, league sponsorship or advertising arrangements.[64]

1.11 WHAT IS A MAJOR OR TOP-TIER ORCHESTRA?

Like sports professionals, orchestral musicians perform in professional ensembles that can be differentiated in terms of size, "reach" and salary. Major or top-tier orchestras are identified by size, reach and salary in addition to music critics' appraisals of that very subjective category, international success. While the RCO was ranked by *Gramophone* magazine as the world's best orchestra in 2008,[65] the winner in 2019 was the Hong Kong Philharmonic, the first Asian orchestra to win such an accolade.[66] For comparative research purposes, less than a dozen critics who often hold strong subjective bias with regard to their "favorites" should not be the final arbiters of the differences between major and "other" orchestras. Perhaps a fairer way to differentiate between orchestras can be taken from the International Conference of Symphony and Opera Musician (ICSOM) consortium of orchestras that differentiate between the orchestras that offer tenured full-time employment to musicians and part-time orchestras that offer per-service payments to a core of musicians and freelancers.[67] Again, the

61. *Heinz Muller v. 1. FSV Mainz 05* 7 AZR 312/16 (January 16, 2018).
62. Conversation with David Bazen, former RCO Director Business Affairs and Media.
63. Conversations with Kees Dijk, Manager RFO and RKF, 2008-2013.
64. Leanne O'Leary. *Employment and Labour Relations Law in the Premier League, NBA and International Rugby Union*. TMC Asser Press 2017, 10.
65. "The World's Leading Critics Rank the World's Leading Orchestras" *Gramophone*, December 2008 available at, https://www.gramophone.co.uk/editorial/the-world%E2%80%99s-greatest-orchestras.
66. Of interest, the music director credited with raising the Hong Kong Philharmonic to its exalted level is the Dutch conductor Jaap van Zweden.
67. https://icsom.org/orchestras/.

definition of what constitutes "full time" is open to further delineation[68] but does serve as a better point of departure than the subjective *Gramophone* criteria.

The Amsterdam-based RCO operates under a unique governance system. Although Dutch legislation mandates the formation of a works council for all enterprises with 50 or more employees,[69] the RCO, "unique in many ways,"[70] is organized as an independently operating foundation, "outside of but respectful of" the codeterminative system in place at all other Dutch orchestras. Unlike all other Dutch orchestras, RCO members do not elect colleagues as representatives on a works council: RCO musicians are empowered through board membership. Eleven members take their places on the Board (Verenigingsbestuur) with three positions occupied by musicians elected by their fellow orchestra members. At the top of the operational pyramid, a triumvirate of administrators, a Managing Director, a Director of Business Affairs and Media, and a Director of Artistic Affairs take charge of managerial, financial, and artistic duties.[71]

1.12 ONE LAST SPORTS-MUSIC-RELATED STOPOVER WITH RELEVANCE TO COLLECTIVE BARGAINING

In the US, multiple employer bargaining encompasses employment situations in which several (a minimum of two) independent employers collectively bargain or negotiate jointly through an agent, committee, or association with one or more labor organizations who represent all of the employees of the "multiple" employers regarding the mandatory subjects of collective bargaining. Before considering if the non-statutory exemption could be reinterpreted to apply to collective bargaining in the orchestral field, a definition of the term will be followed by a discussion of a leading US precedent, *Brown*.[72] The following paragraphs attempt to scrutinize and reassess a particular labor exemption, the non-statutory exemption that is commonplace in the US when multi-employer bargaining takes place. Within sports leagues such as the Major League Baseball Players Association (MLB), the union that represents major league baseball players, and the National Football League (NFL), the bargaining units engaging in collective labor agreements usually do not reach beyond an organization or company's employees/staff members. Rarely do bargaining units embrace multiemployer bargaining, which involves simultaneous bargaining actions with multiple employers.

As an antidote to antitrust, the non-statutory labor exemption entered the sports arena, thanks to the judiciary: the brightest star in that constellation was *Brown*.

US courts had long struggled to delineate the boundaries of the non-statutory labor exemption as it relates to the sports sector where leagues have been embroiled in long-standing litigation related to multiemployer bargaining units. *Brown* involved

68. The number of weeks is less significant than the annual minimum salary as some 52-week orchestras pay less than 40-week season orchestras, *see* https://www.americanorchestras.org/.
69. Article 2, Dutch Works Councils Act (*Wet op de ondernemingsraden*) [WOR] 1998.
70. Conversations with Joel Fried, former Artistic Director RCO.
71. http://www.concertgebouworkest.nl/en/orchestra/Staff/.
72. *Brown v. Pro Football, Inc.*, 116 S. Ct. 2116 (1996).

groups of rookies (recruits), taxi squads (TSs),[73] and professional football players who collectively rejected a proposal by the powerful NFL management to cap their salaries. The NFL team owners proposed to cap salaries at $1,000 a week, a 75% salary cut for most of the players. Despite protests and threatened legal actions on the part of the rookies, the NFL imposed the salary cap. The rookies sued, claiming that the NFL was conspiring to restrain trade in violation of federal antitrust law. In a country where football is the lifeblood, it came as no surprise to legal pundits that the Supreme Court of the United States (SCOTUS) granted certiorari. The majority holding went to the core of national non-statutory exemptions. Justice Breyer opined:

> [t]he non-statutory exemption has its source in the strong labor policy favoring the association of employees to eliminate competition over wages and working conditions. Union success in organizing workers and standardizing wages ultimately will affect price competition among employers, but the goals of federal labor law could never be achieved if this effect on business competition were held a violation of the antitrust laws.[74]

Citing precedents, SCOTUS underlined the relevance of the imperative non-statutory antitrust exemption "that applies where needed to make the collective bargaining process work."[75] Beyond the playing fields, multiemployer bargaining was deemed an efficient, effective, and above all legal means to level the playing field in terms of work conditions and keep what the SCOTUS termed "industrial peace."[76]

Stepping out on a comparative limb, this collective approach of offering employees common contract terms bears similarity to the Dutch system of orchestral bargaining where musician-employees in state-subsidized orchestras are contracted under comparable terms. In the Netherlands, collective bargaining for most orchestras[77] takes place between social partners (unions) and the *Vereniging van Nederlandse Orkesten* (Association of Dutch Orchestras, VvNO).[78] For their US colleagues, collective bargaining for orchestras is individualized and painstaking: "none of us seem to be created equal when it comes to the bargaining table, although rest assured, the top orchestras are all acutely aware of what goes on elsewhere in the country especially when it comes to salaries and benefits."[79] Taking into consideration the distinct nature of orchestral financing in the US that finds one orchestra in solvency and another in financial peril, a consideration of a more collaborative, unified approach to collective bargaining that mirrors the Dutch approach could be beneficial. "Personally, from experience at the

73. In the vernacular of NFL football taxi squads: "ten-man squads where you would place players who are not ready to play on the gridiron. What they gain is valuable practice time with the active roster that helps mold or break them," https://dynastyfootballfactory.com/taxi-squads-and-how-they-improve-your-league/.
74. *Brown*, *supra*, 237.
75. *Connell Constr. Co. v. Plumbers*, 421 US 616, 622 (1975).
76. *National Labor Relations Board v. Truck Drivers Local Union Nr. 449*, 353 US 87 (1957); *Charles D. Bonanno Linen Service v. National Labor Relations Board*, 454 US 404 (1982) at 412.
77. Agreements for the Netherlands Radio Philharmonic Orchestra (RFO) and the Metropole Orchestra are bargained separately from other subsidized Dutch orchestras.
78. https://vvno.nl/english.html.
79. Conversations with Jonathan Sherwin, Cleveland Orchestra contrabassoonist, former chair of the musicians negotiating committee.

bargaining table, this idea seems like another academic exercise; we had several of those at the San Francisco Symphony with consensus-building experiments back in the early years of 2000. I remain skeptical about applying CBAs to more than one orchestra at a time."[80] The *FAQs* to follow describe "how we play," before subsequent *movements* explore how they pay.

1.13 MUSICIANS, MAESTROS, MANAGERS, AND OTHER KEY PLAYERS

A plethora of historians and musicologists have opined on the origins of the modern-day orchestra and put forth different theories as to the when and where of its inception. Several schools of thought bring the orchestra back in time to ancient history, while others focus on the development of the orchestra as a collective post-16th century. Musicologists tend to agree that the "modern" orchestra with its complement of approximately hundred musicians is a product of the 19th century.

To the naked eye and/or ear, the differences between modern US orchestras and their Dutch counterparts are minimal. The 21st-century orchestra consists of between 95 and 110 musicians divided into strings, winds, brass, and percussion sections. Regardless of their geographical location, orchestral musicians fulfill similar roles. Their core business consists of rehearsals, performances, recording sessions and tours. Conductors holding titles such as maestro, music director and/or chief conductor reign over musical matters, while managers and artistic administrators run the daily affairs of the orchestra-as-institution throughout the world. Yet, whereas US orchestras are beholden to corporate and individual philanthropy for funding, the fortunes of their European counterparts depend on state and regional subsidies. Before entering a discussion on "the way they pay" and the labyrinth of issues in the staffing and functioning of the orchestral entity on both sides of the Atlantic—issues that run the gamut from orchestral finances, employment conditions, legislative protection for musicians and the new force of musicians' platforms joining with established unions to promulgate change—I will discuss the inner workings of "the way we play."

1.14 BASIC DIFFERENCES BETWEEN ORCHESTRAS: OF SALARIES AND SERVICES

To fully understand the complexities of employment in orchestras, it is important to understand that regardless of geographical location, there are great differences between full-time orchestras that offer salaries to their musicians and per-service orchestras that pay musicians for the benchmark unit of their work: the service. The term "service" refers to rehearsals, concert performances and recording sessions. To answer the FAQ, "how long is a service?" the simple answer is somewhere between two and three hours, often dependent on the collectively bargained contract between

80. Conversations with Steven Braunstein, San Francisco Symphony contrabassoonist, former negotiating committee member.

the orchestra and its musicians. Both US and Dutch orchestral contracts stipulate the maximum number of services per work week.

In the US and Canada, collective agreements are predicated on a service model under the aegis of the American Federation of Musicians (AFM). An orchestral musician's workweek is calculated in terms of services (rehearsals, as well as performances, constitute services, with contractually defined maximum hours set for each). Generally, according to the definitions provided in orchestral CBAs: "Services are a unit of work upon which wages are based. Each rehearsal as well as each performance constitutes one service."[81] Exceptions to the general "service" definition can be found in combination services such as "back-to-back" educational concerts that take place within a two-and-a-half- hour time period. The current US maximum is eight services per week, comparable to the Dutch maximum. Full-time contracted musicians are paid salaries based on the eight-service week regardless of whether or not all services are accounted for in the work week. While different CBAs show evidence of different forms of daily scheduling, in the USA all CBAs limit the number of services per day to two services.

1.15 DUTCH ORCHESTRAS: HOURS VERSUS SERVICES

An entire dissertation could be devoted to a statistical presentation of the algorithms used to calculate how service minutes/hours are determined. At the time of writing, the Dutch unions are devoting time and energy to negotiate orchestral musicians' CAOs[82] with clearly defined "breaks" and pauses in the rehearsal schedule. "One of the challenges in negotiating Dutch orchestral CAOs is the switch from counting rehearsals within a schedule to what we call 'urenberekening' determining how hours are calculated and paid for."[83] A point of contention for freelancers and substitute players is that they are paid according to the actual number of services played in their "work week." The calculation of what constitutes a service can be a bone of contention for litigation, as illustrated by a mediated dispute, *Kunstenbond v. Netherlands Philharmonic Orchestra* (NedPhO) 2020 in which the assessment of rehearsal hours, pre-concert breaks, dress rehearsals, run-throughs and the appropriate payments for freelance substitute players forms the basis of the legal issues presented.[84]

In recent years, CAOs in the Netherlands have moved from a service model of calculation to an hourly calculation with extra hours calculated for individual preparation (instrumental practice) time, referred to as the *forfait*. Much controversy surrounds this manner of calculation as musicians perceive the hourly model as an excuse for managers to maximize, or in the words of musicians, "squeeze every hour out of us" with their "efficiency" coming at a high cost in terms of musicians' time and

81. Definition taken from US orchestral CBAs generously provided by the American Federation of Musicians (AFM).
82. The Dutch equivalent to a collective bargaining agreement (CBA) is the Collectieve arbeidsovereenkomst (CAO).
83. Conversations with Mark Gerrits, Kunstenbond.
84. The author served as cochair of the independent committee (vastecommissie Nederlandse Orkesten) responsible to mediate resolution of this dispute.

energy. Criticism of the *forfait* and its central role as an employment personnel "filler" abound in the Dutch press showing support for the following viewpoint:

> You have a hard core of permanent employees that you can never get rid of even if they do not do a lick of work because of the nature of rigidly "hammered out" CAOs. And you have a large contingent of hard-working self-employed and flexible workers who you can dump in the event of a setback. They bear, as it were, the business risk that the company itself no longer wants to bear. If these flexible workers lose their work, there is no safety net in place for them.[85]

This inquiry is primarily concerned with salary-based orchestras (the top-tier of US orchestras, and the main state-subsidized orchestras in the Netherlands), but the varieties of highly precarious hybrid and per-service orchestras deserve mention: these so-called pickup groups operate under a variety of flexible agreements and methods of payment. In the US, orchestras in the more protected salary-based category offer a minimum weekly wage to contracted musicians under a CBA regardless of whether or not the musicians perform in that given week. Freelancers who are given short-term contracts are compensated on a per-service basis. In the Netherlands, salary-based orchestras calculate yearly and monthly "work hours" based on the length of services per week, and freelancers fall under a separate collectively bargained agreement to be discussed in detail later in this study.

1.16 PER-SERVICE ORCHESTRAS

Per-service orchestras proffer fixed-rate employment to musicians based on the number of services an individual musician plays and do not offer either the salary guarantees or benefits accorded to musicians who work under CBAs. If a per-service orchestra programs music that necessitates the use of two harp players, these two musicians will be paid for the number of services they play but certainly not for "harp-less" weeks. This differentiation between salaried and per-service orchestras is of considerable import when adding freelancers into the equation: all musicians in a per-service orchestra could be considered freelancers as these orchestras hold no obligation to rehire musicians. The exception in the per-service category is the hybrid orchestra that hires a small core of musicians on salary and the remainder of the musicians on a per-service, on-call basis. Even if legislation stipulates that the employer and the employee must behave in a manner that befits a reasonable and fair employer and a reasonable and fair employee (*see* Article 7:611 Dutch Civil Code (DCC)), there is little security for vulnerable freelance substitutes musicians in a saturated market:

85. Teun van de Keuken. "De flexibele schil is het smerigste begrip uit het bedrijfsleven" *Volkskrant* 14 juni 2020. In Dutch: "je hebt een harde kern van vaste medewerkers waar je door dichtgetimmerde cao's nooit vanaf kunt, ook al voeren ze geen lor uit, en een groot contingent keihard werkende zzp'ers en flexwerknemers die je kunt dumpen bij tegenslag. Zij dragen als het ware het bedrijfsrisico dat het bedrijf zelf niet meer wil dragen. Als ze werkloos worden is er nauwelijks een vangnet" (author's translation).

conducting at Leonard Bernstein's request while serving as concertmaster of the RCO.[92]

1.20 HOW IS THE SIZE OF AN ORCHESTRA DETERMINED? WHAT IS THE "COMPLEMENT"?

Post-2007-2008 crisis, the complement, the term that refers to the size of the orchestra with a focus on the number of players employed to perform in each section, has been bitterly contested as real-life cases in the Netherlands and the United States will demonstrate. The size of the complement featured prominently in the Atlanta Symphony Orchestra's (ASO's) shortlist of problematic issues that figured significantly in labor disputes culminating in the 2012 and 2015 lockouts. In the Netherlands, the size of the complement was a key restructuring factor in the orchestral reorganization at the Dutch Broadcasting Music Center (Muziekcentrum van de Omroep, MCO) in 2012-2013. The parties responsible for making the cuts that resulted in reorganizations in both jurisdictions waxed eloquent on decisions as to "how to cut the number of players efficiently without destroying the orchestra"[93] and put forth theories to back up the assumption that "you can keep an orchestra alive with a core of committed players."[94] Musician responses to the hatchet men and women who make such decisions provide evidence of unanimous antipathy: "whittling down an orchestra whatever the method[95] is an anti-musical and inhumane operation not only on the personal-personnel front but in terms of what actually happens musically to the ensemble, no matter how it is undertaken."[96] Commentary from the US points to the fact that reliance on a "small core" is merely an excuse for the musical ensemble in question to depend on cheaper, freelance labor to fulfill orchestral obligations.

1.21 THE COMPLEMENT THROUGHOUT HISTORY

The following section aims to chart the complement through a consideration of historical, artistic, and pecuniary factors to detail the issues that play into this "hot" bargaining and reorganization-related topic. Musical, technical, and economic considerations determine the number of musicians employed, and there lies the problem: if the Board or in the Dutch variants management dictated by subsidy constraints opt to cut corners and balance the budget, the first cuts usually fall in terms of the number of musicians

92. Jaap van Zweden's first encounter with conducting on Leonard Bernstein's request, *New York Times*, https://www.nytimes.com/2016/01/28/arts/music/new-york-philharmonic-taps-jaap-van-zweden-as-its-next-maestro.html.
93. Conversations with Ella Broekstra HRM Director Stichting Omroep Muziek (SOM) Dutch Broadcasting Foundation.
94. Conversations with Piet van Gennip, formerly senior staffer at Berenschot and Director, Het Ballet Orkest (Dutch Ballet Orchestra) since 2013.
95. In the Netherlands, "kaasschaaf" (cheese slicer) was used to denote a restructuring in which the cuts were equally shared by all sections/departments, the Dutch terms "*pondspondsgewijze*" (a questionable translation, a pound of flesh) has been used to characterize this method of cutback.
96. Conversations with Frans Brüggen, musician extraordinaire.

employed. The Atlanta Symphony, Detroit Symphony, the Dutch radio orchestras, and Holland Symfonia's transition to Het Ballet Orkest provide recent post-crisis examples of dramatic complement cuts. To fully understand the complexity of this issue, it is important to review the changes over time concerning the size of the orchestra.

Throughout history, the question "how large is an orchestra?" has been met with ambiguous answers. Dependent variables such as where the orchestra performs, who pays for the orchestra and the demands of the composer's score are all factors. In addition, there are maestros who attempt to recreate a certain sound that might call for more players as opposed to those who pare down a string section in search of another type of sound. The composer's intention as marked in the score is considered to be the historically sacrosanct point of departure. If a score calls for three flutes and one piccolo, it would be obviously undesirable to perform the piece with fewer musicians. Yet, the situation is not often clear as some composers did not make precise notations, whereas others deliberately left interpretation to the imagination. And more complications arise when we focus on the string section as few composers have specified the exact number of strings intended to perform their compositions. Igor Stravinsky, a 20th-century composer renowned for his meticulous approach to score writing, was notorious for conducting his compositions in totally different ways at each and every performance.[97] Thus, there is a degree of serendipity with regard to a focused adherence to the composer's score-based requirements. How does this translate to the complement? As the brief historical recapitulation below uncovers, this too is open to interpretation. A historically informed performance of a Mozart symphony calls for far fewer string players than a performance of the same symphony in a large concert hall given in modern style.

The growth in terms of the complement from the salon-size orchestras of the 18th century to the large symphony orchestras of the late 19th and 20th centuries is inextricably linked to the rise of the new bourgeoisie: the middle class eager to make its mark in a social context. The call for concert halls as a center for cultural activity in the mid-1800s was heard on both sides of the Atlantic as opera performances and orchestra concerts became the place to be seen and heard. The creation of new performance venues in the form of sizeable concert halls went hand-in-hand with market-related demands that prompted composers to create masterworks to please both the performers and their audiences in increasingly larger spaces. The 19th-century development toward an expanded complement of orchestral musicians continued through the early 20th century. Gustav Mahler conducted the premiere performance of his Symphony No. 8, the *Symphony of a Thousand* in 1910 with a staggering number of performers, 858 singers and 171 instrumentalists onstage. Musicologists are of the opinion that the supersized dimensions of Mahler's colossal composition were based on his exposure to US halls and orchestras. "*Fortissimo*, finally."[98]

97. Erica Buxbaum commenting on Stravinsky's interpretations. "We cannot unquestionably accept either his metronome markings or his own recorded performance tempi as reliable guidelines." *"Stravinsky, Tempo and Le Sacre"* 1998, 11.
98. Reputedly uttered upon experiencing the great falls at Niagara. Alan Ross. *The Rest is Noise* 2006 http://www.therestisnoise.com/2006/01/the_niagara_for.html.

1.22 IS THERE A CORRELATION BETWEEN COMPLEMENT AND OUTPUT?

Economist James Gapinski opined that since audiences do not perceive the difference between the contribution of a single second violin to the total output of an orchestra, the possibility of staging a concert without that second violinist is possible and economically advantageous.[99] To complete his analysis, Professor Gapinski studied the second violin section, frequently maligned within the orchestra for its subservience to the first violin section and role of lesser importance, a viewpoint that carries little weight taking the musical score into consideration. Professor Gapinski's focus on output elasticity leads us down a slippery slope with regard to the size of the orchestral complement. The 2014 lockout at the Atlanta Symphony Orchestra (ASO) spurred headlines such as: "[o]rchestra's size is the big issue."[100] Musicians supported by music directors consider the complement as sacrosanct, within the ambit of artistic decision-making.

Reflecting on the cutbacks and compromises that traumatize orchestral negotiations in today's musical world, is it possible to posit that player reduction is another means to an end in restructuring the orchestra to fit into a pared-down economic structure? In July 2012, the complement demise hit the world-famous Philadelphia Orchestra. Emerging from Chapter 11 bankruptcy, the musicians referred to by classical music fans as the famous Philadelphians accepted a 15% pay cut, a hiring freeze for open positions, and a reduction of the complement by 10 players. This reduction became a common discordant theme in orchestras across the US and Europe, as case studies illustrate.

An ongoing topic of hot debate for orchestras faced with subsidy cuts in the Netherlands relates to the complement. "The trend is not only a US phenomenon, but I fear, here to stay in the lowlands since cuts rather than spending is the way of cultural life."[101] The orchestral constellation in the Netherlands has shrunk from 21 orchestras pre-crisis to 10 subsidized orchestras in 2018. The complement issue was bitterly contested during the most recent reorganization of the orchestras under the aegis of the Dutch Broadcasting Music Foundation as the *Requiem movement* details.

1.23 COMPENSATION, PAY RAISES AND PRINCIPAL PAY

Within most organizations, salary compensation structures are divided into pay scales and pay spines. Pay scales are comparative and show what an employee who performs similar work at a different parallel organization earns, whereas the pay spine shows rates of pay for employees with respect to factors including pay increases over time and pay associated with different levels within an organization. Regardless of terminology,

---

99. James Gapinski. "The Production of Culture" *Review of Economics and Statistics* 62(4) 1980, 578-586 DOI: 10.2307/1924782.
100. https://www.myajc.com/blog/arts-culture/orchestra-size-resonates-big-issue-atlanta-symphony-dispute/3HfL5VSC2dBpXObUQFscpJ/.
101. Comments by Hein Glaubitz.

a closer look at pay spine determinants for orchestral musicians in the US and the Netherlands shows that musicians who enter orchestras as rank-and-file payers (US terminology "section" players as opposed to higher paid "principals," "leaders" or other "named and ranked positions") benefit from limited progression along pay spines. Salary gains might be found if there is a cost-of-living salary adjustment but otherwise pay scales are graded according to years of service and not according to other merit-based components. Even for tenured orchestral musicians, the chances of significant advancement are limited in the orchestral profession. To make the leap from section player to principal involves participation in the highly competitive audition process, and "perhaps the toughest thing a musician could ever undertake is playing for his/her colleagues at an audition, a real 'no mercy' situation. If one fails, you get to face all your colleagues at work at the next morning's rehearsal."[102]

Standard US orchestral CBA and Dutch CAO clauses contain variations that define principal players:

> A "principal position" is defined as "the first chair position in each of the following sections": "first violin, second violin, viola, cello, double bass, flute, oboe, clarinet, bassoon, horn, trumpet, trombone, tuba, tympani, percussion, and harp."[103]

To outsiders, the orchestral workplace might seem confusing in terms of hierarchy and succession. In contrast to the corporate world where the "line of succession" is often clear, orchestra sub-principals hold titles such as associate, assistant and even assistant associate and first associate principals.[104] Importantly, these players do not automatically become principals unless of course they win the audition for a principal position and their salaries do not reach the "personal negotiation" level attained by the principals.

Principals are important not only in terms of their musical responsibilities based on the composer's score but also in terms of their powers as section leaders. Often principals assert leadership when differences of musical opinion such as how to interpret the conductor's demands come to the fore to ensure uniformity of execution and sound within the group. Needless to say, principal players exercise considerable influence as to who is suitable to join "their" section during the audition process. *Of Rowe and Race* underscores that certain individual principal orchestral musicians negotiate separate terms specific to their personal contracts, whereas section players receive CBA-determined scale wages. According to Dutch CAOs, principal pay is regulated contractually and capped at approximately 20% overscale versus section players' pay.

The comparison between US and Dutch orchestras breaks down somewhat when taking pay differentials among state-subsidized orchestras in the Netherlands into consideration. Members of leading orchestras in Berlin and Vienna earn salaries

102. Conversations with a RCO member post-principal audition, anonymity assured.
103. *See*, for example, Art. 3.1.c(1) Colorado Symphony CBA 2017, available upon request at ICSOM.
104. Consult the online rosters of top-tier US orchestras.

commensurate with the top US orchestras,[105] but orchestral musicians in the Netherlands earn substantially less. "The explanation relates to the state and/or municipality's consideration of the orchestra's importance in the largest 'national' sense. For Vienna, its orchestras are its lifeblood. For Amsterdam, its great orchestra is just another cultural jewel, like its museums, opera, etc.; special, yes but not deserving of sizeable extra support."[106] The internationally renowned Royal Concertgebouw Orchestra (RCO) occupies a unique status within the Dutch constellation of orchestras: its musician members earn approximately 20% more than colleagues in the other subsidized (BIS) orchestras.[107] To compare orchestral salaries in the Netherlands to US orchestral salaries becomes even more complicated when taking into account the costs of different taxation schemes, cost-of-living indices and earning potential. As semi-civil servants whose musical activities are state-subsidized, Dutch orchestral salaries are subject to governmental salary controls. "I have been a member (section) for about twenty years. Before tax, my monthly income is €5.040 (US $6,000). Of this, almost half goes to taxes. Extras are €1.000/year (before tax) for recordings and radio/tv recordings, 8% holiday pay (of course that is also taxed), per diem when on tour plus an occasional extra compensation/bonus."[108] Ballpark analysis: RCO members earn less than half of what their major league US orchestral counterparts earn.

Strings attached: the professional orchestral workplace

1.24 *"GOOD LABOR MANAGEMENT IS A PORT IN YOUR STORM."*[109]

In the US, the relationship between orchestral management and orchestral musicians is a contractual relationship set out in a collective bargaining agreement (CBA), often referred to as a master agreement applicable to the contracted musicians and negotiated between the union, representatives of the orchestra and management.[110] Typically a CBA covers a three-year period, and generally the musicians' union represents US musicians with bargaining powers granted to the local branches, referred to as "locals." Virtually all orchestra musicians in the US are employed under the terms of a CBA. The federal National Labor Relations Act (NLRA)[111] governs collective bargaining between unionized employees and employers with notable exemptions such as the "supervisory" exception that will occupy much of the discussion in a subsequent *movement*.

Whereas collective bargaining in Europe is commonly conducted on an industry-wide basis, in the US, SCOTUS has upheld the notion of distinctions between

105. Section players in the Berlin Philharmonic earn a monthly base salary (extra holiday bonuses and many other financial perks including a 13th month payment) just under the equivalent of $10,000 per month.
106. Conversations with Harald Eggebrecht, Munich-based musicologist, and critic.
107. The principal orchestras in the Netherlands are granted a basic infrastructure state subsidy (BIS).
108. RCO's CBA 2016-2017 44, corroborates the quote *Slipped Disc*, https://slippedisc.com/2018/05/what-a-player-earns-in-the-concertgebouw/.
109. Allison Beck, Deputy Director Federal Mediation and Conciliation speech, Federation International Musicians (FIM) Conference, Montreal 2017.
110. US orchestral CBAs are often referred to as master agreements.
111. National Labor Relations Act; NLRA; 29 USC §§ 151-169.

mandatory, permissive and illegal subjects of bargaining as specified in a 1981 holding: "Congress had no intention that the elected union representative would become an equal partner in the running of the business enterprise."[112] The National Labor Relations Board (NLRB) guidelines as to subject matter in each category show that a fine line could be drawn between the three categories and specific rules applied to each category.[113] For example, changes cannot be made to a mandatory bargaining subject on the part of the employer unless the union is given prior pre-bargaining notice. Employers and/or unions cannot refuse to bargain over mandatory subjects related to employment, e.g., benefits and wages, not to mention initiating industrial actions such as lockouts and strikes.

Volumes have been devoted to the many flavors of bargaining in the US workplace.[114] Of special interest to orchestral bargaining in the US has been a focus on what academics and orchestral managers found to be the highly desirable form of "soft-touch" bargaining adopted with the encouragement of Professor Mnookin by the San Francisco Symphony in the bargaining cycle that followed a bitter 10-week strike.[115] From inside the symphony and its committee:

> The 1996 negotiation was extreme, and using Interest Based Bargaining (IBB) was viewed as extreme by many members of the orchestra, and I presume some of the Administration and Board as well. The 2005 negotiation featured a struggle between the orchestra members who wanted to proceed again (as planned) with IBB and the ones who did not trust the process and wanted to dump it. The dumpers won, I was on the committee, and it was the most difficult time of my career... the use of IBB was more or less an aberration: before and after we have used the typical adversarial negotiations with varying degrees of success.[116]

Managers place a great deal of emphasis on management-rights clauses in CBAs. A standard clause such as "[R]etains the sole and exclusive right to manage; to direct its employees; to evaluate performance ... to discipline and discharge for just cause, to adopt and enforce rules and regulations and policies and procedures; [and] to set and establish standards of performance for employees"[117] gives the employer the right to take action on certain terms of employment, thus evading the obligation to bargain with the union. "These clauses are often broad enough to cover situations in which management has to move quickly on a subject, however it is difficult to determine where the permissible management action crosses over into a no-go area."[118] In 2016, the NLRB held that an employer is required to provide considerable specificity in a

112. *First National Maintenance Corp. v. NLRB* 452 US 666 (1981).
113. https://www.usw.org/workplaces/public-sector/2015-conference-material/5-Subjects-of-Bargaining.pdf.
114. Voices from the 19th century, Sidney Webb and Beatrice Webb, *see* "The Method of Collective Bargaining," 1896, 1-29.
115. Robert Mnookin with Gary Friedman and Joel Cutcher-Gershenfeld. "A New Direction: Transforming Relations Within the San Francisco Symphony," *Harmony* 13 2001, 1-26.
116. Conversations with Steven Braunstein.
117. Standard US management-rights clause.
118. Conversations with orchestral employment specialist Kevin Case.

management-rights clause before the Board finds that the union unequivocally waived its right to bargain over the action in question.[119]

As mentioned above and painted with a broad brush, Dutch orchestras have been shaped by a strong tradition of co-determination and employee involvement supported by government and local (both provincial and municipal) subsidies. National sectoral agreements and orchestral CAOs are bargained between union representatives and orchestral management in concert with the individual orchestras' works councils composed of elected musician members. A closer examination of post-2007-2008 financial crisis orchestral cuts on the Dutch front will show that there are marked differences in financing and the role of the Board versus their US counterpart orchestras.

1.25 NO ONE SIZE FITS ALL: DISHARMONY AT THE BARGAINING TABLE

Decision-making in the orchestral setting differs between the US and the Netherlands. In the Netherlands, pay and certain specific benefits exemplified by sick leave, free days and pension are regulated by sectoral agreements. In the US, beyond federal and state legislated minimum requirements, "benefits and pay are the main points of bargaining contention, what makes for fists pounding tables as orchestras negotiate pay, pensions, and all the key employment issues every few years."[120]

In the US, the orchestral CBA sets forth a contract between the employer and the negotiating union, the local affiliate of the American Federation of Musicians (AFM). It came as a great surprise to discover that many US professional orchestral musicians assumed that the CBA arranged the relationship between management and musicians. This particular section heading deserves emphasis as negotiations at the US orchestral workplace have changed and are changing, dependent on financial issues and the introduction of new "players" within the bargaining process. From a "servant of the music, servant to the maestro" pre-1960s, US musicians moved from an invisible role in deciding crucial employment issues to playing a defining role. A summary of high points from the struggle for musicians' participation ensues.

Prior to the 1960s, the watershed decade for US orchestras, orchestral musicians in only one orchestra, the Boston Symphony Orchestra (BSO), took part in contract negotiations alongside union representatives. It was unheard of to have attorneys at the negotiating table, and final contracts were not subject to players' approval. The archives of major US orchestras exemplified by the considerable online offerings available on the New York Philharmonic's library website offer ample documentation to support the statement that musicians were indeed subordinates not only regarding individual employment but also regarding basic collective issues such as salary, work schedules and holidays.[121]

---

119. *Graymont PA Inc.* 364 NLRB No. 37 (June 29, 2016).
120. Conversations with Jonathan Sherwin.
121. *Constitution of the Philharmonic Society of New York* adopted April 1842, https://archives.nyphil.org/index.php/artifact/db938eeb-006a-4c08-b3a5-c5526a251b83-0.1/fullview#page/2/mode/2up.

For US-based orchestral musicians, the role of the NLRB, whose jurisdiction under the National Labor Relations Act (NLRA) covers all establishments whose operations affect interstate commerce, is of paramount importance as subsequent *movements* reveal. With regard to orchestras, "the Board exercises jurisdiction over symphony orchestras which have a gross annual revenue from all sources (excluding only contributions which are because of limitations by the grantor not available for use for operating expenses) of not less than $1 million."[122] The road to collective bargaining for orchestral musicians in the US was rocky to say the least following the amendments to the NLRA under the Taft-Hartley Act (THA),[12329] a subject that will be fully explored in subsequent *movements*. Although orchestras were unionized by the mid-20th century and the closed-shop principle of "no union, no orchestral membership" prevailed, the orchestra as a nonprofit organization was effectively barred from NLRA coverage until the Rochester Symphony was beset by unfair labor practices and the NLRB reversed its previous rulings by deciding to extend its ambit to include orchestras.[12482]

1.26 WHO PAYS FOR AN ORCHESTRA?

> The US is the only country in the world today where the fortunes of most symphony orchestras depend on the generosity, the wisdom, the enthusiasm, indeed the musical tastes and policies of bankers, oil men, meatpackers, merchants and housewives.[125]
>
> In practically all of the civilized nations of the world, the United States excepted, symphony orchestras and opera companies are given government support, and this is a tradition of hundreds of years standing.[126]

Despite the nonpolitically correct notions of "civilized nations" and "oil men," there is more than a grain of truth in the quotes above, which date back to the late 1960s and 1970s. In the *Follow the Money intermezzo,* the financial sources of the orchestra in the 21st century will be examined through several lenses, a criticism of US nonprofit boards during crisis periods at the orchestra, a reconsideration of the Baumol-Bowen "cost disease" theory and its effect on the orchestra and an examination of ephemeral subsidies post-crisis. For a *FAQ* section, other answers are needed to supplement "the way they play" with "the way they pay." Most people who posed the questions that inform this *movement* believe that orchestras pay a good deal of their own expenses.

Yet, statistics supplied by the League of American Orchestras show that top-tier orchestras account for a mere 2 % of the 1,600 orchestras operating in the United States.

122. NLRB Rules and Regulations, §103.2 38 F.R. 6176.
123. 29 USC. §§141-197, the Taft-Hartley Act 1947. The THA restricted the reach of the NRA and set forth a series of unfair labor practices.
124. 82 L.R.R.M. 1519 (1973).
125. Ernest Fleischmann Director Los Angeles Philharmonic, 1969-1998. Quote originally published in *High Fidelity* 1969, requoted in *The Guardian* June 15, 2010.
126. Hope Stoddard. "Subsidy under the American System" in George Albert Seltzer, *The Professional Symphony Orchestra in the United States: An Anthology*. Scarecrow 1975, 390.

US orchestras depend on endowments, corporate sponsorship, and individual donors with a limited amount of funding from municipal and/or state sources; European orchestras are primarily state-funded.

Contrary to the US cultural support system strongly rooted in private and corporate philanthropy, orchestras in the Netherlands like other European cultural organizations are primarily financed through public sector subsidies in a mixed bag of state and municipal subsidies. The principal orchestras gain funding through the basic infrastructure subsidies (BIS) that provide the endowment for an ever-decreasing number of orchestras. Dutch radio orchestras founded at the end of WWII[127] were funded traditionally through radio and tv license fees and the public media budget. The demise of government funding for public broadcasting in the Netherlands is a book unto itself and is the focus of the *Requiem for an orchestra movement*.

Of specific interest within a *FAQ* section are the changes in overall cultural policy related to arts funding in the Netherlands with special regard to orchestral funding. Reacting to the financial crisis with a call for increased "entrepreneurship" on the part of orchestras (and by extension other cultural organizations) and linking national resources to the need for "other players" to step in and support the arts (other players serving as a euphemism for private giving), the approach reflected an Americanization of Dutch cultural policy.[128] One of the leitmotifs that course through this investigation particularly relevant to the *Requiem movement* relates to political changes of heart that devaluated the importance of culture as a public good in the Netherlands, leading directly to massive culture subsidy cuts.

1.27 WHO RUNS THE ORCHESTRAL SHOW: THE TROIKA?

> Orchestras are structured in a rather dysfunctional way.[129]
>
> People do not buy tickets for managers to play concerts.[130]

Henry Fogel, former President of the Chicago Symphony Orchestra, masterminded many instructive articles on orchestral administration for the now-defunct publication *Harmony*. In an article published at the dawn of the new millennium, he likened the orchestral organization to a three-legged stool in which the music director, the executive director and the Board chairman carry equal responsibility for the orchestra.[131] When music directors spend considerable amounts of time with their musicians with an ear for active development, the orchestra's playing and even the musicians' attitude to performance improve, as noted by managers and music critics.

127. The Dutch radio orchestras founded in 1945 have endured multiple reorganizations.
128. *De Staat van Cultuur: Lancering Cultuur-index Nederland*. Boekmanstichting/ 2013 and *Meedoen is de Kunst*, Raad van Cultuur 2014, https://www.cultuur.nl/upload/documents/adviezen/Meedoen_is_de_kunst-def.pdf.
129. Attributed to Peter Pastreich, a US orchestral management insider; CEO/GM for many US orchestras, recently, the San Francisco Symphony.
130. Attributed to Tom Morris, former Chief Executive Cleveland Orchestra.
131. Henry Fogel. "Are Three Legs Appropriate? Or Even Sufficient?" *Harmony* 10 2000, 11-34.

There is consensus concerning the inherent, built-in tension in the relationship between the members of the troika. For example, as many cases taken from the orchestral field illustrate, although a solid board of directors can pledge and guarantee the finances that lead to the musicians' well-being, in many situations, the Board's influence extends to other important areas of the orchestral organization, including operational and artistic decision-making. Turning to the music director in the era of the absentee maestro shows that a knowledgeable and dependable managing director is crucial to set the direction for the orchestral output. The orchestra's leadership troika—the board chair, the music director, and the managing director—are unlikely to be automatically aligned. Adding to troika-musician tensions is a tendency that has been observed within US orchestral management circles in times of financial crisis. Where old-time managers sought to achieve a balance between musical and financial matters, modern-day executive directors opt to "manage up," currying favor with the Board relegating the musicians to second place.[132]

The legal relationship between an orchestra and its musicians is based on the overarching concept of employment, which can be defined fundamentally as the exchange of wages for service provided by an individual employee to the employer. The number of different answers to what appears to be a simple question never ceases to amaze: the dichotomy between the contractually determined legal relationships and the experiences of musicians from inside the orchestra is substantial. "We often feel that although we hold a contract in our hands, the respect for that contract depends on the whim of board members and management."[133]

A comparison of the Dallas Symphony CBA to the NL CAO for the majority of Dutch orchestras uncovers relevant convergences and differences with regard to employment conditions for orchestral musicians. The recently bargained Dutch orchestral freelance CAO will be analyzed on its own merits in a subsequent *movement*, as there is no parallel CBA for freelancers in US orchestras with the exception of the Associates, substitute players at the premier opera orchestra, the Metropolitan Opera Orchestra (The MET), who work under a special contract that provides pay and benefits almost commensurate to the regular MET scale.

Most orchestral CBAs include: audition procedures, benefits such as health insurance and pensions, definitions, and specifications of services (rehearsal/concert length, breaks, scheduling, free days), protection against unfair termination, tour operations and orchestra committee regulations and benefits. By and large, US agreements are massive in terms of length and the degree of detail concerning every aspect of employment, whereas to an American eye, the Dutch agreements resemble framework agreements in terms of depth and the number of issues negotiated and presented. A majority of Dutch orchestra managers interviewed felt that the "CAO is destroying the orchestra's future: it is so inflexible that we have real problems meeting

132. Conversations with Randy Whatley, US based orchestral media advisor.
133. These sentiments are echoed by colleagues on both sides of the Atlantic. This particular quote was given by Evelien, Coprincipal cello (HBO) on season planning that derogates from CAO 2018.

the double demand of financing the organization and taking care of our musicians."[134] Musicians have voiced fears that the so-called inflexibility refers to measures that protect their increasingly precarious employment regulations. An example is provided by the ongoing debates in the Netherlands concerning payment for travel time, different categories of rehearsals and the amount of time that should be allotted for management to be permitted to change a rehearsal-performance schedule.

1.28 BOARDS AND TRUSTEES: US STYLE

> Only a few arts organizations are managed well, with consistent vigor and focus. Too many of them do too little or no real planning....do not know how to market, are governed by weak or ineffective boards.[135]

While US orchestral boards are central to the well-being of the organization in terms of fundraising, governance and general stewardship, their Dutch counterparts are much more behind the scenes:

> Of course, for subsidized orchestras in the Netherlands, fund-raising is not a board responsibility like it is for our colleague-orchestras in the United States. Nonetheless, considering the machinations on the part of board members at the Dutch Broadcasting Foundation when the Radio Symphony was cut in 2005 and of course when the Radio Chamber Philharmonic was offered like a sacrificial lamb in 2012, it is difficult to offer a black-and-white, according-to-the-books picture of how a board operates here. Sometimes, the real powers are hidden from view.[136]

At many US orchestras post-crisis, "we see a trend repeated over and over again in which orchestras with a committed and unified board can ride the storm while orchestras with boards who perceive the musicians and their needs as subordinate or even, irrelevant to the orchestra's future tank."[137] One of the directors of the Canadian musicians' union noted perceptively that orchestral boards have to grapple with governance prerequisites such as accountability, ethics, responsibility and transparency. Accountability for nonprofits rests squarely upon the shoulders of a board of directors, or in the parlance of some US orchestras, a board of trustees. Although the board delegates management authority to the organization's CEO, the board holds both fiduciary and legal duties and responsibilities.[138] A slim volume that attempted to account for the role of governance at Dutch cultural institutions provides evidence that many board members are male and members of a tightly knit old boys' network.[139]

134. Conversations with Piet van Gennip.
135. Michael Kaiser, *Curtains? The Future of the Arts in America*. Brandeis University Press 2015, Preface.
136. Conversations with Kees Dijk.
137. Conversations with Kevin Case.
138. Duties denote the federally imposed tax exemptions as well as restrictions, whereas responsibilities are standards of conduct determined at the state level. *See* Anita Loomis. "US Symphony Orchestra Bylaws: Policy Anomalies and Trends" 2006 https://stars.library.ucf.edu/etd/865.
139. Patricia Maitland. *Directeuren willen meer... directeuren in de cultuursector over de kwaliteit van hun toezicht* privately published 2016.

Governance issues and the disconnect between the key good governance and regulation principles[140] enshrined in the Dutch Governance Code for Culture and the way in which these principles were abjured in relation to the 2018 purported #metoo predicament at the RCO will be revisited in a subsequent *intermezzo*. And as striking examples from recent US-based orchestral debacles confirm, board oversight and even in extremis negligence have contributed mightily to employment woes cross-country. An excellent blog post by Tom Olcott, Financial Vice President of Local 802 AFM, provides ample insight into assorted board-related dramas.[141] Back in the mid-20th century, the US orchestral boards were classified as a mix between a business and a society board: the place to be for savvy social climbing. Corporate and civic leaders mixed with socialites who inherited their board positions from their forebears and donated and raised money for their "pet" orchestra. "All was well and good until orchestral musicians gained and exercised more voice: board members felt a mistrust for the 'unionized' increasingly 'militarized' orchestra."[142] Boards and orchestral managers in both jurisdictions examined criticize restrictive CBAs and the impossibility of raising ever greater amounts of money to meet deficits. "Those who run the orchestra habitually fail to reflect on the primary need to protect our golden assets: the musicians. If we regard the musicians as commodities instead of individual artists of the highest caliber, we can destroy our entire organization."[143] Resentment on the part of orchestral musicians based on perceptions of proliferating mission creep, defined as "the gradual addition of new tasks or activities to a project so that the original purpose or idea is lost,"[144] led to a reassessment of the relationship between board-management and orchestral musicians in recent industrial actions.

1.29 WHAT IS THE ROLE OF THE MAESTRO/CONDUCTOR/MUSIC DIRECTOR?

At the crux of the hierarchical relationship at the orchestra is the relationship between the maestro and the musicians, a thread that runs through subsequent *movements* that focus on history and cases related to unfair employment practices. Music directors are the final authority on artistic matters at the orchestra, from the interpretation of the music to employment-related issues such as hiring, tenure and dismissals. Greater details concerning the complexities of the maestro-musician relations are found throughout case-related analyses and detailed in *Haydn rewrites history*.

140. "Goed bestuur en toezicht" the title of the Governance Code Cultuur report published in 2014 at: www.governancecodecultuur.nl.
141. Tom Olcott. "When Orchestra Boards Fail us," an appraisal of the New York City Opera's final demise November 10, 2013, https://www.local802afm.org/allegro/articles/when-orchestra-boards-fail-us/.
142. Conversations with former Philadelphia Orchestra board chair Peter Benoliel 2015.
143. Conversation with former Cleveland Orchestra Board of Trustees President Frank E. Joseph.
144. *Cambridge Dictionary*, https://dictionary.cambridge.org/us/dictionary/english/mission-creep.

1.30 THE "FOURTH" LEG OF THE STOOL: THE MUSICIANS

While orchestras are characterized by their universal goals of musical performance, variations in size, organizational structure, financial setup, and specific artistic ambitions abound:

> We, as musicians love and make our lives in the art of music. By the nature of things, the compensation for our labors is not in the meager, monetary return, but rather in the excellence of the performances we give, and the fidelity to our art. We feel that no matter how high the purpose of the managerial board might be, nevertheless, it is only natural that the best interests of the orchestra as an artistic institution should be closer to its members than to anyone else.[145]

Conspicuously missing from the troika powers at the helm of the orchestra are the musicians. An article published at the turn of the millennium entitled "Are Three Legs Appropriate? Or Even Sufficient"[146] takes a strong stance on the subject of musician representation. "Musicians cannot, in my view, be excluded from issues of governance or strategic planning, or from any major internal debate and discussion undertaken by orchestral organizations."[147] Admirable in sentiment, two caveats arise. First, 21st-century orchestral musicians in both jurisdictions researched do participate in their organizations on many levels, from the considerable number of orchestra committees in the US to the Dutch works councils as subsequent *movements* will describe. Second, as US case law illustrates, the legal ramifications of representation are all the more complex due to statutory limitations on employees who could be categorized as supervisors-managers, a subject that will undergo scrutiny in *Back in the USA*.

1.31 WHAT IS THE ROLE OF AN ORCHESTRA COMMITTEE?

Aside from the paucity of self-governing orchestras[148] in which members are responsible for every aspect of decision-making, orchestra committee members in both jurisdictions are the musicians' caretakers and advocates.[149] US orchestra committees consist of tenured contract musicians who are elected by their fellow musicians for multifarious tasks ranging from personnel-related issues to calls for collective action. Individual grievances such as discrimination charges or unfair dismissals will be discussed in depth in subsequent *movements*. Committee members liaise with the

---

145. Letter March 4, 1943 "Statement of the Orchestra Committee of the New York Philharmonic Society to the Board" New York Philharmonic Archives, http://archives.nyphil.org/index.php/artifact/94a4f25e-754c-4124-81e2-053612e49c85/fullview#page/48/mode/2up.
146. The article was originally published in the now-defunct publication, *Harmony* 2000 DOI: 10.1107/s2052520620012895/bm5134sup1.pdf.
147. *Ibid.*
148. From the famed European symphony orchestras: Berlin Philharmonic, Vienna Philharmonic to the London-based self-governing orchestras to many chamber orchestras worldwide, self-governing orchestras are the exception to the rule.
149. The names of orchestra committees vary and there is, of course, a variance in types of committees from artistic committees to collective bargaining committees. Some US regional orchestras and European orchestras have one centralized orchestra committee sometimes known as the Player's Committee.

local, serving as the union's "eyes and ears on the job."[150] From participation at the CBA table to conflict resolution with regard to employment grievances, US orchestral committee members are actively involved in protecting musicians by making sure that CBAs are properly administered. A discussion of the role of orchestral works council members in the Netherlands and other European countries with a codeterminative approach is found in *Requiem for an orchestra.*

In legal and practical terms, the orchestra committee, whose mission is to represent the interests of the musicians both collectively and individually, takes on the role of the union's representative in the workplace. Orchestra committees participate in contract negotiations, deal with individual grievances, and play a role in mitigating a range of issues that arise between the musicians and management. "The committees provide boots on the ground, ears and eyes to maintain and update lines of communication with the local [union]."[151] Such a description may lead to the assumption that the relationship between the orchestra committee and the local is symbiotic and harmonious, yet there is an inherent caveat here as the local holds the legal responsibility to negotiate and administer the CBA but has no influence on selecting the members of an orchestra committee. In situations where the local and the committee differ on issues such as bargaining goals or grievances, such differences of opinion can lead to discord. Generally, employees who work under the terms of a collective bargaining agreement are represented by labor unions. In the US, the manifold responsibilities of the union are prescribed by federal law and/or set in the AFM's bylaws.[152] Whereas the relationship between US orchestra committees and the union, represented by locals, can be turbulent as copious reports from interviewees and sources in the ample historical archives of the ICSOM's publication *Senza Sordino* and the AFM's monthly, *Allegro* attest, Dutch orchestras tend to liaise with unions through meetings and communiques between specific orchestra members (*kaderleden*, best translated as *officers*) and union representatives.

1.32 WORKER PARTICIPATION AT THE ORCHESTRA

The orchestral work arrangement in which the conductor controls a mass of musicians with a wave of the baton appears to outsiders as the epitome of an old-fashioned hierarchy in which musicians hold limited powers. "That's just what the audience sees on the outside. Remember, the orchestra is a collective committed to expression, to music-making. Yes, the conductor shapes phrases and gives cues but we contribute not only with our musical abilities but also as real participants in the collective, just wait until collective bargaining for a new CBA begins!"[153] Nonetheless, looking from the outside in, there are differences between US and Dutch orchestras in terms of industrial democracy with respect to worker participation.

150. https://internationalmusician.org/serving-orchestra-committee/
151. Conversations with Jonathan Sherwin.
152. AFM Bylaws, https://www.afm.org/wp-content/uploads/2017/02/AFM-Bylaws.pdf.
153. Conversations with a group of Cleveland Orchestra members.

On the one hand, Dutch orchestral musicians,[154] like all members of companies with more than 50 employees, enjoy a form of democratic representation. "Works councils where elected employee representatives who sit at the table with management go beyond chit-chat to advise and consult. With regard to important management decisions, we hold not only consultation rights but approval rights for issues that affect employees."[155] On the other hand, it could be argued that democratic legitimacy is also built into the US union certification system. "Once they [union] has won an election and are certified as legal bargaining representatives, American unions have the legal right to insist that management bargain with them over ... practically everything covered in the contract."[156]

1.33 THE UNION AT THE ORCHESTRA: US STYLE

Initiated in America's heartland in 1896, the American Federation of Musicians (AFM) first represented three thousand pioneering musicians in search of protection from unreliable employers on the premise that "all men and women playing musical instruments and receiving pay therefore from the public must, in order to get just wages and decent working conditions form a labor organization."[157] By 1913, the union counted 636 groups or "locals" and more than 64,000 members. The pugnacious union boss James C. Petrillo (the AFM's President from 1940-1958) is crucial to a consideration of musicians' empowerment in present-day orchestral relations. Referring to the unfair job displacement in the 1940s engendered by radio broadcasts of recorded works (phonographs) without compensation for the musicians, Petrillo declared:

> Nowhere else in this mechanical age does the workman create the machine which destroys him, but that's what happens to the musician when he plays for a recording. The iceman didn't create the refrigerator. The coachman didn't build the automobile. But the musician plays his music into a recorder and a short time later the radio station manager comes around and says, "Sorry, Joe, we've got all your stuff on records, so we don't need you anymore." And Joe's out of a job.[158]

Since the coming of age of the modern US orchestra in the turbulent 1960s, when collective bargaining and collective representation through powerful orchestral members-only groups such as ICSOM were in their infancy, union membership was the norm for orchestral musicians. To US musicians, the term "the union" refers to the local union in their city, the local union branch affiliated with the AFM. According to AFM statistics, over 80,000 musicians in the US and Canada, approximately 95% of

154. Apart from the RCO that takes its own approach to musician participation, discussed elsewhere in the research.
155. Conversations with Dutch orchestral ondernemingsraad (OR) works council members, *Wet op de ondernemingsraden*, https://wetten.overheid.nl/DCCBR0002747/2019-01-01 in English, https://www.ser.nl/-/media/ser/downloads/engels/2019/works-councils-act.pdf.
156. George H. Strauss and Tove Helland Hammer. *Worker's Participation in the United States*. UC Berkeley Press 1987, 16.
157. The AFM's mission statement, https://www.local802afm.org.
158. James C. Petrillo, quoted by Robert A. Gorman. "The Recording Musician and Union Power. A Case Study of the American Federation of Musicians" 1984, 763.

North America's professional orchestral musicians, were registered as union members in 2019.[159] Almost all US orchestras are union workplaces requiring membership for employees. Even beyond the prerequisite for employment, US orchestral musicians interviewed believe that their membership carries great value. In addition to collective bargaining, the AFM functions as a purveyor of benefits and services for its members. Substitute musicians who freelance also perceive union membership as a positive obligation and do not find that the AFM Bylaws that bar union orchestras from hiring nonmembers for employment are unreasonable.[160]

1.34 NONUNION LABOR GROUPS

In the 1960s, Gino Raffaelli, a Cleveland Orchestra violinist and founding member of the International Conference of Symphony and Opera Musicians (ICSOM), decided that his orchestra's disregard for basic rights for musicians was tantamount to a call for action.[161] "The events in Cleveland in those years, the lawsuits and the counter lawsuits served as the most compelling evidence for the need of an auxiliary organization—one within the union—to represent the interests of the symphony musician, a role so aptly filled with the birth of ICSOM."[162] Another important reason that led to the formation of a lobby group that put the demands of orchestral musicians at the fore went beyond the frustrations of a lack of "voice" at the workplace. "Simply put, most orchestral musicians in the US in the early 1960s did not earn an adequate living."[163] Statistics released by the US census in 1963 disclose that the average orchestral musician's salary was ($4,757 per annum) well below the median salary of other professionals ($6,778).[164]

In 1964, ICSOM was actively involved in an orchestral musicians' employment conflict. Several players with the San Antonio Symphony lost their jobs in retaliation for their active participation on behalf of their fellow musicians. "It was a case of the usual suspects: an autocratic conductor, repressive management and a local that was too weak to stand up to those who ran the only orchestra in town."[165] ICSOM was pivotal in its precursor of a social media campaign, a name and shame operation that put pressure on the San Antonio Symphony. The musicians were never reinstated but did receive $4,000 in reimbursement equivalent to approximately $32,000 in 2018.[166]

159. https://www.afm.org/join/new-members/.
160. Quoting consortium of New York freelancers: "We sense that in the hierarchy of the orchestra, music directors and CEOs could take advantage of their power if musicians did not have strong backup: the union has real clout. If you study the AFM bylaws, you discover that nonunion member musicians cannot participate in orchestra meetings dealing with CBA administration nor do they receive strike fund benefits. It's quite simple: US musicians join unions for protection and power!"
161. *Symposium of Orchestral Delegates* 1962, https://archives.nyphil.org/index.php/artifact/fc4b3540-30dd-4f3b-9819-427d45354cd0-0.1/fullview#page/1/mode/2up.
162. Conversations with Randy Whatley.
163. Conversations with ICSOM pioneer; Cleveland Orchestra violinist, Gino Raffaelli.
164. *See* https://www2.census.gov/library/publications/1963/demographics/p60-41.pdf.
165. *Ibid.*
166. "The Bob Danielson Case" October 1968, 5, https://icsom.org/senza/issues/senza071.pdf.

At present, ICSOM is a thriving representative conference that provides professional orchestral musicians in the top 52 US orchestras with a platform to revisit every conceivable employment-related issue.

The US-based Regional Orchestra Players Association (ROPA) represents approximately 90 orchestras with similar goals and services as ICSOM, whereas the other players' conferences represent three other core groups: theater musicians, recording industry artists and Canadian orchestras. Turning to the Netherlands, there are no players' conferences comparable to the ICSOM/ROPA organizations for Dutch orchestral musicians with one notable exception. The *Platform voor Freelance Musici* (PvFM), founded in the Netherlands in 2018, focuses exclusively on the needs of freelance substitute musicians and shares several notable traits with US players' conferences in terms of visibility and outreach.

1.35 THE DUTCH APPROACH TO ORCHESTRAL UNIONS

In the Netherlands, unions have played and continue to play a significant role in the civic sphere. Post-WWII, sustained union involvement encouraged strong support for collective bargaining with the unions in an ascendant role in upholding workplace rights. The concept of social partnership between the government, expert groups, employers' representatives, and the unions contributes to a highly supportive environment for collective bargaining that can be contrasted to the situation in the US where a clash of interests between "the right of freedom to contract at will" is often juxtaposed against the rights of workers not only in the courts but also in legislation.

Unions in 21st-century Netherlands, however, face similar challenges to their US counterparts as union density is facing decline based on a complex nexus of reasons which find an excellent presentation in Eurofound's ample and thorough documentation.[167] It is important to underline that for all the challenges of maintaining membership density, the coverage provided by collective bargaining is high regardless of a decline in membership as the following statistic illustrates: Dutch union density measured at 18% in 2011 with lower figures in the orchestral sector (estimated 7%), yet collective bargaining coverage in the orchestral sector was estimated at 81%.[168] "The perception that the union bargains for musicians regardless of their union affiliation leads so many Dutch musicians to ask, 'why should I pay to join the union if I do not have to?' The added benefits of union membership have not played a role in musician consciousness for years. This has changed partially because of the most devastating crisis, the COVID-19 pandemic."[169]

167. https://www.eurofound.europa.eu/observatories/eurwork/comparative-information/national-contributions/netherlands.
168. Robbert van het Kaar. *Social Partners Debate Collective Bargaining* 2013 https://www.eurofound.europa.eu/publications/article/2013/social-partners-debate-collective-agreement-system.
169. Conversations with Caroline Cartens, cofounder of the Platform voor Freelance Musici (PvFM).

1.36 WHAT HAPPENS WHEN ORCHESTRAL CONTRACT NEGOTIATIONS BREAK DOWN?

In 2015, of the 14 large-budget US orchestras heading toward CBA expiration dates, only four succeeded in reaching an agreement.[170] In situations where there is a chance of imminent resolution and/or the existence of goodwill between parties, the musicians will continue to perform after the CBA lapses as long as negotiations continue: their continuance is known as a "play and talk" agreement. What are the possible scenarios post-breakdown in negotiation?

(1) Management provides a declaration that negotiations have reached an impasse. Management then enforces the terms of its most recent offer to the musicians. The union can file an unfair labor practice charge with the NLRB.
(2) Lockouts: work stoppages initiated by management in which locked-out musicians do not receive benefits or salaries.
(3) Strikes: work stoppage initiated by the musicians-employees.

The concept of impasse as interpreted by the NLRB has been widely criticized by academics and labor lawyers as well as musicians whose orchestras have gone through protracted "impasse" situations during recent bargaining sagas at the US orchestral workplace. If sufficient good faith efforts are evident yet no agreement has been reached, an employer can declare impasse and implement the last offer presented to the union. Commonly, the union, spurred on by employees, opposes management's offer and/or challenges "good faith" and files an unfair labor practice charge. According to the NLRB guidelines, the Board "will determine whether true impasse was reached based on the history of negotiations and the understandings of both parties."[171] Thousands of cases from the NLRB's archives illustrate the delicacy and difficulty to decipher good faith pursuant to employers' reliance on impasse, which to many legal scholars "promotes the inequality of bargaining power."[172] Moreover, and importantly according to practitioners, impasse has reduced the bargaining process to "a list of words and phrases that unions can never use and employers must always use ... deadlock," "bottom line," "best offer," and "final offer."[173]

If musicians go on strike after their CBA expires, their action is considered to be a "protected concerted activity," fully safeguarded under §7 of the NLRA, which upholds the rights of workers to engage in "concerted activities for the purpose of ...

170. "Does your orchestra have an expired Collective Bargaining Agreement?" *Adaptistration* September 15, 2015.
171. NLRB guidelines, https://www.nlrb.gov/rights-we-protect/rights/employer-union-rights-and-obligations.
172. Considerable academic output by Ellen Danni, Clive Gilson, Joseph E. Kolick, Jr. and Merle M. DeLancey, Jr., leading US-based legal scholars on the impasse inequality.
173. Samuel McKnight. "Impasse Implementation of Final Offers Reviewed by Unionists and Academics" *Collective Bargaining Bulletin* 2, January 16, 1997.

mutual aid or protection." Although management is barred from firing the striking employees, it is under no obligation to pay the strikers. Consider once again that US orchestras are nonprofits: "one does not need to be cynical, just realistic to figure out that the organization that runs the orchestra will save money when the musicians are out on strike: the halls are dark, no concerts take place unless of course the musicians offer free concerts to the community."[174]

1.37 POST-2007-2008 FINANCIAL CRISIS CHANGES AND PERCEPTIONS OF CHANGE

Orchestral musicians in the second decade of the millennium continue to speak of their vocation as a calling, a "must" that is synonymous with their very being. Whether based in Rochester or Rotterdam, they observe that since the 2007-2008 financial crisis, their professional lives have become increasingly gridlocked (a term used by a New York-based violinist). Not only financial issues plague the orchestras: "[O]ur musical lives take place within a hierarchical family—it is no less a profession which is part of a multifaceted musical organization governed by interactions between music director, management and board not to speak of union reps and musicians often with their own objectives and agendas."[175]

Musicians reflecting on the post-crisis orchestral situation where shrinking subsidies and reorganizations/restructuring engendered new budget models based on hours as opposed to weeks of performances speak of heightened stress levels, lack of work/life balance, and, last but certainly not least, diminishing incomes. In addition to these vulnerabilities, the fact that music directors, the maestros who direct the orchestras, are in high demand internationally means that they spend much less time with their home base orchestras with less time for taking care of possible "on-the-job" problems.[176] Orchestras are more likely to work with guest conductors during their seasons, but guest conductors are not responsible for either artistic or organizational continuity. Crucially, the intensified careers of music director-conductors have led to an increase in performance stress for orchestral musicians who once relied on a solid schedule of pre-concert rehearsals.

1.38 DISCREPANCIES BETWEEN RECOGNITION AND REMUNERATION

Individual recognition within the confines of the orchestra is rare, especially for "tutti" players.[177] Yes, the orchestra is a collective led by the maestro; however, the trickle-down of positive rewards is less likely to happen for the tuttis. Traditionally, at the end

174. Discussions with Max Bonecutter, lawyer and former bass trombonist Minnesota Orchestra; Metropolitan Opera Orchestra.
175. Conversations with Judy Nelson, violist New York Phiharmonic, 1983-2019.
176. Statistics gleaned from major European and top-tier US orchestras show that the music director often spends less than 30% of his/her time (between 8 and 12 weeks per season) with the orchestra.
177. *Tutti*, the Italian term is used universally to mean "rank-and-file" (UK) or section players (US), the musicians who make up a larger section of players: the string players.

of each composition performed in a concert setting, the performers stand, face the audience, and accept public approbation. The conductor will ask principal players who excelled in solo parts, often virtuosic or difficult in terms of execution, to take a solo bow. Along with the added accolades, section principals receive overscale pay and other contractual perks. As the *Rowe* lawsuit discloses, principal pay in major orchestras in the US can exceed twice the amount of remuneration as section players.

Above and beyond the remuneration for principals is the issue of conductors' and CEOs' salaries. In both the Netherlands and the US, conductors and managers earn substantially more than orchestral musicians. According to a *New York Times* article aptly entitled, "Baton Inflation,"[178] nine US orchestral music directors earned over $1 million per season in salaries paid by their home orchestras, including orchestras such as the Chicago Symphony Orchestra (CSO) that went on strike to retain pensions and maintain salaries. According to insider information from impresarios, this remuneration tendency is not merely a US phenomenon. Name soloists on center stage charge $30,000-$100,000 for three concerts, analogous to a year's salary for the average orchestral musician:

> Those who manage us are willing to pay top dollar for soloists and guest conductors, perhaps fair enough if you consider that these musicians attract sponsors and are audience magnets. Nevertheless, the discrepancy between a guest conductor who earns more in a weekend than the orchestra's musicians earn in one year is difficult to accept. Where is the balance or at least the consideration of the rank-and-file players?[179]

Unanimous voices from both jurisdictions studied underline that since the financial crisis and its aftermath in the orchestral sphere, "precarity is ever more present for orchestral musicians—the employed witness a diminution of their contracts and the freelancers have to fight harder for work as substitutes in an ever-shrinking number of financially solvent venues in order to survive in the profession. Musicians seem to be becoming increasingly vulnerable."[180]

Turning to the professionals who run orchestras, US top-tier orchestras pay their directors salaries running in the six and even seven figures, with super-fundraiser Deborah Borda earning top dollar following her move from the Los Angeles Philharmonic to the New York Philharmonic in 2017.[181] Even orchestras with small budgets (under $425,000 per annum) reportedly pay approximately 10% of their total costs to managing directors.[182] Musicians accept the fact that those who lead whether in the

178. Zachary Wolfe. "Baton Inflation: American Conductor Salaries Hit a New High," *New York Times* July 27, 2018, https://www.nytimes.com/2018/07/27/arts/music/orchestra-conductors-high-salaries.html.
179. Conversations with Norman Lebrecht author and music blogger (www.slippeddisc.com).
180. Conversations with Mark Gerrits.
181. Borda's Los Angeles $1.8 million salary increased substantially when she left the LA Philharmonic to head the team at the New York Philharmonic, https://www.sfcv.org/music-news/deborah-borda-agrees-to-take-the-reins-of-the-new-york-philharmonic.
182. *See* https://adaptistration.com/2005/04/12/mobile-managers-super-managers-for-tomorrow/.

musical or the management zone are entitled to excellent compensation. The disproportionality, however, between their salaries in "leadership inflation" especially in times of financial upheaval is disconcerting.

1.39 A LACK OF SYNCHRONICITY BETWEEN THOSE WHO RUN THE ORCHESTRAL ORGANIZATION (BOARDS/MANAGEMENT) AND MUSICIANS' EMPLOYMENT NEEDS

Revealing prose from a newly minted tenured orchestral violinist upon joining the BSO "at the tender age of 22" speaks for many:

> It was quite an eye-opener when I saw my first organizational chart of the BSO. Scratching my head, I asked, "Hey, where are the musicians on the chart as for the life of me, I couldn't find us ... In the vast administrative and artistic web of the organization, the musicians of the Boston Symphony, 102-strong, were represented by a diminutive seemingly insignificant orb in the lower right corner of the page, tethered by various lines to other functionaries 'above' us."[183]

From the viewpoint of many orchestral musicians, management, not to speak of the boards, are often out of sync with musicians. Strikes and lockouts past and present along with the rhetoric and media reports that have been disseminated concerning these industrial actions illustrate that boards tend to retrench toward "fiscal responsibility" above and beyond "musicians' needs." We have heard boards refer to the distinguished musicians in their orchestras with the quotes "we don't let tellers run the bank nor do we let prisoners run the prison," denigrating viewpoints at best.[184] Robert Mnookin, the Harvard-based expert, called in to develop a creative solution to CBA woes at the San Francisco Symphony, waxed eloquent concerning differences in basic viewpoints as to how stakeholders identified with the orchestra. "From the musicians' perspective, the name 'San Francisco Symphony' meant the orchestra. From management's perspective, it meant the organization."[185]

1.40 SUBORDINATION AND LACK OF INFLUENCE TO SOLVE WORK-RELATED PROBLEMS

Orchestral musicians in the Netherlands and the US expressed dismay at their lack of autonomy in terms of important artistic and financial choices. Dutch musicians, who were for the most part happy about the participation of colleagues on works councils, also voiced critical opinions concerning participatory decision-making in times of crisis. The musicians who went through reorganization processes during financial crises were critical as to how these processes played out on the work floor:

183. Posted by Gerald Elias (Jerry). *Labor of Love: A Primer in Symphony Orchestra Musician/Management Relations* posted May 13, 2013, http://www.reichelrecommends.com/labor-of-love-a-primer-in-symphony-orchestra-musicianmanagement-relations/.
184. Taken from a string of confidential emails sent by Players Committee members, Grand Teton Music Festival.
185. Robert Mnookin. *Bargaining with the Devil: When to Negotiate, When to Fight* 2010, 298.

> We were being led down the garden path during the reorganization process. The more we were told how fair the process was, the more our suspicions increased that this was really not true. There was little trust between the musicians and management and sadly our works council was highjacked, caught in a difficult position and forced to agree with management.[186]

Similar sentiments were registered by Atlanta Symphony Orchestra (ASO) musicians during their turbulent years, 2012-2014. "Our general director/CEO, his board and the umbrella organization that financed us were definitely not on our side and it was the orchestra, the musicians and the community who suffered for their mistakes."[187]

1.41 VULNERABILITIES EXACERBATED BY A LACK OF COHERENT AND LONG-TERM CAREER PLANNING

Research on employment issues should take workers' including potential workers' expectations into consideration. Musicians interviewed stated that they were often ill-prepared for the challenges they faced in the orchestral workplace. *Of Rowe and Race* considers specific problems and vulnerabilities related to gender, race, misperceptions, and difficult points of entry in orchestras. What do training programs for musicians actually do to prepare musicians for orchestral careers? While there is a great deal of observable variance between different institutions, the majority of music schools and conservatories place the focus of instrumental training on solo enhancement, especially for string players and keyboardists. Although many training institutions have added orchestral studies and course components on what to expect from an orchestral job, "this is the stepchild of the program: we have introduced it but do not take it seriously for musicians who if they are lucky would have orchestral careers in the future."[188]

Contracted orchestral musicians and freelancers speak of a specific lack of career preparation and training with regard to employment-related issues. The International Federation of Musicians (FIM) and *confrères* (and *consoeurs*) at various international unions are taking steps to address this inadequacy. Work-life balance has become a human resources buzzword in recent years with comprehensive systems put into place at the major orchestral institutions to deal with issues associated with the employer's response to performance anxiety, injuries, aging in the orchestral workplace and others. Yet although there is much talk concerning workload and work-life balance, orchestral musicians in both jurisdictions report that stress levels and workaday demands have increased post-2007-2008 financial crisis. Additionally, secondary or regional orchestras lack these mechanisms and substitute players freelancing in both

186. Translated from the Dutch, "om de tuin had geleid," quoted by an RFO musician who did not lose a principal position. The statement was made in reference to how the reorganization was effectuated.
187. An ASO string player looking back at the double lockout period, anonymity assured.
188. A leading violin professor at a major Dutch conservatory, anonymity assured.

jurisdictions are on their own to deal with the downside of injuries and other work-play-related issues.

1.42 SIDELINING AND MARGINALIZATION THROUGH VALUE OF CULTURE DEBATES AND EXPERT ASSESSMENTS THAT QUESTION THE RELEVANCE OF CLASSICAL MUSIC

As media reports recurrently underline, the classical music profession embraces a small, white, and elitist segment of culture. When repeated with frequency, the public and importantly the politicians who make decisions concerning arts subsidies with particular regard to what are perceived as "elitist" orchestras place the sector in a periphery of limited social value. For the orchestral musician, criticism is a central part of performing life. A truism that bears repetition: musicians are highly self-critical, an essential trait to success and reaching the level vital to maintain an exemplary professional standard. Endemic internal critical mechanisms, the scrutiny of musician-colleagues and principals, the maestros' high-powered criticism and the close scrutiny of music critics intensify the pressures that orchestral musicians deal with on a daily basis. When the press and political principals dismiss classical music for its lack of general relevance, musicians who have invested so much in their art feel "abandoned" and "misunderstood" to quote the descriptors used most often by interviewees. The task of identifying with a wider audience and increasing relevance is one of the greatest challenges to orchestras in the US, the Netherlands, and for that matter, worldwide. Add to this mix the fact that management experts hired to advise orchestral managers and boards bandy about the term "talent" to separate "successful" musicians from others who "have not made it," a concept that defies description.[189] Musicians interviewed reacted negatively to the application of the "t-word" to their professional activities. In the lore of musicians worldwide, a story is told of a young conservatory student lost on the streets of New York who stops an elderly stranger to query, "how do you get to Carnegie Hall?" The wise stranger nods his head and answers, "practice, practice." Orchestra players add, "practice, practice and then blend, blend."[190] Musicians agree that the notion of talent spread throughout the literature on orchestras and multiple advisory opinions is eclipsed by years of hard training:

> Consider the subjectivity in highlighting those who supposedly show an incredible spark of originality, "the talented" ones. Now consider that there is no such thing as a standardized measurement of talent, nor are there definable criteria to calibrate performances. So, when Dutch orchestras waived a small number of players deemed indispensable ("onmisbaar") from the lists of musicians slated to lose their jobs during the 2012-2013 reorganizations, how could this determination be fair if there were no established criteria to separate the "saved from the doomed"?[191]

189. The words set apart with quotes refer to a conversation with several faculty members, The Juilliard School.
190. Retold often at master classes in conservatories worldwide.
191. Conversations with former principal player RKF, anonymity assured.

1.43 A LACK OF CLARIFICATION OF ORCHESTRAL FREELANCE SUBSTITUTE MUSICIANS' EMPLOYMENT STATUS

Crucial to freelancers in both the US and the Netherlands is the establishment of employment status. While Dutch cultural unions have worked long and hard to move forward toward finalizing collective bargaining agreements (CAOs, in Dutch) with the major Dutch orchestral employers and freelancers to level the playing field for the most vulnerable,[192] a closer examination of a pair of clauses in the 2021-2022 agreement opens the door to gentle criticism. Under Article 9.2 (a), the Dutch CAO reiterates the Guideline's (both Commission and ACM) central tenet of equal pay for side-by-side workers. Article 9.2 reads in the relevant part:

> a. Upon commencing employment for the first time, a freelancer who is not regularly employed by one of the orchestras affiliated to this collective agreement will be entitled to receive the same salary received by regularly employed orchestra members, the salary that corresponds to the position he/she holds within the orchestra.
> b. Years of relevant experience already acquired will be counted in the salary determination. The years of experience start at the beginning of the career as a freelance player with one of the orchestras to which this CAO applies. Equivalent foreign professional experience also counts in the determination.

Within the Dutch orchestral salary system, a musician's initial salary is determined by several factors: section versus principal pay; years of prior professional experience; and extra salary compensation for doubling instruments. So far, so good. However, Article 9.2. (b) has caused concern on the part of freelance musicians. Its admirable momentum in the direction of equal pay on all levels could inadvertently engender an undesirable discriminatory component. More experienced freelancers, older players, will cost the hiring orchestra more under this equivalence clause. As orchestras are ever-cautious spenders following the impact of the COVID-19 pandemic, the enticement to hire cheaper freelancers could impact directly those who cost more. Comments by Dutch orchestra personnel managers corroborate the aforementioned opinion. The general reflection on their part is that although quality is and should be the most important criterion for hiring a substitute player, the temptation to hire excellent starters, freelancers who have graduated from orchestral academies and/or recent top conservatory graduates is great.

1.44 ORCHESTRAS IN FLUX IN THE NETHERLANDS

The post-crisis picture in the Netherlands is marked by apprehension for a sector that faces a major "rethink" on two fronts. First and foremost, the subsidy shrinkage resulting from the devastating cuts in 2012-2013 has reduced the number of orchestras

192. Freelance Substitute Players CBA Dutch Orchestras negotiated by FNV Media & Cultuur/Klassiek Muziek & Kunstenbond, https://www.fnv.nl/getmedia/c59fbc3a-00a6-4b0b-97a3-bcfc25aa9a70/1393-remplacanten-nederlandse-orkesten-cao-01-01-2021-tm-31-12-2022-v28122022.pdf?ext=.pdf.

and kindled a competitive atmosphere with regard to "who gets how much subsidy." Subsidy cuts in the face of increased production requirements put an incredible strain on the orchestral musicians who are still employed, many with lowered percentages of employment, and orchestral freelancers now compete for work in fewer and fewer orchestras. Second, while Dutch legislation (WAB) that came into effect on January 1, 2020 leveled the remuneration playing field between the self-employed and the regularly employed, the element of change poses enormous challenges to orchestral managers who are caught between a rock and a hard place to balance budgets and meet requirements to increase the pay scales for freelancers.

Relevant to an inquiry on exacerbated vulnerabilities is the added work stress engendered by the changes in scheduling at the Dutch orchestral workplace, where the same rates of production (services) pre- and post-crisis are performed by ensembles that have endured personnel cuts. Freelancers fill many of the gaps, and the "fully" employed musicians suffer from increased work stress with orchestral schedules that call for high rates of production accompanied by a diminution of salaries.

Additionally, the impact of orchestral training academies with volunteer-like schemes is perceived as a direct threat to the livelihoods of orchestral freelancers. At several orchestral academies, the conservatory student interns are not paid professional wages although they perform at regular series concerts. "This creates a problem for freelancers. When I was a student, I and my fellow students got professional experience by playing in orchestras while receiving 'normal' substitute wages, and now, interns receive next-to-nothing and replace freelancers."[193] In the view of union negotiators:

> In our minds aside from the usual jockeying for position to receive subsidies with all that entails, one of the biggest challenges in the sector is that under the guise of flexibility, student interns are pushing the professionals out. Many of the orchestral academies create a supply of fictitious volunteers that encroaches on the paid substitute players "market."[194]

As state and municipal subsidies have shrunk and competition for limited resources has increased since the 2007-2008 financial crisis, the Dutch trade unions active in the orchestral field have opted to move toward correcting the shortfall and the most egregious inadequacies in employment conditions. In the post-neoliberal age, employers in many sectors are tempted to adopt an entrepreneurial business model that grants them the leeway to lower costs and increase output:

> Their other piece de résistance is the ongoing search to develop new revenue models, not in and of itself unacceptable in times of austerity, however when the revenue model flies in the face of the well-being of orchestra musicians, it is unacceptable. A revenue model in its purest form projects an organization's potential for growth and profit. In the orchestral sphere, survival is key, no orchestras fall within the classic definition of profit-making enterprises. A model that cuts forfait hours, adds extra services to "free days" leads to a slippery slope

193. Conversations with Dorine Schoon, cofounder Platform voor Freelance Musici (PvFM).
194. Conversations with Martin Kothman.

for employees as demands for more work/less pay are made with an appeal to the musicians' commitment and professionalism.[195]

Employers are demanding even more flexibility from the musicians, and musicians are not willing to move forward on flexibility issues because their workload has already reached a high, almost untenable level.

1.45 FACTS AND FIGURES: DUTCH CUTBACKS AND US LOCKOUTS/STRIKES

The majority of Dutch orchestras remaining after the major culture cuts (2012-2013) have undergone cutbacks in employment for the full complement of players. As the examples cited in the appendices highlight, musicians under contract are now receiving "partial contracts" for full-time work. The Dutch Ballet Orchestra (Het Ballet Orkest) has witnessed another variation on the merger/reorganization theme: a combination of part-time contracts and personnel cuts. It is fair to note that maximum-scope CBAs are losing out to part-time contracts in the orchestral sector. *Epilogue: Appendix 1* offers a status quo update on the contractual vulnerabilities at Dutch orchestras prior to the COVID-19 pandemic. A concise review of recent US orchestra lockouts and strikes post-2007-2008 financial crisis can be accessed in *Epilogue: Appendix 2.*

1.46 ATONALITY IN ATLANTA: TWO LOCKOUTS IN THE SPACE OF FOUR YEARS

It may seem unorthodox to present a pair of mini case studies in a *FAQ movement* intended to answer basic questions that feed into a discussion of the orchestra and challenges following the 2007-2008 financial crisis. The justifications for examining several case studies of US-based orchestral labor disputes are trifold. First, the reader will be introduced to a large cast of characters ever-present in orchestral labor disputes. Second, the complexity and the many layers of legal, organizational, and cultural issues will allow the reader to delve deeply into the ups and downs of orchestral management, musician concerns and the realities of a labor crisis unfolding through social media in a "breaking news" approach. Lastly, while it may be unorthodox to quote from social media and certainly irresponsible to assess the impact of Twitter, Facebook, and Instagram on labor disputes in the orchestral workplace without the proper tools to measure impact, a brief presentation of social media reporting deserves some attention as it has led to victories on the part of musicians in some of their industrial actions as we soon shall discover.

Upon closer examination of the ASO's 2013 compromise CBA, which diminished the orchestra's complement from 95 to 88 musicians after contentious attempts at

195. Conversations with Martin Kothman. The wonderfully descriptive term "paradepaardje" was used.

reconciliation, the 2012 lockout and the musicians' acceptance of a much-disputed salary cut bring this point home.[196] For the ASO musicians, these cutbacks were a portent of things to come. A second wave of disruptions took place in 2014 when the orchestra was locked out for the second time in two years.

The crisis at the ASO that escalated in the 2010s with a record of two lockouts within two years was attributable to a variety of factors. In terms of governance and financial control, the ASO fell under the aegis of the Woodruff Art Center (WAC), a nonprofit organization that ran the Woodruff Concert Hall and several other resident organizations including the Alliance Theatre. Major parties within the dispute were entrenched in positions that made it increasingly difficult to offer concessions without losing face among peers and followers. The lockout timeline below illustrates the lack of commitment toward the orchestra on the part of WAC executives. "For the musicians of the ASO, this sounded like a declaration of war when WAC's President/CEO Virginia Hepner declared that ASO musicians had to take a 'flexible approach to her attempts to set artistic and financial priorities for WAC, priorities that meant cuts in the ASO's complement and budget.'"[197]

Referring to comments made by CEO Hepner, in which balanced budgets were emphasized at the cost of orchestral personnel, an ASO violinist retorted:

> this, in a nutshell, is the root of the orchestra's problem. So glad Virginia has come out so soon to voice her opinion so that we can understand why there has been such a fundamental shift in policy, since 2012, from nurturing world-class quality to simply keeping the books tidy and the money flowing. I think it's time for a public debate.[198]

America's top-tier orchestras list hundred musicians as a minimum on their rosters. The ASO, which was trimmed from 95 to 88 full-time players in the 2012 collective bargaining agreement, began the delayed 2014-2015 season with 77 remaining musicians. The "complement" is contracted to grow to 84 by the end of year three and 88 by the fourth year. Commenting on the fight for the complement, Danny Laufer, cellist and head of the ASOs orchestral bargaining committee, underscored: "We fought like dogs to maintain our complement in 2014 having lost that battle in 2012 when we lost seven players."[199]

The ASO's Music Director Robert Spano and Principal Guest Conductor Donald Runnicles took the unprecedented step of breaking the conventional maestros' omerta by publishing a widely circulated open letter that warned the greater Atlanta community and orchestral aficionados worldwide that "there are artistic lines that cannot and must not be crossed."[200] Remarking on this unusual advocacy a few months later, he observed: "there are times when one cannot stand by and watch a great orchestra

196. https://members.afm.org/uploads/file/20130510_Atlanta Symphony.pdf.
197. Conversations with Juan de Gomar, ASO contrabassoonist.
198. In response to Denis O'Hayer's interview with Paul Murphy, President ASO Players Association, and Virginia Hepner aired on WABE FM 90.1 an Atlanta-based radio station September 9, 2014, http://wabe.org/post/aso-lockout-puts-season-opener-jeopardy-conversations-both-sides.
199. Conversations with ASO associate principal cellist Danny Laufer.
200. https://www.artsatl.org/2014/09/breaking-news-spano-runnicles-express-fear-aso-quality-compromised-2/.

suffer injustice."[201] A comment made by the ASO's Board Chair, Douglas Hertz, scion of a culturally aware philanthropic family, speaks volumes concerning not only his frustration levels at the money-raising board level but also the abject contempt on the part of the spokesperson for the orchestra's caretakers: "maybe Robert's feeling a little bit guilty because he's getting paid and the musicians aren't."[202]

Across the Atlantic, conductors registered their dismay at the proposed cuts suggesting that an orchestra with less than 90 players moves into "a danger zone in terms of the repertoire they can handle not to speak of reputation."[203]

The dilemma concerning the complement opens another question that weaves its way through the *movements* devoted to freelance substitute orchestral musicians: is it not possible to substitute high-level freelancers to bolster the complement, especially following cutbacks? "Yes and no! This is of course the solution most orchestras that have been reduced are obliged to take. With all respect for the excellent level of freelancers who substitute in great orchestras, there is a great difference between our guest players and those who grow and are nurtured by the orchestra's culture year-in-year-out."[204] Another observation points to general malaise and the standoff between the "haves" aka board members and the "have nots" or workers in general, orchestral employees specifically. A particularly savvy US-based orchestral musician waxed eloquent on what many musicians find to be a valid appraisal of the "bigger picture":

> We here in the New World are crippled by an irrational toxic religious cult with no discernible tie to any known reality. Of course, I am referring to Free Market Fundamentalism. Our leaders in the world of business by and large have utter contempt for the fine arts which cannot pay its own way in the "market." Even worse, US musicians are unionized, which is a foul sacrilege unto all that is virtuous in the eyes of Milton Friedman and his minions. So, you get circular firing squads such as we saw last year in Minnesota and are seeing in Atlanta. Your charming little country has a significant advantage which also gives it a leg up in pretty much everything else.[205]

The ASO's delayed opening night gala was given a grandiloquent name, *Ode to Joy*. All signs for a grand opening were in place: the hall was sold out, and the crowd was enthusiastic and the orchestra was more than elated. On stage, 71 musicians were euphoric to return to perform and put the stress and strain of the lockout behind them. Of the complement, 40 musicians were fully contracted ASO players, and 31 were substitute players hired for the week. The opinions expressed by ASO musicians show

201. Conversations with Sir Donald Runnicles.
202. Howard Pousner. *Atlanta Life and Culture Blog* October 4, 2015, https://www.ajc.com/blog/arts-culture/woodruff-arts-center-board-leader-takes-stands-atlanta-symphony-crisis/bvsW0IJrkI0R183N0ryK9J/
203. Conversations with Sir Mark Elder.
204. Conversations with Maestro Edo de Waart.
205. This sharp-witted musician quoted anonymously as promised.

that concerted (word choice intentional) efforts involving a united community of musicians, audiences, municipal leaders, and union reps are key to influencing management and boards to change approach and method related to financially driven challenges:

> I guess what I boil down from all of this is that it takes a decision from the highest levels of boards-management. In a right-to-work state having a CBA is not an easy sell for powerbrokers. Move the leaders, influence their choices and yes, you can make change happen. It's incredible to look back and see how our situation has turned around in the past few years. First and foremost, it came from an understanding from our highest levels of board leadership that they were heading in the wrong direction: what starves the musicians, starves the community. Certain key board members took leadership roles and fired senior staff wholesale—those who plummeted us into the 2014 lockout. Lots of public pressure and negative PR helped as well as in all this, our parent organizations (WAC) looked inept and even vindictive especially after locking us out twice within two years![206]

Another member of the orchestra alluded to differences between US orchestral financing and European models in her response:

> It seems like private philanthropy and our dependence on that, and corporate support sets us apart from orchestras in Europe. In Atlanta, our pillars of support had a special history going back generations to several leading families. In 1962, there was a horrible plane crash in which 103 of Georgia's leading arts patrons were killed at Orly airport Paris. Their families banded together to create a strong legacy in memoriam and spearheaded a new arts center and many initiatives. Back in that era of the 20th century reports predicted that US orchestras would go the way of the dinosaurs, nevertheless our Atlanta community proved that culture was important for all. During our 'one-after-the-other' lockouts, the musicians made a strong case for our role as a leading part of the city's identity, on equal footing and just as important to the civic image as our sports teams. Our motto became: "The ASO, a world-class orchestra for a world-class city." We were mocked for this by the CEO of the WAC, Virginia Hepner who ended up agreeing with us before she stepped down! When organizations turn a corner, the momentum starts to tilt, a sort of domino effect takes place—the WAC received an infusion of $38 million, the orchestra received the promise to endow 11 chairs and a renovation of the Alliance Theater was scheduled. The drumbeat shifted and we have received a new lease on our orchestral lives.[207]

The Atlanta Symphony case with its ultimately happy ending after years of discord and strife shows that for US orchestras, it is vital for the Board to place the orchestra and the musician's employment needs at the center of their mission. The complement, the number of work weeks and solid pension plans are in no way superfluous but an integral part of what constitutes institutional success for a musical operation that enriches an entire community.

---

206. Conversations with Juan de Gomar.
207. Conversations with Judy Cox, ASO violinist.

Figure 1 Baltimore Symphony Musicians on the Picket Line

Source: Photo credit: Geoff Robertson. *The Washington Post* June 17, 2019.

1.47 CRISIS AT THE BALTIMORE SYMPHONY ORCHESTRA (BalSO)

In 2019, another major US orchestra, the Baltimore Symphony Orchestra, fought for its future following a board announcement of the cancelation of the orchestra's summer season, a cutback from a 52-week to a 40-week season with concomitant pay cuts (Figure 1). Editorial comments on the crisis in Baltimore intimated a change from a fully employed orchestra to a pay-per-service model to solve immediate financial woes. Cutting to the heart of the complement issue, a cogent reader posted: "a symphony can't reduce staff because it can't, for example, play a piece of music written with three trumpet parts using only two trumpeters."[208]

Founded in 1916 by patrons with significant support from the municipality of Baltimore, the BalSO was privatized in 1942. Beyond the many recordings, tours and significant artistic endeavors that have garnered great respect for the orchestra worldwide, its importance as a social and cultural force within the community is particularly noteworthy. Maestro Marin Alsop, the first woman appointed to conduct a major US orchestra, was appointed as music director in 2005 and has engaged and

208. Charles T. Downey. "BSO Bids Reluctant Farewell" *Washington Post* June 9, 2019, https://www.washingtonpost.com/entertainment/music/bsobids-a-reluctant-farewell-with-mahlers-ninth-symphony-at-strathmore/2019/06/09/efaee61e-8974-11e9-a870-b9c411dc4312_story.html?utm_term=.3aaf3af3f827.

revitalized forgotten communities with year-round music and social mentoring through OrchKids and other related programs.[209]

In 2018, the BalSO management proposed a drastic cut in the musicians' contracts, from 52 to 40 weeks and a decrease in the number of paid vacation days. A cut in weeks lowers the orchestra's status and fuels the fear that the ensemble will not be able to attract superlative musicians who are wont to audition for orchestras with better employment contracts. While negotiations were ongoing, the musicians' union and the orchestra's management agreed to a contract extension through January 2019, entering into a talk-and-play scenario: as musicians were participating in rehearsals and performances for the 2018-2019 season, they were engaged in collective bargaining negotiations. While "talk and play" might point to a US phenomenon, it is common practice in the Netherlands during bargaining season, as orchestras there continue to perform while social partners discuss and flesh out the finer points of employment CAOs.

In May 2019, management canceled the BalSO summer season, including its community blockbuster: the annual Star-Spangled Spectacular Fourth of July concert. The municipality's Artscape, the most extensive free arts festival in the US, was forced to announce that the BalSO musicians would not be able to participate. On June 11, 2019, management locked out the musicians: neither salaries nor benefits were paid out until the lockout ended in November. An estimate of $2.5 million was "saved" by the orchestra's management/administrators in terms of musicians' wages and benefits during the canceled summer season, an observation that shows some cynicism as the savings came at the cost of the musicians' none-too-deep pockets.[210] "It was not as if this was the first time we were hit by concessions, we have moved backwards to the financial level we were at a decade ago and that really hurts all of us."[211]

In an extraordinary move of support, the Maryland General Assembly, the state's legislative body approved House Bill 1404 to appropriate $1.6 million in funds to the orchestra. While locked out, the musicians offered countless concerts at venues throughout the region. Symbolically, the musicians replaced the canceled Star-Spangled Spectacular with another iconic performance that same day. Deep insights into the BalSO's challenges, provided by the former Baltimore-based arts critic Tim Smith, crystallize many facets of the musicians' viewpoints and expose their willingness to sacrifice hard-earned salaries as part of a compromise deal. His observations on the problems of applying business models to cultural organizations are instructive not only for US orchestras but also for Dutch orchestras facing similar financial quandaries.[212]

209. https://www.bsomusic.org/education-community/young-musicians/orchkids.aspx.
210. Brian Prechtl, cochair Baltimore Symphony Musicians, shared comments detailing the musicians' plight.
211. *Ibid.*
212. https://bytimsmith.com/f/a-few-more-thoughts-about-the-bsos-woes.

1.48 CLOSING OBSERVATIONS

#1 the 52-week season, full-time employment

History teaches us that the move from part-time contracts to a full 52-week season for US orchestras took place in the 1970s.[213] The post-2007-2008 financial crisis moves to cut seasons that have shaved off weeks in Atlanta, Detroit and St. Louis are a reminder that a 52-week season at least for US orchestral musicians is not to be taken for granted. Although the state-subsidized orchestras in the Netherlands offer year-round employment, as mentioned above, orchestras have been "downsized" as a result of post-crisis budgetary cuts. One of the most disconcerting consequences of downsizing as it plays out in the Netherlands is the extensive pressure placed upon those musicians who "remain." Employers expect the "remaining" musicians to produce the same number of services (concerts/recordings, etc.) and thus maintain the same level of production as before the implementation of the cuts. The health and welfare of the "working" orchestral musicians have deteriorated in terms of a rise in burnouts and requests for sick leave. This affects not only the quality of employment for the individual orchestral musician but also ultimately the artistic quality of the orchestra.

#2 cross-cultural considerations

European musicians including of course Dutch musicians were mystified by their US counterparts' industrial actions, lockout after lockout and strike after strike in rapid succession. Pre-crisis, Dutch colleagues viewed their colleagues' actions in the United States as "over the top," "exaggerated" and even "unnecessary."[214] "We really do not understand why these Americans are picketing their own orchestras not because we feel they shouldn't but because we are of the view, where will all this disorder lead to? Will they really gain something other than mistrust on the part of their managers?"[215] Well-documented information concerning strikes at US orchestras from the first major musicians' strike in Philadelphia in 1966[216] to the recent seven-week Chicago Symphony Orchestra (CSO) strike ending in April 2019 proves that strikes can benefit musicians by attaining greater leverage in terms of collective bargaining for specific employment benefits.[217]

The previous statement should be taken with a grain of salt as public opinion needs to be taken into consideration during work stoppages, and public opinion does not always take kindly to strikes. The aforementioned CSO strike 2019 gleaned responses published in media reports such as: "the impression of most of the concert-loving audience appears to have gradually shifted over the last four weeks—from vague sympathy

213. *Senza Sordino,* ICSOM's monthly publication provides a great deal of material on the march forward from shorter seasons to a full-time, fully remunerated orchestra job as its 1970s editions attest.
214. Gleaned from conversation with Dutch orchestral musicians fully employed as well as freelancers.
215. Conversations with Jan Spronk, RCO former principal oboe.
216. *Senza Sordino, supra,* provides ample historical evidence from US orchestras since 1963.
217. Ending on April 27, 2019, the CSO musicians' longest strike centered on pensions.

to dismay, impatience, frustration, anger and even outrage. Words like 'unrealistic,' 'out of step,' 'spoiled,' 'childish,' 'pampered,' and 'selfish' are increasingly being voiced."[218] The recurring theme of the "overpaid top-tier US orchestral musician" voiced infamously by Ivan Hewett, "why should musicians be paid so well for doing what they love?"[219] and recast in *The Guardian* one year later was replayed countless times in commentaries concerning the CSO strike.[220] The tenor of this commentary ran as follows: these musicians should be grateful to play in such a jewel of an orchestra and to receive salaries (minimum salary 2019: $181,000) that most people, not only musicians, could only dream of. Comparisons between well-paid US orchestras (the Los Angeles Philharmonic) and Manchester's notoriously low paid Hallé Orchestra were brought forward to support the argument that US orchestral musicians should reconsider their demands for competitive wages and compensation packages as they are "too high and unreasonable." Of all comparisons, the mention of the Hallé is painful at best. An article published in *The Guardian* reporting on the miserable wages received by British orchestral professionals prior to the salary slam bore the subheading "The money's terrible, the stress is awful ... No wonder so many of Britain's orchestra players are choosing to hang up their bows."[221] Its closing quote brought home the exigencies of working in Britain's underpaid orchestras: "People say to you, 'Oh, you play in the Hallé, how wonderful. What's your day job?'"[222]

A comparison of successful well-paid orchestral employees with those who face penury is damaging and sadly pervasive in media reports on key issues in the orchestral world. From the US examples mentioned above and the buzz about adequate wages for musician freelancers in the Netherlands, there is a tendency to judge the value of musicians' output and gloss over many of the pressing issues that engender lockouts and financial allocation crises. If critics were to take a more celebratory stance by applauding the fact that orchestras enrich communities and deserve remuneration for these services, such observations could contribute mightily to the ongoing discussion of the orchestra's importance in terms of impact and value. The Los Angeles Philharmonic, cast in a negative light as overpaid, deserves a quick revisit. In its celebratory centennial year, the orchestra, feted for its financial stability and superlative musician remuneration, is noteworthy for much, much more than that. A musical organization that puts social justice and community building smack in the middle of an ambitious musical mission to promote 50 new commissions in one year and has nurtured a cadre of young professional players from underprivileged areas of the city is an inspiration for orchestras worldwide.

218. Lawrence Johnson. "CSO Musicians, Management Need to End Strike Now: For the Good of Chicago and Themselves." *Chicago Classical Review* April 19, 2019.
219. Ivan Hewett. "US Orchestras Are Greedy and Overpaid." *The Guardian* October 2, 2013, https://www.telegraph.co.uk/culture/music/classicalmusic/10350252/US-orchestras-are-greedy-and-overpaid.htm.
220. Tom Service. "Why Are Salaries So Markedly Different Between British and U.S. Orchestras?" *The Guardian* June 26, 2014, https://www.theguardian.com/music/tomserviceblog/2014/jun/26/orchestra-salaries-higher-in-america-than-uk.
221. Anna Price. "Pit of Despair" *The Guardian* February 2, 2006, https://www.theguardian.com/music/2006/feb/02/classicalmusicandopera3.
222. *Ibid.*

2

Haydn Rewrites History

> Orchestral musicians not only contribute to the perpetuation but to the creation of musical works, while the limelight is usually taken by composers, soloists and conductors, let us not forget the musicians who play the music, integral cogs in the musical wheel.[223]

> The truth is that our present-day symphony orchestra is not basically different in concept or composition from that of 1910, in spite of the tripling or quintupling of wind instruments, or the addition or invention of the plethora of percussion instruments which seem to be invading the whole stage.[224]

In our quest to contextualize vulnerabilities within orchestral musicians' employment and make sense of the changes wrought by recent crises on the work lives of orchestral musicians, a trip down a historical lane sets the stage for an examination of issues as relevant in the 21st century as they were at the dawn of orchestral history. *Haydn rewrites history* takes a narrative path to share details on the nature of orchestral musicians' contracted work in one of the great early orchestral collectives, the Esterházy orchestra in the second half of the 18th century led by Joseph Haydn, one of the giants in the pantheon of Western classical composers. We will also travel to other musically relevant locations and time periods to provide a better understanding of the inner and outer workings of the orchestra and its musicians in its formative years.

This movement's section 2.1 moves back in time to the guilds and medieval precursors of the modern orchestra with special emphasis on emergent contracts in medieval France and London.

Section 2.2 studies the orchestral situation in the Austrian empire of the 18th century, with special emphasis on contractual obligations and the role of patronage and its influence on musicians' contracts during Haydn's lifetime. This section provides a

223. Conversations with Christopher Keene, former Music Director of the New York City Opera.
224. Leonard Bernstein. *The Future of the Symphony Orchestra* speech American Symphony Orchestra League 1980, https://leonardbernstein.com/lectures/speeches/the-future-of-the-symphony-orchestra.

closer look at the 18th-century maestro-Kapellmeister in charge of creative and administrative activities to open the discussion on the development of the conductor as a major influence not only on musicians' musical lives but also on their employment situations. The story of a velvet revolution, the first recorded musical labor protest dating back to November 1772, will also be told.

Section 2.3 examines Haydn's later life ventures in London as pivotal in bridging two worlds of orchestral employment. Leaving the protection of princely patronage to voyage to London in the 1790s brought the Kapellmeister Haydn to the epicenter of the English entrepreneurial music scene. We also focus on the freelance musicians who performed at the city's burgeoning theaters. Musical performers in London moved frequently between jobs at various venues much like modern-day freelancers: London musicians did not make their homes under the aegis of protection of the agents and theaters who offered employment, unlike their confreres in European courts and chapels (Kapelle).

Section 2.4 reviews Leipzig's civic academies to provide information on another form of orchestral organization that relates to contemporary orchestral freelancers' vulnerabilities.

Section 2.5 leads to the 19th century to study the impact of societal changes on orchestral musicians in terms of patronage and employment.

Section 2.6 charts the ascendancy of the US orchestra.

Forging ahead from a discussion of Haydn's role as conductor-administrator, the *movement* sketches the cult of the larger personality to continue the discussion on the role of the maestro as a controlling force at the orchestra. The live-in onsite Kapellmeisters of the 18th century, the 19th-century roots of the cult of the maestro, and the personality-maestros of the 20th-21st centuries are considered in the context of their influence on their musicians and the orchestral organization.

2.1 MONTEVERDI'S MOJO

In the early years of the 17th century, a performance of the operatic drama *Orfeo* changed the course of music history. The prolific composer Claudio Monteverdi took the radical step to insert vocal musical outbursts, the term first associated with arias, to fully exploit the emotional impact of the text. A division of labor between the sung word and played accompaniment revolutionized the market for musicians in a soundscape in which singers and orchestral musicians were indispensable.

By the mid-18th century, the orchestra as an essential part of operatic performance and in its own right became an indispensable focal point for culture and cultural entrepreneurship.[225] The social history of the orchestra can be read in terms of shifts in patronage and changes in social structures tied to political and economic changes. The public concert, a precursor to today's orchestral mega-performances at parks and large arenas, became a forum for lavish display that gave rulers across the European continent the opportunity to enhance their popularity through mass entertainment.

225. Adam Carse, *The Orchestra in the XVIIIth Century*, on orchestral patronage, 1940.

Vivid accounts of the open rehearsal of George Frideric Handel's *Music for the Royal Fireworks,* composed to celebrate King George II's victory in the War of the Austrian Succession, mention an extraordinary traffic jam in London as 12,000 people fought their way to the Vauxhall Spring Gardens. The premiere would have been the envy of any modern rock band. An eyewitness reported, "what contributed to the awkwardness of the whole was the right pavilion catching fire and being burnt down in the middle of the show."[226] Inferno notwithstanding, the show did go on for a record nine hours, a triumph for the performers and George II, whose popularity rose considerably thereafter.[227]

The orchestral musicians who provided musical entertainment at courts, chapels, theaters, and other musical venues during the 18th century are an excellent point of departure for a study of present-day vulnerabilities. A considerable number of orchestral performers found employment in three settings with differences in employment situations akin to the protected, contractually employed orchestral musicians versus their modern-day freelance colleagues. To deepen our understanding of the somewhat singular employment context within the orchestral world, we will discuss the historical antecedents of the modern orchestral workplace in Europe, the cradle of orchestral civilization.

A diversity of roles played by freelance as well as fully contracted orchestral musicians characterized employment in the formative years of the modern orchestra, with a special focus on the well-documented Esterházy Kapelle orchestra under the inspired leadership of Joseph Haydn. The focus on this extraordinary "band" of musicians informs a discussion of the interactions between musicians and a hierarchy of conductors, impresarios, and patrons who exercised control over musicians' lives.

2.2 EARLY ORCHESTRAL TYPOLOGIES

Three variations on the orchestral theme in the 18th century are noteworthy: the protected Kapelle,[228] civic orchestras, and the freelance bands of trained musicians who traveled from gig to gig in search of work. In terms of employment protection, two of the three types of orchestral employment, the Kapelle and the civil service orchestras, involved a modicum of protection for those employed. For the Kapelle musicians, contractual ties to patrons, and for the civil orchestral players, contracts to perform music at civic occasions, provided some security. Akin to modern-day freelance orchestral musicians, a third category of 18th-century orchestral players were the freelancers employed by impresarios to perform in London theaters. Charles Burney, chronicler par excellence, immortalized one ensemble of peripatetic independent players, "That prodigious orchestra, which never before had existence on the earth and

226. Eyewitness accounts of the premiere, preface, http://www.hogwood.org/archive/composers/handel/introduction-to-facsimile-edition-of-handels-music-for-the-royal-fireworks.html.
227. *Ibid.*
228. *Merriam Webster Dictionary* definition:

1. The choir or orchestra of a royal or papal chapel.
2. A musical organization; especially: orchestra.

which by its admirable arrangement seemed like Music itself, to descend from the skies."[229]

2.3 MUSICIANS' GUILDS IN MEDIEVAL EUROPE: INSIDERS AND OUTSIDERS ON THE FREELANCE SCENE

Bands of itinerant musicians were part of the European social landscape since early recorded history, ranging from small musical troupes to individual musicians who joined others on-location.[230] Although a staple source of entertainment at county fairs and city festivals, their lives were beset by haphazard work and living conditions and fraught with vicissitudes such as negligible (or total lack of) payment and low societal status. Viewed as idle ne'er-do-wells by rulers, city fathers and even their fellow musicians who were more successful in finding patronage, itinerants were subjected to bans and other legislative restrictions documented in France, England, and Germany with roots in the 12th century.[231] A closer examination of these early-day musical freelancers is useful as the closer the scrutiny, the more similarities can be found with modern-day musicians and the vulnerabilities they face.

One of the few recorded examples that offer insights into the work lives of musical itinerants pre-17th century takes us back to the reign of English King Edward IV, just prior to the War of Roses (1484). The monarch was keen to organize what he perceived to be unruly bands and presented traveling musicians under his jurisdiction with a quandary: refrain from plying your trade or join the Guild of Royal Minstrels.[232] The protectionist measure was taken at the instigation of the King's personal musicians who sought to keep "certain ignorant rustics" and "foreigners" from taking the work of genuine, skilled minstrels. The guild gave its members the power to examine and control membership and delimit the competition. Whether or not the guild's Charter provided genuine protective measures to further artistic goals or was simply a way to maintain a status quo in which unwelcome (politically, religiously, socially) individuals were deemed to be societal pariahs remains unclear.[233]

The Charter itself was not long lived: 30 years after its entry into force, a localized charter was enacted in the City of London. In the City, membership was key as the Charter determined participation in coveted paid musical activities. The members of the Minstrels and Freemen of the City of London were referred to as waits, servants who performed musical entertainments at municipal fairs and official holidays. The London guild favored an extreme, patriotic membership in which foreigners were barred from "any Minstrelsy, singying or playeing upon any instrument (sic)" within

229. Charles Burney. *An Account of the Musical Performances in Westminster-Abbey and the Pantheon 1784 in Commemoration of Handel* 117, 1785, https://books.google.nl/books?id=DdFbAAAAQAAJ&pg=RA1-PA24&source=gbs_toc_r&cad=4-v=onepage&q&f=false.
230. Walter Salmen. *Der fahrende Musiker im europaäischen Mittelalter* 24-25, 1960.
231. Nigel Wilkins. *Music in the Age of Chaucer* 143, 1979.
232. Charter Musicians' Company 1604, https://www.wcomarchive.org.uk/--company-charters.
233. Heretics and Jews were prohibited from guild membership; questionable means were relied upon to ascertain faith.

City or its franchises.[234] A breach on the part of a foreigner or another type of unwanted musician was subject to a hefty fine.[235]

2.4 ALLONS ENFANTS: THE CONFRÉRIES IN MEDIEVAL FRANCE

The French historian Jacques Le Goff[236] underlined that although many professions gained legitimacy in medieval France, two métiers were excluded from the ranks of proper Christian society: prostitution and the category encompassing musicians (la jonglerie). Yet, despite this dire marginalization, musicians trade organizations were active in several medieval urban centers. The first documented guild, an offshoot of a religious group that opened its doors to both women and men, the *Confrérie des Jongleurs et des Bourgeois d'Arras,* dates back to 1175.[237] Historians stress that religious hocus-pocus more than musical professionalism was the binding factor for a guild that centered its activities on combining an enactment of legends with music, a precursor to the present-day musical.[238]

According to the wise essayists who initiated the essential encyclopedia of music known as *Sir George Grove's Dictionary of Music and Musicians* (revised multiple times since its original publication in 1879), Paris was the most important hub for organized musicians and individual freelancers in search of employment as evidenced by tax records going back to the 13th century.[239] By 1328, the members of the Parisian musicians confrérie had established a hospital and a chapel to attend to members' spiritual and physical needs. Prospective members were required to be "faithful to the Church" and had to pass a mandatory musical examination—the precursor to the modern audition. "*Etrangers*" (foreigners) and non-church adherents were barred from entry into the protected society. Profit sharing was an important part of membership in these arrangements as evidenced in notarial deeds and the 1407 statutes. The statute remained in force until the mid-17th century when Louis XIV reverted to a more authoritarian approach to cultural personnel.

2.5 ORCHESTRAL MUSICIANS' PROFESSIONAL POSITIONS PRE-18TH CENTURY

A musician's professional life in pre-18th century Europe can best be described as a peripatetic existence that entailed moves in search of gainful employment. At the high end of the supply chain, performance entrepreneurs *avant la lettre,* the performing

234. "The Musicians' Company" *Musical Times* November 1, 1919 586-588.
235. *Ibid.*
236. Jacques Le Goff. "Métiers licites et illicites dans l'occident medieval" *Pour un autre Moyen Age,* 1978.
237. Kay Slocum. "'Confrérie, Bruderschaft' and Guild: The Formation of Musicians' Fraternal Organisations in Thirteenth- and Fourteenth Century Europe " *Early Music History* 14 1995, DOI: 10.1017/s0261127900001480.
238. *Ibid.*
239. Paris, *The New Grove Dictionary of Music and Musicians* 184-169, 1980.

musicians who acquired a high level of training and had the right connections, sought the protection of a residential position that provided protection against the vagaries of nonemployed musicians' lives. In contrast to the present day, when music conservatories are the center for musical training and career connections, Europe's first orchestral musicians were more often than not members of the same extended family.[240] Regardless of geographical location, from the Austrian Kapelle to the corps of free-market musicians in Amsterdam, London, Paris, and Venice, family connections were an important commonality. The musical craft was passed on through family tradition, more often than not, from father to son (although there is documentary evidence that points to a few famed daughters who worked in early-day European music ensembles).[241] While many orchestras throughout mainland Europe consigned musicians to servant status,[242] their leaders were granted a higher status leading to complex intra-orchestral hierarchies resulting in the maestro-musician disparity in terms of salary and status found in the modern-day orchestra. Armed with essential information concerning orchestras pre-18th century, we will lift the curtain on the first documented orchestral protest: the premiere performance of Haydn's "Farewell" Symphony.

2.6 THE CURTAIN OPENS: AN UNLIKELY PROTEST IN THE 18TH CENTURY

About 250 years ago, when the lives of orchestral musicians were controlled by the whims of their patrons, the celebrated Austrian composer Joseph Haydn[243] devised an ingenious musical ruse to grant rights for his musicians. Haydn's introduction of a discrete but effective form of industrial action into a musical score provides insights into the role of musicians, maestros, and their supporting patrons on the eve of the century of orchestral development, the 19th century.

Although great composers such as Joseph Haydn (1732-1809) and his younger compatriot Wolfgang Amadeus Mozart (1756-1791) brought the classical period in music history to exceptional heights in terms of musical invention, their quests for economic stability within a profession characterized by uncertainty posed substantial professional challenges.[244] It was, with the notable exception of London's commercial theaters, the church and the aristocracy that provided the primary support system for

240. John Spitzer and Neal Zaslaw, *The Birth of the Orchestra: History of an Institution, 1650-1815*. Oxford University Press 2004, 404.
241. More details in the movement, *Of Rowe and Race*.
242. A wealth of literature written by 18th-century diarists including Charles Burney, Samuel Pepys, and Leopold Mozart provides indispensable information on the trials and tribulations of musicians.
243. Joseph Haydn, born the same year as George Washington and politically savvy in his own right (1732), was applauded not only for his genius as a composer but also for his affable demeanor. *See* H.C. Robbins Landon's *Haydn Chronicle and Works*. Indiana University Press 1976 and Grout's encyclopedic source.
244. Wolfgang Amadeus Mozart (1756-1791) was born 24 years after Joseph Haydn. *See* Charles Rosen's monograph *The Classical Style: Haydn, Mozart, Beethoven*. W.W. Norton 1971 for more background information on this extraordinary period in musical history.

Europe's successfully employed musicians until the 19th century. The rise of publicly supported concert halls and concert series that made the London music scene so unique resonated with Enlightenment and subsequent revolutionary ideas that swept Europe in the late 18th century. The success of London's various public subscription series became a cultural export product and influenced cultural activities in European capitals and subsequently US cities in the 19th century.

2.7 MOZART VERSUS HAYDN: THE QUEST FOR FINANCIAL STABILITY

Haydn's stable musical career as a composer-conductor stands in sharp contrast to the trials and tribulations that Wolfgang Amadeus Mozart suffered in his unsuccessful attempts to find a harmonious balance between musical creativity and financial stability. His short life as a composer-performer extraordinaire was hampered by his constant and oft-futile attempts to attain a modicum of economic stability. From earliest childhood, the wunderkind crisscrossed Europe to seek remuneration for feats of musical prowess. Mozart's correspondence provides evidence of increasing frustration on finding sponsorship and brings to the fore the difficulties of coming of age: young prodigies were apt to strike gold, whereas "older" talents became quickly passé. His multiple attempts to gain financial support from his Masonic brothers reveal an early creative attempt to engage in marketing, similar to crowdfunding initiatives employed by some musicians today. Ample correspondence bears witness to the pressures of the habitually penniless genius in search of handouts. The tone of Mozart's letters toward the end of his short life borders on desperation as he begged a diminishing circle of friends and fellow Freemasons for funds to cover basic living expenses. "Without your help, the honor, peace of mind and perhaps the life itself of your friend and brother Mason will perish."[245]

Passed over by the Austrian Emperor Joseph II for a Kapellmeister position as head of court music, Mozart's bid for a stable position was thwarted by the clever Antonio Salieri (1750-1825), whose place in history remains tainted by unfounded albeit well-popularized accusations of jealousy and even murder.[246] Unlike Haydn, Mozart did not have a "home-based" orchestra under his supervision. Mozart's freelance artistic collaborations with existing orchestral ensembles the length and breadth of Europe were dependent on the orchestral ensembles hired by aristocrats, archbishops, or on occasion, civic orchestras.

Of great musical and cultural historical interest, Mozart's artistic and financial history is but ancillary to this research because his fortunes, or more aptly financial misfortunes, while closely related to changes in artistic support models, were not

245. *The Letters of Mozart and his Family* vol. 3, https://archive.org/stream/lettersofmozarth000640mbp/lettersofmozarth000640mbp_djvu.txt, Letter to Freemason brother Michael Puchberg July 1789.

246. No less a literary light than Alexander Pushkin wrote *Mozart and Salieri* shortly after Antonio Salieri died in 1825, adding a theatrical twist to the rumor concerning Mozart's untimely demise.

directly related to the ups and downs of life within the orchestra. What is pertinent are Mozart's fundraising attempts and his efforts to ally himself with a community of patrons-musicians. In subsequent *movements*, we will discover that the success of the 21st-century orchestra often lies in its ability to build a relationship with audiences, patrons, municipal leaders, and the community at large. Without such ties, the ensemble is doomed to extinction.

Centuries later, locked-out US musicians took to social media and crowdfunding to popularize their efforts in attempts to maintain financially solvent status. Tellingly, examples taken from the prolonged Minnesota Orchestra lockout of 2013 illustrate that the Mozartian method of direct contact with patrons helped pave the way to move forward from industrial conflict to resolution. "One of the major learning points during the long lockout [almost 17 months] was the realization of how important relationships with committed patrons of our art were to the eventual success of our mission: to get the orchestra back on stage. Careful grooming and constant reminders to those who influence, cannot be overestimated."[247] Hold that thought for later *movements*, as Haydn's long tenure at Esterházy will now be discussed to provide more depth in our discussion of orchestral musicians' employment.

2.8 HAYDN: OF GENIUS, PROTECTION, AND STABILITY

Among the most prolific composers of all time,[248] Haydn's musical life and professional maneuvers suggest diverse points of departure to examine the role of the orchestral musician within a nexus of interconnected employment relationships. Under his aegis as Vice-Kapellmeister and in due course Kapellmeister for the Esterházy aristocrats, Haydn auditioned, selected, conducted, rehearsed, and organized every aspect of orchestral operations at the individual and collective level. Germane to research that examines orchestral crises, the first recorded act of protest with regard to musicians' employment that took place during the première performance of Haydn's Symphony No. 45 (known since its premiere as the "Farewell" Symphony) opens the door to a discussion on how orchestral musicians interact with their "patrons"/employers, their maestros/directors, and their audiences.[249]

2.9 THE SEEDS OF THE MODERN ORCHESTRAL ORGANIZATION

The first chronicled industrial action in the orchestral workplace took place in the closely controlled Esterházy Kapelle under Haydn's creative direction. As total subordinates, the Kapelle's contracted musicians were expected to be loyal servants who

247. Conversations with Marcia Peck, Minnesota Orchestra cellist and orchestra committee chair.
248. Haydn's output was exhaustive, for starters: 108 (!) symphonies, 68 string quartets, 19 operas, 32 chamber divertimenti, 29 piano trios, multiple masses, and oratorios.
249. James Webster's *Haydn's "Farewell" Symphony and the Idea of Classical Style: Through-Composition and Cyclic Integration in His Instrumental Music*. Cambridge University Press 2004.

would "contract their entire person to the Prince."[250] Their services were remunerated by Princely protection and salary payments.[251] Wages, clothing, housing (including housing for musicians' immediate families), candles, wood, food, wine, and health services were granted to the lucky few who agreed "to appear diligently ... and to participate as long as We shall please."[252] Certain instrumentalists with seniority and several virtuosic players received higher wages than the rest.[253] According to conventions established in earlier centuries, singers were seen as high-status musicians whose name recognition and stage-performance skills lent them a privileged place above the orchestral rank-and-file. Records prove that salaries for Kapelle singers were generally higher than those of orchestral players.

Haydn's patron, Prince Nicolaus, in full cognizance of the impact an impressive residence would add to perceptions of his wealth and power, set about to build a vast domain in the hinterlands of the Austro-Hungarian region.[254] The Prince was so partial to his grand palace that he opted to spend the greater part of the year there. This in turn meant that his servants, including Haydn's orchestra members, were required to sojourn and perform at this preferred residence. Their work was intensive, requiring early morning chapel accompaniments, music at mealtimes (Tafelmusik), and late-night performances. Although the opulent summer palace was replete with hidden gardens, trompe l'oeil creations, and a shell-encrusted grotto, it certainly was not an ideal performance space: the residence was surrounded by mosquito-infested swamps. More importantly, musicians were obligated to live far away from their families; overworked, they grew restless.

While no written records extant bear witness to the Esterházy musicians' communiqués with Haydn, the Vice-Kapellmeister kept journals that documented many aspects of orchestral protestations. Haydn decided to assuage the tension between the Prince's policies and the players' reasonable demands. According to his contract of service, he held the responsibility to "influence his subordinates to preserve such harmony" (*see* clause #3 in the 1761 contract below) and to keep the peace at all times; all musician-related problems were to be kept "far from his Serene Highness" (*see* clause #6 below). Haydn's choice for musical diplomacy proves inspirational centuries later, as orchestral musicians face recurrent impasses in terms of their employment conditions.

Rather than engage in verbal intercession with his esteemed patron, Haydn devised a sophisticated musical solution to bring the musicians' demands to the Prince's table. Haydn's Farewell Symphony revolves around the capricious F-sharp-minor key, a deliberate and highly original choice. Whereas this quirky choice of a key, which is rarely used in 18th- and early 19th-century classical music, might not seem

250. John Spitzer & Neal Zaslaw, *supra*.
251. János Harich. "Das Haydn-Orchester im Jahr 1780." *Haydn Jahrbuch* 8 1971, http://www.haydn13.com/Inhaltsseiten/Das-Haydn-Orchester.
252. Author's translation above. "Manche Instrumente waren finanziell bessergestellt als andere. Sänger bekamen noch mehr Geld."
253. *Ibid.*
254. Geographic boundaries in the region changed as the result of numerous wars and power shifts; in Haydn's day, the Esterházy territories were part of the Habsburg Empire.

obvious to today's listeners due to a lack of enhanced musical education, the Prince and his entourage would have taken note, literally, of the subtlety of Haydn's choice of key and the uncommon musical turn of affairs aurally evident in the first movement. Adding to the unusual nature of the last movement, Haydn closes deliberately with a slow section that adds an unexpected twist, a measured aftermath following a rousing opening section. Farewell Symphony anecdotes abound, but rather than continue down the storytelling path, the score should suffice as a means of explanation. Haydn indicates that the musicians should play until they exit the stage, one by one. Last but certainly not least, the first two violinists from the orchestral complement calmly finish the symphony en duo, the very last to leave.

Haydn's musical maneuver brought instant success. According to his biographers, the Prince took the musicians' cues in stride, reputedly uttering the words, "well, if the musicians have gone, we had better leave as well."[255] Haydn's orchestra members were commanded to return home for a brief sojourn with their families. Did Haydn's cleverly packaged musical act of protest yield any long-term effects? Did the walkout resonate throughout the centuries to inspire other acts of protest? Do orchestral musicians who are dissatisfied by present-day work situations band together and stage protest actions? The simple answer to the first question is "yes." The second and third questions will be addressed in *movements* on orchestral industrial actions and Dutch orchestral reorganizations, which occupy the bulk of this book.

The orchestral walkout written into Haydn's score has been repeated as a musical joke to the delight of audiences worldwide since its 1772 premiere. Inside the orchestra, the Farewell action is certainly not forgotten. Faced with an overtime call in which an orchestra rehearsal had reached its CAO set time limit, the Dutch conductor Hans Vonk offered his musicians the opportunity to "walkout like in Haydn's time" or stay put for a few minutes to finish the movement of music they were rehearsing. "Had it been one my American orchestras, I would not have thought to ask, however I thought that the (Netherlands) Radio Symphony musicians would agree affably—they did."[256]

Protest actions on the part of orchestral musicians who took to more militant means of showing dissatisfaction in the 20th and 21st centuries will be discussed in subsequent *movements*. On to a closer examination of Haydn's Kapellmeister experience as it illuminates several significant factors that are imperative to the story of orchestral musicians' employment. Subordination, a key factor in determining workers' status in the employment relationship, was certainly essential to Haydn's contractual relationship with the Prince as well as central to his musicians' relationships with both the Prince and Kapellmeister.

2.10 THE KAPELLMEISTER

Haydn stood at the helm of musical activities for the culturally active Esterházy clan from 1761 until 1791. As chief of musical affairs, he was subservient only to his

255. David Wynn Jones, *The Life of Haydn*. Cambridge University Press 2013, 84.
256. Conversations with Maestro Hans Vonk.

employer, the Prince. Starting as a Vice-Kapellmeister to the paterfamilias Prince Peter Paul, Haydn's early-day experiences as a composer-musicians' manager and princely go-between shed light on the working lives of performing musicians before revolutionary social and political upheavals later in the century would sweep orchestral musicians into more precarious employment situations. A closer examination of Haydn's contract signed months before Peter Paul's brother Nicolaus the Magnificent[257] took over the position as head of the powerful Esterházy family shows that indeed subordination to the Prince was of paramount importance.

Haydn was contracted to provide compositions ranging from Tafelmusik (performed at tableside) to sizeable compositions for Sunday masses and additional chamber music compositions, symphonies, and operas. Part and parcel of his duties was the organization and management of the resident orchestra, capable of performing at flexible hours amplified by a coterie of singers, brass fanfare specialists, and, if the Prince requested, special performers (referring to itinerant bands of freelancers).

A closer examination of Haydn's contract of service provides evidence that supports the notion that Haydn enjoyed a special relationship with Nicolaus. He was able to spread his musical wings with a superlative orchestra at his disposal and an international as well as discriminating royal audience who showed their approval of his prodigious compositions with great regularity at the Esterházy residences. Unlike many a patron who claimed ownership of a subordinate's productions, the Prince broke with the conventions set down contractually by his predecessor (*see* clause 3, 1761 contract)[258] and permitted Haydn to accept commissions from international venues.

2.11 HAYDN'S INITIAL CONTRACT SIGNED ON MAY 1, 1761

> The said Joseph [Haydn] shall be considered and treated as a member of the household. Thus, his Serene Highness is graciously pleased to place confidence in the belief that he will conduct himself in a fitting manner, as becomes an honorable official of a princely house. He should be mild, temperate, not showing himself overbearing toward his musicians, but straightforward and composed. He should never treat his musicians in a brutal manner.

A close reading of paragraph 2 offers remarkable insight into the personality traits considered appropriate for the Prince's preferred chief musician. The chosen one, i.e., the Kapellmeister, was expected to be accommodating, courteous, and above all, respectful. Haydn would aggrandize the Princely fortunes through his gift of music as a highly esteemed member of the Prince's inner circle.

Examples of poorly run musical Kapelle that contrast to Haydn's abode abound: an interesting study of the Viennese Imperial Court (1705-1711) at the time of Joseph

257. Prince Nicolaus Esterházy (1714-1790) epithet "the Magnificent" refers to his substantial aesthetic interests, love of luxury and investment in architecture, art and above all, music.
258. Documents on contractual matters, *Haydn-Studien* III:2. Further, Griesinger reproduced parts of Haydn's contracts. *See gettyimages-164071604-594x594-2.jpg.*

I and Joseph II[259] provides copious examples of misuse of funds, musicians' squabbles, reductions in the numbers of musicians employed (in today's orchestral reorganization parlance, cuts in the complement), problems in finding suitable musicians, as well as the efficient organization of orchestral musicians and singers.[260] The Esterházy Kapelle did not suffer from a shortage of musicians; performers competed for positions in the well-known and greatly esteemed ensemble. Haydn proved to be the ideal Kapellmeister: his endless musical production put the Esterházy palaces on the cultural map of Europe. A place on the cultural map helped maintain the Esterházy position of power accrued through wealth, military prowess, and political savvy—vital to the continuation of the dynasty of fame and fortune.

A return to the contract underlines the significance of fairness and equal treatment in this early example of a musician's employment contract. The manner in which Haydn responded to the dissatisfaction expressed by his musicians in the Farewell episode points to his diplomatic skills. Within the contract, the instruction that "he should not treat his musicians in a brutal manner"[261] provides a contractual caution to protect musicians from the whims of a callous, hard-handed Kapellmeister (music director). Countless tales of musical woe at the hands of authoritarian and even "brutal" maestros pepper the pages of accounts of orchestral musicians' tales from the pit, as the *movement* devoted to discrimination on the part of music directors elucidates. The aforementioned contractual warning could well serve as a model for conductors' conduct in modern times:

> 2. When the orchestra is summoned to perform before company, the Vice-Kapellmeister and all the musicians shall appear in uniform, and the said Joseph [Haydn] shall take care that he and all the members of his orchestra follow the instructions given, and appear in white stockings, white linen, fully powdered, and with a tie wig.

The fact that the uniforms were paid for by the Prince gives credence to the influence of enlightenment ideas that emphasized that an aristocrat's leadership and wealth should inspire a sense of obligation toward all those who contribute to his well-being:[262]

> 3. Whereas the other musicians are referred for directions to the Vice-Kapellmeister, he shall therefore conduct himself in an exemplary manner and abstain from unnecessary familiarity and common behavior in eating, drinking, and conversation, not dispensing with the respect due to him, but acting uprightly and influencing his subordinates to preserve such harmony as is becoming in

259. Joseph II coruled as Holy Roman Emperor over the extensive Habsburg lands with his mother Empress Maria Theresa, 1765-1780; and as sole ruler, 1780-1790.
260. *See* Alison Dunlop "Forgotten Musicians: Documenting Musical Life at the Viennese Imperial Court in the Eighteenth Century" *Musicologica Brunensia* 47(1), 2012, 93-112.
261. *See supra*, 8.2.2.3 Haydn's initial contract signed on May 1, 1761.
262. Thought-provoking insights connecting Nicolaus' cultural patronage to Enlightenment ideals, *see* Kristóf Faster, "Taste Inequalities in the Art Consumption of Prince Nicolaus I Esterházy 'the Magnificent'" in *A Taste for Luxury in Early Modern Europe: Display, Acquisition and Boundaries*. Johanna Ilmakunnas and Jon Stobart (eds.) Bloomsbury 2017.

> them. He must take heed that any discord or disputes would displease his Serene Highness.

The thought-provoking clause 3 that underscores Haydn's responsibility as a role model and mediator recapitulates the importance of proper norms of behavior as part of the modus operandi at a well-functioning workplace. Conceptualize for a moment a relation between "to abstain from unnecessary familiarity" and the #metoo complications that plague the orchestral world at the present time.[263] The Kapelle contract sought to mitigate the problematic relationships that could impact musicians' ability to work effectively, cognizant of the temptations of the musicians' lifestyle with its inherent late nights, hard-work, and hard-play way of life. Putting the Prince at the top of the chain of command as a peace-loving ruler ("disputes ... would displease his Serene Highness") underscores the value of a harmonious workplace to the employer:

> 4. The Vice-Kapellmeister shall be bound to compose such music as his Serene Highness commands, and neither to communicate such compositions to any other person, nor to allow them to be copied, but he shall retain them for the absolute use of his Serene Highness, and not compose for any other person without the knowledge and permission of his Highness.

Composers' rights to their creations were as important in the 18th century as they are in the age of internet dissemination. Haydn's princely patrons were aware of the production and exchange of value inherent in the creation of original works. While this clause shifts the ownership of the composition from the creator (Haydn) to the patron, the actual situation with regard to "ownership" and "dissemination," not to speak of the "legal moment," in artistic production went far beyond clause 4.[264] Manuscript specialists hired by the Prince under the supervision of Haydn copied the Kapellmeister's compositions. In the 18th century, piracy was commonplace: at least 43 symphonies and 51 chamber music compositions were published in Amsterdam, London, and Paris without Haydn's permission between 1764 and 1780.[265] The assumption that he was unaware of these pirated copies might well be farfetched; his diary entries show that he was pleased with his growing acclaim.[266]

Aware of his contributions to the Esterházy court, Haydn succeeded in negotiating a substantial salary raise. Haydn insisted on not only an increase in monetary remuneration but also payment of 515 liters of wine per annum and complete coverage for his substantial medical costs and apothecary bills.[267] Over and beyond financial remuneration, artistic freedom was essential for Haydn. Although Haydn lived in a backwater location far from the delights and distractions of urban life, he was relieved

263. The Royal Concertgebouw Orchestra (RCO) and the Cleveland Orchestra (CO), both world-renowned orchestras, have been at the center of #metoo allegations in recent years, a theme that will be taken up in *Singing the classical #metoo blues*.
264. The concept of intellectual property was still in its infancy, first steps taken post-French Revolution, *see* Roland Barthes' "From Word to Text" in *Image, Music, Text* 161, 1977.
265. A treasure trove of information on issues concerning dissemination and piracy G.A. Griesinger. *Biographische Notizen über Joseph Haydn (1810)* (A.C. Dies edition 1963) https://books.google.nl/books?id=sGhDAAAAcAAJ&printsec=frontcover-v=onepage&q&f=false.
266. *Ibid.*
267. Haydn, *The American Cyclopaedia: A Popular Dictionary of General Knowledge* 540-542, 1883.

to follow his musical pursuits far from the crowded city and wrote frequently about the joys of splendid isolation. Thanks to Nicolaus' largesse, he built a first-rate orchestra and was the third highest-paid staff member at the Prince's court:

> My Prince was satisfied with all of my work, I received applause. as chief of the orchestra, I could try experiments, observe what produced the right effect and what weakened it; could therefore improve, add, cut out, venture, I was separated from the world, nobody to meddle with and plague me, and so I was perforce original.[268]

Haydn received permission not only to compose for any patron he chose but also to publish his works at will according to his revised contract in 1779:[269]

> 5. The Vice-Kapellmeister shall on a daily basis in whatever territory his Serene Highness resides consult with said Highness both morning and afternoon to inquire whether a concert should take place that day. If so, Haydn will be responsible to notify all musicians necessary for performance to ascertain that they will be prepared to perform. He will take duly note of any tardiness or attendance issues.

Outlining the nuts and bolts of a Kapellmeister's daily managerial duties, this clause makes no mention of the creative content of Haydn's obligations. Akin to the relationship between today's orchestra directors and management, common practice at the orchestra teaches that while managers might be free to offer suggestions, they should not question artistic decisions, the provenance of the music director. For Haydn, consultation was the tip of the iceberg during his long workdays: the Kapellmeister had to choose and compose the works to be performed, a creative process that took place while he addressed more mundane organizational issues such as tardiness and attendance issues. Often, the lead violinist (Konzertmeister) would receive additional delegated responsibilities and remuneration for his assistance in these matters.[270] Like contemporary concertmasters, Haydn's leader was granted extra privileges and pay:

> 6. In case of a dispute or complaint concerning the musicians, the Vice-Kapellmeister will resolve these matters to keep them far from his Serene Highness, not to disturb the peace. Only if dispute resolution is impossible to achieve should his Serene Highness be alerted in order to settle the matter... .

Haydn's biographers report that "with the players and singers, Haydn was on the best of terms. They vied with each other in carrying out his intentions, simply to show their gratitude and affection for him."[271] True to his nickname, Papa Haydn took care of his flock, and as his multiple biographers note, he was frequently involved in petitioning the Prince in an act of supplication on behalf of musicians' extra salaries, pensions, and/or sick pay.

---

268. *Ibid.*
269. Griesinger, *supra.*
270. *Ibid.*
271. *Grove's* vol. 4 5th edition (Eric Blom ed.) 151, 1961.

2.12 AT YOUR SERVICE: MUSICIAN'S ENTITLEMENTS AT THE ESTERHÁZY COURT

Haydn's musicians were privileged in terms of position and employment when compared to their compatriots in other European consorts and orchestras.[272] Holding a status that placed them above common servants, Haydn's orchestra members were easily identifiable as officers of the household entitled to wear livery uniforms. They received contracts that outlined their duties and a decent salary of 240 florins per year that held excellent purchasing power given the price of food, wine, and other necessities. Interestingly, in an early parallel to today's health-care coverage demands, the musicians demanded coverage for their apothecary bills—the 17th-century approach to health insurance. Their request for complete coverage was met with Princely refusal; such a request would only be granted to their leader, not to the rank-and-file musicians. The Prince was clever at economizing with regard to his personnel as the musicians' families were known to run up considerable charges:[273]

> 10. the Vice-Kapellmeister will make sure that the orchestra is on such an excellent level that it will bestow honor to himself and he will be remunerated with princely benefits accordingly.

According to Haydn's letters, "the prince gave unusually high salaries" not only to the Kapellmeister but also to the top-level musicians employed, a situation that parallels the elevated salaries of principal players nowadays, which will be given greater attention in *Of Rowe and Race*.[274] The comparatively low turnover within Haydn's core orchestra and the high number of superstar international musicians within the orchestra's ranks can be attributed to the inspiration gleaned from working with Haydn, the pleasant (albeit oft-stressful) work sphere, and favorable terms of employment.

A trip down musical memory lane teaches us that high salaries "so startlingly out of line that one might wonder if it could be a misprint or a wild rumor" were commonplace for 18th-century operatic celebrities.[275] Salary reports from Kapellmeister Haydn's Esterházy musicians show that while certain celebrity vocalists received competitive fees, their remuneration did not reach the heights of London theaters. The highest-paid member of the orchestra, the Konzertmeister Tommasini, earned less than 50% more than other contracted musicians. Well-remunerated, yes, but certainly not exorbitantly paid, considering his additional responsibilities.[276]

A glance at an orchestral musician's contract dated and signed by Nicolaus Prince Esterházy is useful not only as a marker to compare to the Kapellmeister's contract but also as an early and telling example of musicians' employment agreements. It shows

272. C.F. Pohl. *Joseph Haydn*, vol. 1. Verlag von Sacco Nachfolger, 1875, https://archive.org/details/bub_gb_wp6yAAAAIAAJ.
273. Documents on contractual matters, *Haydn-Studien* III:2, 1974.
274. For contemporary parallels, *see FAQs*.
275. Judith Milhous and Robert D. Hume, "Opera Salaries in Eighteenth-Century London" *Journal of the American Musicological Society* 46(1) 1993, 71-73, http://www.jstor.org/stable/831805.
276. *Haydn-Studien* III:2, 1974, *supra*.

how much, or more accurately, how little leeway they had to negotiate individual demands and how much control their patrons exercised. The live-in musician was paid, housed, and assured of light and heat—no small matter in the hinterlands of 18th-century Europe:

> We take Carl Schiringer into our Service as a double bass player, and We graciously authorize a yearly provision or salary, namely:
>
> In cash every month....20 Florins[277]
> For parade money, daily (the same amount as
> the other musician...17 Kreutzer)[278]
> Lodging, candles, wood
> One suit of clothes each year or two suits every two years.[279]

In return, the musician will perform the following duties:

(1) He will perform assiduously with choral and instrumental music at the hours designated, early and/or late, and to perform as long as we determine. We shall order that the musician shall provide diligent service not only at Eisenstadt but also in other locations where his services are required.
(2) To show total obedience to the Kapellmeister and to perform without any form of verbal remonstration that which the Kapellmeister commands in his service to the Prince.
(3) He shall conduct himself with quietude and grace as is suitable to a respectable part of the Prince's household, and he shall not engage in any sort of disorder or disturbance.
(4) He shall not take leave of his duties without Our[280] permission from Eisenstadt, Vienna or any other location at which the court is sojourning for a period of time. Nor shall the musician miss any performance of instrumental and/or choral music. He must report in a timely fashion for all musical activities to the Kapellmeister.

The second clause underlines the Kapellmeister's powers, while the third clause outlines grounds for dismissal. Records from Haydn's preeminence as Kapellmeister attest to cases of excessive drinking as cause for discharge from service.[281] Several hundred years later in the new world (US), evidence to support the notion of orchestral musicians as subordinates emphasizes the importance of maintaining respectful

277. The Holy Roman Empire (seat of the ruling Habsburg monarchy in the Austro-Hungarian region) used several standards of coinage. Here the f (or Fl) refers to Florins, divided into 60 Kreutzer, http://www.pierre-marteau.com/currency/converter.html.
278. *Haydn-Studien* III:2, *supra*.
279. *Ibid.*
280. The use of the royal "we" is used throughout the document. However "Our" could also refer to the joint permission of Prince and Kapellmeister.
281. H.C. Robbins Landon's *Haydn Chronicle and Works*, 1972.

silence during rehearsals, the ultimate sign of "quietude and grace."[282] The fourth clause finds articulation in contemporary Dutch and US orchestral collective bargaining agreements.

Comparing the individual Kapelle musician's contract to Haydn's 1761 contract, there is a contrast between the Kapellmeister's freedom to give notice and the orchestral musician's lack of freedom concerning the termination of the contract. Haydn was obliged to give six months' notice, while the individual musician had to ask for leave from services with permission determined on a case-by-case basis:

> 12. ... if the Vice-Kapellmeister should wish to test the waters elsewhere, he must provide his Serene Highness with six months' notice.[283]

The musicians' contracts did not allow for the half-year leeway granted to the Kapellmeister, which speaks to the importance of the latter's position. Haydn's loyalty to his employer remained undiminished throughout Nicolaus' reign. Although besieged by offers to perform throughout Europe, Haydn did not entertain any such offers until "his" Prince's death and the subsequent coercion to reduce the size of the exceptional orchestra.

A brief comparison of the salaries of the Esterházy musicians to other employed persons in mid-late 18th-century Austria-Hungary shows that the Prince's musicians were certainly not underpaid. The Prince's musicians received an average of 300-350 Florins per annum, except for the Konzertmeister (concertmaster/orchestra leader), who received 520 Florins. A hired coachman earned 20 Florins per annum, a schoolteacher 120-150 Florins, and a government civil servant (Ambtsdiener) 400 Florins per annum.[284] With cradle-to-grave guarantees for social and economic benefits as well as a solid salary, the Kapelle musicians were more than adequately paid in kind and cash. Their wives and children were clothed, housed, and entitled to pensions. They had a powerful interlocutor in the form of their beloved Papa Haydn, who championed their rights at regular intervals and petitioned for clemency in dismissals.[285]

A precarious employment situation ensued after the death of Prince Nicolaus in 1790. Prince Anton decided that if he disbanded the orchestra, he would have extra financial resources to serve other purposes. Only a small group of wind players remained employed to accompany hunting ventures and provide Tafelmusik tableside accompaniment. Perhaps at least in spirit, the last member of the 18th-century Esterházy dynasty embraced the philosophy behind the culture cuts that dismantled the Dutch arts scene more than two hundred years later.

---

282. *See Lancaster Symphony Orchestra v. NLRB* 822 F.3d 563 (2014) discussed in A long and winding road.
283. C.F. Pohl. *Joseph Haydn I* 391-394, 1878, author's translation, https://archive.org/details/bub_gb_wp6yAAAAIAAJ.
284. *See* R. Sandgruber, "Wirtschaftsentwicklung Einkommensverteilung und Alltagsleben zur Zeit Haydns." In Katalog: *Joseph Haydn in seiner Zeit*. Eisenstadt 72, 1982, also cited by Spitzer and Zaslaw 403.
285. *See* H.C. Robbins Landon's *Haydn Chronicle and Works, supra*.

2.13 TO LONDON TOWN: HAYDN'S ENCOUNTER WITH THE FREE MARKET AND FREELANCERS

The prolific composer's reputation caught the attention of the London-based German violinist-entrepreneur Johann Peter Salomon, who was eager to introduce Haydn and his compositions to London and, of course, earn hefty percentages for his services. Haydn declined the impresario's offer at first: taking leave of his trusted home for decades and the "well-loved prince" was not part of his life planning. As if fate intervened, at a precarious juncture in terms of Haydn's future following the death of Prince Nicolaus, the impresario redoubled his efforts to encourage Haydn to leave the Esterházy court for an extended visit to England in 1791. With some panache and a great deal of wit, the entrepreneur approached Haydn with a tantalizing proposal, not to speak of play on words (accord refers to a chord in music and an agreement in regular parlance): "I am Salomon from London who has come to fetch you. Tomorrow we shall make an accord."[286] That accord turned out to be lucrative for both parties. An adoring London public and an enormous fee (£2,000) was the perfect antidote to the problematic musical situation back home. As Haydn's Scottish biographer J. Cuthbert Hadden (1861-1914) reported, "it is only in England," said Haydn, "that one can make 4000 gulden in one evening."[287] To quote one of Haydn's primary biographers, Carl Ferdinand Pohl: "He often said afterwards that it was not till he had been to England that he became famous in Germany; by which he meant that although his reputation was high at home, the English were the first to give him public homage and liberal remuneration."[288]

2.14 LONDON INDEPENDENTS: THE RISE OF THE CONCERT HALL AS A CULTURAL HUB

London had a less stratified social world in which orchestral musicians mingled with their noble patrons after performances, a concept that would have shocked the persons who moved in the much more hierarchical Kapellen circles.[289] The metropolis counted more venues, more patrons, and a greater diversity of musical activities than any other European capital in the 18th century. Musicians were not tied to one court or one patron but were free to move from one venue to another. Forerunners of modern-day gig musicians, the London performer could play for large audiences at one of London's massive gardens, perform in a private royal band of musicians, accompany theatrical performances at one of the many theaters at Covent Garden, or with luck join the ranks

286. Class notes taken by the author, Professor Leon Plantinga's "Music History of the Classical and Romantic periods" Yale University 1981.
287. J. Cuthbert Hadden. *Haydn*, https://www.gutenberg.org/files/3788/3788-h/3788-h.htm.
288. C.F. Pohl. *Joseph Haydn, supra.*
289. Simon McVeigh's contribution replete with salient details on the social scene in London, "Italian Violinists in Eighteenth-Century London" in *The Eighteenth-Century Diaspora of Italian Music and Musicians*, Reinhard Strohm (ed.), 2001, 139-176.

of the *King's Band of Musick* in which musicians benefited from lifelong appointments without signing an exclusivity contract.[290]

In England, the professionalization of orchestras was part of a well-developed cultural scene that revolved around theatrical performance. Although contracting orchestras was the prerogative of the violinist-leaders (Konzertmeister), the London theater orchestral players were known to exercise their rights of protest. When a manager at the King's Theatre attempted to lower the salaries of the orchestra's wind players (who apparently had less to play than the string players), the entire collective of musicians took action to overrule him.[291] These late 18th-century musicians wielded more power to affect a management decision than their contemporary counterparts in Dutch and US orchestras, as future *movements* will illustrate.

Flexibility and entrepreneurship were the keys to success in a market teeming with opportunity and excellent wages. Significantly, entrance into the musical circus was not only open to English musicians, as lists of musicians with Italian and German names prove.[292] A constant stream of singers and instrumentalists arrived from the continent to perform at London's two Italian opera houses; these glamorous divas commanded exorbitant salaries.[293] Yet, as foreign musicians entered the mix of the lower-level musical supply chain (the orchestral/opera pit musicians), London's scandal sheets provoked xenophobia that led to a diminution of opportunities for foreign orchestral musicians. Promoting local culture also became a cause célèbre for master-pamphleteer Daniel Defoe:

> Our nobility and gentry have shown their love ... by supporting at such prodigious expense the Italian opera, improperly called an academy. but they have at the same time shown no small partiality in discouraging anything English and overloading the town with such heaps of foreign musicians ... Would it not be a glorious thing to have an opera of our own, in our own most noble tongue, in which the composer, singers and orchestra should be of our own growth.[294]

The call to take to the stage with national music has echoed from Defoe's time to the present day in many musical meccas including the Netherlands[295] and the US.[296]

290. Information gleaned from Chapters 4, 7 and 10 of Deborah Rohr's excellent monograph *The Careers of British Musicians 1750-1850: A Profession of Artisans* Cambridge University Press 2004.
291. For a full description, *see* Curtis Price. *Italian Opera in the Late Eighteenth-Century London* Vol. 1: The King's Theatre Haymarket 1778-1791, 187, 1995.
292. Thomas McGeary, *The Politics of Opera in Handel's Britain*, 2013, DOI: 10.1017/cbo9780511842559.
293. E.J. Dent, "Italian Opera in London" in Proceedings of the Royal Musical Association 71st Session, 1944-1945, DOI: 10.1093/jrma/71.1.19.
294. Daniel Defoe. *Augusta Triumphans: Way to Make London the Most Flourishing City in the Universe: A Proposal to Prevent the Expensive Importation of Foreign Musicians* J. Roberts 1728, http://name.umld.umich.edu/004843563.001.000.
295. Kaspar Jansen, "de Nuis-norm" *NRC Handelsblad* 8 november 1996 https://www.nrc.nl/nieuws/1996/11/08/de-nuis-norm-7331090-a1191461.
296. "American music for American audiences" was spearheaded by the National Endowment for the Arts in the 1960s.

2.15 A CONSIDERATION OF THE CIVIC MUSICIANS IN LEIPZIG

One of the world's most famous orchestras, the Leipzig-based Gewandhausorchester, regales online visitors:

> The earliest roots of the Gewandhausorchester can be traced as far back as 1479. In this year Leipzig City Council appointed musicians—Kunstpfeifer—as municipal employees. The musicians played a central role in Leipzig's cultural life.[297]

Another important step on the road to the professionalization of the orchestra took place in Leipzig with a direct relation to the city as an educational center. Many student-musicians trained in other fields of study performed in student orchestras and freelanced as musician-trainees in professional ensembles. The formation of orchestral academies added to freelancers' woes in the 18th century, just as these academies are impinging upon the scarce amount of work available to 21st-century orchestral freelancers. Regardless of their place in time, these academies showcase excellent students who receive low honoraria and willingly took and take the place of bonafide professionals. To fill the employment-related gaps between the civic employees[298] and the free-market performers who received little or no social benefits, the students formed a collective, the Orchestral Institute (Orchesterinstitut) in 1786. Perhaps by coincidence, or just merely historical happenstance, most of these student-musicians were law students. The Institute's bylaws included significant controls placed firmly in the hands of the orchestral musicians themselves: the power to hire, fire, rule on dismissals, and establish a pension fund.[299] The seeds of the powerful Gewandhaus musical tradition sown in the 15th century sprouted into an institution in which musicians were seen as employees worthy of protection by the end of the 18th century.

2.16 BEETHOVEN: THE MANTLE OF REVOLUTION

While Haydn's many letters do not speak of encounters with the Leipzig orchestras, they do reveal another encounter that foreshadows musical change in the widest sense of the word. En route to London in 1790, Haydn stopped in Bonn to meet the young grandson of a Flemish Kapellmeister, the pianist/composer Ludwig van Beethoven whose unorthodox approach to professional life galvanized fellow musicians as they shifted from subservience to entrepreneurship in the 19th century. It was not only Beethoven's astonishing gifts that moved the masses; the force of his persona changed the course of the conductor's role, and for the purposes of present research, the orchestra.[300] To paraphrase Roland Barthes' perceptive prose inspired by Beethoven's mix of the heroic and the tragic: "he won for artists the right to reinvent themselves."[301]

---

297. https://www.gewandhausorchester.de/en/orchester/history/.
298. *Kunstgeiger* and *Stadtpfeifer*, above.
299. Hans-Joachim Nösselt. *Das Gewandhausorchester* 52-57, 1943.
300. Of the many excellent resources on Beethoven: Jan Swafford, *Beethoven: Anguish and Triumph—A Biography*. Faber & Faber 2015.
301. Quoted by Ivan Hewett. "The Irresistibility of Beethoven." *Regina Leader-Post* November 2, 2019.

As the first bona fide freelance composer, Beethoven was highly dependent on concert ticket sales at newly created venues. He spent much of his musical life in Vienna during the turmoil of the Napoleonic Wars, and his compositions bore witness to the events of the day as exemplified by his Eroica (Heroic) Third Symphony, originally dedicated to Napoleon Bonaparte. The composer's choice to remove the dedication after Napoleon declared himself Emperor in late 1804 was decisive; for Beethoven, the people who upheld ideas of freedom and equality were heroic, not the newly proclaimed monarch. Like the messages posted on new media platforms nowadays, his rejection of Napoleon's actions carried persuasive power.[302] This musical detour from Haydn to Beethoven is intended to introduce another level of thinking about orchestral musicians, the music they play, and the fruits of their labor. Within Haydn's lifetime, the role of the highest rank musician, the Kapellmeister-leader with his administrative and compositional demands, changed definitively. The section to follow outlines several reasons why.

2.17 THE ADVENT OF SOCIAL CHANGE: PUBLIC SPACE AND CONCERT SPACE

The currents of social and industrial change that followed the revolutions in the late 18th century brought significant change to the lives of musicians in the 19th century. The rise of a middle class hungry for access to forms of musical entertainment (previously reserved for church and court) and a new-money urban elite eager to show its wealth in public places changed the course of orchestral history. The transfer of the orchestra from royal courts to the public domain brought about changes in how orchestral musicians sought employment. Although the main sponsors of musical activity in Europe's 18th century were still the court and the church, entertainment entrepreneurs and a burgeoning music publication industry answering to increased audience demand were to transform the music industry. As emerging patronage spread its largesse, composers took the opportunity to experiment. Haydn composed his late symphonies (1791-1795) upon invitation by the impresario-composer Johann Salomon for public subscription concerts at London's Hanover Square Room. The popularity of this series inspired similar formulas across the continent with reverberations in newly minted US concert halls. As detailed earlier in the *movement*, at the age of 59, Haydn not only expanded his use of orchestral forces but also became a globetrotting musical celebrity creating an example for many a 20th-century counterpart.

2.18 BIGGER IS BETTER: THE GROWTH OF 19TH-CENTURY ORCHESTRAS

In the 19th century, orchestral musicians transitioned from the status of subordinates serving the aristocracy, the church, or the municipality to become vulnerable free

302. Recall a quote attributed to Metternich, "A single newspaper article is worth to Napoleon more than a battalion of thousands of men."

agents, performing in the public domain in fledgling orchestral organizations under oft-spurious contracts controlled by impresarios. Collective organization in the form of union activity would have to wait until the second half of the 19th century. Regardless of precarity in terms of employment protection, the number of orchestras in Europe and the United States increased rapidly.

As a result of the demands of inventive composers such as Ludwig van Beethoven and the eccentric genius Hector Berlioz, orchestral forces underwent expansion and instruments underwent seismic changes (think of the differences between the 18th-century delicate fortepianos and the powerful metal-framed, double action 19th-century pianofortes, the precursor of today's concert grand pianos). By the last quarter of the 19th century, large-scale symphonies, operas, and tone poems were standard fare and the numbers of musicians in opera house pits and onstage at newly minted halls grew exponentially.

Musical genius was not the only fuel to fire the demand for grand halls and great orchestras. Large buildings signified power, a new urban power emanating from a rising middle class eager to set forth and make their mark in hallowed urban centers once the provenance of the landed aristocracy. The origins of Amsterdam's premier music venue, Het Concertgebouw (literally, Concert Building), provide a good example of an urban initiative in the hands of a newly empowered middle class. Prior to raising money for the new hall in 1882, concertgoers had to content themselves with closed concerts at the Felix Meritis Society located on the posh Keizersgracht (King's Canal).[303] Until the mid-1860s, the society was restricted to not only those with money (yearly subscription fees were steep by local standards) but also those who professed Christian faith: Jewish civic leaders and merchants were excluded. When a limited public company (Naamloze Vennotschap) was set up in 1882 to invest in a "temple dedicated to musical performance" on the outskirts of the city, "all citizens" were invited to purchase shares regardless of religious affiliation, and monies were raised for the creation of het Concertgebouw within months.[304] Expanding upon the metaphor of a concert hall as the apotheosis of civic pride and bourgeois patronage, maestro Willem Mengelberg[305] associated the orchestra's concert hall with an ideological revolution:[306]

> The concert hall is a product of the middle-class culture of the 19th century.
> The entire symphonic oeuvre and style reflect the spirit of a society that grew from the ideology embodied by the French Revolution (author's translation).[307]

303. Loes Gompes and Merel Ligtelijn, *Spiegel van Amsterdam: Geschiedenis Van Felix Meritis*. Stichting Felix Meritis en Rozenberg Publishers 2007 (author's translation).
304. *Ibid.*
305. Willem Mengelberg, principal conductor of the Concertgebouw Orchestra, maintained cordial contacts with the Nazi occupiers following the German invasion of the Netherlands. In 1945, the Dutch authorities banned Mengelberg from conducting in the Netherlands, https://www.naxos.com/person/Willem_Mengelberg/30349.htm.
306. http://www.businessinsider.com/best-concert-halls-in-the-world-2016-10?international=true&r=US&IR=T/-2-symphony-hall-boston-usa-2.
307. Rudolf Mengelberg. *50 Jaar Concertgebouw 1888-1938* "De concertzaal is een product der burgerlijke beschaving der negentiende eeuw. De geheele symphonische kunst en de stijl harer beoefening weerspiegelt den geest eener maatschappij, voortgekomen uit de ideologie der Fransche revolutie" 33.

The lauded musicologist Charles Rosen speaks of a concomitant expansion of musical style that embraced the "sweep" of operatic melodies underpinned by accompanying harmony as a radical musical march forward. Succinctly put, the change from Bach's ingenious counterpoint to the symphonic structures of the unique constellation of talent- Haydn, Mozart, Beethoven—whose compositions called for larger musical gestures. The classical symphony was born, and with it, the modern orchestra.[308] The transformation of the orchestra from civic or Kapelle ensembles to larger symphonic orchestras in the 19th century brought fundamental changes in the size of the complement, leadership, and organization—all of which were connected to the social changes sketched above. European and US orchestras soon to be described metamorphosized into organizations formed to provide music for a paying audience in a commercial venue—a far cry from the audience elites invited to the Esterházy palace.

2.19 MUSICIANS AS HEROES: THE RISE OF THE SUPERSTAR

Post-Beethoven, the hunger for musician superstars on the part of new audiences led to the hero worship of solo performers as well. The Italian violinist Nicolo Paganini (1782-1840) was compared to the devil and caused audience frenzy long before he placed his bow on the string. Appearances by the virtuoso pianist/composer Franz Liszt (1811-1886) caused "women to throw their clothes onto the stage and taking his cigar butts and placing them in their cleavages."[309] Equally prolific as a writer and music educator and with a talent for self-promotion, Liszt was also a pioneer in his use of music to achieve political aims. Beyond their stage shenanigans and celebrity status, artists exemplified by Paganini and Liszt commanded exorbitant fees which in turn inspired conductors to pressure their impresarios for equal treatment. Later in the 19th century, the cult of the great conductor, the musical genius whose special powers to control musicians and mesmerize audiences, took shape. By the early 20th century, these lions of the podium had achieved celebrity on par with soloists and orchestral musicians were eclipsed by the clamor for stardom, a subject of interest to a discussion of financial issues that face rank-and-file orchestra musicians past and future.

2.20 MUSICAL BRIDGE TO THE SUPERSTARS AND ARBITERS OF MUSICAL TASTE: THE MAESTROS

Our scrutiny of the orchestra, its inner workings and outer trappings continues with an analysis of the role played by the maestro—the musician responsible for guiding the orchestral collective toward a unified artistic goal and the final arbiter on the concert podium. In order to comprehend the hierarchy within the orchestra, and orchestral musicians' tacit acceptance of a conductor/maestro's authority that can even engender questionable workplace practices, attention must be paid to the kingpin at the top of the orchestral hierarchy.

---

308. *See* Charles Rosen. *The Classical Style, supra.*
309. Conversations with pianist-historian Steven Hough.

In a letter penned during the period Haydn was in musical command at Esterházy, Mozart received invaluable advice from his father-mentor Leopold. To be a well-respected conductor, "you must make every effort to keep the whole orchestra in a good mood, to compliment them and keep the players well disposed towards you by means of a little flattery ... even the worst violist is most touched if one gives him a little praise privately."[310] In Haydn and Mozart's time, the conductor was more often than not a time-beating lead violinist or keyboard player who could only hope for the goodwill of the orchestra, especially if he was a visiting guest. Until the mid-19th century, a conductor was part of the orchestra, most often leading from the concert-master seat or sitting behind a keyboard instrument in the midst of the orchestra.

It was the French mastermind composer and prolific essayist Hector Berlioz's 12-page pamphlet entitled *L'art du Chef d'Orchestre* that instructed the conductor not to sit in the midst of the orchestra as in the 18th century but to actually turn his back to the audience and focus on the musicians.[3111855] To Berlioz, technical proficiency such as score analysis and a sixth sense for listening were but points of departure. A maestro must also "possess other indefinable gifts without which an invisible connection between the conductor and those whom he leads will not occur. Without those gifts, he will not be able to communicate feelings to the musicians and consequently his authority ... his ability to shape the musicians through his directions will fade away totally."[312]

2.21 A TRIUMVIRATE OF SHOWMANSHIP

The triumvirate of Hans van Bülow, Richard Wagner, and Franz Liszt, all renowned as conductors (and in the case of the latter two, composers), revolutionized the profession by superimposing their supersized personalities on orchestral musicians, singers, and audiences. Descriptions of the virtuoso traveling maestro Hans van Bülow, who toured Europe's cultural capitals with his Meiningen orchestra in the late 1880s, provide a litany of traits that soon became associated with maestros of note. Masters of the pen and arbiters of public taste, the ever-powerful music critics observed that van Bulow personified "all the virtues and vices subsequently associated with that species: a talent for discipline and skillful rehearsing, conducting from memory, a picturesque histrionic presence, personal readings, speeches from the stage, and public idolatry."[313] Critics, the likes of George Bernard Shaw, were soon to lament that the conductor's personality and egocentricity often outweighed musical integrity, and the simple ability to keep the orchestra in motion:[314]

> I never go to hear a work without fearing that, instead of exquisite threads of melody, wonderful in their tenuity and delicacy, and the surpassingly strange and

310. Letter from Leopold Mozart to Wolfgang Amadeus concerning rehearsals for the younger Mozart's opera *Idomeneo*, Christmas 1780. Mozart *Briefe und Aufzeichnungen*, Vol. III 70 (author's translation).
311. 1855 version, in French http://www.hberlioz.com/Scores/Chefdorchestre.htm.
312. *Ibid.*
313. *Ibid.* (314).
314. George Bernard Shaw (1856-1950) wrote under the pseudonym *Corno di Basetto*.

> curious sounds and measures, ghostly in touch and quaint in tread, unearthly, unexpected, unaccountable, and full of pictures and stories ... for Heaven's sake don't stop to think about what you are doing, gentlemen, or we shall never keep the thing together.[315]

A permanent fixture of present-day top-tier orchestral activity, the phenomenon of the touring orchestra was aided by the great railway expansion mid-19th century and fed by media hypes concerning the conductor's magical powers both onstage and offstage. Media hype in the 21st century will be discussed in a different context in the *intermezzo* devoted to the effects of the *#metoo movement* on the orchestra.

2.22 FANFARE FOR THE COMMON MUSICIAN: THE ASCENDANCY OF THE US ORCHESTRA[316]

> Europe gave America the gift of music and America, in return gave Europe the music business.[317]

In the late 20th century, the American musicologist Philip Hart conjectured that orchestras in the US are a hybrid combination of their European predecessors with a uniquely American mission and structure.[318] Although Europe provided the model and the repertoire to form the foundation of the American orchestra, the US orchestra developed along different lines from its venerable European predecessors. The first mention of public concerts in the new world dates back to 1729, just about one hundred years after the religious sect, the Pilgrims, sailed from Leiden to establish their settlements on the east coast of the country.[319] Although the old-time religion of the Protestant founding fathers frowned upon secular music-making, religious convictions could not inhibit the positive social and economic value of the music trade: instrument making and music printing thrived alongside public and private performance. Reviews of concerts given by European-trained newcomers in Boston bear witness to the popularity of these ventures in the mid-1730s.[320] With a rapidly increasing population base and the expansion of urban centers, old-world culture prospered along the eastern seaboard.[321] From the onset, organized ensembles in early America did not benefit from the support of power brokers on any level, from the municipal to the state or eventually federal levels post-1787. Paying the piper was relegated to the whim of the individual patron or more

315. George Bernard Shaw, July 9, 1889. *London Music in 1888-89 as Heard by Corno di Bassetto (Later Known as Bernard Shaw) with Some Further Autobiographical Particulars*. Constable and Company Limited, 1950, 155-156.
316. Reference to Aaron Copeland's masterpiece, *Fanfare for the Common Man*.
317. Norman Lebrecht, *Who Killed Classical Music?* 58, 1957
318. Philip Hart, *Orpheus in the New World: The Symphony Orchestra as an American Cultural Institution*. W.W. Norton 1973, xiv, xv, 1-3.
319. New World, in *Mundus Novus: Letter to Lorenzo Pietro di Medici* (George Tyler Northup translation) 1-13, 1916.
320. *See* Richard Crawford's introduction "A Historian's Introduction to American Music." Speech revised 1979, http://www.americanantiquarian.org/proceedings/44539323.pdf
321. John Henry Mueller, *The American Symphony Orchestra: A Social History of Musical Taste*. Indiana University Press 1951.

often the ingenuity of the musicians themselves. The distance between the musician and the nucleus of power and wealth stood in sharp contrast to the established sponsorship that had promoted European collective music-making for centuries. Thus, with regard to musical culture, state-supported funding lagged behind artistic aspirations from the earliest days of the fledgling republic to the present time.

The nation's oldest professional music organization, the United States Marine Band, affectionately dubbed "the President's Own" due to its command performances for the presidents, was founded in 1798. While the stage could have been set for cultural subsidy at the twilight of the 18th century at least for that special ensemble, no move was made to create centralized support for the arts on the part of the US government. With the notable exception of schemes set up during the Great Depression of the 1930s, and the National Endowment of the Arts (NEA) grants first initiated in the 1960s supported in principle by President John and First Lady Jackie Kennedy,[322] subsidies akin to the European models of structural state support for the arts have been lacking. Since its initial golden years, the NEA has suffered ups and sadly in recent years, dramatic downs based on eroding political support from the Trump Administration that defunded superfluous cultural projects that detract from important mainstream and "real American" projects.[323]

Conversations with orchestra directors in Europe revealed their affirmations of a "Europe first" outlook concerning the orchestra's golden period of development in the mid-19th century. Yet, although Europe was the "cradle of orchestral evolution" pre-19th century, the major US orchestras developed at the same time as the great European orchestras with a parallel growth in concert hall construction.

Like their European counterparts, America's nouveau riche embraced the idea of building concert halls, and funding performances to build a civic legacy.

Social stature and wealth were the musts—the commodities in a brave new world where Europeans were startled by new social realities in which "coachmen shared tables with gentlemen."[324] According to Napoleon's effusive Consul, Louis Auguste Félix de Beaujour, America was in the sway of a "frantic love of money" that had its roots in "the political equality which reigns ... leaving people no other distinction besides wealth."[325] Civic pride turned backwater towns into cities, and musical performance was considered to be a means to refine the new nation's rough and tumble cities. A lack of distinction based on birth or military rank encouraged a novel type of philanthropist thrilled by the possibility of making his/her mark through legacies intended to sponsor educational institutions and the arts. Orchestras as collective protagonists were at the vanguard of a movement to remake a nation of rough and ready entrepreneurs, in the

322. President and Mrs. Kennedy's friendships with musical luminaries exemplified by Aaron Copeland and Leonard Bernstein sowed the seeds for a favorable political climate for arts funding.
323. For the demise of funding, *see* Naomi Adiv, "Goodbye to the NEA?" *Arts Journal* February 7, 2018, https://theartsjournal.net/2018/02/07/goodbyenea/.
324. Louis Auguste Félix de Beaujour. *Aperçu Des États-Unis ... Depuis 1800 Jusqu'en 1810 Cahiers 3*. Republished by Nabu Press 2010.
325. *Ibid.*

words of Alexis de Tocqueville—the "ultimate pragmatists"—into culturally aware consumers ready to use music as a vehicle for community enhancement.[326]

The city of Chicago and its cultural ambassador, the Chicago Symphony Orchestra (CSO), provide a prime example of how important music has been to augment civic identity in the US. By the mid-1800s, this boomtown had become a cultural hotspot with a fine arts museum, a state-of-the-art public auditorium, and many theaters. Before the turn of the 20th century, Chicago was the world's fastest-growing city with a population of over 1.5 million. The author of a famed 19th-century history of Chicago opined, "one of the most powerful civilizers is Music."[327] Fast forward to 2019. Stressing that the orchestra was vital to the well-being of the city on multiple levels, Mayor Rahm Emmanuel brokered peace during the CSO strike[328] (*see FAQs*).

2.23 A BRIEF RECAPITULATION OF EARLY DAYS IN US UNIONS

One of the most feted of all European 19th-century composers, the musical whiz Jacques Offenbach (1819-1880), who was credited with singlehandedly creating the popular operetta genre, visited the United States in 1877. Of the many remarkable discoveries he made during his trip, he was most impressed by the extraordinary power of musicians' representation. "The musicians in this country are supported by a large and greatly powerful organization, a type of society that if one is not inside it, there is no salvation. All individual musicians who want to play in an orchestra must firstly join and become a member."[329] Parallel to the growing union movement in other areas of labor, the US musician unions first formed as locals before their end-of-century national unification.

The trials and tribulations of a power struggle that engendered a split between the two main pre-20th century musicians' representation groups, the National League of Musicians (NLM) and the American Federation of Musicians (AFM), were reported in national newspapers as a fundamental difference of opinion concerning the identity of the working musician, a question of relevance to a meaningful modern identity.[330] Yet, while broadsheets and tabloids ramped up the dispute as a clash between artists versus wage slaves, the real differences were essentially linked to the core mission of the two organizations.

Reflect for a moment on the industrial foment in late 19th-century America. In 1887, the year Samuel Gompers, the American Federation of Labor's President, extended an invitation for musicians to join the AFL, there were 1,486 strikes across the country that often led to brutal actions on the part of employers, strikebreakers, and riot police.[331] To some musicians, the AFM's hard-core approach to labor and its

---

326. Alexis de Tocqueville, *Democracy in America*, Vol. 2 Chapter XI "In What Spirits Americans Cultivate the Arts," 1835, https://www.gutenberg.org/cache/epub/815/pg815-images.html.
327. I.D. Guyer. *History of Chicago; Its Commercial and Manufacturing Interests and Industry*. Church, Goodman & Cushing Book 1862, 180.
328. *See* http://www.chicagosymphonymusicians.com/press-for-cso-musicians-strike.html.
329. Jacques Offenbach. *Offenbach en Amérique: Notes d'un musicien en voyage* 1877, 2013.
330. James P. Kraft. "Artists as Workers: Musicians and Trade Unionism in America 1880-1917" *Musical Quarterly* 7(3), 1995, 512-543, DOI: 10.1093/mq/79.3.512.
331. *Ibid.*

support of collective bargaining brought musicians dangerously close to turbulent industrial actions. Under the weight of Gompers' influence, the two groups eventually merged in 1896, as the artist versus worker question was subsumed in a struggle for adequate wages. More than a century later, the apposition that characterized the NLM-AFM debate could be found in the musician disagreements that caused a rift between Dutch orchestral musicians[332] who sought to take real action against reorganization-dismantlement plans in 2012-2013 and their more recalcitrant colleagues, a subject that will be distilled in the *movement, Requiem for an orchestra.*[333]

The big takeaway from a passing glance at the early history of US musicians' unions that is of relevance to 21st-century challenges facing today's unions and their members can be encapsulated as follows:

(1) Closed-shop nature of unions
(2) Importance of the "local" in bargaining
(3) Price lists
(4) The strongmen: leaders.[334]

The first two listed subjects will be further fleshed out in reference to specific cases and disputes later in this book. While a savvy observer may comment that the last two subjects on the list bear little direct relevance to contemporary union-musician issues, both are of importance. The price lists, the rate schedules for musical engagements published by unions starting in the 19th century, are highly relevant to discussions that are taking place in the Netherlands at the present time in relation to proposals for a minimum wage for freelance musicians.

2.24 THE US MUSICAL COMMANDER-IN-CHIEF ON THE PODIUM

> I never use a score when conducing my orchestra. Does a lion tamer enter a cage with a book on how to tame a lion?[335]

Taking a closer look at US orchestras mid-19th century shows evidence that the role of the conductor as a central, authoritarian figure at the helm of a musical organization was in a nascent state. For example, during the first five years of New York Philharmonic history well documented in online archives, the conductor's position of leadership rotated between several different musical leaders. The *Founding*

332. Particularly the musicians of the Dutch radio orchestras and the Holland Symfonia players [eventually Het Ballet Orkest (Dutch Ballet Orkest)] forced to reorganize in 2012-2013 were divided between those who were desirous of real actions, those who preferred ludicrous actions such as carrying a coffin into the Concertgebouw Hall to signify the death of an orchestra, and those who were against action.
333. Conversations with Dutch composer Reinbert de Leeuw.
334. Although female musicians were permitted to join unions, they did not hold leadership roles. *Of Rowe and Race* provides more information on this subject.
335. Dmitri Mitropoulos stood at the helm of the Minneapolis Symphony prior to leading the New York Philharmonic Orchestra in the 1950s, https://www.quoteswave.com/authors/dimitri-mitropoulos.

Constitution of the Philharmonic Society of New York ratified in April 1842 stipulated that a conductor should be chosen democratically, one distinct individual per concert.[336] By the early 20th century, that egalitarian approach to maestros had all but disappeared. The great personalities of the first half of the 20th century can be epitomized by Leopold Stokowski, the charismatic music director of the Philadelphia Orchestra (1919 to 1936), who was also a hit in Hollywood as the music director of Disney's *Fantasia.* Equally renowned was the electrifying Italian maestro Arturo Toscanini whose political principles exiled him from fascist Italy to make musical furor in his new home in the US. Both maestros achieved heroic status augmented through the mass marketing of their numerous recordings.[337]

2.25 THE ECONOMY OF SCALES: CONDUCTORS, FAME, AND MONEY

A dichotomy between conductors' salaries and the salaries of the orchestral musicians who produce the music has always been a bone of contention for orchestral musicians especially during periods of economic crisis as interviews and information presented in the *FAQs* present. The British cultural commentator Norman Lebrecht sharpened the debate with the publication of a critique of what he dubbed "the Maestro Myth": a bold exposé of a music impresario-led international conspiracy of price-fixing that leads to an outrageous salary scale for conductors and controls on soloists who will appear with the maestro, tacitly increasing the conductor-music directors' powers. The impact of the conductors' cartel of heavyweights and the inflated fees for 20th-century superstar conductors has had an indelible impact on orchestral finances. But, according to the wisdom of managers, "to compete at the highest levels, an orchestra has to engage big name conductors and those individuals cost a small fortune. There is no way to bargain with the major league music managers, you either join them or you lose out."[338]

In the Netherlands, in the midst of the 2007-2008 financial crisis, the Dutch Parliamentarian Jasper van Dijk (SP Socialist Party) submitted a series of questions to the Minister of Education, Culture and Science with specific regard to conductor's salaries. Basing his queries on concerns expressed in a leading Dutch newspaper, van Dijk's questions noted that if the state subsidizes culture, it was only fair to ascertain the extent of an imbalance in payment between orchestral musicians and their musical leaders.[339] Although the question has been reframed by labor groups and politicians ever since, no further action to mitigate the inflated salary issue has been undertaken to date.[340]

---

336. New York Philharmonic The Leon Levy Digital Archives, https://www.nytimes.com/2018/04/23/arts/music/new-york-philharmonic-archives.html.
337. One of Stokowski's many experiments involved switching the traditional placement (seating) of wind and string groups visually and audibly challenging. For details concerning Toscanini's contributions, *see* Harvey Sach's biography, *Toscanini: Musician of Conscience*, 2017.
338. Conversations with Rob Groen, Dutch impresario.
339. Kamervraag 14 august 2008 kenmerk 2070825550, in Dutch http://www.volkskrant.nl/archief/dirigenten-kosten-ons-te-veel-geld~a921230/.
340. For that matter, although the subject of inflated salaries for maestros, soloists and CEOs is discussed with great frequency in the US as well (*see* Adaptistration; ICSOM posts) no

2.26 CLOSING THOUGHTS

This *movement* leaves the reader to ponder a number of substantial themes with variations based on historical reflection. Haydn's Kapellmeister role combined the functions of composer-in-residence, music director and personnel manager, a position unparalleled in scope when we consider the orchestral organization in the centuries that follow. But perhaps of more merit than a précis of Haydn's numerous roles is an emphasis on how he was able to excel in a variety of roles with various skill sets. A Papa to his much-loved musicians, a diplomatic interlocutor on behalf of these musicians, a composer of consummate originality, and a true friend to the Esterházy princes whose status did not imply equal footing with a musician maestro changed the role of musical leader into a Kapellmeister. In later life, Haydn was, indeed, a Kapellmeister nonpareil.

Can one picture the famed American contemporary composer John Adams taking roll call as a personnel manager? Or for that matter, any eminent composer regardless of nationality pleading with management to desist from docking pay and initiating dismissal charges against a section player who arrived late to a concert in a state of inebriation? The aforementioned examples reflect actions that Papa Haydn carried out on a regular basis during his decades at the Esterházy court. Even the most beloved "contemporary" maestro of them all, Leonard Bernstein,[341] called Lenny by musicians as a sign of affection, would not be bothered by the daily quibbles and quandaries so inextricably linked to the ups and downs of orchestral life, dismissing troubling issues with a wave of the hand, and the comment, "try not to make your problems mine." To most musicians, a successful relationship with a conductor is based on mutual respect, and to quote Thorsten Veblen, an "instinct of workmanship" at rehearsal.[342]

Music directors in the 21st century could be characterized as jet setters who spend more weeks as guest conductors than leading their "own" orchestras. Another issue associated with maestro-musician issues that goes beyond pay disparities and conductors' absenteeism from home orchestras relates to the legendary autocratic personality type associated with the great 19th- and 20th-century conductors who spent decades with their orchestras: from Leopold Stokowski in Philadelphia to Arturo Toscanini at the Metropolitan Opera and NBC Symphony; Fritz Reiner at the Chicago Symphony (CSO), George Szell at the Cleveland Orchestra (CO) and, perhaps the most authoritarian of them all (and according to biographers, by far the richest), Herbert von Karajan of the Berlin Philharmonic[343] who reputedly declared: "there are two places where democracy is not helpful: in music and in the army."[344]

Endemic to the era of the all-powerful maestro with his power to hire and fire at whim are the power struggles between strong-willed orchestral musicians, principal

resolution is in sight. Similar to discussions of highly inflated commercial CEO salaries, "they will leave us for another position elsewhere" is oft cited as a reason to perpetuate the system.

341. Leonard Bernstein's conducting career spanned from 1943 to 1990.

342. Adopted from the title of Thorsten Veblen's *The Instinct of Workmanship*, 1914.

343. von Karajan's death net worth was estimated at over €250 million https://www.welt.de/kultur/article1573132/Das-Privatleben-des-Herbert-von-Karajan.html.

344. Requoted by the Boston Symphony Orchestra's Music Director Andris Nelsons, https://www.egonzehnder.com/insight/interview-with-conductor-andris-nelsons.

players who "took the heat" and triumphed. From the annals of the CSO under the irascible Fritz Reiner era, a story illustrates the battle of wills between the tyrannical maestro and an affable albeit iron-willed principal trumpet player, Adolph (Bud) Herseth:

> It was during our first series of recordings with Reiner. We did *Ein Heldenleben* all day Saturday and *Zarathustra* (two of the major Richard Strauss tone poems known for difficult orchestral writing, author's note) the next. When we came to the exposed high octave in the middle of the piece, I played it. Reiner looked at me with a little bit of a smirk on his face, and everybody knew what was going to happen ... He looked at me and said in his thick Hungarian accent, "May I do it again?" We did it six more times and it was clear he was waiting for me to miss it. Fortunately for me, shall we say it was one of my lucky days and I hit it every time ... I ended up playing it eight times in a row for him.[345]

Herseth told Reiner he might as well let the rest of the orchestra go home; he was not going to miss the passage. And with that, at the intermission break of the recording session, Herseth played the infamous "lick" over and over again while he strolled off the stage.[346] Bud Herseth was a star in his own right: he held the position of principal trumpet with the CSO for over five decades of incomparable performances (1948-2001). Needless to say, most orchestral musicians did not fare as well as the unusually gifted and strong Herseth in their encounters with authoritarian maestros. For the ultimate degradation for love of music, take a listen to the immortal Arturo Toscanini at work in the 1940s, decimating his least-favorite section, the bass section, at https://youtu.be/tg5GPaUJ3aw.

For all the tales of immediate dismissals, public humiliation and fear and loathing at the symphony hall at the whim of despotic music directors (George Szell fired 22 of the 94 musicians his first year at the CO in 1946), there are many who applauded the musical results gleaned by the absolute maestros. Yet, if media reports by the likes of the *Wall Street Journal* are to be trusted, the passing of the much-feared, much-revered Szell engendered a backlash on the part of militant musicians who felt that their path to a more democratic orchestral institution was a possibility.[347] After 24 years of what critics called the greatest orchestral achievements, CO musicians went on strike for better employment conditions. "It was as if the yoke of the great master was lifted, and we could raise our voices for freedom and more realistically a better working life. Although our musical lives were often tense, Szell was a visionary, as strict with himself as he was with us. He admired Toscanini who said, 'democracy in politics, aristocracy in music.' We were not militants, we were democrats."[348]

345. Retold by Bud Herseth, National Public Radio (NPR) interview https://www.npr.org/sections/deceptivecadence/2013/04/15/177335679/appreciating-a-pillar-of-the-chicago-sound-trumpeter-bud-herseth.
346. *Ibid.*
347. Quoted by Julie Ayer, *More than Meets the Ear: How Symphony Musicians Made Labor History*, 2005
348. Conversations with Kurt Loebel, Cleveland Orchestra violinist; chairperson of the strike committee.

The legacy of strikes in the latter part of the 20th century took its toll on orchestral organizations as managers became estranged from the employment-related demands of newly empowered musicians. As music directors began to spend less and less time with their home orchestras, a power vacuum once filled by the maestro became more and more evident "especially at bargaining time [when] a musician vs. management tug of war ensued. Just maybe, if music directors could have shown more care for the institutions they represented, we might have been able to agree on important terms with less controversy."[349] A new breed of maestros who stand up for orchestras in turmoil includes Donald Runnicles (Atlanta Symphony lockout 2014), Robert Spano (Atlanta Symphony lockout 2014), and Riccardo Muti (CSO strike 2019) discussed in the *FAQs*. Indeed, not all maestros past and present are or have been martinets and/or superstars. Most conductors are hardworking servants of music intent on bringing home transcendent messages. The Dutch recorder virtuoso Frans Brüggen (Figure 2) founded an orchestra based on friendship and a commitment to historically informed performances. Their communal effort, the internationally acclaimed *Orkest van de Achttiende Eeuw* (Orchestra of the Eighteenth Century), was respected not only for its musical output but also for its leader's total lack of egocentrism—an antidote to the portrait of the vainglorious mega-maestro. For more than a decade, Brüggen inspired the RKF (Netherlands Radio Chamber Orchestra) as Artistic Director and Principal Guest Conductor: he conducted their final Concertgebouw concert on July 14, 2013. Words to the wise, upon taking on the position of music director at the RKF in 1992, long before subsidy cuts were to silence the orchestra, Brüggen (the term "maestro" was anathema) presented the orchestra members with priceless advice for their musical collaboration. His "geloofsbrief" (a statement of intent) offered to the orchestra on February 25, 1992 is reproduced from the author's original copy in *Epilogue: Appendix 3*.

Figure 2 Frans Brüggen 1981

Source: Author's photo.

349. Conversations with Marcia Peck.

Remaining in the Netherlands for another universalist podium view, the internationally treasured maestro Bernard Haitink had three secrets for conducting success:

(1) Trust the musicians
(2) Talk as little as possible
(3) Every once in a while, ask them to play a bit more softly.[350]

2.27 HAYDN'S LAST WORDS OF WISDOM

Music historians have mused as to how Haydn could have accomplished so much musically while relegated to spending the bulk of his time managing and organizing several ensembles of musicians who were often required to perform several times a day. His unfettered musical genius leads to questions on the role of the conductor, the maestro as the musical and "spiritual" leader for modern-day orchestras. Haydn's personal and orchestral patron while paternalistic in demeanor was munificent in terms of largesse: Prince Nicolaus' unwavering support for the arts he believed in could provide a model for contemporary orchestral financiers whether governmental subsidy decision-makers or corporate sponsors, who tend to kowtow to the whims of cultural politics. The controlled musical employment in the Esterházy Kapelle juxtaposed with the free-for-all lifestyle of the well-paid cadre of London freelancers in that capital's thriving theaters in the late 18th century provides food for thought as we move forward in a portrayal of musician vulnerabilities and present-day orchestral challenges.

It would be academically naive to assume that Haydn's orchestral musicians working under the protection of a benevolent Kapellmeister were better off than orchestral employees contracted by impresarios and symphonic organizations in subsequent centuries. There is no documentary evidence to support such a notion, yet it is tempting to look back in admiration at what Haydn was able to accomplish in tandem with his magnanimous supporter, Prince Nicolaus. That said, it must be underlined that as soon as Esterházy power moved from one generation to the next, musical and musicians' fortunes waned. As cultural servants responsible to serve their master, the Esterházy orchestral musicians were totally dependent on a successor who paid no heed to musical excellence. From a coveted position in one of the most renowned orchestras of the 18th century to a precarious freelance existence was the fate of most members of Haydn's magnificent band after the newly appointed Prince shut down musical operations. The orchestra was disbanded in 1791, as France was on the revolutionary path destroying all vestiges of the aristocracy in its wake. A contract, the likes of the Esterházy orchestral contract, which had offered a buffer against arbitrary behavior on the part of the employer, was not to appear on the orchestral scene until the 1960s when musicians' unions supported by a community of activist orchestral players at top-tier US orchestras called for improved employment rights.

350. Recounted in an email May 28, 2014 from CSO violist, composer, and writer Max Raimi. Bernard Haitink passed away in 2021 leaving an immense void.

II Symphonic Variations: Orchestral Employment, Freelancers and the Law

3
Intermezzo: Follow the Money, Economics at the Orchestra

> In the performing arts, crisis is apparently a way of life.[351]

> The economic argument is attractive for its elegant parsimony. The artists who remain in artistic occupations despite low earnings and highly uncertain prospects gain something else that has to be taken into account in order to preserve their rational occupational choice frame.[352]

> At the end of the day, it's all a question of purse strings, of cost and so-called public will. If the general consensus is "we need this orchestra or this dance company" the cost will not become central to the debate. We are sadly moving backwards to a discussion of "do we really need these things called art?"[353]

The future of orchestras as employers and musicians as employees in the 21st century is indelibly linked to the financial condition of their musical organizations. As described in the previous *Haydn rewrites history movement*, wages and budget-related issues have been central to musicians' misfortunes from the earliest recorded days in musical history as evidenced by diary entries and letters from the likes of Haydn, Mozart, and other prominent musicians. The *movement* further touched upon the principal pillars of orchestral support: the church, the state, and philanthropists in various incarnations. During the orchestra's period of rapid growth in the 19th and 20th centuries, development and financing were closely tied to the expansion of urban centers and civic culture within these centers. The concert hall became not only a place in which to listen to music but also a place to be seen as new elites vied for social standing through philanthropy. The importance of the orchestral institution to national culture contributed to a golden period of growth for symphonic institutions in the 20th century during which the expansion and popularity of the recording industry and orchestra tours led to innumerable

351. William Baumol and William Bowen. *Performing Arts: The Economic Dilemma* 1966, 3.
352. Pierre-Michel Menger. "Artistic Labor Markets: Contingent Work, Excess Supply and Occupational Risk Management" in *Handbook of the Economics of Art and Culture* 2006, 558.
353. Discussions with Ronald Wilford, founder Columbia Artists, New York.

cultural exchanges and a heightened demand for classical music. Integral to a favorable notion of cultural value is the concept of culture as a "national good," an enhancement for the nation, a hypothesis that has been shaken to its core in the post-financial crisis 2007-2008 era in both countries studied. The weakness inherent in a dependency on the value of culture arguments and the impact of cultural economic hypotheses on the orchestral sector are central to this *movement.*

3.1 ORCHESTRAL MALAISE IN THE US: THE RUN-UP TO 2007

In the absence of state subsidies, the funding that provides European orchestras with their financial lifeline, US orchestral budgets depend on endowments, private donations, and institutional investments. The 1990s marked a period of rapid expansion for US orchestras. Studies backed up by the American Symphony Orchestra League speak of a heyday in terms of budget increases, community outreach and orchestral staffing.[354] Yet, under the surface of the golden decade, trouble loomed. The S&L crisis (Savings and Loan) in which over one-third of small banking institutions in the United States collapsed[355] was a portent of future disaster as mortgage lending associations buckled under the pressures of a noxious combination of corruption at the highest levels, risky junk bond investments, and lack of fiduciary control.[356] "Once banking institutions shake, US cultural institutions are soon to follow."[357] The dramatic downward turn in orchestral finances in the United States in the 21st century was rooted in several factors: the first shock wave of general financial setback followed the September 11 attacks and the 2002 recession, which was minor compared to what was to come in 2008. "When the stock market plummets, philanthropy walks out the front door."[358]

3.2 FINANCIAL CRISIS 2007-2008: PERCUSSIVE REPERCUSSIONS

Even the savviest orchestral insiders could not have predicted the full force the financial crisis 2007-2008 would have on their industry. It led to increased precarity in the orchestral sector not only in turns of season cancelations but also more critically in terms of bankruptcies and marked upsurges in industrial action and the call for increased concessions as musicians bore the brunt of budgetary losses. "Frozen salaries, the demand for musicians to cover more and more of health plans and pensions are the signs of disturbing financial times."[359] Diminished donor finances and decreasing endowments accounted for the demise of an alarming number of orchestras across the US and

354. https://americanorchestras.org/symphony-magazine/archive/older-issues.html.
355. The bailout came on the back of the taxpayer, *see* the succinct analysis at, https://www.investopedia.com/terms/s/sl-crisis.asp.
356. For a solid analysis of the S&L crisis, *see* Paul Z. Pilzer's *Other People's Money: The Inside Story of the S&L Mess*. Simon and Schuster 1989.
357. Conversations with Professor John Montias (Yale).
358. Cleveland Orchestra Board member, anonymity assured.
359. Conversations with Jonathan Sherwin.

Europe post-financial crisis 2007-2008.[360] Yet, notwithstanding plummeting fortunes, orchestral organizations in both countries studied set store in reliance on *temps perdus*, past sources of success. A realization that orchestral organizations may have exacerbated their financial problems is troubling in light of the cost disease theory discussed below. What critics perceive as resistance to change within the orchestral organization fed into orchestral malaise post-financial crisis 2007-2008 exemplified by one of the most expensive components within an orchestral budget: tours.

3.3 ON THE ROAD, OFF THE ROAD

In the pre-crisis era, leading orchestras were treasured as cultural ambassadors worthy of support, a theme that permeated arguments to exempt the Royal Concertgebouw Orchestra (RCO) from subsidy cuts inflicted on other subsidized Dutch orchestras. Economists doubt whether today's orchestras earn money on tour in comparison to the 20th century when capacious recording contracts and reputational spinoffs brought groups such as the Philadelphia Orchestra and the New York Philharmonic international renown and lucrative recording sales.[361] Presently, the recording business is "a shadow of its former self and a lion's share of musical dissemination takes place online."[362] One year after resolving a bitter 17-month lockout, the Minnesota Orchestra toured Cuba (2015), politically high-profile, yet economically irresponsible. Skeptics who observed the bitter labor struggles at the Baltimore Symphony (2019) observed that within a year of a successful London Proms debut and European tour, the orchestra was on the verge of bankruptcy. Despite the allure of the tour, realists inside the orchestral business concur: "[t]icket sales, tours and recording contracts, the magic trio that spelled out success in the mid-20th century has been in total obsolescence in the 21st century; we have yet to find formulas to replace them."[363]

3.4 VALUE OF CULTURE DEBATES

While an analysis of theoretical debates on the value of culture is not central to this inquiry, a quick discussion is nevertheless relevant. Several strands within the debate have swayed public and political views, with a direct effect on if and when policymakers, sponsors and subsidy purveyors opt to spend the taxpayer's money for artistic endeavors. Many a present-day orchestral musician is perplexed by the post-financial crisis backlash against embracing the arts as a common good. Interviews with

360. US orchestras including the Albany Symphony, Honolulu Symphony, New Mexico Symphony, Syracuse Symphony and Tampa Symphony declared bankruptcy or were forced to shut down as a direct result of the crisis. The San Jose Symphony declared bankruptcy during the 2002 recession.
361. Robert Flanagan. *The Perilous Life of Symphony Orchestras: Artistic Triumphs and Economic Challenges*. Yale University Press 2012 and further orchestral economics-related publications by the Stanford economist.
362. Conversations with Ab Sengupta, Artistic Planning Carnegie Hall and professional violist.
363. Conversations with Bruce Coppock, former Executive Director, Saint Louis Symphony; former Managing Director, Saint Paul Chamber Orchestra.

musicians on both sides of the Atlantic displayed a disturbing consensus of disbelief expressing "there must be something wrong within our profession, as we are forced to spend so much energy defending its very existence."[364]

The media feeds into the mix by posing questions that revolve around the theme "is the orchestra relevant? Is it dying?" when reporting on financial and labor-related struggles in the field.[365] Economists joined by social commentators and politicians debate whether funding culture is essential to a flourishing society. Suffice it to say, classical economists have not always been friends of the arts. Adam Smith, the founding father of economics, placed musicians in the category of "frivolous" workers whose contribution to production was the antithesis of value: in a word, "unproductive."[366] Smith's emphasis on consumption and the interests of the consumer as the be-all and end-all of production finds its echoes in speeches by politicians in both countries studied with respect to "lazy" artists, "culture as a left-wing hobby" and other negative slogans used to dismiss creative output.[367]

3.5 A CONSPECTUS ON CULTURAL ECONOMICS

Leaving Adam Smith and the 18th century to fast-forward two hundred years takes us squarely to the late 20th century when the Dutch economist Arjo Klamer advocated a total rejection of Smith by calling for unabashed support for the arts: a "life form" interwoven in the fabric of society, a basic need whose value should not be assessed by the rules of the marketplace.[368] Cultural economics, a field that has steadily gained academic popularity since the early 1960s, marked an attempt for academics to develop theories on the characteristics of production and distribution relevant to artistic endeavors.[369] Realizing that the "culture has value, so support it" argument rests on exceedingly thin ice in times of economic crisis, David Throsby convincingly linked cultural and economic values in order to devise a rationale for allocations in which culture is a contributory factor to economic growth.[370] Whether applied to the case of the Netherlands where culture (read orchestras) are funded primarily through state subsidies, or the US model of indirect funding through tax-exempt contributions by corporations and individuals, Throsby put forward two recommendations as benchmarks. First, cultural output should be an integral part of a nation's cultural heritage.

364. Paraphrasing responses given by Dutch and US-based orchestral musicians.
365. Google search on the decline of classical music nets over 20,400,000 hits in a matter of seconds while a similar search on the ascendency of the arts less than 6 million hits.
366. Adam Smith. *The Wealth of Nations*. "Like the ... tune of musicians, the work of all of them perishes in the very instant of its production," http://www.gutenberg.org/files/3300/3300-h/3300-h.htm.
367. Senator Jesse Helms rants against the National Endowment of the Arts in 1989 and Dutch State Secretary for Education, Culture and Science Halbe Zijlstra's "art is a left-wing hobby," 2012, comes to mind.
368. Arjo Klamer. *The Value of Culture: On the Relationship Between Economics and Arts*. Amsterdam University Press 1997.
369. Paraphrasing the words of pioneer Ruth Towse. Also, Introduction *A Handbook of Cultural Economics* 2d ed. Edward Elgar 2013, 1.
370. David Throsby, *The Economics of Cultural Policy*. Cambridge University Press 2010, 7 DOI: 10.1017/cbo9780511845253.

Second, teams of experts should be employed to influence financial decision-makers to make the right decisions to benefit the public good. Throsby did not enter into a discussion of the possible negative repercussions from expert opinions, a subject for further discussion in the *Requiem movement*.

3.6 BAUMOL'S CURSE: COST DISEASE

More than 50 years have passed since the Princeton-based experts William Baumol and William Bowen shared their findings on the economic challenges faced by US arts organizations with special focus on orchestras, "by far the nation's longest-lived performing organizations."[371] Their findings proved seminal not only in terms of methodology but also in reframing the narrative concerning orchestral survival regardless of financial sources. Following a discussion of Baumol and Bowen's theory and its predictions, this *movement* moves toward a discussion on how Baumol and Bowen's cost disease theory influenced generations of cultural economists and cultural policy-makers post-financial crisis 2007-2008.

A prophetic *New York Times* article at the beginning of the 20th century reported: "[t]he permanent orchestra season has, as usual, been financially a bad one all over the country ... [T]here is always a deficit, which public spirited guarantors are called upon to pay year after year. A permanent orchestra, it seems pretty well established by American experience, is not at present a paying institution and is not likely immediately to become so."[372] The quote could well have been written one hundred years later, considering the financial precarity in many orchestras worldwide and the vulnerabilities faced by orchestral musicians. Why do symphony orchestras seem destined for financial failure?

According to Baumol and Bowen's analysis, the success of the US economy in the post-WWII period was based on productivity increases that stemmed from a combination of factors, including technological advances, improved workers' education, and an expansion of economies of scale. In their analysis, the performing arts, exemplified by symphony orchestras, would be unable to benefit from such an increase in terms of productivity, and are thus doomed to suffer from cost disease.[373] Two primary motives lead us to take a closer look at how this theory continues to play out in the realm of the orchestra in the US and the Netherlands. First, imperfect market forces in the cultural sector influenced not only the discourse on cultural economics but also actions taken by decision-makers with regard to financing cultural organizations. It is vital to delve into their investigation to bolster comprehension of the rationale behind cultural policy decisions in a beleaguered sector. Second, in order to craft answers to labor-employment problems within a vulnerable sector, a rudimentary understanding of root causes is indispensable.

---

371. William Baumol and William Bowen. *Performing Arts-The Economic Dilemma* 1966, 3.
372. Richard Aldrich. "Permanent Orchestra Season a Bad One" *New York Times* May 3, 1903, https://query.nytimes.com/mem/archivefree/pdfres – F6OC16FD34591B728DDDAA0894DD 405B838CF1D3.
373. Baumol and Bowen, *supra*, 1.

The essential labor requirements, the bottom line as to what an orchestra produces, are set by the composers whose works are selected for performance. While there is some interpretational variance as to exactly how long a Beethoven symphony might take to perform as well as exactly how many players (*see* discussions on the complement in the *FAQ movement*), no technological efficiency-oriented improvements can change the total amount of performance time. "From an engineering point of view, live performance is technologically stagnant"; the mechanics of a violin and the notation of a score have changed little since the time of Johann Sebastian Bach. Accordingly, the "hourly output yield" of performers has not changed over time.[374] While "[h]uman ingenuity has devised ways to reduce the labor necessary to produce an automobile ... no one has yet succeeded in decreasing the human effort expended at a live performance of a 45 minute Schubert quartet much below a total of three man-hours."[375] At the very heart of the cost disease hypothesis lies the intrinsic nature of artistic performance: it cannot be measured or improved upon through efficiency. Furthermore, and importantly, there is little or no equilibrium between supply and demand: the oversupply of artists in comparison to the amount of employment on offer is a given within the orchestral sector. Following the Baumol and Bowen line of thought, the wage-standard of living in the orchestral sector falls into a regressive pattern when compared to industries that are able to progress because of technological change. In other words, the orchestra is doomed to financial failure based on a combination of high-performance costs and low reliance on technological know-how to increase efficiency as well as the aforementioned imbalance in supply and demand.

Disturbingly, the orchestra becomes linked to what the economists refer to as a sector rife with productivity stagnation. In a sector that stagnates, when labor costs rise and musicians earn higher wages, their orchestral organizations will be forced to accept increased deficits in order to continue operation. Baumol and Bowen argue that where there is no productivity gain, the cost to produce the concert will rise exponentially compared to the revenues gained to pay the musicians. Increasing costs compounded by the post-financial crisis 2007-2008 market forces have prevented orchestras from increasing their revenues, and a noxious mix of stagnating subscription/ticket sales and philanthropic falloffs have ravaged the sector with bankruptcies, reorganizations, and shutdowns.

Consumers purchasing the latest smartphone do not pay attention to the number of hours related to the development and production of the product: they want a device that works and is relatively affordable. To Baumol and Bowen, a symphonic performance is fundamentally different from other products on the marketplace: the musicians' labor/the performance is the product. If symphony orchestras existed in a vacuum, inherent productivity stagnation would not be an issue of concern. Equating the orchestral workplace to the factory floor places a burden of unfair comparison on the orchestra and its musicians. High productivity in other sectors of the economy leads to wage increases and more favorable employment conditions according to Baumol

374. *Ibid.*, 163-164.
375. *Ibid.*, 164.

and Bowen.[376] Do vulnerable musicians deserve extra protection as they are the cogs in the wheels of a sector that suffers from productivity loss?

To recapitulate, because orchestras cannot increase their productivity and because the cost of performance increases, cost disease cannot be cured and the "real quantity of artistic production will decline."[377] Rising fixed costs, exemplified by the cost of renting halls and increasing salaries, cannot be offset by productivity growth. The race against the clock of diminishing returns focuses on the intractability of fixed costs and, if Baumol and Bowen are to be believed, the income gap will widen further with the passage of time. Three decades after the publication of the cost disease bomb, William Baumol gave his answer to the question: "in a free market economy, is organizational death the natural ultimate theoretical result of cost disease?" His answer circumvented the worst-case scenario "because it involves foretelling the future" as he warned, "current trends in support of the arts and prospects for tax laws and other incentives to giving are not encouraging."[378] Relating the cost disease that plagues orchestral organizations to cost disease in other vital sectors such as health care and education, Baumol remained pessimistic concerning general trends in general public welfare, as "many of the services that we associate with quality of life will become relatively more expensive while mass-produced things become cheaper and cheaper."[379] The incurable cost disease has permeated the rhetoric on orchestral demise, but is it relevant or beneficial? If cultural sectors are implicitly stagnant by virtue of their disposition, why focus on efficiency? Looking closely at Baumol's *weltanschauung*, questions arise if economic growth is aligned with technological advances in a vulnerable sector. To paraphrase the master, it is difficult to apply cost disease to music performance: even with the advent of technological advances, efficiency does not make a string quartet more efficient.

3.7 AN UNLIKELY SOURCE OF VULNERABILITY: PRESSURES AT THE BARGAINING TABLE

> Every year, our musicians go into a cave and begin.[380]

A critical assessment of the cost disease emanates from union insiders who have frontline experience in collective bargaining on behalf of orchestral musicians. Union officials in both the US and the Netherlands have countered the cultural economists' cost disease critique with a counterproposal. "Instead of viewing the orchestra as a pariah, it should be considered as a real service provider, which benefits the

376. Baumol and Bowen, *supra*, 168.
377. Tyler Cowen. "Why I Do Not Believe in the Cost-Disease" 1996, 207-214.
378. Interview, William J. Baumol *Harmony* 1996, https://www.americansforthearts.org/by-program/reports-and-data/legislation-policy/naappd/harmony-forum-of-the-symphony-orchestra-institute.
379. William Baumol. *The Cost Disease: Why Computers get Cheaper and Health Care Doesn't* 2012.
380. International Conference of Symphony and Opera Musicians (ICSOM) members discussing collective bargaining ICSOM Conference 2016.

community-at-large through the dissemination of art, creative performance. A change of attitude in the mindset could work wonders at the bargaining table."[381]

Reports from US orchestras in the post-2007-2008 financial crisis era, ranging from top-tier orchestras to regional orchestras, provide ample evidence to support the statement that managements come to the bargaining table with proposals that impact musicians negatively.[382] "These days management arrives at the bargaining table with multiple proposals that involve variations on the theme of proposing fewer work weeks, cutting back the number of musicians (the complement) but neglect to address the financial pressure that the exorbitant costs of paying conductors, soloists and the ever-increasing administrative and marketing support staff exerts on the orchestral budget."[383] In comparison to US orchestral collective bargaining traditions characterized by the legendary Len Leibowitz as "pugilistic,"[384] Dutch orchestral bargaining is much less adversarial. "Certainly, no cadres of lawyers on opposite sides at Dutch orchestras or for that matter European orchestras,"[385] yet, nonetheless, as finances shrink, Dutch orchestral problems grow. A quick glance at the websites of major orchestras in the US and the Netherlands shows a dramatic increase in the number of administrative staffers on payroll. A tally of staff members shows that staff members slightly outnumber musicians at top-tier US orchestras, whereas the leading Dutch orchestras make do with roughly 50% fewer staff members.[386] Are the Dutch orchestras simply more efficient or does the answer lie elsewhere? As cogently clarified by a member of the RCO management team, "Dutch orchestras like other European counterparts while always on the lookout for creative ways to increase funding do not have to operate huge marketing and fundraising initiatives as still to this day, government and municipal subsidies account for most of our costs. However, as culture cuts increase, we are emulating our American colleague orchestras by turning to marketing and social media with an increase in staff members."[387]

3.8 WHAT IF THE COST DISEASE THEORY WAS WRONG?

What if Baumol and Bowen were wrong? Perhaps the concept of cost disease does not have any business meddling in the orchestral nonprofit world. A metaphorical

381. Conversations with Martin Kothman, Senior Director FNV Media/Culture.
382. Information gleaned from ICSOM and ROPA on multiple occasions enhanced by discussions with delegates at the 54th ICSOM Conference Washington DC August 24-27, 2016, where bargaining issues and cutbacks were covered in multiple sessions and individual meetings; ROPA information clarified by Naomi Bensdorf Frisch, ROPA Board member. Discussions with AFM President Tino Gagliardi amplified by information presented at the 4th FIM International Conference, Montreal 2017.
383. Conversations with Randy Whatley.
384. Leonard "Len" Leibowitz, legendary legal counsel at ICSOM Symphonic Services Division AFM, Local 802 New York City. *See* "The Myth of the Structural Deficit" https://www.local802afm.org/allegro/articles/the-myth-of-the-structural-deficit/.
385. Conversations with Jan Willem Loot, former Director RCO.
386. Compare, for example, the New York Philharmonic staff versus musicians to the Rotterdam Philharmonic staff versus musicians, available at, https://nyphil.org/about-us/meet/philharmonic-staff to https://www.rotterdamsphilharmonisch.nl/nl/het_orkest/team.
387. Interview, David Bazen, former RCO Director of Business and Media.

association with disease invokes and perpetuates negative scenarios that point to a sector predestined for financial failure. Internationally, researchers and thinktanks not to speak of the Dutch Council for Culture (RvC) and ministerial departments concerned with subsidies have relied heavily on Baumol and Bowen's theory in their policy recommendations for culture cuts, going back to the late 1990s. To recall, economist and Minister of Culture and Media (1998-2002) Rik van den Ploeg's proposals linked subsidies to organizational efficiency under the aegis of a functional approach to state support.[388] It is interesting to note that van der Ploeg was critical of the cost disease theory; he presumed that Baumol and Bowen's hypothesis was not persuasive when applied to the subsidized arts world. According to van der Ploeg, just because an orchestra could not increase its efficiency quotient, it would nevertheless benefit from progress in other sectors. "Jobs in the cultural sector are not destroyed, since technological progress elsewhere boosts purchasing power just enough to maintain spending on culture despite rising prices of culture."[389] Unfortunately, the mere fact that purchasing power increases does not directly relate to increases in cultural consumption, nor does it relate to an increase in orchestral support simply because personal taste, popular trends, and the marketplace govern how money-for-culture is distributed. Developments in the Netherlands post 2008 prove that orchestras are no longer a high priority in a cultural support climate that attaches great value to efficiency and an organization's ability to raise its own funds. Professor Throsby pleads for a rethink in which the intrinsic value of artistic production moves to the center of economic decision-making, arguing that cultural institutions possess inherent intrinsic worth. "[They are] separate from the hard numbers of the economic value, from the dollars and cents. That means it's a different sort of value they're creating, which we can call cultural value or artistic value."[390]

Although the differences between cultural funding ideologies in the Netherlands and the United States are considerable, with the former relying mainly upon state subsidy, an independent arts council and ministerial responsibility, and the latter highly dependent on corporate and private patronage, the similarities in post 2007-2008 financial crisis effects are remarkable. Post-crisis cultural policy in the Netherlands, as RvC reports corroborate, sang a new tune: reduce dependency on government funding and require orchestras to seek their own income from the marketplace.

Respected economists writing post Baumol and Bowen, exemplified by Robert Flanagan, have focused on structural deficit and cost disease avoiding what orchestral musicians have long hailed as a larger elephant in the room: the spiraling cost of CEO salaries, the marked expansion of administrative staffers with their concomitant costs and the rapid escalation in soloist and conductor salaries. What Baumol's cost disease

388. Former Minister van der Ploeg's "functionele benadering van subsidies" (functional approach to subsidies) stimulated policy in the years that followed. *See Cultuur als confrontatie: Uitgangspunten voor het cultuurbeleid 2001-2004.*
389. Rik van der Ploeg, "The Making of Cultural Policy: A European Perspective" in *Handbook of the Economics of Art and Culture*. Victor A. Ginsburgh and David Throsby (eds.). Elsevier 2006, 1207.
390. David Throsby. Australian Broadcasting Radio (ABC), "Why no symphony orchestra in the world makes money" April 4, 2017.

neglects to consider is the positive aspect of technical performance advancement in the orchestral sector. Simply, the technical advancement of musicians' training and performance levels has skyrocketed in the late 20th-21st century. In terms of the cost disease theory, better trained players master the compositions they are required to perform more efficiently than their illustrious predecessors. "Just think of how many great composers in past centuries wrote concertos for soloists who were unable to meet the composition's technical demands! Nowadays, young performers are playing at a technical level that only a few could dream of a half-century ago. Perhaps (laughing) our teaching has improved but more realistically the easy access to old recordings and the cultural shift that has made classical music professions desirable in parts of the world (China, Japan, Korea) where the art form was inaccessible has had an incredible impact, certainly for string players and thus orchestras worldwide."[391]

Turning to economic assessment, James Heilbrun pointed out that Baumol and Bowen had neglected to consider the fact that at least in the US, orchestral finances depend more on donations than market earnings, debunking part of the earning gap argument. He argued that it should be possible to include both donations and subsidies, so crucial to the European orchestral landscape, into the earning side of the equation.[392] Another layer of critical comment can be found in the fact that Baumol's cost disease considers the salaried, contracted members of the orchestra as the sole producers of orchestral labor. Closer inspection of "who" performs in orchestras on a weekly, monthly, and seasonal scale proves that there is a fallacy to this assumption as a considerable number of performers in the orchestral workforce are freelancers, often self-employed. Statistics show that freelancers' wages have not risen at the same rate as musicians under collective bargaining agreements, with many reports showing an actual decline in orchestral cost disease partially due to the increase of freelance labor at lower wages.[393]

3.9 REPLACEMENT SCENARIOS

Disturbingly, following an analysis of the first empirical evidence related to orchestral cost disease, Bowen asserted, "the only way an orchestra can avoid it [cost disease] is by substituting amateurs for professional musicians, or simply cutting down steadily on the number of musicians."[394] The "cut down" in terms of complement is an ongoing bone of contention for orchestras in both countries studied as the FAQs already revealed: consider the central role it played in the Atlanta, Minnesota and Baltimore Symphony lockouts and the bitter contentions around the complement cuts at the Netherlands radio orchestras' debacle in 2013.

The consequences of hiring an amateur are mentioned in Figure 3.

391. Conversations with famed violin pedagogue Boris Kuschnir.
392. James Heilbrun. "Baumol's Cost Disease" in *Handbook of Cultural Economics* 2d ed., Ruth Towse (ed.) Edward Elgar 2013.
393. Conversations with Ruth Towse concerning Baumol's cost disease and British orchestras in the late 20th century.
394. *See* Interview William J. Baumol, *Harmony, supra.*

Figure 3 Hire an Amateur

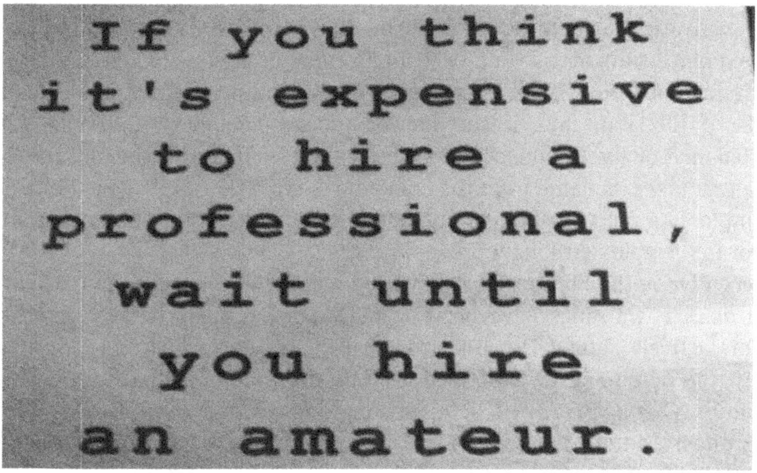

Source: Author's collection since 1998.

Although orchestras in the US and the Netherlands have not resorted to hiring amateurs to replace professional musicians, there have been moves to replace professionals with advanced student "interns" and other trends that cause consternation on the part of professional freelance musicians. Within the past decade, several orchestras in the Netherlands have introduced academies in which conservatory students receive training through various "side-by-side" initiatives: the students play alongside seasoned orchestral players as part of a "learn to adapt by doing" scheme. While exemplary in objective, practice discloses that several of these academies do not offer training above and beyond performance practice. The differences between the academies associated with the Royal Concertgebouw Orchestra, the Vienna Philharmonic Orchestra and other major European orchestras are incredible when compared to some of the newer ventures that proliferate in the Netherlands. The academicians are expected to take part in public performances but are not paid accordingly:

> I hold advanced degrees in my instrument from a leading US college and started in on a second master's degree at the Codarts Conservatory Rotterdam. Deliriously happy to win an audition to join the Academy at an excellent Dutch orchestra in 2018, I soon learned that I was expected to play all rehearsals and public concerts for less [than] 400 euros per month! Had the orchestra hired me as a regular freelancer, I would have been paid at least that per week. The training? Simply, sit next to a regular member of the viola section and play. Something tells me that this particular academy is just an excuse to hire cheap labor.[395]

395. Conversation with a violist who won a position at a leading Dutch orchestral academy, anonymity assured.

The second escape valve for orchestras seeking to replace paid professionals with cheap labor is exemplified by "strike breaking" attempts on the part of orchestral managements. Infamous scab hiring attempts at the Louisville Symphony Orchestra not only were alarming in terms of "strike breaking" and a breach of solidarity with the contracted players but also set a precedent for other orchestras to take similar steps to thwart industrial action if necessary. Although the right to strike is a fundamental principle of US labor law, it can be constrained and even undermined by the counterbalance of the employer's right to replace workers. In the US, the *MacKay* doctrine that takes its name from the eponymous SCOTUS case[396] gave pride of place to an employer's right "to protect and continue his business" without requiring the employer to reemploy striking workers.[397]

Recently, on the European scene with direct implications for the German-Dutch musical market, warnings have been posted on social media after several German orchestras actively sought Dutch-based musicians to replace striking musicians. In Germany, the right to strike is derived from the freedom of association. The German Constitution (*Grundgesetz*) Article 9, Section 3 sets forth a general guarantee of the freedom of association. The right to strike derives from the right to organize; strikes must be authorized by unions. Although hiring foreign strikebreakers is not illegal, the action was widely condemned by musicians reacting on social media. The original text disseminated on Facebook, Twitter and other social media platforms as captured in a screenshot is followed by the response from the Platform voor Freelance Musici (PvFM), the Netherlands, reproduced below (Figure 4).[398]

396. *NLRB v. MacKay Radio & Telegraph Co.*, 304 US 333 (1938).
397. *Ibid.*, at 345.
398. Text taken from the Platform voor Freelance Musici (PvFM) Facebook page with Twitter links, April 11, 2019 "GERMAN ORCHESTRA VIOLATES EUROPEAN SOCIAL CHARTER BY HIRING SUBSTITUTES DURING STRIKE: By the European Social Charter, during a lawful strike the employer is not permitted to hire any other person in substitution for a striking worker. A German orchestra, however, is now trying to do exactly this, by contacting Dutch orchestras. We hope that all Dutch and other European instrumentalists and orchestra managers will take a stand in solidarity with their German colleagues. Please, do not give contact information about your workers (which also violates privacy laws) and share this message with other instrumentalists!"
#Europe #EuropeanCharter #EuropeanSocialCharter #EU #Solidarity #Artbutfair #strike #classicalmusic #musicians #music #laborlaw.

Figure 4 Strikebreaking

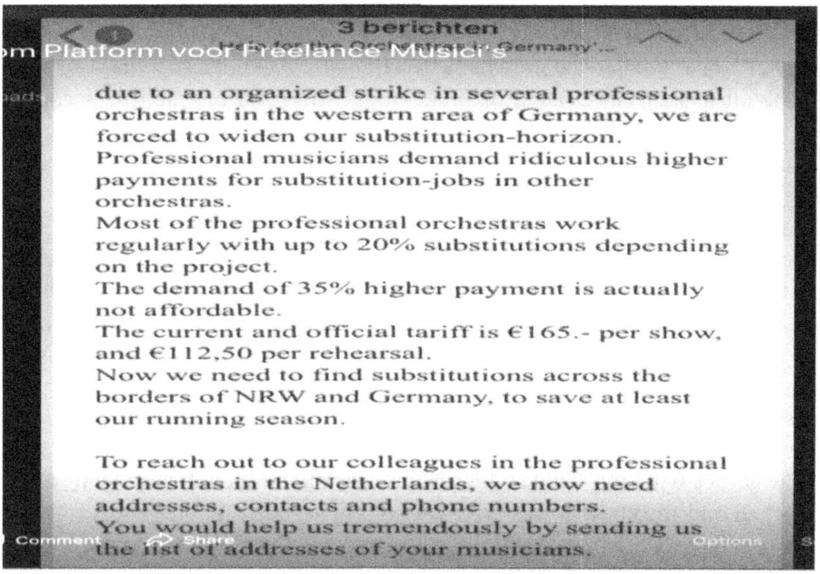

Questionable practices linked to strike-breaking and the erosion of solidarity among orchestral musicians have taken place throughout history. With increased easy access to musicians through social media and the increased precarity in the orchestral freelance sector, "the temptation to think of oneself and not one's colleagues is real and hard to avoid."[399] The Louisville Symphony was placed on the AFM's International Unfair List for a short period of time, the most serious "name and shame" reprimand.[400] In an article penned by the author on the Louisville labor infringements, I emphasized that it is the musicians rather than the orchestra who were in need of support.[401] As both the German-Dutch and Louisville orchestral examples show, the right to strike versus the right of a worker to return to the workplace after a strike is laden with emotional complications that can impact a legally condoned action.[402]

3.10 QUANTIFYING ARTISTIC OUTPUT

Last but certainly not least, the question as to what the real justification might be for quantifying the output of an artistic performance should be posed. Might we not

399. Dutch freelance orchestral musician response to the German ads, anonymity assured.
400. In accordance with Art. 8, section 3 AFM Bylaws, "Members shall not render musical services for organizations, establishments or people who have been placed on the International Unfair List. Any member who violates this Section shall be subject to penalties."
401. Heather Kurzbauer. "Help Wanted" *The Strad*, December 11, 2011, https://www.thestrad.com/help-wanted/2786.article.
402. These complexities underpin the need to overturn *MacKay*. Julius G. Getman, *The Supreme Court on Unions: Why Labor Law Is Failing American Workers*, Cornell University Press, 2016.

hearken back to Joseph Schumpeter and his belief in entrepreneurship as the most significant, change-inducing source of improvement along with his distinctions between three types of innovations: process, product and organizational? Schumpeter would nod in approval if he were to consider the multiplicity of advances in orchestras that have curbed unbalanced growth as described by Baumol's cost disease.

The misfortunes associated with operating with persistent deficits according to analyses by Baumol, Bowen and later, Robert Flanagan are a direct consequence of wage inflation and organizational inflexibility. As the analysis of the orchestral complement in the *FAQ* movement revealed, a healthy, well-functioning orchestra calls for a certain number of musicians who are highly skilled and "should be quite expensive" according to musicians and union representatives in both countries studied. If the aforementioned economists are right, salaries in the orchestral workplace account for wage inflation deficits that are impossible to curtail especially as subsidies and/or sponsorship diminishes. Can the cost disease problem be bucked without cutting musicians' salaries? Is there a way to increase revenues to meet rising costs? Increasing ticket prices is tricky business as these prices are market sensitive: the Dutch government's brief flirtation with a VAT tax increase on ticket prices in the cultural sector was met with the valid criticism that the public would stay away from the concert hall and theater if prices were raised. Orchestras rely on "nonperformance" income, monies donated by corporate, governmental and/or private sponsors as well as investments related to long-term endowments. Government support in the US accounts for approximately 5% of a US orchestra's revenue while accounting for over 80% of the revenues in Dutch orchestras.

"Repeating the mantra that the financial foundations of US orchestras are built on quicksand is not constructive but steeped in detriment."[403] Instead of emphasizing cost disease, accepting the fact that any large-scale cultural endeavor demands considerable expenditure and merits support is necessary to ensure that not only private/corporate sponsors but also governments/municipalities provide support. Placing the blame for financial inadequacy on lazy boards, careless management or clueless musicians is counterproductive. To paraphrase Pierre Audi's bold statement of his views on the subject at the 50th anniversary of Dutch National Opera, "opera is extravagant, opera is expensive, opera is worth it: it takes us to emotional and experiential spaces that we have never travelled to before. Its reach is beyond our individual capabilities, it deserves our every support."[404]

Beyond a positive mindset as advocated in the paragraph above, several noteworthy reports present data to support orchestras' positive economic impact on the urban centers and outlying communities they serve. In the US, the Ford Foundation and the National Endowment of the Arts (NEA) research in the late 20th century and 21st century revealed data that backs up the hypothesis that orchestral organizations contribute more than prestige to their hometowns: the spinoff revenues are of

403. Conversations with Randy Whatley.
404. Speech, Gala Celebration, 50 Years Dutch National Opera, September 25, 2015.

significant economic benefit to their greater communities.[405] Some of the findings from a 2012 NEA report paint a positive picture of cultural production in relation to other sectors. That year, cultural production contributed over $698 billion to the US economy, over 4.3% of the US GDP, considerably more than the construction sector ($586.7B) or even the transportation sector ($464.1B).[406]

The same report notes "a ripple effect on the overall economy" that has a positive effect on the creation of new jobs in sectors related to cultural consumption. Recently, a report undertaken by academics in Cleveland, Ohio, found that: "The orchestra alone generated $135.4 million in spending at both Severance Hall and Blossom Music Center. Of that, $19.4 million came from visitors outside Northeast Ohio, primarily in the form of dining, travel, and lodging."[407] In terms of enhanced employment opportunities, the Cleveland Orchestra and directly related derivatives were responsible for over 1,200 jobs in the 2017-2018 season alone.

Similar observations can be found in a comprehensive joint opinion presented by the Dutch Social and Economic Council and the RvC, which presented concrete suggestions for improving the future of cultural workers and their organizations in the Netherlands.[408] The study emphasizes the contribution that the cultural sector in its totality provides to the Dutch gross domestic product, estimated at 2.25% in terms of direct contribution over a 20-year period.[409] In addition, the Dutch study emphasized the important added value of culture to the nation's well-being for its citizens, the greater business community, and the multitude of tourists who flock to the Netherlands to avail themselves of its rich cultural life.[410]

3.11 PROFESSOR FLANAGAN STRIKES BACK

The Economic Environment of American Symphony Orchestras, commissioned by the Andrew Mellon Foundation in 2008, became influential beyond academic circles: collective bargaining initiatives cross-country felt the impact of the ominous predictions of cost disease-related failure in the sector.[411] Cogently, Professor Flanagan hypothesizes that orchestral economic instability can be attributed in part to the history of its organization. He was fascinated by the shift from a self-organized cooperative to a professional establishment ("the three-legged stool"), in which a board employs

405. National Endowment for the Arts, and United States Department of Commerce. Arts and Cultural Production Satellite Account 1998-2017, DOI: 10.3886/ICPSR36357.v6.
406. For a useful infographic, *see* https://www.arts.gov/sites/default/files/nea-infographics-economic-value.jpg.
407. Zachary Lewis "Cleveland Orchestra Economic Impact Report Details Large Financial Footprint." *Cleveland Plain Dealer* September 26, 2019.
408. In Dutch, *Passie gewaardeerd: advies over versterking arbeidsmarkt culturele sector*. SER-advies 17/07, 21 april 2017 https://www.ser.nl/-/media/ser/downloads/adviezen/2017/passie-gewaardeerd.pdf.
409. *Ibid.*, at 43 with a reference (fn. 1) to statistics in *Cultuur in Beeld* 2016 [Culture at a glance] Den Haag, 2016.
410. *Ibid.*, §3.
411. Robert Flanagan "The Economic Environment of American Symphony Orchestras." *GIA Reader* 19(2) 2008.

third-party management to run the orchestral operation. His findings show that negative economic conditions that he refers to as "cyclical influences" exacerbate entrenched structural problems inherent to that organizational model. Alas, a lack of insider information and a lack of sensitivity to the concessions made by US orchestral musicians form a leitmotif throughout the study. Focusing on "the extent to which the economic difficulties faced by symphony orchestras reflect collectively bargained wage increases and work rules,"[412] the study deflects academic focus away from the important role of inflated CEO/executive director salaries, expanded administrative staff costs, and the ever-rising fees claimed by conductors and soloists.

In 2012, Flanagan published a volume considered by orchestral managers worldwide as the definitive study on orchestral finances: "whether you are running an orchestra in Capetown, in the US or in the Netherlands, this book is the go-to volume for all stakeholders in the music business."[413] While this writer does not purport to lock horns with an economist's methodology, there are many disturbing elements within his research. Consider the following statement: "[m]ost alarming for the size of an orchestra's structural deficit, pay change shows little sensitivity on average to the financial balance of orchestras."[414] Unfortunately for those who care to base hypotheses and policy on Flanagan's extensive data, his study came to fruition just before the crisis; thus, it was impossible to fathom the extent of financial problems that ensued in the cultural sector. His focus on the performance income gap,[415] the difference between performance revenues and performance expenses, can be regarded as another iteration of cost disease. Calculating the cost of mounting concerts is a challenging exercise if one considers the number of variables involved. Relying on data collected from 50 major orchestras in the US compared to the *Producer Price Index*, an indicator that measures the average changes in prices producers receive for their output, Flanagan concluded that the cost of orchestral performances increased a whopping 300% in the period between 1987 and 2005 as compared to commercial sector gains of approximately 40%.[416] A slippery slope of comparisons to say the least and a questionable manner of calculation with regard to the cost of mounting concerts can be noted. Data from orchestras locked out by management since 2012 including data supplied by the Atlanta Symphony and the Minnesota Orchestra show that per-concert costs did not increase as a result of the financial crisis of 2007-2008, but did increase dramatically after management chose to schedule fewer concerts in the 2010-2011 season.[417] In addition, a computation of the financial sacrifices borne by orchestral musicians who accepted pay cuts to aid their organizations' quest for healthy recovery post 2008 is missing from Flanagan's analysis. Once again, no mention is made of the exorbitant fees paid to guest conductors and soloists, not to speak of the steep salaries of orchestral CEOs and music directors.

412. Robert Flanagan. "Symphony Musicians and Symphony Orchestras" Stanford University Graduate School of Business Research Paper No. 1989, revised 2008.
413. Jeff Woodruff, CEO diverse US orchestras.
414. Robert Flanagan, *The Perilous Life of Symphony Orchestras* 2012, 173.
415. Robert Flanagan, *supra*, 3.
416. *Ibid.*
417. *Save our Symphony Minnesota* "Unlocking the Truth" 2013 www.saveoursymphony.org.

Flanagan proposed a three-prong solution for orchestral survival: increase performance revenues, reduce growing expenditures, and raise nonperformance income. While all three proposals could well be applied to any organization seeking financial advice, their application to the plight of orchestras post-crisis is problematic. Of special application to the research, the second proposal with regard to expense reduction has a direct effect on musicians' salaries and related employment benefits. Numerous discussions with orchestral musicians involved in collective bargaining in the US illustrate that musicians and union representatives' cross-country are highly attuned to the need for cooperation and acceptance of belt-tightening salary proposals while recognizing that there are points of no return, as the Atlanta and Baltimore lockouts discussed in the *FAQs* highlight. Had Flanagan spent more time in discussion with stakeholders instead of interpreting statistics supplied by the League of American Orchestras, an organization criticized for supplying unreliable data, his findings could have reflected greater nuance.[418]

According to his view, orchestral cuts in terms of finances, season diminution and a reduced complement are part of a historical reversal, an about-face to the extraordinary growth US orchestras experienced in the second half of the 20th century. As the recession took hold, "basically, orchestras are trying to change labor from being quite as fixed a cost into a more variable cost."[419] Thus, the financially troubled orchestra is a reactive organization: shedding players, cutting weeks, and acting like factories in trouble when finances are at stake. Musicians, conductors, and even savvy managers beg to differ. "Keep in mind, orchestras are not factories that produce something tangible, musicians are in the business of magic, of making dreams tangible, of putting sound into the hearts and minds of listeners, it pains me to think that those who put their minds, bodies and hearts into acts of creation turn into flimsy shards whose futures can be shaken and even destroyed by flighty managerial decisions."[420]

In 2014, the League of American Orchestras disseminated the news that US orchestras have been forced to rely more on their unearned (read investment income and donations) than on earned income (read ticket sales and assorted fee-related services such as educational concerts, or in the case of orchestras who own their halls, venue related income such as rental fees).[421] Where do these findings lead the 21st-century orchestra? Is the dinosaur doomed to extinction as a broker for elitist art consumed by the privileged few? Or can the musicians, "soldiers of the future,"[422] build a new future based on community engagement and the thrill of artistic participation? Are there actionable means to serve orchestral ends when follow the money seems to be at the root of orchestral problems? Actionable responses to the myriad of problems

418. Former ICSOM President, Bruce Ridge, led the critique regarding League data, discussions at the 2016 ICSOM Conference Washington D.C.
419. Robert Flanagan, quoted by Michael Cooper "Roll over Mahler: US Orchestras are Shrinking," *New York Times* November 22, 2014.
420. Conversation with Michael Schønwandt, former principal conductor, Netherlands Radio Chamber Philharmonic.
421. Michael Cooper, *supra*.
422. Paraphrasing statements by Yo Yo Ma and the New York Philharmonic's President CEO Deborah Borda, May 16, 2017, https://nyphil.org/whats-new/2017/may/deborah-borda-curtis-commencement-address.

presented by cultural economists are few and far between. What steps can stakeholders from within the orchestral organization to unions and politicians take to build a stronger future? Is part of the post-crisis orchestral dilemma tied to mismanagement, weak governance and ramped up patterns of corporate cluelessness and greed as multiple stakeholders discussing recent US orchestral lockouts have reported?[423]

3.12 THE LEGACY OF BAUMOL'S CURSE: EXPERT REPORTS AND ASSESSMENTS

The presentation of The Wolf Report in 1992 at a meeting of the American Symphony Orchestra League underscored Baumol's curse message to a new generation of US orchestral managers and administrators. Challenging orchestral leaders to embrace a paradigm shift or sink into oblivion as a result of aging audiences and increased deficits, the dismal prognosis at the core of the report attempted to solve cost disease by downscaling the orchestral complement, reducing the number of concerts performed per season, and reorganizing municipal orchestras into regional performance groups.[424] Questionable conclusions such as "can orchestras continue to produce more product than their consumers want?" were coupled with fallacious reasoning exemplified by the connection between increased numbers of orchestral services/concerts and the requirements of unions to strive for wage increases as a part of collective bargaining processes. "The problem for orchestras has been that in order to pay musicians a reasonable wage, the decision has been made to schedule more concerts than the market will easily bear."[425] Gloom and doom permeate the report, with statements such as: "many financial approaches have been tried over the past fifty years to improve the financial condition of orchestras. Yet, the industry as a whole appears to be in the worst financial shape it has ever been in."[426]

Several worthwhile suggestions appear on the pages of the Wolf Report, including a call for greater racial integration and talent development as well as a call for a more transparent and inclusive system of collective decision-making. However, the point remains that Wolf's economic analysis was flawed. Taking two decades of statistics from US orchestras reported by the American Symphony Orchestra League as a point of departure, the report shows that in 1971, US orchestras ran an operating deficit of $2.8 million. Twenty years later, the deficit reached $23.2 million with a budget deficit of $64 million predicted by 2000.[427] History would show that the Wolf Report was incorrect in its economic analyses as the predicted $64 million deficit was happily superseded by an $85 million surplus in 2002.[428] Yet, then again, moving forward to the post-financial crisis 2008 era characterized as the Great Recession, the

423. *Song of the Lark* blog https://songofthelarkblog.com/; weekly reports *Adaptistration* www.adaptistration.com.
424. The Wolf Report. *The Financial Condition of Symphony Orchestras* 1992, http://www.polyphonic.org/wp-content/uploads/TheFinancialCondition of SymphonyOrchestras.pdf.
425. *Ibid.*, A-18.
426. *Ibid.*, A-17.
427. *Ibid.*, A-13.
428. League of American Orchestras 2002, https://www.americanorchestras.org/.

rhetoric of Baumol, Wolf and Flanagan echoed through orchestral halls as nonprofits struggled to attract donors in a climate of lackluster philanthropy.

3.13 DUTCH EXPERTS INTERPRET DATA

A closer examination of expert reports on orchestral survival in the Netherlands finds mantras of doom and gloom and their impact on decisions imperative to orchestral futures. Berenschot, a well-respected Dutch public and private sector consultancy firm, and other experts in the Netherlands circle around the subject of whether or not it is desirable to maintain a high degree of subsidy for an industry that cannot sustain itself economically. Borrowing heavily from Baumol, Bowen and Flanagan's findings, the Dutch experts conclude that unless there is a public social policy exception made for cultural endeavors, it is increasingly challenging to mount reasons to grant the subsidies integral to sectoral survival. Interestingly, expert reports on both sides of the Atlantic show that despite the pessimistic prognosis in various cultural sectors, there is no dearth of musicians and other cultural actors competing in the market. In a report on new models for Dutch orchestras in response to 2008 data regarding the comparatively low pay scales for orchestral musicians,[429] Berenschot reported that pay scales for orchestral musicians in the Netherlands are considerably lower than those for other professionals at a comparable level of training.[430] However, the experts did not utilize an analogous factor to determine a comparable level of training. The Berenschot logic runs as follows: the average orchestral musician holds a conservatory degree. Conservatories in the Netherlands (as opposed to the US where conservatory training is considered to be on par with college education) are considered to be HBO studies, the Dutch equivalent of the vocational level of higher education lower in terms of future salary determination than an academic university degree (WO).[431] On average, employed HBO diploma recipients earn markedly less than their WO counterparts both immediately post-graduation and five years thereafter.[432] If experts compare an orchestral musicians education—a lifelong, singular focus on perfecting instrumental skill akin to the highest level of sports training—to a three-year vocational course of study, musicians' salaries will remain low and musicians will have to continue the struggle to justify higher salaries.

Moving forward in the Berenschot Report, a single sentence speaks volumes: "we have not received any signals that point to the fact that it is difficult to attract musicians

429. Berenschot *Naar nieuwe prestatiemodellen voor orkesten* (Towards new performance models for orchestras) 29 april 2011 https://www.parlementairemonitor.nl/9353000/1/j9vvij5epmj1ey0/vip1eantjlxu.
430. In Dutch, "De inkomenspositie van musici is gebleken dat de primaire salarissen van orkestmusici lager zijn dan bij andere functionarissen die op Hbo-niveau in de muziek zijn opgeleid." *Research voor Beleid* 2008.
431. HBO (university of applied sciences) and WO (academic university education) with vocational degree (HBO) versus academic degree (WO).
432. https://mens-en-samenleving.infonu.nl/opleiding-en-beroep/26187-gemiddelde-salaris-na-hbo-of-wo-studie.html.

on the basis of their remuneration" (author's translation).[433] Market saturation as Berenschot's experts observe leads to the stark fact that for every musician, hundreds are waiting in the wings to rush on stage, implying, "we often do not even dare to think about let alone stand up for the financial aspects of our employment because we have been taught to internalize the fact that we are lucky to be able to work at any level in the music profession, let alone hold down an orchestra job."[434] From the musician's acceptance of the fact that their métier is characterized by an overabundance of qualified professionals for a small number of positions to the policymaker's observation that low salaries do not deter musicians creates a self-fulfilling prophecy as this laconic statement indicates: "if you think you should earn more, I strongly suggest a career switch. This is an orchestra, and your salary will remain more or less the same with some small cost-of-living adjustment for the duration of your days."[435]

3.14 THE X FACTOR: TALENT AS AN OBJECTIVE FACTOR TO SURVIVE ORCHESTRAL CUTS

Many of the hypotheses presented by cultural economists and subsequently policymakers are colored by misperceptions. To exemplify, Berenschot considers talent as a measure of key performance indicators (KPIs) in the orchestral sector.[436] Is talent an appropriate indicator? And even more fundamentally can talent be measured? Hearken back to Baumol's assertion that the "cost of talent rises in a growing economy yet the unit productivity of the performers in stagnant service industries does not,"[437] and consider talent in relation to musical success, a term that wends its way through position papers, reports and assessments regarding orchestral subsidies and other musician-related subjects. Infamously, talent was linked to a special status that shielded certain players from dismissal during the reorganization that decimated personnel at Dutch radio orchestras (2012-2013), a topic of focus in the *Requiem for an orchestra movement*. Is it not possible to cast some aspersions on the legitimacy of empirical fact-finding if talent is an objective criterion?

3.15 MORE BERENSCHOT: EXPERT SUGGESTIONS

In a study commissioned by the Dutch Ministry of Education, Culture and Science in 2011,[438] a team of eight benchmark and organization experts investigated the state of Dutch orchestras in order to advise the Ministry on how to restructure the sector on the basis of cost-efficiency. Starting off with a baseline measurement ("nulmeting") of the

433. Berenschot, *supra*. "We hebben geen signalen gekregen die erop duiden dat het moeilijk is om musici aan te trekken of te behouden op grond van de beloning," 52.
434. Conversations with Laurie Niles, founder www.violinist.com.
435. Jan Willem Loot in a contract negotiation with the author. Former Managing Director, Netherlands Philharmonic Orchestra, he was soon to move to the top management position at the Royal Concertgebouw Orchestra in 1998.
436. Berenschot, *supra*.
437. William Baumol. "Children of Performing Arts, the Economic Dilemma" 1996, 183-206.
438. Berenschot, *supra*.

status quo for Dutch orchestras in 2009, the experts noted that the RvC called for far-reaching changes in the entire system of orchestral organization and subsidies: orchestras would receive subsidies in accordance with their "results" and not according to the number of employees per province (formatieplaatsen per landsdeel).[439] Their conclusions indicated that several changes were necessary to serve these ends. Berenschot advised, in unranked order:

(1) Reduce the number of orchestras: allow remaining orchestras to take on the performance activities of "redundant" ensembles. Berenschot advocated a separate cluster category in which orchestras combine forces post-personnel cuts.
(2) Reduce the complement (vaste formatie), the infamous cheese cutter ("kaasschaaf") method in which a slice of the orchestra is removed and replaced by flexible workers (flexibile schil), freelancers.
(3) Administrative mergers on management and support staff levels.
(4) Create pools of orchestral musicians who travel throughout the country to fill open positions, or alternatively are assigned to specific provinces to perform in orchestras.

Discussing these points with Dutch orchestral stakeholders was not only an emotionally charged exercise but also valuable in terms of valid criticism from the insiders who perform orchestral duties on a daily basis. The cluster category suffers from a fundamental misconception related to the value of what US orchestras refer to as "crucial community building."[440] "Redundant ensembles are not mere throwaways, they are living, breathing cultural entities that interact with real audiences. Certainly, if you look at the orchestra from a distant, economist lens, all orchestras, all players are replaceable. What makes each cultural organism distinct, however, is just that: they are marked by individual personalities and characters. Cutting and reshuffling at random destroys artistic cohesion."[441] Additional criticism of the cheese cutter method (point 2 above) can be found in a protest manifesto by the author on the eve of orchestral cuts in the Netherlands in 2004.[442]

While cynics may observe that musicians would be enthusiastic to learn that their ranks remain unscathed while management bears the brunt of a reorganization (point 3 above),[443] the premise behind this efficiency maneuver ignores the fact that staff members with little or no direct link to a home orchestra can complete routine

439. *Ibid.*
440. League of Symphony Orchestra https://americanorchestras.org/learning-leadership-development/diversity-resource-center/best-practices-in-orchestras-arts-organizations/audience-development.html.
441. Conversations with Netherlands Television Radio producer Anita Wijnen.
442. Heather Kurzbauer. "Kaasschaaf en Cultuur: Culture on the Cutting Board." February 20, 2004. *Epilogue: Appendix 4.*
443. Initially musicians interviewed chuckled at this proposition but then realized that it entailed a geographic merger akin to the reorganization that created PhilharmonieZuid Nederland (PZN), *see FAQs.*

assignments, but cannot presume to take on the myriad tasks that call for personal commitment and identification with the organization.

The fourth observation, the creation of freelancer pools of orchestral musicians, hearkens back historically to the freelance bands of unaffiliated troubadours described in *Haydn rewrites history*. Remarkably, a Dutch-based freelancer presented a proposal to the now-defunct *Cultuur in Beeld* (Culture in Focus) Dutch-based culture conference in 2017.[444] The proposal however differentiated itself from the Berenschot proposition in that it was intended to give orchestral freelancers additional work in small chamber ensembles. "A freelance pool of musicians could enrich each province by presenting chamber music concerts in a variety of venues including nonstandard locations. This idea helps to solve two problems—the high degree of unemployment amongst excellent conservatory graduates and the need for 'door-to-door' music in areas of the country where there is no direct access to Dutch orchestras."[445] The Berenschot proposition could aggravate orchestral employment crises unless freelancers in the pools were well remunerated for travel time and performance-related activities.

3.16 CAO FLEXIBILIZATION

Without any discussions that involved orchestral musicians, Berenschot came to the conclusion that the orchestral CAOs were much too inflexible. "To introduce flexibility into the terms of employment is of the greatest importance."[446] Prophetic words indeed when one reads the name of the third Berenschot expert listed among the eight assigned to the task: Piet van Gennip. Two years after lending academic expertise to the report, van Gennip was appointed to the position of General Director, Het Balletorkest (HBO). His steadfast adherence to CAO flexibility could be related to his previous employment at Berenschot; it has led to frequent differences of opinion with the orchestra's representatives on the Works Council. To highlight, a close reading of the work schedule of a fully employed musician at HBO shows that the schedule stretches the CAO to its limits in terms of free days for musicians, creating additional work stress in a job in which 70% contracts are closer to 100% work. "Everybody in the orchestra was hurt by the reorganization in 2012-2013, we lost a preponderance of players. The core that was left works longer hours, gives more performances than ever before, and all that for less money. We were told that those who remained were the lucky ones, they at least get to perform, this is the classic dilemma for musicians—you have to accept less because you want to be a part of the performance."[447] Another HBO member added a philosophical note to a discussion of more work, less pay at the orchestra. "It is the classic divide, the 'them' and 'us' of manager and musician. They

444. *Culture in Focus* discontinued 2018, https://www.vnpf.nl/nieuws/congres-cultuur-in-beeld-stopt.
445. Discussions with Tiziana Pintus, violinist and creative project initiator, 2017. Her quest for a position in the RCO is the focus of *A long and winding road*.
446. In Dutch: "Het allerbelangrijkste is dan ook om flexibiliteit in de arbeidsvoorwaarden te brengen." Berenschot *supra*, 54.
447. Conversation with former HBO violist, Andrew Faughnan.

look at the cash flows, the schedules, the possibilities to cut and we experience overfull schedules, shrinking salaries with less time for other enriching musical activities."[448]

The list of interviewees who submitted information to bolster Berenschot's findings contains the names of cultural economists, human resource professionals, and managers along with the name of one, and only one, musician. Adding insult to injury, the sole musician, violinist Frederieke Saeijs, never sought nor gained employment as a member of a professional orchestra in the Netherlands or beyond.[449] If experts seek stakeholder advice from managers and other insiders, is it too much to ask for information from those who operate at the center of their inquiry, the musicians?

3.17 THE NEGATIVE IMPACT OF THE COST DISEASE THEORY ON ORCHESTRAS

There is nothing novel in the statement that orchestras have been plagued by financial hardships throughout the centuries. What is novel is that a reliance on theories such as the cost disease can lead financial decision-makers down a dangerous path in terms of orchestral futures. An attorney with vast experience in negotiating US orchestral contracts, Len Leibowitz acknowledges the realities of financial challenges but makes the point that US boards use cost disease theory and structural deficit arguments to excuse their negligence in making commitments to raise money, enhance and expand community relations, and other supportive endeavors. He notes, "managers are often unwilling to negotiate and throw up their hands and say, 'that's it.' Where is the end of the road? Managers and boards have abdicated their responsibility by saying the structural deficit is built in, it can't be fixed."[450]

Going back to Adam Smith, is it not possible to posit that whatever economic theory policy decisions in times of crises are based upon, the central issue should be what is the concept of the individual, the stakeholder, the employee who is about to lose his/her job? Peter Benoliel, a forward-thinking music business insider with decades of board experience, opines, "most economists take a sanguine view of their own study of inquiry. I preferred philosophy to economics during my formative years and nevertheless learned much related to economics through life experience. Boom and bust are the vernacular of many economists. For orchestras to navigate treacherous waters and deal with real-time deficits, they need board members with a special understanding of these challenges but more importantly, a connection to the vital necessity of having an orchestra grace one's life, one's city."[451] Looking carefully at the signals presented by cultural economists, managers, and panels of experts epitomized by Berenschot reports, the Dutch RvC and across the ocean, the Wolf and Flanagan report, the following quote sets the tone for discouragement with regard to orchestral

448. Conversation with HBO associate principal cellist Evelien Prakke.
449. Berenschot Bijlage: "betrokken personen," 60, https://www.frederiekesaeijs.com/.
450. Len Leibowitz, *supra*.
451. Former CEO Quaker Oil Peter Benoliel served as board chairman of the Philadelphia Orchestra and held board positions at the Curtis Institute of Music, the Grand Teton Music Festival and Marlboro Music Festival.

finances, "because of the economic structure of the performing arts, financial pressures are here to stay, and there are fundamental reasons for expecting the income gap to widen steadily with the passage of time."[452]

3.18 TIMES THEY ARE A-CHANGING?

David Throsby posed the daring question: "how appropriate is it to ask how far an economic approach to policymaking might be able to incorporate culture within its frame of reference?"[453] Probing further, one might ask: how can culture be accommodated within free-market economic thinking that guides most states in their approach to funding cultural activity? The post-WWII purposive approach to arts funding has undergone a major shift, a destabilization in terms of public sector spending, and a withdrawal of state involvement as public budgets have decreased dramatically. The Thatcher-Reagan neoliberal support of market liberalization, deregulation and the rules of the market economy has caused a shift in states' conclusions concerning whether or not the arts are worthy of funding not only in the US but "[i]n Europe the market and the arts are often unhappy bedfellows."[454] The impact of these changes in cultural support sowed seeds of destruction in the Netherlands as the *Requiem for an orchestra movement* describes.

3.19 NEOLIBERALISM: THE NEMESIS OF CULTURAL SPENDING?

The neoliberal approach was characterized by minimum intrusion on the part of big government to set acceptable standards in capital and labor markets. Countervailing forces of strong unions and labor market regulation were undermined by a balance of power shift from workers to employers. Market-driven solutions severed from the protection of government intervention became the accepted norm. This mini reflection on the fruits of the neoliberal revolution bears repetition as it seeps through the cracks in most cases of orchestral crisis. From reports of mismanagement and faulty orchestral board judgments in Atlanta, Minnesota and the 2019 Baltimore lockout to the disregard for musicians' rights to structure free time experienced by an increasing number of Dutch orchestral professionals whose 70% pay jobs closely resemble 100% work-jobs, the screws are tightening in the profession. An offshoot of Pareto's famed principle of equilibrium conditions holds that in order to ensure that some workers/colleagues will be better off in the future, others must suffer, and become worse off.[455] "After the golden years of the last quarter of the 20th century, orchestral managements view us more like commodities, not as performing artists. We are constantly reminded that we

452. Hyman R. Faine. "Cooperative Bargaining in Nonprofit Arts Organizations." *The Journal of Arts, Management and Law* 1985.
453. David Throsby. *Economics and Culture* 2001, 138-39.
454. Rik van der Ploeg, "The Making of Cultural Policy: A European Perspective" *supra*, 1.
455. The Pareto Efficient named after the early 20th-century Italian economist Vilfredo Pareto spawned numerous studies on redistributive transfer. *See* Ravi Kanbur. *Spatial Inequality and Development* 2005.

are the privileged few to even hold jobs in the field as if it is our good luck to experience various levels of exploitation in the profession."[456]

The observations presented by Los Angeles Philharmonic violist and ICSOM President Meredith Snow at a national convention in 2019 sound yet another alarm in terms of orchestral survival. Even though her comments are based on US orchestral experiences, a parallel shift distilled through the rhetoric of Dutch cultural policymakers can be detected in the post-financial crisis decade:[457]

> As the majority of wealth in our national economy flows upwards into the hands of a few, ICSOM is seeing a change in the balance of power in our non-profit sector of the music business. As orchestras continue to generate less earned income, we become increasingly dependent on endowments and donations. This is changing the leverage points we have traditionally used in negotiations. Boards and managers seem to have no qualms about leaving musicians locked out until they come to heel. There is no commitment to the orchestra and no commitment to the music we provide to our communities. The bottom line is their idol, with little care for their underlying civic duty to the public and to our non-profit arts.[458]

Perhaps the last messianic words should come from the brilliant pen of Deirdre McCloskey with her global challenge: "Using the arts is the way that anything changes in a free society."[459] And while we are at it, add a tall order of healthy national cultural policies and good governance in orchestral management.

The question remains that if the odds are stacked up against orchestral survival as cost disease is much more of a reality than a fear, how can the orchestra persevere? Answering the question with the retort, orchestras have always faced these challenges and survived falls short of providing a real answer. We need to reinterpret the question to ask if there is another paradigm, another manner to cut costs while delivering the unique orchestral product: such paradigms have already found homes in the increasing number of self-governing orchestras and flexible models found in the smaller orchestra, the chamber orchestra sector in which expensive administrative and management positions are replaced by musician-leaders who take on these posts.

The translation of the UK self-governing model common to the major London orchestras[460] to the United States has not been met with great success. The Louisiana Philharmonic Orchestra, which formed after the dissolution of the New Orleans Symphony Orchestra in 1991, is a notable exception, as the full-time complement of musicians are its corporate members. Yet with a small complement (less than 70 musicians) and comparatively short (36-week) season and comparatively low salaries,[461] it could be argued that the Louisiana Philharmonic does not offer a viable means of evaluating success as a self-governing US orchestra. "Every decade brought

456. Conversations with Rebekah Johnson, New Jersey Symphony violinist.
457. Dutch RvC statements and pronouncements following State Secretary Halbe Zijlstra's infamous "culture is a left-wing hobby" remark.
458. ICSOM Chairperson Meredith Snow's address, AFM Convention Las Vegas June 17, 2019.
459. Deirdre McCloskey, "Battles to Be Won" *Windy City Times* September 17, 2014.
460. The Royal Philharmonic Orchestra, London Symphony, London Philharmonic and the Philharmonia are self-governing, with players holding shares in the company. All players are paid on a freelance basis.
461. Section violin salaries (2012) listed at less than $13,000, www.glassdoor.com.

challenges to the classical musicians in New Orleans. We survived the loss of the New Orleans Philharmonic, we survived Katrina, we fought for the survival of classical music in our city and to some extent we won as we still exist, however the price we had to pay was high and our earnings are low."[462]

Many self-governing orchestral initiatives are to be found within the realm of chamber orchestras: Orpheus, the storied New York-based chamber orchestra founded in 1972 and the Dutch-based Ludwig, a forward-thinking ensemble founded in 2012 provide stellar examples of musician-operated startups. Closer analysis shows that Orpheus elects 3 of its 34 musician members to the Board of Trustees, and another trio to the Artistic Director positions which means in essence that although musician members have input into decision-making, the three-legged stool classical management hierarchy described in the *FAQs* is still in operation.

3.20 RATIONALES FOR ARTS FUNDING: THE BIGGER PICTURE

"How can we find the freedom to use our imaginations as musicians without constantly thinking of the commercial impact of our output?"[463] In an eye-opening piece in the Arts and Leisure section of the *New York Times*,[464] A.O. Scott critiqued a new era of social inequality and cultural change, a world in which "museums chase dollars with crude commercialism aimed at the masses and the slavish cultivation of wealthy patrons. Symphonies and operas chase donors and squeeze workers (that is, artists) as the public drifts away."[465] Scott analyzed the clash between high and middlebrow culture through the lens of Thomas Piketty's blockbuster, *Capital in the Twenty-First Century*, a political economics tour-de-force that describes inequality in terms of the rapacious increase in economic disparity between the very top of the financial pyramid, the 1 % in Piketty's terms, and the middle class. Whereas the specific elements in terms of taste and spending patterns that define allocation according to class are not relevant to an analysis of the ups and downs in orchestral funding, what it does add to a consideration of funding in the new millennium is Scott's unmasking of a new twist to patronage. According to Piketty, prior to WWI, the 1% received approximately 20% of total income garnered in both the US and the UK. The post-WWII period measured by US statistics in the 1950s showed a decrease of 10%. The rush forward took place in the 1980s, the decade of the big earners and sky-is-the-limit bonuses: US millennials experienced a dramatic upturn to 20%. To Piketty, inherited wealth and the conspicuous lack of progressive taxation in the US resulted in exacerbating economic inequalities and led to the "erosion" of the middle class.

462. Conversation with Louisiana Philharmonic harpist Rachel van Voorhees.
463. Freelance musician's comment, *Platform voor Freelance Musici* meeting Splendor Amsterdam, June 2019.
464. A.O. Scott. "The Squeeze on the Middle Brow" *New York Times* August 3, 2014.
465. *Ibid.*

3.21 A TAX ON CULTURE?

Progressive taxation mitigated by philanthropy would make donations to cultural (and other) nonprofits attractive. In reality, however, Piketty makes it clear that public policy can make an enormous difference. Even if the underlying economic conditions point toward extreme inequality, what Piketty calls "a drift toward oligarchy" can be halted and even reversed if the body politic so chooses.

Conversations with orchestra managers and musicians across America shed light on another dimension of the philanthropy issue. As a newly minted wealthy class rises, the desire to support "art for art's sake" vanishes as a new generation of dot.com billionaires eschew outdated traditions of cultural philanthropy, preferring market-place investments (read art or culture that makes money for them) and feel good investments to advance greater goals such as erasing poverty, curing AIDS. And, on the corporate front, many of the more established national foundations—Ford, Rockefeller, Pew, Gates, etc.—are "edging politely but firmly away" from institutions "that cannot demonstrate a significant contribution to solving or soothing specific social or economic traumas."[466] Dr. Harald Falckenberg, a cultural scholar and renowned art collector, tied art investment in the "plastic arts" to major world investment strategies. He offended theorists and policymakers with a statement that was perceived as short-sighted and crass: "every era gets the art it deserves."[467] Yet, a closer look at the impact of subsidy cuts in the Netherlands and philanthropic reductions in the US indicates that there is some merit to his observation. "Offerings in the cultural section have become leaner and meaner as funds diminish; too many believe that if we don't cater to the crowd, we will face extinction. Our challenge is to shout from the rooftops that art matters."[468] Does this imply that we can only acquire the culture we can afford to pay for?

The discrepancy between the number of students attending professional training programs at conservatories and the places of employment available upon graduation sparks regular discussions concerning the necessity to close training institutes or, conversely, create job opportunities for music students.[469] A discussion on the quality of conservatory training or the necessity thereof in the face of dismal employment opportunities goes beyond the scope of this book; however, the intensity of the debate following the latest round of cutbacks raises the question: where will highly trained young musicians find work when orchestras are disappearing steadily as a result of financial cuts in both countries studied? "We are told, be creative, artists have always faced great financial instability, this is not a new phenomenon. However, such

466. Mike Scutari. "From Mahler to the Masses" *Inside Philanthropy* May 5, 2017, https://www.insidephilanthropy.com/home/2017/4/6/orchestras-symphonies-grants-foundations.
467. Harald Falckenberg. "The art world we deserve?" *Financial Times* April 11, 2014, https://www.ft.com/content/498f5cca-bfce-11e3-b6e8-00144feabdc0.
468. Conversation with Erin Roy, theater producer.
469. "Nederlanders gezien als tweederangs muzikanten schaf conservatoria af" (The Dutch are considered second-rate musicians, decrease the number of conservatories) *Volkskrant*, August 11, 2011 http://www.volkskrant.nl/vk/nl/2676/Cultuur/article/detail/2845625/2011/08/11/Nederlanders-gezien-als-tweederangs-muzikanten-schaf-conservatoria-af.dhtml.

statements do not bode well for progress. We read about the evils of precarious work in other sectors only to discover, that we are very vulnerable as well."[470]

The shift from support for the arts as a vital investment in a country's future to support as a charitable donation to lend a helping hand to cultural institutions has given way to a profit-model view toward culture that reads: "if culture can make money, it deserves support." Does this mark a messy descent to a piecemeal cultural environment in which only the fittest survive? The competition between cultural organizations on the macroscale and the battle for subsidies/support for orchestras on the microscale calls for structural solutions. Do we need to determine calculated return on public investment in cultural products in order to attract philanthropists? Across the channel in the UK, it can be observed that the language of state grant giving has undergone a shift in terminology from giving grants to investment. Such a terminology shift implies a refreshing approach as to how orchestras could work toward a turnaround. If managers start to cooperate, rather than compete with one another for funding, if musicians, whether freelance or fully employed, rise up to express the cultural and monetary value of their artistic endeavors with strength and unity, we can make the case for our services. To paraphrase Churchill, "if we don't fight for our culture, what is there to fight for?"[471]

470. Round table discussions with Juilliard School of Music graduates.

471. Benoît Machuel, Secretary General, Federation International Musicians (FIM), referring to a famous remark by Sir Winston when asked to cut the arts budget to support the WWII war effort replied, "then what are we fighting for?"

4 Requiem for an Orchestra

> The Cabinet needs to restore sound public finance ... the credit crisis and the European debt crisis have made it imperative for us to deal with this situation.[472]

> On the first of August 2013, the employment contracts of 174 employees came to an end, either in whole or in part as a result of the reorganization at the Netherlands Broadcasting Music Foundation (MCO).[473]

> The process may have been blessed by the stamp of legality, however it never felt right.[474]

> Our belief is that no arts organization can cut itself to success.[475]

A saga replete with collective angst and personal drama influenced by encroaching vulnerability, this *movement* retells narratives related to the breaking and remaking of Dutch radio orchestras in the 21st century. From politically motivated budgetary machinations to media politics, from questionable governance to internal strife, this *movement* is motivated by the stories of those who chose or were forced to leave the orchestras and those who were approved to stay and play—their realities and perceptions under the watchful eyes of unions, works councils, and the regulatory mechanisms within Dutch dismissal law. Many stories remain untold at the behest of stakeholders and their valid privacy concerns. Regardless of certain poignant omissions, this *movement* endeavors to let the musicians take the lead. Mediated by political

472. "Vrijheid en verantwoordelijkheid" Regeerakkoord VVD-CDA (Freedom and Responsibility, VVD-CDA coalition agreement) September 20, 2010, 15 "Het kabinet wil de overheidsfinanciën weer gezond maken ... door de kredietcrisis en de Europese schuldcrisis is het saneren een harde noodzaak," https://rijksoverheid.archiefweb.eu/#archive.
473. "Als gevolg van de reorganisatie is per 1 augustus 2013 aan de dienstverbanden van 174 medewerkers van de Stichting Muziekcentrum van de Omroep geheel of gedeeltelijk een einde gekomen." Financieel Jaarverslag 2013, 37 https://www.omroepmuziek.nl/content/uploads/2019/04/SOM-jaarverslag-2013.pdf.
474. Conversations with Cyril Scheepmaker, RSO and RKF bass trombone; member MCO Works Council.
475. Bruce Ridge, former President, International Conference of Symphony Opera Musicians (ICSOM).

and legal constructs that influenced the reorganization, it is their voice that resounds through these pages. One orchestra in particular, the now-defunct Netherlands Radio Chamber Orchestra (RKF) is granted a last hurrah.

The handwriting was on the wall for numerous Dutch artistic endeavors in the post-2007-2008 financial crisis years when massive subsidy cuts led to the ruin of many venerated institutions including the dismantling of prestigious Dutch radio orchestras.[476] An agreement entitled *Freedom and Responsibility*, reflecting the views of the Dutch political coalition in power, showcased its efficiency in the choice of a mere seven words to announce: "the Broadcasting Music Center will be abolished."[477] Three major orchestras (Netherlands Radio Philharmonic Orchestra, further RFO; Netherlands Radio Chamber Philharmonic, further RKF; the Metropole Orchestra), a renowned chorus (Groot Omroepkoor, further GOK) and a prized library employed by the Broadcasting Center (Muziekcentrum van de Omroep, further MCO) were slated for demolition.

In 2011, the Dutch State Secretary for Culture, Halbe Zijlstra finalized plans for a €200 million cultural subsidy cut that led to the "kaalslag" or destruction of a sector known worldwide for its extraordinary range of performances and productions.[478] Commenting on the impact of the 2012-2013 culture cuts at a convocation in the Valhalla of Dutch culture—the Concertgebouw's Great Hall—Bastiaan Vinkenburg, a senior consultant in the Dutch cultural field, indicated that detrimental effects would increase over time: "compared to 2010, the Ministry of Education, Culture and Science spent a total of 225 million euros less per year on culture. This means a decrease of 24% in 2013 compared to 2010. And the biggest blow is yet to come after the municipalities make further cutbacks."[479]

Writing what is a partially personal narrative in the context of a book is complicated as it calls for removing subjectivity to answer to the demands of academic objectivity. It has taken years to be able to approach the subject without letting emotions run away and tarnish the narrative with personal feelings. The reorganization process left its tracks not only in the lives of the orchestra's former musicians but also on the music world at large. Listeners at home and abroad lamented the RKF's passing. "An orchestra with a real adventurous spirit from its historically informed

476. Inventory of culture cuts (in Dutch), https://nos.nl/artikel/251291-bezuinigingen-kunst-en-cultuur-een-overzicht.html; Achtergronddocument "Bezuiniging op cultuur. Realisatie en effect" Algemene Rekenkamer 12 februari 2015 https://opmaat.sdu.nl/hulkStatic/SDU/OP/blg-464461/sharp_/ANX/blg-464461.pdf.

477. "Vrijheid en verantwoordelijkheid." "Het muziekcentrum voor de omroep wordt afgeschaft." "Vrijheid en verantwoordelijkheid" Regeerakkoord VVD-CDA (Freedom and Responsibility, VVD-CDA coalition agreement) 20 september 2010, 34. https://rijksoverheid.archiefweb.eu/#archive.

478. The term "kaalslag" trended in 2011. Henny de Lange "Het wordt een kaalslag in de kunst" *Trouw* 14 juni 2011, https://www.trouw.nl/cultuur-media/het-wordt-een-kaalslag-in-de-kunst~b5dd25c1/.

479. Announcement June 22, 2015. "De bestedingen van het Ministerie van OCW aan cultuur zijn ten opzichte van 2010 in totaal 225 miljoen euro per jaar minder. Dat betekent een afname van 24% in 2013 ten opzichte van 2010. En de grootste klap komt nog als de gemeentes verder gaan bezuinigen."

readings of the early classical period to the wildest 21st century premieres, gone."[480] US-based orchestral insiders assume that subsidized European orchestras are protected from the vicissitudes of financially driven reductions. "We always thought that you Europeans had it made, that orchestras were not precarious like US orchestras because you have enjoyed such a long history of government support for culture, without struggling to justify an orchestra's cultural value."[481]

This *movement* resounds in a minor key. Following general observations concerning radio orchestras, it describes dark days in the history of the Dutch radio orchestras before moving to a closer examination of policy themes underlying the decisions to cut orchestras. Interviews with musicians on both sides of the Atlantic demonstrated that not only US-based musicians but also Dutch musicians were largely unaware of the influence the push/pull of policy agendas have on their sector, forces that feature strongly in the RKF story. The final demise of the RKF is a mere story within a story that touches upon questions of cultural validation and fundamental financial decision-making in the light of substantial subsidy cuts post-2007-2008 financial crisis. For those who might ask "what's law gotta do with it?" a myriad of issues centering on collective redundancy processes heightened by the employers' application of dismissal regulations mix with contract interpretation (both individual contracts and collective bargaining contracts),[482] general governance-related questions and most importantly, the interaction between policy and dismissal affected musicians.

4.1 CREEPING BACKWARD INTO DARKNESS

Prior to WWII, four different broadcasting associations within the Dutch radio system funded and operated their own orchestras. From dance music to mainstream classics, these ensembles answered the needs of an ever-expanding radio audience throughout the 1930s. Following the German occupation of the Netherlands in 1940, the radio orchestras were consolidated under the Rijksradio De Nederlandsche Omroep with a twofold purpose: general entertainment and the transmission of Nazi propaganda.[483] Disturbingly, reports emphasized the positive economic impact of cultural occupation: "the organization of musical life went on smoothly" ... "[the] German occupiers tripled our salary."[484] A paucity of reports make mention of the demise of Jewish colleague-musicians "who played in our orchestras and were required to wear a yellow star."[485] Not only their livelihoods but also their lives were endangered.[486]

480. The Dutch radio orchestras enjoyed worldwide diffusion from pan-European stations including BBC Radio 3 and radio stations in North America. Quote, Edo de Waart, former Music Director, RFO.
481. Conversations with Alabama Symphony violist Lucina Horner.
482. Collective bargaining agreements in US parlance (CBAs); collectieve arbeidsovereenkomsten (CAOs) in Dutch.
483. P. Micheels. *Muziek in de schaduw van het Derde Rijk: de Nederlandse symfonieorkesten 1933-1945*. Walburg Pers 1993.
484. *Ibid.*
485. *Ibid.*
486. Fewer than 10% of the Jewish community of Hilversum survived during 1942-1944, https://jck.nl/en/page/hilversum.

Looking back, Ben Janssen, former MCO General Director, remarked: "today's radio orchestras were preceded by musical organizations with a tainted history, something we never really have come to terms with. During the war, the mayor of Hilversum was a notorious Nazi sympathizer, you can imagine what that meant to the radio orchestra's employees. We talk about how to interpret history; however, we have not dealt with the terrible inequality that is part of our history." Although it might be confrontational to draw a comparison between the disproportionate treatment of certain musicians during the dark days of occupation to the personnel reductions that destroyed an orchestra in 2013, it is the musicians themselves who brought forth this comparison to accentuate their vulnerability. "A terrible feeling of who was permitted to stay in the orchestra and who was not, all the lists of and the interminable selection process hearkened back to darker days."[487]

4.2 QUESTIONING LEGITIMACY: IS A RADIO ORCHESTRA UNIQUE? DOES IT DESERVE PRESERVATION?

Radio orchestras have long had a particular identity both sonically and creatively. The ever-present microphone that signals that an ensemble is ready to record inspires "a quickness of attack, a flexibility and a penchant for learning quickly."[488] In terms of repertoire, radio orchestras traditionally present national musical treasures and other lesser-known works from the repertoire including contemporary commissions and premieres of new works.[489] Yet despite these contributions, proposals to shift specific radio orchestra responsibilities to regional and municipal orchestras have chipped away at Dutch radio orchestras' identities since the 1950s.

4.3 MORE LEGITIMACY ISSUES: UNFAIR COMPETITION?

In a markedly direct challenge to the raison d'être of the radio orchestras, Ronald Plasterk, State Secretary for Culture, Science and Education (2007-2010), wrote: "The broadcasting orchestras function almost entirely separately from the other ten orchestras. The RFO in particular has in recent years increasingly entered the playing field of regular orchestras as it goes on tours, organizes educational projects in the region and plays standard repertoire on its CD releases. This raises the question of whether a separate position for broadcasting orchestras is still legitimate."[490]

An additional claim of false competition was advanced by the Director of the Amsterdam-based Netherlands Philharmonic Orchestra (NedPhO): "A different form of financing accentuates the competition between top-level state subsidized orchestras

487. Conversations with former RFO violinist Peter Weimar.
488. Conversations with Maestro Edo de Waart.
489. V. Schouten. "De Orkesten van het MCO: Artistieke selectieprocessen" Master's Thesis, University of Utrecht 2010.
490. Ronald Plasterk. "Advies over het orkestenbestel aan het Raad voor Cultuur" 23 april 2009. Response RvC 18 februari 2010, 9 (author's translation).

and the radio orchestras when they give concerts in major halls; the cost of presenting a radio orchestra is much cheaper than the costs of presenting my orchestra, for example. We have to pay for the use of concert halls, broadcasters defray these substantial costs for their radio orchestras. Not really fair in a financial climate when budgets are particularly tight."[491] Considering the reexamination of the role of radio orchestras on the part of advisory groups and influential politicians' intent to implement austerity measures, the conscious move from recording to a combination of recording and live performance could have been partially responsible for the orchestras' final demise in 2012.

4.4 BROADCASTING AND BROADCASTING MUSIC: AN UNEASY ALLIANCE

The history of Dutch radio orchestras from their post-WWII resurrection to cuts and reorganization in 2012-2013 has been turbulent. None of the radio orchestras under the aegis of Dutch broadcasting foundations escaped the threats of multiple austerity plans. Part of a larger story on changes within broadcasting systems, the saga of Dutch radio orchestras is weighed down by external and internal conflicts, from a lack of political commitment to broadcasters' alacrity to divert funds away from the music sector. Uncertainty in terms of orchestral identity and shifting patterns of cultural decision-making at governmental and expert council levels prompted unfortunate competition between the orchestras as the end was in sight.

For those who might dismiss broadcasting imbroglios as a mere tempest in a teapot, keep in mind that the downfall of the Dutch cabinet in 1965 was attributed to political conflicts prompted by intense differences of opinion concerning commercial broadcasting and the regulation of advertising.[492] In contrast to the weak role of public broadcasting in the US, public broadcasting in the Netherlands, like many of its European counterparts,[493] has enjoyed a long history as a distinctive institutional form strongly supported by the government. Present-day debates with regard to state support for public broadcasting substantiated by highly critical reports on dubious spending practices show evidence of long-standing cracks in Dutch Public Broadcasting (Nederlands Publieke Omroep, the NPO). "The NPO's performance is compromised by doubts and divisions within the organisation about what its role should be."[494] Such doubts and divisions elaborated upon in the 2019 report were part and parcel of the demise of the radio orchestras under the aegis of the NPO, an organization that was never wholly committed to its musical branch.

491. Conversations with Rob Streevelaar NedPhO Managing Director.
492. The Marijnen Cabinet fell due to sharp differences of opinion concerning commercial broadcasting and allocation of airtime https://www.parlement.com/id/vh8lnhronvwd/kabinet_marijnen_1963 1965.
493. Many other European countries have similar broadcasting traditions.
494. "Hilversum in View." Netherlands Court of Audit 2019, https://english.rekenkamer.nl/publications/reports/2019/12/10/hilversum-in-view.

4.5 CULTURAL POLICY TRENDS APROPOS DUTCH CULTURE

To achieve an understanding of the bigger picture within Dutch broadcasting, it is helpful to review several important points. A frequently quoted principle attributed to one of the founding fathers of the Dutch Republic, Johan Thorbecke, "the government may make no judgement with regard to science or the arts," signals the positive value of detachment on the part of the state within the realm of culture. By the second decade of the 20th century, however, the Dutch government emulated several other European states in supporting cultural activities.[495] Expert panels were established to play a vital role in advising the government concerning expenditure since the 1950s,[496] a phenomenon that this *movement* will examine on hand of the many recommendations put forward concerning the radio orchestras both pre- and post-2007-2008 financial crisis.

Several important trends in Dutch cultural policy took hold in the 1980s and have held sway in cultural policies ever since. Previous decades had embraced cultural policy as a priority within a concept of general well-being, a beneficial component of social welfare policy. Severe economic recession in the late 1970s and early 1980s led to a reassessment of cultural policy. While culture was still considered to be of great importance, budget cuts were deemed even more essential. Cultural institutions were encouraged to consider commercial ventures to decrease their reliance on government subsidies. Concurrently, the concept of a market for culture based on public demand grew in importance. A four-year subsidy cycle was put in place giving power to an advisory board of experts, the Raad voor Cultuur (Dutch Council for Culture, RvC) for subsidy determination. On more than one occasion, Minister Elco Brinkman sharply criticized the RvC's subsidy recommendations labeling their choices as "elitist, aloof, and one-sided (or "unilaterally biased," author's translation)."[497] Efficiency became a constant in the rhetoric and actions taken by politicians and policy advisors at the end of the 20th century. A secondary result of the Great Efficiency Operation 1990 (Grote Efficiency Operatie) was to encourage the RvC to align its subsidy-related decision-making to embrace political aims. If austerity was called for in other areas of national expenditure, culture was certain to take a "lion's share"[498] of the burden.[499]

495. Dutch Ministry of Education, Arts and Science (Onderwijs, Kunst, Wetenschap) dates back to 1989.
496. Information gleaned from the Raad voor Culture (Dutch Council for Culture) www.Raadvoorcultuur.nl.
497. Elco Brinkman. *Afscheid van de Raad voor de Kunst* 19 december 1995. In Dutch: "elitair, afstandelijk en eenzijdig."
498. Frans Brüggen, former principal conductor, RKF, until its dissolution in 2005.
499. State Secretary for Education, Culture and Science Aad Nuis' documents sent to the Dutch Council for Culture (Raad voor Cultuur). No mention is made of decision-making according to artistic value, but rather the accent is placed on a link between the Council's advice and relevant policy decisions. *Adviesaanvragen cultuurnota 1997-2000* and *Pantser of ruggengraat: Uitgangspunten voor cultuurbeleid, Handelingen* 11 1994-1995 24247 nr. 1 9.

4.6 A NEXUS OF CULTURAL POLICY DECISION-MAKERS

> Before the large assortment of austerity measures were applied in 2012, consultants were hired to give advice on how to apply austerity measures. Here at the orchestra, when we saw them (in this case the Berenschot "men in suits") enter our rehearsal space to spend but a few minutes watching us, we couldn't help but think, quoting Judy Collins, they "sent in the clowns." Clowns on a mission. Their world of efficiency and management-speak had little to do with our performance, art.[500]

While ministers/state secretaries hold the power to change policy directions, it is the Dutch Second Chamber of Parliament (Tweede Kamer) that puts the final stamp on policies. The Specific Cultural Policy Act 1993 created the obligation for the government to delegate the preparation of cultural policy memoranda to the ministries with a mandate to enumerate subsidies in four-year cycles.[501] In an amendment proposed to the Second Chamber in 2004, rather provocatively titled, "Making a Difference: A Recalibration of Cultural Issues," submitted by State Secretary Medy van der Laan, several changes to the Act were put forward.[502] Additional amendments included *inter alia*: a retraction of the obligation for the ministry to provide a subsidy policy memorandum on a four-year basis and the possibility for a limited number of cultural organizations to receive direct subsidies.[503] These amendments are very relevant to the story of the dismantlement of the radio orchestras.

4.7 A COUNCIL OF CULTURE OR A COUNCIL FOR CULTURE?[504]

> And finally, one last recommendation: profile yourself as a true Council **for** Culture with respect to your dealings with a minority government (and its shadow political partner) a government that clearly opts **against** Culture.[505]

Formed in 1996, after mergers between several arts advisory organs, the Dutch national cultural advisory board is the principal legal advisory body to the government and Parliament in the field of arts, culture, and media. Readers will soon discern that the RvC vacillated from support to objective distance and silence during different periods

500. Conversations with Peter Weimar.
501. *Wet op het specifiek cultuurbeleid* (Specific Cultural Policy Act) https://wetten.overheid.nl/DCCBR0005904/2016-07-01.
502. Medy van der Laan, "Verschil maken. Herijking cultuurnotasystematiek," aan de Tweede Kamer aangeboden, met daarin de contouren voorde nieuwe cultuurnotasystematiek (Kamerstukken II 2004/05, 28 989, nr.22).
503. Kamerstukken II 2004/05, 28 989, nr.22, 11 juli 2007.
504. The play on words is intentional and reflects the oft-posed question as to whether the RvC acted in such a way as to deserve the title, Council for Culture. Hans Hierck and other pundits have suggested the contrary.
505. Hans Hierck letter to the Council for Culture 15 februari 2011. "En echt tenslotte, een laatste aanrader: profileer u als een ware Raad **voor** Cultuur ten opzichte van een minderheidskabinet (en gedoogpartner daarvan) dat overduidelijk **tegen** Cultuur kiest" (emphasis added by Hans Hierck) www.opusklassiek.nl.

of radio orchestras in crisis. An independent commission, the Hierck Commission,[506] was formed to research efficiency recommendations in the orchestral sector at the beginning of the millennium. The interplay of advice provided by external experts and the final measures taken at the ministry level highlights the significant amount of influence experts wielded. A 2003 report commissioned by the Dutch Parliament to investigate the possibility of austerity measures prepared by the experts at McKinsey recommended: "cutting two to three radio orchestras" in order to effectuate savings of €12-16 million.[507] The McKinsey rationale had a questionable premise: "the idea that a regional orchestra could move in and take over the unique repertoire-rich territory of radio orchestras began to be accepted based on reports that were based on efficiency rather than artistic output."[508]

4.8 DESTRUCTION OF THE NETHERLANDS RADIO SYMPHONY ORCHESTRA (RSO)

Prior to the cuts that destroyed the RKF in 2013, a 55% personnel reduction at the Netherlands Broadcasting Music Centre (MCO) led to the destruction of the distinguished RSO in 2005. To quote one of its principals, the RSO became partially submerged into a new orchestral entity: the Netherlands Radio Chamber Philharmonic (RKF, new style).[509] Faced with the loss of the RSO, the MCO and public broadcasters responded with an alternative: integrate the RSO into the RKO to create a new, flexible chamber philharmonic, a super chamber orchestra. State Secretary Medy van der Laan objected as she calculated that this variant would neither enhance efficiency nor provide enough savings.[510]

4.9 THE 2005 RADIO ORCHESTRA CUTS: REACTIONS FROM THE PRESS AND POLITICIANS

Protests to the RSO reorganization echoed in Dutch media, augmented by vociferous protests from the Hierck Commission and the RvC. Proposals were made to cut either the RSO or the RKF; the RvC weighed in on the side of the RKO, citing the orchestra's "clear and differentiated artistic profile" while turning its back on the RSO.[511] Members of the left-wing opposition vehemently opposed the plan, venting frustration at the fact that a mere €7.5 million could save an ensemble whose performances promoted Dutch

---

506. Headed by Hans Hierck, former coordinator of Radio 4, the commission was entrusted to research orchestral efficiency recommendations in 2001.
507. *Efficiencymaatregelen bij de publieke omroep*, McKinsey report commissioned by the Ministry of Education, Culture and Science, June 26, 2003, 86 https://www.parlementairemonitor.nl/9353000/1/j9vvij5epmj1ey0/vi3aglvq64rs.
508. Conversations with Ben Janssen.
509. Conversations with former RSO principal cellist, Arturo Muruzabal.
510. Medy van der Laan. "Vaststelling van de begrotingsstaat van het Ministerie van Onderwijs, Cultuur en Wetenschap 2004" 14 november 2003.
511. Raad voor Cultuur, Muziekcentrum van de Omroep "Brief aan Staatssecretaris Medy van der Laan" 22 april 2004, 7.

cultural aims, but a majority in the Second Chamber of the Dutch Parliament supported the merger.[512] Socialist Party chair Jan Marijnissen countered with solid arguments supporting the validity of the RSO's raison d'être with an enumeration of quality and mission-related characteristics supplemented by the orchestra's contribution to diversity through its cross-over series at the Vredenburg concert hall in Utrecht. Prophetically, when we consider the quintessential catchphrase "left-wing hobby" applied to culture in the Netherlands following Halbe Zijlstra's announcement of crippling cuts in 2010,[513] Jan Marijnissen presumed that a direct link between an enlightened country and its cultural budget should persuade the Dutch government to increase its cultural budget rather than sink into a pattern of unremitting culture cuts.[514] "A civilized country spends at least one percent of its national budget on culture. That's not a left or right ideal, it's a measure of enlightenment."[515] State Secretary Medy van der Laan held on to the aforementioned McKinsey line of reasoning in its totality: in her opinion and according to her mandate to cut the broadcasting budget by €5.5-7.5 million, the RSO had no chance for survival.[516] Labeling the MCO reorganization plans as "unworkable," MCO Director Ben Janssen resigned, commenting that the merger between the MCO orchestras would weaken the MCO, eventually to a point of no return.[517] His proposal supported by cultural celebrities including Maestro Edo de Waart was to merge the splintered classical broadcasting entities into a centralized unit under the aegis of the Dutch classical radio station, Radio 4. "Pardon my language, hell would have frozen before the broadcasting organizations would have given up any of their turf not to speak of their funds. Their 'pillars' were still in place; all the broadcasting organizations were trying to maintain their importance, their positions."[518]

4.10 A NEW ORCHESTRA IS ... CONSTRUCTED: RSO + RKO = RKF (RADIO KAMER FILHARMONIE)

The RSO was discontinued in its entirety. The result was a "void both artistically and on the collegial level a significant artistic void. Rehearsals and of course concerts were deep musical experiences in an orchestra filled with so many musical characters such as legendary Russian section leaders (RSO concertmaster Valentin Zhuk previously

512. Tweede Kamerdebat Publieke Omroep, Debat naar aanleiding van een algemeen overleg op 23 juni 2004 over bezuinigingen 1 juli 2004.
513. First introduced as an expression by the populist PVV and centrist VVD parties that advocated budget cuts in the arts. The slogan gained iconic word status in 2011, when Halbe Zijlstra laid out his plans for €200 million plus culture cuts.
514. Jan Marijnissen "Opdoeken Radio Symfonieorkest grenst aan barbarij" www.sp.nl. "een beschaafd land besteedt minimaal één procent van de rijksuitgaven aan cultuur. Dat is geen links of rechtsideaal, dat ik een kwestie van beschaving."
515. *Ibid.*
516. Van der Laan, *supra*, 8-10.
517. "Directeur Ben Janssen van MCO legt functie neer" *NRC Handelsblad* 18 mei 2004. "De keuze voor een fusieorkest tast alle ensembles aan, met een onvoldoende sterk MCO als eindresultaat." https://www.nrc.nl/nieuws/2004/05/18/directeur-ben-janssen-van-mco-legt-functie-neer-7686701-a19763.
518. Conversations with Hans Quant, former Director Music Department Radio Netherland (Nederland Wereldomroep).

held that position at the Moscow Philharmonic and principal bass Boris Kozlov led the section in the legendary Leningrad Philharmonic), and great conductors over the years. Irreplaceable."[519] Although the artistic consequences for the RSO were dramatic, the impact on personnel in terms of statistics related to the number of musicians who were dismissed was certainly no less dramatic. The decision was taken to offer, or to quote many employees interviewed, force early retirement for radio orchestra musicians over the age of 55 in order to make space for younger colleagues. The remainder of the RSO's musicians swelled the ranks of the newly expanded RKO in its Radio Chamber Philharmonic incarnation with a few players filling openings in the RFO. "Sounds like a humane solution to the 'problem' of an orchestra, doesn't it? For those of us who were faced with forced retirement at 55, this was certainly a drastic move—remember, many musician careers, certainly if you take a look at US orchestras continue on for decades after that age."[520]

To infuse the newly created Radio Chamber Philharmonic (RKF-new style) with confidence following the debilitating period of deconstruction, a celebrity within the classical music world, Jaap van Zweden (former Concertgebouw Orchestra concertmaster and rising star conductor) was chosen as artistic director for the ensemble. For the musicians, the merged orchestra was challenging in many ways. "It was in a sense an exercise in cultural change. The contrast between playing in a large orchestra used to perform large-scale repertoire and the delicacy of a chamber orchestra in which a smaller group of players performs the repertoire is really a significant difference. We mixed two very separate musical cocktails to try and achieve a satisfying blend."[521] Despite excellent musical results, changes in the RKF contract with a direct impact on workload were noted by orchestra members. Part-time employees were quick to observe that the new contracts and accompanying work schedules reflected an increase of 8% in terms of obligations without an increase in remuneration.[522] The situation was resolved eventually to the satisfaction of management and the disillusionment of employees who were reminded that they should be grateful for their privileged positions as employed musicians in times of financial crisis.

Cuts and reorganizations are certainly not new in the history of radio orchestras in the Netherlands. "The seeds of austerity were sown long before the most drastic of all reorganizations affected the radio orchestras. Can you imagine, 2001 predates the destruction of the illustrious RSO (2005) and already efficiency was equated with the ability to cut personnel."[523] Rik van der Ploeg, former State Secretary for Culture and Media, 1990-2002, championed diversity and modernity in his polemic "Culture as confrontation."[524] He decried the fact that Dutch orchestras "continued to focus mainly on the classical-romantic repertoire. While the orchestras present themselves as

519. Conversations with Cyril Scheepmaker.
520. Conversations with former RFO cellist Michael Feves.
521. Conversations with former co-principal cello RKF Teije Hylkema.
522. The author and other RKF members repeatedly submitted letters and emails to management with regard to this issue starting in 2005.
523. Conversations with Eri Klas, former Chief Conductor, RSO.
524. Rik van der Ploeg. "Cultuur als confrontatie" *supra*, referenced by the Tweede Kamer vergaderjaar 2000-2001 27 432 nr. 30.

guardians of the musical heritage ... we are still far away from the starting point that 'a healthy musical life presupposes an important place for contemporary music in the total musical use.'"[525] Prophetic words or misplaced observations? Had Van der Ploeg focused his sharp analysis on the offerings of the NSRO; he would have discovered a brave new world of contemporary compositions in weekly performances and broadcasts. After the RSO dissolution in 2005 and the recession that followed had impacted the Netherlands, the RvC found itself in "a dark political corner"[526] in which the very premise of cultural funding was challenged by a government that prided itself on its anti-culture stance post-2007-2008 financial crisis.

It is important to reiterate that although culture cuts "were almost accepted as a given within the four-year subsidy cycles especially at times of economic crisis,"[527] the culture cuts pre 2007-2008 financial crisis were certainly not out of proportion in comparison to austerity measures across all sectors of government spending. According to materials published by the Court of Audits, the 2011 cuts reflected an entirely different norm: both culture and media were slashed by more than 20%, whereas the cuts in other sectors reflected in total government spending measured approximately 10%.[528]

4.11 OBSTACLES WITHIN THE MCO SYSTEM: GOVERNANCE

An article in a leading Dutch newspaper published in 2009 referred to governance in greater radioland as a fictional concept. The MCO's parent company, NOS, which received hundreds of millions of euros from the government, was likened to a fiefdom in which nepotism reigned supreme and integrity and/or control were nonexistent.[529] In terms of governance, the NOS Board of Trustees was presided over by a chairman and an additional 32 members: one-quarter of the members were appointed by the government, one-quarter by cultural organizations, with the remaining half by the broadcasting organizations. "Chickens in a very hierarchical coop constantly engaged in finding ways to climb up the ladder at another's expense," according to Ben Janssen. Remarkably, the MCO did not benefit from an independent board of trustees (Raad van Toezicht, further RvT) until its crisis year 2011.[530] "Am I too cynical to report that their

525. Rik van der Ploeg *supra*. Author's translation above: "de orkesten bleven zich hoofdzakelijk toeleggen op het klassiek-romantische repertoire. Terwijl de orkesten zich profileren als hoeders van het muzikale erfgoed ... zijn we nog steeds ver verwijderd van het uitgangspunt dat 'een gezond muziekleven een belangrijke plaats veronderstelt van de eigentijdse muziek in het totale muziek gebruik," 9.
526. Conversations with impresario Marco Riaskoff.
527. Conversations with Hein Glaubitz.
528. "Bezuiniging op cultuur, Zicht op bezuiniging." Algemene Rekenkamer Den Haag 2015, www.rekenkamer.nl/bezuiniging.
529. Joep Dohman "Bij ons in Hilversum" *NRC Handelsblad Weekblad*, 13-19 juni 2009. "In Hilversum hing een ons-kent-ons sfeer...toezicht was zwak en integriteitsregels ontbraken," https://www.nrc.nl/nieuws/2009/06/13/bij-ons-in-hilversum-11740541-a288500.
530. Information gleaned from internal communiqués to MCO employees, 2011.

motto, or perhaps mandate could be summarized as 'stand by and watch the boat sink.'"[531]

4.12 MORE MCO OBSTACLES: AN "INCONVENIENT SYSTEM"[532]

If governance caused frustration, "that was nothing in comparison to the constant friction that was the very personification of artistic life in broadcasting land."[533] A factor that contributed to the demise of the radio orchestras in the Netherlands was the orchestras' lack of independence not only with regard to controlling their finances but also with regard to artistic decision-making.[534] The exacting German composer-conductor Hans Zender achieved iconic status as an interpreter of esoteric contemporary music.[535] Feared and respected by his RKO musicians (Maestro Zender was music director, RKO, 1987-1990), his criticism of the lack of artistic control at the MCO was forceful. Opining that "nine broadcasters, adds up to quatsch nine times over,"[536] his dissatisfaction with a system in which the music director had little freedom to make important artistic decisions such as the selection of soloists and repertoire led to his premature severance in 1990.

Years later, a Berenschot report observed en route to the final RKF dismantlement, "at the present time, the administrative relations between the MCO and the broadcasters are particularly tense. This is mainly due to the diffuse division of powers and responsibilities between the MCO and the broadcasters. The announced cutbacks put further pressure on relations."[537] In separate interviews, MCO Director Anton Kok and RKF orchestra manager Kees Dijk alluded to relationships that frustrated any hopes of concrete support from the governing board of trustees to add to the malaise.

In late 2011, the MCO's Works Council (OR) reacted positively to the Minister's proposition, backed up by RvC advice to appoint an independent MCO RvT (Supervisory Board). Yet another factor related to governance frustrated the OR and the musicians they represented. As the threat of cuts drew near, the fact that Monica Damen, the Director of the GOK (Groot Omroepkoor) chorus, served in tandem with Anton Kok at the top of the MCO's Management team was incomprehensible. How could good governance and impartiality be guaranteed if the Director of one of the ensembles threatened by impending cuts held a top decision-making function? An announcement circulated on the MCO website attempted to dispel any misgivings:[538]

531. Member Works Council MCO, anonymity assured.
532. Jan Zekveld, Artistic Programmer Matinee op de Vrije Zaterdag.
533. Conversations with Hans Quant.
534. Until 1994, decisions concerning repertoire and performing artists were controlled by broadcasters based on a profile promulgated by Radio 4.
535. Hans Zender, RKF principal conductor, 1987-1990.
536. The author witnessed the maestro's rare break with composure during the Holland Festival, June 1990.
537. Berenschot, *supra*, 9. "Op dit moment zijn de bestuurlijke verhoudingen tussen het MCO en de omroepen gespannen. Dit heeft hoofdzakelijk te maken met de diffuse verdeling van bevoegdheden en verantwoordelijkheden tussen MCO en de omroepen. De aangekondigde bezuinigingen hebben de verhoudingen verder onder druk gezet."
538. "Bericht Raad van Toezicht" October 17, 2011.

1. With her extensive experience, especially in the previous round of cutbacks, Monica Damen stands for continuity. Monica has an attitude that stands completely above the parties. She appears to be very capable of fulfilling her duties and powers for the management and for the Groot Omroepkoor ... should it ever turn out to be biased, which the Supervisory Board considers highly unlikely, there are enough compensating forces in the form of Anton Kok and the members of the Supervisory Board themselves.
2. The Supervisory Board is of the opinion that the management is functioning well and does not wish to change this at a time when the MCO is facing large and difficult tasks. Reducing the management to a press ... is not justified.

Throughout the long, drawn-out reorganization process, a growing number of MCO orchestral musicians voiced their concern at this perceived conflict of interest. Regardless of Damen's experience and professional qualities, good governance would have mandated a decision to step down from one of the highest posts within the MCO's decision-making hierarchy.

Initially, MCO General Manager Anton Kok announced his intention to file suit against Marja van Bijsterveldt, Minister for Education, Culture and Science (2007-2010), due to inconsistencies in her argumentation and the use of questionable statistics with regard to impending MCO cuts. In the words of her parliamentary webpage, "she did not run away from painful cutbacks during the Rutte I cabinet."[539] For many in the cultural sector, her lack of affinity with the sector coupled with the determination to carry out austerity plans added to the frustration of those who thought they could reason with politicians. Her proposal to redirect funds primarily intended for the MCO to the broadcasters who in turn would have greater freedom of choice as to which orchestra would be at their disposal for programming was met with dismay on the part of insiders.[540] They feared in-fighting on the part of the broadcasters who had their own tenuous finances to think of.[541]

4.13 AN ATTEMPT TO SAVE THE RADIO ORCHESTRAS: RvC RECOMMENDS SUBSIDY CONVERSION

In order to safeguard the radio orchestras from far-reaching austerity measures and ensure that the subsidy system was adequately balanced, the RvC recommended that the radio orchestras should be incorporated within the basic subsidy infrastructure (BIS) post-RSO cuts. "The Council sees little difference between the tasks of the RFO/RKF and other Dutch subsidized orchestras principally because the broadcasting orchestras manifest themselves as regular orchestras who perform concerts in the major municipalities and regions, undertake educational activities, lend their services to the National Opera, and embark upon international tours. Thus, the broadcasting

539. "Liep tijdens het kabinet Rutte-I niet weg voor pijnlijke bezuinigingen." https://www.parlement.com/id/vh091adpnkt8/j_m_marja_van_bijsterveldt_vliegenthart.
540. *Ibid.*, 5.
541. Conversations with Kees Dijk, RKF RFO Manager, 2008-2013.

orchestras are inextricably linked to the ten orchestras already in the BIS subsidy structure."[542]

4.14 CONSULTANTS WEIGH IN: UNFAIR COMPETITION BETWEEN SUBSIDIZED ORCHESTRAS AND RADIO ORCHESTRAS?

On December 3, 2010, Marja van Bijsterveldt announced her intention to investigate whether it would be possible to retain the MCO at least in part, keeping in mind the irreproachable level of its orchestras and the mission they fulfilled in the service of public broadcasting. A Berenschot consultancy bureau report put forth several arguments to support the preservation of the MCO:

(1) The ongoing and high demand for adventurous, distinctive repertoire from broadcasters.
(2) The significance of the radio orchestras for the regional Dutch music infrastructure with specific emphasis on the RKF and RFO's popular series in the city of Utrecht (The Utrecht Symphony Orchestra was disbanded in 1985).[543]

Crucially, the report pointed out that despite its recommendations to save the MCO in its entirety, only two of the five radio ensembles could be financed if the Minister insisted on a reduction in subsidy, from approximately €30 million to €12-14.[544] In a worst-case scenario in which only two ensembles could be financed, Berenschot opted for the GOK, the MCO's sole choral ensemble and a "streamlined version of the RFO and the RKF, a new RFO."[545] "Really King Salomon's worst nightmare: where was the logic to destroy a chamber orchestra as there are so few of them on the orchestral scene worldwide?"[546] For Berenschot, the tipping point that led to a preference for the RFO was "its size, international stature and high-level productions" that made it indispensable to Dutch music life and in broadcasting.[547]

Van Bijsterveldt supported the Berenschot expression of preference wholeheartedly, paraphrasing their advice in a letter to the Second Chamber of the Dutch Parliament.[548] She advised keeping the RFO within the media budget while "slowly phas[ing] out the RKF."[549] Paradoxically, the RFO's international tours criticized by the

542. RvT comments cited by State Secretary Ronald Plasterk, "Letter to the Council for Culture concerning Dutch orchestras": "Advies over het orkestenbestel aan het Raad voor Cultuur" 23 april 2009 (author's translation).
543. Bart Drenth, Gerard Putman for Berenschot. "Toekomstscenario's voor het Muziekcentrum van de omroep: Keuzes in gezelschappen, programmering en positionering" 2011, 8.
544. At 27.
545. Berenschot Report, *supra*. "Komen we tot de conclusie dat er in ieder geval ruimte zou moeten zijn voor een gezelschap dat in staat is bijzonder werk voor een grote bezetting uit te voeren. Dit kan een afgeslankte combinatie zijn van RFO en RKF" 30.
546. Conversations with Reinbert de Leeuw.
547. Berenschot, *supra*. "Voor een budget van maximaal €14 miljoen kunnen hooguit twee gezelschappen (met subsidie) overeind worden gehouden."
548. Marja van Bijsterveldt. "Uitwerking regeerakkoord onderdeel media" 2011.
549. *Ibid.*

RvC in their 2010 recommendations as activities that impinged upon the playing field of other major Dutch orchestras had become, in less than a year's time, a critical factor in the Minister's decision to save the RFO at the expense of the RKF.

4.15 CURTAIN FALLING: HALBE ZIJLSTRA REMAINS STEADFAST

With the appointment of Halbe Zijlstra to the highest post in the Dutch cultural hierarchy, "we had the sinking suspicion that the show would not go on."[550] Openly proud of his lack of affinity with the sector, Zijlstra's first published interview as State Secretary was peppered with such quotes as "[i]f you opted for a mere 6% cut, the cultural world would just try to absorb the cuts within its existing framework. To effectuate change, drastic measures are needed" (author's translation).[551] His mission to bring about the most significant cuts in the history of Dutch subsidized culture (€200 million in four years) was accomplished by applying the ax to the performing arts. Echoing Prime Minister Rutte's mantra, "the arts have their backs to the audience and an open wallet towards the state,"[552] Zijlstra was more than eager to excel in austerity challenges. To bypass the advice given by the RvC was but a small step in that direction. Where his predecessor Ronald Plasterk had at least paid lip service to the notion that the government bears a responsibility to subsidize culture, Zijlstra was eager to set off in the opposite direction.

4.16 BROADCAST FUNDING PREDICAMENTS: "WHEN IN DOUBT, KICK AN ORCHESTRA OUT"[553]

"It did not matter if the institutions changed names, kowtowed to the ministry, or consolidated their operations in the name of efficiency into one organization (Muziekcentrum voor de Omroep [MCO]). The struggle over funding and artistic concerns as the threat of funding cuts not only from the Ministry but from the broadcasting bosses was nonstop. By the time the Stichting Omroep Muziek (SOM) was set up in August 2013, the fate of the radio orchestras hung on a thin thread, tied to publicly supported classical radio station (Radio 4) and the ongoing fight for funds for what the bosses called the real broadcasting goals far from adventurous music programming. Once everything linked to classical music became elitist in the minds of politicians, the handwriting on the wall grew larger and larger."[554]

550. Conversations with Mark Gerrits, Kunstenbond.
551. Thijs Broer, Thijs Niemantsverdriet "Niet Raad voor Cultuur maar publiek moet bepalen wat goede kunst is" *Vrij Nederland*, 12 januari 2011."Als je zou kiezen voor maar zes procent, zal de culturele wereld proberen de bezuinigingen op te vangen binnen de bestaande kaders. Als je écht een omslag wil maken, is een onsje eraf niet genoeg." https://www.vn.nl/halbe-zijlstra-niet-raad-voor-cultuur-maar-publiek-moet-bepalen-wat-goede-kunst-is/.
552. http://www.simber.nl/2011/06/dutch-arts-cuts-explained/.
553. Conversations with Michael Feves.
554. Conversation with Maestro Hans Vonk.

4.17 FOR WHOM THE BELL TOLLS I: THE RKF WHITTLES DOWN ITS COMPLEMENT

The first cuts in the complement impacted sub-principal string players eligible for placement in the new orchestral organization. "These musicians would have excellent chances to audition and win a place in another orchestra as many were still young and at the top of their careers."[555] While several sub-principals found their way to orchestras in Australia, Germany and other Dutch orchestras, several colleagues met with misfortune and never found employment in a professional orchestra. "And then there was silence, no colleagues, no great concerts, and no chance to continue a career. Follow-up? My musical path can now be described as a dead end. How could our management think that it would be easy to replace a leading position in one orchestra with a parallel position elsewhere? There are age limits placed on auditions and of course, if you are tied to the Netherlands because of family obligations musical migration was unthinkable."[556] This observation is particularly cogent as it points to the fact that subsidy cuts at the radio also affected the "fusieorkesten" (literally, fusion orchestras), the orchestras that were slated to be forcibly merged due to austerity measures. "Less is never more: following the radio cuts, it became normal to talk of culture cuts in a scenario of less political support and shrinking subsidies. The labor market is shrinking fast for musicians, a fact that has all but destroyed the chance for musicians to make a living, from formerly employed orchestral musicians to vulnerable freelancers."[557]

4.18 FOR WHOM THE BELL TOLLS II: EMPLOYMENT TERMINATION

Under amended provisions of the Media Act intended to modernize the Dutch broadcasting system,[558] the Rutte II cabinet did not carry out the previous Cabinet's (Rutte I) agreement to abolish the MCO in its entirety: a limited budget (€14 million of the original MCO budget of €30 million) was allotted to finance a part of the MCO.

The Second Chamber of Parliament voted in favor of maintaining one symphony orchestra and the sole broadcasting vocal ensemble (GOK). "Really, this decision smacked of a move to keep up appearances. To intimate that a slash in funds concomitant to the destruction of fine radio ensembles is necessary to continue to 'maintain the high quality of classical music' is a farce."[559] In January 2012, the last RKF calendar year, a newsletter reported proudly: "2012 started jubilantly for the Radio Chamber Philharmonic (RKF). Members of the orchestra were invited to play during Queen Beatrix' state visit to the United Arab Emirates and Oman 8-12 January."[560]

555. Conversations with Kees Dijk.
556. Conversations with a former principal string player RKF, anonymity assured.
557. Conversations with Reinbert de Leeuw.
558. *Wijziging van de Mediawet 2008 teneinde het stelsel van de landelijke publieke omroep te moderniseren*, 33541 2012-2013, https://zoek.officielebekendmakingen.nl/kst-33541-3.pdf.
559. Conversations with Kenneth Montgomery, former principal conductor, RSO; principal conductor, GOK. Quote Tweede Kamer vergaderjaar 2012-2013, 33 541 nr. 3.
560. *MCO Nieuws* online 14 januari 2012.

Regardless of triumphs in far climes, the fate of the RKF was inevitable: with each concert, the final dissolution of the orchestra was inevitable.

By early April 2013, the MCO was engaged in "exit gesprekken," the final termination-of-employment meetings with 110 musicians and singers whose employment as proud radio musicians was soon to vanish. "With 14 million left of our €31 million subsidy, we were placed against a terrible wall. No choices, but to cut personnel from our excellent orchestras, first based on 'vrijwillig vertrek' (voluntary severance)."[561]

4.19 TOO MUCH SMOKE, TOO MANY MIRRORS: INTERNAL INCONSISTENCIES

Interviews with musicians and OR members support the observation that throughout, the RKF crisis was amplified by internal issues impaired by a marked lack of robust and effective communication that exacerbated musicians' vulnerability. "Angst and more angst, too much information was withheld. We read about cuts in the newspaper before our management talked to us."[562] To further illustrate this criticism on the part of musicians concerning the MCO's crisis management, an email correspondence sent by the author to the management team and all RKF musicians related to what management referred to as "an unfortunate press leak" in a leading Dutch newspaper (*NRC Handelsblad*) deserves mention.

MCO management insinuated that the journalist, NRC music critic Mischa Spel, had published articles based more on rumor than fact. The RKF's management reply to queries on the part of RKF musicians, formulated by the author read in relevant part (translation by the author): "sometimes, however, we trail behind the facts, especially if journalists apparently gather and publish unverified facts gleaned through the grapevine."[563] This denunciation, specifically directed toward a published statement that foretold the RKF's extinction, was difficult to swallow as it spelled out the truth. Additional examples of managerial ineptness resulted from an email sent to MCO employees written by the MCO Director Anton Kok: "The proposed Decision is that we will make offers for voluntary severance based on, among other things, quality (individual and group) and social cohesion."[564] Writing on behalf of RKF colleagues, the author responded, "the designate social cohesion derives from the Durkheim's theories: how is such a term applicable to an orchestral musician's suitability to stay on the job. Musicians were told in group meetings and in section breakaways that the leading factor in determining who stays and who leaves would take place according to

561. Conversations with former MCO director Anton Kok.
562. Conversations with former section leader RKF, anonymity assured.
563. Kees Dijk email March 8, 2012 11:02 AM, "soms lopen we echter achter de feiten aan, met name wanneer journalisten kennelijk vanuit de wandelgangen niet geverifieerde feiten weten te vergaren en ook nog publiceren."
564. Anton Kok "Het voorgenomen Besluit is dat wij op grond van o.a. kwaliteit (individueel en groepsmatig) en sociale cohesie aanbiedingen zullen doen voor vrijwillig vertrek."

strict proportional rules based on Dutch dismissal law with quality as another primary determinant. Who establishes what quality and social cohesion are within the orchestra? Will conductors who we have rarely encountered decide our fates?" Indeed, the changing of the guard at the RFO's artistic helm was troubling for vulnerable musicians: Markus Stenz took on the responsibilities of principal conductor late in 2012-2013 as the reorganization process was in full swing. "Many players never worked under his baton, how could he possibly bear the responsibility to decide who would remain in the orchestra, who might be spared from the cuts?"[565]

Durkheim's concept of social cohesion found its derivation in collective conscience and has been used to reframe new forms of societal integration. A reliance on a diffuse concept aroused fear and suspicion among the musicians facing job loss. As an RKF concertmaster observed, "all of our current members successfully completed the trajectory of auditions and a trial period before receiving permanent contracts. They all have gone through assessments—social cohesion or the lack thereof, would only play a role if a musician was disruptive, and that rarely ever happens. Otherwise, everything we do in performance is based on real cohesion. It builds an orchestra and now it is being used to break it apart."[566] MCO Music Director Jaap van Zweden put it more succinctly, "linke soep" (risky business).

4.20 REDUNDANCY SELECTION METHODS: THE LAST IN-FIRST OUT PRINCIPLE AND AGE COHORTS

To promote objectivity in the dismissal process in the event of a request for employee dismissals due to economic reasons, strict rules must be followed. Article 4.2 of the *Ontslagbesluit* (Dismissal Decree) regulates the order in which employees should be selected for dismissal.[567] To facilitate the process, the Dismissal Decree further stipulates that employees whose jobs are interchangeable should be grouped according to age cohorts. "This called for a selection process for each subsection within the string sections. Within each of those sections, age cohort lists were prepared that showed the date each musician entered into their contractual relationship with the RFO and/or the RKF. That date was all-important as in some cases we had accepted several musicians for the same section, at the same audition. And it did come to pass that one musician signed a contract on a later date than the colleague who had won the audition on the same date."[568] In the interest of procedural fairness, the Dismissal Decree mandates that after the process has been completed, the age ratios in the new organization within interchangeable function categories should reflect the same proportionality within age cohorts.

565. Conversations with former RFO violinist Anna Korpalska.
566. Conversations with former associate first concertmaster RKF Quirine Scheffers.
567. *Ontslagbesluit* (Dismissal Decree) Art. 4.2.
568. Conversations with Ella Broekstra, Human Resources Manager, 2009-2021, Stichting Omroep Music (SOM).

4.21 RKF AND RFO SEEK LEGAL ADVICE TO DETERMINE PRIORITY

The reorganization situation descended into a quagmire of apprehensive and even aggressive actions as the two principal classical music orchestras, the RKF and the RFO, sought legal advice in hopes of guaranteeing their survival. "Firstly, could members of the RFO derive rights from Minister Bijsterveldt's letter to the MCO and the Parliament (the Second Chamber) on the basis of which they could claim a place in the newly reorganized orchestra, overlooking the members of the RKF in similar circumstances? Secondly, could members of the RFO claim priority once the redundancy measures were put in place based on their existing MCO contract?" (author's translation).[569]

In the opinion of the MCO's legal advisors, an appropriate reading of the legal question suggested an emphasis on the first step in the dismissal decision process, with extra importance given to a sub-question that centered on whether the two orchestras, the RFO and the RKF, were each acting as an independent unit in the company.[570] The sub-question of whether the MCO's musicians were employed by separate organizational entities or jointly employed by the MCO was of importance.[571]

4.22 SEVERAL OBSERVATIONS NECESSARY FOR A CORRECT APPLICATION OF THE LEGAL FRAMEWORK

Although both orchestras were radio orchestras under the aegis of the MCO, the RFO and the reorganized RKF (2005) worked as separate performing entities, from rehearsal preparation to final performances. Numerous broadcasts, concerts, and CD recordings not to speak of orchestra schedules attest to the existence of two separate orchestras. The orchestras rehearsed in different studios in the MCO building and even had their own fan club organizations whose members attended special events and produced newsletters. The orchestras shared a management and financial administration team, but to add a bit of confusion, the personnel managers responsible for hiring freelance substitute players and stage managers were not shared. "This showed a logical division of labor: the two orchestras in the MCO's classical division rehearsed in different spaces simultaneously and had different concert and recording schedules."[572]

The contracts of RKF and RFO musicians under a collective bargaining agreement (MCO CAO and Employment Regulation 2005) provide ample evidence that following the RSO reorganization (2005), all MCO musicians were employed by one department,

569. Allen & Overy, Memorandum Unit Klassiek inzake uitvoering bezuinigingsplannen, 29 september 2011. In Dutch, "Kunnen leden van het RFO, rechten ontlenen aan de brief van de minister aan MCO en aan de Tweede Kamer op basis waarvan zij een plek claimen in een orkest met voorbijgaan aan leden van de RKF en vergelijkbare omstandigheden?" and the second question, "Kunnen leden van de RKF op basis van het bestaande contract een plaats claimen in een afvloeiingsvolgorde?"
570. "Elk in de maatschappij als zelfstandige eenheid optredend organisatorisch verband." *Staatscourant* 27 december 2001 nr. 249/42.
571. Allen & Overy *supra*, at 2.9.
572. Conversations with former personnel manager RKF Anne-Marie Boeke.

the MCO Unit Klassiek. Further specification as to the musicians' positions as members of the two classical MCO orchestras is found in Article 4.2 (a). Under the heading *Employment*, the article reads in relevant part:

> a. The employee is employed within the department MCO Classical ... Within the department MCO Classical there are 2 orchestras, where the employees are placed in 1 orchestra or in both orchestras. Apart from this formal placement, employees can be deployed in both orchestras of MCO Klassiek.[573]

Originally employed in the first violin section of the RKF (1987-2005), the author received a "contractomzetting" (contract conversion) letter on September 28, 2005, which announced: "We hereby confirm a number of contractual changes that will take place because of the reorganization within the MCO. Starting 1 August 2005, you will be a part of the Classic Unit of the MCO. You will work part-time as a 1st Violinist for an indefinite period of time. As your position will remain the same in terms of content, no changes will be made to the employment conditions."[574]

Although one could debate the validity of information disseminated in a newsletter as a basis for legal argument, Allen & Overy relied on the information in one particular MCO newsletter sent to all musicians on September 22, 2005, regarding the reorganization that created MCO Nieuw (the new MCO post-RSO dismantlement) for both fact-finding and decision-making. In its new MCO Nieuw incarnation, musicians formerly employed by the RSO, RFO, or RKF would not be entitled to decline placement in one or both of the newly reorganized orchestras, the Radio Philharmonic (RFO new style) and the Radio Chamber Philharmonic (RKF). Taking the complement requirements of the orchestras into consideration, the MCO musicians had to adjust to flexible schedules that could translate into one week performing with the RKF and the next week in the RFO.[575]

Of significance to Allen & Overy's considerations, the aforementioned newsletter presented the viewpoints of the MCO directors concerning the question of MCO musicians' legal status in the case of an eventual future reorganization. "The handwriting was on the wall for the radio musicians: we were cut and reshuffled so many times in recent memory that we wanted some reassurance concerning our job security, or to quote our RKF first violin colleague Nico (ed. comment, Nico Brandon), job insecurity."[576] An MCO newsletter promulgated the basis for equal treatment: (in the

573. MCO CAO Art. 4.6 (a): "a. De werknemer wordt tewerkgesteld binnen de afdeling MCO Klassiek ... Binnen de afdeling MCO Klassiek is er sprake van 2 orkesten, waarbij de werknemers geplaatst zijn in 1 orkest of in beide orkesten. Los van deze formele plaatsing kunnen werknemers in beide orkesten van MCO Klassiek worden ingezet."
574. The contract conversion letter September 28, 2005: "Als gevolg van de reorganisatie binnen het MCO zullen er voor u een aantal contractuele wijzigingen plaatsvinden die wij u hierbij bevestigen. Met ingang van 1 augustus 2005 zult u deel uitmaken van de Klassieke Unit van het MCO. U zult voor onbepaalde tijd parttime als 1ste Violiste werkzaam zijn. Daar uw functie inhoudelijk gelijk blijft zullen er geen arbeidsvoorwaardelijke wijzigingen plaatsvinden."
575. MCO orchestral planning schedules (2005-2012) in the possession of the author provide evidence of orchestra switches and flexible scheduling.
576. Conversations with RKF former violinist Laszlo Tuscni.

author's translation): "To prevent the suggestion, in the event of unexpected new austerity targets, that austerity could simply mean the cancellation of one of the classical orchestras, all musicians were given a new contract, although this could have been communicated in the form of a unilateral confirmation from the employer."[577] A manifestation of symbolic value or a contract that can be relied upon?

4.23 A SECOND OPINION

Unhappy with Allen & Overy's conclusions, the RFO's orchestra committee sought a second opinion from the distinguished Dutch law firm, Loyens & Loeff. Did the MCO pass the test of a sole business establishment within the meaning of Article 4:2 Dismissal Decree 2012,[578] or did the fact that the RFO and the RKF operated separately substantiate the claim that the orchestras were two separate business establishments? Contrary to Allen & Overy's findings pointing to two orchestral subdivisions, the RFO argued that the two orchestras were substantially differentiated from one another.[579] The RFO and RKF not only rehearsed in separate studios and performed as independent musical organizations under the names RFO and RKF but also listed photos and names of their musicians on separate web pages. An organizational chart included in the orchestras' policy plans listed separate conductors, production managers, and orchestra assistants. Further, the RFO claimed that only a few musicians rotated between the two orchestras, most musicians operated from one orchestra, either the RFO or the RKF. In addition, the RFO claimed that many musicians had never signed the MCO (2005) contract; thus, the original RKF contracts prevailed. If the proportionality principle were applied to MCO musicians regardless of their home orchestra, the RFO new style would lose its initial complement, and it would take years to reach its then-present high level of accomplishment.[580] The Loyens memorandum emphasized that it was the intention of the Minister to maintain the RFO in its present state of distinction; personnel changes—in other words, the introduction of musicians from the RKF—would undermine its protected status. Thus, the RFO musicians deserved priority to keep their positions post-reorganization and to acquire priority in the all-important proportionality process.[581]

577. MCO Nieuwsbrief 22 september 2005: "Om te voorkomen dat bij een onverhoopte nieuwe bezuingingstaakstelling ooit nog de suggestie gewekt zou kunnen worden dat bezuinigen kan inhouden het simpelweg schrappen van een van de klassieke orkesten, is besloten voor iedereen een nieuw contract te maken, daar waar het ook in de vorm van een eenzijdige bevestiging vanuit de werkgever gecommuniceerd had kunnen worden. Voor veel mensen heeft een nieuw contract een symbolische waarde."
578. Ontslagbesluit *supra*.
579. Loyens & Loeff Second Opinion memorandum Unit Klassiek inzake uitvoering bezuiniging-splannen 17 october 2011 at 2.2.1.
580. *Ibid.*, at 4.14.
581. *Ibid.*, at 4.3.2. Here reflection seems more appropriate in translating afspiegeling than either balance or proportionality.

4.24 MINISTERIAL CLARIFICATION SETTLES THE QUESTION OF PRIORITY

Allen & Overy's conclusions sought to settle the difference of opinion as to priority within the redundancy procedure. Based on the considerations spelled out above, they concluded that the musicians of the RFO and the RKF were on equal footing. To bolster their arguments and those of their legal advisers, the MCO requested Minister Bijsterveldt to prepare a letter of clarification (in Dutch, "verduidelijkingsbrief") to answer the $64,000 question of whether RFO musicians could claim priority. Her response: "To further clarify the character of the orchestras, I added their names in brackets in the text of my letter dated 16 September. It was certainly not my intention to interfere in the employment law relations between the musicians and the MCO."[582] Thus, RFO musicians could not rely on Minister Bijsterveldt's letter to both the MCO and the Second Chamber to claim priority. Allen & Overy's memorandum reiterated that the musicians of both orchestras (RFO and RKF) would be entitled to equal treatment within the redundancy procedure.

4.25 A THIRD ADVISORY PATH: HOUTHOFF BURUMA

The RKF turned to yet another well-known Dutch law firm, Houthoff Buruma, for an interpretation of the Allen & Overy and Loyens & Loeff memoranda. Emphasizing the import of an answer that was key to establishing dismissal rankings in the proportionality (afspiegeling) regime, Houthoff sought to mitigate its response by first presenting ancillary information. "For the sake of completeness, I would like to point out that it is also conceivable to implement possible dismissals by means of settlement agreements in which the employment contract is terminated by mutual consent."[583] In other words, while the priority of musicians in the dismissal process was of great import, it was only one factor of importance within the wider scope of dismissal. As alluded to earlier in the *movement*, the MCO eventually opted to offer voluntary severance opportunities (vrijwillig vertrek) to musicians who had reached the age of 59,[584] "to partially relieve the burden of musician reductions."[585]

The Houthoff Memorandum listed significant external characteristics they felt pointed to the existence of one central organization (MCO) with separate, subordinate sub-orchestral establishments:

(1) Both RFO and RKF are recognized Dutch radio orchestras.
(2) Both RFO and RKF are registered at the same address.

582. Minister Bijsterveldt's clarification reprinted in MCO-toekomst (future) communiqué Anton Kok, 14 november 2011. "Om het karakter van de gezelschappen nader te verduidelijken zijn in mijn brief van 16 september tussen haakjes de namen van de huidige gezelschappen vermeld. Het is echter niet de bedoeling geweest om mij te mengen in de arbeidsrechtelijk verhoudingen tussen musici en het MCO."
583. Houthoff Memorandum Unit Klassiek inzake uitvoering bezuinigingsplannen 31 october 2011.
584. The age of 59 was an age variable indication: the author was 58 when the voluntary severance offer (vrijwillig vertrek) was made.
585. Conversations with Ella Broekstra.

(3) The orchestras do not submit independent financial/tax reports.
(4) The orchestras are not registered as separate legal entities.
(5) The orchestras shared the same chief conductor, Jaap van Zweden (2005-2010).
(6) The orchestras shared the same Manager, Kees Dijk (2008-2013).
(7) RFO and RKO had separate artistic committees although there was evidence of shared artistic coordination.
(8) RFO and RKO were represented jointly on the Works Council.

Houthoff emphasized that although the RFO and RKF performed their own concerts, the two radio orchestras shared audiences: "a significant portion of their audience subscribes to concert series performed partially by the RFO and partially by the RKF" (author's translation).[586] The internal organizational characteristics of the two orchestras merited the designation of a single business enterprise.

4.26 AID AND ABETMENT: THE SOCIAL PLAN

Dutch dismissal law operates on one basic principle: to offer extra protection to the weaker party, the employees. In addition to protection, consultation between employer and employees is encouraged to alleviate the consequences inherent to dismissal. The explanatory memoranda that provide background on collective dismissal regulations call for employers and works councils to consult on a post-dismissal social plan.[587]

To US orchestral colleagues, the very notion that employers and trade unions with added input from the OR devise a social plan to alleviate former employees' redundancy traumas is a dream come true. "We do not have much of a safety net. If an orchestra is struck down by financials, no play, no pay. Musicians can apply to the union's emergency relief fund, which certainly does not offer the cushion of a social plan."[588] Although the contents of the Social Plan met with the approval of most musicians interviewed, how voluntary severance was communicated led to agitation and confusion as the following sections illustrate.

4.27 RELEVANT PRINCIPLES OF DUTCH DISMISSAL LAW: *AFSPIEGELING*

The "afspiegelingsbeginsel"—literally, the reflection principle, translated with some regularity as the "proportionality" or "balance" principle—is one of the central pillars within the ample body of Dutch dismissal regulations related to reorganizations due to

586. Houthoff Memorandum at Ad. 4. "Ik denk niet dat sprake is van een eigen klantenkring of doelgroep ... een groot deel van de klanten afnemer is van een serie concerten is, die deels door het RFO en deels door de RKF worden gespeeld. Alleen daar blijkt al uit dat niet sprake is van een strikt separate doelgroep."
587. Memorie van Toelichting Kamerstukken II 1974/75, 13 324, nr. 3.
588. Conversations with Tino Gagliardi. President and Executive Director AFM, Local 802, New York.

economic necessity. According to the principle, employees with interchangeable positions are grouped into categories according to age. Under a "last in, first out" regime, the employees with the least number of years of service within each age group are the first to be dismissed. Furthermore, and importantly, the principle requires that job losses must be proportionally distributed between age cohorts. Another germane legal protected requirement that impacted the RKF reorganization and how musicians interpreted the process related to the concept of *uitwisselbaarheid van functies*, the exchangeability factor.[589] The instructions given in the policy rules on dismissal provide instructions on how to eschew decision-making based on employees' qualities as opposed to strictly defined job descriptions. "The problem with orchestral positions is exactly within that straitjacket of a definition: what is the difference between an associate and an assistant concertmaster (plaatsvervangende 1ste en 2de concert-meester)? Or, for that matter, a second flautist who doubles on piccolo and a second flautist who is a superlative player but does not double? The law does not answer these questions."[590]

4.28 THE OCCASIONALLY INVOLUNTARY NATURE OF VOLUNTARY SEVERANCE

Musicians whose positions were about to be phased out, orchestral members facing redundancy (boventallig) exemplified by the secondary principal string players, were given the chance to opt for voluntary severance as specified in the Social Plan.[591] The musicians received letters dated June 19, 2012 with "Employment" (dienstverband) in the subject line. Summarizing the reasons for austerity, the letter mentioned that although the OR was not positive concerning all of the personnel-related cuts and how these cuts would be effectuated, the OR did agree to individual meetings between MCO management and employees most likely facing redundancy. The opening of the following paragraph raised consternation: "As communicated verbally to you on Monday 25 June 2012, we are proposing to you a personal offer of voluntary severance."[592] "Really, although there was nothing funny about this whole business, a letter dated 19 June about communication on 25 June made us wonder -if our bosses could not get dates straight, how would they deal with the legal documents to follow?"[593] Confusion of dates aside, there was another major point of contention written into the text of the letter: "if we do not receive a response before the deadline, we will assume that you do not intend to accept the offer and we will proceed to employ an alternative method to determine reduction (redundancy)."[594]

Disillusionment set in as musicians shared accounts concerning the personal meetings. "There was very little of that word 'voluntary' in this option, it was more like

589. Ontslagbesluit, *supra*.
590. Conversations with Catharina Kat, Catlaw, Amsterdam https://catlaw.nl.
591. Sociaal Plan, Art. 10 and Art. 11.
592. The author's Dienstverband (Employment) letter *Epilogue: Appendix 5*.
593. Conversations with former RFO violinist Jill Bernstein.
594. Employment Letter, "Ontvangen wij voor die datum geen reactie, dan gaan wij er van uit dat u het aanbod niet accepteert en zullen wij overgaan tot een alternatieve formatiereductie."

leaving with a gun to your head, that is what the decision to annul my leadership position really meant. The distant, cold, and yes, calculating manner in which I was told that my job was disappearing came as a shock. No thanks, no personal message. That is when I realized that playing your heart out for all those years was a gift to the public, certainly not to our managers."[595] The final statistics concerning voluntary severance reveal that 24 musicians left the orchestras and chorus as a result of age-related criteria, 46 musicians suffered partial job loss with 12 of these musicians reduced to 50% employment, 20 musicians lost their jobs due to complement cuts (positions dismantled) and 15 musicians resigned citing nonpublicly disclosed reasons.[596]

4.29 ANOTHER RELEVANT DISMISSAL CONCEPT: THE INDISPENSABLE EMPLOYEE (*ONMISBAARHEID*)

> With regard to your client and his/her objection to redundancy within the MCO reorganization, the MCO conducted meetings with musicians. The conversations were of an informative nature, i.e., they were not yet conversations in which staff members were definitively declared superfluous. The decision-making process (e.g., request for advice from the Works Council regarding the reorganization) has not yet been completed and is expected by January 2013.
>
> Because these were informative talks with 170 MCO musicians we only dealt with the situation of the musician in question during the talks and deliberately did not discuss concrete criteria and assessments during these talks. We opted to inform all those involved first, without giving any further information about colleagues.
>
> We can imagine that your client is angry and disappointed that we have informed him/her that he/she will be foreseeably redundant because a direct colleague has been deemed to be indispensable.
>
> Should this situation become definitive, your client will be informed no later than January 2013 and will be free to formally object to dismissal as well as ask for insights into the criteria applied.[597]

Under Dutch dismissal policies, an employee with knowledge and skills that are deemed indispensable to the organization can be specially exempted from the dismissal procedure.[598] "This was for many of us musicians the most difficult thing to swallow, especially as we were not aware of the criteria our management used to determine how they decided who was exceptional. Obviously, the guiding hand of the maestros must have been determinative but then again, some of us had never played under the baton of the conductors who were making these all-important choices. Was there an element of nepotism [in Dutch, 'vriendjes politiek']? Especially concerning certain wind instruments, there were too many dubious decisions in the minds of

595. Conversations with former associate concertmaster RFO Micho Dimitrov.
596. Corroborated by Ella Broekstra.
597. Response (email) sent to RKF musician in advance of dismissal. The colleague sought legal advice and sued the MCO. Email in the possession of the author, anonymity assured.
598. https://www.rijksoverheid.nl/onderwerpen/ontslag/afspiegelingsbeginsel.

many."[599] The MCO based its indispensability criteria on highly subjective talent criteria defined maladroitly in communiques to its musicians as: "talent is a natural ability to do something right, an innate ability or suitability for something."[600] Renamed Berenschot's folly as a reference to the expert source of the definition, musicians were unanimous in their rejection of the premise that their futures could be based on a decisive factor with no measurable benchmark. "To emphasize talent made a mockery of our years of service, our musical commitment, our proven worth to our orchestras. It led to confusion and even anger not only from those directly affected by so-called talent-based decisions but from all musicians who know that success in an orchestra is more about the ability to blend, and work hard to reach musical goals than it is about talent!"[601]

Several musicians opted to litigate, challenging the specific indispensability choices made by the employer. Conversations with advocates active on behalf of MCO-related claims and follow-ups with several ex-RKF and RFO colleagues emphasized the complexity and personal distress that characterized these cases.[602] Although the ex-colleagues discussed their issues in openly shared emails, the author respects her promise not to publish any further details concerning situations shared in confidence. Several years post-reorganization 2012-2013, many affected musicians were acrimonious concerning the "indispensables." "Yes, some of us sued and got nowhere, one or two who were awarded some extra financial compensation and others are now performing as members of the RFO in their essential, indispensable function. It's better to move on and not speak about what happened. Talking does not remove the sense that although we know the reorganization was certainly not the fault of our managers, the decisions to allow certain musicians to stay and to dismiss others were not always fair. Do the math. How many of the players who got that indispensable status were a part of the RSO? It seemed that protected status was reserved for RFO players."[603]

Given the opportunity to respond to these allegations, the MCO's HRM Director maintained that the process proscribed by Dutch law was followed meticulously. "Remember, musicians often do not see the difference between who they are and what they do. As a professional, I do not take my position home with me but once a musician, always a musician. Firstly, there is little separation between the workplace, the concert hall, and the home. Secondly and regrettably, musicians have almost no social hygiene. They hear a rumor and spread it around as soon as possible, which means that sooner or later, the fabricated or re-personalized story becomes the whole truth. There were hundreds of examples in the 2013 MCO reorganization files of secret agendas and lists of inside players or of a powerful conductor getting rid of certain RSO players to the advantage of RFO players. Indispensability revolves around one factor: who is the most

599. Conversations with RKF principal players, anonymity assured.
600. "Talent is een natuurlijk vermogen om iets goed te doen, een aangeboren handigheid of geschiktheid voor iets." OR Adviesaanvraag met betrekking tot de gevolgen van de aangekondigde bezuiniging (MCO call for advice) 27 April 2012, 13.
601. Conversations with four RKF section leaders, anonymity assured.
602. Conversations with Catharina Kat (Catlaw) and Bart de Vroe (Vestius Advocaten).
603. Conversations with a former RSO principal not granted "onmisbaar" status.

outstanding player in their group, who deserves this special advantage?"[604] Cogent commentary, yet taking the first point concerning musicians' identity to heart, the MCO should have taken its duty of care more seriously concerning how sensitive aspects of reorganization, from voluntary severance to indispensability, were conveyed as multiple interviews with musicians confirm. In conclusion, six musicians were granted the coveted indispensable status, and several musicians whose jobs were cut as a result of that special status took action. The final scorecard, deeply confidential in nature, reveals that several succeeded in receiving additional financial compensation although none of these musicians were reinstated to their former positions within RFO.

4.30 ADDING INSULT TO INJURY? INTERACTIONS BETWEEN MANAGEMENT AND MUSICIANS

Two words, "massale broedermoord" ("unmitigated fratricide"), were repeated by colleagues who endured the drawn-out RKF dismissal process. Although communiqués were distributed regularly, the malaise of the musicians was exacerbated by the lack of specific information and the tone taken by a distanced management team "who seemed to retreat from us while resorting to communication with newly hired lobbyists and HRM interims. One of the most distressing features of the long, drawn-out reorganization process was not the fact that the RKF would disband but the how and when. Too many of our colleagues did not know whether they would be able to stay on as a part of the new orchestra, or whether their careers as orchestral musicians were on the line. The last-minute phenomenon caused so much confusion, so much pain."[605] This viewpoint was corroborated by the MCO's OR presenting its opinions clearly in the Advies (Advice) presented to management and disseminated to all MCO employees: "The Works Council has suffered greatly from information disseminated from management-director that changed constantly, not to speak of changing circumstances. This had a major effect in its contacts and communication with orchestral stakeholders, the musicians at the MCO."[606]

A last-ditch attempt on the part of the MCO to make a counterproposal to a Minister intent on effectuating cuts was doomed to failure. "The MCO proposes substantial improvements in the efficiency of the financial agreement by taking away a symphony orchestra's funding, making cuts at the GOK, RFO, RKF, and Metropole Orkest, and abolishing the Music Library and MCO Education."[607] MCO musicians and staff members were not surprised when this particular message fell on deaf ears.

604. Conversations with Ella Broekstra.
605. Conversations with Peter Weimar.
606. "in de contacten met de achterban heeft de OR veelvuldig last gehad van de voortdurend en snel wisselende informatie en situaties," author's translation.
607. MCO Newsroom reprinted on the MCO website, June 11, 2011. "Het MCO stelt voor een forse efficiencyslag te maken die financieel overeenkomst met het wegbezuinigen van een symfonieorkest, door te bezuinigen bij het GOK, RFO, RKF en Metropole Orkest, en door de muziekbibliotheek en MCO Educatie op te heffen."

"Using the language of management to curry the favor of the decision-making politicians, especially when it spelled out the annihilation of a treasured library, was cursed from the very onset. An analogy to reprehensible behavior exhibited during wartime comes to mind—betray one to save another."[608] Music critics in the Netherlands and pundits abroad reflected on "the paradoxical situation that the musicians of the RKF, whose jobs are seriously under threat, can still make such joyful music."[609] To the musicians, this behavior fell in line with custom; like the musicians on the Titanic, they play until the last note sounds, no matter what transpires.

See Figure 5 for RKF's final VARA Matinee rehearsal at the Concertgebouw Hall.

Figure 5 Final RKF Saturday Matinee Rehearsal Concertgebouw Hall (June 15, 2013)

Source: Photo credit: Ben Bonouvrier. Janine Jansen soloist, Michael Schønwandt conductor. Author pictured in the first violin section.

608. Conversations with Frans Brüggen.
609. Frits van der Waa. "Andrew Manze" *De Volkskrant* 13 juli 2012. "Dat de musici van de RKF, wier banen ernstig op de tocht staan, nog zulke vreugdevolle muziek kunnen maken blijft een bijna paradoxale gewaarwording."

4.31 SOLIDARITY? CONTRAST TO ORCHESTRAS UNDER FIRE IN THE UNITED STATES

Responses to the culture cuts came swiftly from media reports in leading newspapers, journals and radio broadcasts worldwide.[610] The MCO musicians sought support from fellow musicians around the globe, a tradition that rested upon actions taken on the eve of the RSO cuts in 2005.[611] Dutch cultural leaders called for protest actions epitomized by the *Schreeuw voor Cultuur* (Scream for Culture) and the *Mars der Beschaving* (March for Civilization) June 26-27, 2011 (Figure 6).[612]

Figure 6 Mars der Beschaving *Sets Forth from Rotterdam (June 26, 2011)*

Source: Author's photo.

A reoccurring theme that came to the fore in multiple interviews concerned intra-orchestral solidarity. US orchestral musicians and their organizations are known for their vocal support for colleagues in need. When the Dutch radio orchestras faced their last-ditch battle for survival in 2012-2013, audience support was massive; however, the officials, as well as managers and musicians from subsidized regional and municipal orchestras, were reticent to speak out. Conspicuously missing from the march and other calls to action were statements from the country's leading orchestra, the Royal Concertgebouw (RCO). "It was worse than quiet, musicians in the orchestra were told by the board not to participate in any of the cultural strikes and calls for

610. Beyond reporting in the Dutch media, the MCO cuts were reported in newspapers and journals in the UK and the US. For a report in *The Guardian* https://www.theguardian.com/music/tomserviceblog/2010/oct/05/dutch-arts-cuts-orchestra.
611. Musicians' letter sent to 75 internationally acclaimed musicians in 2004 *Epilogue: Appendix 6*.
612. *Mars der Beschaving* took place on June 26-27, 2011. Approximately five thousand actors, artists, musicians, and cultural sector aficionados walked from downtown Rotterdam to the Hague's Malieveld.

action. Our management felt that protests on behalf of others would be detrimental to our organization as we might alienate those who grant future subsidies."[613]

4.32 SECRET WEAPONS? THE MYTHICAL POWERFUL LOBBY

Speaking of paying attention to the boss, MCO employees were reminded of the possible negative impact of even the most reasonable calls to action at many points in the reorganization trajectory. Without providing any salient details, MCO Director Anton Kok alluded to a powerful lobby in his communiqués, emails, and speeches. "The lobby that we have deployed is listening to us now, thus I would urge you not to take action as this could harm this allegiance."[614] In retrospect, the wisdom of these precautions can be questioned as the oft-referenced lobby employed by the MCO to deliver its message to the appropriate politicians was ineffective at best. "The OR actively questioned management about what these lobbyists were doing, or more importantly, what they were not doing but we never received convincing answers. Politicians and lobbyists frequently swim in the same pond (vijver, in Dutch) which makes vulnerable outsiders skeptical."[615] In an internal MCO memo, the Director encouraged musicians to opt for solidarity as the best line of defense in troubled times, yet solidarity with no tangible external support amplified employee vulnerabilities.[616]

A different story emerges across the Atlantic. Under the motto, "we are all one," pride of place was given to locked-out musicians of the Fort Worth Symphony at the annual meeting of the International Conference of Symphony and Opera Musicians (ICSOM) in Washington D.C. in 2016.[617] Orchestral representatives of orchestras cross-country joined in solidarity pledging emergency funds, buying t-shirts, and joining in media campaigns. "We don't even think twice: if our orchestral colleagues are in trouble, wherever, whenever, we join to support them. It certainly would not be uncommon to witness New York Philharmonic musicians sporting Fort Worth t-shirts to get the message out: when one orchestra bleeds, we share the pain collectively."[618] In addition, US orchestras are often on the lookout to hire substitute players from the ranks of orchestras in dire straits. "When Detroit was in deep crisis, the Dallas Symphony saved my life by offering me a musical home and a financial safe haven."[619]

See the representatives from across the US stand up for their striking Fort Worth Symphony colleagues in Figure 7.

613. Conversations with RCO bass player Carol Harte.
614. Email Anton Kok, June 17, 2011, in the possession of the author, "de lobby die wij nu ingezet hebben luistert erg nauw. Ik wil jullie daarom met klem verzoeken geen acties op touw te zetten. Dit kan onze inzet schaden."
615. Conversations with MCO OR member, anonymity assured.
616. "Ik roep iedereen op om de saamhorigheid vast te blijven houden" (I call open everyone to band together in solidarity, author's translation) Internal communique 15 februari 2011.
617. The ICSOM annual conference August 24-27, 2016. Washington D.C.
618. Conversations with New Jersey Symphony violist Martin Andersen, active ICSOM representative.
619. Conversations with former concertmaster Detroit Symphony Emmanuelle Boisvert, at present associate concertmaster Dallas Symphony Orchestra.

Figure 7 Representatives of Pan-US Orchestras Sport Their Support for the Musicians of the Fort Worth Symphony ICSOM Conference Washington D.C. 2016

4.33 POSTMORTEMS IN DUTCH REORGANIZED RADIO ORCHESTRAS

Looking back on the emotional roller coaster that accompanied the dismissal procedure, the closing chords for the RKF, it is telling to note that almost no attention was paid to the fate of the radio orchestras' cadre of freelance substitute players. "Although our work lives suffered a major downturn after each and every reorganization, our lot was not of concern to official bodies such as the ministry nor was it of concern to the advisors. The unions did try to put up a fight to save the radio orchestras and made specific mention of the significant number of freelancers negatively affected. However, that was a lost fight from the very beginning. If the orchestras could not be saved, how would the freelancers have been spared?"[620]

620. *FNV Kiem Nieuws online* 17 september 2013 "Prinsjesdag: FNV slaat alarm over cultuur in gemeenten en bezuinigingen publieke omroep." The specific quote "FNV is niet gerust op te toekomst van zzp'ers ... die worden direct in hun bestaan bedreigd door de miljoenen bezuinigingen" (the FNV is quite distressed about the future of freelancers ... whose employ ment is directly threatened by the millions in cutbacks). Socialist Party leader Jan Marijnissen made mention of the plight of the freelancers.

5 En Route to *FNV KIEM*: Of Musicians and Labor Law[621]

> Competition law must be tough with the strong and gentle with the weak.[622]
>
> The initial thinness of social policy provisions within the EU integration project was premised on a consensus that the creation of a common market would not require harmonisation of labour standards or national systems of labour law.[623]

That jurisprudence lies at the heart of much of legal research is a given; however, what laypeople such as orchestral musicians push to ascertain is: can case law help resolve employment-related challenges in the here and now? If any case could begin to fulfill the wishes of orchestral freelancers desperately seeking improved employment status, *FNV KIEM* (further, *FNV*) fits the bill. FNV is indisputably a crown jewel among the cases considered here, particularly as it is the only piece of ECJ jurisprudence to spotlight orchestral freelance substitute musicians as a particular class of workers. Literature concerning the case is extensive and ranges from laudatory appraisals that hailed a new era in the struggle against disguised self-employment to critical assessments of the ECJ's restraint.[624] The ECJ's pronouncement that focused on the "false self-employed" deserves repetition as the jury is still out as to whether the court opened new doors of protection or merely offered a smoke screen in the guise of social protection:

621. *FNV Kunsten Informatie en Media* C-413/13 [2014].
622. Thiébaut Weber, Confederal Secretary, European Trade Union Confederation (ETUC).
623. D. Asiagbor, "Unravelling the Embedded Liberal Bargain: Labour and Social Welfare Law in the Context of EU Market Integration," 307.
624. For thought-provoking examples: Martin Risak and Thomas Dullinger, "The Concept of 'Worker' in EU Law: Status Quo and Potential for Change" ETUI Research Paper-Report 140 2018 https://ssrn.com/abstract=3190912 and Eva Grosheide and Beryl Ter Haar, "Employee-Like Worker: Competitive Entrepreneur or Submissive Employee?" *Law and Social Rights in Europe: The Jurisprudence of International Courts. Selected Judgements*? Reflections on ECJ, C-413/13, FNV Kunsten Informatie. University of Gdansk Press 2018.

> On a proper construction of EU law, it is only when self-employed service providers who are members of one of the contracting employees' organisations and perform for an employer, under a works or service contract, the same activity as that employer's employed workers, are "false self-employed", in other words, service providers in a situation comparable to that of those workers, that a provision of a collective labour agreement, such as that at issue in the main proceedings, which sets minimum fees for those self-employed service providers, does not fall within the scope of Article 101(1) TFEU. It is for the national court to ascertain whether that is so.[625]

Did a seminal piece of European Court of Justice (ECJ) jurisprudence create a solution for Dutch orchestral freelancers seeking a resolution to employment status questions? Has it inspired more comprehensive legislative and/or policy-related solutions? Brought by a Dutch union on behalf of orchestral freelance substitutes whose terms of employment were regulated under a collective labor agreement, the ECJ decision paved the way to success for other types of self-employed workers under similar bargaining agreements, as exemplified by the Irish experience.[626] For those who engaged in the long uphill battle to achieve equal pay for freelance Irish voice-over actors, the *FNV* decision was inspirational, "it provided us with a beacon of light, a reminder never to give up."[627] Before analyzing *FNV* within the push-pull of competition law, this *movement* offers an overview of EU policies and a concise lineup of EU jurisprudence with relevance to key aspects of *FNV*.

5.1 A NAGGING DICHOTOMY

A conventional view on the fundamental differences between the employed and the self-employed has shaped European jurisprudence, legislation, and social policies for decades. "The reason for the distinction drawn by the draftsmen of the Treaties between workers and the self-employed persons is rather straightforward: as a general rule, the ways in which the professional activities of those two groups are organized and exercised differ profoundly."[628] At the crux of *FNV* is the nagging dichotomy between who is/is not an employee and importantly who holds the power to make that call. Although nonstandard employment has greatly outstripped standard contracted employment in both countries examined, there is little consensus as to where orchestral freelance substitutes fit within definitions of employment found in legislation and case law.

It should be emphasized that the differences between the employed and the self-employed are not merely a matter of semantics. In the Netherlands, for example, until the Balanced Labour Market Act (WAB, enacted in 2020) leveled the playing field

625. *FNV KIEM* at 42.
626. Referencing The Irish Bille, Competition (Amendment Bill) 2017.
627. Conversations with Karan O'Loughlin, Services, Industrial, Professional and Technical Union (SIPTU) Sectoral Organizer, Arts and Culture.
628. Opinion Advocate-General Wahl at para. 43. C-413/13 *FNV Kunsten Informatie en Media (KIEM)* [2014]. ECREU:C:2014:2411.

between employees and "zzp'ers" (the Dutch abbreviation for self-employed/independent contractors), conspicuous disparities in terms of compensation, levels of protection and benefits were discernable. An employee is by definition dependent on his/her employer for protection against work-related risks, including income protection in case of inability to work. Article 7:660 Dutch Civil Code (DCC) describes this subordinacy fully.[629] The self-employed are deemed to be entrepreneurs who exercise greater freedom in their employment choices. In the current global orchestral marketplace, shrinking opportunity resulting from financial crisis has diminished occupational choices for musicians in extremis.

En route to *FNV*, several key elements of the employment relationship with regard to European national and transnational reactions to the dramatic changes in the nature of work should be noted, keeping in mind that self-employment has outstripped traditional employment models in the 21st century. First, EU law set forth in the Treaty (TFEU) does not define the term "worker." Second, although the TFEU regulates worker-related rights such as the freedom of movement (Article 45 TFEU), other social-economic rights are regulated through directives and national legislation. Third, the hierarchy between the EU's fundamental rights and freedoms is neither set in stone nor established in black letter law. Frustrated by the perception that economic concerns take precedence over social matters, a growing number of legal scholars find that the relationship between the EU's economic and social pillars has created more tension than compatibility.[630]

5.2 A SIDE-STEP TO EUROPE'S FLEXICURITY POLICY

A side-step to flexibilization is warranted. Also referred to as flexicurity, the policy vigorously pursued first in Denmark and subsequently in the Netherlands was promoted actively by the European Commission from the 1990s onward and played a major role in public policy embraced by Member States before, during, and even after the financial crisis of 2007-2008. Flexicurity has been described succinctly as "an integrated strategy to enhance, at the same time flexibility and security in the labour market."[631] After a decade of windfall, the 2007-2008 financial crisis prompted a sharp rise in unemployment levels, and for many EU countries, negative growth.[632] The underlying liberalization concepts that depend on a flexible workforce to answer to the needs of economic efficiency did not, according to critics, answer calls for increased social justice. Instead, they heighten the conflict between free competition imperatives

629. Article 7:660 DCC Warendorf translation: "An employee must observe the rules governing the performance of work and those designed to promote order in the undertaking of the employer issued to him, by or on behalf of the employer, whether or not at the same time as issued to other employees, within the limits of generally binding provisions or of a contract."

630. Twenty-first-century contributions by Catherine Barnard, Brian Bercusson, Guy Davidov, Simon Deakin, Miriam Kullmann, and Fritz Scharpf for starters.

631. COM(2007) 359. "Towards Common Principles of Flexicurity: more and better jobs through flexibility and security" adopted on June 27, 2007, 2.

632. *Ibid.*

and social protection measures.[633] A double bind in which greater labor market flexibility corresponds to success in the globalized competitive market must be accompanied by high-level employment security according to those who believe in integrated social and economic justice.[634] Advocating a holistic take on flexicurity, the Dutch approach called upon social partners to provide the balance between labor market needs and social protection reflecting the prescriptions found in Article 152 TFEU.[635]

The two-faced character of the EU, or as Martin Potuček fittingly labels it, its "Janusian" face, singles out a rift between flexibility and efficiency.[636] Flexicurity was crafted as a response to economic and policy issues associated with globalization. Its critics observe that its excellent track record in times of economic stability and/or growth is curbed markedly during the recession and post-recession phases that followed the crisis. Christopher Hermann, inspired by research undertaken by the European Trade Union Confederation (ETUC) in 2007,[637] asserts that flexibility has developed into an excessive means to an end that leads to heightened precariousness.[638] A selection of explanatory documents including *travaux préparatoires* reinforced the notion that economic and social aims were intended as mutually supportive, not contradictory.[639] The strong link between the social and economic strands of European cooperation was underlined in a proposal for a motion for a European Parliament resolution on flexicurity:

> Whereas flexicurity, therefore, should be seen as an important component of the European social model fostering competitive and adaptable businesses and workforces; whereas the term "flexicurity" arouses strong concerns among European workers, who fear increased job insecurity, and whereas, therefore, this term, and the firm principles it covers, should be defined as precisely as possible.[640]

633. Critical notes expressed on the European Trade Union Confederation (ETUC) website https://www.etuc.org/IMG/pdf/Depliant_Flexicurity_EN.pdf, and scholarly articles by: Astrid Sanders, "The Changing Face of 'Flexicurity' in Times of Austerity?" in Nicola Countouris and Mark Freedland (eds.) *Resocialising Europe in a Time of Crisis* Cambridge University Press 2013, 314-332. Heyes, J. "Flexicurity in Crisis: European Labour Market Policies in a Time of Austerity." *European Journal of Industrial Relations* 19(1) 2013, 71-86. Also, Sonja Bekker, "Flexicurity in the European Semester: Still a Relevant Concept" 2018 DOI: 10.4324/9781351025621-3, https://www.cambridge.org/core.
634. M. Nardo and F. Rossetti. *Final Report on Flexicurity in Europe*. European Commission 2013, 2.
635. Article 152 TFEU takes into account the diversity of national systems. "It shall facilitate dialogue between the social partners, respecting their autonomy."
636. *See* Martin Potuček, in Zlatica Zudová-Lešková, Emil Voráček et al., eds., *Theory and Practice of the Welfare State in Europe in 20th Century*, 2014, 143, http://www.hiu.cas.cz/en/download/open-acces-online-research-cutputs/2014/theory-and-practice-2014.pdf.
637. ETUC, *supra*, 2007.
638. Christoph Hermann, "Crisis, Structural Reform and the Dismantling of the European Social Model." *Economic and Industrial Democracy, Economic and Industrial Democracy* 38(1) 2014, 51-68, DOI: 10.1177/0143831X14555708.
639. European Economic and Social Committee's exploratory opinion on "Flexicurity (internal flexibility dimension—collective bargaining and the role of social dialogue as instruments for regulating and reforming labour markets)" of July 11, 2007 (SOC/272).
640. Motion for a European Parliament Resolution on Common Principles of Flexicurity (2007/2209 (INI) at B.

The European Commission presented an explanation of the aim of Article 3(3) TEU as an expression of the need for balance and sustainability in the model that is based on two complementary pillars: "on the one hand, the enforcement of competition, and on the other, social policy measures to guarantee social justice by correcting negative outcomes and bolster[ing]social protection."[641] Nevertheless, flexibility and economic efficiency and competitiveness are increasingly at odds with the ideals of social justice and social rights, participative prosperity and the fight against poverty and social exclusion. Flexicurity has not led to the promised land of healthy employment and adequate labor benefits for freelance musicians. A survey of several landmark ECJ cases shows that social rights have rarely trumped economic rights. Of the EU organizations that could answer the question as to "how" the EU's social market economy objective could and should be fulfilled, it is the European Court of Justice (ECJ) that was called upon to tackle conflicting Treaty on European Union (TEU) provisions.

5.3 *ALBANY*: RESTRICTIONS ON COMPETITION?[642]

Albany is one of a trio of 1999 decisions in which the ECJ tackled the fault line between competition law and social protection.[643] Challenging the legality of compulsory participation in a pension fund that had been organized in-house by a company with the intention to increase social protection for employees, the *Albany* court argued that this measure restricted competition notwithstanding its original intent.[644] The ECJ did not doubt that "certain restrictions of competition are inherent in collective agreements" but followed the line of reasoning that "the social policy objectives of such agreements would be seriously undermined ... subject to EC competition law."[645] Stressing the tensions between social policy and competition, the ECJ emphasized, "the social policy objectives pursued by (collective) agreements would be seriously undermined if management and labour were subject to Art. 81(1) of the Treaty."[646] In principle, *Albany* instructs: if a collectively bargained agreement contains clauses that improve work and employment conditions, the contract should not fall within the reach of the competition law, Article 101(1) TFEU. The ECJ ascertained that an exception to competition law could find its basis through collective agreement provisions that led to "a direct improvement of working conditions."[647]

641. Article 3(3) TFEU.
642. *Albany*, at 60.
643. *Albany, Brentjens and Drijvende Bokken*: and Joint Cases C-115/97, C-116/97 and C-117/97, *Brentjens' Handelsonderneming BV v. Stichting Bedrijfspensioenfonds voor de Handel in Bouwmaterialen*, and Case C-219/97, *Maatschappij Drijvende Bokken BV v. Stichting Pensioenfonds voor de Vervoer- en Havenbedrijven*, September 21, 1999.
644. *Ibid.*, at 97.
645. *Ibid.*, at 59, 60.
646. *Ibid.*, at 59.
647. Ibid., at 60; Brentjens at 57 and Drijvende Bokken at 47.

5.4 THE SELF-EMPLOYED AS UNDERTAKINGS

Article 101(1) TFEU prohibits all agreements between undertakings, decisions by associations of undertakings and concerted practices within the EU that have as their object or effect the prevention, restriction or distortion of free competition. Notwithstanding the stated prohibitions, the Treaty does not offer a definition of "undertakings." Although the ECJ avoids engaging in definitions, it lent its support to a broad conception of undertakings in *Höfner*: "undertakings encompass every entity engaged in an economic activity, regardless of the legal status of the entity and the way in which it is financed."[648] Thus, in EU-speak, an undertaking is an entity engaged in economic activity and encompasses individuals who offer goods and/or services on the market and bear financial risks associated with the performance of these services. Significantly in *Becu*, the ECJ reasoned that employees should not be categorized as undertakings because they do not engage in autonomous economic activity and do not bear the risks as such.[649] However, the ECJ positioned self-employed workers, especially those who engage in "liberal professions" within the "undertaking" category in *Pavlov*.[650] In what could be seen as a rehearsal for issues central to *FNV*, the ECJ showed its reticence to extend exceptions to competition law to a group of self-employed Dutch-based medical professionals who intended to top-up their pensions by contributing to a supplemental pension scheme set up under a collective agreement. "A fund entrusted with the management of a supplementary pension scheme set up by a collective agreement concluded between organizations representing employers and workers in a given sector...was an undertaking within the meaning of Art. 85 et seq. of the Treaty."[651] Strict compliance with stringent competition rules was the ECJ's strong message.[652] Decisively, the ECJ pointed out that the Treaty was silent with regard to advancing "the members of the liberal professions" to enter into agreements to improve their work conditions.[653] The ECJ stopped short of blocking the pension scheme in question as it did not distort competition through the abuse of a dominant position.[654] The ECJ's construal of core concepts such as agreement, undertaking and the all-important restriction of competition suggests an interpretational divide between *Albany* and *Pavlov*.[655] The narrow interpretation of undertakings in *Pavlov* might have indicated a roadblock to a more open interpretation of the concept of the self-employed as undertakings: *FNV* was to reroute that course, at least for the false self-employed.

648. Case 41/90, *Höfner and Elsner v. Macrotron* (1990), at 21. ECLI:EU:C:1991:161.
649. C-22-98 *Criminal proceedings against Jean Claude Becu, Annie Verweire, Smeg NV and Adia Interim NV* (1999) ECLI:EU:C:1999:419.
650. Case C 180-184/98 *Pavel Pavlov and Others v. Stichting Pensioenfonds Medische Specialisten* (2000). ECLI:EU:C:2000:428.
651. *Ibid.*, at 11.
652. *Ibid.*, at 84-89.
653. *Ibid.*, at 69.
654. *Ibid.*, at 120.
655. Mark Freedland and Nicola Kountouris. "Some Reflections on the 'Personal Scope' of Collective Labour Law" *Industrial Law Journal* 46(1), March 1, 2017 DOI: 10.1093/indlaw/dww041.

5.5 SETTING THE STAGE FOR *FNV*: IN THE SHADOW OF BUDGET CUTS

A reliance on a sizeable number of freelance substitute musicians is a given in the orchestral profession: "without freelancers, there would be no performances, it is really that simple."[656] Worldwide orchestras were adversely affected by the 2007-2008 financial crisis with personnel cuts at best, and in many worst-case scenarios collective dismissals. "When the institution is threatened by downsizing and subsidy reductions, the most precarious workers, the freelancers are even more threatened and unfortunately the slippery slope became non-negotiable."[657]

Dutch orchestral musicians are bound by employment contracts negotiated between various consortia of orchestras[658] and the unions: collective labor agreements known as CAOs in Dutch (collectieve arbeidsovereenkomsten). To improve employment conditions for freelance musicians, two Dutch musician's unions, the FNV KIEM (Dutch Trade Union Confederation Art, Information and Media) and the Nederlandse Toonkunstenaarsbond (Dutch Musician's Union) collaborated with the Vereniging van Stichtingen Remplaçanten Nederlandse Orkesten (Association of the Foundation for Substitute Players in Dutch Orchestras, further VSR) to formulate a CAO on behalf of the substitute players. The musicians' CAO set forth minimum fees in a mixed membership agreement comprised of substitute orchestral musicians hired on the basis of employment contracts and substitute orchestral players hired under contracts for services. The latter group was considered by employers as self-employed substitutes as opposed to the former who were deemed to be employed substitutes. Under a provision put forward in the CAO's Annex 5, the self-employed substitutes were entitled to receive the same minimum payment for rehearsals and concerts as employed substitutes augmented by 16%.[659]

The FNV's[660] attempt to level the freelance playing field for freelance substitutes was brought to the attention of the Dutch competition law administrative body, the Nederlands Mededingingsauthoriteit, Dutch Competition Authority, further NMa. In opposition to the CAO that set minimum rates for substitute musicians, the NMa observed: "a union bargaining on behalf of self-employed members is an association of

656. Conversations with Angela Garland, Artistic Coordinator, Netherlands Philharmonic Orchestra.
657. Conversations with Martin Kothman, Senior Director Audiovisual media & classical music sector, FNV Media & Culture.
658. The majority of subsidized orchestras are members of the Association for Dutch Orchestras (VvNO Vereniging van Nederlandse Orkesten).
659. CAO Remplaçanten Nederlandse Orkesten 1 november 2006-31 augustus 2007. Annex 5: "Aan de zelfstandige remplaçant, d.w.z. remplaçanten waarmee een overeenkomst van opdracht en geen arbeidsovereenkomst wordt aangegaan, wordt tenminste het in bijlage 2 genoemde repetitie- en concerttarief betaald plus 16%. Bedoelde zelfstandige remplaçant is geen werknemer in de zin van artikel 1 c van deze CAO," https://adoc.tips/collectieve-arbeidsovereenkomst-remplaanten-nederlandse-orke.html.
660. Although the acronym FNV is used throughout the book, it bears repetition that the parties who bargained collectively on behalf of the substitutes were the FNV, the Dutch Musicians Union (Nederlands Toonkunstenaarsbond, NTB) and the Foundations for Substitutes in Dutch Orchestras (VSR).

undertakings and is not permitted to take advantage of the social exception."[661] Apprised of the FNV's bargaining activities on behalf of the self-employed substitute players, the NMa initiated an informal inquiry to ascertain the CAO's legality. Their findings were published in a Vision document, "CAO fees for self-employed in light of Dutch Competition Law" (author's translation).[662] According to the Vision document, the CAO's Annex 5 could restrict competition on the Dutch market, which is prohibited under Article 6 (1) Mw (Mededingingswet/Competition Act):

> Agreements between undertakings, decisions by associations of undertakings and concerted practices between undertakings, which have as their object or effect the prevention restriction or distortion of competition on the Dutch market or on part of it, shall be prohibited.

The FNV maintained that both categories of orchestral substitutes under the aforementioned collective labor agreement were entitled to receive negotiated minimum rates outside the reach of competition law, and additionally, "the NMA's actions went much too far by singling out the lawful collectively bargained agreement. We felt that **their** actions, not ours were unlawful."[663] At the Hague District Court (Court of First Instance), the FNV sought a declaration that competition law did not preclude the mixed membership CAO, "an agreement had the strong mission to protect the weakest of all parties within the freelance orchestral sector."[664] The Hague Court rejected the FNV claim finding that the FNV failed to prove that fixed fees directly contributed to improving labor conditions for the freelance substitute musicians.[665] Subsequently, the FNV applied to the Gerechtshof s'Gravenhage (The Hague Regional Court of Appeal) for a correct interpretation of Article 6 Mw. According to the Court of Appeal, the soundest approach to national legislation largely influenced by EU legislation, Article 101 TFEU, was to initiate a request for an ECJ preliminary ruling based on the following two questions:

> (1) Does Art. 101 TFEU apply if a collective labor agreement sets minimum fees for self-employed workers performing the same functions under a contract for services as employed workers and,
> (2) If so, would the collective labor agreement fall within the Art. 101 (1) regime if the agreement was intended to improve the working conditions (either directly or indirectly) of all of the workers within the scope of the agreement?[666]

Holding steadfastly to that cardinal concept of the split between employees and undertakings, the ECJ acknowledged that in principle social dialogue should benefit

661. Visie Document, "CAO-tariefbepalingen voor zelfstandigen en de Mededingingswet," December 12, 2007, https://www.sdu.nl/content/staatscourant-2007-241-visiedocument-cao-tariefbepalingen-voor-zelfstandigen-en-de-mededingingswet.
662. *Ibid.*
663. Conversations with Mark Gerrits.
664. Conversations with Martin Kothman.
665. *FNV Kunsten Informatie en Media v. De Staat der Nederlanden,* Rechtbank 's-Gravenhage October 27, 2010. ECLI:NL:RBSGR:2010:BO3551.
666. *FNV Kunsten Informatie en Media v. Staat der Nederlanden* (C-413/13) July 9, 2013, subsequently referred to the ECJ.

employees but not independent service providers, the self-employed. Carefully applying a checklist of employment characteristics, the court found that substitute musicians who play alongside member musicians were workers who could be classified as false self-employed, a category that could benefit from the *Albany* exception to Article 101(1) TFEU.[667]

In a narrow interpretation of how the benefits of a collective labor agreement between unions and orchestral freelancers should be interpreted, the ECJ noted that the substitute musicians should be classified as undertakings under EU law: they perform services in a specific market (orchestras); receive remuneration (fees for rehearsals/performances) paid by the employer and importantly, perform the aforementioned activities as independents in relation to their employers. A labor organization that negotiates on their behalf does not function as a bona fide social partner representing the interests of these musicians but rather as an "association of undertakings." While the provisions within the TFEU encourage social dialogue to answer to the social objectives (*see* Articles 151, 153 and 155 TFEU), the intent of the legislation is to ameliorate employment situations for employees, not for entrepreneurial self-employed persons unless of course these persons can be classified in a special category, in *FNV*, the "false self-employed":

> That being said, it must be held that the minimum fees scheme put in place by the provisions in the collective labour agreement directly contributes to the improvement of the employment and working conditions of those substitutes, classified as "false self-employed". Such a scheme not only guarantees those service providers basic pay higher than they would have received were it not for that provision but also, as found by the referring court, enables contributions to be made to pension insurance corresponding to participation in the pension scheme for workers, thereby guaranteeing them the means necessary to be eligible in future for a certain level of pension.[668]

The ECJ held that, according to Dutch law on collective labor agreements, a Dutch independent service provider (self-employed person) has the right to join a trade union. Furthermore, trade unions are within their rights to negotiate collective labor agreements on behalf of employees including the self-employed whose services are provided to the employer.

As *Albany* instructed, a collectively bargained agreement created to improve employment conditions does not fall within the scope of Article 101(1) TFEU. However, according to superficial appraisals, the self-employed substitute orchestral players who play their instruments as part of an orchestral collective in return for remuneration could be construed as entrepreneurs, in the parlance of competition law, undertakings competing in a specific market. What is the relationship between a substitute player and his/her employer? Did the FNV and partners negotiate a collective bargaining agreement (CAO, in Dutch) for these musicians in good faith in order to improve the employment situation for individual substitute players or was the union negotiating on behalf of an association of undertakings? If in fact the FNV's collective

667. *Albany* at 60.
668. *FNV* at 39, 40.

bargaining activities were undertaken on behalf of an association, the resulting agreement was subject to competition law under Article 101(1) TFEU. What requirements did the court set to define self-employed service providers who fall within their newly defined category of "false self-employed" workers? To meet the requirements of this hybrid category, the worker must be dependent on the employer, possess no ability to determine his/her market-related conduct, and not bear any responsibility for the employer's financial risks.

Confusion as to attribution reigns if we consider that a worker can be qualified as self-employed according to the national law of Member States, and the same worker could be classified as an employee according to tax regulations. In the ECJ's view, if the substitute musicians would be classified by national courts as genuinely self-employed, the collectively bargained agreements concluded by their representative organizations would not be exempt from the long reach of Article 101 TFEU. However, should national courts ascertain that these substitute musicians were employees according to national and EU definitions, then their collectively bargained agreement would merit exemption under *Albany*. In the ECJ's consideration, a self-employed substitute musician reaps the benefits of more independence and flexibility than regularly employed musicians who perform the same activity with regard to work schedules, the location of the work and manner of performing the tasks assigned, in other words, the rehearsals and concerts. Further, recalling *Albany*, the ECJ emphasized that the collectively bargained agreement would have to contribute to the improvement of the employment and working conditions of the substitute musicians. Turning its attention to the employment relationship, the ECJ looked back to its past holdings: "The essential feature of an employment relationship, however, is that for a certain period of time a person performs services for and under the direction of another person in return for which he receives remuneration."[669]

5.6 *FNV* HAS LEFT MANY QUESTIONS OPEN

The ECJ took a conservative approach to the FNV's expansion of collective bargaining activities to include all of its self-employed members. In essence, the court demoted social dialogue on the part of trade unions on behalf of these self-employed members to a lower level than collective bargaining between bona fide employers and employees.[670] The case was certainly not resolved at either the EU or the national level, keeping in mind the ruling at the Hague Court of Appeal with its admonishment (loosely translated): "we cannot give judgment on the question of whether self-employed other than substitutes (such as self-employed workers without employees in general or working in another sector) could be categorized as false self-employed." As mentioned above, a victory for competition exceptions with regard to certain categories of self-employed workers led to legislative change (WAB). No solid definitions of the

669. *Lawrie-Blum* at 42.
670. Social dialogue in its European iteration commonly refers to either tripartite consultations between public authorities, employers, and employees or consultations/negotiations between employers and trade unions, https://ec.europa.eu/social/main.jsp?langId=en&catId=329.

false self-employed were provided, and despite the hopes of legal certainty in terms of definitions, the "false self-employed" in the freelance orchestra sector still face challenges in terms of employment, as they are to quote a Dutch union representative, "vis noch vlees."[671]

5.7 THE ECJ MOVES BEYOND EUROPEAN BORDERS: US JURISPRUDENCE AND ANTITRUST

In his quest to find a balance between worker's rights and competition law concerns in *FNV*, Advocate General (AG) Wahl referenced three pieces of US Supreme Court (SCOTUS) jurisprudence as a basis for an Opinion submitted on September 11, 2014.[672] His choice focused on cases that date back more than half a century[673] and included a case that involved the specific concerns of musicians. These US precedents will be considered briefly.

In *Allen Bradley*, a New York-based electricians' union took closed-shop agreements with equipment manufacturers to a new level. To protect local suppliers, New York City manufacturers agreed to boycott contractors who used equipment that was not produced locally. Non-New York City manufacturers claimed that such activities not only quashed competition but also denied them access to operate freely in the market. The question posed to SCOTUS: is there evidence of a violation of the Sherman Antitrust Act of 1890 if labor unions and their members unite with employers and manufacturers of goods to restrain competition to monopolize the marketing of such goods with the aim of improving the wages of local workers?[674] Recognizing the difficulty of balancing market competition with the rights of workers, the SCOTUS majority explained:

> Our holding means that the same labor union activities may or may not be in violation of the Sherman drawing legislation primarily aimed at trusts and monopolies so that it could also be applied to labor organizations without impairing the collective bargaining and related rights of those organizations has been emphasized both by congressional and judicial attempts to draw lines between permissible and prohibited union activities.[675]

Importantly, the court recognized that granting free rein to the union to effectuate secondary boycotts could obstruct legitimate public policy concerns and could further

671. Literal translation "neither fish nor meat," the category is ambiguous, quote by Mark Gerrits, Kunstenbond.
672. Opinion Advocate General Nils Wahl, Case C-413/13 *FNV KIEM* December 4, 2014, at para. 99.
673. *Allen Bradley Co. v. Electrical Workers*, 325 US 797 (1945).
674. Sherman Antitrust Act of 1890 15 U. S. C. §§1-7, in relevant part: "Sec. 2. Every person who shall monopolize, or attempt to monopolize, or combine to conspire with any other person or persons, to monopolize any part of the trade or commerce among the several States, or with foreign nations, shall be deemed guilty of a misdemeanor." Other relevant antitrust legislation: Clayton Antitrust Act, 15 U. S. C. §§ 12-27 and the Norris-LaGuardia Act 29 USC. §§ 101-115 specifically exempt trade unions from antitrust law "provided they act in their own interest."
675. *Allen v. Bradley*, 25.

put the court in the sacrosanct place reserved for the legislator.[676] Soon thereafter, the US Congress passed the Taft-Hartley Act (THA) in which secondary boycotts were categorized as unfair labor practices:[677]

> Section 8(b)(4) of the Act makes it unlawful for a labor organization "(i) to engage in, or induce or encourage any individual employed by any person engaged in commerce or in an industry affecting commerce to engage in, a strike or a refusal in the course of his employment to use, manufacture, process, transport, or otherwise handle or work on any goods, articles, materials, or commodities or to perform any services,"[678] and more generally, "any activity, business, or industry in commerce or in which a labor dispute would hinder or obstruct commerce or the free flow of commerce and includes any activity or industry affecting commerce" is prohibited.[679]

In *Pennington*, the second US case that AG Wahl cited, agreements between the union and a major mine operator met with SCOTUS' disapproval.[680] In the opinion of the majority, the impact of a union that joined forces with a nonlabor group exerted undue pressure on the activities of smaller mine operations and their employees. Although wages were rightly viewed as a legitimate subject of mandatory collective bargaining that fall outside the reach of antitrust, the impact of such bargaining on competition within the sector was decisive, according to the SCOTUS majority.

5.8 AT THE HEART OF THE NEW YORK GIG SCENE

While precedents concerning antitrust behavior abound, *Carroll* was the only case of judicial weight in the musical sphere to reach SCOTUS.[681] Posing the question as to whether price lists— also designated as price floors—a group-imposed minimum charge set by orchestra leaders, were designed to protect musicians or merely an excuse to increase the leaders' powers, SCOTUS was challenged to ascertain whether or not the powerful musicians' union, the American Federation of Musicians (AFM) Local 802, had conspired with orchestra leaders to violate federal antitrust laws of relevance. The THA defines industry affecting commerce as: "any activity, business, or industry in commerce or in which a labor dispute would hinder or obstruct commerce or the free flow of commerce and includes any activity or industry 'affecting commerce' within the meaning of the Act."[682] Taking us to the heart of the New York gig scene in its 1960s heyday, the courts were challenged to differentiate between gig contractors or "leaders" and hired musicians: "subleaders" and "sidemen." Lucrative New York City engagements were closed-shop gigs. Working musicians were required to join the union, and club owners were required to hire local unionized musicians and required

676. *Ibid.*
677. Labor Management Relations Act, 1947 [LMRA, the Taft-Hartley Act]. §8(b)(4). Title 29, USC § 402(c).
678. *Ibid.*
679. *Ibid.*
680. *United Mine Workers v. Pennington*, US 657 (1965).
681. *American Fed'n of Musicians v. Carroll*, 391 US 99 (1968).
682. Title 29 USC. § 402(c) *Taft-Hartley*, the *Labor Management Act* 1947.

to pay fees set in a "Price List Booklet." According to Carroll and three other orchestra leaders (the claimants), these union practices were tantamount to "conspiracy with a nonlabor group."[683] Their claim asserted that the AFM Local 802 violated the Sherman Act as its fee-setting activities "created a combination with a nonlabor group."[684]

Under a doctrine established by SCOTUS during WWII, unilateral actions undertaken by a union can be exempt from the long arm of antitrust laws under two conditions set forth in *Hutcheson*.[685] First, there must be proof that the union has acted in its own self-interest, and second, the union is not permitted to have joined forces with a nonlabor entity. The reach or more appropriately lack thereof when applied to pit orchestras performing in New York clubs was decisive within the context of *Carroll*.

Before the case reached SCOTUS, the United States Court of Appeals for the Second Circuit had found that such price-setting practices were direct infringements of the Sherman Act.[686] The majority opined that since the *Carroll* leaders were in competition with their fellow musicians (subleaders and sidemen), they were entitled to establish price lists. Following a precedent set by *Jewel Tea* "the crucial determinant is not the form of the agreement—e.g., prices or wage—but its relative impact on the product market and the interests of union members."[687] The union's activities were exempt from antitrust limitations because protective actions such as price floors to protect the wages of subcontracted players were well shielded by existing legislation.[688] Although *Carroll* marked an attempt to establish a justification for anticompetitive schemes devised by the unions and employers that could benefit union members, SCOTUS chose not to define "labor group." Critics are more than reasonable in their skepticism concerning the expansion of the AFM's powers as a result of a firm reliance on the value of promoting "greater union interest." It could be argued that the AFM, as the strong and sole union representing US musicians' interests, already exerted far-reaching control over musicians' employment with a specific focus on adequate pricing, without the additional allowances put forth in *Carroll*. Equally questionable is the court's avoidance of a central tenet within the object and purpose of the National Labor Relations Act (NLRA): the support of collective bargaining at the workplace.[689] The imposition of price lists under union bylaws and other regulations gives the union the power to take charge of a vital job condition setting the price for labor, without discussing this condition within the collective bargaining process. "By combining with a nonlabor group, the musicians' union has obtained effective control of the entire

683. *Ibid.*
684. *Allen Bradley Co.* The union was disallowed an exemption from antitrust laws if the union combined with a nonlabor group to achieve a commercial restriction.
685. *US v. Hutcheson*, 312 US 219, 232 (1941).
686. *Carroll v. Associated Musicians of Greater New York*, 183 F.Supp.636 (S.D.N.Y. 1960), affirmed 284 F.2d 91 (2 Cir. 1960).
687. Local 189, *Meat Cutters v. Jewel Tea Co.* 81 US 676 (1965).
688. Norris-LaGuardia Act § 13, 29 USC. § 113 (c) (1964)."The term labor dispute includes any controversy concerning terms or condition of employment or concerning the association or representation of persons in negotiating, fixing, maintaining, changing, or seeking to arrange terms or conditions of employment, regardless of whether or not the disputants stand in the proximate relation of employer and employee."
689. National Labor Relations Act (NLRA) 29 USC. §§ 151-169 (1935).

club-date industry ... The Court treads dangerous ground ... to deny a particular industry the normal competitive conditions envisioned by the antitrust laws, conditions usually viewed as essential for maintaining services and prices at satisfactory levels."[690] Acutely aware of the differences between the workings of competition law versus antitrust in their respective EU-US contexts, AG Wahl relied on the aforementioned SCOTUS examples to encourage the ECJ to employ restraint when applying the *Albany* exception to self-employed workers. In his view, the ECJ held the responsibility to gauge "whether the provisions at issue directly improve the employment and working conditions of employees, by genuinely and effectively preventing social dumping and not going beyond what is necessary to achieve that objective."

5.9 SOCIAL DUMPING: DIFFERENTIATIONS BETWEEN AG WAHL AND ECJ FINDINGS

Concerned with the effects of social dumping,[691] AG Wahl reasoned that minimum rate provisions for self-employed workers are in the interests of employees because otherwise, it becomes more attractive for employers to exchange employees for self-employed workers who may cost less than employees. In his opinion, the prevention of social dumping falls squarely within a category of direct and legitimate objectives to be pursued in collective bargaining provisions concerning self-employed workers. The element "direct" is reinterpreted in such a way that it does not exclude the possibility of including collective agreement provisions relating to self-employed workers that improve the employment and working conditions of employees.[692] The ECJ did not opt to either call social dumping by its name or allude to it in passing. Instead, the court underlined that minimum rate provisions make a positive contribution to the employment and working conditions of the false self-employed and further enable this specific category of workers to avail themselves of collective pension insurance.

5.10 U-TURNS AND OTHER CONSIDERATIONS INSPIRED BY *FNV AND CARROLL*

Legal scholars Mark Barenberg and Eva Grosheide developed a theory that applies US legal interpretation principles that could lessen the restrictions of European competition law with regard to the rights of the self-employed to negotiate minimum fees.[693] According to these scholars, it is advisable, at least conceptually, to advance concepts

690. Dissent William O. Douglas, *see Carroll*.
691. In some jurisdictions, "wage dumping," relegating workers to substandard pay or employment conditions with regard to local laws and/or CBAs, https://home-affairs.ec.europa.eu/networks/european-migration-network-emn/emn-asylum-and-migration-glossary/glossary/social-dumping_en.
692. Opinion of AG Nils Wahl *FNV Kunsten Informatie en Media v. Staat der Nederlanden* September 11, 2014. In particular, conclusion *FNV KIEM*, paras. 74-94.
693. Mark Barenberg and Eva Grosheide, "Minimum Fees for the Self-Employed: A European Response to the Uber-ized Economy." *Columbia Journal of European Law* 22 2016, 193-236.

tested by US courts to come to grips with employment-related issues in European cases with similar fact patterns. They suggest creative paths to elude competition law restrictions via legal maneuvers, about-faces or in their preferred vernacular, "U-turns." Pushing aside the oft-cited differences between common law and civil law, one of their U-turn examples extends the US concept of a "labor group" to an amalgamation of employee associations comprised of self-employed persons. If such an extension could reach Europe, they argue, it could provide a workable solution to problems faced by freelancers and self-employed workers keen to gain fair remuneration through collectively bargained agreements akin to the substitute musicians in *FNV*. According to Barenberg and Grosheide, the *FNV* court "dodged the question" of whether the minimum fees bargained for on behalf of the substitute musicians met the *Albany* exception standard. The ECJ did not step up to the plate and free self-employed persons from the shackles of undertakings that perform economic activities by opting to remand the issue back to the Hague Court of Appeal for a final status appraisal as to whether the substitutes were "false self-employed."[694]

Their third U-turn examines the theoretical possibility for fee scales to be set through a system of government mandates with the caveat that EU Member States would bear the responsibility to monitor fee-setting independent bodies. These independent bodies would be mandated to set fees in the public interest and maintain distance from the beneficiaries such as the self-employed in privileged professions (the medical professionals in *Pavlov* come to mind).[695] Their far-reaching fourth and final U-turn calls upon the ECJ to consider SCOTUS' adoption of the concept of the "labor group," an intermediate category that includes associations-groups of self-employed persons akin to the labor group considerations in the *Carroll* case.[696]

5.11 WINDS OF CHANGE? *FNV* MEETS THE FUTURE

In a controversial Dutch case in 2015, several categories of nonstandard, self-employed workers in the mail delivery branch employed by PostNL organized a strike and a blockade which they publicized through social media. PostNL sought judicial relief for these actions claiming that they were illegal because some of the striking workers were self-employed. The judge who oversaw the interlocutory proceedings afforded the entire group of workers including a group he described as "false self-employed"[697] defined in *FNV* the right to strike under Article 6 (4) European Social Charter (ESC) extending the right to strike to the newly minted false self-employed.[698]

694. Pavlov, *supra*.
695. *Ibid.*, 236.
696. *See Carroll v. Associated Musicians of Greater New York*, 183 F.Supp.636 (S.D.N.Y. 1960), affirmed 284 F.2d 91 (2 Cir. 1960). Debates concerning whether or not the decision was correctly reasoned still rage.
697. To quote the Dutch term, *schijnzelfstandigen*.
698. Article 6 (4) ESC revised 1996 upholds: "the right of workers and employers to collective action in cases of conflicts of interest, including the right to strike, subject to obligations that might arise out of collective agreements previously entered into," https://rm.coe.int/168007cf93.

Yet, despite the promise of legal certainty implied by *FNV*, the false self-employed in the freelance orchestra sector face challenges in terms of employment. Take the case of a saxophone player engaged to perform with a leading Dutch orchestra. Common knowledge of an orchestra's repertoire informs that saxophone players are not regular members of an orchestra as their services are only needed on rare occasions. If a self-employed saxophone player is hired for a short series of rehearsals and concerts, would the union be permitted to fix a price for the musician's services, or would that action involve illegal price-fixing as it is impossible to determine the degree of disguised employment for a musician who does not technically take on a "side-by-side" role in the orchestra? To quote a Dutch union negotiator, "de laatste loodjes wegen het zwaarst"(loosely translated by the author: the last mile is the longest).[699]

In keeping with the ECJ's answers to the pair of prejudicial questions posed in *FNV*, the Hague Court of Appeal ruled that the freelance substitute orchestral players should be categorized as false self-employed persons.[700] As subordinates, the substitutes worked "side-by-side" performing the same tasks as regular orchestral employees and did not have the option to determine the particulars of their work schedules like true self-employed persons. Crucially, the Court of Appeal rejected the State's counterargument that a self-employed orchestral substitute could "execute or execute only partially the assignment; in other words, the musician could opt out and not attend some of the rehearsals.[701] In a correct assessment of an orchestral freelancer's dependent status, the Hague Court observed that "even if such freedom existed in a strictly legal sense, it must be assumed that it is unlikely that such a substitute will be hired a second time by the orchestra .... Real freedom does not exist."[702] The court did not go beyond the boundaries of the ECJ ruling to consider if false self-employed persons who are not bona fide self-employed under the competition law regime could be categorized as employees under Dutch law, Article 6:610 DCC.[703]

A number of determining questions come to mind when considering the effects of *FNV* in practice. Yet beyond the inspirational value of FNV, the union advanced arguments to support the idea that freelance substitute musicians are employees, not entrepreneurs or undertakings whose fees prompt price fixing. Difficulties in classification arise when considering a substitute musician's activities beyond the orchestral sphere. Contemplate the fact that a freelance musician often switches roles between orchestral performance under contract, private teaching, teaching at a music school and/or conservatory, performing as a member of a chamber music group and engaging as a freelance performer in other musical enterprises. Are these musicians then "false self-employed" as orchestral musicians when they play alongside their contracted musical colleagues and simultaneously bona fide self-employed when performing chamber music concerts with, for the sake of argument, a string quartet? Which specific criteria should be taken into consideration?

699. Conversations with Mark Gerrits.
700. *FNV Kunsten Informatie en Media v. De Staat der Nederlanden*, Case 343076/HA ZA 09-2395, September 1, 2015.
701. *Ibid.*, at para. 2.8.
702. *Ibid.*
703. *Ibid.*, at para. 2.3.

If false self-employed workers who are hired to perform under contracts of services are regarded as employees under domestic law, should they be covered by collective bargaining agreements? Is the national authority sufficiently competent and well versed in the nuances within freelance situations and self-employment to fairly determine if an employee is false? Professor Evert Verhulp has never wavered from his conviction that substitute musicians in an orchestra are employees *pur sang*. "Unthinkable, how can an orchestral musician be classified as self-employed? The conductor directs and controls what an orchestral musicians does. The musician follows those orders and is totally dependent in every aspect of work." Musicians chime in wholeheartedly. "What does an orchestral musician do? We breathe together, become one with the music, recreate the conductor's gestures into musical magic and join together to create a performance experience based on notation, that is what an orchestral musician does."[704] Orchestral substitutes must perform their duties, as an individual within a collective, in perfect synchronization with their regularly contracted colleagues. "They certainly are not entrepreneurs who run a business, direct a staff, or share in any sort of commercial endeavor—they are musicians!"[705]

Setting minimum fees breaches European competition law when applied to the "real" self-employed but allows the false self-employed to benefit from the *Albany* exception. Following that line of logic, when the FNV engaged in social dialogue on behalf of the orchestral substitutes, the trade union bargained for employees, not self-employed persons. The court stayed clear of true legal innovation as it certainly did not depart from the binary distinction between employees and self-employed entrepreneurs. The question remains as to how, if and when the *FNV*-doctrine could be expanded to include self-employed persons in collective agreements who are not categorized as "false self-employed" but for all intents and purposes work in disguised employment situations.

5.12 NATIONAL REGULATORY ACTION IN THE NETHERLANDS POST-*FNV*

The ACM changed its tune in the aftermath of *FNV* by allowing independent contractors the freedom to set prices within the framework of collective bargaining agreements as articulated in its 2017 *Leidraad: Tariefafspraken voor zzp'ers in cao's* (Guidelines: Rate agreements for freelancers in collective agreements).[706] Crucial to the exceptions outlined in the Guidelines is that self-employed persons work "side-by-side with employees and are therefore not an undertaking within the meaning of the Competition Act." Thus, like the orchestral substitute who performs alongside orchestral members, these self-employed persons are indistinguishable from regular employees in terms of their work and should not be placed into the category of entrepreneurs (frequently translated from the Dutch as undertakings) within the meaning of the Competition Act.

704. Conversations with Maestro Christopher Keene.
705. Conversations with Sir Mark Elder.
706. *Leidraad: Tariefafspraken voor zzp'ers in cao's*. Autoriteit Consument & Markt, 24 februari 2017 www.acm.nl.

Under the Guidelines, this special category of self-employed persons is permitted to work under a collective labor agreement that sets minimum fees for their labor.

Martijn Snoep, Chair of the Authority for Consumers & Markets Board (ACM), showed enthusiasm for this relaxation of the strict application of competition rules "to show consideration for more than one million independent contractors at work in the Netherlands."[707] The cumulative requirements for the competition exception in the Guideline's text adopted in Article 6(3) Competition Act (author's translation):

> The agreements ensure that the parties involved work more efficiently, as a result of which the advantages outweigh the disadvantages, and
>
> - a fair share of these advantages accrues to customers, and
> - these benefits can only be achieved through the agreements and the agreements interfere no more than necessary, and
> - there is still sufficient competition in the market after the agreements have been made.[708]

In the 2007 NMa Vision Document discussed earlier, the ACM's precursor, the NMa had rejected this line of reasoning based on the contention that fixing fees for self-employed workers would exceed necessity in the pursuit of social objectives to benefit workers. Fortunately for substitute musicians, a particularly vulnerable category of freelancers in need of a safety net in terms of social benefits, the formalism of the NMa old-style, has made way for a creative new approach to the competition-social benefit dichotomy.

5.13 THE LIVING LEGACY OF *FNV*

The question remains: did *FNV* move into bold protective territory expanding upon the *Albany* exception with its designation of a special category, the false self-employed? With its closed, circle-the-wagons approach to limit the reach of minimum fees through collective bargaining for this restrictive category of false self-employed substitute musicians, it could be argued that the ECJ created a stranglehold on the very notion of bargaining freedoms. By circumventing the wide options for workers to bargain collectively in Article 28[709] in the EU Charter on Fundamental Rights and the ILO Convention Article 98 and turning a blind eye to the European Court of Human Rights' (ECtHR) expansive interpretation of these rights in *Baykara*,[710] the ECJ underlined its conservative approach to workers' rights. Are dancers, photographers or for that matter self-employed house cleaners protected under *FNV*? Or for the sake of accuracy,

707. Conversation with Martijn Snoep, Board chair Authority for Consumers & Markets (ACM).
708. Quoted on page 4, *Leidraad*. Artikel 6, lid 3 van de Mededingingswet.
709. Article 28 of the EU Charter on Fundamental Rights: "Workers and employers, or their respective organisations, have, in accordance with Union law and national laws and practices, the right to negotiate and conclude collective agreements at the appropriate levels and, in cases of conflicts of interest, to take collective action to defend their interests, including strike action." https://fra.europa.eu/en/eu-charter/article/28-right-collective-bargaining-and-action.
710. *Demir and Baykara v. Turkey* [GC]-34503/97. Judgment 12.11.2008 [GC] [2008] ECHR 1345, (2009) 48 EHRR 54, https://hudoc.echr.coe.int/fre#{%22itemid%22:[%22002-1864%22]}.

what about orchestral musicians who perform as ensemble players at the behest of non-orchestral employers in the various manifestations of recording including streaming companies? Can these performers set minimum rates as false self-employed persons?

The judicial ruling established a pattern of understanding and acceptance of the concept of the false self-employed status of orchestral freelance musicians. But where does that lead for those who work in the sector? Union organizers valiantly attempt to pave the way to collective bargaining for cultural workers regardless of dependence and classification. Academics ponder ways to transmute hybrid employee-worker categories into positive legislation. In both the Netherlands and the US, the boots on the musical ground are increasingly concerned by continued austerity on the part of employers with regard to freelancers. "Orchestras nowadays tend to hire fewer freelancers in an attempt to cut costs and have found creative ways to mitigate the costs of employment by taking on student-apprentice players, members of in-house training academies who replace seasoned freelancers at reduced rates of pay."[711]

A deeper consideration of the legal landscape as it impacts the most vulnerable workers post-*FNV* is invaluable. Comments provided by a Dutch-based bass player who, in her own words, "mustered the courage" to take her former employer to court in 2020 underscores this observation. "The litigation I was involved in was so much larger than my personal situation that the very idea to go to court struck fear in my heart. I am a bass player and a woman, that says a lot in a corner of the orchestral profession that is full of powerful men. Until the budget cuts (2012) I was a regular employee in my orchestra. Immediately, less than a few weeks following the cuts and my dismissal, 'my' orchestra hired me as a guest player (freelance substitute), and I worked happily for several more years until I was told that I was not needed anymore. How could a former colleague who had proved themselves for years be not needed? I went to court in the name of all those freelancers who are afraid to stand up for their rights. A win for me is a win for all."[712]

5.14 A PATH TO EMPOWERMENT: THE *PLATFORM VOOR FREELANCE MUSICI*

> Organizing freelancers is like organizing cats. Or maybe, more like giving a cat a bath.[713]

711. Conversations with Angela Garland.
712. Conversations with former Het Ballet Orkest bass player Annemieke Marinkovic who won her case in July 2020. According to the Amsterdam Court, the conditions of her employment may have been given another contractual wording (guest player post-dismissal; employee for 10 years prior to the staff reductions), but her work as a bass player in the section remained the same. The fact that she worked in the orchestra as an independent contractor post-dismissal was not a matter of personal choice: it was her only option. According to the judge, she was an employee *pur sang*.
713. Thérèse Boutin, former CEO Orchestre Symphonique du Québec, Federation International Musiciens (FIM) International Conference, Montreal 2017.

The ongoing push to address and readdress the protection of freelancers, the most vulnerable and often difficult to define category of workers, will continue to set the agenda for unions and fueled the formation of an alt-labor group, the *Platform voor Freelance Musici* (PvFM) in the Netherlands. The phenomenon of the free concert as a means to showcase new talent became its first cause célèbre after musicians woke up to the fact that performing for free even at such renowned venues as Amsterdam's Concertgebouw Hall was not an appropriate modus for future success as a professional musician. "No pay, no play" became the clarion call for the alt-labor group. Since its first *Facebook* invitational in 2018, the PvFM has attracted more than three thousand members from the ranks of freelance musicians ranging from its core cadre of orchestral musicians to music teachers, vocalists, and most recently spinoffs that include musicians representing other genres. Its trio of aims: to negotiate for better working conditions for freelancers; to increase mutual solidarity among cultural stakeholders and government decision-makers; and to generate societal support for musicians. The collective's leaders join with union representatives at the bargaining table, monitor the actions of orchestral employers and offer support to members on a multiplicity of issues associated with freelance vulnerability such as how to persuade employers to pay within a reasonable timeframe; how to galvanize momentum for fair practice, issues recently codified in the Dutch Fair Practice Code. To reach fair pay for those who play, the true path forward could become a reality if legislation enacted in the name of fair practice was enforceable. In 2022, a consortium of Dutch creatives including the PvFM under the aegis of Platform ACCT[714] subsidized by the Dutch Ministry of Education, Culture and Science has engaged in a series of round table discussions to develop practical tools, including the establishment of salary scales for freelance musicians and additional proposals to strengthen enforcement of fair pay policies.

Breaking news in March 2023 from across the channel brings a dire message to the sector from orchestral colleagues in the UK: the BBC announced plans to slash the salaries of its fully employed orchestral musicians by 20% and cut the distinguished BBC Singers entirely.[715] In a reaction to swift and sharp criticism of the planned cutbacks, the BBC's Head of Orchestras and Choirs commented, "[we] want to be able to work with more musicians, and broadcast from more venues, in all parts of the country. That will mean more opportunities for freelance musicians in our English orchestras, and fewer salaried posts. It's a change that keeps the BBC in line with the industry standard, freelance and salaried musicians working together, but it also realigns us with the founding spirit of the BBC ensembles as flexible performing groups."[716] Adding insult to injury, the BBC musicians learned of the cuts and redundancy plans through social media; no BBC-initiated consultation took place before the announcement hit the headlines. The insinuation of an industry standard in

714. Platform ACCT, Platform Arbeidsmarkt Culturele en Creatieve Toekomst (Platform for a Future Cultural and Creative Labor Market).
715. There are five BBC orchestras; cuts were announced on March 7, 2023, https://www.thestage.co.uk/news/bbcs-plan-to-cut-orchestras-by-a-fifth-devastating-union-warns.
716. Simon Woods' comments, https://www.classical-music.com/news/simon-webb-the-bbcs-head-of-orchestras-and-choirs-comments-on-its-2023-classical-review.

which the employed suffer the loss of one-fifth of their salaries to make way for freelancers in the name of flexibility is preposterous. Formerly fully employed BBC musicians will be forced to replenish lost income by joining a sizeable cadre of freelancers that will result in an even larger pool of vulnerable freelancers. In the current global orchestral marketplace, shrinking opportunities resulting from financial crises and a preponderance of management decisions that forefront efficiency to the detriment of honest employment practices has diminished occupational choices for orchestral musicians in extremis.

Professor Ruth Dukes has convincingly argued in many of her writings that even well-publicized successes at the highest courts will not fill the vacuum of advocacy at the grassroots level. In a paper that brought to the fore real concerns of a particularly vulnerable sector, it is only fair to give the last word to a Dutch *FNV* advocate, "[w]hile many find the *FNV* case to be a landmark and we were pleased after the case was settled in the Hague, we realized that we still had a long way to go—the road to make sure that the playing field is level is long and arduous. The Court limited its findings on the false self-employed to substitute musicians in orchestras. What we really need is more judicial distinction and of course more enforcement of *FNV* principles in the names of all self-employed who deserve protection. We will continue to strive for equality off stage as well as onstage."[717]

717. Conversations with Martin Kothman.

6

A Long and Winding Road: Freelancers in a Tale of Two Countries

Figure 8 A Gig Musician

Source: Author's photo.

Outsourced workers exemplified by Uber/Lyft drivers and Deliveroo food service workers have attained significant media attention in their quest for employee status at the heart of the independent contractor versus employee debate. Their fight for employee recognition has given face and place to the debate concerning the evolution of work, where atypical has become the new typical in the context of accepted modes of employment in the 21st century. Employment patterns in the developed world now mirror the patterns of precarity that traditionally plagued the developing world. Shifting between such world of work terms as "atypical," "contingent," "nontypical," "precarious" and last but certainly not least, "gig" workers abandon those who do this type of work to the whim of nomenclature (*see* Figure 8 for a cynical view of gig musicians' livelihoods). These vague determinations show little regard for the transformative structures of employment that dominate the world of work not to speak of the needs for protection on the part of vulnerable workers.[718]

Although the work lives of freelance musicians bear little direct relationship to outsourced app-dependent delivery workers, both types of workers suffer from similar vulnerabilities and share in a quest for a living wage with "all that frosting on the cake, that good stuff that sweetens the dream of adequate employment."[719] Freelance musicians customarily fashion a portfolio career or what some interviewed refer to less euphemistically as a patchwork career in which musicians will work at different jobs often simultaneously in an attempt to earn a living. These musicians face a precarious and competitive labor market characterized by a diversity of ensembles that contract musical services for varying time periods with varying degrees of call back success. To disseminate the stories told by freelancers in both countries examined, not all orchestras are created equal, and not all gigs are paid at a rate that comes close to a minimum wage. Many freelance musicians are forced to take on underpaid work in the hopes that it will lead to something better, that it will widen their circle of possibilities and lead to improved work prospects. More often than not, the improved prospects are illusory.

6.1 GIG WORKERS IN THE ORCHESTRAL SECTOR

Where does the term "gig" come from? A survey of encyclopedias netted an interesting etymological source moving back in history from the jazz musicians' patois that gave the term so much of its pizzazz since its first usage in the 1930s. One of the earliest chronicled meanings of gig was "a combination of numbers in betting games."[720] For a more exact etymology, music historians point to the swinging 1920s when gig was an acronym for jazzers, jazz musicians, the "cats" who intoned alternatively "God is

718. Contingent workers include those who are independent contractors, who work less than full time, or whose jobs are structured to last only a limited length of time.
719. Conversations with bass gig-master, Buell Neidlinger, former principal bass Warner Brothers studio orchestra.
720. Purportedly dating back to 1847, *see* origins of the term "gig" at, https://www.etymonline.com/word/gig.

Great" when receiving work or, "Git it Going" to raise the musical temperature and rev up the band.[721]

To open the floodgates inherent in an exploration of the asymmetrical nature of freelancing and its dependence on the largesse of employers would be counterproductive to an inquiry that seeks to make things better for gigging musicians. For those looking for a legal solution, regulation and inclusion might offer the key to improving conditions for all workers, whether freelance or fully employed. However, for some freelancers who earn an excellent living by working at will, there is some reticence to support any type of restriction on their freedom to operate. "You might say that our solidarity moves directly towards our pocketbooks, as long as regulation is good for our earnings, we support it. If not, we would rather be as elusive as possible, that is how giggers are, chameleons who move from gig to gig; sometimes present and when the taxman comes around elusive."[722]

6.2 TYPES OF FREELANCE ORCHESTRAL MUSICIANS

In the orchestral vernacular, there are several varieties of freelancers who are called upon to perform side-by-side with contracted orchestral members. Substitute players "on call" replace regular members who have taken ill, or are off on sabbatical, or for that matter, any mutually and contractually acceptable reason for missing work.[723] Another group of freelance players are the extras, the musicians who are called in to augment the complement when the musical score demands extra special musical reinforcement. Extras are vital as performers in massive pieces within the orchestral repertoire that call for a large number of players. To recall, Mahler's Symphony No. 8 *Symphony of a Thousand* mentioned in the *FAQs* is a prime example of an XXL orchestral complement. A performance of George Gershwin's *Rhapsody in Blue* would be unthinkable without a soprano sax and a banjo, instruments not commonly found within the orchestral complement. Much of my research examines the vulnerabilities of freelance substitutes, the musicians who play side-by-side with regularly contracted colleagues in an orchestra. The most vulnerable of all freelance musicians however are those who perform in pickup orchestras with more often than not, a pittance in terms of payment:

> One of the guys I play with is musical director for a small church ...he recruited me to play. My question for those who play these kinds of gigs is whether any of you are getting paid and, if so, what's the general rate. He is paying barely enough to make it worth setup time, but I do enjoy playing ... and it's a church.[724]

721. Retold by famed bandleader, Skitch Henderson, during a Stamford Symphony rehearsal.
722. *Ibid.*
723. Illness, pregnancy leave, other forms of personal leave are the most common reasons to hire substitutes. In the last several decades, it has become common practice to hire substitutes to fill a position left open following auditions if no player(s) is (are) hired when a vacancy is not filled post-audition.
724. https://www.talkbass.com/threads/questions-about-church-gig.1335924/.

6.3 WHAT IS IN A NAME: INTERIM MUSICIANS, EXTRA MUSICIANS, ET AL.

Adding to the external complexity of classifying freelance musicians is the contract-driven internal complexity that differentiates orchestral performers and the benefits they may receive. An examination of a US orchestral collective bargaining agreement (CBA) reveals no less than four categories: "musician"; "interim musician"; "part-time musician" and "extra musician" within the Dallas Symphony Orchestra (DSO). A musician is "a person employed by the Employer as a playing member or Librarian under full contract with the DSO."[725] Two categories are classified by the number of services contracted: "extra musician" performs 64 or more services "not under full contract"[726] and "part-time musicians" are employed for 63 or fewer services per season.[727] It does make sense that the latter two categories are classified as "interim musicians" defined under the CBA as nontenure track members who are "ineligible to receive a contract for a third consecutive Season ... cannot serve on committees but [are] otherwise entitled to all benefits and rights of a Musician."[728]

6.4 HOW DO YOU GET AN ORCHESTRAL GIG IN THIS TOWN?

The lack of a system for hiring substitute players in orchestras relates to different practices within orchestral organizations. To outsiders, the freelance classical music world seems haphazard as the distribution of work does not follow any particular coordinated structure. Perhaps the very nature of a profession centered on public performance calls for a flexible system or lack thereof. "Other professions warrant more control before a replacement employee shows up to work, we often work with a lead time of a few hours, even less if last-minute debacles occur right before a concert. We can't be held accountable for not following a prescribed list: our first priority is to reassure the conductor that an empty seat is filled as soon as possible, the show must always go on."[729]

Substitute wind, brass and percussion players in major orchestras are either known entities, professional musicians who hold jobs in other top orchestras free to perform in their "off" weeks or stellar recent conservatory graduates recommended by leading orchestral players. To confuse matters further, despite officially organized auditions for substitute string players in Dutch orchestras, the list of those who pass any given audition is often not adhered to. "I have won places as a 'remplaçant' in three Dutch orchestras and am still waiting for the phone to ring while one of my closest

725. Section 8.14 CBA Dallas Symphony Association and Dallas/Fort Worth Professional Musicians Association, Local Union No. 72-147 American Federation of Musicians 2015.
726. *Ibid.*, Art. 8.5.
727. *Ibid.*, Art. 8.18.
728. *Ibid.*, Art. 8.11.
729. *Ibid.*

friends from my student days plays regularly in two of those orchestras without ever having gone through the audition process. Why? It's a mystery!"[730]

6.5 PINTUS VERSUS CONCERTGEBOUWORKEST: A FREELANCER CLAIMS EMPLOYMENT

Maria Tiziana Pintus, an Amsterdam-based Italian violinist, received her advanced performance diploma at the Utrecht Conservatory in the early 1990s and became active on the orchestral freelance scene shortly thereafter. Pintus was hired under a series of fixed contracts and took part in all performance-related musical activities: rehearsals, concerts, recording sessions, and tours. Preparation for these musical activities was not compensated: substitute musicians are responsible to be prepared fully by the time the first rehearsal begins. But unlike regularly employed players, substitutes do not benefit from the forfait,[731] nor do they receive pension benefits, instrument insurance and/or holiday payment.

6.6 DUTCH EMPLOYMENT LEGISLATION AND *PINTUS*: CONSECUTIVE FIXED-TERM CONTRACTS

The articles of Dutch employment legislation relevant to the *Pintus* case are found in the Dutch Civil Code (DCC) *Section 7.10.9. End of an employment agreement*. Under the terms set forth in Article 7:667 DCC, an employment agreement is terminated when either the time period that has been contractually agreed upon or the time period agreed upon by law or "common usage" expires.[732] The subsequent Article 7:668 DCC *Tacit continuation of a fixed-term employment agreement* and Article 7:668a DCC *the chain of fixed-term employment agreements* were the deciding factor.

According to Pintus' understanding of the chain of contracts rule expressed in Article 668a DCC, she was legally entitled to proceed from a fixed contract to an open-ended contract starting on March 12, 2002. Several points call for further clarification. First, as a substitute player at the RCO, she had signed contracts with Stichting Remplaçanten van het Koninklijk Concertgebouworkest (the Foundation for Substitute Players Royal Concertgebouw Orchestra, further: RCO Foundation)[733] and not the RCO. Second, the collective agreement for substitute players, the CAO voor Remplaçanten van Nederlandse Orkesten (CBA Substitute Players in Dutch Orchestras),[734] carved out an exemption to the applicability of Article 7:668a in the CAOs Article 3(2) stipulating that Article 668a DCC was not applicable "waardoor in geen enkel geval een arbeidsovereenkomst voor onbepaalde tijd onstaat" (thus without

730. Interview, Dutch freelance string player waiting for a breakthrough, anonymity assured.
731. *Forfait* refers to compensated preparation hours.
732. Author's translation, Art. 7:667 DCC (entry into force January 1, 1992).
733. KCO refers to the Dutch, Koninklijk Concertgebouworkest, whereas RCO refers to the English translation, Royal Concertgebouw Orchestra.
734. In Dutch, Collectieve Arbeidsovereenkomst (CAO) Remplaçanten Nederlandse Orkesten 1 november 2000-31 october 2001, ongewizgd verlengd tot en met 31 maart 2002.

exception [literally: in no case] an employment contract for an indefinite period of time does not exist).[735] Pintus and her legal advisors were of a different opinion based on the nature of the work performed under contract. "Even though we (my legal advisor and I) knew about that exception, we wanted to prove our point that this loophole was simply not fair to orchestral substitutes who perform exactly the same work as the regularly contracted musicians."[736] It is the inner workings and outer applicability of this series of contracts, the duration of the work completed and the differences in performing in a first and/or second violin section that lie at the crux of the litigation. Pintus claimed that her regular freelance work following a fourth employment contract entitled her to a permanent contract.[737] Yet, without winning an audition for a specific first or second violin position, what type of contract would have answered to her claim?

6.7 THE SPECIAL CASE OF VIOLINISTS AS ORCHESTRAL FREELANCERS

For extra insight into some of the motivations behind Pintus' claims, it is important to take note of the difference between the roles she fulfilled within the orchestra. The largest section in the orchestra (the violins) offers the greatest amount of freelance employment per capita based simply on the number of players per orchestra and the chance that tenured violinists may be unavailable for work. In the weeks that she was employed with the RCO, her position as violinist rotated between playing in the first violin section and playing in the second violin section. While both roles call for a high level of professionalism, first and second violin positions are not interchangeable in most professional orchestras. Interestingly, for violinists at the New York Philharmonic, for example, "we are very strict about who gets to play in a string sections with a tradition of freelance substitutes playing in the second violins and our own players, second violinist moving into the first violins if substitutes are called for."[738] With regard to the "interchangeability" of the two positions within the orchestra, the Amsterdam court held:

> The parties disagree about the question about the interchangeability of the functions of first and second violinist. This question is important to the extent that if it must be concluded that these functions are so far apart that the employment contracts with which the performance of this work has been agreed cannot be regarded as a successor to the previous contract, there is no way to arrive at an adequate application of Art. 668a DCC. The Court of Appeal finds that Pintus has worked alternately as first and second violinist in the period indicated under 3.3 iii and on the basis thereof—assuming evidence to the contrary—assumes that both functions are interchangeable to a large extent and that consequently there are subsequent employment contracts. The Court noted that successive employment

735. *Ibid.*, Art. 3(2).
736. Excerpts taken from discussions with Tiziana Pintus and her claim *(Maria Tiziana Pintus/1. Stichting Remplaçanten van het Koninklijk Concertgebouworkest)* Gerechtshof Amsterdam 26 juli 2007 JAR 2007/243.
737. In Dutch, "arbeidsovereenkomst voor onbepaalde tijd," an employment contract of "infinite duration" or "permanent contract."
738. Conversations with Judy Nelson.

contracts could only be refuted if there was a substantial difference between the work agreed in the contracts.[739]

A closer look at what these differences might be and whether or not orchestras equalize the functions is merited.

6.8 ROTATING VERSUS FIXED SEATING VIOLIN SECTIONS

Dutch orchestras do not opt for a system of rotation between sections in contrast to the New York Philharmonic. The violinists who audition for that particular top-tier US orchestra perform first violin parts during their entrance exam. "Violinists hired by major orchestras usually go directly into the second violin section. Our string sections have rotation, so all second violinists actually end up playing in the firsts at some point during every season—all except the frozen players, who sit on the first two stands of the seconds."[740] According to the traditions of the profession in the Netherlands, a violinist auditions for either first or second violin, plays the appropriate section's parts at the audition, and if successful, wins a seat in one of those sections. Although the court did not expressly refer to the difference between the player's functions as a first versus second violinist, Pintus adamantly insisted that the fact that she had worked in two sections was a detrimental factor with regard to gaining fixed employment. "From the employment point of view, I worked in the orchestra for many years as a violinist, my training was to play the violin, certainly not to play the first or second violin. In the context of the law I am wondering, did the section I played in or the chain of sections that I played in matter?"[741] Yet, objectively the question of equivalence is not based on training: first and second violinists in a professional context receive the same training. The difference in positions is found in the score, the notes of the musical parts. To gain any permanent position in an orchestra, to earn the right to play those notes in a protected professional organization, a musician must make the grade at auditions and pass tenure hurdles successfully.

6.9 DEFINING EQUIVALENT POSITIONS TO DETERMINE EQUAL PAY

Under the legal principle of equal work = equal pay enshrined in Dutch jurisprudence, the *Agfa* case[742] and, most particularly, the *Parallel Entry/KLM* case at the highest court (Hoge Raad HR) deserve mention.[743] The latter case concerned differences in seniority benefits between airline flight personnel who worked for KLM City Hopper (KLM's short flight subsidiary company) versus KLM, a fact irrelevant to the divergences between playing first violin versus second violin. What is relevant, however, is the

739. *Pintus* at r.o. 3.11.
740. Former New York Philharmonic concertmaster Glen Dicterow, https://www.latimes.com/archives/la-xpm-2009-may-17-ca-violins17-story.html.
741. Conversations with Tiziana Pintus.
742. *Agfa* HR April 8, 1994, JAR 1994/94.
743. *Parallel Entry/KLM* HR 30 januari 2004 JAR 2004/68.

HR's observation that "even if it must be assumed that employees perform the same work in the same circumstances, without the appearance of any objective justification for a difference in pay, this cannot necessarily lead to the conclusion that these employees should receive equal pay."[744] Thus, it was possible to assume that flight personnel performed different tasks at the two companies. Turning to the relationship between good employer practices[745] and the equal-pay-for-equal-work principle that played a role in *Agfa* 10 years earlier, the court held that unequal pay must be tested against other factors, including the fact that the flight personnel operated under a valid CAO, to determine if the employer was fair. This dalliance to HR cases on equal work might shed light on the strict application of criteria used to determine what constitutes equal work, not to speak of the fact that good employer practice rests upon many criteria.

Another issue important to a correct reading of the *Pintus* case relates to the intention of the employer. Was there any form of intent on the part of the RCO, or its subsidiary, the SRNO to offer permanent work to Pintus? Or, for that matter, does any highly specialized professional organization with defined points of entry (the audition; the trial period) intend to hire a freelance substitute as a permanent member? Could Pintus rely on "stilzwijgend voortzetting" (tacit continuation) of her numerous contracts as a substitute violinist? Employers and certainly the Dutch courts are cautious about the application of tacit continuation in the context of a service contract.[746] Ruling in *Emergis*, the HR held that an employer cannot be held accountable to offer an employee a permanent contract without evidence of an explicit expression to do so.[747] The Amsterdam court held that the series of employment contracts between the Pintus and the RCO Foundation must be qualified as temporary employment contracts. Parties were asked to submit additional information in order to determine the correct amount of payment that Pintus was to receive taking the relevant statute into account. Although she received some remuneration, Pintus was never to perform in the RCO again.

6.10 ALTERNATIVE INTERPRETATIONS TO *PINTUS*: THE POTENTIAL OF PRIORITY VIA ARTICLE 17 CAO REMPLAÇANTEN

Could Pintus at least have claimed some sort of advantage to gain admission into the orchestra by way of a priority audition? An updated version of the CAO Substitute Players contains an article that offers a freelance substitute musician who intends to audition in the orchestra where he/she substitutes regularly the prerogative to play in

744. *Ibid.*, Hoge Raad "ook ingeval op zichzelf moet worden aangenomen dat werknemers gelijke arbeid in gelijke omstandigheden verrichten, zonder dat voor een verschil in beloning een objectieve rechtvaardigingsgrond valt aan te wijzen, kan dit nog niet zonder meer tot de slotsom leiden dat zij een gelijke beloning behoren te krijgen."
745. *Ibid.*, in Dutch: "goed werkgeverschap."
746. *See* ECLI:NL:HR:2007:BA6755 JAR 2007/284, Hoge Raad, 19-10-2007/ C05/333HR.
747. *See* Evert Verhulp's cogent commentary (in Dutch) in *JAR-Verklaard* 14 oktober 2006, 3-4.

the second round.[748] The requirement for the advantage for a substitute player to pass automatically through the preliminary round is that the musician has to have worked a minimum of 50 days with the orchestra.[749] In retrospect, had the 2000 version of the CAO contained such a clause, Pintus would have deduced that if a frequent substitute could gain priority to compete starting in the second round of an audition under a provision of the collective bargaining agreement, it would be logical to assume that the audition, and not the consecutive fixed terms, was the prerequisite for permanent employment.

The court's holding in *Pintus* paved the way for a ministerial exception in the form of a regulation that set the stage to change the treatment of specific groups of special employees regarding the chain of fixed-term employment agreements.[750] "This exception is necessary due to the intrinsic nature of the industry. Thus, it is necessary to perform the work solely on the basis of fixed-term employment contracts, not employment contracts specified as temporary employment contracts referred to in Art. 690."[751] The regulation grants an exception to contracted football professionals, and importantly for the scope of this research, to various categories of performers and employees in the cultural sector. *Section sub e.* reads in relevant part: "the following are designated as positions referred to in Art. 668a(8)(e) Book 7 DCC: substitute players employed by the SRNO or the Dutch Broadcasting Music Center."[752] How the exception will play out at the orchestral workplace remains to be seen, as many freelance substitutes share the concern "although one might think that we gain security through an exception, we fear that our orchestral employers might prefer to switch between freelancers in the large pool of available players than stay true to a core of reliable, long-term players."[753] A freelance substitute player's fear is reinforced by statements made by an orchestra manager who reflected, "this puts us in what might become a difficult place in terms of decision-making as to who we hire and for how long, the personnel issues are tricky to begin with and do not seem to find resolution through legislation."[754]

6.11 *PINTUS* REDUX 2019

The *Pintus* case took on new meaning almost 15 years after Pintus' hopes of permanent employment at the RCO were dashed. Fearful of a significant rise in the cost of hiring

748. COLLECTIEVEARBEIDSOVEREENKOMST REMPLAÇANTEN NEDERLANDSEORKESTEN 1 februari2 019 tot en met 31 maart 2020 Artikel 17, https://www.sfpk.nl/wp-content/uploads/2019/05/cao-remplacanten-2019.pdf.
749. *Ibid.*
750. Regeling van de Minister van Sociale Zaken en Werkgelegenheid van 22 december 2016 tot wijziging van de Regeling ketenbepaling bijzondere functies Staatscourant 2017, 132, in force the day following publication, January 2, 2017, https://zoek.officielebekendmakingen.nl/stcrt-2017-132.html.
751. Article 7:668 DCC para. 8, author's translation.
752. In Dutch: "Remplaçant in dienst bij de door de Nederlandse orkesten opgerichte Stichtingen Remplaçanten of het Muziekcentrum van de Omroep."
753. Conversations with freelance substitute violinist Gideon Nelissen.
754. Conversations with Roland Kieft, former artistic director Hague Philharmonic.

substitute players, the RCO sought to formulate a distinction between the employment relationship of a permanent musician and a substitute player in 2019, showing a complete disregard for jurisprudence and legislation that reinforces the notion of orchestral substitutes as false self-employed: musicians who perform the same duties as their regularly employed colleagues.

The Dutch Minister of Social Affairs and Employment (2017-2022) Wouter Koolmees alluded to the *Pintus* case in his answer to an urgent letter sent by the RCO: "what are the consequences of the *Wet arbeidsmarkt in balans* (WAB) (Balanced Labor Market Act) in specific relation to the employment regime of substitute players hired at the RCO?"[755] In a sparsely researched response, he reflected that in order to answer the question properly, the RCO would have to determine whether the orchestra and/or its Foundation of Freelancers (Stichting Remplaçanten, earlier referred to as the RCO SRNO) engaged in payrolling. Explaining the two requirements to establish payrolling under the law, he underlined:

> Firstly to satisfy the payrolling requirement, the formal employer (hirer) cannot engage in allocation in which selection and hiring are undertaken by the employer. You state in your letter that the recruitment and selection of substitute players are carried out by the Concertgebouw Orchestra (hirer) ... What is key to making a proper determination is the question of whether the RCO's Foundation (SRNO) renders the "employee" exclusively available to the Concertgebouw Orchestra or whether it offers the services of the "employee" to other employers to work under different supervision. If both conditions are met, the conditions of payrolling are satisfied.[756]

The RCO stated that it is the orchestra itself, and not the SRNO, that engages in recruiting and hiring. According to common orchestral practice discussed earlier in this inquiry, the custom at work mandates that certain key musicians, often principal players, recommend substitute players. And, sometimes, orchestras hire substitutes from lists of those who "almost" won a previous audition. "The selection of players should be based on musicianship and 'fit' that can only be determined by musicians, not a Foundation."[757] The RCO emphasized that its SRNO could not be construed as a clearinghouse for musicians; it does not engage in offering services of substitutes/freelancers to other orchestras. Rather, the SRNO is "an intermediary between the orchestral foundation and the part-time players."[758] With regard to the second factor, "exclusivity," the RCO's SRNO allocated freelance musicians solely to the RCO, an exclusive activity by definition.

To answer the crucial question as to whether the RCO's substitute players are entitled to receive the same employment benefits as permanent members of the RCO, the Minister relied on the provisions of the WAB legislation:

> If payrolling has been established, the WAB legislation will have effect as the law equalizes the position of the freelancer and the regular employee. To quote: a

755. RCO brandbrief October 18, 2019, *Epilogue: Appendix 7.*
756. Author's translation, original *see*: *Epilogue: Appendix* 8 Koolmees December 11, 2019.
757. Conversations with Joel Fried, Artistic Director, Royal Concertgebouw Orchestra (2017-2020).
758. *See* RCO brandbrief, Epilogue: Appendix 7.

freelance worker is entitled to the same legal position and employment conditions as employees **in the same or equivalent positions** (In Dutch, gelijkwardige functies) who are directly employed by the hirer. If the position of substitutes is indeed to be seen as a separate function and is therefore not equivalent to that of permanent orchestra members of the Concertgebouw Orchestra, then a derogation in the CAO for substitute players is permissible.[759]

Have we come full circle to the slippery sands of *Pintus* in which the first violin-second violin functions were never specified, or can we infer that freelance substitutes are entitled to the same employment conditions as permanent members? Any musician would comment that the fact of the matter is that indeed, a substitute player is required to blend, join in, and play the same notes at the same time, etc. Yet if the other requirements that lie within an orchestral CAO are taken into consideration, a "permanent member" does have to fulfill other requirements related to their membership in the orchestral organization. Musically speaking, reiterating what colleagues noted in discussions of orchestral tradition, the long-term expectations associated with a tenured musician's performance requirements point to admittedly subjective yet distinctive requirements within the realm of orchestral musical participation.

6.12 AUDITION PRACTICES AND DISGUISED INCOMPATIBILITY: ORCHESTRAL MUSICIANS' SHOWTIME COLLEAGUES

I am not the first, several colleagues met the same fate.[760]

Turning to litigation in which a Dutch musician took on a powerful employer is warranted as it is one of a small number of cases that reached the courts, in comparison to an extensive US-based caseload discussed subsequently.

A keyboard player in his mid-40s, Bernard Goovaerts, enjoyed a busy career performing in the musical ensembles associated with the successful long-run musical productions mounted by Dutch entrepreneur Joop van den Ende's internationally acclaimed production company, Stage Entertainment. Importantly, Stage Entertainment holds a veritable monopoly on musical productions in the Netherlands and exports its acclaimed theatricals worldwide.[761] After performing regularly for over two decades, Goovaerts was not hired (rehired) to perform in a musical, according to his assertions due to discriminatory behavior related to Stage Entertainment's audition procedures. Further, and interestingly in terms of a link to US cases involving discrimination found in other *movements*, Goovaerts claimed that Stage Entertainment was engaging in a recognizable pattern of questionable employer behavior as it

759. *See* Minister Koolmees response *Epilogue: Appendix 8*. Author's translation, above.
760. Goovaerts: "Ik ben de eerste niet, diverse collega's trof hetzelfde lot."
761. On its website, Stage Entertainment provides details concerning its multiple national and international productions https://www.stage-entertainment.nl/shows/musical/.

systematically "traded in" its permanent hires for "flex workers."[762] Stage Entertainment disputed these assertions avowing that the employment contract was terminated due to a "seriously compromised" relationship between Goovaerts and certain production directors. Part of the case revolved around Stage Entertainment's legally unsound dismissal application, which impacted Goovaerts benefits allocated by the Dutch employees' insurance agency (UWV). The specific details of this aspect of the case have been omitted as they do not relate directly to what the court considered to be "culpable actions by the employer with regard to the method of assessing employees during auditions."[763]

As an experienced showtime keyboard professional, Goovaerts took part in the normal procedures to gain a position in Stage Entertainment's many musicals. Conventionally, a "musical supervisor" listens to auditions and chooses his/her preferred musician from among the candidates invited to audition. According to veteran musicians, these lists are often closed lists where a few are invited, and more often than not, excellent performance in one show, especially a musical with a long run (i.e., a great number of performances) guarantees employment in subsequent shows.[764] This description holds for Goovaerts' employment track record as a preferred keyboard player for Stage Entertainment for over 20 years.

Welcome to a new age of music supervisors, "young cats replace the older experienced musicians and need to get their own people on the payroll, sometimes at the expense of really great players."[765] Following company rules, Goovaerts took the audition to take part in *The Lion King,* a musical blockbuster based on the Disney hit film, scheduled for a long run in the Netherlands. To his utter amazement and dismay, the musical supervisor rejected him summarily stating that his style was "jazzy" and not "groove."[766] Goovaerts took the brave step of suing for reinstatement and/or damages. The Hague Court reasoned that the employer was free to choose musicians at will while noting that there is a substantial measure of subjectivity in that decision-making process. Significantly, the court disputed the fairness of the process, observing: "this method of selection, including a subjective assessment deprives the employee of the possibility to prepare for and/or improve, if necessary, which puts him in a disadvantageous and undesirable position."[767] Importantly for the outcome, the court found that an audition conducted in such a one-sided manner was directly related to the denouement of the employment relationship between Goovaerts and Stage Entertainment. Of relevance:

> The manner in which, however, should be such that the result of an audition can be measured in a certain way and that feedback and comparison of the measured factors are possible ... The written statements submitted in that context are also

762. *See* https://uitspraken.rechtspraak.nl/inziendocument?id=ECLI:NL:RBDHA:2018:2361 for Goovaerts in Dutch.
763. *Ibid.,* r.o. 5.6.
764. Conversations with New York-based Broadway musicians and Dutch-based *Soldaat van Oranje* musicians.
765. Conversations with Richard Feves, freelance bassist, Los Angeles studios.
766. *Goovaerts* r.o. 5.12.
767. *Ibid.*

> very short, not specific and do not provide any clarity regarding the rejection. It was precisely that short rejection based on subjective elements that formed the basis for the disturbed relationship, which is largely attributable to the employer.[768]

Taking Goovaerts' distinguished and unusually long track record as a Stage Entertainment employee into consideration, as well as his diminished chances, or better put, nonexistent chances for further employment, the court ordered Stage Entertainment to pay a transition allowance, "an equitable remuneration for gravely culpable actions"[769] totaling just under €80,000.

6.13 FREELANCERS IN A TALE OF TWO COUNTRIES: BACK IN THE USA

One of the many reoccurring questions that freelancers in both jurisdictions pose is: "should we care about our status, isn't it more important just to go about getting gigs?" The short answer, a resounding yes backed up by legislation and case law in the US, the Netherlands, and the EU underlines the fact that employee status is certainly desirable. Under US law, the rights of an employee include the NLRA-protected rights to form a bargaining unit, paving the way to collective bargaining, to flesh out terms of employment and additional benefits/protection. Workers who are classified as independent contractors do not share in these protections, as they are considered to be of equal standing to the employer, another "agent" in a free-market conception of workers.

The previous section showcased a Dutch freelancer's attempt to gain employment. On the other side of the Atlantic, National Labor Relation Board (NLRB) decisions that show little consistency have impacted the musical workspace for the most vulnerable category of orchestral musicians. This section narrows the focus to musicians who work as freelance substitute players in US orchestras and their attempts to litigate in order to mitigate precarious employment situations.

6.14 HISTORY AS A GUIDEPOST

The brief historical inquiry that follows is centered on the US experience in coming to grips with worker classification. To contextualize classification in the case of orchestral musicians, it is vital to gain an understanding of some of the most important legal and regulatory battles in broader employment contexts. Formulae developed by administrative agencies, US courts and the NLRB point to a variety of paths to establish worker classification. In the interest of reaching consensus on appropriate and stable regulatory treatment, it is paramount to examine these paths. This *movement* also gives pride of place to cases that center on musicians working at the most precarious end of the orchestral musician spectrum: the orchestral musicians who perform in per-service,

768. *Ibid.*, r.o. 5.13.
769. In Dutch: "Het musicalbedrijf heeft ernstig verwijtbaar gehandeld."

regional orchestras. We will discover how different courts and NLRB panels have come to different conclusions in classifying these musicians as independent contractors or more desirably, employees when assessing parallel facts. While Dutch jurisprudence and regulatory frameworks have moved toward an acceptance of orchestral substitutes as false self-employed workers, the same workers in the US fall within a regulatory grey zone. It is important to note that while the European (and Dutch) focus has centered on side-by-side musicians, performers who play alongside regularly employed musicians, many of the US musician-related cases discussed in the pages to follow center on a different type of orchestral musician: the professionals who perform in per-service, regional orchestras. We aim to open our inquiry by giving priority to orchestral musicians' worker classification in an area in which legal norms and rules are still evolving.

6.15 US WORKERS' RIGHTS IN THE PRE-NLRA ERA

To opine that workers' rights are redefined through the responses of courts and legislatures due to a synthesis of economic, political, and social factors borders on cliché. A journey back to a 40-year stretch at the cusp of the 20th century (1897-1937) conveys deeper insights into an incongruous zone between employers and employees to expose the push and pull between individual and corporate economic-related activities. The state's regulation of social rights adds relevance to this brief historical reflection as we come to grips with flexible/gig workers' present-day vulnerabilities.

During the *Lochner* era, SCOTUS struck down well-nigh two hundred federal and state laws in the realm of employment legislation. "The doctrine that private commercial activity should be confronted with a minimum of public interference"[770] not only influenced the courts but also swayed legislative policy. This turbulent period in US labor law history revealed the substantial extent of influence peddling by the elites, industrialists, and early-day US robber barons who feared the force of the union to empower workers. Although the facts of *Lochner v. New York* (1905)[771] relate to a particular subject matter, its impact shaped the lives of working Americans for decades. In short, Joseph Lochner, the owner of a small bakery in upstate New York, was fined $50 for requiring an employee to work more than 60 hours per week. On appeal, Lochner challenged the constitutionality of the Bakeshop Act 1897 (the Act) because it violated the right of employers and their employees to exercise genuine "liberty of contract": "to make contracts regarding labor upon such terms as they may think best, or upon which they may agree."[772]

Resting on the established doctrine of a legitimate exercise of state powers to benefit the people, the State of New York, representing the employee, stressed that the Act was construed to alleviate the common practice of forcing workers to work 12-hour days, 7 days a week. The impact of *Lochner* was as swift as it was far-reaching:

770. William Finley Swindler, *Court and Constitution in the Twentieth Century: A Modern Interpretation*. Bobbs-Merrill 1969, 37.
771. *Lochner v. New York* 198 US 45 (1905).
772. *Lochner*, at 54.

legislation in support of any form of redistributive justice for workers met with judicial wrath. Legislation prohibiting anti-union "yellow-dog" contracts in which future employees were required to sign an oath that they would not join the union as part of their employment contract was struck down by the conservative SCOTUS majority in 1915.[773] A minimum wage law to level the wage playing field for women working in Washington D.C. suffered a similar fate in 1923; SCOTUS held that a wage board to monitor the payment of minimum wages restricted the individual's right to freely contracted labor.[774] Referring to *Lochner* as the "whipping boy" of judicial misguidance, Ronald Dworkin noted, "[t]he stench ... does not lie in jurisdictional vice or judicial overreaching ... The vice of bad decisions is bad argument and bad conviction; all we can do about those bad decisions is to point out how and where the arguments are bad."[775]

6.16 THE NLRA: THE TIDE REVERSES

History in the form of crisis, the dreadful economic downslide following the stock market crash of 1929, was to reverse the *Lochner* tide. In the midst of the Great Depression, New York Senator Robert F. Wagner and a noteworthy cohort of congressional colleagues penned the National Labor Relations Act (NLRA), referred to in much of the literature as the Wagner Act. Establishing a legal framework for collective bargaining and a wealth of union activity, the NLRA reflected an attempt to mitigate the democratic deficiency in industrial America that was crumbling under the pressure of economic stagnation and the iron grip of *Lochnerian* policies. To quote its preamble, the Act articulates a large step forward to achieve "industrial peace." The impact of the Great Depression in which unemployment averaged 20% in the 1930s, and farms and factories lay fallow, fostered a belief that recovery could only take place if massive reforms including labor reform took a prominent place on the national agenda; collective bargaining formed the core of these reforms.[776] A legislative antidote to *Lochner* coupled with an attempt to balance the power between worker and employer, the NLRA reshifted national policy and heralded a move toward reinforcing union power. Of particular importance regarding the establishment of worker's rights, NLRA § 7 authorizes:

> Employees shall have the right to self-organization, to form, join, or assist labor organizations, to bargain collectively through representatives of their own choosing, and to engage in other concerted activities for the purpose of collective bargaining or other mutual aid or protection.

773. *Coppage v. Kansas* 236 US 1 (1915).
774. *Adkins v. Children's Hospital* 261 US 525 (1923).
775. *See* Ronald Dworkin. Dworkin, Ronald. "Pragmatism, Right Answers and True Banality" in *Pragmatism and Law* Michael Brint and William Weaver (eds.) Westview Press 1991, 359.
776. Although a full discussion of the sociopolitical and economic impetus leading to the NLRA goes beyond the scope of this research, these two sources provide a good point of departure: Mark Barenberg "The Political Economy of the Wagner Act" 1993 and Ellen Danni, "NLRA Values, Labor Values, American Values." *Berkeley Journal of Employment and Labor Law* 26 2005.

As set forth in NLRA §8, unfair labor practices include any interference with the formation or administration of a labor union, any form of discrimination against employees who aspire to union membership, refusals to bargain collectively with the legally recognized employee representatives, and any attempts to interfere with the administration and/or formation of a labor union at the workplace.

The National Labor Relations Board (NLRB), established under the NLRA, is the principal administrative and adjudicative organ for the NLRA. At the very top of the NLRB's administrative pyramid, a three-member board appointed by the President, with Senate approval, oversees the administrative, economic, legal, publication, and trial divisions. The NLRB has the authority to resolve disputes about the scope of a bargaining unit as well as the claims of unions to representation. Accordingly, the Board has the power to "certify" a particular union as the "exclusive representative" of a bargaining unit's employees. The Board's General Council heads the legal division whose trial examiners and administrative law judges (ALJs) are to quote SCOTUS "functionally comparable" to US District Judges.[777] To ensure that the NLRA would be adhered to across a substantial jurisdictional space, regional offices of the Board were established to investigate and prosecute unfair labor practice claims in their specific geographic district. Politics at the core of NLRB appointments will pass muster in the context of several cases under scrutiny, further on in the *movement*.

Tomes have been written on the consolidation of union power and the increase in worker's rights as reflected in legislation and jurisprudence post-NLRA enactment.[778] Union membership, measured by union density rates, grew from just over 13% to 34.7% from 1935 to 1955.[779] Early NLRA jurisprudence reflects the push and pull of New Deal industrial relations. Importantly, the labor contract solidified rules to govern the workplace. Getting to "yes" in those contracts became a struggle between employers and unions, with the latter wielding power through the threats of work stoppages and strikes. The stage was set for amendment.

6.17 THE TAFT-HARLEY BACKLASH

Within less than one year from the annus horribilis of widespread strikes (1946), a strong, anti-labor backlash gained political and legislative power. Although President Truman voiced his strong support for union protection, politicians in both houses of Congress penned a bill to correct runaway union powers that had their legal base in the NLRA. With the passage of the Labor Management Relations Act 1947, commonly referred to as the Taft-Hartley Act (THA), several core NLRA tenets were "rectified": workers holding managerial and supervisory functions were barred from NLRA protections, and the "right to work" initiated by the THA gave states the power to

777. *Butz v. Economou*, 438 US 478, 513 (1978).
778. *See* Ellen Danni, *supra*.
779. Michael Goldfield. *The Decline of Organized Labor in the United States*. University of Chicago Press 1992, 10, Table 1.

outlaw union shop clauses and the "right to refrain" from the NLRA's Section 7 rights to "self-organize."[780]

6.18 WHO IS AN EMPLOYEE UNDER THE NLRA?

NLRA §2 (3) specifically excludes "any individual having the status of an independent contractor" from NLRA protection raising the question as to who is responsible for ascertaining the status of an individual or group of individuals as independent contractors or employees. In its consideration of multiple factors leading to a final assessment, the NLRB has opted for a case-by-case analysis, as the weight linked to a factor shifts from one case to another.[781] Ultimately, in 2001, the Board, backed by court approval, determined that the party claiming independent contractor status holds the burden of proof.[782] In an interesting twist at the state court level that clarifies the issue as to whether the description or labeling of a worker as an "independent contractor" could be a factor in final status determination, the United States District Court for the Northern District of California held that "the determination of independent contractor or employee status is a determination of fact and that the label the parties place on the relationship is not dispositive."[783]

Many questions come to mind when considering the tests, factors, and deliberative points that courts and NLRB use to reach decisions on worker status.[78429] Yet, with an increase in factors, still, no 100% watertight consensus has been reached. Is it possible to posit that language including the "language of the law" is too limited to provide a "one size fits all" formulation to answer to the variety and nuance of employment-related cases? And, to complicate matters further, different administrative entities rely on different tests: the all-important US tax administration service, the Internal Revenue Service (IRS), relies upon a 20-factor evaluative test to evaluate "employee" versus "independent contractor" status for payroll and withholding tax purposes.[785]

6.19 DIVERSE DEFINITIONS AND TESTS TO ESTABLISH THE EMPLOYMENT RELATIONSHIP

In the US, courts have grappled with defining "employee" devising several tests to come to grips with the status of workers "in the borderland between employers and

780. Taft-Hartley, §14(b) 29 US Code § 164(b).
781. *BKN, Inc.*, 333 NLRB 143, 144 (2001) citing *Roadway Package System*, 326 NLRB 842, 850 (1998).
782. *BKN, Inc.* and further at the court level, *NLRB v. Kentucky River Community Care Inc.*, 532 US 706, 710-712 (2001).
783. *Besag v. Custom Decorators, Inc.*, N.D. Cal. February 10, 2009, No. CV08-05463 JSW.
784. 29 USC § 152 Definitions.
785. The IRS 20-factor test https://www.irs.gov/businesses/small-businesses-self-employed/independent-contractor-self-employed-or-employee.

non-employers"[786] and to extend the former SCOTUS Chief Justice Wiley Blount Rutledge's description, the "borderland" between workers, employees, and quasi-employees in a changing landscape marked by the rise of the 'self-employed.'[787] Commentators have put forward that "the law is in a complete state of disarray with regard to the definition of employee."[788] US courts have devised tests to aid in defining "who is an employee" with a theory of dependency as a point of departure. Employees are dependent on the employer they "serve," while an independent contractor's work is primarily involved in his/her own business. The complications built into this characterization will be elaborated upon in the cases that follow. The four most commonly applied tests are the common law agency test, the statutory purpose test, the economic reality test, and unsurprisingly, a "combination" test referred to as "the hybrid test." Several of these tests will be discussed with specific regard to their application in cases involving orchestral musicians.

6.20 EMPLOYEES ACCORDING TO THE RESTATEMENTS (SECOND AND THIRD)

While not considered to be a binding source of law, the American Law Institute's Restatements of Law are strong secondary sources that summarize leading cases and put forth trends in black letter law based on a broad selection of cases and subjects. No less a legal light than Benjamin Cardozo noted:

> It will be invested with unique authority, not to command, but to persuade. It will embody a composite thought and speak a composite voice. Universities and bench and bar will have had a part in its creation. I have great faith in the power of such a restatement to unify our law.[789]

Richard Posner and fellow proponents of the Law & Economics line of thinking along with Critical Legal Studies advocates are highly critical of Restatements, as in their opinion, this "source" does not take the interdisciplinary nature of law-in-action, and its intersections with economics and public policy, into consideration.[790] Scholarly critique notwithstanding, courts across the US, from the Supreme Court to the lower courts, take the Restatements seriously and frequently rely on their persuasive authority.

The Restatement (Third) of Agency § 7.07(3) stipulates that "[a]s a general matter, a hired party is the employee of the hiring party when the hiring party controls

786. Chief Justice Rutledge delivered the opinion of SCOTUS in the influential case *NLRB v. Hearst Publications., Inc.*, 322 US 111, 121 (1944).
787. Terms such as "bogus self-employed," "fictive self-employed" and "fake self-employed" have been put forth by courts in the US and Europe.
788. Mitchell N. Rubinstein. "Employees, Employers, and Quasi-Employers: An Analysis of Employees and Employers Who Operate in the Borderland Between an Employer-and-Employee Relationship" *University of Pennsylvania Journal of Business Law* Spring 2012.
789. The eminent Benjamin Cardozo opined with optimism concerning the powers of Restatements in: *The Growth of the Law* 1924, 9.
790. *See* Richard A. Posner. "The Problematics of Moral and Legal Theory" *Harvard Law Review* 111 1997, 304-307.

(or has the right to control) the manner and means of the hired party's performance of work. The fact that work is performed gratuitously does not mean that the hired party is not an employee." In contrast, a hired party is an independent contractor when she "is not controlled by the other nor subject to the other's right to control with respect to his physical conduct in the performance of the undertaking."[791] The benchmark to consider is the amount of control the employer/hiring party exerts over the work of the party who has been hired. The term "independent contractor" was eliminated in the Restatement (Third) of Agency:

> The common term "independent contractor" is equivocal in meaning and confusing in usage because some termed "independent contractors" are agents while others are nonagent service providers. The antonym of "independent contractor" is also equivocal because one who is not an independent contractor may be an employee or a nonagent service provider.[792]

6.21 THE US DEPARTMENT OF LABOR (DOL) RESTRICTIONS TO THE DEFINITION

As leading US practitioners have observed, "an increasing number of US federal and state government agencies led by the Department of Labor (DOL), are heavily invested in restricting the use of independent contractors and increasing the number of workers classified as employees. Some jurisdictions have limited application of the traditional "right to control" test, which looks primarily to the degree of control exerted or retained by the company to determine if a worker is an employee. Many courts have relied on a more expansive "economic realities" test, which looks at multiple factors, including whether the work is integral to the business, the worker's opportunity for profit and loss, the relative investments of the company and worker, the permanency of the relationship, and the company's degree of control. Under this test, the ultimate question is whether the worker is economically dependent on the company (an employee) or is in business for him or herself (an independent contractor)."[793]

To add to the categorization protocols used by courts, several states have adopted what is arguably the most difficult standard to overcome: the "ABC" test, which presumes an individual is an employee unless the employer can prove the worker's autonomy and independent nature of services in a three-prong test (*see* **A-B-C** below).

(1) **A**bsence of control: does the worker perform tasks independently?
(2) **B**usiness of worker: does the worker engage in specialized tasks?
(3) **C**ustomarily engaged: does the worker have his/her own business identity? Does the worker rely mainly on one employer?

791. Restatement (Second) of Agency § 2(3).
792. Restatement (Third) of Agency § 7.07(3).
793. Discussions with US attorneys summarized here, https://www.skadden.com/insights/publications/2016/01/restrictions-on-use-of-independent-contractors.

6.22 DIFFERENT STROKES FOR DIFFERENT FOLKS: THE FLSA

Sifting through the main legislative acts that set forth the employment relationship of workers in the US is a tricky business, as different acts bring forth different standards needed to reach employee status, with a confusing amount of variation between the various acts. For example, the Fair Labor Standards Act (FLSA), the US legislation that provides minimum wage and overtime wage regulations originally promulgated in 1938, provides a wide, remarkably circular definition of the term "employee": "an individual employed by an employer."[794] It also contains the requirement that an employer-employee relationship exists for a worker to be covered by the Act's provisions, which require employers to pay minimum wage and overtime wages to employees who work a minimum of 40 hours a week.[795] Leaving the door open to the courts and Congress to fill in their own interpretations as to who is an employee with its remarkably circular definition of "employee," the FLSA sets specific requirements for minimum wage, overtime and other standard work-related regulations.[796] Under the FLSA, the verb "employ" is defined somewhat archaically as "to suffer or permit to work."[797]

With a modicum of wit and savvy, legal scholar Richard Carlson delves into the problems of using a verb-based definition in the statutory quest to define "employee" in an article bearing the droll title, "Why the Law Still Can't Tell an Employee When It Sees One and How it Ought to Stop Trying."[798] Taking the reader on a detailed voyage through reams of jurisprudence since the enactment of the NLRA where SCOTUS, lower courts and Congress attempt to define "employee," he reaches the conclusion that "the borders of any test of employee status are destined to remain forever vague."[799] Noting that the courts offer holdings to answer to specific situations, Carlson joined by a chorus of international scholars calls on legislators to draft basic rules of coverage for **all** workers regardless of status.[800]

Judicial interpretation with regard to worker status has led to a great deal of uncertainty and disagreement. Is employee status, the exclusive domain for coverage, the soundest manner to determine statutory coverage? In the best of all scenarios, Carlson contemplates, with hope, that workers would best be served if Congress and the states exercised their powers on behalf of workers' rights. However, considering the politics of such legislation, are his hopes realistic? Neil Komesar's comparative institutional analysis theories presented through the lens of property law in a pair of thought-provoking books could provide guidance along a thorny path of definition:

794. *See* Fair Labor Standards Act 29 US Code § 203.
795. *Ibid.*, 29 US Code § 206.
796. *Ibid.*,§§ 201-219, establishes minimum wage, overtime pay, recordkeeping, and other standards affecting employees in the private sector and in federal, State, and local governments. *See* https://www.dol.gov/whd/flsa/.
797. *Ibid.*, §203 (g).
798. *See* Richard Carlson "Why the Law Still Can't Tell an Employee When It Sees One and How it Ought to Stop Trying." 2001.
799. *Ibid.*, 368.
800. For example, Miriam Cherry, Matthew W. Finkin, and Breen Creighton to mention a few scholars who focus on the subject of worker classification.

Komesar returns time and time again to underline the notion that real rights deserve more than flimsy, en passant solutions. Many argue that the different definitions of employee, not to mention exclusion from NLRA coverage, have encouraged conflicting court and board decisions.[801]

SCOTUS brought several factors to the fore to separate employees from independent contractors under FLSA, recommending the economic reality test. Under FLSA, the courts have examined the issue of misclassification by applying the economic realities test and making case-by-case determinations as to whether the workers are employees and thereby covered by the Act. To test the relationship between "worker and boss," the courts underlined the importance of considering the entire activity within a broad reading of work, not merely isolated factors.

6.23 NLRB TESTS TO DEFINE EMPLOYEES

Although the NLRA grants employees the rights to organize and bargain, there are limits as to who can benefit from these rights. The scope of the NLRA is open to determination by the NLRB, which has held that there is a difference between employees who are protected by the Act and independent contractors who are excluded from the protections of the Act. Furthermore, to benefit from the Act, there must be a recognized group of workers, a defined "nexus" in employment terms and conditions common among employees to avail themselves of NLRA stipulated rights. The community of interest test applied by the NLRB to determine the commonality necessary to form a group relies on factors: the degree of interaction among the job titles in the proposed bargaining unit, the management structure at the workplace, and the location at which the employees work. Without this shared commonality, the NLRB will not allow union representation elections to take place. The NLRB determined a formula to delimit the eligibility of part-time employees to form a bargaining unit in *Davison-Paxon*.[802] According to the original *Davison-Paxon* formula, a part-time or on-call employee must meet the requirement of four or more hours of work per week for a three-month period to demonstrate "a sufficient regularity of employment to demonstrate a community of interest" with employees who are part of the employee bargaining unit, unless "special circumstances" exist.[803] These circumstances, often widespread in many variations within the entertainment industry, prompted the creation of other eligibility formulae (*Juilliard* and variations):

> **29 CFR § 103.2: Symphony orchestras**
>
> The Board will assert its jurisdiction in any proceeding arising under sections 8, 9, and 10 of the Act involving any symphony orchestra which has a gross annual revenue from all sources (excluding only contributions which are because of

801. *See* Neil Komesar. *Imperfect Alternatives—Choosing Institutions in Law, Economics, and Public Policy 1994 and Law's Limits—The Rule of Courts, the Rule of Law and the Supply and Demand of Rights*. Cambridge University Press 2001.
802. *Davison-Paxon* 185 NLRB 21, 24 (1970).
803. *Ibid.*

limitation by the grantor not available for use for operating expenses) of not less than $1 million.[804]

The case law developed by the NLRB on the composition of the bargaining unit has revealed a flexible approach to eligibility standards for freelance musicians in their quest for employee rights. The intermittent nature of their employment was not an obstacle, but on the contrary, a key to resolution in a series of leading cases. The eligibility standard first set out in the mid-1970s in *Juilliard*[805] shows a strong pro-union bias with its inclusive eligibility standard. The case centered on the bargaining rights of intermittently employed theater workers at the famed Juilliard School of Music, a renowned educational institution that offers top training to highly skilled young musicians. Such leading *Juilliard* facts as the type of work, the amount of control and supervision the employer exercised over its workers, and the infrequency of "call backs" parallel several orchestra-related cases to be considered in the pages to follow.

6.24 HOW ARE TEMPORARY EMPLOYEES DEFINED IN CASE LAW? *JUILLIARD* SETS THE TONE

In *Juilliard*, a central argument to support the temporary workers' hopes to form a bargaining unit was that these skilled workers could rely on a reasonable expectation of reemployment for another "temporary" term. A bargaining unit is a key component within the collective bargaining process as it delimits the group of employees included within the unit, the specific group of workers entitled to union representation. Here, and in other parallel cases, the temporary employees were hired on a defined date, yet the termination of their employment had not always been stipulated contractually. The workers in *Juilliard* could be categorized as ultra-contingent: stagehands and other experienced backstage theater professionals with a varied history of regular employment. While some of the workers were hired for a mere two productions per annum, they relied on this employment year after year. Interviews with freelance musicians hired to work as temporary employees in US regional orchestras attest to similar expectations and similar employment patterns as the plaintiffs in *Juilliard*. To prove reliance, the *Juilliard* Board examined the level of "repetitive" employment:

> The record shows that many of these employees work for periods of time which indicate repetitive employment, and which permit them reasonably to anticipate reemployment in the near or foreseeable future. The Employer hires from the same labor market and some of these "per diems" work for as long as 35 weeks. Although it uses no rehire list, we find that the Employer makes a practice of hiring employees who are experienced with the facilities at Juilliard and have proven through past performance their capacity to perform their job functions.[806]

804. NLRA 29 USC. §§ 151-169 Section 8 Unfair Labor Practices; Section 9 Representation and Elections; Section 10 Prevention of Unfair Labor Practices.
805. *The Juilliard School* 208 NLRB 153 (1974).
806. *Ibid.*, at 154.

In the entertainment industry, where employees are often hired to help on a day-by-day or production-by-production basis, the Board found that the irregular patterns of employment presented a special circumstance warranting deviation from the *Davison-Paxon* formula. Under *Juilliard,* a widened notion of employment was advanced: workers who perform in two productions for a minimum of five days in one year, or a minimum of 15 days in two years, should be granted access to the benefits of union organization and collective bargaining.

When employees are temporary or seasonal, however, the Board devised alternative formulae calculated to take the special conditions that are inherent to the field of theatrical employment to heart. Citing an obligation to study the particular facts of a case before making a determination as to which formula to use, the Board has shown its creativity in developing variants on the *Davison-Paxon* theme. In one of those variants, the Board emphasized the importance of ascertaining whether workers show a "reasonable" expectation of being hired by the employer in the future. In *American Zoetrope,* the Board underlined the importance of their independence to develop a formula "compatible to our obligation to tailor a general eligibility formula to the particular facts of the case."[807] Further, the Board opted to limit the voting benefits to workers who "average four or more hours of work per week during the quarter preceding the election eligibility date."[808] The *Juilliard* flexible deviation from *Davison* received additional confirmation beyond the music-related sphere from the landmark *Trump Taj Mahal* decision.[809] Expanding on the *Juilliard* standard to embrace intermittent workers in the entertainment sector without an ongoing employment contract, the NLRB reiterated in *Trump Taj Mahal* that *Juilliard* afforded freelancers a benchmark that: "permits optimum employee enfranchisement and *free choice* (emphasis added by the author) without enfranchising individuals with no real continuing interest in the terms and conditions of employment offered by the employer."[810]

6.25 *FLORIDA GULF COAST SYMPHONY* PLAYS A CONSERVATIVE TUNE

In the *Florida Gulf Coast Symphony* case in 1980, freelance musicians employed by the orchestra were found to be independent contractors. The court relied on the common law test to demonstrate that these musicians earned more than two-thirds of their income from sources beyond the control of the orchestra.[811] Additionally, the musicians' distinct occupation placed them within the context of independent contractors, and their employer paid them on a per-service basis. Most importantly, the musicians were free to pursue other sorts of work: "[a]s to the interdependent relationship that exists between petitioner and musicians, we agree that the services of musicians

807. *American Zoetrope Productions, Inc. v. Association of Film Craftsmen* 207 N.L.R.B. 621 (1973).
808. *Ibid.*
809. *Trump Taj Mahal Casino* 306 NLRB 294, 296 (1992).
810. *Ibid.*
811. *Florida Gulf Coast Symphony v. Dep't of Labor & Employment Sec.,* 386 So. 2d 259 (Fla. App. 1980).

constitute work. Although this element is persuasive, it is not inconsistent with the interdependent relationships which may exist between a principal and an independent contractor."[812] The veracity of such an observation rests upon the availability of musical work in that particular geographical area, and, as a leading musician who has worked in the successor orchestra of the Florida Gulf Coast Symphony noted, "many fine musicians in this area compete for a small amount of quality work in the classical music profession. Free to pursue other sorts of work is a demeaning way to intimate that those musicians should supplement their income with more lucrative employment."[813]

6.26 *OGUNQUIT* UPHOLDING *JUILLIARD*: HOW FAR SHOULD THE TEST REACH TO DESIGNATE UNUSUAL EMPLOYMENT PATTERNS?

In *Ogunquit*, the Board applied *Juilliard* to a small group of musicians who performed in two musical productions in two seasons at a summer stock theater in Maine.[814] Of the 28 musicians hired in the 2008 and 2009 seasons, most performed in only one or two shows, and approximately half of the musicians had been rehired in 2009. Widening the eligibility for workers to "gain free choice,"[815] the Board expanded further upon its interpretation of the eligibility test first developed in *Davison-Paxon*. The NLRB Regional Director relied on the time-honored Restatement test to ascertain whether freelance musicians were employees or independent contractors in *Ogunquit Playhouse*.[816] The Board found that the musicians' risk of employment loss was too minimal to confer independent contractor status; the "unusual" employment features at the playhouse merited a departure from *Davison-Paxon*. Operating on a seasonal summer basis, alternative eligibility for a union representation protocol was called for as the playhouse operated for 21 weeks yearly. The Board developed minimum criteria under which musicians who had worked for two productions during the previous two seasons were eligible to participate in union activity.

6.27 DEVIATING FROM JUILLIARD: STEPPENWOLF THEATER C.,

To ascertain whether a deviation from *Davison-Paxon* is warranted, the critical consideration is the employment pattern resulting from the total number and incremental length of the employer's stage productions. In *Steppenwolf Theatre Co.*,[817] the

812. *Ibid.*
813. Conversations with Mary Corbett, violinist in the Florida Gulf Coast Symphony's successor orchestra, the Florida Symphony.
814. The term "summer stock" refers to summer season theater companies. The *Ogunquit* theater offered musicals from late May to early October.
815. *Trump Taj Mahal Casino, supra*.
816. *Ogunquit Playhouse Foundation and Boston Musicians' Association, A/W American Federation of Musicians Local Union* No. 9-535 1-RC-22423 (Reg. Dir. Dec. and Direction of Election, March 11, 2010).
817. *Steppenwolf Theatre Co.*, 342 NLRB 69,71 (2004).

Board examined the degree to which the theater relied on different categories of workers including permanent staff as well as per diem employees who worked during the theater's long season. The theater mounted 14 productions each season, equivalent to 500 performances in a 48- to 50-week season. The Board concluded that the theater operated like a regular employer; its musicians and staff members were deemed to be employees. Even though the freelance musicians employed by Steppenwolf Theater were seasonal, they could demonstrate a community of interest with fellow theater unit employees, the group of production staffers who held permanent employment contracts. The NLRB took the stance that the strict requirements of *Davison-Paxon* applied, abjuring the more relaxed *Juilliard* standard.[818] The NLRB held that "an employee is deemed to have a sufficient regularity of employment to demonstrate a community of interest with unit employees if the employee regularly averages four or more hours of work per week for the last quarter prior to the eligibility date."[819] Thus, for entertainment industry employees who work on a regular, year-round basis, the standard *Davison-Paxon* formula was favored.

A similar focus on the frequency of employment led to the affirmation of employee status in *Columbus Symphony Orchestra*. During the 2002-2006 seasons, the orchestra operated for 46 weeks on a regular performance schedule, averaging over 170 concerts per year. Such an employment schedule contained the regularity needed to achieve the coveted status, and thus, the musicians were employees. Once again, the NLRB bowed to the "spirit" of free choice within the entertainment industry, in which a group of employees who work infrequently and show strong evidence of an irregular pattern of employment could constitute a collective bargaining unit.

6.28 KANSAS CITY REPERTORY THEATRE INC.: THE NLRB MITIGATES JUILLIARD

An analysis of *Juilliard*'s progeny highlights the NLRB's interest in giving freelance musicians the safety net provided by employee status. Turning to a group of "on call" freelance musicians in *Kansas City Repertory Theatre Inc.*, the NLRB majority found that the musicians formed a unit. Under the *Juilliard* doctrine, although the musicians are temporary employees who work intermittently, they shared a community of interest that leads to employee status:

> The spirit of Juilliard allows for the optimum employee enfranchisement and free choice that is sought by the Board in just this type of case: an entertainment industry employer with a group of employees who, but for an irregular employment pattern, would otherwise constitute an appropriate unit for the purpose of collective bargaining.[820]

818. *Davison-Paxon, supra.*
819. *Ibid.*
820. *Kansas City Repertory Theatre Inc.*, 356 NLRB No. 28 (2010) at 8.

But was *Juilliard* correctly applied in *Kansas City*? The answer lies in a further analysis of "who" the workers were. The *Juilliard* workers were mainly "rehires"—workers asked to return because of their familiarity with the theater and the demands of the job. Successful "past performance" played a significant role in the rehiring process. In the case of the freelance musicians in *Kansas City*, there is no proof that the same musicians returned as rehires, as these freelancers were deemed to be "more itinerant" than the *Juilliard* workers. The *Kansas City* musicians would show up when work became available. Under the NLRA's requirements for a legitimate bargaining unit, would these "itinerant" musicians share in the "legitimate bargaining interests of the regular employees"? Or were their interests short-term, sporadic like the nature of their work? Taking another tack, perhaps the court was interested in supporting all workers regardless of the irregularity of their work. As discussions with freelance musicians have illuminated, "we care deeply about every aspect of our employment and most certainly, the terms and conditions on-the-job."[821] Temporary employment, the gig story, continues to pose a paradox for courts seeking an appropriate formula of determination with regard to NLRA-related rights to unionize and collectively bargain.

6.29 NEW DEVELOPMENTS, THE ON-DEMAND US CASES: IMPACT FOR ORCHESTRAL MUSICIAN STATUS?

Can we make a case for classifying freelance orchestral musicians as employees based on court decisions in an increasing number of US-based cases related to the "on-demand" economy? After all, a freelance musician is the original "gig" economy worker: the specific term "gig" has been deeply embedded in the music profession since the 20th century. US courts have flip-flopped[822] as to whether orchestral musicians are self-employed independent contractors or employees entitled to receive benefits and file class-action suits. And, in the US, the debate concerning the misclassification of workers has intensified, from the halls of government and courts to the main streets of public debate fueled by frequent media reports. An analysis of relevant cases and tests to determine employee status will follow the more direct answer to the second question. Simply put, the determination of "employee" opens the door to a wealth of economic and social benefits under legal regimes that include pensions (Social Security Act), minimum wage, and FLSA. As the cases below show, determination follows increasingly complex tests, some set forth through a judicial process, others set by agencies. The Internal Revenue Service (IRS) uses a "common law control test" consisting of 20 factors with a strong focus on the employer's level of "control over the employee."

Before examining relevant legislation and leading cases, the precedent-setters that shape the course of further judicial decisions, it is important to consider the crucial

821. Conversations with Kristin Linfante, successful US-based freelance violist.
822. In US politics, a term used since the Nixon era with reference to an ideological U-turn. William Safire waxed eloquent on the sources of the "flip-flop" during a Yale College seminar attended by the author.

issue of policy, politics and how changes in political stripe can influence the very definitions of terms such as "employee" and "independent contractor." Reporting on changes during the first months of the Trump Administration in 2017, Department of Labor (DOL) insider David Weil, author of the telling, *The Fissured Workplace: Why Work Became So Bad for So Many and What Can Be Done To Improve It*,[823] reports that a guidance document that provided clear definitions to help employers avoid the pitfalls of misclassification was discredited by President Trump's minions at the DOL. The press release, dated June 7, 2017, announced:

> **WASHINGTON**—US Secretary of Labor Alexander Acosta today announced the withdrawal of the US Department of Labor's 2015 and 2016 informal guidance on joint employment and independent contractors. Removal of the administrator interpretations does not change the legal responsibilities of employers under the Fair Labor Standards Act..., as reflected in the department's long-standing regulations and case law. The department will continue to fully and fairly enforce all laws within its jurisdiction, including the Fair Labor Standards Act.[824]

On the one hand, it is possible to argue that the retraction is not worthy of concern. After all, the press release clearly states that such removal does not "change legal responsibilities" under legislation and legal precedent set by SCOTUS case law. It is the issue that rises to the fore, on the other hand, that raises uncertainty.

6.30 THE ECONOMIC REALITIES TEST

On July 15, 2015, the DOL's Wage and Hour Division issued guidelines on the economic realities test, giving credence to the observation that a majority of America's workers who fall within the grey zone of "independent contractors" would be deemed to be employees. Of paramount importance according to the 2015 DOL analysis is that no single factor should be taken as dispositive; all factors should be considered in relation to one another to engender a "qualitative" instead of a "quantitative" analysis:

(1) The extent to which the work performed is an integral part of the employer's business.
(2) The worker's opportunity for profit or loss depending on his or her managerial skill.
(3) The extent of the relative investments of the employer and the worker.
(4) Whether the work performed requires special skills and initiative.
(5) The permanency of the relationship.
(6) The degree of control exercised or retained by the employer.

823. Head of the US Department of Labor's Wage and Hour Division under President Obama, May 2014-January 2017. For Weil's theory on the "fissured workplace," *see*, https://hbr.org/2017/03/making-employment-a-fair-deal-in-the-age-of-contracting-subcontracting-and-temp-work.
824. *See* https://www.dol.gov/newsroom/releases/opa/opa20170607.

6.31 SHARING IN THE SHARING ECONOMY? *UBER*, *DYNAMEX* AND BEYOND

In the central battleground of independent contractors versus employee status, the on-demand companies epitomized by Uber and Lyft, in which customers and service providers are linked through smartphone apps, have engendered increasingly acrimonious regulatory battles at federal and state agencies and led to a spectacular number of cases in the United States.[825] The circuit split on the status of Uber drivers is reflected in the problematic delineation as to who is an employee in the sharing economy sector.

In a round of Uber-related decisions emanating from the United States District Court of Northern California,[826] Judge Edward Chen upheld the plaintiffs' class-action status. A major victory for the entire "class," his holding potentially permits approximately 240,000 California-based Uber drivers to bring their claims in front of a jury. In January 2017, SCOTUS granted certiorari to address a trio of cases that center on how the interaction between the Federal Arbitration Act (FAA) and the National Labor Relations Act (NLRA) impacts the enforceability of class- and collective-action waivers in arbitration agreements. The future of the Uber cases is uncertain until the court decides on the future of employers relying on waivers.

Framing the central question in its certiorari petition, the NLRB inquired:

> Whether arbitration agreements with individual employees that bar them from pursuing work-related claims on a collective or class basis in any forum are prohibited as an unfair labor practice under 29 USC. § 158(a)(1), because they limit the employees' right under the National Labor Relations Act to engage in "concerted activities" in pursuit of their "mutual aid or protection," 29 USC. § 157 and are therefore unenforceable under the saving clause of the Federal Arbitration Act, 9 USC. § 2.

Of relevance to the Uber cases and incumbent issues of classification is the claim in the 2016 Ninth Circuit case *Ernst & Young LLP v. Morris*.[827] In *Ernst*, the respondent Morris maintained that the well-known accounting firm *Ernst & Young* had violated the FLSA through a deliberate misclassification of employees resulting in the withholding of overtime wages. On appeal, the Ninth Circuit court, commonly regarded as the most liberal of the US Courts of Appeal, held that *Ernst* was in violation of the NLRA. The plaintiff-employees had been required to sign a concert action waiver that precluded their rights to enter into a class-action suit and were required to file separate arbitration proceedings in case of a dispute. According to the Ninth Circuit, if a waiver mandated such separate proceedings, it violated not only the intrinsic nature of the plaintiffs' claims but also the object and protective purpose of the NLRA.

---

825. Uber was involved in more than 70 federal lawsuits in US courts in 2016.

826. US District Court Northern California *O'Connor v. Uber Techs.*, Inc., F. Supp. 3d, 2015 WL 1069092 (N.D. Cal. 2015); *O'Connor v. Uber Techs., Inc.*, No. 13-cv-3826-EMC, 2014 WL 1760314 (N.D. Cal. May 2, 2014); *Mohamed v. Uber Techs., Inc.*, F. Supp. 3d 2015 WL3749716 (N.D. Cal. 2015).

827. *Morris v. Ernst & Young LLP* No. 13-16599, 2016 WL 4433080 (9th Cir. August 22, 2016).

6.32 A STEP BACKWARD: *LEROHL* LEAVES MUSICIANS IN THE DARK

In *Lerohl v. Friends of Minnesota Sinfonia*, two musicians fought dismissal by bringing gender and disability claims against their employer, the Minnesota Sinfonia.[828] The Sinfonia was an ensemble entirely comprised of freelance musicians. The case revolved around the central question of whether the pair of freelancers could be considered employees or independent contractors in an ensemble that was by its very nature, part-time and freelance. Citing the element of control as key to a status determination, the court did not consider "control" to be a key factor that determines the conductor's authority over the orchestra, nor did the court find that the Sinfonia's control of scheduling and other performance-related matters was sufficient to hold that the Sinfonia exerted considerable control over its musicians. Perplexing but true, the court opted for an interpretation in which control does not refer to how the workplace controls the musician, but rather, the amount of control freelance musicians retain to accept freelance work in other venues. The court placed a high degree of persuasive authority in a factor that previous courts tended to gloss over: the Minnesota Sinfonia did not deduct withholding taxes, a fact that the *Seattle Opera* court found irrelevant to the employee versus independent contractor debate.[829]

To freelance musicians actively pursuing careers in the here and now, this interpretation is incomprehensible as "control" beyond the workplace bears no relevance to what really goes on during rehearsals and concerts. Although the court showed some realization of the difficulties inherent to taking a decision with regard to an unfamiliar set of professional circumstances such as those encountered by freelance substitute orchestral musicians, their decision-making certainly provided no music to any listener's ears, rather a cacophony of chaos.[830] Yet, instead of considering the *Seattle Opera* decision in terms of the majority finding, the *Lerohl* court opted to take heed of Circuit Judge Randolph's sole dissenter view as detailed above.[831]

6.33 *LANCASTER* TO THE RESCUE

In the waning days of 2011, the NLRB held that musicians playing for community orchestras in three states, Pennsylvania, Massachusetts, and Texas, were employees, not independent contractors. The musicians of the Lancaster (PA) Symphony Orchestra took a brave step pinning their hopes on the benefits of union membership: the regional, part-time orchestra with a small core of "regulars" contacted the local union to start the procedure. The orchestra's management resisted, maintaining that the musicians were freelancers, independent contractors who did not meet the requirements of employment under US law.

The Regional Director's first instance decision in *Lancaster* was based on a weighing of factors that the orchestral musicians shared with independent contractors.

828. *Lerohl v. Friends of Minnesota Sinfonia* 322 F.3d 486 (8th Cir. 2003).
829. *See Seattle Opera, supra.*
830. *See Lerohl, supra,* here the court cites both *Darden* and *Reid.*
831. *Ibid.*

The amount of personal control freelance musicians maintain over their work schedules à la *Lerohl* and the fact that musicians are highly skilled professionals who themselves provide the tools of their trade to perform the tasks required within their employment as performers swayed the pendulum in favor of independent contractor classification. In a 2-to-1 decision in *Lancaster*,[832] the Board reversed the Regional Director's decision that the orchestra's musicians were independent contractors, remanding the case back to the regional board for action.

Both the NLRB and the Circuit Court relied heavily on the significant amount of control the orchestra exerted on the way in which musicians' performance at the workplace is controlled. Several examples, starting with the conductor's power to determine how musicians perform the score is a strong expression of control. "Musicians participating in an orchestra are, by necessity, subject to the control and scheduling of the conductor because such control allows the symphony to perform as a single unit."[833] Further, the court noted that the orchestra, as controlling employer, requires musicians to give their full attention, to "be attentive" throughout both rehearsals and performances, to show respect by not "crossing their legs" or conversing with one another during rehearsals, thus enhancing the notion of employer control. While the outside world might take this to be unusually strict and authoritarian behavior, the musicians do not see it as an example of unusual control but as a normal part of the status quo of expected behaviors in rehearsal. Even at the onset of the rehearsal, musicians are expected to keep quiet, and as the court noted, reprimands are in order if a musician leaves her chair to talk to a colleague (even if the conversation relates to the music). The orchestra's meticulous specification of the ensemble's concert dress code was interpreted as another example of "strict control." Although musicians have some control over their work by choosing whether or not to bid on programs, "once they are selected to work in relation to a particular program, the musicians' control over their work time ends." The Board noted that the orchestra management exerts significant control over the musicians: it sets work hours, payment schedules, dress codes, and standards of musician conduct during rehearsals and concerts.

In its consideration of entrepreneurial opportunity factors key to the independent contractor status, the *Lancaster* court found that, beyond the confines of their employment, the symphony's musicians were free to engage in teaching activities and attempt to find random freelance work such as church service work and wedding gigs. However, unlike the freedom associated with deputy players in the UK (the musicians could not deputize fellow musicians to replace them if they had to miss a concert), no recruitment opportunities existed whatsoever. The court concluded that although the musicians could avail themselves of "limited entrepreneurial opportunity," they did not gain additional meaningful work because of their particular employment with the symphony, a point that tipped the scales in favor of "employee." On appeal at the Washington D.C. Court of Appeals, the court opted for the Restatement factors that

832. *Lancaster Symphony Orchestra and the Greater Lancaster Federation of Musicians, Local 294 AFM 357* NLRB No. 152.
833. *See Lerohl, supra.*

inspired what came to be known as the "economic realities test" seminal within the determination in the high-profile *FedEx case*.[834]

Board member Brian Hayes' dissent provides food for thought. Applying a multifactor analysis, Hayes argued that his colleagues on the Board erred by basing their judgment on an incorrect assessment of relevant factors. He also asserted that the factors that swayed the decision were of insignificant relevance to the bigger picture of orchestral employees working for the Lancaster Symphony. In Hayes' opinion, the central question in the case was "whether the musicians retain discretion to accept or decline to work with the employer and to play elsewhere." Concluding that freelance musicians hold that freedom meant that they could in theory work for multiple employers and take or reject jobs at will. Thus, freelance musicians demonstrate entrepreneurial characteristics that are part and parcel of the definition of an independent contractor. Considering the job opportunities for freelance classical musicians within a 100-mile radius of Lancaster, he concluded that the musicians were able to expand their work opportunities to reap the benefits of working as professional musicians in "nearby" cities including the mid-sized metropolises Allentown, Harrisburg, and Philadelphia.

On appeal in *Lancaster*,[835] the United States Court of Appeals for the Circuit of the District of Columbia scrutinized the NLRB decision. In a King Solomon-esque "share the wealth" ruling, the court acknowledged that although the "relevant factors point in different directions" and both sides brought sound, albeit "conflicting," positions to the fore, deference was shown to the NLRB's decision. To reach the fragile tipping point favoring "employee" status, the court reapplied the 10-factor test that had been recently put forth in two leading cases related to delivery services.[836] This limited entrepreneurial opportunity, however, provides only minuscule support for independent contractor status; the Lancaster musicians could only increase their gig income by accepting jobs with other employers, scarce at best in the greater Lancaster area. And, according to the court's reasoning, if the musicians opted to renege on a Lancaster Symphony performance contract, they would effectively have shut down their opportunity to earn a living as a musician. Had this quite minor entrepreneurial opportunity been given much weight, it might have engendered an almost automatic classification of many part-time workers as contractors. Yet as the Board explained, "[p]art-time and casual employees covered by the Act often work for more than one employer."[837]

On the one hand, control was construed as a regulatory factor that allowed the musicians little leeway for personal opinion or action. According to testimony and the contractual obligations signed by musicians, the conductor exercised virtually "dictatorial control" over the musicians in terms of how they play, at what volume, and pitch. Furthermore, the orchestral management exercised great control over the musicians in terms of scheduling but also in minute details concerning "where and what they

834. *See FedEx Home Delivery v. NLRB* 563 F3d 492.
835. *Ibid.*
836. *See FedEx Home Delivery, supra*; *Corporate Express Delivery Systems v. NLRB* 292 F.3d 777 D.C. Cir. 2002.
837. *Lancaster, supra.*

played, whether they could cross their legs, their posture and even what they could talk about during rehearsals. Work was part of the orchestra's regular business."[838] On the other hand, the relatively short period of real employment was taken into consideration: the orchestra engaged the musicians for a very short time period, in the relevant case, a mere 140 to 150 *hours* per calendar year. The agreements signed voluntarily by the musicians allowed them to work for all or part of the concert season without employment repercussions. Ostensibly, the musicians exercised some sort of entrepreneurial freedom as they could accept other music-related work, for example, devoting time to teaching activities or accepting itinerant, occasion-based gigs such as playing at private parties and community events.

6.34 TWO UNPUBLISHED NLRB DECISIONS UPHOLD *LANCASTER*

Lancaster is not a stand-alone case; the NLRB issued parallel decisions in cases involving regional orchestras in other areas of the United States. Interestingly enough, in two unpublished decisions issued the following day, citing *Lancaster*, an NLRB Board held that the musician members of the *Cape Cod Symphony* (Massachusetts) and the *Plano Symphony Orchestra* (Texas) should be categorized as employees.[839] The freshly settled *Lancaster* case was cited as the leading precedent, as the same analysis was used to determine employee status.

Taking a closer look at a freelance/gig musician's work life, do *Lancaster* and the related *Cape Cod* and *Plano* decisions provide fair precedents within the sector? We could argue that musicians are free to take the work they accept, or, of course, turn down. Musicians traditionally use their own instruments to perform, with the possible exception of orchestral pianists who rehearse and perform on instruments provided by the employer. Should this factor apply to the orchestral professional, would there be a classification difference between the orchestral violinist and the orchestral pianist? Should this factor into the equation of the "independent contractor" line of argumentation?

Quo Vadis? As the only two federal court cases about the status of orchestral musicians, *Lerohl* and *Lancaster* leave the orchestra in dissonance as to what the status of musicians might and even should be. Admittedly, the *Lancaster* court mentioned the discrepancy between the two decisions presenting two main reasons for differentiation. First, *Lerohl* was a discrimination case, while *Lancaster* was an employment definition case. Second, the standard of review (*see de novo* above) was different in the two cases. Do economies of scale play a role in an evaluation? Major orchestras, from the US top-tier to the BIS orchestras in the Netherlands, offer (or in the case of Dutch

838. *Ibid.*
839. Board member Brian Hayes referred to *Lancaster* in his next-day *Cape Cod* determination, "Consistent with my dissent in *Lancaster Symphony Orchestra*, 357 NLRB No. 152 (2011), I would grant the Request for Review, reverse the Regional Director, and find that the symphony orchestra musicians are independent contractors. Thus, I find it unnecessary to address the other issues in this case."

orchestras, used to offer) competitive salaries, paid vacation weeks, and other important benefits. However, unionized regional orchestras, from the ROPA members in the United States to the quickly decreasing number of Dutch regional orchestras, bargain for contracts at significantly lower pay scales than the top-tier ensembles and enjoy fewer benefits. Managers and freelancers at the lower end of the pay scale have opined that the "employee" status significantly increases the financial burden on the smaller orchestras. Is it possible to validate such arguments? Inevitably, to deny the musicians protection as employees would legitimize a race to the bottom. Yet, if orchestras are faced with the terrible dilemma of closing down or continuing with less, which option is actually the best? How do musicians respond at the end of the juridical day?

6.35 *FIDDLEHEAD* JOINS IN TO PLAY THE SAME TUNE AS *LANCASTER*

A regional board's 2016 decision in *Fiddlehead*, regarding musicians who performed intermittently at a Boston-based theater, played the same tune as *Lancaster*.[840] Fiddlehead, the name of a theater company, not a reference to a stringed instrument, revolved around the issue of whether musicians who worked temporarily were entitled to the full array of NLRA's entitlements or whether these musicians were independent contractors. To support the assertion that the musicians were in fact independent contractors, the company brought four factors to the fore:

(1) Musicians were hired and performed on a show-by-show basis; those hired for one show were not necessarily employed at subsequent shows.
(2) Musicians are highly skilled workers.
(3) Musicians supply their own tools, instruments.
(4) Musicians were contracted at a flat fee per-service rate for rehearsals and performances as differentiated from a weekly or monthly salary.

The NLRB's Regional Director, however, weighed the factors differently, holding that the musicians were in fact employees, relying heavily on a different set of factors, namely:

(1) The employer exercised recognizable and substantial control over the details of the musicians' work.
(2) Musicians had negligible input with regard to rehearsal and performance schedules.
(3) Musicians were required to follow a company-established dress code.
(4) Musicians did not have the potential for entrepreneurial gain based on their relationship with the theatre company (*Fiddlehead*) that had employed them.

840. *In the Matter of Fiddlehead Theatre Company, Inc., and Boston Musicians Association et al.*, Case Number 01-RC-179597 (July 26, 2016).

At the ideal end of the employment spectrum, orchestral musicians, whether freelance or employed under CBAs, *should* be eligible for the benefits and protections of federal and state laws. And, to receive these benefits, musicians, including all categories of contingents, should be recognized as employees, not independent contractors. It appears as if the NLRB espoused this all-embracing, pro-labor stance in the Obama and other Democratic presidential years. Indeed, the regional board decision reflected the Obama administration's oft-stated desire to expand NLRA protections to an expanded pool of workers previously shut out. However, drifting to a devil's advocate stance, the question arises: does the fact that the common law factors used to determine whether a worker is an employee are not weighted add to the politicization of Board findings? Is it not possible to posit that, had the *Fiddlehead* et al., boards considered the first four factors as superior evidentiary aspects of a gig musician's working life, the musicians would have been excluded from the NLRA?

The NLRB, the IRS, and the DOL rely on their own sets of factors, adding to the complexity of how to reconsider the already complex work and work relationships in the 21st century. As can be expected of workers within the cultural sector, freelance musicians do not tick all the boxes, nor do they fit uniformly into the prescribed categories. Courts and government agencies developed these categories to serve other classifications of workers. Pundits in the music business were worried about the direction board decisions would take as President Donald Trump's NLRB took shape. This raises the question as to whether the DOL and NLRB's expansive stance in favor of employees during the Obama years does justice to the peculiar and precarious freelance musician world. Depending on how the analysis is shaped, freelance orchestral musicians' work shows elements of employment and elements of independent and entrepreneurial contracting. Considering the all-important and leading factor, control, the balance should weigh in the favor of the musician as employee because a theatrical and/or orchestral organization directs all the terms of employment, from scheduling and attendance requirements to performance dress codes.

The political nature of presidential discretion in appointing NLRB members bears repetition, as it led to the overruling of the 2014 *FedEx Home Delivery* case referred to in regard to *Lancaster* above. Briefly, resulting from President Trump's pro-employer, anti-labor appointments at the NLRB, the pendulum swung back from freelance-workers-as-employees protected under the NLRA to precariously unprotected workers, as the *SuperShuttle* case illustrates.[841] The *SuperShuttle* Board determined that the business opportunities afforded to franchise shuttle bus driver-owners granted van operators the chance to generate revenue, even in the face of SuperShuttle's substantial control over the franchise agreement and the noncompete clause limiting franchisees from seeking and taking work at similar companies. Critics found that the comparison of SuperShuttle drivers to genuine entrepreneurial opportunists was unsubstantiated.

841. *SuperShuttle DFW, Inc., and Amalgamated Transit Union Local 1338* No. 16-RC-010963 (January 25, 2019).

6.36 THE IVIES WEIGH IN ON EMPLOYEE STATUS

At Yale and Columbia Universities, two prestigious Ivy League universities where doctoral students have become increasingly vocal with regard to "employee" status, graduate students are of the opinion that the "doctoral students" assist faculty.[842] Their teaching responsibilities, according to Yale sources, take up approximately one-sixth of their time and are a part of their rigorous academic training.[843] Graduate students do not pay tuition and are remunerated with annual stipends (depending on the university, approximately $32,000) and health insurance benefits. The principle that graduate students are indeed students who hold an academic rather than economic relationship with the educational institution was upheld in the much-discussed *Brown University*[844] case where the NLRB held that this particular group are not employees but "primarily students and have a primarily educational, not economic, relationship with their university."[845] At both universities, graduate students protested many aspects of their subordinate status including their right to unionize.

In an amicus brief submitted by nine leading US colleges and universities,[846] the academic institutions distinguished between public and private educational institutions. The argument advanced: "[although the] economic model of graduate assistant service may well be true in the public sector where restricted public funding forces institutions to value the per capita cost of educating undergraduates and where doctoral candidates are not granted the level of support characteristic of preeminent private sector research universities."[847]

Significant to freelance orchestral musician cases, a closing question in *Columbia* is of interest: "If the Board concludes that graduate student assistants, terminal master's degree students and undergraduate students are statutory employees, what standard should the Board apply to determine whether they constitute temporary employees?"[848] Ivy hopes ran high that the Board would be sympathetic to the universities' contention that granting employee status would be impractical in an academic setting, where the time limit of employment is traditionally understood as the graduation date.

The Board overruled *Brown University*, determining that graduate students are indeed employees who hold the right to unionize. Turning to the temporary nature of employment that could have provided a bar to exclude student assistants from

842. Although the term "graduate students" is used to denote the category of "students" seeking employment status, doctoral students is more appropriate for the category as master's degree students are also "graduate" students.
843. Information gleaned from a conversation with Karen Peart, Yale Office of Public Affairs & Communications: opac@yale.edu.
844. *Brown University* 342 NLRB (2004).
845. *Ibid.*, at 487.
846. Brown University, Cornell University, Dartmouth College, Harvard University, Massachusetts Institute of Technology, University of Pennsylvania, Princeton University, Stanford University, and Yale University joined to submit the brief on February 26, 2016.
847. *The Trustees of Columbia University in the City of New York and Graduate Workers of Columbia–GWC, UAW* Case 02-RC-143012 *Brief of Amici Curiae*, 20.
848. *Trustees of Columbia, supra.* 2 (4).

employee status, the NLRB rejected the university's assertion that the finite nature of the employment was determinative for status. Rather, the Board considered that, even if the master's and undergraduate student assistants' positions were comparatively short in tenure, these groups held a "community of interest with the unit or their ability to engage in meaningful bargaining." The "critical nexus between an employee's temporary tenure and the determination whether he shares a community of interest with the unit employees" as underscored by a 2003 precedent was the deciding factor.[849]

Relying on *Kansas City* as a point of departure, the Board underlined that it had never ruled out the inclusion of temporary employees from the Act. "The logical consequence of the Employer's argument is that temporary or intermittent employees cannot exercise the rights vested in employees by §9 of the Act. However, no such exclusion appears in the definition of employees or elsewhere in the Act."[850] The sole dissenter, Philip Miscimarra, who was soon to become President Trump's nominee for NLRB Chairman, raised the specter of disruption. In his opinion, if students were permitted to unionize, the potential for strikes and lockouts would "wreak havoc" on their education.[851]

Contemplating the wealth of NLRB cases with a locus within the orchestral arena, most have pointed toward a wide interpretation of employee, granting that status to musician-workers in the plethora of cases discussed here. Yet, taking the politically sensitive nature of the NLRB into consideration, the triumph for musicians as employees is certainly not memorialized in black letter law. To quote the ever-astute Kevin Case, a legal expert in the field of US orchestras, "such determinations are made on a case-by-case basis, however, and can ebb and flow with the political winds depending on which presidential administration appoints the five Board members of the NLRB who adjudicate cases under the NLRA."[852]

6.37 *WANG*: VARIATIONS ON A THEME WITH A JOINT-EMPLOYER ELEMENT

A 2016 NLRB decision regarding musicians who performed intermittently at a Boston-based theater Wang (WTI) transposed *Juilliard* into yet another key.[853] Like *Juilliard* and *Kansas City*, *Wang* revolved around the issue of whether or not a freelancer who performs services intermittently "on call" at a theater is an independent contractor or an employee able to benefit from NLRA entitlements. Citing both aforementioned cases to establish the special eligibility test for irregular employment, the NLRB Board

849. Quoting *Marian Medical Center* 339 NLRB 127, 128 (2003).
850. *Ibid.*, citing *Kansas City, supra*.
851. *Ibid.*, dissenting opinion Philip Miscimarra.
852. Posted in Kevin Case's enlightening blog *Bargaining Notes* http://www.caseartslaw.com/CAL/2019/11/28/festivals-behaving-badly/?fbclid=IwAR1Q_CLBhvmOA-WotY3XUtKP3OYdelNMS1iMbxmCDXdD64n1qx6hq5G0TP.
853. *The Wang Theatre, Inc. d/b/a Citi Performing Arts Center and Boston Musicians Association, a/w American Federation of Musicians Local Union No. 9-535, AFL–CIO* Case 01–CA–179293, November 10, 2016.

(Region 1) was consistent in its support of employment status for "on call" freelancers, no matter how irregular their employment patterns seemed to be. WTI argued that the irregularity and unpredictability inherent to freelance work engenders a situation in which different musicians perform for each and every performance, thus obliterating any notion of a pattern of stable work. Basing their decision on *Juilliard* in which, as a memory refresher, a mere two productions for a total of five days over a one-year period or 15 days in two years was the baseline to establish employment, the Board found that it was precisely this "special circumstance," this unpredictability and lack of regular income characteristic of entertainment industry employees, whose "irregular employment patterns" that needed rectification. The small group of 17 freelance musicians should suffer a denial of the benefits afforded by NLRA protection "simply because they have not worked in a year."[854]

Beyond the aforementioned points, *Wang* marks an interesting variation within the context of musicians' employment cases in terms of a theater's control and responsibility with regard to freelance musicians hired to perform. Customarily, the show's producer, not the theater, is deemed to oversee all employment-related issues, most importantly hiring and firing. If the local union and musicians sought bargaining rights, the theater was not the sole employer. At best, a case could be made for a joint-employer relationship between Wang and the individual producers of the shows presented. The Board disagreed, citing precedent that was based on *Wang* and the erstwhile 2004-2007 bargaining agreement with the very same union that sought to *reestablish* bargaining rights for the musicians who were hired to perform at the theater.[855]

6.38 THE SUPERVISORY-MANAGERIAL EXCLUSION

As reiterated in the brief survey of NLRA history above, the US Congress sought to protect workers' rights by granting them the right to "self-organize," join and assist in the formation of labor organizations and bargain collectively with the aid of representation. Indeed, the 1935 NLRA had lofty ambitions with its expansive definition of "employees." We have seen how politically motivated follow-up legislation and SCOTUS has whittled away at that definition. In a sharply focused article written in 1949,[856] Robert Leaner points an accusing finger at the court for denying certiorari in *Foreman's Association*, a case that focused on the "third arm" of US labor, the supervising "foremen" in the 1940s.[857] According to Leaner, the THA and the recasting of "employees" broke the powerful Foreman's Union (FAA) and weakened industrial relations significantly post-WWII.

854. *Ibid.*
855. *Ibid.*
856. Robert D. Leiter. "Supervisory Employees and the Taft Hartley Law." *Southern Economic Journal*, 1949, 311-320 DOI: 10.2307/1054128.
857. *Foreman's Association of America v. L. A. Young Spring & Wire Corp.*, 21 LRR 168 in response to *L. A. Young Spring & Wire Corp. v. NLRB* 163 F. 2d 905 1947.

"Foremen unionized because they saw the necessity of doing so. Although some industries were achieving advances in wage scales and improving conditions, the spread between production workers and foremen was narrowed as gains by supervisors lagged behind. When it became clear to the subordinates, they turned to collective bargaining. A large number of employers bitterly resisted organization of their supervisors."[858]

In 1947, taking heed of what Polanyi would dub "neo-liberal dystopia" and the demands of "big" business, the previously discussed THA was passed. To reiterate, the THA not only excluded supervisors from the definition of "employee" but also changed the NLRB's two-part requirement that a supervisor *both* direct the work of other employees *and* perform another stated function to permit direction alone to suffice for supervisor status.[859] Thus, in one fell legislative swoop, workers who had enjoyed the protection of the NLRA lost their power to unionize and bargain collectively. The NLRB and US courts have grappled with the definition of "supervisor," and excluded many categories of employees along the way ever since.

Turning to the category of orchestral musicians, the question arises as to whether certain sub-categories in an orchestra, namely principal players and/or section leaders, fall within the "employee" or "supervisor" category. In recent years, some US orchestras have experimented with joint management-musician committees, variations on the theme of works councils and codeterminative labor-management paradigms, taking inspiration from their European counterparts.[860]

Does this departure from the classic US industrial labor-management model impact the status of these musicians as employees under the NLRA? In 1975, "[f]rom the Rochester Philharmonic Orchestra, usually a source of harmonic strains of Mozart or Sibelius, comes the dissonant chord of a labor dispute" relating in part to the "supervisor" question.[861] Much of the case in which a conductor purportedly attempted to dismiss musicians essentially focused on the union's attempt to organize. It provides a clear reference to the "reservoir doctrine" that was set aside in the *Florida Power & Light* decision in 1974.[862] The rationale of that doctrine is that supervisors are a "reservoir of manpower available and likely to be chosen" to take on eventual leading positions as collective bargainers or grievance adjusters:

> The conclusion is thus inescapable that a union's discipline of one of its members who is a supervisory employee can constitute a violation of § 8(b)(1) (B) only when that discipline may adversely affect the supervisor's conduct in performing the duties of, and acting in the capacity as, grievance adjuster or collective bargainer on behalf of the employer.[863]

858. *See* Robert Leiter, *supra,* 313.
859. Karl Polanyi. *The Great Transformation*. Beacon 1957.
860. Discussed at some length in the *FAQs*.
861. *NLRB v. Rochester Musicians Assn.*, 514 F.2d 988, 922-993 (CA2 1975).
862. *Florida Power & Light Co. v. I. B. E. W. Local 641* 417 US790 (1974).
863. *Ibid.*

Since the demands inherent to "union discipline" could affect the supervisor's loyalty to the employer, the employer would be restricted in his choice of future representatives.

6.39 JURISDICTIONAL STANDARDS APPLICABLE TO SUPERVISORS IN ORCHESTRAS

Leading cases revealing circuit splits and NLRB cases (a 2006 lineup for starters) that turn on the definition of "supervisor" will pass further review. An added variance in the typology of employer-employee relationships in the orchestral world brings other NLRA-related questions to the fore. In 2016, a principal player from the then-locked-out Saint Paul Chamber Orchestra (SPCO) took on an additional position as senior artistic director with that organization.[864] One of the most noteworthy orchestral venues in terms of experimental models of labor organization, the SPCO may well have taken its novel appointment from the pages of European orchestral history where shared supervisory/performing positions are not uncommon.

Reacting swiftly, the AFM moved to file charges with the NLRB against the SPCO for unlawful interference with a labor organization. Is this NLRA employment "edifice" still standing for musicians employed in the United States in light of the "supervisor" exclusion and this recent SPCO issue? And further, do interpretations of the NLRA uphold the Act's original and lofty goals: to level the employer-employee playing field, to bring equality into the employer-employee relationship? Or are courts' interpretations of the NLRA contributing to its demise?

In *NLRB v. Kentucky River Community Care Inc.* (*Kentucky River*), the Board's attempt to lend a categorical exception to 12 registered nurses (RNs) at a community nonprofit mental health care facility failed to convince SCOTUS.[865] The NLRB argued that nurses-as-clinic-subordinates act in the interest of the patients, and not the employer. In a close (5-4) decision, SCOTUS decided against the NLRB. The court was particularly critical of the Board's assertion that employees do not use "independent judgment" if their employment calls upon technical decisions in order to direct subordinates to perform services. The NLRB was ordered to realign its test for ascertaining the supervisory status of workers who rely on professional or technical judgments in directing less skilled workers. Dissenter Justice Stevens vociferously disagreed with his colleagues, warning that this decision could bar professionals from the right to organize:

> Thus, under the Court's view, it is impermissible for the Board to attach a different weight to a nurse's judgment that an employee should be reassigned or disciplined

864. The SPCO announced on its website, with effect 2013-2014 season "Kyu-Young Kim, principal second violin of the SPCO as well as the orchestra's Senior Director of Artistic Planning, is one of the most versatile and accomplished violinists of his generation. His appointment as the SPCO's head of artistic planning marks the first time an SPCO musician has served in a senior management role." At present, Kim has been promoted to SPCO's Artistic Director in January 2016 https://content.thespco.org/people/kyu-young-kim/.
865. *NLRB v. Kentucky River Community Care Inc.*, 532 US 706, 721 (2001).

keeping in mind that the reason to keep supervisors beyond the reach of the NLRA was to circumvent any possibility of a conflict of interest engendered by the supervisor's authority to take action on colleagues within the same bargaining unit. In 1994, SCOTUS exacerbated the situation in a case that deeply divided the court: *NLRB v. Bell Aerospace Co.*[875]

As explained in the *FAQ movement*, the conventional orchestral structure consists of a "three-legged stool"[876] in which a nonpaid board of directors (or trustees), CEO (or President) and music director all play important roles in the organization's governance. To reiterate, the Board is legally responsible for the orchestra and deputizes artistic responsibilities to the music director and administrative concerns to the CEO and his/her staff members. Musicians, according to this practice, much like Haydn's Esterházy star performers, are to be "heard not seen," holding limited powers beyond the exhibition of their musical talents.[877]

The sharply delineated hierarchy that appears to exclude musicians, however, is not a correct reflection of reality within most 21st-century orchestras, where musicians serve on audition committees, artistic advisory committees, dismissal review committees, and, importantly, represent their colleagues in collective bargaining. Select US orchestral musicians exercise authority parallel to the university faculty members who had engaged in supervisory activities at Yeshiva University. These musicians serve on peer review committees, engage in binding decision-making concerning renewals, and, in some cases, serve on a governing board, a position that remains controversial for its potential for conflicts of interest.[878] Perusing the trajectory of SCOTUS cases highlighted by the Kentucky trilogy regarding the managerial-supervisory exclusion of professional workers from NLRA protection, one finds that the court has broadened the exclusion. The *Yeshiva* court held that the exclusion applies not only to the professionals in that specific case but also to those employed by "any mature educational institution."[879] Such a sweeping exclusion embracing a wide class of professionals who "use independent judgment to ... responsibly direct the work of other employees' leads to a union-free workplace for this 'separate' class of managers-supervisors."[880] The broad prohibition affects the orchestral workplace in two ways: principal players could be classified as professionals and members of "decision-making" committees (such as audition, dismissal, and artistic committees) and could also be construed as holding supervisory powers. Before proceeding to a discussion of principal players and the "exclusion" possibility, it is important to mention that SCOTUS was split 5-4 in these leading cases. Although dissents are certainly not binding, their influence on the trajectory of the managerial-supervisory exclusion has not been ignored in the literature and may well influence future cases weighing in on the difference between

875. *NLRB v. Bell Aerospace Co.*, 416 US 267, 276-277 (1994).
876. With a tip of the hat to Henry Fogel, former President, League of American Orchestras.
877. Reference to comments made by Maestro Christopher Keene who supported an increased role for musicians as participants in artistic matters, as a true "fourth leg" of the orchestral stool.
878. wagechart.afm.org ICSOM Wage Scales and Conditions in the Symphony Orchestra.
879. *Yeshiva, supra*, 27.
880. *Oakwood Healthcare, Inc., supra*, 589.

managerial professionals and practicing professionals, the latter of which is deemed deserving of NLRA protection.[881]

6.42 PRINCIPAL PLAYERS: SUPERVISORY ACTIVITIES

As the subsequent inquiry into the *Rowe* case will spell out in the *movement, Of Rowe and Race,* principal players in orchestras engage in supervisory activities as part of their unique position within the orchestra and their respective sections. Interviews with musicians from orchestras in both countries studied show that there is no consistency in how principals work as "supervisors" within their sections. Aside from their musical performance-related functions, principals bear the responsibility of maintaining the quality of their sections, a multifaceted role that involves setting specific musical standards and providing artistic guidance related to the conductor's demands. Are these principals within the orchestra then supervisors who should be excluded legitimately from the NLRA's protection? If principals, as members of the orchestral complement, are excluded from the protections afforded to their peers in the same section, i.e., the nonprincipals, this double standard of protection within one organization engenders an unsound labor environment. According to SCOTUS' findings in the *Oakwood Healthcare, Inc.*, and *Kentucky River* cases, principals are barred from NLRA protection, as they hold the authority to delegate responsibility within their sections and can set performance schedules for their subordinates.

Henry Fogel and other orchestral insiders advocate for increased participation of musicians in the ways and means of running their performance organizations. While provisions for employee involvement in Europe provide for orchestral members' participation in works councils and other forms of player boards, the US has lagged in terms of widespread player involvement. The advent of a "fourth leg" of the "three-legged stool" was proclaimed by several renowned conductors in the 1980s with orchestral musicians seeking a greater voice, more say in their employment. Musicians took up the gauntlet shortly thereafter.[882] Henry Fogel himself argued that the advent of the modern-day maestro, an absentee music director who spends but a few weeks with his/her home orchestra (the orchestra they ostensibly lead), fueled the fires of orchestral discontent. The jet-setting maestro who takes on guest appearances the world over with little time for the daily artistic matters in his/her home orchestra is the rule rather than the exception since the 1980s, according to the well-known music critic and author Norman Lebrecht.[883] In a number of US orchestras, the solution to the power vacuum caused by the absentee maestros has been to grant musicians increased powers.

881. David Rabban. "Can American Labor Law Accommodate Collective Bargaining by Professional Employees?" *The Yale Law Journal* 99 1990, 689, DOI: 10.2307/796636.
882. Interestingly, the jet-setting maestros Leonard Bernstein and Pierre Boulez led the clarion call in the 1980s.
883. *See* Norman Lebrecht's *The Maestro Myth* (1991) placing responsibility for the pursuit of power and enhanced career opportunities firmly in the hands of avaricious impresarios.

6.43 COMMITTEES WITH POWER AND INDIVIDUAL ORCHESTRA MEMBERS IN MANAGERIAL POSITIONS: THE SPCO UNDER SCRUTINY

One of the most striking examples of an orchestra in which the members participate closely with management in a range of functions is the Saint Paul Chamber Orchestra (SPCO). To quote former CEO and mastermind behind the winds of change, Bruce Coppock, "savvy insiders with a wealth of information, our musicians are a veritable untapped resource ripe for effective and efficient use to effectuate real teamwork with 'management.'"[884] The SPCO experiment merits further investigation to establish whether it "breaches" the NLRA requirements or whether its actions merit a call for an orchestral exception. Importantly, although the NLRA classifies "professional employees," the Act does not delimit the term "professional workers," instead relying on the open-ended characterization of workers whose "decision making is limited to the routine discharge of professional duties in projects to which they have been assigned."[88529]

As touched upon earlier, orchestral musicians, regardless of location, can avail themselves of participation on various "subject-based" committees exemplified by artistic advisory boards, audition committees, community outreach committees, and conductor search committees. In the US, the composition of these committees varies, and functions are often defined within orchestral CBAs, as much of the orchestral musicians' occupation is channeled by the master agreement. In Europe, orchestral musicians are elected by their peers to serve as members of works councils, employee-run bodies that promote the interests of employees at the company level. In the Netherlands, consultation rights concerning management decisions and approval rights related to the organization's employment policies are stipulated by legislation through the *Wet op de ondernemingsraden* (WOR) Work Councils Act.[886] The significance of this form of representation was discussed with specific reference to the Dutch radio orchestras' 2012-2013 reorganization, as described in *Requiem for an orchestra.*

6.44 SPCO: UNFAIR PRACTICE OR A PROGRESSIVE ORCHESTRAL PARADIGM?

There are hundreds of fine chamber orchestras in the US. However, most operate on a per-service, part-time, and/or ad hoc basis.[887] Formed in 1959, the SPCO is one of a handful of professional US-based chamber orchestras in which musicians enjoy a permanent status as orchestral employees. The Minnesota-based SPCO consisting of 35 members went through a soul-searching process in the early part of the millennium to

884. Interviews with Bruce Coppock, former president and CEO SPCO (1999-2008 and 2013-2015).
885. 29 USC § 142(12).
886. *Wet op de ondernemingsraden* (WOR) English translation, Work Councils Act, available at: http://www.or.nl/entree/naar/wenrtekstendb.cgi?db = wenrteksten&uid = default&Document naam = wcacontent&view_records = 1.
887. Information gleaned from the League of American Orchestras https://www.americanorchestras.org/.

discover how to meet the challenges of a new era. In consort with board members and management, the musicians formed a Contract Renewal Group (CRG) and engaged in contract renewal plans enumerated in a Strategic Planning Process.[888] Prior to making the commitment to adopt an innovative governance and business model for the SPCO, the chamber orchestra had operated according to the same top-down organizational archetype as almost every other orchestra in the nation. Interviews with the orchestra's former CEO/President netted a wealth of inside information concerning the arduous process to take the first steps toward orchestral independence and give musicians more say in more matters related to their employment:

> Prior to the millennium "new road", the SPCO went through a painful self-recognition process. In 1994, orchestra members attended a retreat to discuss their situation, their future and most fundamentally, what was wrong with the orchestra and how to fix it. All comments were written down and distributed to all orchestra members post-retreat. In the name of openness and transparency, even the most painful, personally directed comments were published. Imagine reading that your colleagues think nothing of your contribution to the collective. Bloodletting became part of the SPCO culture, not a healthy development to say the least. And now imagine that the commentary becomes quite explicit. How will this impact your present and future performance not to speak of the manner in which you regard your colleagues and your orchestra from that moment on? We had a long way to go toward recovery. The orchestra was divided by a coalition to get out and experiment with a new vision, to enlarge the box and take a look at what other leading international chamber orchestras such as the Australian Chamber Orchestra, Mahler Jugendorchester and the Chamber Orchestra of Europe were doing and the coalition to recreate the past.[889]

The 2004-2005 season marked the initiation of the SPCO experiment: the orchestra took the bold move of incorporating aspects of the strategic plan into the SPCO's CBA. At the top of the artistic pyramid, the music director signed off on artistic decisions ranging from repertoire to hiring/firing. The SPCO's new style repositioned the music director's sole powers to an artistic committee comprised of a triumvirate of musicians and a pair of artistic managers. A group of five held the responsibility for every conceivable facet of artistic operation: musician selection and tenure reviews, repertoire and programming, touring, and planning/scheduling. Innovative in terms of financing, the new plan called for the distribution of funds to orchestral employees only if the SPCO posted a profit at the end of the season.

The SPCO's Artistic Vision Committee (AVC) programmed, selected conductors and guest artists, and met with management to decide on the number of performances, all conceivably supervisory activities according to *Yeshiva* standards. Other SPCO committees, such as the Artistic Personnel Committee and an Artist Vision Committee, put musicians in the "driver's seat" in concert programming, tour development, artistic choices and most notably the disciplinary, hiring and firing roles traditionally reserved for management. "The [committee members] sit where the buck stops. Musicians will

888. SPCO Strategic Plan September 2000 https://iml.esm.rochester.edu/polyphonic-archive/wp content/uploads/sites/13/2012/03/spcoStrategicPlan.pdf.
889. Interviews with Bruce Coppock.

make decisions about every program we play, every soloist, every conductor. Musicians will think about touring not in terms of their own careers but in terms of the orchestra's career. Musicians will think about recording in the same light. That's what makes this a revolutionary document."[890] Perhaps less revolutionary is the fact that the SPCO musicians did not elect their committee members themselves: the members were selected by management.

A controversial clause in the 2003 agreement concerning peer review and dismissal, as stated in the SPCO's 2010 Agreement (a projection of the SPCO's 2003 Agreement in its 50th Anniversary Year), disseminated by the CRG reads:

> This process addresses those situations when an individual's artistic performance jeopardizes the integrity of the whole … . The intention of this process is to assist the individual in reestablishing the high standards of the SPCO. If unsuccessful … the initiation of the dismissal process may be recommended.[891]

To a sizeable number of SPCO musicians, this clause and several others detailing the wide-ranging powers held by musician-colleagues indicated that the orchestra's inner circle had crossed a line. "There was a great deal of pain and bewilderment when long-term, committed SPCO members were confronted with a committee of so-called experts to decide on competence. A suspicion of an inner circle of favored players who were granted the 'ear' of President Bruce Coppock was held by many faithful SPCO players."[892] SPCO members voted 19-15 in favor of ratification of the 2003 Agreement. "Because the ratification vote was close, there is a hazard that morale will suffer. But status quo is not good enough. We cannot get to a different place if we don't take some risks including financial risks."[893]

6.45 THE POSSIBLE IMPACT OF NLRA EXCLUSION ON US ORCHESTRAL MUSICIANS

A strict reading of *Yeshiva* would determine that committee members who serve on audition, dismissal and/or peer review committees would fall under the *Yeshiva*-delineated exclusions. "The touchstone of managerial status is thus an alliance with management, and the pivotal inquiry is whether the employee is performing his duties represents his own interests or those of his employer."[894] And *Yeshiva* specifies the authority to dismiss as a major factor in determining supervisory authority—all powers that certain SPCO musicians hold. The NLRA-protected processes are the cornerstone of established and durable labor relations. Senza protection, management could justify

890. Bassoonist and CRG member Chuck Ullery quoted by Lowell J. Noteboom. "Good Governance for Challenging Times." *Harmony* October 2003.
891. Clause IV.D. Intervention Process Description SPCO 2010 Vision Statement http://www.polyphonic.org/harmony_archive/issue-no-16-october-2003.
892. Conversations with a former SPCO member who opted for early retirement in 2012, anonymity assured.
893. Herb Winslow, principal horn, SPCO joined the ensemble in 1981, as quoted in *Harmony*, *supra*.
894. *Yeshiva*, *supra*, 686.

barring SPCO musicians from participation in collective bargaining. The musicians' hard-won say in matters relating to employment could be thus threatened. In the US, the post-financial crisis proliferation of lockouts and strikes gives evidence of a pattern of increasing industrial action and often bears witness to sharp differences of opinion between management-boards and orchestral musicians. "Moving forward as independent thinkers and actors in the orchestral sphere is risky, but if the SPCO, a self-reliant type of smaller organization did not take the risk, who would?"[895]

Yeshiva addressed the issue of whether faculty members had taken on supervisory roles and stepped into the realm of management. As the SPCO moved toward embracing their collaborative model of orchestral organization, all parties concerned concurred that the *Yeshiva* holding should not influence the status of their CBA. AFM negotiator and ICSOM advisor Len Leibowitz was approached to draft a waiver clause that would protect the SPCO musicians from *Yeshiva* repercussions. "The question with regard to *Yeshiva* arose as to whether peer review alone would be considered a managerial function sufficient to satisfy *Yeshiva*. The SPCO CBA has many more functions that could be considered to be managerial and 'intent' per se has no legal legs."[896] Leibowitz expressed his concern about the possibility of unfair labor practice charges regarding the SPCO situation. "It was all well and good that President Coppock and his Board were on one line with regard to the functions held by musicians, but what if a future executive and board would take the tack that the union was not in line with the organization. They (the CEO board) could refuse to bargain and subsequently the union could file an Unfair Labor Practice charge. Here's the rub, the board could respond that the musicians were in fact managers and not employees under the NLRA and under *Yeshiva*."[897]

Taking into consideration the fact the faculty members at Yeshiva were originally classified as nonsupervisory personnel by the NLRB regional office before they moved forward with a petition for certification to unionize, the SPCO musician-"managers" might well operate in dangerous waters in terms of their employee classification, considering the results of *Yeshiva*. Perhaps the fact that all orchestral musicians are by definition "supervised strictly" in their fundamental performance roles under the direction of a music director/conductor might lead to an exception to the *Yeshiva* holding. Yet, while this possible exception might provide support for the SPCO musicians-as-employee argument, the elephant in this particular room is the fact that the SPCO's new model eschewed the role of a single supervisory music director. The position of music director was eliminated during the 2004-2005 season, replaced by an elite group of Artistic Partners chosen by the SPCO's artistic committee. Thus, there was no one central figure who held the reins at the orchestra, no music director, no sole authority.

895. Conversation with Chuck Ullery, principal bassoon, member of the SPCO's Contract Renewal Group (CRG).
896. Conversations with Len Leibowitz.
897. *Ibid.*

III Dissonance: Orchestral Workplace Discrimination

7 Of Rowe and Race

> In my younger days, I never saw an opera where an orchestra had female players. Then someone had the bright idea to drop the curtain between those auditioning and the panel, and things changed overnight. I wish we could have a drop curtain in every field of human endeavor.[905]

> When all is said and done, there is a problem, and it lies in the very nature of the symphonic orchestra, an organism that was formed at the onset of industrial revolution and has resolutely resisted egalitarianism, and multicultural values.[906]

To answer the question as to what a *movement* that appraises issues of gender bias in orchestras contributes to research that examines the vulnerability within employment-related struggles in the orchestral workplace, it is important to underscore two points. First, the research is not intended to offer a comparative study of US and NL orchestral cases to generate an inventory of differences and/or similarities. Rather, one objective is to provide a compendium of concerns that shape not only the employment of orchestral musicians but also the perceptions thereof. Second, as many of the stakeholders interviewed emphasized, employment embraces a broad panoply of issues that in turn impact status and even as the *Rowe* case indicates, wages. Hence, the inclusion of gender bias and #metoo-related topics is not only justified but also indispensable to gain a broader perspective on additional vulnerabilities at play in the sector. Notably, the number of cases in which orchestral musicians in the Netherlands have turned to litigation for a solution to pay-disparity issues has increased rapidly with musicians deriving inspiration from US colleagues. This *movement* is dedicated to the musician-plaintiffs who have shown the courage to represent themselves to make their voices heard.

On July 2, 2018, Elizabeth Rowe, the principal flautist in the storied Boston Symphony Orchestra (BSO), claimed that her employer had engaged in gender-based

905. Justice Ruth Bader Ginsburg #RuthBaderGinsburg January 1, 2019.
906. Norman Lebrecht. "Still All White on the Night" posted August 7, 2002. Available at: http://www.scena.org/columns/lebrecht/020807-BL-equality.html.

pay discrimination.[907] Massachusetts was the first state to prohibit employers from seeking salary history and using that information to formulate a salary offer for a prospective employee under the Massachusetts Equal Pay Act (MEPA).[908]

That a news story with an orchestral flautist[909] as protagonist would hit major media outlets was news in and of itself in 2018.[910] As this musical journey has shown, orchestras operate in a niche market that rarely captures the attention of a wide audience either on or offstage. US-based pundits suggested that Rowe's action could open the floodgates for further litigation in other discriminatory orchestral scenarios. Some voices from inside orchestras registered astonishment with regard to the claim, "when I read that Ms. Rowe earns $236,303 per year at the BSO, I almost fainted as this is three to five times more than a principal flutist earns here in the Netherlands. She probably had every right to sue her employer. Yet, at the same time, I can't but think about all those fellow musicians, who do not have the leeway to negotiate such salaries."[911]

As previous *movements* have described, orchestras have their own codes of conduct and exhibit the characteristics of a particular culture. These guild-like characteristics have helped to perpetuate discriminatory practices still ongoing. What contemporary researchers reference as the gender gap is difficult to measure and equally difficult to come to terms with, as it is rooted in long-seated practice.[912] Women have performed in a limited capacity in orchestras for centuries, yet the gender gap evident in terms of the restricted positions women have held, the instruments designated as female friendly, and the pay discrepancies women have endured form a complex mélange of gender bias-related topics.

In a *movement* devoted to women in orchestras, the introduction places gender-in-orchestras issues in a wider context of general historic/contemporary bias and socio-economic factors. A historical review including gender-based instrumental stereotyping and the role of women as leaders leads to the second section that introduces the women's orchestra as a distinct species that legitimately segregated women from playing alongside their male counterparts. To usher in an analysis of the capstone case in this *movement*, a discussion of the audition process with specific regard to principal positions will be reviewed. Subsequently, a comparative component is added with the introduction of an infamous, at least in musical circles, gender-related orchestral musician's suit in Germany that expands on the notion of discriminatory practice related to gender-based instrumental stereotyping. Next, Rowe's lawsuit is set in the context of relevant legislation and precedent. The intriguing issue of tainted variables in court interpretations of employment discrimination will be touched upon as well. A brief evaluation of Dutch legislation and relevant cases vis-à-vis equal-pay-for-equal-work

907. Elizabeth A. Rodgers, lawyer for the plaintiff, sent an email copy of the complaint to the author on July 11, 2018. *Elizabeth Rowe v. Boston Symphony Orchestra* https://www.scribd.com/document/383285548/Rowe-v-Boston-Symphony-Orchestra.
908. https://malegislature.gov/Laws/GeneralLaws/PartI/TitleXXI/Chapter149/Section105A.
909. "Flautist" and "flutist" are used interchangeably to denote a flute player.
910. Coverage on CNN, Associated Press, Reuters, major US newspapers, and widespread social media postings between July 2 and 14, 2018.
911. Comment given by a principal wind player in a major Dutch orchestra, anonymity assured.
912. The *Global Gender Gap Report* measuring gender equality in 144 countries was first published by the World Economic Forum in 2006.

precedes the conclusion. The *movement* closes with a consideration of the possible repercussions of Rowe's claim to equality issues in the orchestra.

7.1 FROM SAINT CECILIA TO MODERN-DAY MUSICIANS: THE MYTH AND THE MESSAGE

Before an attempt is made to unwrap how gender impacts orchestral employment, a paradox is highlighted here. From Saint Cecilia, the patron saint of music to pop divas strutting their stuff on YouTube, there has been no paucity of female musicians throughout history. However, their acceptance and fame were often based on appearances or perceptions thereof. The ancient Greeks chose Euterpe, translated as "pleasing" for the muse/goddess who represents music. "These stereotypes have lasted for centuries! To please and to be pretty in the heat of performance and to stay as young as possible, this is the message that haunts female musicians as they hear repeatedly."[913] To the feted violinist Nadja Salerno Sonnenberg, oft represented in the press as the bad girl rock star among classical musicians, "women are supposed to act according to submissive roles set forth by males and accepted dominating hierarchies for centuries ... exceptions were made for exotic female singers whose diva status brought fame and great sums of money. They have little in common with female orchestral musicians who had to fight every step of the way for equality."[914]

Marin Alsop,[915] the first woman to be appointed music director (MD) of a major US orchestra and recently, the first to ascend the podium as MD of one of Vienna's elite symphonies, advocates the destruction of all barriers to musicians in terms of gender or for that matter any other disadvantaged category. Through word and deed, her rise to the top of the conducting profession, traditionally a bastion of male dominance, is a testimony to perseverance and excellence. Put in the spotlight with the question, "why aren't there more female conductors?" Alsop's quick response, "why ask me, why not pose that question to the men in the business?" Turning to the Netherlands, the leading violin pedagogue for youngsters, Coosje Wijzenbeek,[916] proposed a new twist on a commonplace Dutch expression, "vioolmeisje" (literally, violin girl), an expression that colloquially refers to a goodie two-shoes. In the headline of a press interview "Vioolmeisje is geen doetje" (a violin girl is no pushover),[917] Wijzenbeek observed that although most of her young students (over 75%) are female, this phenomenon could be attributed to their "fijne motoriek" (dexterity, motor skills) and "aanleg" (physical aptitude). To be a "real violin-playing girl" takes more discipline and guts than the expression infers.

913. Interview with Kyung-Wha Chung, the first superstar among a galaxy of Asian female violin soloists.
914. Interview with soloist/violinist Nadia Salerno Sonnenberg, originally conceived for *The Strad*.
915. Marin Alsop, Music Director of the Baltimore Symphony Orchestra, and the Vienna Radio Symphony Orchestra.
916. Coosje Wijzenbeek was an internationally recognized pedagogue who specialized in training young violinists. Her string ensemble, Fancy Fiddlers and individual students exemplified by Janine Jansen attained international recognition, interviews with Ms. Wijzenbeek supplement quotes in this section.
917. *Volkskrant* interview https://www.volkskrant.nl/cultuur-media/-vioolmeisje-is-geen-doetje-~bd25b9aa/.

Gender discrimination in the orchestral workplace has been exacerbated by the general assumption that women are more suited to play specific instruments regardless of their aspirations. The same cultural and social norms that kept women out of the workplace to begin with are highly evident in the orchestral world through the ages. When finally admitted to orchestral violin sections in the 20th century, women customarily played second fiddle to men.[918] And, stereotypically, softer instruments exemplified by flute, harp and the violin were deemed appropriate for the gentler sex. "Women cannot possibly play brass instruments and look pretty, and why should they spoil their good looks?" was an observation penned in 1904 that could well have applied to Abbie Conant's tribulations to maintain her principal position in a major German orchestra in the 1980s.[919] While female cellists broke through the ranks in the 19th century Great Britain, they were required to emulate female equestrians and ride their cellos side-saddle; a woman placing an instrument between her legs was looked upon as either immoral or provocative, or both.[920] As the following paragraphs illustrate, instruments have transmitted gendered meanings for centuries.

Figure 9 The Ecstasy of St. Cecilia, Raphael (Circa 1515-1516)

Source: https://en.wikipedia.org/wiki/The_Ecstasy_of_St._Cecilia_%28Raphael%29#/media/File:Saint_Cecilia_by_Raphael.jpg.

918. Jane M. Bowers, Judith Tick. *Women Making Music: The Western Art Tradition, 1150-1950* 1987.
919. Gustave Kerke. "Musical Standard" 1904 cited by Carol Neus-Bates. *Women in Music: An Anthology of Source Readings from the Middle Ages to the Present.* Harper & Row 1982, 202.
920. M. Cowling. *The Cello* (2d ed.). Batsford Press 1983.

7.2 OF PATRON SAINTS AND EMPOWERMENT

Moving back through the annals of history, a closer analysis of music's female patron, Saint Cecilia, shows that even a patron saint's affiliation with a metaphorical art form is ambiguous. An early secret Christian whose past is swathed in mystery, Cecilia's rise to posthumous fame is an early example of public relations through storytelling and art, precursors of modern-day advertising. To bring the message of sacrifice home to the people and underscore church values, ecclesiastical storytelling through painted images transmitted approved messages. Cecilia is no flesh-and-blood musician; her relationship to music is as ephemeral as her upward gaze far removed from the broken instruments at her feet (Figure 9).

7.3 WOMEN IN EARLY-DAY ORCHESTRAS

Although female singers were a fixture in court, city and Kapelle musical life,[921] the domain of the orchestra was predominantly male until the 20th century. Only the daughters of famous professionals could study music, thanks to benevolent male family members. Another notable example of an exception takes us to 18th-century Venice where orphaned girls were trained in music. That tradition resulted in wide-spread acclaim for such compositional stars as the virtuosic composer-conductor Antonio Vivaldi (1678-1741), who crisscrossed Europe with his superstar female orchestra.[922] The novelty of young women attracted adoring crowds. As the French pundit Charles de Brosses observed, "[The girls] are reared at public expense and trained solely to excel in music. And so they sing like angels, and play the violin, the flute, the organ, the violoncello, the bassoon."[923]

In the 19th century, a heady mix of post-Enlightenment factors combined with the rapid changes wrought by capitalization, industrialization, urbanization, and the marked rise of a moneyed middle class led to great transformations in the cultural sector described elsewhere in this book. Although gender equality was one of the expected outcomes of the revolutions of the late 18th century, the wheels of change turned slowly. Even the watershed French Revolution with its calls for Rousseauian emancipation[924] did not open the floodgates to wash away restrictions on women's chances for equal participation. The Napoleonic Code that influenced legal systems throughout Europe affirmed the basic precepts of the Revolution, *inter alia*: equality before the law and freedom of religion. Yet, in terms of women's rights, the Code

921. *See Haydn rewrites history* for more information on pre-19th-century orchestras.
922. The genial "Red Priest," Antonio Vivaldi served Venice's Ospedale della Pietà for almost 40 years beginning his professional career as a violin instructor in 1713.
923. Charles de Brosses. *Lettres familières écrites d'Italie en 1739 et 1740*. E. Perrin 1885 https://archive.org/details/lettresfamiliere01brosiala/page/n7.
924. Keep in mind Jean-Jacques Rousseau's adage: "women's education should be relative to that of men."

advanced the idea that a married woman was her husband's property, a subordinate barred from entering into property-related transactions.

Orchestras in the United States benefited from European economic migrants who traveled to the United States in the 1800s. Almost all of these musicians were men: women of good reputation would compromise their social standing if they left their homes. Class differences might well be key to an appreciation of the finer points here as the exploitation of women in the factories of the Industrial Revolution is a sharp contrast to the portrait of the middle-class woman, an angel in the house responsible for maintaining domestic harmony. The instrument of choice for ideal middle-class ladies was the cottage piano, depicted here by a popular Belgian parlor painter.

Figure 10 Woman at the Piano with Cockatoo Gustaphe de Jonghe 1870

Source: https://commons.wikimedia.org/wiki/File:Gustave_L%C3%A9onard_de_Jonghe_-_Woman_at_the_Piano_with_Cockatoo.jpg.

The young woman surrounded by exotic allusions to affluence (tiger skin at her feet; a beckoning cockatoo) does not play the instrument: her relationship to it is passive, suitable for a docile female who takes no action independently (Figure 10). Countless paintings and prints *à l'époque* show women in rapturous poses behind the piano often with adoring males standing nigh. To enter the public eye as an instrumentalist performing on stage was a rarity. To move out of the protection of home to sit alongside men in an orchestral setting strayed far beyond accepted social conventions until the 20th century.

7.4 THE SOLO EXCEPTION

During the course of the 19th century, audiences gained familiarity with exceptional female soloists such as the pianist-composer Clara Schumann (1819-1896) for whom a career was "the very breath of my body."[925] Married to the mercurial and catastrophically suicidal musical genius Robert Schumann, she not only toured extensively as a piano soloist but also composed prolifically while serving as the principal breadwinner for her large family.[926] Another prominent exception to the stereotype of female musicians off stage was the American violin virtuoso Maud Powell who broke every convention of the time to leave the hinterlands of Illinois for Europe. Unlike orchestral musicians who form part of a collective relatively indistinguishable as individuals, these women were soloists who occupied center stage and commanded respect for their unusual virtuosity and star status.

Another change along the path to equality of the sexes within the orchestra lies in the realm of education and the professional drill. The efforts of Julius Eichberg, the founding father of Boston's Conservatory of Music (1867), factored prominently into the integration of women into a male-dominated field. A vociferous champion of equal rights, Eichberg, accepted and showcased talented pupils regardless of gender. Comments in the news of the day:

> Twenty-five years ago, a girl appearing upon frequented streets with such a burden would have been subjected to much staring ... if not downright persecution. But a good many things may happen within 25 years, and under the modern view of things girls may aspire to almost any attainment of which humanity is capable.[927]

7.5 WOMEN'S ORCHESTRAS: IF YOU CANNOT JOIN THEM, BEAT THEM AT THEIR OWN GAME

Cultural stereotyping was a major factor that kept well-trained women musicians out of orchestras and led to the search for other, more acceptable outlets for musical talent. In the 19th and early 20th centuries, women's orchestras were a popular hybrid form of entertainment; hundreds of women's orchestras toured Europe and the United States to great acclaim. At first blush, a positive move forward to provide employment for professional musicians barred from entering the men's club of professional orchestras, the ladies' orchestras could be viewed as the perfect economic solution to the predicament of what to do with the well-trained women entering the profession? The succinct answer in two words: segregate them.

925. *The Letters of Clara Schumann, and Johannes Brahms 1853-1896* (Berthold Litzmann (ed.). Vienna House 1971, 168.
926. Nancy Reich. *Clara Schumann: The Artist and the Woman* 2001.
927. "Girl Violinists: An Innovation that has been followed by Good Results" *Boston Herald* January 20, 1888 (microfiche).

Figure 11 Fadette Women's Orchestra

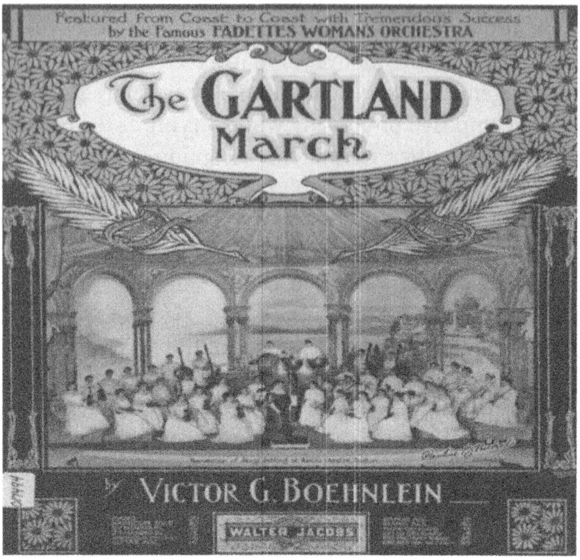

Source: https://commons.wikimedia.org/wiki/File:The_Gartland_March.png.

One of the most popular late 19th-century women's ensembles, the Boston-based Fadette Orchestra (Figure 11), toured throughout the United States for over three decades. Despite their popularity, the women's orchestras were secondary to male-dominated symphony orchestras in two ways: their repertoire was limited to suitably light music and their financial remuneration was significantly less than the fees earned by male musicians.[928] Female musicians could delight and entertain but serious music-making was an impossible dream:

> If I had the chance to substitute for a man I should do so in a minute and should look for more and better opportunities to follow. Now we are limited to concert work or to musical organizations composed entirely of women. I am sure, a great many of us could hold our own with the majority of men.[929]

In 1898, the English composer-pianist Mary Wurm founded a women's orchestra in Berlin. A protégé of Clara Schumann and encouraged by no less a musical force than the composer Johannes Brahms, she went down in history as the first woman to be engaged to conduct the Berlin Philharmonic Orchestra. However, honors aside, Wurm had to finance the concert herself; she engaged and paid for the orchestra to showcase

928. Ralph P. Locke and Cyrilla Barr, eds. *Cultivating Music in America: Women Patrons and Activists since 1860*. University of California Press 1997, 35.
929. "Opinions of New York Leaders on Women as Orchestral Players" *Musical Standard* April 2, 1904.

her prowess as a piano virtuoso. Her contract made allowance for her to conduct the program's opening overture, a token gesture. The remainder of the program was led by the "real conductor," Gustav Kogel.[930]

Of the many women's orchestras throughout history, the last of the extant all-female US orchestras was the Cleveland Women's Orchestra (CWO). Founded by Cleveland Orchestra violinist Hyman Schandler in 1935 until it disbanded 55 years later, the group gave women a chance to prove their orchestral prowess. "The perception that women belong in the kitchen and not on stage was unfortunately one of the reasons that led me to create an ensemble where women could show that they can perform as well as men."[931] Again, it was the male-dominated music world that relegated the ensemble to a periphery where housewives were permitted to dabble in their hobbies.

Reviews of the CWO's premiere concert refer to the conductor's skills as workman-like while admonishing the orchestral players to adopt "a more masculine touch in the exalted society of Brahms and Beethoven they cannot afford to be too ladylike."[932] To disparage equality in the name of Brahms would have made the mighty lion roar.[933]

7.6 UNIONS AND REGULATION

Where, may you ask, was control or regulation in the form of legislation or the regulatory initiatives of organized labor? Legislation with regard to the employment of musicians would have to wait for the 20th century with dilemmas surrounding fair work hours and fair pay not to speak of nondiscrimination between the sexes and a ban on racial discrimination. If regulation lagged behind discriminatory reality, fledgling unions were not much better at leveling the playing field between genders in the late 19th and early 20th centuries.

In the 18th and early 19th century, regulation in terms of employment was restricted to the venue's respectability in terms of municipal acceptance rather than the labor conditions for musicians; gender equality was a nonissue. In the US, the Musicians Union, a precursor of the American Federation of Musicians (AFM), kept women from performing in all union-run public orchestras until the union officially became affiliated with the powerful American Federation of Labor (AFL) in 1904. Of the 4,500 musicians who joined the AFL in New York City in those early days, 31 were women.[934]

Far from reaping the wide-ranging benefits of membership, women were often ostracized by the conductors and managers who held hiring powers. Consider the following quote that shapes an understanding of the same preconceived notions that play a role in both the Abbie Conant and Elizabeth Rowe claims, respectively mounted in the 1980s and in 2018:

930. https://www.berliner-philharmoniker.de/en/titelgeschichten/20172018/female-conductors/.
931. Conversations with Hyman Schandler.
932. *See* Herbert Elwell's review *Cleveland Plain Dealer* "Women Score in First Debut Concert" November 18, 1936, http://www.clevelandwomensorchestra.dreamhosters.com/wp-content/uploads/2016/11/Severance_Debut_Review.jpg.
933. An allusion to the 2016 BBC 3 *Great Composers* series: *The Great Lion (Johannes Brahms) and the Little Leopard (Hans von Bülow)* https://www.bbc.co.uk/programmes/b07lfzv2.
934. Christine Ammer. *Unsung: A History of Women in American Music* 2016, 5.

> Woman, lovely woman is always to be admired except when she is playing in an orchestra.
>
> In a little while men will wake up to find that they are closely and successfully being pushed in one more sphere by the fairer sex... fewer and fewer positions will be waiting for them.
>
> Women cannot possibly play brass instruments and look pretty.
>
> Women ... are content to be paid what is offered.[935]

The dream of mutual protection was shattered by the perpetuation of a male-dominated, closed hierarchical guild. Musician union alliances forged in the latter part of the 19th century certainly did not pursue nondiscriminatory goals in terms of either gender or, as we shall soon discover, race.

7.7 WOMEN AS SIDE-BY-SIDE ORCHESTRAL COLLEAGUES

One of the most iconic conductors of the 20th century, hailed not only for his prodigious musical abilities but also for his witticisms uttered during rehearsals,[936] Sir Thomas Beecham professed, "I do not like, and never will, the association of men and women in orchestras. As a member of the orchestra once said to me, 'If she is attractive, I can't play with her and if she is not, I don't want to.'"[937] The words of this revered maestro added grist to the women as second-class musical citizens' mill.

Academics dispute which 20th-century orchestra deserves kudos for paving the way to emancipation: a US orchestra or perhaps the London-based Queen's Hall Orchestra under the direction of Sir Henry Wood? Wood's orchestra might win the day: in 1913, his Queen's Hall Orchestra gave equal contracts to 6 female violinists; by 1918, 15 women had joined the orchestra. The increase can also be attributed to the dwindling number of males available to perform due to WWI conscription.[938]

In the US, the Cleveland Orchestra added four ladies to its professional roster in 1923. Several decades later, the parents of the Emerson Quartet's violinist Philip Setzer won auditions as members of the orchestra. Fellow musicians characterized Marie Setzer as humble and quiet. Quiet was perhaps the best reaction to taking one's place in a man's world. In 1937, Otto Klemperer hired Ellen Stone to play the first horn in the Pittsburgh Symphony Orchestra. She was the first female brass player to hold a principal position in a major orchestra worldwide.

935. Jane M. Bowers, Judith Tick, *supra*, quoting Opinions of New York Leaders on Women as Orchestral Players, *Musical Standard* April 2, 1904.
936. Sir Thomas Beecham. *Beecham Stories: Anecdotes, Sayings, and Impressions of Sir Thomas Beecham* 1993.
937. Mary Brown Hinley. "The Uphill Climb of Women in American Music: Conductors and Composers." *Music Educators Journal* 1984, 34, DOI: 10.2307/3400740.
938. This argument has been raised regarding increases in the number of female musicians contracted to work in US orchestras during WWII as well. While it is interesting to consider, it is difficult to find evidence to back up the assumption.

7.8 THE MAESTRA SYNDROME

The reoccurring theme of gender stereotyping of musical instruments silenced women and barred them from competing for a chance to work as orchestral musicians in the Netherlands until the middle of the 20th century. The Dutch cinema box office offering, "De Dirigent" portraying the trials and tribulations of Antonio Brico[939] to gain acceptance as a conductor in the 20th century, reminds us that orchestral direction was a bastion of male dominion, a theme central to the Hollywood blockbuster TÁR in 2022.

The Dutch cellist Frieda Belinfante immigrated to the United States in the 1950s, in the hopes of New World success. She was the first female conductor appointed to direct a fully professional orchestra, the Orange County Philharmonic in 1954. Nevertheless, despite her victory at the US regional level, her attempts to break into the major leagues as an orchestral conductor were not successful.[940]

Despite the breakthroughs by female conductors highlighted by Marin Alsop's career, often the esteemed masters who train conductors disparaged women's chances for success. Remarks by such greats as Mariss Jansons[941] and the most famous of all maestro-trainers Jorma Panula underscore their remarkable disdain. When Panula was asked if he thought that female conductors marked a positive step forward, he retorted, "I do not."[942]

Nonetheless, the "times they are a-changin"[943] applies to certain segments within the top echelons of the conductor's world. In 2013, the Director of the Conservatoire de Paris commented: "conducting is too physically demanding for women."[944] Just two years later, Nathalie Stutzman received the prestigious Chevalier de l'Ordre National du Mérite for her contributions to operatic conducting; Marin Alsop has continued to amass distinctions in her international career and in 2018, Karina Canellakis was appointed music director of Netherlands Radio Philharmonic, the first woman to take on such a position of leadership at a major Dutch orchestra.

As the "women in orchestras" section underlined, the gender inequality in orchestras is historically generated and deeply rooted in long-accepted traditions. The role of the conductor as the definitive arbiter of authority, power, and leadership on the podium takes on a masculine representation with women belittled in their attempts to join the "men's club." To quote Harold Schonberg, the Pulitzer Prize winning *New York Times* music critic: "as for women conductors, a musician knows when the upbeat starts, because that is when the slip starts to show."[945] The road has been long and

939. *De Dirigent* charts the career of Antonio Brico, 1905-1989.
940. Toni Bauman. *Een Schitterend Vergeten Leven: de Eeuw van Frieda Belinfante* 2015.
941. Maestro Jansons opined "I grew up in a different world, and for me seeing a woman on the podium .... well, let's just say it's not my cup of tea." Ivan Hewett's interview with Jansons on November 23, 2017, *The Telegraph* at: https://www.telegraph.co.uk/music/concerts/mariss-jansons-women-podium-arenot-cup-tea/.
942. The interview and quote reprint, https://www.limelightmagazine.com.au/features/jorma-panula-claims-women-should-not-be-conductors/.
943. Quoting the Bob Dylan hit, 1964.
944. Bruno Mantovani, quoted by Jessica Duchen. "Why the Male Domination of Classical Music Might Be Coming to an End." *The Guardian* February 28, 2015 https://www.theguardian.com/music/2015/feb/28/why-male-domination-of-classical-music-might-end.
945. Harold Schonberg. *The Great Conductors*. Simon & Schuster 1967.

winding toward orchestral gender integration. The fact that musicians enter into lawsuits with regard to discrimination in the 21st century informs us that prejudices still hold sway in the orchestral workplace, and on a positive note, these musicians might not accept discrimination.

7.9 THE LOW BRASS CEILING: ABBIE CONANT'S STRUGGLES IN MUNICH

The case of the American trombonist Abbie Conant's struggle to keep the job she won at the distinguished Munich Philharmonic (MP) in 1980 is an example of one of the most blatant gender discrimination cases on record. Although the author attempts to refrain from excessive personal asides, it should be mentioned that I was privileged to play in the Spoleto Festival Orchestra where Conant played principal trombone prior to her Munich audition. Like many members of that celebrated summer orchestra, she decided to test the audition scene in Europe after the summer festival ended. Of the 11 orchestras she applied to, only one invited her to participate in the audition, and her invitation to compete for the first trombone position at the MP was addressed to "Herr" Conant.

The Abbie Conant story is endemic to an understanding of the brass ceiling, which has kept women out of mainstream orchestral brass sections regardless of location (with the notable exception of horn sections).[946] Her story not only sheds light on German patriarchal orchestral traditions but also illuminates the uphill battle female lower brass players have faced worldwide.

See Figure 12 for a pictorial representation of the all-male Munich Brass Connection.

Figure 12 The Munich Brass Connection 2018[947]

Source: No limits program, agent granted permission.

946. Examples of notable female horn players in the last quarter of the 20th century include: Julia Studebaker RCO, first horn, 1974. Gail Williams joined the Chicago Symphony Orchestra in 1978, holding the position of Associate principal horn from 1984 to 1998; Julie Landsman became the first female brass player at the MET winning the first horn audition in 1984.

947. A link to Abbie Conant's troubling story is pictorial. Reproducing the evolutionary pun that showcases the Munich-based ensemble's male players relates to Conant's story without any criticism of this fine ensemble.

Conant's audition for the principal spot in Munich was legendary: 32 male candidates competed for the coveted position, and she was the only American and, of course, the only woman to participate in the blind audition. After two rounds behind a screen, number 16 was allowed to step forward as the only candidate selected for the unscreened final round. "There was an audible gasp when I came out."[948] It was not to be the last gasp.

Conant won her position when Sergio Celibidache, the iconoclastic, ultra-authoritarian maestro, was transitioning from principal guest conductor to music director. It is important to note that had the maestro held the role of music director at the time of the audition, he would have held full veto power, and Conant would not have stood a chance to have won the audition. In a field where mystery and authority construct a heady mix, Celibidache attracted a cult following. Part and parcel of his almost supernatural standing came from "the projection of an unobstructed masculine aura that is not corruptible."[949] Convinced that no woman could play the trombone in his orchestra, the newly minted music director demanded that complaints concerning Conant's playing should be recorded during her probationary year. Although no complaints were filed, she was demoted to the position of second trombone.[950] The MD's control was absolute: there was no outcry, nor was there any form of administrative support for Conant to take her rightful place as principal.

Conant's quest for justice led to a series of lawsuits in German courts and garnered international support. After four years of proceedings, she won back the right to play first trombone; five years later, she won the right to equal pay. Due to a statute of limitations in German law, she was only able to regain five years of back pay. The ongoing humiliation, unfairness, and nonstop litigation took its toll: "it was slow drip insanity the whole time, and institutionalized male hysteria."[951] Thirteen years after Conant first filed a discrimination suit against the MP and the municipality, the German courts found in her favor and granted her back pay to compensate for the loss of the principal position. The victory was hollow, as it was impossible for her to return to the MP to claim her rightful position.[952] A tradition of male domination turned the glass ceiling into an upper limit of impenetrable brass: there was simply no place for a foreign female in a German brass section at the end of the 20th century.

Conant's struggle for basic acceptance contributes to the discussion on discrimination making headway toward an in-depth description and analysis of Rowe's 2018

948. Abbie Conant's interview on WQXR, New York, replete with quotes, https://www.wqxr.org/story/trombonist-got-job-munich-philharmonic-then-she-fought-them-court-13-years/.
949. Quote by former MP chairman, cellist Jörg Eggebrecht as retold by his brother, musicologist and critic Harald Eggebrecht. The complete text can be accessed at *Philharmonische Blaetter* February-March 1992.
950. Maestro Celibidache, "you know the problem, we need a man for the principal trombone." Quoted by William Osborne "Art Is Just an Excuse." *International Alliance of Women in Music Journal* October 1996, 6-14.
951. Abbie Conant's interview WQXR, *supra.*
952. *See* Abbie Conant. "The Status of Women in German Orchestras: A Report Based on Practical Experience" 1998 http://www.osborne-conant.org/status.htm.

claims against the BSO. Almost three decades earlier, Conant had to fight, first for her position, and then for equal pay. Whereas Conant discovered female-male salary discrepancies by chance and eventually claimed those losses, her litigation centered on the more rudimentary issue of the right of a woman to work as a first trombonist. Fast forward to 2018: the BSO agreed that Rowe's value to the organization was undisputed.[953] No such affirmation was ever afforded Conant by the Munich Philharmonic.

7.10 HIGH VISIBILITY POSITIONS: US ORCHESTRAS AND GENDER

As discussed in other *movements*, the practice of blind auditions in which a screen conceals the candidate's identity from the audition panel (jury) was instrumental in changing orchestral demographics. A study isolating the blind audition variable undertaken by American economists in the late 1990s focused on the orchestra as a test ground for discriminatory practices. Their data showed that the placement of a screen increased the probability for a woman to advance from the preliminary to the second round by an astounding 50% after the blind audition process became standard practice at US auditions starting in the 1970s.[954] While women accounted for fewer than 5% of orchestral musicians in 1970, they accounted for over 25% of employed orchestral musicians just 30 years on.

7.11 HIGH VISIBILITY POSITIONS: FEMALE LEADERS IN THE "HOT SEAT"

A description of the challenges faced by female concertmasters feeds the discussion on orchestral gender bias. Conversations with Emmanuelle Boisvert, the first female concertmaster in a major US orchestra,[955] square with Marin Alsop's observations on trailblazers. Both leading ladies prefer to dwell on their core business rather than comment on the discrimination they encountered along the way. A striking blonde who sports the latest fashion, Boisvert spoke out: "Why should we label a woman who leads an orchestra as a female leader? I have spent decades working hard to become the best musician I could possibly be, never to become the best female musician."[956] The international superstar conductor Jaap van Zweden, former concertmaster of the Royal

953. Diverse media reports in Boston newspapers and materials on the BSO's website bolster Ms. Rowe's claim as "the poster child of the BSO."
954. Claudia Goldin and Cecilia Rouse. "Orchestrating Impartiality: The Impact of Blind Auditions on Female Musicians" *The American Economic Review* 2000, 715-741 DOI: 10.3386/w5903.
955. Following a stint as a section violinist in the Cleveland Orchestra, Ms. Boisvert took the lead position at the Detroit Symphony Orchestra in 1988. She left to take an associate concertmaster position with the Dallas Symphony Orchestra during the Detroit Symphony's prolonged labor conflict and strike in 2011.
956. Interview with Emmanuelle Boisvert.

Concertgebouw Orchestra,[957] a man of many deeds and few words, agrees wholeheartedly: "taking a position as leader rests on excellence and has nothing to do with gender, color, or any other factor." Yet, for all of these rose-colored observations, discriminatory practices have flourished for over 150 years at the very heart of the orchestral world, at its veritable Valhalla, Vienna, Austria.

7.12 HIGH-PROFILE STATISTICS FROM EUROPE: *WIEN BLEIBT WIEN*

A world leader in the orchestral world since 1842, the ur-traditional Vienna Philharmonic Orchestra (VPO) rigorously excluded women from full membership until 1997.[958] A plethora of arguments was mounted in support of the Viennese traditionalists: the acceptance of women would lead to lower standards, the prestigious Musikverein (home to the orchestra) did not have proper backstage facilities to accommodate women, young women were bound to get pregnant and take long leaves of absence from their orchestral duties, and last but certainly not least, women would distract male musicians onstage, and the audience in the hall.

The VPO's operating system is a democratic self-administration model in which the orchestra's 126 members vote on every issue of concern to the collective.[959] Daily operation is delegated to 12 elected musician members of the administrative committee.[960] The musicians who commit to upper echelon administrative positions are multitaskers in extremis. Consider Dieter Flury, who served as the orchestra's artistic director, general manager, and principal flute from 2005 to 2014. As a principal player, his performance pressures were substantial; concomitantly, he was responsible for negotiating with conductors, concert promoters, and media programers.

In accordance with Philharmonic statutes, only a member of the Orchestra of the Vienna State Opera can become a member of the VPO. Following three years on probation, the aspirant is deemed eligible to apply for membership to the Association of the Vienna Philharmonic and can compete for a place in the VPO elite ensemble. As Flury explained, "we create a family in a system that has been in place for 172 years."[961]

See Figure 13 for a picture of the Vienna Philharmonic Orchestra taken at the traditional New Year Concert 2015.

957. Jaap van Zweden is concurrently Music Director of the New York Philharmonic, the Hong Kong Philharmonic and the Seoul Philharmonic.
958. The first female member of the Vienna Philharmonic, harpist Anna Lelkes performed with the orchestra for 26 years. She was paid less than the male members of the orchestra and received no mention in programs.
959. *See* http://www.wupromotion.com/en/about-us/the-company/983-wiener-philharmoniker-austria-2017-2021.
960. *Ibid.*
961. Dieter Flury. Revolutionär war im Wiener Vormärz die Idee einer demokratischen Künstlervereinigung, die später die noch heute gültige Rechtsform eines Vereines bekam, https://blog.lucernefestival.ch/blog/2017/09/09/im-gespraech-mit-dem-schweizer-solofloetist-der-wiener-philharmoniker-di/.

Figure 13 Vienna Philharmonic (New Year Concert 2015)

Zubin Mehta conductor

Women and minorities few and far between

Source: Anonymous iPhone photo taken in the hall.

A shimmer of light in terms of progress fell on the VPO shortly after the celebrated institution received ongoing international criticism for its lack of a female onstage presence, which intensified in the 1990s. With the threat of canceled concerts in the prestigious Carnegie Hall, New York and in Los Angeles, the VPO voted in 1997 to accept and induct one female player, the harpist, who had performed as principal harp in the orchestra for over 26 years.

The infamous moniker, "we are a white male orchestra playing the music of dead white males," articulated by Flury in the late 1980s has been replaced by a clarion call for equality. After a 2014 round of VPO auditions failed to deliver a suitable candidate in the final round, the orchestra announced an additional concertmaster audition to take place in mid-February 2015. Notably, the Orchestra of the Vienna State Opera website stated: "All rounds, apart from the last, will take place behind a screen. The Vienna State Opera aims at increasing the share of women in the orchestra." Next challenge: the racial barrier, an issue to be tackled later in this *movement*. It is somewhat ironic that the first orchestra to introduce the blind audition in 1952 was the defendant orchestra in the *Rowe* case; the blind audition practice spread to other US orchestras in the 1970s and 1980s. The European orchestral reaction to blind auditions was recalcitrant until the cusp of the 21st century. "If we feel that we need to see a player in order to hear that player, this is our prerogative. It shows our esteem for our orchestral culture."[962]

7.13 THE MET SETS THE STAGE FOR ASSESSMENT WITHOUT BIAS

The news on the beat emanating from orchestral auditions at one of the world's leading opera houses, the New York-based Metropolitan Opera (MET), shows that it is possible to be a leader not only in terms of quality but also in terms of how that quality is hired. The MET's audition system confirms an institutional commitment to neutrality on many fronts, including the prior salary issues central to Rowe's claims. All applicants regardless of ethnicity or background, prior-held position, or education, are invited to play.[963] Importantly, the MET fills all its positions at the first audition call, a radical departure from the tradition of a great number of orchestras on both sides of the Atlantic that keep vacancies open for years. Conversations with Bruce Ridge shed light on the financial aspect of that practice. "It can be a money saver as we all know that subs cost much less than tenured players in top orchestras. If a budget has to meet certain criteria in a season, jobs are held open from one season to another."[964]

The fact that the MET puts applicants behind a screen for all rounds gives credence to the notion that sex and race-blind adjudication leads to an increase in both women and minorities on stage at a major orchestra. This policy has reaped positive results not only in terms of filling positions but also in terms of increasing diversity.[965]

7.14 POTENTIALLY TAINTED VARIABLES

Within the larger field of compensation equity, the analysis of whether or not employees who perform the same tasks are paid differently based on ambiguous reasons, the issue of tainted variables sets off alarm bells and whistles. Legal scholars in ivy towers as well as "boots on the ground" human resource managers have presented compelling evidence in US courts with regard to flawed determinations of membership in a class of protected individuals and how underpayment is determined. Studies have shown that the gendered stereotypes of male versus female instruments visible in the literature and paintings of previous centuries were still evident at the end of the 20th century.[966] And as present-day reports cited in previous paragraphs confirm, there is a marked difference between the percentage of women versus men within different instrumental groups in orchestras reflecting bias. The question that plays into a legal assessment that applies indirectly to Rowe's case and directly to a discussion of gender discrimination in orchestras is: does the fact that there is a

962. Conversations with (former) personnel manager Nederlands Kamerorkest (Netherlands Chamber Orchestra) Wim van Loon.
963. Reports of orchestras turning down players with Asian last names after "too many Asians" fill the sections have been noted in the US and Europe.
964. Bruce Ridge commentary at the ICSOM Conference Washington D.C. August 26-27, 2016.
965. Information gleaned from http://www.metorchestramusicians.org/.
966. H. Abeles and S. Porter, "The Sex-Stereotyping of Musical Instruments." *Journal of Research in Music Education 26* 1978, 65-75.

significantly higher female-to-male ratio in violin sections and a lower percentage of brass players reflect nondiscriminatory market forces, gender discrimination or both? Moving on to *Rowe*, what of the fact that women are not only typecast as flute players but also their flute sections within professional orchestras are predominately female? Does this fact make Rowe's quest for equal pay discussed in the pages to follow even more worthy of attention?[967]

7.15 SUING FOR GENDER PAY DISCRIMINATION IN THE US: THE EPA & TITLE VII

Pay discrimination has played an important role in the march for equality in US legislation and case law since the late 1930s. The Equal Pay Act 1963 (EPA),[968] amending the Depression era Fair Labor Standards Act 1938 (FLSA), established "the principle of equal pay for equal work regardless of sex"[96929] into the ambit of the law. Six months after President Kennedy signed the EPA into law, Congress passed Title VII of the Civil Rights Act of 1964.[970] Title VII provides broader coverage than the EPA with prohibitions on discriminatory employment practices based on enumerated protected traits, including race, religion, sex and national origin.[971] While these pillars of antidiscrimination legislation seek to protect employees from gender-based wage discrimination, statistics confirm that women were paid 53 cents to the dollar men earned in the 1960s.[972] In 2017, the gap had narrowed to 80 cents to the dollar with wider discrepancies reported for minority women.[973]

Of relevance, the statutes have been interpreted in fundamentally different ways by federal courts, a situation that results in dramatically different outcomes.[974] In 1981, SCOTUS recognized the problems endemic to EPA-based discrimination suits, "the language and legislative history of the provision are not unambiguous."[975]

The EPA is subdivided into two parts: the initial prohibitory and the subsequent affirmative defense section in which employers can differentiate in pay under specific categories. To create a balance between claims and defenses, the Act allows the employer to submit four permissible affirmative defenses. An employer's assertion that compensation rates are based on a publicized job classification system does not in and of itself count as a valid justification for gender-based pay discrimination. The

967. Corroborated by statistics, most professional flute players at least in US top 20 orchestras are female, *see* O'Bannon R. "Boys play trumpet and girls play flute, but why?" 2017 https://www.bsomusic.org/stories/boys-play-trumpet-and-girls-play-flute-but-why.aspx.
968. Equal Pay Act 1963 (EPA) (29 USC., Movement 8 sec. 206(d)).
969. 29 USC. § 206(d)(1) §6 (2000).
970. Civil Rights Act of 1964 § 7, 42 USC. § 2000e et seq. (1964).
971. Section 703(a)(1), 42 USC. §2000e-2(a)(1) (2000) … .
972. *See America's Women and the Wage Gap*. Available at: http://www.nationalpartnership.org/our-work/resources/workplace/fair-pay/americas-women-and-the-wage-gap.pdf.
973. *See* https://www.census.gov/data/tables/time-series/demo/income-poverty/historical-income-people.html.
974. For clear analyses, *see* Peter Avery. "The Diluted Equal Pay Act: How was it Broken? How can it be Fixed?" 2004 and Debra H. Goldstein. "Sex-Based Wage Discrimination: Recovery Under the Equal Pay Act, Title VII, or Both." *Alabama Law Review* 56 1995.
975. *County of Washington v. Gunther* 452 US 161 (1981).

employer must prove that the job classification system accurately reflects job duties and job-related employee qualifications. Moreover, the job classification system must be uniformly applied to men and women. It is this defense that employers have used quite ingeniously to evade claims of discrimination. Another key EPA clause stipulates that the assertion that a compensation differential is attributable to a collective bargaining agreement does not constitute a valid defense. The following section discusses a suit mounted under the EPA and Title VII, which led to the enactment of federal legislation that moved beyond the restrictions that SCOTUS placed upon employees seeking remedies for discrimination.

7.16 LILLY LEDBETTER'S FIGHT FOR EQUAL PAY AND THE WORKINGS OF TITLE VII

When Lily Ledbetter first took a management post at the Goodyear Tire and Rubber Corporation, she was renumerated at the same pay rate as male managers. However, once Goodyear introduced a performance-based wage system, she received between 15% and 40% less pay compensation than her male counterparts.[976] After opting for early retirement, Ledbetter filed discrimination claims at the EEOC under the EPA and Title VII.[977] She presented evidence that her supervisors had not only given her poor evaluations based on gender but that these evaluations had a direct link to pay. The jury agreed, and Ledbetter was awarded compensatory and punitive damages in the amount of $3 million. On appeal, the Eleventh Circuit reversed the decision, holding that evidence of two pay decisions taken within a 180-day time span was insufficient to prove Goodyear's discriminatory intent.[978] Litigation continued; Ledbetter petitioned SCOTUS:

> Whether and under what circumstances a plaintiff may bring an action under Title VII of the Civil Rights Act of 1964 alleging illegal pay discrimination when the disparate pay is received during the statutory limitations period, but is the result of intentionally discriminatory pay decisions that occurred outside the limitations period.[979]

In a close-call decision,[980] the court affirmed the Eleventh Circuit unwilling to grant deference to the argument that the 180-day time bar contributed to a discriminatory practice. Reconsideration according to the majority would "jettison the defining element of the legal claim on which her Title VII recovery was based."[981] Reading for the majority, Justice Samuel Alito stated, "current effects alone cannot breathe life into prior, uncharged discrimination."[982]

976. Lilly Ledbetter, Equal Pay for Equal Work: Hearing before the Senate Judiciary Committee 110th Congress.
977. *Ledbetter v. Goodyear Tire & Rubber* 421 F.3d (2005) 2162, 2165.
978. *Ibid.*
979. Lilly Ledbetter's Petition for Certiorari https://www.oyez.org/cases/2006/05-1074.
980. Indeed, a SCOTUS close call at 5 4.
981. *Ledbetter v. Goodyear Tire & Rubber Co.*, 550 U.S. 618 (2007).
982. *Ibid.*

Justice Ruth Bader Ginsburg and her fellow dissenters' criticism of the majority was portentous as it paved the way for the Lilly Ledbetter Fair Pay Act.[983] The dissent was vociferous and scathing, labeling the majority's ruling out of tune with the realities of wage discrimination while accusing the majority of "a cramped interpretation of Title VII, incompatible with the statute's broad remedial purpose."[984]

Following heated debate in congressional halls in the wake of the decision, several legislative attempts were made to give credence to the dissenters' criticism. In 2008, President Barack Obama signed the Act proclaiming: "there are no second-class citizens in our workplaces ... it is bad for business, to pay someone less because of their gender, age, race, ethnicity, religion, or disability."[985] The Act ensures that ongoing pay discrimination at work can be challenged regardless of when the discrimination began. Yet, despite the swathe of admirable legislative initiatives that followed on the state level as an antidote to wage disparity, prior history checks, and other discriminatory labor practices, recent statistics show that in the US, women still earn less than men and often face insurmountable challenges in terms of effort and expense to prove wage discrimination in court.[986] To quote Lily Ledbetter, "employers still rely on job applicants' salary history to set pay, they will be forced to carry these depressed wages throughout their career and into retirement."[987]

7.17 BROOK FERGUSON: A FLAUTIST (PRE-*ROWE*) ATTEMPTS TO GAIN EQUAL PAY

As mentioned previously, the difficulties in mounting an EEOC claim are significant. The bar to meet EPA standards is high as the following statistic illuminates: of the 996 gender pay discrimination complaints reviewed by the EEOC in 2017, 65.1% were found to have "no reasonable cause for action."[988]

In a case that came to light in a *Washington Post* article in 2018, the Colorado Symphony's principal flutist, Brook Ferguson, spoke about an EEOC discriminatory pay complaint filing that she attempted to pursue after discovering that male colleagues in principal positions earned 28% more than she did.[989] Ms. Ferguson presented the Post's reporter with evidence to prove that the Colorado Symphony offered her a salary increase if and only if she would waive some legal rights. Ultimately, she dropped her

983. Lilly Ledbetter Fair Pay Act of 2009. 123 Stat 5 (West 2009).
984. *See Ledbetter*, dissenting opinion of Justice Ginsburg, with whom Justice Stevens, Justice Souter, and Justice Breyer join, https://supreme.justia.com/cases/federal/us/550/618/-tab-opinion-1962369.
985. Timothy Kneeland. *Today's Social Issues: Democrats and Republicans*. ABC-Clio 2016, 113.
986. Bureau of Labor Statistics and the Census Bureau, The Simple Truth about the Gender Pay Gap https://www.aauw.org/resource/the-simple-truth-about-the-gender-pay-gap/.
987. Lily Ledbetter's public post via CNN on the eve of a bipartisan congressional reintroduction of the Paycheck Fairness Act, January 30, 2019, http://lite.cnn.com/en/article/h_d81be4a73dcf52aaffd3b3f1b240fce0.
988. EEOC Equal Pay Act Charges Filed 1997-2017, https://www.eeoc.gov/eeoc/statistics/enforcement/epa.cfm.
989. Geoff Edgers. "A Star Flutist Has Sued the Boston Symphony Orchestra" *Washington Post* December 11, 2018.

EEOC claim for several reasons, the series of explanations most often cited by would-be claimants according to the EEOC: the high costs of litigation and the difficulties inherent in suing the boss in terms of work relationships with fellow employees and management.

Of interest, the NLRB examined the right of the union to investigate pay scale information as it related to Ferguson.[990] The NLRB held that the time of filing was irrelevant because the union was entitled to investigate pay scale information as a legitimate part of its justifiable CBA obligations. Further, this entitlement was of a broad nature: thus, even if a CBA did not expressly contain a pay transparency nondiscrimination provision, the union could request and must receive the relevant information.[991] *Ferguson* marked a substantial expansion of the scope of requested information, a welcome addition to the arsenal of legitimate weapons in the struggle to achieve equal pay and eradicate gender pay discrimination.

7.18 FLUTE FOIBLES

A bit of institutional memory serves as an analysis of the *Rowe* case well. In 1952, the BSO welcomed a new member to the position of first flute, Doriot Anthony Dwyer. Headlines in the local press revealed: "Woman Crashes Boston Symphony,"[992] and if the point was not clear enough, the *Springfield Morning Union* placed the headline, "Flutist, 30 and Pretty, Here with Boston Symphony" (October 10, 1952). Announcements of male principal appointments made no such mention of physical attributes in the 1950s or thereafter. The headlines show evidence of a disturbing tendency to single out a principal player with regard to gender, not performance abilities.

With considerable background material to consider, it is time to turn to the 2018 headliner case that pitted a star player against her renowned employer. Elizabeth Rowe joined the BSO after winning the principal (first) flute audition in 2004. Immediately prior to that triumph, she held the position of second flute in Washington D.C.'s National Symphony Orchestra. Her counterpart in the BSO's wind section, principal oboist John Ferrillo, joined the orchestra in 2001 after what nonmusicians termed a buyout from the prestigious MET, the highest-paid orchestra in the United States.

990. *Colorado Symphony Association and Denver Musicians Association, Local 20-623*, 366 NLRB No. 60 (April 13, 2018) https://www.nlrb.gov/search/all/Colorado Symphony Association.
991. An example of a pay transparency nondiscrimination provision: "xxx, will not discharge or in any other manner discriminate against employees or applicants because they have inquired about, discussed, or disclosed their own pay or the pay of another employee or applicant. However, employees who have access to the compensation information of other employees or applicants as a part of their essential job functions cannot disclose the pay of other employees or applicants to individuals who do not otherwise have access to compensation information, unless the disclosure is (a) in response to a formal complaint or charge, (b) in furtherance of an investigation, proceeding, hearing, or action, including an investigation conducted by the employer, or (c) consistent with the contractor's legal duty to furnish information." 41 CFR 60-1.35(c).
992. Reported by Cyrus Durgan, *The Boston Sunday Globe* October 12, 1952.

According to statistics publicly accessible in the BSO's tax filings,[993] Ferrillo was offered compensation at 200% above the BSO's base pay rate to sweeten the deal and persuade him to leave the MET for the BSO. Using the same calculation, Rowe was offered compensation at 154% above the base when she was hired three years after Ferrillo. Did gender discrimination play a hand in the BSO's individual compensation schemes? Or is there a genuine difference between the roles played by the principal oboe and the principal flute that would obviate the necessity to pay a male principal in the wind section considerably more than a female principal in the same section?

Is it possible to explain the disparity between the two salaries because of Rowe's lack of leverage power when she negotiated? After all, the second flute position at the National Symphony Orchestra, a less musically prestigious organization than the world-renowned MET, has less trade-in value in the salary negotiation game. Perhaps she simply did not drive a hard-enough bargain to reach Ferrillo's higher level of compensation. Is this a telling circumstance that adds to the noxious mix of discrimination, or just one of many factors in this complex case? Or does this show an unfair and illegal reliance on prior compensation?

Rowe brought up another thought-provoking point of contention at §49 in her complaint: "the BSO discriminated in compensation by providing additional assistance to reduce the physical demands required of the principal oboist ... in addition to the overscale pay, [the BSO] provides and pays for the use of an assistant for approximately 6-12 weeks per season to assist the male principal oboist." Although Rowe was responsible for playing the principal flute part in as equally demanding repertoire as Ferrillo and played more solos than her illustrious colleague did on a per-season basis, she was not offered the luxury of relief by way of an associate/assistant principal player. Associate-assistant players offer the principal player respite from a particularly difficult program. The tradition of hiring assistants to alleviate the burdens placed on principals is common practice in European orchestras where two musicians share premier positions; principals hold 50% of positions and are paid 100% of salaries. The logic behind this model is that the principals are rewarded for their extra duties and performance pressures by receiving more free time than rank-and-file players.

Back to Rowe at the BSO: there are several issues that clouded her demand for an assistant player. First, it is possible that management could have supported Rowe's demand for an associate if she had made this demand because of the arduous nature of her position rather than as part of a discrimination claim. Further, the BSO's orchestra committee could have been in opposition to the creation of a newly created contracted position within the orchestra in the form of an associate flute player.

993. Like all US orchestras, the BSO as a nonprofit organization is required to file salary information. *See* Form 990 schedule J https://www.guidestar.org/profile/04-2103550.

7.19 DIFFERENT STROKES FOR DIFFERENT FOLKS: SECTION VERSUS PRINCIPAL PAY

According to US industry practice, principal players negotiate their own salaries, often for an amount considerably higher than CBA negotiated scales for section players. To understand another important nuance within Rowe's claims of unequal pay and gender discrimination, the reader needs to understand a distinction within the audition process for principal players at major US orchestras where high-profile players are often recruited from the ranks of other top orchestras. As principal positions are not controlled by collectively bargained pay scales, Ferrillo's previous position at the MET granted him leveraging power in negotiations with his prospective future employer (BSO) both in terms of payment and other employment-related benefits. Rowe's claim is instructive in many ways as it shows that leverage power in a highly competitive field can prompt contractual gaps in which similar players do not operate within a system of controllable bargaining positions.

7.20 BSO DEFENSES

The BSO brought to the fore the argument: "the flute and the oboe are not comparable instruments, nor are they treated as such by most orchestras in the United States."[994] To analyze a bit further, there is some merit to this argument. Oboe players spend a great deal of time engaged in making reeds for their double reed instrument. The peculiarity and difficulty of not only playing a technically demanding instrument but also the responsibility of making a part of the instrument endows oboists with extra responsibilities. While an academic endeavor does not frequently bow to the level of the light bulb joke, it is impossible to resist this telling portrait of the oboist in enlightened terms. "How many oboists does it take to screw in a light bulb? Only one, but they must go through at least five bulbs before they find one to fit."[995] Witticisms aside, the oboist does have an extra burden that is not shared by flute players who do not have to physically craft a part of their instrument.

Whereas US orchestral musicians negotiate for these additional expenses, European contracts exemplified by Dutch orchestral contracts take these expenses into consideration within the framework of the negotiated CAO. Wind and brass players in Dutch orchestras and symphonies across the continent and in the U.K. are also granted extra pay for dental costs related to the performance vicissitudes of their wind instruments. The Dutch system of including these benefits in the general CBA is more transparent than the individual negotiations that a principal undergoes to receive remuneration.

The BSO argued that Rowe's compensation package put her in fifth place within the ranks of the highest-paid musicians in the orchestra: higher than nine other BSO male principals. Rowe maintained that her position was unusual among BSO principals

994. *Rowe* court filing, August 31, 2018.
995. Click to discover the "life cycle of the oboist" https://goo.gl/images/ci5MKP.

because of her prominence as a "marketable asset."[996] Her combination of musical excellence, professionalism, and charisma supplied her employer with benefits above and beyond the requirements of her principal position. Undeniably, she was the poster child, the face of the orchestra, featured conspicuously on the BSO website and its official Facebook page.

7.21 BSO MAKES MOVES

On August 25, 2018, the BSO offered to raise Rowe's salary to $250,149. That would have narrowed the pay gap to $64,451 from the original $70,497. Representatives of the BSO repeated the truism "to determine compensation for each musician, particularly principals, is a nuanced process involving many factors." If that statement is weighed at face value, the question arises as to what is a fair way to contract principal players? And, importantly, does gender discrimination hide behind that nuanced process to perpetuate a system in which a woman's contribution to the orchestra is valued less than a man's contribution?

One of the orchestra's key defenses rested on the fact that solo instruments in other top orchestras are paid according to differentiated scales: principal oboists often command higher salaries than principal flutists. However, information requested from the League of American Orchestras regarding the highest-paid orchestral musicians proves that there is no prescribed modality to ascertain the salaries of principals as some orchestras pay the principal flute more than the principal oboe and vice versa. For example, in Cleveland and Philadelphia, the principal flute earns considerably more than the principal oboist, whereas in New York, the situation is reversed. Gender at least in terms of compensation does not enter into this reflection, as the four principals in the aforementioned orchestras are male. It could well be argued that Ferrillo, who is 18 years older than Rowe, could have received extra remuneration based on an age-experience differential. Yet, a closer look at the facts verifies that after an adjustment for seniority was taken into consideration, Rowe still earned approximately 25% less than Ferrillo.

7.22 FLUTE VERSUS OBOE: APPLES VERSUS ORANGES?

Turning to the letter of the law, MEPA defines comparable work as work that requires substantially similar skill, effort, and responsibility and is performed under similar working conditions. How should comparable work be defined in the orchestral context? Both wind players held endowed chairs, and both bore great responsibility to perform major solos. Orchestral insiders would be quick to point out that the two instruments within the orchestra hold equivalent musical responsibility within much of the repertoire, to quote *Rowe* at §24: "the prominence of their contributions"[997] is

996. *Rowe* §56.
997. *Rowe* §164.

analogous. Furthermore, flute and oboe sections are similar in the number of players, pointing to additional comparability.

The question arises: who should be the arbiter for this similarity question? Andris Nelsons, the BSO's MD, could have provided testimony with regard to Rowe's claim. While the MD sits at the helm within the complex nexus of relationships within the orchestra, the notion that he/she would discuss the equivalence of positions may not be advisable as it borders on making a quality call. What if he felt that one of the principals was superior to the other in terms of artistic merit, regardless of gender?

How adequate and legally satisfying is Rowe's claim of pay discrimination when we take into consideration the fact that the oboe is the second most important instrument in the orchestra, the veritable leader of the woodwind section who stands up and tunes the orchestra at the concertmaster's bidding? In the hierarchy of the orchestra, each section has a principal player as well as the "overall" principals. Generally, aside from the conductor who plays the top leadership role, an orchestra's concertmaster is the leader, second in command, while the principal oboe is third in command. Is it germane to query if the principal flute were male and the principal oboe were female within the ranks of the BSO, would the Rowe-Ferrillo pay discrepancy have been a hot issue?

7.23 RESPONSE ON THE PART OF JOHN FERRILLO

What of Rowe's oboe colleague, John Ferrillo? Claiming that the pair plays the Floboe, a combination flute-oboe, he spoke highly of his orchestral neighbor, a "peer and equal," signing a statement that Rowe attached to her complaint that emphasized their outstanding musical teamwork. However, he did not go so far as to speak out about leveling the compensation playing field with Rowe.

Beyond the overarching obligation of good faith, is there any form of obligation for orchestras not to engage in this type of individualized bargaining? US managers and musicians respond by underlining the realities of the marketplace. "If you want the best players possible for a top-tier orchestra, you must do everything possible to attract and keep them. Ultimately this is not as individualized or as some might think, 'elitist' as an outsider may think, because a great principal shapes the sound of his/her section and thereby contributes greatly to the collective."[998] If orchestras are "only as good as their weakest player,"[999] traditional logic holds that compensation for the strongest is warranted. Orchestral CBAs with allowances for individualized bargaining for solo-principal positions provide a means to achieve this end.

Elizabeth A. Rodgers, the attorney who guided Rowe in her lawsuit, reached out to the author to discuss a particular matter with regard to one of Rowe's predecessors, Jacques Zoon. Serving a four-year tenure from 1997 to 2001, the Dutch virtuoso chose

998. Conversations with Ronald Wilford, founder and motivating force at Columbia Artists Management (CAMI)
999. Much repeated adage quoted by conductors ranging from Leonard Bernstein who believed in raising the level of the weakest to a plethora of contemporary maestros who believe in getting rid of the weakest link.

to leave the BSO to pursue a variety of projects. Rodgers was interested to discover if I had any insights concerning Zoon's BSO salary. A musician of prodigious creativity, Zoon had performed frequently with Dutch orchestras where I played. Rodgers was taken somewhat aback when I told her that although I was privy to no inside information, it would have surprised me if Zoon had negotiated for a high overscale salary.[1000] An American lawyer working for an American client in the context of one of the most high-powered orchestras in the country could not believe that this would have been the case. Zoon most likely took his culture with him to Boston: a section player in the highest-paid Dutch orchestra (RCO) in the late 90s would have earned a salary of 75,000 Dutch florins per year, 50% less than BSO colleagues.

7.24 MEDIATION AND SETTLEMENT

The *Rowe* case went to mediation in early December 2018; the final settlement was announced in February 2019. In the initial claim, Rowe had requested a jury trial and damages resulting from unlawful nonpayment of wages with an award that would be doubled along with costs. The BSO responded to the settlement with a reference to the orchestra's honorable past as the first to introduce the screen for blind auditions in 1952 and emphasized that the orchestra continues to strive to be an industry leader in furthering the role of women at every level of its organization. Both parties asserted, "the matter has been resolved to the mutual satisfaction of the parties."[1001] In a joint statement, Rodgers and the BSO emphasized the confidentiality of the mediation and stated that Rowe would continue to perform as principal flautist. Regrettably, the nondisclosure agreement mandatory to resolution closed the door on the details of the settlement. It would have been beneficial not only for academic research but also for musicians in similar positions to ascertain what their chances for equal remuneration could have been. Keeping *Ferguson* in mind, it would have been equally instructive to have access to the role played by the local union to request information related to the overscale contracts at the BSO unavailable through nonprofit reporting channels.

As mentioned above, pay gaps between the sexes can find no justification in past salary history under MEPA. To further such a laudable goal, the employer can be found liable for double the amount of unpaid wages at the high end of the scale unless the employer can provide proof of reasonable self-evaluation of its compensation schemes over a period of three years prior to the claim.[1002] It would have been instructive to discover whether any of the BSO's affirmative defenses were accepted. With characteristic acuity, industry expert Drew McManus remarked, "the missed opportunity here is the potential for creating a set of best practices that help prevent bias and demand the

1000. The direct quote emailed to Ms. Rodgers on July 11, 2018: "It would not surprise me if Zoon would not have bargained for a mega-salary ... between you me and the lamppost, he lived more or less simply, think bicycle no Lexus. He really truly does not care about money. Just a hunch that Zoon's salary might not be as telling as other 'males with flutes' (Cleveland Orchestra) or fellow BSO players."

1001. Malcolm Gay. "BSO Flutist Settles Equal-Pay Lawsuit with Orchestra." *Boston Globe*, February 14, 2019.

1002. MEPA, M.G.L. c. 149 § 105A.

processes used to determine individual agreement terms free from implicit bias and subject to routine oversight."[1003]

A more academic critique of *Rowe* circles around two separate issues. First, to what extent should the state or for that matter the federal government hold the right to meddle with regard to a one-on-one contract (i.e., an overscale individual contract entered into by a single performer with his/her orchestral employer)? For those who ponder the constitutionality of this situation and hope for an answer from the highest court, rest assured the chance that SCOTUS would potentially grant certiorari to a case that pits a highly paid musician against her nonprofit orchestral employer is slim. Second, but no less important, if Rowe was not able to prove that a solo orchestral player is a member of a protected category, was her salary differential compelling enough to prove discrimination? Casting this uncertainty aside, the key to Rowe's success in a MEPA claim can be found in her assertion at §26 that "upon information and belief, the BSO had a policy of considering prior salary earned by an applicant."[1004]

7.25 THE EUROPEAN APPROACH: LIMIT SALARIES TO CBA LEVELS

The European approach teaches that wind and brass players as well as some key strings (concertmaster, principal cello) are doubled, meaning that two principals share the job, each usually working 50% of the time.[1005] Musicians interviewed in the US are split into two camps with regard to their reactions to the issue of discretionary overscale payment particularly with regard to orchestral finances as a whole. Predictably, most orchestral musicians interviewed felt strongly that the salary inflation for principals as well as the exorbitant level of MD and CEO salaries is of great concern, especially in times of financial crisis. Perhaps even the high discretionary overscale payments could undermine the collective bargaining process that leads to section players' CBAs. "If our board and management want to revisit the issue of personnel reduction, they often bring up principal salaries. Interestingly enough, they never talk about the MD's salary, the top of the orchestral hierarchy is immune to salary critique."[1006]

In the US system where the union is key to negotiating scale (the minimum pay for section players), it is absent when individual principals negotiate exclusive overscale contracts. In Europe, while there is an allowance for extra remuneration, this allowance is held under the surveillance of the bodies responsible for orchestral subsidies, the state, the province, and/or the municipality. This control precludes the level of individuation in contracts with regard to creating a new position to alleviate the workload of a principal player.

1003. Drew McManus, *Adaptistration*, available at: https://adaptistration.com/2019/02/19/rowe-lawsuit-settles/?utm_source=Adaptistration+Weekly+Email+Summary&utm_campaign=49bbba437e-.
1004. *Rowe* §26.
1005. Contrast personnel listings at the RCO and the BSO https://www.concertgebouworkest.nl/en/musicians and https://www.bso.org/brands/bso/about-us/musicians/bso-musicians/woodwinds.aspx.
1006. Conversations with Cleveland Orchestra contrabassoonist Jonathan Sherwin, former chair negotiating committee.

Rowe's claim with its focus on pay differentiation among equals opens the floodgates to another issue of consequence in a comparative inquiry: orchestral remuneration. The differences between US top-tier orchestras' and the second and third-tier orchestras' salaries are eye-watering, with differences best illustrated by the contrast between a six-figure salary in the top eight US orchestras[1007] and salaries well below $50,000 a year in the remainder (and majority) of US professional orchestras.[1008]

Of relevance to a comparative study are the differences in compensation between top-tier US orchestras and the RCO. Every few years, the RCO's general manager will take to the press to plead for more funding for the orchestra, bringing forward the argument that as a world leader in the field, it is impossible to attract and keep top players without offering remuneration commensurate to other top orchestras elsewhere in the world.[1009] Benchmarks gleaned from statistics on compensation at top orchestras worldwide show that RCO section members earned 135% less than their colleagues in top orchestras abroad.[1010] The discussion of comparative cross-border salaries takes the reader down a slippery slope: after all, these are the discussions that have led top banks and investment corporations to offer outrageous bonuses at times of financial crisis. The argument "if we can't offer highly competitive salaries, who will want to work here" rings false for several reasons. First, the RCO has not suffered in terms of the level of its players in the last few decades (take note, the same article quoted a salary discrepancy of 100% in 1998 when comparing RCO section players to the highly subsidized Berlin Philharmonic). Second, as other excellent orchestras within the Dutch subsidy constellation struggle for a piece of the competitive subsidy pie in an economic environment of continued cutbacks, the RCO's appeal for more subsidy monies caused consternation among other top-level Dutch ensembles.

7.26 ENFORCEMENT POLICY FOR BEST PRACTICES

As noted in a previous *movement*, endowments and other forms of gifts and donations account for a large part of US orchestral financing. Good patronage should rest on principals of supporting institutions committed to fair employment practices. Thus, from a basic governance point of view, orchestral organizations should support real best practices policies that rest on transparency in all areas of orchestral employment, starting with nonbiased hiring and compensation policies. And, as a MET principal player perceptively reflected, the orchestra owes its audience the assurance that the workplace is not only of the highest artistic standard but also of the highest standard in terms of fairness.[1011]

1007. In terms of salary, the Chicago Symphony, Los Angeles Philharmonic, San Francisco Symphony, Boston Symphony Orchestra, New York Philharmonic, National Symphony Orchestra, Cleveland Orchestra, and Philadelphia Orchestra all offered six-figure base pay to section players in 2017.
1008. More information on Adaptistration, https://adaptistration.com/.
1009. Hilda Bouma "Concertgebouw wil lonen verhogen" *Financieele Dagblad* 25 februari 2019.
1010. *Ibid.*, also *see FAQs* for more information.
1011. Interview with William Short, principal bassoon, Metropolitan Opera Orchestra (MET), http://www.metorchestramusicians.org/blog/2014/4/16/auditioning-for-the-met-orchestra.

It comes as no surprise that there is no evidence of specific gender pay gap jurisprudence within the orchestral profession in the Netherlands. As the discussion on overscale in the US versus CAO-regulated wage scales in the Netherlands highlights, the variance in principal players' salaries is controlled in a system that rewards seniority in terms of years, not previous employment.

7.27 A LEAP OF FAITH? A BRIDGE FROM CONANT TO FERGUSON AND ROWE

Linking *Conant, Ferguson* and *Rowe*, what remains to be seen is how far a union will go to protect its female members from gender discrimination and how much information the NLRB will require an employer to provide on nonmandatory subjects of bargaining relating to possible discrimination. As Conant's fight to maintain the position she won in Munich in 1980 and Rowe's equal pay lawsuit in Boston 2018 underline, the influence of male stereotypes has had a marked impact on hiring practices and overscale compensation in the orchestral workplace up and to the present day. Rewriting the history of orchestras with women as equal musical partners remains a test for orchestras to pass. As long as conductors turn to a brass section and address them as "Gentleman" or as long as a conductor asks the violins to play like "female angels,"[1012] orchestral gender bias persists.

7.28 DIVERSITY, ETHNICITY AND RACE AT THE ORCHESTRA

> Orchestras are a "bastion of whiteness" performing predominately white male music in a very white setting.[1013]
>
> While the economic downturn is certainly having a negative impact on racial discrimination in the world of work, the truth is that even before 2008 progress in this area was limited.[1014]

Major studies point to the fact that racial discrimination increases during periods of economic malaise, high time to consider the state of diversity at the orchestral workplace.[1015] Leave it to Hollywood, not a traditional center of orchestral activity but a hotbed for activism and social media hashtags to fuel the fires of the #metoo movement. On the heels of that combustible movement to be discussed in the following *Intermezzo*,

1012. Comments at rehearsals in professional Dutch orchestras 2013-2018, conductors' identities protected.
1013. Chi-chi Nwankoku. "Classical Music Is Overwhelmingly White and Male." *The Guardian* July 26, 2019.
1014. Lisa Wong, Senior Declaration Officer in the ILO's Programme on Promoting the Declaration on Fundamental Principles and Rights at Work, remarks prefacing *World of Work Magazine* n°72, August 2011 https://www.ilo.org/global/publications/world-of-work-magazine/issues/WCMS_160434/lang--en/index.htm.
1015. Amy R. Krosch and David M. Amodio, "Economic scarcity alters the perception of Race" June 25, 2011, https://www.pnas.org/content/pnas/early/2014/06/04/1404448111.full.pdf.

the #Oscarssowhite debate led the call for more racial diversity on the silver screen.[1016] Musicians interviewed are concerned about the future of their orchestras not only in terms of solvency but also in terms of social relevance and longevity. Beyond the call for equal pay for equal work, these two concerns are of primary importance:

(1) Repertoire traditionally centered on the traditional canon of classics must be expanded to include new voices.
(2) The bridge to a better orchestra is built on gender balance and greater inclusivity. Orchestras should strive to include a multiplicity of ethnicities both on and offstage (administration, board, and management).

A heightened awareness of diversity issues provides fuel for the fires of the next section of a *movement* devoted to equality. Although a thorough discussion of diversity in repertoire and orchestral programming falls far beyond the core issues in this inquiry, it bears mention as what we hear mirrors what we see. Of the hundreds of concerts performed within the eight weeks of concerts (two-four on average per day) broadcast worldwide on the BBC in the Proms concert series 2019, less than four hours of music was composed by a non-white male. And, in terms of total broadcast time, "less than 20 minutes from black and minority ethnic composers, throughout the whole season."[1017] If an orchestral organization eschews egalitarian and multicultural values notwithstanding appeals for modification, what the orchestra plays can appear to be representative of who the orchestra hires.

Recent statistics published by the League of American Orchestras in a study entitled *Racial/Ethnic and Gender Diversity in the Orchestral Field* provide somber facts with regard to US orchestras.[1018] Whereas blacks and Hispanics were represented respectively at 1.7 % and 1.8 % in 1980, the 2018 percentages weighed in at a mere 1.8% and 2.5%. The fourfold increase reported in the aforementioned study on onstage diversity in American orchestras was generated by the rapid rise in successful candidates from a specific ethnic group: Asian and Asian-American musicians.[1019] Off center stage, the statistics show that orchestral administration and board membership is a white bastion in which gender is less of an issue than race.[1020] "Sad but true, the only place where we actually find a significant representation of any sort of minority participants of color at the orchestra is if we look at our stage hands and the cleaning crews."[1021]

1016. Meme #oscarssowhite started to protest the Oscar awards in 2015, a superlative article explores the movements' legacy; *see* https://www.newyorker.com/culture/cultural-comment/is-the-era-of-oscarssowhite-over.
1017. *Ibid.*
1018. *See* "Racial/Ethnic and Gender Diversity in the Orchestral Field: A report by the League of American Orchestras" Research and data analysis by James Doeser September 2016. Available at: https://americanorchestras.org/learning-leadership-development/diversity-resource-center.html.
1019. *Ibid.*
1020. A tradition of women on boards was long established in the US (*see* for more) and several leading ladies sit at the helm of major US orchestras, New York Philharmonic CEO-President, Deborah Borda and Deborah Rutter at the helm of the Kennedy Center in Washington D.C. since 2014 to name but two.
1021. Comment made by minority string player, member of a major US orchestra, anonymity assured.

7.29 THE ASIAN INVASION

If a picture really is worth thousand words, the image below says it all. A poster announcing performances at the prestigious Baden-Baden festival in Germany depicts the polemic, nationalistic German composer Richard Wagner with slanted eyes. To portray Wagner in Asian guise implies that a foreign interpretation of the ur-German master's music will ensue (Figure 14).

Figure 14 A Culturally Questionable Poster Announces Concerts Led by the Japanese-American Conductor Kent Nagano in 2006[1022]

For those who may not find anything questionable at best or reprehensible at worst in this depiction, a reminder of Wagner's overt anti-Semitism can be found in his ample correspondence. "I hold the Jewish race to be the born enemy of pure humanity and everything noble in it."[1023] The fact that the greatest interpreter of Wagner's music, the German-Jewish Wagnerian Hermann Levi, conducted the premiere of *Parsifal* at Bayreuth has intrigued historians, musicians and psychiatrists for over a century.[1024] Armed with a bit of background on Wagner and his racial rantings, the Nagano portrayal is especially alarming considering the difficulties Asian musicians have faced in their quest to enter the European orchestral territory as several disturbing examples from the Vienna Philharmonic Orchestra (VPO), perhaps the most iconic of great European orchestras, illustrate.

1022. Image: Festspielhaus Baden-Baden, referenced at: https://www.dw.com/en/anti-racism-groups-slam-german-ads/a-1649145.
1023. References to Wagner's letters in Richard Wagner (translation W. Ashton Ellis) vol. 3 *Judaism in Music and Other Essays* 1995.
1024. Laurence Dreyfus. "Hermann Levi's Shame and Parsifal's Guilt: A Critique of Essentialism in Biography and Criticism." *Cambridge Opera Journal* 1994, 125-45.

Otto Strasser, a violinist, and former VPO GM, presented his take on the matter of how to deal with increasing competition by superlative Asian musicians in the 1990s when Vienna's legendary conservatories welcomed hundreds of superlative Asian music students:

> I hold it incorrect that today the applicants play behind a screen; an arrangement that was brought in after the Second World War in order to assure objective judgments. because I am convinced that to the artist also belongs the person that one must not only hear, but also see, in order to judge him in his entire personality. [...] Even a grotesque situation that played itself out after my retirement was not able to change the situation. An applicant qualified himself as the best, and as the screen was raised, there stood a Japanese before the stunned jury. He was, however, not engaged, because his face did not fit with the *Pizzicato-Polka* of the New Year's Concert.[1025]

Ten years later, in 2000, the Viennese press broke the news of the acceptance of a half-Japanese violinist into the ranks of the VPO. In an article entitled "A Heaven full of violins," readers learn that the aforementioned violinist was the son of a VPO member, thus more acceptable as one of the elites. Strikingly, the report reiterated the view that such a move would have been unthinkable in the past as the worldwide VPO broadcasts of the New Year's Concert, Mozart masses and Beethoven symphonies were a greeting to the whole world and should be seriously considered as representative of middle-European bliss without the intrusion of other cultures.[1026] In 2003, the Japanese tubist Yasuto Sugiyama was let go before the end of his first trial year. The VPO's chairman Dr. Clemens Hellsberg stated that Mr. Sugiyama was one of the world's best tuba players; however, "even when sitting in the audience, I could hear how differently he played compared to the rest of the orchestra."[1027] This begs the question: did Dr. Hellsberg see or hear the difference? "It's out of the question to say that our orchestra does not accept Japanese musicians. It is just that we have never found any whose musical approach fits in with our special style of playing."[1028]

1025. Otto Strasser. *Und dafür wird man noch bezahlt. Mein Leben mit den Wiener Philharmonikern*. DTV Deutscher Taschenbuch 1990.
1026. *Focus* Dezember 31, 2000, "Ein Himmel Voller Geigen." Quote in original German, "Sogar ein Halbjapaner, Sohn eines Philharmonikers, darf jetzt mitgeigen. Das galt lange als undenkbar, weil die Fernsehbilder von Neujahrskonzert, Mozart-Messen und Beethoven-Symphonien als Grußkarten nostalgischer Mitteleuropa-Seligkeit in alle Welt gesendet wurden."
1027. Francesca Jakes. "All White on the Night: Why Does the World-Famous Vienna Philharmonic Feature So Few Women and Ethnic Minorities?" *The Independent* March 4, 2010, https://www.independent.co.uk/arts-entertainment/music/features/all-white-on-the-night-why-does-the-world-famous-vienna-philharmonic-feature-so-few-women-and-ethnic-1915666.html.
1028. News (Issue 13, 1998) "Es ist keine Rede davon, daß wir keine Japaner nehmen. Es war nur bisher keiner dabei, der vom Spielstil zu uns gepaßt hätte. Wer den nicht hat, wird nicht genommen, und in Wien studiert zu haben, ist noch keine Garantie. Unsere Musiker kommen aus 10 Nationen, viele aus der früheren Donaumonarchie, unser neuer Solocellist, zum Beispiel von der Budapester Oper. Das ist auch eine Sache der kulturellen Tradition."

7.30 ASIAN MUSICIANS DIVERSIFY US ORCHESTRAS

According to a recent study of racial/ethnic diversity in US orchestras, approximately 10% of musicians in major US orchestras identify as Asian in terms of ethnicity, an increase of 80% between 2012 and 2016[1029] with higher percentages reported in the string sections of major US orchestras.[1030] The New York Philharmonic website shows that at the violinist's port of entry, the second violin section, 12 of the 14 second violinists are Asian/Asian-American with similar statistics at other top-tier orchestras.[1031] The answer as to how and why are not central to this research; however, a cursory response can be found in a combination of factors starting with the fact that music study and discipline not to speak of parental involvement in a child's development is given pride of place in many Asian cultures. In the 2011 bestseller, *Battle Hymn of the Tiger Mother*, Yale Law professor and supermom Amy Chua's methods to enforce her daughter's daily piano practice considered mainstream by Chinese parents were deemed abusive by American peers.[1032]

Glen Kwok, Executive Director of the International Violin Competition of Indianapolis and former President of the Board of the World Federation of International Music Competitions, dreams to empower a new generation of Asian orchestral members to find their voices as participatory orchestral committee members keeping in mind that orchestral musicians often face collective financial-organization crises in the course of their careers:

> Winning the audition is just a first step. Afterwards, the challenges really kick in. You have to be savvy on so many levels—to become the best musical "citizen" in the broadest sense makes the whole orchestra better. And let's face it; I can speak for the Asians coming from a Korean background myself. Humility and high level playing are great, but in the modern orchestra you need participation on many fronts.[1033]

Who will guard against bias and subjective decision-making that does not have the best interests of equal opportunity in mind? To gain a broader perspective on this issue, the question was posed to several well-known conductors and key decision-makers with regard to personnel decisions in orchestras.[1034] Marin Alsop, one of the most successful musicians to break the gender barrier among conductors, adds: "[h]ow can we approach

1029. *Racial/Ethnic and Gender Diversity in the Orchestra Field* League of American Symphony Orchestras https://americanorchestras.org/knowledge-research-innovation/diversity-studies.html.
1030. For example, 20 of the 27 violinists (including principal players) listed on the roster of the New York Philharmonic in 2021 are of Asian background https://nyphil.org/about-us/meet/musicians-of-the-orchestra.
1031. *See* Chicago Symphony viola section https://cso.org/about/performers/cso-musicians/ and Philadelphia Orchestra string sections https://www.philorch.org/your-philorch/meet-your-orchestra/musicians/.
1032. Chua threatens her daughter during a piano practice session, "If the next time's not perfect, I'm going to take all your stuffed animals and burn them!" Many successful musicians who claim that their disciplined childhoods led to future success reported similar experiences.
1033. Multiple conversations with Glen Kwok.
1034. As the *FAQs* elucidate, the gateway to the orchestra is the audition. In some orchestras (the Cleveland Orchestra for example), conductors have the final say over candidates. In others, conductors exercise one vote.

what the media dubs an Asian invasion without sounding 'racist'? This challenges all of us in the profession who know that to win an audition and pass through the hurdles to join an orchestra is a superhuman act of perfection and artistry. Today's Asian musicians show the commitment and discipline, fantastic training and individual talent that leads to audition success. Their culture supports classical music as ours once did."[1035] In order to address what appears to be excellence, anti-Asian backlash and racist behavior must be addressed at the pre-audition stage. A recent report from an Asian musician who attended Amsterdam's renowned conservatory (CvA) went viral on social media (Figure 15).[1036]

Figure 15 Racial Stereotyping at the Amsterdam University of the Arts

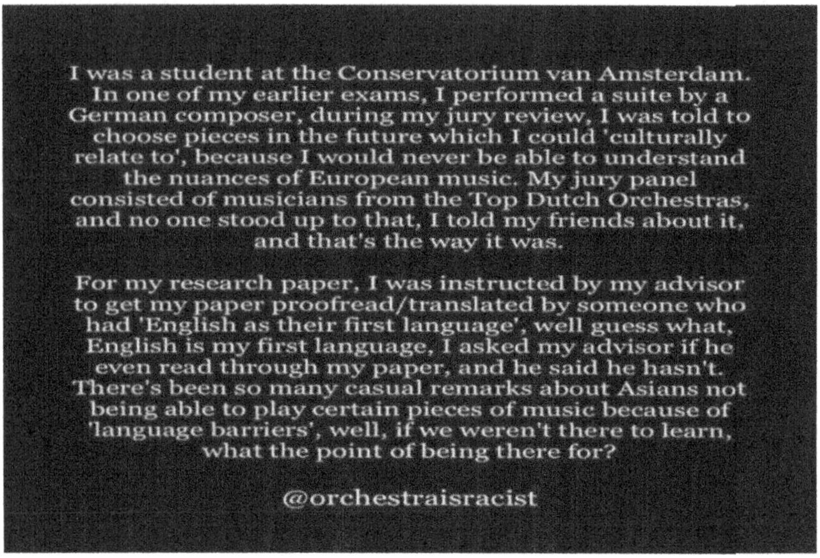

Source: @Orchestraisracist, https://www.instagram.com/orchestraisracist/.

Discussions with a significant pool of CvA graduates corroborated the shocking disclosures. Probing further, several CvA pedagogues disclosed that the offensive allegations were in all probability true, based on frequent, behind-the-scenes comments relating to Asian musicians.[1037] Repeated attempts to get answers from CvA authorities were stonewalled.

1035. Conversations with Marin Alsop.
1036. Conservatorium van Amsterdam (the Amsterdam University of the Arts) https://www.conservatoriumvanamsterdam.nl/en/.
1037. "The look alike, they play alike" was the oft-repeated comment, anonymity assured to the CvA pedagogues.

7.31 CALL IT BY ANOTHER NAME? FINANCIAL BARRIERS

> At first it was kind of awkward, and I think it was awkward for the other players too because I got some strange comments. One guy came up to me and said, "You must fry some mean chicken."[1038]

Music commentator and blogger Norman Lebrecht is one of many who have explored the subject of the white orchestra with particular emphasis on the fact that although the orchestral color barrier has been broken by Asians, the paucity of black and other minority musicians is striking. "To diversify orchestras, the social aspects have to be taken into consideration. Too few blacks can afford a tertiary musical education."[1039] His observation is supported by the award-winning black oboist Althea Ifeka: "the lack of black orchestral musicians is about money, not colour."[1040]

Tellingly, a significant part of orchestral integration takes place long before the audition stage. The cost of studying music, purchasing/renting an instrument, and receiving professional training audition is massive for any entrant into the field. For economically disadvantaged aspirants of any background, these costs much like the costs associated with advanced education are real and insurmountable obstacles. The road to a competitive career means the young musician has to be nurtured by excellent teachers, summer programs that promote musical excellence, and instruments that motivate the student to improve—all components that cost money.

For all the difficulties that musicians face en route to professional careers, the worst is yet to come for skilled black musicians. The record shows that several black musicians who passed US auditions struggled with another hurdle: tenure requirements. Take the saga of Elayne Jones, a black timpanist in the San Francisco Symphony. An audience favorite, she was denied tenure within two years of winning an audition.[1041] While Jones was denied tenure by a vote by her orchestral peers based on specific performance, the taint of discrimination came to the fore. To quote one of her former colleagues:

> To prove a player is incompetent is practically impossible. But it happened with Elayne Jones. No, she wasn't fired, she didn't get tenure. For tenure all the musicians are asked. After you have your two probationary years, there must be a consensus of people who have knowledge, and with Elayne Jones people complained that her tympanies were not in tune. Was it true? No, the people have no

1038. Ann Hobson Pilot, the sole black musician in the Boston Symphony for decades, interview *Senza Sordino* June-August 1989, 5.
1039. *Ibid.*
1040. Althea Ifeka, quoted by Elizabeth Day. "Why Are Our Orchestras So White?" *The Guardian* September 14, 2008 https://www.theguardian.com/culture/2008/sep/14/music.classical musicandopera.
1041. William Duncan Allen. "An Overview of Black Concert Music and Musicians in Northern California from the 1940s to the 1980s" *Black Music Research* 9(1) Spring 1989, 81-92 DOI: 10.2307/779433.

> sense of pitch… most of us do not even know where the tympanies were. I wasn't asked about Elayne Jones, but why I wasn't asked, I don't know.[1042]

7.32 TALES FROM THE NEW YORK PHILHARMONIC

In 1969, as the civil rights movement gathered momentum in the United States, two black musicians who had freelanced regularly in the New York Philharmonic, bassist Arthur Davis and cellist Earl Madison, accused the orchestra of discriminatory hiring practices and subsequently filed suit at New York's Commission on Human Rights.[1043] The Philharmonic's superstar MD Leonard Bernstein was a vociferous supporter of civil rights. Putting deeds to back up his words, Bernstein was a founding father of the Symphony of the New World, a completely integrated orchestra founded just after the Civil Rights Act came into effect in 1964. Yet, when queried about the lack of integration in his orchestra, he retorted: "the New York Philharmonic is not in the social rearmament business."

Perhaps the most shocking statistic to emerge from the case revealed that during the period of a decade (1960s), 277 substitutes and extra players performed a total of 1,773 weeks with the Philharmonic. Among those musicians was a black musician who was hired only for one week.[1044] Reacting to the claims presented by the two musicians including evidence of a structural lack of racial integration at the workplace, the National Urban League called on the orchestra to put affirmative action in place. Charges against the Philharmonic were dismissed, as "discrimination in matters involving artistic judgment is, in the very nature of the case, most difficult to prove."[1045] Davis was called back to substitute a few more times post hearings, however within a few months he lost his freelance work at the Philharmonic. And, Sanford Allen, a violinist who held the distinction of being the only black member of the New York Philharmonic, left the orchestra after 15 years of service in 1977. In a *New York Times* interview, he stated that he was "simply tired of being a symbol."[1046]

Another illustrative story tells the tale of many thousands of careers in the shadow of success in New York, "a haven of opportunity for all musicians":[1047]

> When I began my career in 1941, it was almost unthinkable for a black musician even to ask for an audition with a symphony orchestra. I did get a job as a bassist with the National Youth Administration orchestra, but after it was disbanded, I couldn't even get an audition with Phil Spitalny's all-girl orchestra, and that's no

1042. Listen to Felix Khuner. *A Violinist's Journey from Vienna's Kolisch Quartet to the San Francisco Symphony and Opera Orchestras: An Oral History Transcript/1996*. Available at https://archive.org/details/violinistsjourn00khunrich.
1043. *Ibid.*
1044. Archives of the New York Philharmonic, Black Musicians Human Rights Commission Hearings 1969, July 30, 1969-September 26, 1970 (ID: 011-03-22) https://archives.nyphil.org/index.php/artifact/abb6b2d1-5a2e-4a0d-888d-6ba897f038e6-0.1/fullview#page/1/mode/2up.
1045. *Ibid.*
1046. https://www.nytimes.com/1977/08/29/archives/only-black-in-philharmonic-is-resigning-after-15-years.html.
1047. Repeated by the New York Philharmonic's exuberant Music Director (1978-1991) Zubin Mehta.

> kidding. It was then that I began playing primarily with jazz groups, as so many black musicians have done when they had no alternative.
>
> Yet years later, I did ask Leopold Stokowski [distinguished US-based conductor, started his legendary career at the Philadelphia Orchestra, author's comment] for an audition, citing two awards I had won from the National Orchestral Association. He auditioned me despite my relatively advanced age for a symphony orchestra beginner and told me that was acceptable and that there would be a job for me in his orchestra in the fall. Yet when the fall came, I learned that the musicians for his orchestra had already been chosen and I was not included among them.[1048]

More troubling, when a black musician finally makes it in the white, white world of classical music performance, he/she might discover that there are other barriers that show themselves at the front door to the concert hall, "a shored-up sonic refuge of whiteness."[1049] A jaw-dropping blog written by maestro Brandon Keith Brown reports on "Why Blacks don't go to concerts." Before engaging the reader in tales from the concert crypt replete with jibes and nasty comments, he observes:

> Classical concerts are racially traumatic experiences. It's why we don't go. Why pay to sit stone-still, quiet, cooped up with white folks who don't want us there? Does this sound like a relaxing Saturday night to you?
>
> Artists on stage—and the composer(s)—rarely look like us. Instead of masterworks on subscription concerts, Black artists are mostly relegated to ethnically pigeonholed variety shows during Black history month or other auxiliary dates white administrators choose to look and feel less racist.
>
> As a Black male, I'm not afforded the option to express the same range of emotion white men can. I'm required to be demure, mitigate my speech, be overly gracious and smile like a Cheshire cat at all times. At concerts, I should think, "Gosh oh gee, I'm SO privileged to sit with all you white people after years of legalized segregation!"
>
> I don't. It makes folks nervous and mad. Not my problem.
>
> So, what does a ticket cost when Black?
>
> Our dignity.
>
> The concert hall is white people turf, another space where I'm not wanted.[1050]

7.33 AFFIRMATIVE ACTION AND PROTESTS AGAINST DISCRIMINATION

Despite calls for greater diversity within contemporary orchestras, affirmative action as a means to serve this end is as controversial in 2023 as it was in 1989, as an example from the Detroit Symphony (DSO) foregrounds. The Michigan state legislature warned that it would withhold further funding unless the DSO changed its tune and hired more black musicians. With a DSO total of two black musicians in 1989 in a predominantly black city (75% of Detroit's population was black as confirmed by census reports in

1048. Lucille Dixon. "Is It Artistic Judgment or Is It Discrimination?" *New York Times* August 1, 1971. A version of the archives appeared on August 1, 1971, on Page D11 of the New York edition with the headline: Music.
1049. Brandon Keith Brown's blog, https://medium.com/@maestrobkb/smile-for-white-supremacy-no-more-ad78df59c42c.
1050. *Ibid.*

1990, up from 63% in 1980), the orchestra chose not to screen auditions in order to expedite the legislature's demands. This incurred the wrath of DSO musicians who threatened to file unfair labor charges and troubled new hires who were concerned that they would be scorned by their colleagues for entering the orchestra on a fast track.

7.34 RAISE A FIST AGAINST DISCRIMINATION: GEORGE SZELL SETS AN EXAMPLE

In the gallery of "musicians in power" along the road to integration, there are heroes who attempted to foster integration: among the heroes, the Cleveland Orchestra's legendary MD, Szell, hired the orchestra's first black musician, cellist Donald White in 1959. White who performed in the orchestra for 39 seasons recounted, "Szell would pass by and put his hand on my shoulder" as if to say, "I know what you are going through."[1051] In March 1961, two months before the Freedom Riders were attacked in Birmingham, Alabama,[1052] White was denied entry to the city's concert hall. A municipal regulation that forbade blacks and whites from appearing together in a public place was enforced at the hall's artist entrance. In a crucial gesture of solidarity, Szell announced that the entire Cleveland Orchestra would boycott the concert unless White was granted his right to enter the hall. The show did go on, with White joining his colleagues in the cello section.[1053]

7.35 THE DUTCH TOUCH: IMBALANCED BUT NOT RACIST

Missing among these tales of discrimination in orchestras is an appraisal of the Dutch touch, the orchestral landscape in the Netherlands. Do these lacunae bear witness to an ideal multicultural state of affairs or is it possible that a discussion of discrimination in Dutch orchestras is not applicable to the orchestral status quo? Debates concerning multiculturism, a buzzword of sorts within political as well as cultural debates, include discussions on pluriformity, the recognition and inclusion of a multiplicity of cultures into the mainstream culture. This entails a change of direction from encouraging and enhancing awareness of the Western canon toward embracing all cultures as part of a larger conception of poly-national culture.[1054]

Indeed, it is difficult to attribute the paucity of minorities in Dutch orchestras to direct discrimination. Interviews with stakeholders corroborate the hypothesis that racism in Dutch orchestras has not been as overt as the anti-Asian sentiments expressed by the VPO in past years, and according to reports, many German orchestras until the 2020s. The RCO's caretakers report, "our orchestra welcomes the players who succeed at auditions: we have Asians, two foreign concertmasters and many other representatives of foreign countries. The musicians of color issue, or lack thereof, is more related to

1051. Listen to Mr. White: https://www.youtube.com/watch?v=pDCCcEsW1bVw.
1052. The Heinous KKK Attack on the Freedom Rides captured on video, courtesy the Smithsonian, https://www.youtube.com/watch?v=J8WnT6v_W3o.
1053. Recounted in Michael Charry's biography, *George Szell: A Life in Music* 2011, 174-175.
1054. Adri Schreuder. *Multiculturele variaties in muziekeducatie*. 2008.

who auditions, who even gets to that point in terms of training."[1055] Once again, maintenance and sustenance issues tied to early training, parental support, and financial sponsorship crucial to enable young musicians to begin and continue the arduous process that leads to an orchestral career are central to changing orchestral color.

In terms of cultural differences, minority classical musicians brought forward the point that there is a marked tendency to dismiss or disregard nonmainstream national culture. "Many minorities who are Dutch nationals (Surinamese, Antillean, Turkish and Moroccan) have rich cultures of their own; the link to the Western classical music tradition is tenuous at best. For some there might even be a stigma to get involved in white man's music as that means you turn your back on your roots."[1056] To others queried "do not forget the political considerations that relate to the fact that at orchestras non-EU candidates must wait in line for auditions, as EU candidates and those holding work permits are given a first chance to play. This means that many fine non-European nationals are effectively barred from winning auditions as many orchestral vacancies are filled before they get a chance to play. This might not be viewed as a discriminatory policy, but it certainly keeps the orchestras in Europe-first mode."[1057]

7.36 POSITIVE NOTES: A CALL FOR COMMITMENT AND ACTION

The ups and downs of affirmative action aside, the number of contemporary orchestras that fund and actively support diversity initiatives is becoming a structural part of an orchestra's status quo. Many US orchestras have announced Minority Fellowships[1058] and pledge nondiscrimination on their websites. As this *movement* illustrates, inclusive texts on websites and antidiscrimination black letter law are commendable but nevertheless inconsequential unless followed up by action. Suggestions for tangible improvement on the orchestral integration front should reach out on three fronts. First, orchestra budgets should earmark funds to initiate local educational projects for young students. Subsidized Dutch orchestras are now required to implement fair pay regulations; why not pair subsidy grants with educational fulfillment requirements to benefit those who have little or no access to classical music? Second, whereas orchestras in the past were required to showcase national repertoire, the modern orchestra should add minority voices to programs. Third, orchestras should collaborate actively with conservatories to develop programs geared to aspiring performers/composers with the aim of fostering professionalism. From the Amsterdam-based combination "music and social project" *Leerorkest*[1059] to the Los Angeles Philharmonic's showcase youth

1055. Conversation with Joel Fried, Artistic Director RCO 1999-2020.
1056. Conversations with Ernst-Paul Fuchs, pianist.
1057. Conversations with a South American national on the Dutch audition scene, anonymity assured.
1058. For example, the Cleveland Orchestra and the Detroit Symphony announced special fellow ships 2016-2017 https://www.dso-org.
1059. *See* www.leerorkest.nl, as of 2019 the Netherlands Philharmonic Orchestra cooperates with Leerorkest projects.

orchestra YOLA (with its own youth center),[1060] and the pan-US *Sphinx* initiatives,[1061] social justice through classical music training startups modeled on the Venezuelan El Sistema "tocar y luchar" (to play and to struggle) are transforming the classical music scene at least at the rudimentary training level.[1062] Whether this will alleviate discriminatory practices and vulnerabilities remains to be seen and heard. Let the closing kudos go to a classically trained top-tier orchestral musician who has devoted a significant portion of her life to developing classical music programs for disadvantaged children. "Communication through music is defined by give-and-take. We learn, they learn. Start small, dream big: music captures the imagination and takes root" (Figure 16).[1063]

Figure 16 Hands-On Training, Consuelo, Dominican Republic 2017

1060. https://www.latimes.com/entertainment/arts/la-et-cm-yola-center-commentary-20180815-story.html.
1061. https://www.atlantasymphony.org/community/ ~ /media/b7d970f28422427a9caceff25f908405.ashx and http://www.sphinxmusic.org/our-history/.
1062. A critical note on the hierarchy within El Sistema and its inability to reach the most precarious, https://www.theguardian.com/music/2014/nov/11/geoff-baker-el-sistema-model-of-tyranny.
1063. Visionary violinist Isabel Trautwein, member Cleveland Orchestra; founder El Sistema@Rainey; initiator music startup in Consuelo, Dominican Republic (2017), where the author and her daughter Yaël Kurzbauer coached.

8

Intermezzo: Singing the #metoo Classical Blues

This *intermezzo* juxtaposes how two top-tier orchestras in the United States and the Netherlands reacted to serious allegations of sexual harassment brought against leading figures at the workplace. While one may argue that this topic does not figure within an inquiry on the vulnerable state of orchestras and their workers, post-financial crises, musicians voiced great concerns with regard to on-the-job functionality if #metoo issues were not addressed properly, and even pointed to possible ramifications beyond the work floor. "Think about it: if an orchestra cannot come to grips with such a critical matter that shakes its credibility and has a negative impact on our safety, should that orchestra merit significant financial support no matter whether it emanates from individuals, corporations and most certainly, the state?"[1064]

The news concerning the two cases that involved top-ranked orchestras in the US and the Netherlands broke in the *Washington Post* on July 26, 2018, causing a sensation in international and social media.[1065] Citing a significant number of sources both on and off the record, reporters confirmed: "the *Washington Post* spoke to more than 50 musicians who say they were victims of sexual harassment. These artists, many of whom shared their stories for the first time, described experiences ranging from sexual harassment to sexual assault, at every level from local teachers to international superstars."[1066] We begin in Cleveland, Ohio home of the famed Cleveland Orchestra (CO), before crossing the ocean to Amsterdam, home of the legendary Royal Concertgebouw Orchestra (RCO). Even though the cases are markedly different in terms of substance and outcome, they foreground crises of impropriety at the orchestral workplace.

1064. Musician member RCO#1, anonymity assured.
1065. Anne Midgette and Peggy McGlone. "Assaults in Dressing Rooms. Groping During Lessons—Classical Musicians Reveal a Profession Rife with Harassment." *Washington Post* July 25, 2018.
1066. *Ibid.*

8.1 CLASSICAL BLUES IN CLEVELAND

Since winning the concertmaster audition at the world-renowned CO in 1995, Bill Preucil was prized not only for his playing but also for his superlative rapport with Music Director (MD) Franz Welser-Möst. CO musicians spoke openly with respect concerning Preucil's impeccable performance skills and clear leadership. Yet, for years a shadow marred this perfection. Deleterious observations portending a darker side had been relegated to the back pages of social media, local newspapers and the "we know but don't talk" rumor mill. Preucil's soft spot for female students at the Cleveland Institute of Music (CIM) where he was a star faculty member was the stuff of much speculation after specific allegations surfaced in 2007. A local rag, the *Cleveland Scene*, broke a story that detailed accusations of sexual improprieties.[1067] The article focused on a specific incident in which Preucil's unwanted advances led to a deal and a cover-up: in exchange for silence, a female violin student was transferred to a top musical institution far from Cleveland and received a cash payout for the inconvenience. In response to the situation, the CIM's President responded:

> The Cleveland Institute of Music is thoroughly committed to providing a safe and comfortable working and learning environment for all of its constituents ... When any issues are brought to the attention of the CIM administration, it has consistently taken prompt, immediate and decisive action to gather the facts and confidentially resolve the matter in full accordance with CIM's published policies.[1068]

The reader might clamor for a stronger choice of words; however, the actions of the CIM in this case of sexual harassment showed a desire to protect the institution and the alleged perpetrator from negative publicity. "It was a real nightmare and a total cover up. I was close to the woman in question who only wanted to be handled with decency and within the boundaries of the law."[1069] Silence and a quick-fix response protected the reputation of not only the prestigious CIM but also, Preucil's principal employer, the CO. Cleveland's musical institutions were not the only examples of tarnished silence: in the months and years to follow, leading conservatories and institutes of higher learning were exposed as complicit partners unwilling to condemn illicit actions on the part of their famed pedagogues.[1070] An ongoing saga at London's Royal College of Music in 2023 centers on a violin pedagogue who had been previously

1067. Rebecca Meiser. "Sour Notes." *Cleveland Scene* February 14, 2007.
1068. Prominent violin pedagogue David Cerone served as CIM President (1985-2007); his recalcitrance to handle the abuse situation was endemic to institutional reactions at the time. As a matter of full disclosure, the author studied violin with David Cerone and received this email in 2016.
1069. Discussion with a former CIM violin student, close friend of the anonymous victim, anonymity assured.
1070. Published reports from *inter alia*: Indiana University, University of Michigan, Eastman School of Music, the Berklee College of Music, and the Curtis Institute report similar stories of abuse and coverups https://www.theatlantic.com/education/archive/2020/01/conservatories-sexual-harassment-abuse/604351/. *See* also, reports from the Chetham's School of Music in Manchester https://www.bbc.com/news/uk-england-manchester-49907386.

implicated while teaching at the Conservatory of Amsterdam (CvA), Chetham's School of Music and the Royal Northern College of Music.[1071]

En route to the Grand Teton Music Festival in 2018 and the long-awaited chance to experience Preucil's artistry, orchestral participants at the festival received the following email from Festival management:

> Many of you saw the unfortunate article in today's *Washington Post* concerning sexual harassment in classical music. In that article, there were allegations of sexual misconduct by William Preucil, concertmaster of the Cleveland Orchestra. Mr. Preucil was scheduled to be concertmaster for Festival Orchestra during Week 6. Earlier this evening, the Festival rescinded its invitation to Mr. Preucil.[1072]

Had the *Washington Post* discovered something that smacked of predatory behavior? Cringing in the aftershock of Harvey Weinstein's #metoo bevy of film star casualties, a growing number of classical musicians held their collective breaths wondering when other incidents of abuse on and offstage would capture media attention. "It had a sort of *veni, vidi, vici* feel to it—all of us, musician members of great orchestras as well as colleagues who teach at conservatories, had long lists of names, some secret and some not-so-secret, of perpetrators. That list was never shared with the outside world, nevertheless, we knew who was misbehaving and worse."[1073] For decades, such stories were more apt to escape media attention or fuel *Mozart in the Jungle* scripts than reach courtroom scrutiny.[1074]

Within days of the *Washington Pos*t revelations, Preucil resigned from the faculty of the CIM and was suspended from the CO.[1075] On August 16, 2018, the CO announced that it had hired a leading New York-based law firm, Debevoise & Plimpton, bolstered by a committee of five members of the CO's Board of Trustees to investigate the claims brought against Preucil. A *Report to the Special Committee of the Board of Trustees of the Cleveland Orchestra* (Report) contained enough information to lead to the suspension and eventual dismissal of another orchestra member accused of harassment, principal trombonist, Massimo La Rosa. In the Preucil case, the committee interviewed over 70 people, including Preucil. He admitted to "engaging in sexual contact with three female students during or after lessons" but offered no additional comments.[1076] On October 24, 2018, 11 years after the allegations of impropriety were reported in *Cleveland Scene*, Preucil was fired by the CO. Stating that "the independent investigation speaks for itself."[1077] Sections IIIA.2-IIIa.5. of the Report spell out:

1071. https://www.thestrad.com/news/former-violin-professor-denies-two-counts-of-sexual-assault/16234.article.
1072. Email received July 27, 2018.
1073. Conversations with Judy Nelson, violist New York Philharmonic (1983-2019).
1074. Blair Tindall's *Mozart in the Jungle: Sex, Drugs and Classical Music,* first appeared in book form in 2005 (Atlantic Press) before its reincarnation as a popular Amazon Prime series in 2014.
1075. Michael Cooper. "Cleveland Orchestra Suspends a Star After Allegations of Assault" *New York Times* July 27, 2018.
1076. Anastasia Tsioulcas, "Cleveland Orchestra Fires 2 Leading Musicians after Sexual Misconduct Investigation." National Public Radio October 24, 2018.
1077. Justin Holden, Senior Director of Communications, the Cleveland Orchestra, *Adaptistration* November 14, 2018.

> Two then-members of the executive committee of the Board were separately approached by members of the Orchestra who were concerned about the allegations in the Cleveland Scene article. During at least one of those discussions, a musician raised concerns about...sexual misconduct at CIM and reported that Preucil had made unwanted verbal sexual advances to a female player in the Orchestra... Neither former Orchestra management nor former Board leadership took steps to investigate or otherwise act upon the sexual misconduct allegations in the *Cleveland Scene* article or the additional allegation of sexual misconduct that was reportedly relayed to a Board member in 2007. Former Orchestra leadership should have done more to investigate the reports about Preucil's behavior following the *Cleveland Scene* article.

What is missing regrettably from the Report as well as from the CO's website is any form of apology for more than a decade of silence. Tellingly, it took the clout of a *Washington Post* article and the swift, damning responses in media and practice to motivate changes in Cleveland.

8.2 SUPERSTAR PREDATORS: ARTISTIC LICENSE

Like the infamous Weinstein and others in the film business, classical musicians of fame and power are often free to engage in abusive behavior. Historically, the notion of the riveting musician who possesses superpowers to transform all within earshot was personified by several superhuman 19th-century performers, most notably Franz Liszt and Niccolò Paganini. Their well-documented performances and behavior both on and off the podium challenged the accepted social mores of self-control, especially when it came to the behavior of female audience members. "Devout women lost their simplicity of faith ... and become filled with sinful agitation."[1078] Performances interrupted by mass hysteria and stories of personal downfall filled the pages of scandal sheets and in the case of the charismatic Franz Liszt convinced Heinrich Heine to coin the term "Lisztomania" to characterize the audiences' "veritable insanity, one unheard of in the annals of furor."[1079] The myth of the larger-than-life musician who wields control over the collective orchestral instrument created the image of the genius whose often incontrollable behavior was condoned in the name of art. "As long as the persons in question are great musicians, so-called geniuses, they receive a kind of carte blanche for misbehavior. There is this perverse idea that greatness can excuse the inexcusable and that if you do not play along with it, either your career will be ruined or that there is something wrong with you. These disturbing patterns run through music schools and continue on into the professional circuit."[1080]

1078. Anatoli Vinogradov, *The Condemnation of Paganini* (translation) Stephen Garry. Hutchinson & Co 1946, 816.
1079. Heinrich Heine. "Florentine Nights," *Works of Heinrich Heine* vol. 1 Charles Leland translation, 71-72.
1080. Conversations with several graduates of Manchester's storied Chetham's School of Music post Independent Inquiry into Child Sexual Abuse (IICSA) hearings October 1-2, 2019, anonymity assured.

8.3 THE PHYSICAL NATURE OF MUSIC LESSONS

Music lessons are one-on-one, deeply personal, and to a substantial degree, physical in nature. Karen Tuttle, a force of nature among 20th-century viola educators, insisted that her students pull their shirts uncovering the left shoulder in order to place the instrument on bare skin to expose the body to the unique contact and the vibrations of "a piece of wood." Memory lane takes the author back to a master class with the legendary concertmaster-soloist-conductor Joseph Silverstein, in sweltering Sarasota, Florida. Hands-on demonstration was key to unlearning bad habits. Silverstein pummeled and pushed in an attempt to coax some modicum of relaxation as sweat poured down my face. In the context of the #metoo epoch, Tuttle and Silverstein's physical interactions could have attracted criticism as examples of impropriety.

Where do we draw the line between inappropriate behavior and criminal actions? What happens when the #metoo floodgates open and a domino effect of accusations gathers momentum? Enter the grey zone between victim and accused, a zone in which institutions pray for silence and the media clamors for more dirt. Preucil and others who have been placed in classical music's #metoo limelight are celebrities whose status helps grab headlines: scandal sells. And, as the celebrated Weinstein actress-accusers proved, some victims keep these experiences quiet for decades as accusations, especially those pinpointed against celebrities, roam in rough terrain. No apologist for behavior that crosses into the legal no-fly zone and a vociferous opponent of inappropriate behavior at work or school, legal beagles (pun intended) plead for a dogged investigation of the bad, i.e., predatory actions/criminal behavior coupled with true caution regarding actions that fall within an acceptable spectrum of behavior.

8.4 BE CAREFUL OF WHAT YOU WISH FOR: PRESUMPTION OF INNOCENCE

Our screens transmit nascent buzzwords that mold public opinion as commentary shared on social media platforms obviates. As with all movements, both off and online, the #metoo movement has revolutionized the thinking on sexual harassment. Not only was awareness raised but also on a more questionable side a tsunami of politically correct disclosures followed initial outrage. From the legitimate consciousness-raising exercise to the ensuing witch hunt of public figures, especially in the media-ripe turf of the performing arts, cries of "he is guilty" negated real proof. "It was as if we all had our personal #metoos to share, overnight. Some doubtlessly legitimate hidden by a noxious combination of angst and bad memories however, as distressful as it might seem, I can't help but think that some of these articulations are based on unproven states of affairs."[1081] To critics, #metoo had the power to create a disconcerting herd mentality, replacing fact-finding with a thought police without any regard for questions of a legal

1081. Conversations with a female musician at the Curtis Institute of Music after allegations pointed to inappropriate behavior on the part of several distinguished faculty members, anonymity assured.

nature. To disregard the sacrosanct principle enshrined in the presumption of innocence smacks more of a witch hunt and less of a movement committed to improving the lives of the abused. A still small voice begs for caution before we enter the stone-throwing arena. Until the parameters of appropriate behavior at workplaces and schools are subject to open discussion first and rulemaking second, the temptation to sit back and applaud as another one bites the dust prompts smug hypocrisy or as the Royal Concertgebouw (RCO) situation described below illustrates, questionable accusations.

8.5 THE WHOLE TRUTH OR JUST PLAIN JUMPING THE GUN? #METOO AT THE ROYAL CONCERTGEBOUW

On August 2, 2018, the RCO's MD, Daniele Gatti, the seventh MD in the illustrious lineup at the Royal Concertgebouw Orchestra (RCO), was fired following the aforementioned *Washington Post* allegations of inappropriate behavior. Gatti had served a mere two years at the helm of the famous orchestra. Reports had surfaced alleging unwanted sexual advances on the part of the maestro at opera houses in Italy back in 1996 and 2000 compounded by accusations reportedly made by three female members of the RCO. Yet, unlike the well-documented case that put the CO's concertmaster into the shadows, *#gattigate* (to quote the hashtag that trended in the Netherlands)[1082] was based on cries, whispers, and as hindsight teaches, unproven allegations. The justifications for Gatti's fall from grace have occupied the thoughts and minds of many beyond the hallowed halls of the Concertgebouw. Months of speculative newspaper articles, punctuated by television appearances in which direct questions concerning the nature of the inappropriate behavior were deflected by the RCO's General Manager Jan Raes, increased the uneasy speculation that there was something egregiously wrong with the dismissal. A star-studded lineup of conductors voiced support for their dismissed colleague, and several well-known conductors refused to accept invitations from the RCO to replace the deposed Gatti. The prestigious Rome Opera took the bold move of hiring Gatti as MD in December 2018.[1083] Speculations in the Dutch press regarding overly rash decision-making on the part of RCO management lingered for more than a year.

Frustration leaked to the press and social media brought to the fore an orchestra divided by musicians in disagreement over "the affair," with consensus supporting the view that the situation was "something of a nightmare. Instead of Gatti we get to work with conductors who fill the weeks he was forced to drop; the majority of these conductors are totally unsuited to lead this great orchestra. And, in the meantime, our management demands that we obey a no comments order. We were told to rely on the care and expert judgment of our management and board with regard to the issue."[1084]

1082. #gattigate surfaced within minutes of the *Washington Post* article and remained as a much-cited tag.
1083. As reported internationally by *Associated Press* et al., *see*, https://www.insider.com/ap-rome-opera-hires-gatti-who-lost-job-over-metoo-allegations-2018-12.
1084. Musician member #2 RCO, anonymity assured.

Sworn silence on the part of the musicians led to robust criticism from deep inside the orchestra, "we were told that three women had brought forward charges, yet, if any of us knew who these colleagues were or for that matter, what they alleged, that remained a mystery for the rest of the orchestra."[1085]

Another musician voiced discomfort at the speed with which purported harassment could change into a definite condemnation. "Yes, Gatti was the stereotype of an Italian macho flirt, yet this does not mean that his gauche remarks are tantamount to sexual harassment, at least from what I observed at the hall. How far should we dig into the past is another question: if allegations from 20 years ago that were not criminally charged can lead us to fire a conductor, how many others would be brought down?"[1086]

8.6 THE #METOO LEGAL LANDSCAPE: DEFAMATION IN THE GREY ZONE

Although the RCO refused to comment on Gattigate,[1087] several insiders[1088] affirmed that his defense team could have pressed for defamation charges. For women and men on both sides of #metoo, defamation lawsuits have provided the chance to triumph on the legal and media battlegrounds where accusations of sexual misconduct are at issue.[1089]

Regarding the Gatti accusations, Anne Midgette, the principal journalist who wrote and researched the *Washington Post* article that caused consternation and retaliation, was "frankly shocked by [Gatti's] dismissal."[1090] In a YouTube interview, she clarified that in order to publish such damning information in the US she needed two sources to come forward and allow identification by name. After these sources were vetted, the decision to publish was made. With regard to the fact-checking elements on the part of the RCO, Midgette articulated, "the RCO only consulted me once and that was after the article was running. They wanted to know whether I knew when Gatti had known about the article."[1091]

In an initial response, Gatti released a statement to clarify that he had never engaged in any illegal or offensive behavior and that he was accused of purported behavior that had taken place "a long time ago." Following the advice of the Reputation Doctor, a public relations crisis advisory firm, the media-beleaguered conductor released an apology to all women: "I would like to say that if I have hurt anybody, I am very sorry."[1092] Clumsy at best, his apology backfired: Gatti was subjected to massive

1085. Musician member #3 RCO, anonymity assured.
1086. Musician member #2 RCO, anonymity assured.
1087. The author, not to speak of the mainstream Dutch press, was left in the dark despite numerous attempts to gain clarity concerning the allegations.
1088. Two individuals close to the RCO board, anonymity assured.
1089. Much has been written on actress Ashley Judd's defamation charges and the link to the sexual Harvey Weinstein harassment cases against Harvey Weinstein https://www.courthousenews.com/ashley-judd-defamation-suit-against-harvey-weinstein-advances/.
1090. Anne Midgette at https://www.youtube.com/watch?v=ZIXE4PaGkWg.
1091. *Ibid.*
1092. https://reputationdoctor.com/.

amounts of ridicule on social media and intensified speculation in the press as to why he was apologizing for actions he had distanced himself from.

8.7 SILENCE AND INSTITUTIONAL ACCOUNTABILITY

How could an orchestra with such a strong, protective structure have failed so utterly with regard to Gattigate? As illuminated in the *FAQs*, the RCO's organizational structure differentiates itself from other Dutch orchestras. In a move to ensure that the musicians have a voice at the most centralized level of decision-making, three members of the orchestra serve on the RCO's governing board.[1093] "Our system ensures that the musicians have more powers than other Dutch orchestras that operate on a standard state system in which a works council cooperates with management to give employees a voice."[1094] Yet, even with musicians advising at the highest echelons, the perceived unfairness inherent to Gatti's guilty-until-proven-innocent situation reflected poorly on the RCO.

RCO fans worldwide and the scores of individuals who commented in Dutch national newspapers and on social media[1095] expressed great uneasiness with what was considered to be a cavalier approach to the presumption of innocence enshrined in European law in Article 6, para. 2 of the European Convention on Human Rights (ECHR).[1096] Rumors reached fever pitch as the press speculated on the fact that the orchestra was looking for an excuse to get rid of an MD who had been hastily chosen. Speculation abounded that the hasty decision to terminate Gatti's contract masked a very different decision: any hint of #metoo provides a perfect excuse to dispose of an employee who might not meet the approval of the Board for other reasons. "We were not permitted to know why he was actually fired so quickly without a thorough review of what he had or had not done. The very notion that #metoo accusations could be used for other means is inexcusable."[1097]

In April 2019, the RCO announced that Gatti and the RCO had come to an agreement, the contents of which were not disclosed to the orchestra members, the public, and certainly not to the press.[1098] In what many perceived as a gratuitous gesture, the orchestra's website subsequently heralded, "the return of Daniele Gatti,"

1093. *FAQs* for additional information.
1094. Conversations with David Bazen, RCO director of Business and Media.
1095. For example, Peter Glesen. "Daniele Gatti werd haastig geofferd op het altaar van het reputatiemanagement" *Volkskrant*, February 27, 2019.
1096. Article 6 (2) ECHR "Everyone charged with a criminal offence shall be presumed innocent until proved guilty according to law." https://www.echr.coe.int/Documents/Convention_ENG.pdf.
1097. Musician member #2 RCO, anonymity assured.
1098. Press Release, RCO website April 23, 2019. "Het Concertgebouworkest en Daniele Gatti zijn verheugd te melden dat het ongenoegen tussen beide partijen na uitvoerig overleg is opgelost. Het Concertgebouworkest is Daniele Gatti erkentelijk voor zijn artistiek leiderschap van het orkest en de bijdrage die hij heeft geleverd aan de positie van het orkest in de wereld van de klassieke muziek." Author's translation: The Concertgebouw Orchestra and Daniele Gatti are pleased to report that the disagreement (literally, displeasure, dissatisfaction) between the two parties has been resolved following extensive consultation. The Concertgebouw Orchestra is grateful to Daniele Gatti for his artistic leadership and the contribution he has made to

wished him well in the future and as a token of bygones-be-bygones, announced the release of three recent Gatti-RCO recordings.[1099] All is well that ends well?

8.8 DUTCH TOUCH #METOO RULINGS

It is interesting to note that since the #metoo revolution, Dutch court rulings on situations in which employers terminate employment contracts of those who have been accused of sexual harassment at the workplace do not show massive support for the victims of harassment. Case law in recent years shows that at least at the district courts in Amsterdam and the Hague, the employer bore a great deal of the responsibility to put procedures in place that would have precluded such actions on the part of the employee. In 2017, the Amsterdam district court[1100] held that a university lecturer[1101] who was accused of sexual intimidation and lost his job was nevertheless eligible to receive €10,000 plus the customary transition payment stipulated by statute. The university had failed in its duty of care to apply specific internal procedures that may have mitigated the offense.

The same court emphasized the importance of internal anti-harassment regulations at the workplace in a 2018 case.[1102] An inebriated employee was suspended after inappropriate sexual advances at a corporate Christmas celebration. The employee was suspended and dismissed by his employer who defended the decision as "fitting in the context of the current #MeToo discussion."[1103] The court demurred, finding that dismissal was disproportionately severe because the employee should have been notified of his right to seek counsel, and had been denied the right to react to the accusation within 48 hours. Thus, although the employee's misconduct was actionable, the measures taken were too severe.

An important lesson to take from these decisions is that employers should be prepared to re-evaluate how the organization's sexual harassment-related protocols and investigations are implemented and monitor the procedures actually followed after a claim is brought forward. In most countries, including the Netherlands and the United States, the employer bears the responsibility to ensure that the workplace is free of any form of discriminatory behavior including unlawful harassment. The CO's Preucil story is a sad reminder of how employers attempt to ignore such claims: 12 years is an unforgivably long time to wait for an investigation. It is essential that

---

the orchestra's position in the world of classical music, https://www.concertgebouworkest.nl/nl/concertgebouworkest-en-daniele-gatti-sluiten-hoofdstuk-af.

1099. Toef Jaeger. "Danielle Gatti en Concertgebouworkest bereiken 'overeenkomst'" *NRC Handelsblad* 23 april 2019.
1100. ECLI:NL: RBAMS: 2017:9966. Rechtbank Amsterdam, 08-12-2017/ 6216391 EA VERZ 17-728. Available in Dutch at: https://linkeddata.overheid.nl/front/portal/document-viewer?ext-id=ECLI:NL:RBAMS:2017:9966.
1101. Amsterdam University of Applied Sciences (Hogeschool van Amsterdam) is named, the lecturer's name is not, in keeping with privacy regulations.
1102. ECLI:NL:RBAMS:2018:3327. Rechtbank Amsterdam, 01-05-2018/ 6656369 EA VERZ 18-136, https://uitspraken.rechtspraak.nl/inziendocument?id=ECLI:NL:RBAMS:2018:3327.
1103. *Ibid.*, author's translation.

employers develop and strengthen their complaint procedures with proper confidentiality safeguards. In addition, procedures and protocols must be brought to the attention of all employees with great regularity. Last, but certainly not least, training programs and awareness campaigns need to be revisited in order to protect employees. Although the #metoo movement accelerated awareness of orchestral harassment, most musicians agree that their institutions as well as their fellow musicians have a long path to tread. For different reasons, both the CO and the RCO were poles apart in handling similar claims. Both the CO's initial choice to ignore claims in 2007 and the RCO's hasty decision that sullied a conductor's good name before adequate fact-checking took place gave rise to substantial reputational impact. It can be argued that the RCO still carried a stigma of shady dealings post-Gattigate as it took four years for the orchestra to appoint a new MD.[1104] Adding to widespread speculation of managerial misjudgment, the RCO's Jan Raes stepped down as general manager in December 2019.

As the dust settles on #metoo claims, will those who have really suffered at the hands of #metoo perpetrators, the voiceless and vulnerable benefit? Real change moves slowly, is totally unspectacular, and its legalistic detail will not make headlines or even the media back pages. The power of the #metoo narrative will dissipate unless the discourse widens to analyze and take steps to change the culture that has permitted pervasive abuse and continues to turn a blind ear to skewed power relationships and protected hierarchies. Without respect and trust, without tight protocols administered by trustworthy custodians, the music profession and all professions for that matter will drift into a witch-hunting frenzy where individuals lose their careers and discriminatory behavior persists leaving the vulnerable out in the cold.

1104. Klaus Mäkelä was appointed Artistic Partner of the RCO in 2022 and will take on the responsibilities of Chief Conductor in 2027, https://www.concertgebouworkest.nl/en/stories/klaus-makela-the-eighth-chief-conductor.

9

Greener Pastures: Coming of Age in the Orchestral Workplace

> "Musicians don't retire, they just decompose."[1105]

> We are in a situation in which the older generation is enjoying all the securities while even the very best young musicians have to fight it out for scraps.[1106]

> Age discrimination cases are not slam dunks by any means.[1107]

This *movement* explores health and age-related challenges in the orchestral workplace, in terms of both employment issues faced by tenured orchestral players and parallel issues faced by freelance substitute players entering into the grey-ing zone.[1108] Aging and age-related vulnerability such as the angst of diminished performance ability in orchestras are closely tied to internal issues. Although age-based challenges at the workplace are not directly related to the 2007-2008 financial crisis or the COVID-19 crisis at the center of this project, research demonstrates that as the orchestral profession shows signs of increased precarity related directly to financial instability, traditional challenges such as age-related issues in performance have become amplified. This amplification takes several forms as the cases to follow illustrate. "If an orchestra replaces an older player with a younger musician, crassly put, there is a savings component, as the older player unquestionably costs more according to

1105. Dave Lee, Chairman, Musicians' Union (UK).
1106. Hugo Shirley, "Is Germany's Orchestra Paradise as good as it seems?" *The Strad*, April 4, 2019 https://www.thestrad.com/debate/is-germanys-orchestral-paradise-as-good-as-it-seems/8782.article.
1107. Harvey Mars, legal counsel to Musician's Local 802 American Federation of Musicians (AFM).
1108. The pun on grey zone is intentional as a greying zone refers to the coming of old age, while a grey zone according to the *Oxford Dictionary* is a "situation not easily defined."

contractual obligations that entail seniority pay and pension-related benefits."[1109] What might be perceived as a preposterous observation contains more than a grain of truth in light of jurisprudence that highlights situations in which tenured older musicians were unduly pressured to leave their jobs.

This *movement* presents background on age-related issues in orchestras while giving voice to those who have endured age discrimination and/or "combination" discrimination in its many forms. It opens up a space in which to consider age-related issues, including the right to play and pension payments from the perspective of musicians, employers, and courts. Starting off with a general consideration of age-related physical and stress-related challenges, pensions and pension diminution in the post-crisis age will be discussed with special attention paid to industrial action in US orchestras in which musicians opted to strike for the right to maintain pension entitlements. Relevant US jurisprudence in which orchestral musicians attempted to (re)claim their positions by relying on age discrimination legislation will be explored in an attempt to bring these cases to life for vulnerable musicians of all types who face similar issues in other jurisdictions.

In a much-debated article published in *The Atlantic* in 2008, one of the magazine's editors, Megan McArdel, commented on the vicissitudes faced by young entrants into the workforce, as the generation known as the "Baby Boomers" approached retirement age.[1110] In a *movement* devoted to aging orchestral musicians whose concerns run the gamut from age discrimination with regard to enforced early retirement on the one hand to efforts to bargain for seniority pay and secure pensions as well as the right to continue playing on the other hand, a particular quote rings true:

> But it's also the perverse result of a social bargain we've made with our workers: you accept slightly lower wages than you're worth when you're young in exchange for steady increases as you age. The problem is, this makes older workers expensive compared with young people, and harder to reemploy if they lose their jobs. Wages are what economists call "sticky": they rarely adjust downward, except after long agony. The *sticky wage* theory hypothesizes that pay of employees tends to have a slow response to the changes in the performance of a company or of the economy ... . Specifically, *wages* are often said to be *sticky*-down, meaning that they can move up easily but move down only with difficulty.[1111]

The issue of aging in orchestras is, to dip into Ms. McArdel's terminology, particularly sticky, as it calls into question the worth of a musician decades after passing the double whammy of the competitive entry auditions and demanding tenure stages that lead to permanent orchestral employment. Orchestral musicians in the Netherlands register astonishment when they learn that some of their US counterparts litigate. To Dutch musicians, "court action is a bridge too far. Our society is not litigious

1109. Conversations with Allison Beck, director of the Federal Mediation Agency appointed by President Obama in 2015.
1110. Baby Boomers is used to describe persons born in the post-WWII period of increased prosperity in the developing world (1946-1964), *see* https://www.investopedia.com/terms/b/baby_boomer.asp.
1111. Megan McArdel, "No Country for Young Men," *The Atlantic*, January/February 2008, https://www.theatlantic.com/magazine/archive/2008/01/no-country-for-young-men/306578/.

like American society. Then again, as my orchestra heads into crisis, maybe if we think our case is important, we should go to court."[1112]

9.1 AGE-RELATED ISSUES IN THE ORCHESTRAL WORKPLACE

Septuagenarian, and even octogenarian, conductors and classical music soloists might be sought after as star performers at international concert halls; yet, this status does not necessarily trickle down to positively impact the life of the aging orchestral musician. For some, the process is painful and humiliating. The psychological pressures of maintaining a career in which a musician's output is under constant aural scrutiny are not, contrary to what nonmusicians often posit, a matter of experience and routine. "Setting a standard, rehearsal after rehearsal and concert after concert, takes a tremendous amount of mental and physical stamina which in many cases takes its toll on the individual musicians."[1113] And, maintaining that standard of excellence as age-related physical issues impact performance ability is a challenge that bears further research and on-the-job support.

Whereas recent music graduates are wont to express the view that seasoned old-timers with connections get the best gigs in town,[1114] those very same seasoned players shed light on another aspect of the precarious freelance domain. While the connection between the aging musician's woes and the crisis-ridden orchestral musician's world might not appear to be direct at first blush, the quote that follows and the messages received from working musicians corroborate the fact that orchestral life has gotten even tougher since 2008. "Speaking for many of us who are between 50-65 now, we left conservatories with diaries bursting with diverse gigs and tours far and wide. Inevitably, the precarity of freelance orchestral life kicks in. Conductors often prefer the younger kids eager to enter the market and who never complain about adverse work situations. And, if a conductor makes disparaging comments about an older player, younger players tend to look away in the hopes that it will never happen to them. To make matters worse, after the crisis hit, orchestras started to disappear. The older freelancer has been hard hit on all sides."[1115]

9.2 LONGEVITY IN THE ORCHESTRA: FREELANCERS VERSUS CONTRACTED REGULAR ORCHESTRAL MUSICIANS

For a complete discussion of the nuances related to growing older in the orchestral environment, one turns to the German researchers Heiner Gembris and Andreas Heye, writing for the impressively titled journal *Musicae Scientiae, who* provide ample

1112. Conversations with Maurits Wijzenbeek, RKF violist and orchestra committee member.
1113. Remarks made by Esther van Fenema, psychiatrist, Leiden University Medical Center author of *Het ontstemde brein, psychiater op de Muziekpolt (The Untuned Brain)* 2018.
1114. Viola graduate, the Juilliard School of Music interviewed May 2016.
1115. New York-based veteran of 30 years of freelance work at over 25 orchestras who noted that her work-base shrink to 2-3 orchestras in 2016 from the earlier 20 + .

perspectives for consideration.[1116] Their sensitivity to the nuances of how musicians juggle the challenges of what the researchers delicately refer to as the "largely inescapable declines in musical peak performance due to aging"[1117] run counter to "unchanging high expectations and increases in retirement age."[1118] The difference between the experience of older professional orchestral musicians who enjoy stable careers under the protection of collective bargaining agreements and the experiences of aging freelancers is substantial. In the run-up to freelance collective bargaining (CAO) sessions in the Netherlands (2020), an oft-articulated line of reasoning centered on the conundrum as to how true equivalence between the standard and the freelance CAO could be reached with regard to pay scales related to years of experience and age. "For true equality, the clauses in both agreements should be the same, however, older freelancers fear that employers will not hire them if they must be paid more than less experienced, younger freelancers with fewer years on the pay scale."[1119]

Some of the many questions that come to the fore when the older musician becomes the focus of discussion include: how can musicians best manage their orchestral careers to guarantee employment longevity? What are best practices taken from the experiences of orchestras in the Netherlands and the US? Are there any gaps between the protections embodied in legislative texts regarding the position of older musicians in orchestras? Is there a role for additional legal regulations beyond generic antidiscrimination legislation to come to the aid of musicians in need or do collectively bargained agreements provide enough protection? Should there be a boilerplate "one size fits all" clause incorporated in orchestral contracts with regard to age-related departures or should orchestras consider individual players, as just that—individuals who face different challenges at different points in their careers? Discussions with musicians and human resources (HRM) specialists in the Netherlands and the US point to a mix of the aforementioned options, although this mix does not solve the issue of abuse of powers as exhibited in the jurisprudence discussed below. "The law provides a basis for employee protection, but the orchestra must craft a plan for musicians as their careers mature."[1120]

Questioned about decisions taken with the goal to reshape the Rotterdam Philharmonic, where a considerable number of players faced demotion and even forced early retirement in the 1970s, Edo de Waart, its then Chief Conductor, remarked: "music is a calling that necessitates inhuman amounts of discipline and self-criticism. What is fair is that which is fair to the music, all of us have to make sacrifices. In the name of quality and artistic commitment, the tough but honest reality is that sometimes a player must step down."[1121] Artistic concerns outweighed employee protection;

1116. Heiner Gembris, et al. "Health Problems of Orchestral Musicians from a Life-Span Perspective: Results of a Large-Scale Study." *Music & Science* January 2018 DOI: 10.1177/2059204317739801.
1117. *Ibid.*, 385.
1118. *Ibid.*
1119. Conversations with *Platform voor Freelance Musici* active member, harpist, Saskia Rekké.
1120. Interview, Ella Broekstra HRM advisor.
1121. Conversations with Maestro de Waart.

without protest on the part of the Works Council, the employee's workplace watchdog, the maestro had free rein to hire and fire in the name of quality.

While some US orchestras welcome pensionable players to remain in the orchestra, there is no "set in stone" policy. Retirement in US orchestras is, according to many managers, a variable to be dealt with on an individual basis. "The decision to stay or leave is often under the discretion of several key musicians, not the least the individual, his or her section leader and the music director."[1122] A peek down under into the pit at New York's prestigious Metropolitan Opera Orchestra (MET) shows viola section players respectfully performing alongside living viola legend Marilyn Stroh, who was the second woman contracted in the orchestra back in 1960.

Stroh's orchestral longevity is unheard of in the orchestral landscape in northern Europe where musicians are contractually obliged to stop performing at a statutory retirement age, even if they are more than capable of performing their musical duties. For example: "The Vienna Philharmonic will hire no musician over 35 years of age; the mandatory retirement age is 65."[1123] Dutch orchestras do not post such information but follow similar retirement regimes. Interviews with Dutch professionals show that the desire to stay in the orchestra past retirement age felt by many US colleagues does not appear to exist in the Netherlands. "We have a feeling of obligation to our colleagues: when it is time to go, it is time to make room for younger players."[1124] Yet, even in the Netherlands, some orchestral musicians feel that a legally proscribed career termination date is not fair. "As they age, some orchestral musicians seem able to perform better: a lifetime of concentrated practice and rehearsal activity that combines hearing and hand-to-eye conditioning can keep a player in top form. The legendary former concertmaster of the Leningrad Philharmonic and the Netherlands Radio Symphony Orchestra, Valentin Zhuk is still going strong as a freelance concertmaster as he approaches the age of ninety."[1125]

Colleagues with jobs at US orchestras express: "if older colleagues play well, they can mentor the new 20-something hotshot players, they belong here. Our orchestra has a great history of longevity: Michele Zukofsky just retired from playing clarinet after 54 years in the orchestra."[1126] The list of "longest served" in US orchestras includes such renowned characters as the Metropolitan Opera Orchestra (MET) timpanist Richard Horowitz, who performed in the New York pit from 1946 to 2012 until the age of 88. The longest-tenured US orchestral musician, the diminutive bass player Jane Little, collapsed on stage just before the final bars of "There's No Business Like Show Business"; she performed for 71 years as a member of the Atlanta Symphony.[1127] Of

1122. Conversations with Jeff Woodruff, executive director of the Harrisburg Symphony Orchestra.
1123. Exceptions can be made for certain leading positions. James R. Oestrich, "Even Legends Adjust to Time and Trend, Even the Vienna Philharmonic." *The New York Times*, February 28, 1998.
1124. Conversations with former RCO principal bassoon, Brian Pollard, who retired at 65 after 40 years in the orchestra. Post-retirement, Pollard played in the Hague Philharmonic.
1125. Concertmaster Kam-Lung Cheng commenting on tour with co-concertmaster Valentin Zhuk, Chengdu, China 2017.
1126. Conversation with Stacy Phelps and Mick Wetzel, Los Angeles Philharmonic members.
1127. Norman Lebrecht's *Slipped Disc* blog offers a list of long-lived orchestral members http://slippedisc.com/2011/09/new-longest-serving-orchestral-players-the-ultimate-list/.

comparative interest, orchestral musicians in Russia and the United Kingdom serve much longer tenures than Dutch musicians.

A study based on a sample of 14 US retired musicians representative of various sections within the orchestra boasted its conclusion in the title: "The great symphony orchestra—A relatively good place to grow old."[1128] However, even a cursory analysis of the author's hypothesis that "obsolescence was not a problem" puzzles the reader.[1129] A small sample could very well skew the results, and the differences between the career paths and longevity within the orchestra are markedly different between the fully employed at top-tier, well-financed organizations and freelancers who compete for limited access to employment.[1130] Finances aside, the individual struggles of US musicians such as Louis Kampouris, whose litigation woes will be discussed subsequently, prove that not all aging professional orchestra players experience the "orchestra as a warm bath of happy colleagues supporting the elder colleague through thick and thin."[1131]

9.3 THE ROLE OF PENSIONS

Pension payments in post-employment years have been a major bone of contention for workers in the US both in and beyond the orchestra. In March 2019, the world-renowned Chicago Symphony Orchestra (CSO) went on strike, canceling seven weeks of season concerts. Orchestras across the US held their collective breaths: a leading orchestra taking on a board intent on curbing expenses, especially with regard to pensions, resonated with the struggles of musicians in less fortunate positions than the top-tier Chicagoans.[1132] And, when music director Ricardo Muti broke the silence so often associated with an esteemed maestro to join the musicians on the picket line, his gesture became an iconic cultural news item. "Conductors usually do not take sides, they are careful and usually abide by the motto, 'I am a musician, not a politician.'"[1133] A digression to highlight the CSO strike's central issue is germane, as it breathes life into the issue of life after the orchestra.

One of the key issues to ignite the headline catching CSO strike centered on the Board's proposals to diminish pension benefits. This diminution is embedded within the larger issue of what Americans refer to as mission creep,[1134] a shift in the Board's interpretation of its all-important role.[1135] A tangible example of creeping change was

1128. David Smith, "The Great Symphony Orchestra: A Relatively Good Place to Grow Old." *The International Journal of Aging and Human Development* 27(4) December 1988, 233-247.
1129. *Ibid.*, 233.
1130. Observation based on a compilation of interviews with musicians at all ranges of the "financial success" spectrum.
1131. Paraphrasing a 55-year-old orchestral professional in the Cleveland Orchestra.
1132. Thousands of comments on the Musicians of the Chicago Symphony Orchestra blogsite corroborate this statement, http://www.chicagosymphonymusicians.com/.
1133. Conversations with Max Bonecutter, former bass trombonist Minnesota Orchestra, The Metropolitan Opera, attorney-at-law Illinois, USA.
1134. Since the early 1990s, the term can be interpreted as an expansion of the initial objectives of an organization.
1135. *See FAQs*, the role of the board.

the CSO Board's insistence on shifting the orchestral musicians' retirement plan from a guaranteed benefit plan to an individualized risk model,[1136] a proposal that would engender a sharp diminution of benefits. Importantly, according to the musicians, "pension problems are not of the Orchestra's making but reflect the Board's decision to not fully fund the plan over the last years. We would also fault their decision to spend nearly two-thirds of revenues on the building and non-Orchestra employees and allocate little more than 1/3 of revenues to the Orchestra itself. After all, it is the music that people come for."[1137] Seniority pay is but one element in a larger package of orchestral health and pension benefits that has not caught up with the realities of aging. "If an organization starts fiddling around (pun intended) with the financial stability of its elder statesmen and women who have given decades of artistic service to the public, it shows a lack of commitment to a basic right, retirement with dignity."[1138] Although defined-benefit pensions are being phased out in the private sector, "unions have fought long and hard for defined-benefit pensions as customary for America's top orchestras."[1139]

Pensions are less of a controversial issue for orchestral employees in the Netherlands, as tenured musicians are covered by mandatory sector-wide pension funds. Dutch occupational pension schemes are direct benefit schemes, with stringent solvency requirements imposed on these funds. In the last decade, Dutch pension funds' levels of protection have been placed under increased scrutiny, and the threat of lowered pension payments has hit the headlines yearly since the recession and stock market debacle that followed on the heels of the 2007-2008 financial crisis. Simple answers to a question of great complexity that puzzles many an economist is that the Dutch system is based on a concept of inter-generality, in which each generation is partially responsible for shouldering the burden of economic downturns as opposed to "the American practice of shielding the current generation of workers, retirees, and taxpayers while pushing costs and risks into the future, where they can metastasize unseen."[1140]

Another contrast to the US pension system lies in the fact that employers' contributions to pensions are capped, which in times of market depreciation precludes the sort of frantic cash call-ins that have led many US employers and many orchestral organizations to stop offering defined-benefit pensions. Last, but certainly not least, the Nederlandsche Bank (DNB, Dutch Central Bank) maintains a watchdog role to make sure that pension funds can pay out the pensions promised.[1141] "American public

1136. For a thorough analysis of the defined-benefit versus the defined contribution plan, consult the Adaptistration website: https://adaptistration.com/2004/08/18/pension-plans-and-negotiations-part-1/.
1137. Posted on Facebook March 10, 2019; statements released on the CSO musicians official website http://www.chicagosymphonymusicians.com/.
1138. Conversations with Peter Benoliel.
1139. Conversations with Tino Gagliardi, President, American Federation of Musicians, Local 802.
1140. Interview with Keith Ambachtsheer, Dutch economist and pension specialist at the University of Toronto's Rotman International Center for Pension, https://www.nytimes.com/2014/10/12/business/no-smoke-no-mirrors-the-dutch-pension-plan.html.
1141. Funds are granted a three-year turnaround recovery period if they do not meet the requirements set by the Central Bank.

pension funds have no such minimum requirement, and even if they did, there is no regulator to enforce it. Company pensions are bound by federal funding rules, but Congress has a tendency to soften them."[1142]

While litigation in the Netherlands is rare in the orchestral field, and even rarer with regard to age discrimination, the number of lawsuits in the sector increased after major cultural subsidy cuts were announced in 2012. And, with the rise of human resource management (HRM) initiatives to provide solutions for workplace issues related to longevity in employment, new clauses dedicated to well-being have found their way into collectively bargained agreements in the Netherlands to give legal muscle to a healthy work life for musicians.

9.4 FACTORS THAT ADD INJURY TO AGE

An important consideration that feeds into deliberation on musicians' exacerbated vulnerabilities relates to a heady mix of psychological and physical stresses and strains. Compounded by age, these factors "are massive at the best of times, and for older musicians additionally traumatic."[1143] The expenditure of physical energy and chances for injury associated with playing orchestral instruments varies considerably between different instrument groups. Brass and wind players can suffer from embouchure issues, ranging from trembling lip to focal dystonia.[1144] String player maladies are central to the *Kampouris* case discussed subsequently.

The aging musician who suffers from a performance-related disorder is apt to suffer in silence. From the onset, music teachers pass on the suffer in silence message as the show must go on no matter what. The famed Dutch violin pedagogue, Coosje Wijzenbeek, instilled a performance ethic by teaching pre-teens to "never miss a lesson or certainly not a concert unless your fever reaches 41 centigrade."[1145] This message retranslates into a musician's omerta, an unsettling vow of silence. "Nothing seems to be more shameful than to admit that something is wrong; this instantly undermines your position not only in your eyes, but in the eyes of your colleagues."[1146]

Until the late 20th century, the cause of overuse injuries in musicians was largely undiagnosed, and few accepted the fact that maladaptive playing patterns lead to incurable muscular strain or irreparable neurological injury. After the internationally renowned soloists, pianists Leon Fleischer and Gary Graffman[1147] came out in the open to share the truth behind their suffering and performance impediments, both insiders within the profession and outsiders began to face the facts with regard to a profession

1142. Keith Ambachtsheer, *supra*.
1143. Conversations with Dr. Boni Rietveld, orthopedic surgeon and musician. Founder, Medisch Centrum voor Dansers en Musici, The Hague.
1144. Steven Frucht. "Embouchure Dystonia: A Video Guide to Diagnosis and Evaluation" *Journal of Clinical Movement Disorders* 3, June 18, 2016 DOI: 10.1186/s40734-016-0035-x.
1145. Translated from Dutch, Wijzenbeek's generations of talent attest to variations on the quote.
1146. Interview, Dr. Boni Rietveld https://www.haaglandenmc.nl/nieuws/boni-rietveld-promoveert-in-de-dans-en-muziekgeneeskunde.
1147. Both Leon Fleischer and Gary Graffman were preeminent piano soloists who suffered from focal dystonia cutting short, distinguished careers in the late 20th century. Leon Fleisher made a much-publicized comeback in 1982 after 18 years of "one-handed" performances.

replete with occupational hazards. Yet, although a great deal of sympathy and media attention was garnered by the retelling of Messrs. Fleischer, and Graffman's struggles to overcome music-related injuries, the trickle-down effect for orchestral players was minimal. "The famous soloists were both pianists who were individual stars, quite unlike orchestral principals, or heavens forbid, section players who are viewed from the outside as 'group players,' not individuals. If orchestral musicians make a mental leap to regard their performance craft like athletes favor their chosen sport, perhaps we could gain professional focus for needs in times of distress."[1148]

Before delving further into how psychosocial pressures in playing can lead to orchestral drama, one notable exception bears mention. Adolph (Bud) Herseth, the protagonist of brass lore, reigned for 53 years as principal trumpet in the Chicago Symphony Orchestra. Musicians interviewed repeatedly made mention of the largest elephant in the room, the conductor and his/her influence with specific reference to aging musicians. Stories of abusive behavior on the part of celebrated conductors abound, with similar tales told regardless of the prestige of the orchestra. A brass player recalls a particularly painful series of Tannhäuser rehearsals,[1149] in which a celebrated conductor humiliated the orchestra's bass trombone player, a respected musician rapidly approaching retirement. "It did not seem to matter to the illustrious maestro that our colleague who was soon to end his great career was belittled and bullied in front of his colleagues during consecutive rehearsals. He had to repeat the most difficult passages over and over again; it became a sort of maestro power trip as if the prize would have been to break the musician. Nobody dared speak out against such a famous conductor."[1150] Yet, for all those amassed stories of woe, only a handful of players opted for any form of legal action. The orchestral musicians' level of empowerment to take action to stand up against harassment is surprisingly limited and often highly individualized.

9.5 PROTECTING THE WEAK: PROTECTED CLASSES IN US LEGISLATION

To frame a discussion of select US orchestral musician cases carefully, a brief description of US legislation applicable to discrimination cases follows. In its first incarnation, the Civil Rights Act of 1866, passed by Congress on the heels of a legislative override of President Andrew Jackson's veto, purported to prohibit discrimination "in civil rights or immunities ... on account of race, color, or previous condition of servitude."[115114] A commentary on its failure to protect any of the enumerated

1148. Esther van Fenema, *supra*.
1149. A Wagner opera completed in 1845, Tannhäuser is infamous for demanding brass parts.
1150. The story was retold at a FIM conference on Musicians and Health Issues, Amsterdam, November 2018; the specific orchestra and conductor's name have been omitted.
1151. 14 Stat. 27 (at 31).

classes goes beyond this research but deserves mention and a link to in-depth analysis.[1152]

The number of protected classes increased substantially under the Civil Rights Act of 1964 (the Act) in which Title VII Act prohibits discrimination in employment on the basis of race, color, national origin, sex, and religion.[1153] A number of bona fide exceptions to the seemingly broad coverage include the fact that the Act covers workers between the ages of 40 and 64. Further, federal government employees and employees in enterprises with less than 20 employees are excluded from the ambit of the Act. Numerous antidiscrimination protections are afforded by state legislation which will be discussed where relevant to a particular case under scrutiny. Independent contractors are not covered by the Act, as we soon shall learn from a closer inquiry into jurisprudence in the freelance orchestral sphere.

9.6 THE EEOC AND THE ADEA

An independent federal agency, the EEOC, was established under the Act to administer the enforcement of Title VII and other civil rights acts that apply to workplace discrimination. To take action against an employer in a US discrimination case, an employee is required to file a charge with the EEOC within 180 days from the time the alleged discrimination took place. Most commonly, claims are filed under the Age and Discrimination in Employment Act of 1967 (ADEA).[1154] Following a fact-finding process, the EEOC decides whether the charge will withstand a high procedural bar and decide if the claim is trial worthy.[1155] Yet, as the jurisprudence discussed in this *movement* confirms, the EEOC system has not been set up to tackle a large case load; the vast majority of EEOC cases are found to be lacking in merit, and do not meet the high bar set for probable and direct cause. Thus, whereas a high percentage of claims receive an EEOC Notice of Right to Sue, a very low percentage moves forward to litigation. An eye-opening article written at the beginning of the millennium records the same mitigating issues that 2016 federal records corroborate.[1156] According to these records, employees filed 97,443 charges, and the EEOC issued 81,129 Notices to Sue (83.3%) according to records in the fiscal year 2016 (October 1, 2015, through September 30, 2016). Yet less than 10% (7,239 cases) proceeded to court. Of the complaints that did reach federal courts, 87% were antidiscrimination claims.

After receipt of the Notice of Right to Sue, claimants can prepare for battle in court. The term "battle" is chosen carefully as scholarly research and federal records corroborate that employment discrimination plaintiffs fight an upward battle to win their cases at any level, from pre-trial motion to appeals, especially with regard to

1152. *See* George Rutherglen. *Civil Rights in the Shadow of Slavery: The Constitution, Common Law, and the Civil Rights Act of 1866.* Oxford University Press 2013.
1153. Civil Rights Act of 1964, Pub.L. 88-352, 78 Stat. 241 (1964).
1154. The Age Discrimination in Employment Act of 1967 (ADEA at 29 USC. §621 to §634).
1155. *Ibid.*
1156. Michael Selmi. "Why Are Employment Discrimination Cases So Hard to Win?" *Los Angeles Law Review* 61 2001, 574-575.

burden of proof encumbrances that will be discussed in the following pages. "Navigating the system is challenging: the local (union) can provide help for an orchestral claimant but the local must have the legal resources and time to assist. These factors vary cross-country depending on the experience and finances the union local has. To find decent representation for people with little knowledge of the law, limited resources leads to a thorny path toward resolution."[1157]

Another possible hindrance with regard to EEOC discrimination litigation is the promotional aspect at play. The EEOC does not take on cases purely on merit; it seeks cases that will broaden its impact.[1158] The EEOC website boldly reaches out to potential class-action "clients" with a text that reads like a tv ad: "Are You Affected by an EEOC Lawsuit or Settlement? We are looking for people who may have been affected by the unlawful discrimination alleged in these suits."[1159] Musician discrimination cases certainly do not have the societal impact or "reach" that is key to profile-raising success at the EEOC. From the aforementioned statistics on actual cases litigated, one would hope that the EEOC would practice more of what it preaches by extending its enforcement reach without paying undue heed to public relations. In order to bring forward a claim of intentional disparate treatment under the ADEA, a plaintiff has to show that discrimination was the predominant factor that caused the injurious employment decision, or, under the 1991 amendments to the Civil Rights Act, that discrimination was a motivating factor.[1160] The ADEA only applies to individuals aged 40 and older, and the federal courts have customarily interpreted it narrowly over time.

Is it possible to argue that Congress tacitly approved of a mandatory retirement age and approved of discrimination against workers who might have wanted to continue to work past the age of 65? Or is a more sensitive reading of the ADEA as part of progressive civil rights legislation in order? A brief foray into background documents supports the argument that Congress envisioned protection for the most vulnerable group who would otherwise be unable to enjoy the benefits of social security.[1161] Age discrimination legislation at the state level proliferated since the passage of the two aforementioned acts in the 1960s: exceptions to the scope of coverage will be discussed in relation to the cases selected below. An intriguing state-by-state comprehensive analysis points to gaps in protection for certain groups and opens the door to further study.[1162]

The two aforementioned examples of US rights-protection legislation were products of a great move forward with regard to legislating equal rights in direct reaction to the sweeping civil rights movement of the 1950s and 1960s. More than a

1157. Conversations with Morris Shanker, Professor Case Western Reserve School of Law.
1158. Harvey Mars. "Musicians Fight Age Discrimination" *Allegro* April 2018.
1159. *See* www.eeoc.gov.
1160. Civil Rights Act of 1991 Pub. L. No. 102-166, § 107(a), 105 Stat. 1071, 1075 (1991) (codified at 42 USC. § 2000e-2(m)); The Age Discrimination in Employment Act of 1967 (ADEA); codified at 29 USC. §621 to §634.
1161. For further consideration regarding the scope of the ADEA, *see* Bryan Woodruff, "Unprotected Until Forty: The Limited Scope of the Age Discrimination in Employment Act of 1967." *Indiana Law Journal* 73 1998.
1162. Jerome Hunt. "A State-by-State Examination of Nondiscrimination Laws and Policies." *Center for American Progress* June 2012.

half-century later, jurisprudence on employment discrimination has shown more discord than harmony with regard to the goal of alleviating workplace discrimination as cases discussed as the *movement* unfolds confirm. As articulated earlier, Congress struck down the mandatory retirement age in 1978, and follow-up federal legislation in 1986 rendered mandatory retirement at the age of 70 illegal.[1163] Many orchestral managers were caught "unawares" by the importance of this issue as a bargaining point for musicians as the *Henrickson* case illuminates.

9.7 *FRANCES HENRICKSON V. ATLANTA ARTS ALLIANCE INC.*

In 1973, *Senza Sordino*, the official publication of the International Conference of Symphony and Opera Musicians (ICSOM), published a disconcerting report in its volume XI. The report provided details about a civil suit in which violinist Frances Henrickson claimed both age and sex discrimination against the Atlanta Arts Alliance Inc., the corporate umbrella organization that operated the Atlanta Symphony Orchestra (ASO).[1164] Henrickson joined the ASO in 1965 at a comparatively late age (mid-50s) after a rich musical life as a performer and pedagogue. According to the *Senza Sordino* account, "her problems began with a series of actions on the part of Music Director (MD) Robert Shaw, and the personnel manager, Martin Sauser." In February 1972, she was demoted from her initial placement on the fifth stand first violin to the last stand of the second violin section. Although section members of the two violin sections receive the same financial remuneration, there is a significant difference in the parts played by violinists in the two sections. While modern-day violinists interviewed in major orchestras are proud to play in the second violin section recognizing the importance of every individual with a coveted orchestral contract, the old school players often cast aspersions on second violin positions, hence the allusion to inferiority, as in "to play second fiddle."[1165]

In June 1972, Henrickson called in sick; the ASO docked pay after she exceeded the 10-day sick leave maximum stipulated in the ASO CBA by two days. Subsequently, the ASO granted her an official leave of absence so that she could recover fully (at least, that was her reading of the leave). To her amazement, she received a letter of contractual termination from the ASO's outgoing manager during what she perceived as her recuperation period. In the relevant part:

> We, therefore, have decided that we will not be able to offer you a contract for the next season. In accordance with Article XX of the master agreement, which deals with physical incapacity, you will be granted severance pay in the amount of $500 at the conclusion of the season.

1163. Retirement age was abolished under the 1989 ADEA amendments 29 USC. §§621-634.
1164. "Francis Henrickson: A Study in Calumny." *Senza Sordino* August 1973, 1-3.
1165. The same expression in Dutch, "de tweede viool spelen," is used in exactly the same way as the English expression. The *Cambridge Dictionary* defines "to play second fiddle" as "to be less important or in a weaker position than someone else." https://dictionary.cambridge.org/dictionary/english/play-second-fiddle.

Stunned by her unexpected job loss, Henrickson sought immediate reinstatement. Procedurally, the ASO's actions were questionable, perhaps illegal, lacking due process: Henrickson had not been served notice, nor did she receive a mandatory hearing in the presence of union officials and at least one member of the orchestra committee. Although the ASO's local union Atlanta Federation of Musicians Local 148-462 advised her to seek arbitration, she opted for litigation. Before filing suit for discrimination on the basis of age and gender, the purportedly wronged violinist met with the ASO's newly appointed manager, Mr. Ratka, who agreed to grant her a contractual extension until the end of the 1972-73 season in return for a signed letter of resignation. Henrickson presented a bill of good health from her attending physician and signed the extension-for-resignation offer, albeit unwillingly. She continued to plead her case during the course of the new season, this time with the renowned Robert Shaw, who appeared to be sympathetic to her cause.

Bowing to majority rule, Shaw requested the entire orchestra to vote in order to ascertain whether or not there was support for Henrickson's reinstatement. "The orchestra by a vote of 53-5 showed support for Henrickson upholding her view that she was 'illegally dismissed without consideration for her illness, and unduly persuaded to resignation in a coercive manner.'"[1166] Nonetheless, Henrickson received no reply from either management or the MD concerning the continuation of her employment. It is interesting to note that no mention was made of her age in the claim report, a salient fact crucial for success in an age discrimination case. Archival research netted the following document that shows evidence of her debut as violin soloist, age 17, with the Boston Pops Orchestra in 1935; thus, she would have been between the ages of 55 and 56 at the time of the dispute.[1167]

The US Department of Labor's Wage and Hour Division[1168] took notice of Henrickson's claims. The Division that serves as an enforcement agency for a long list of labor-related laws ranging from worker protection to wage laws mounted an investigation to ascertain if Henrickson's allegations of discrimination were an isolated case, or if her claim could point to general discriminatory actions forming a recognizable pattern at the ASO. Perhaps the fact that Henrickson opted to sue for both age and gender discrimination diminished the plausibility of her case. Henrickson had not proffered hard evidence of harassment as a core determinant leading to her demotion, nor could she prove that her advanced age was the tipping point factor that pushed her employer to curtail her employment. Even though the case generated media support in favor of Henrickson,[1169] the ASO never reinstated Henrickson. She settled out of court agreeing to accept one year's salary and reimbursement for legal fees and court costs.

1166. *See Senza Sordino*, Henrickson, *supra*.
1167. The Boston Pops Archives contain a copy of Henrickson's debut performance with the orchestra in 1935, https://archive.org/stream/bostonpopsorches1935bost/bostonpopsorches1935bost_djvu.txt.
1168. Responsible to enforce federal wage laws, the US Department of Labor, Wage and Hour Division was established in 1938 under the Fair Labor Standards Act (FLSA).
1169. A microfiche survey of *Atlanta Journal-Constitution* articles reported on the case, http://www.af.public.lib.ga.us/.

Hypothetically, had the dispute taken place two years later, the union could have played a more significant role as a result of the SCOTUS decision in *NLRB v. Weingarten*.[1170] The seminal case established an employee's right to union representation if the employee is required to participate in an inquiry that could result in disciplinary (or more serious) actions on the part of the employer. Yet, although the ASO did not follow a defined inquiry protocol, even *Weingarten* might not have offered Henrickson recourse. Is there another possible explanation for her dismissal?

Digging beneath the surface of the case, a different storyline emerges. The MD had earned his stripes as choral director for the authoritarian maestro Arturo Toscanini and had served as Associate Conductor to the exacting taskmaster, George Szell. By the time Shaw arrived in Atlanta, he had a taste for greatness having experienced the sound and fury of Szell. A man with a mission, Shaw wrote prolifically on the subject of his quest to catapult the ASO into the ranks of top-tier US orchestras. Within just a few years, Shaw not only raised the orchestra's standards dramatically but also the musicians received considerable employment perks including competitive salaries and a 30-week performance season. Such a solidification of benefits meant that the ASO could attract and retain high-level players. Once a sleepy town part-time regional orchestra, the maestro grew the ASO to its stature as the premier orchestra in the southern United States. For a man with such an artistic vision, there was no choice but to retire or fire personnel who could not meet the challenges of excellence.[1171]

Decades later, the letters he wrote to these dismissed musicians show that he was not only forthright but also on occasion remorseful.[1172] If Shaw crossed the boundaries of unfair treatment in Henrickson's situation or if he was acting out of purely musical interests to raise the level of the organization is a question that crosses into a grey zone. Is the pursuit of a collective goal of excellence at the price of players who cannot meet the high bar expected unreasonable? The famed Dutch maestro Edo de Waart would have shown solidarity with Shaw: "we sink or swim as a result of our whole team, if there are too many weak players, the collective sinks."[1173]

9.8 DAVID VERSUS GOLIATH: *KAMPOURIS V. THE SAINT LOUIS SYMPHONY*

The contours, or more appropriately, the ups and downs of the *Kampouris* case,[1174] in which a long-standing member of the St. Louis Symphony Orchestra (SLSO) sued his employers for discrimination on the basis of disability, serves as a blueprint for subsequent cases in which musicians have litigated on grounds of discrimination in US orchestras. The facts of *Kampouris*[1175] cannot be presented without reiterating the

1170. *NLRB v. J. Weingarten, Inc.*, 420 US 251 (1975).
1171. With special thanks to archivist Richard Boursy at the Yale Music Archives who shared documents from the Robert Shaw Papers, https://archives.yale.edu/repositories/6/resources/5898.
1172. *Ibid.*
1173. Conversation with Maestro de Waart.
1174. *Kampouris v. Saint Louis Symphony Soc.*, 52 F. Supp. 2d. 1096 (1999).
1175. *Ibid.*

difficulties inherent in making the call as to when a musician should stop playing. Soloists, who spend their performing lives in front of the orchestra, face particular challenges. "Please realize, it is our lifeblood this music making, to take this away from us is like cutting out our hearts" observed superstar violinist Ivry Gitlis (95) after a live performance on the Dutch TV show *Podium Witteman* in 2017.[1176] Performance in the classical music world, whether solo or orchestral, calls for great mental and physical stamina that is not within the traditional provenance of old age. New York-based orchestral musicians were particularly happy to back up Isaac Stern in recording sessions toward the end of his illustrious career, as the aging violinist insisted on numerous takes for each phrase of music as technical challenges mounted during the recording process. To "earn with Stern" was synonymous with high paychecks. Far from the glitter and glamor of the solo world, cases such as Louis Kampouris and John Wetherill's 2017 suit bring the drama of aging in the orchestra to the fore.

Violinist Louis Kampouris joined the SLSO in 1949 and performed faithfully in the violin section for 45 years. In 1989, after 40 years of service, he experienced mobility problems in both arms and sought professional advice from a neurologist. By December 1994, he was forced to take a leave of medical absence because of several neurological abnormalities that impeded him from functioning at full capacity. During his disability leave, Kampouris received benefits from his employer's (Saint Louis Symphony Society's (SLSS')) insurance provider, as stipulated in the orchestra's collective bargaining agreement.

Eager to return to the orchestra, he sought a variety of medical treatments to alleviate his symptoms. The list of medical practitioners he consulted is significant in terms of numbers and the wide-ranging nature of the remedies. He was able to return to work in the spring of 1997 participating in all SLSO rehearsals and concerts from mid-May to early August 1997. A medical professional, Dr. Gelberman, sent a note to Mr. Neville, the orchestra's personnel manager expressing his opinion that Kampouris was improving rapidly. Fast forward: within a few months. Kampouris' disability benefits were discontinued in June 1997 based on reports by an independent medical practitioner who had reported to the SLSO that Kampouris suffered from "[s]evere atrophy of [the] ulnar musculature in both hands."

At the very start of the new season in September, the orchestra informed Kampouris that he was not ready to return to work. His salary was not paid, and he was barred from returning to his seat. The decision taken by Executive Director Bruce Coppock and personnel manager Neville was based on the firm conviction that the independent specialist's appraisal of Mr. Kampouris' ailment was leading. Looking back on the situation from a vantage point of posterity, Coppock commented: "such a decision is most challenging for a director. The outside world and many of our musicians unfortunately thinks that we are heartless automatons. They forget that it is our responsibility to put the collective first, to do what is good for the symphony."[1177] The court concurred:

1176. Performance link, October 30, 2017, https://www.youtube.com/watch?v=fClh4hqYJAM.
1177. Conversations with Bruce Coppock.

> There exists no evidence of any motivation other than skepticism that plaintiff's deteriorated physical condition permitted him to play to the Symphony's requirements of stamina and artistry, the circumstances do not suggest unlawful discrimination.

Orchestra committee members corroborate that the orchestra with the support of the union (Local 2-197) mandates that a musician who wants to return to the orchestra following a legitimized disability leave must demonstrate the ability to perform full time within 24 months. Mere physical ability to play was not considered a full return to the orchestra's heavy work schedule of 7-8 services per week. A long-standing member of the orchestra, hornist Kaid Friedel, sought arbitration to settle a dispute concerning disability benefits in 1991, during Kampouris' tenure in the orchestra. Of relevance, two clauses from the Kaid Friedel Arbitration Decision:

1. a disabled musician is treated like an active employee and remains covered by the Society's group medical and dental plans as long as he/she receives long-term disability benefits.
2. a disabled musician's position can be filled permanently when the disabled musician is determined to be totally disabled from any occupation, and never to return to the Orchestra.

The SLSO applied a 24-month rule in which a player who was unable to perform his/her duties would relinquish the right to play in the orchestra, and the position would be open for audition.

Kampouris maintained that the 24-month policy breached the orchestra's CBA, as there was no proof that it was a bargained part of the employment contract. Shortly thereafter, Kampouris launched an appeal against the district court's decision to grant summary judgment.[1178] The Eighth Circuit Court held that the employer's decision-making processes were nondiscriminatory, and not based on age per se. Perhaps the most vital strike against Kampouris was that the court found that although he had partially returned to perform in the orchestra, he did not prove that he was able to perform full time.

In an attempt to gain reinstatement, Kampouris added age discrimination to his litigated claims. On the record in court, Neville attested that the music director was the sole arbitrator with regard to a musician's playing quality. Hans Vonk, the distinguished Dutch maestro, was MD at the SLSO; his tenure was sadly cut short by amyotrophic lateral sclerosis (ALS). Vonk's limited presence during Kampouris' performance weeks in the spring and summer of 1997 and Kampouris' physical distance from the maestro could not have afforded the maestro the opportunity to evaluate the situation. If Kampouris' colleagues, violinists in his immediate proximity, did not complain about his ability to play and the music director was not available for commentary, how could the orchestra stand by its decision to fire Kampouris?

Could it be possible that *Kampouris* provides a textbook example of a failed case under the 1990 Americans with Disabilities Act (ADA) to provide redress for "unfair

1178. *Kampouris v. St. Louis Symphony Society* Case no. 99-2704210 F.3d 845 (8th Cir. 2000).

and unnecessary discrimination and prejudice" against persons with disabilities?[1179] Was this a classic example of a case in which the perceived discrimination claims bolstered Kampouris' fundamental right of trial by jury? Or was the court correct in opting for a summary judgment dismissal?

9.9 SUMMARY JUDGMENT: A PROTECTIVE MEASURE OR A STUMBLING BLOCK?

Freelance orchestral musicians in the Netherlands have shown interest in their US counterparts' attempts to rectify employment inequalities through litigation. The protagonist of a previous *movement*, Tiziana Pintus, opined, "in the Netherlands you start out with a strike against you if you are a musician in court, in my time it was just not done."[1180] To diffuse the notion that the litigation grass is greener on the US side, the paragraphs that follow examine summary judgment, one of the major stumbling blocks to success in employment discrimination cases.[1181]

The rule of summary judgment did not exist in common law until its introduction in England in the mid-1800s.[1182] Across the Atlantic decades later, the US legal scholar, Charles E. Clark, fought hard for the implementation of the infamous Rule 56, arguing in favor of its expediency and success rate at the state level.[1183] His views were immediately contested in the literature and in the courts, notably by the illustrious Judge Jerome Frank, a proponent of the fairness inherent in the right of trial by jury. As the advisory notes that prefigured Rule 56 elucidate, summary judgment was envisioned as a "method for promptly disposing of actions in which there is no genuine issue of material fact."[1184] Judicial idealists hoped that the Rule would increase efficiency at state and federal courts swamped by an overload of cases. A quick check on the background of summary judgment in its English embodiment shows that the US incarnation of summary judgment bears scant similarity to the English procedure. Two principal differences deserve mention. First, the English procedure was not available to defendants.[1185] Second, it was limited to cases in which a debtor could not dispute the existence of an agreement and could not pay his/her bills.

Tracing the jurisprudence that burgeoned since the early days of summary judgment, an ideological discord exists between judges who sought to take a new procedural opportunity to resolve as many cases as possible in a quick and efficient manner versus those who continue to be apprehensive that litigants would be denied their constitutional right for their day in court if summary judgment became a means to an end with regard to pruning heavy caseloads. Certain areas of the law, including,

1179. Americans with Disabilities Act of 1990 (ADA). 42 USC. § 12101(a) (9).
1180. Conversations with Tiziana Pintus.
1181. Federal Rules of Civil Procedure 56, https://www.law.cornell.edu/rules/frcp/rule_56.
1182. For a complete background check on summary judgment in England, *see* Charles Clark & Charles Samenow. "The Summary Judgment" 1929.
1183. For personal views on summary judgment, *see* Charles E. Clark "The Federal Rules of Civil Procedure: 1938-1958" 1958.
1184. Federal Rules of Civil Procedure 56, Advisory Committee Notes, 1937.
1185. Charles E. Clark, *supra*.

but not limited to antitrust, civil rights cases, negligence, and patents were considered initially to be no-go areas for a motion of summary judgment.[1186] However, the increasing use of summary judgment in age and gender discrimination cases as well as civil rights cases in the last decades of the 20th century raised a red flag even among jurists who advocated a handle-with-care approach to prevailing summary judgment discourse.[1187] Motions to dismiss were infrequent at US courts until well into the 1980s and were not perceived as overextending the boundaries of fairness until the millennium.

It is fair to pose the question: is summary judgment granted disproportionately or wrongly in employment discrimination cases? The aforementioned high rates of failure are not enough to make that call and answer the question. And, to make the question more difficult to answer, discrimination cases are, pardon the pun, rarely black versus white. Factors such as the employer's state of mind or intent are difficult to evaluate. In the subtle legal arena that encompasses a wide description of what constitutes discrimination, "the smoking gun, evidence of discrimination," can be elusive.[1188] Before attempting to flesh out an answer to the question with particular regard to orchestra-related cases, mention must be made of the positive aspects of summary judgment, as it would be unfair to give this form of judicial procedure an exclusively negative reading. Summary judgment can be a valid tool to separate the wheat from the chaff in terms of long-winded, time-consuming cases that would fail due to claims without merit. In any legal system, and with special consideration for the litigious US system with its high concentration of civil suits per capita,[1189] it can be advantageous to rely on procedures to separate the cases that should go to trial from those that should not. Yet, discrimination cases are particularly susceptible to misinterpretation, as the bulk of evidence on the employer's side is often managed more efficiently than the evidence provided by the "injured" employee.

One of the three appeal judges and the sole dissenter in *Kampouris*, Judge Mark W. Bennett, vociferously expressed his disappointment at the decision to affirm the summary judgment. He as well as other bench practitioners lamented a hardening of the legal profession, a cultural change in which Rambo-style litigation was favored over solution-seeking, a move "from trial by jury into a litigation by the summary judgment legal industry."[1190] Bennett's dissent brings forward the contention that there were real issues, genuine issues of material fact, that should have swayed the court to dismiss

1186. *Ibid.*

1187. Most notably, Judge Richard Posner's observation: "there is not a separate rule of civil procedure governing summary judgment in employment discrimination cases," however, courts should "be careful" before they grant summary judgment in such cases. *See Wallace v. SMC Pneumatics, Inc.*, 103 F.3d 1394, 1396 (7th Cir. 1997).

1188. *Richards v. New York City Bd. of Education* 668 F. Supp. 259 S.D.N.Y. (1987).

1189. Consider in this light, the illustrious British judge Lord Denning's observation: "As a moth is drawn to the light, so is a litigant drawn to the United States." *Smith Kline & French Labs Ltd. v. Block*. [1983] 2 All E.R. 72, 72 (End. C.A. 1982).

1190. Hon. Mark W. Bennett, US District Court Judge, Northern District of Iowa. "Essay: From the 'No Spittin,' No Cussin' and No Summary Judgment Days of Employment Discrimination Litigation to the Defendant's Summary Judgment Affirmed Without Commend Days," 2012, 660.

summary judgment in favor of trial by jury with its full consideration of relevant facts. In Bennett's opinion, the court erred not only in its holding but also in its entire approach to the case:

> Indeed, that decision undoubtedly states the conclusion I would have reached on the record presented, had I been the trier of fact. However this case was not before the district court as the trier of fact. Rather, it was before the district court on a motion for summary judgment.[1191]

Bennett disputed the holding on two grounds: pretext and the presentation of genuine issues of material fact. Underlining his support for a judiciously cautious application of summary judgment, he concluded that Kampouris was short-changed by judicial intent on getting to the bottom of the case. Bennett relied on the importance of the 1986 trio of cases, referred to in the literature as the *Celotex* trilogy (*Anderson, Matsushita* and *Celotex*)[1192] in which SCOTUS emphasized that standards for summary judgment called for judges at the district court level to engage in gatekeeping, not in taking the law into their own hands. The nuances within *Kampouris* are found in the inferences, insinuations and perceptions, and/or misperceptions that colored the relationship between an aging employee and his employers.

Coming to grips with Bennett's sharp criticism, one can ask: what were the issues of genuine fact that passed into the mist in *Kampouris*? The crux of the matter centers on the question: was the orchestra's legitimate, nondiscriminatory reason for denying Kampouris a performance contract pretextual; in other words, did it cover up the employer's true motives?[1193] According to Judge Bennett's line of thought, this reasoning trumps a grant of summary judgment as "the record undoubtedly generates a genuine issue of material fact as to Kampouris's ability to play to the required standards."[1194]

Upon his return to the orchestra after extensive treatment, Kampouris performed during the orchestra's spring and summer seasons. In court, the SLSS highlighted that these seasons were not as rigorous as the fall and winter seasons, and there was disagreement as to the quality of Kampouris' level of performance. A disturbing pattern in *Kampouris* is that sworn depositions by members of the orchestra and its personnel manager were rife with conflicting observations that led to questionable conclusions. Beyond the cynicism shown by managers who echo the sentiment "bring me four musicians and you will find 40 opinions,"[1195] the court should have taken these discrepancies into consideration. With regard to the adverse employment action, the

1191. The full text of Judge Bennett's dissent, http://media.ca8.uscourts.gov/opndir/00/04/99270 4P.pdf.
1192. *See*, for example, Eric K. Yamamoto et al., "Summary Judgment at the Crossroads: The Impact of the Celotex Trilogy." *University of Hawaii Law Review* 12 1990, 3-33.
1193. Examined under the lens of employment law, pretext refers to a false reason proffered in an adverse employment action; the reason serves as a cover up for the employer's real motives. Proving pretext is of particular importance in litigation at the motion for summary judgment stage. The possibility to prove pretext is by mounting evidence that attacks the credibility of the employer's reasoning and points to discrimination that motivated the employer.
1194. *See* Judge Bennett's dissent, *supra*.
1195. Observation brought to the fore by Ben Janssen, former director Dutch Broadcasting Music Center.

SLSS' move to fire Kampouris showed a changing tune, a wavering set of inferences leading up to the action. The consistency vital to persuade the court that summary judgment is indeed viable and desirable in the pursuit of justice was questionable on several fronts. Did the orchestral personnel director believe that Kampouris was disabled within the ADEA's definitions, that is not only disabled from violin performance in the orchestra, but also disabled in the widest sense, unable to take on any form of employment? Or did he believe that Kampouris was totally disabled because of the SLSS' insurance company's findings? Neville either suffered from amnesia or perhaps could not hold to one line of inference, as he admitted to the court that there were other reasons to change his mind along the way.

Should the documentation supporting evidence in *Kampouris* have been left up to opinions stated in insurance company reports and/or the personnel director's perceptions? Or should the court have required evidence from Kampouris' fellow section players, his concertmaster and the music directors with whom he performed? The SLSS was vitally interested in ridding itself of Kampouris and his problematic health issues without taking into consideration his mental condition, his willingness to play as much as possible, and his actual condition. The manner in which the SLSS presented its evidence was questionable enough to merit Kampouris' claim of pretext.

Where should the line be drawn between discrimination and the practical issues associated with keeping an orchestra running? According to a recently published dissertation entitled, *Musculoskeletal Health in Musicians,*[1196] not enough institutional attention is paid to the debilitating musculoskeletal problems that accrue from the functional demands of a profession with high physical demands. What could have happened if the orchestra had a system in place to deal with the physical issues that plagued Kampouris and several of his colleagues, including the former principal second violinist, Cara-Mia Antonello (mentioned in *Kampouris*) whose physical ailments led to early retirement from the SLSO at the age of 40?[1197]

A Dutch Works Council member and principal player reflected on the importance of HRM elements within the process of coming to grips with reasonable measures. "Without a water-tight system in place in which management puts fair protocols in place and enforces them, we descend further into unfairness and frustration."[1198] Adding another spin, a Dutch HRM manager noted that many of the changes wrought in the Netherlands were influenced not only by workplace necessity but also by changes in the sector stemming from US initiatives. "It was decided that we needed more budget to encourage life learning, and the development of personal portfolios. We could not just let the musicians take care of themselves as the musicians grew older. The challenge became, would management, the men making decisions, take us seriously?"[1199]

1196. Laura M. Kok. *Musculoskeletal Health in Musicians: Epidemiology & Biomedics*, Leiden University Medical Center, 2018, thesis defended November 20, 2018.
1197. For more details, Janet Horvath, "Cara Mia's Story," in *Playing Less Hurt*, Hal Leonard Books 2010.
1198. Interview with a Dutch principal player, major orchestra and Works Council member, anonymity assured.
1199. Interview, Ella Broekstra.

A true wake-up call for orchestras is that relevant health-related appraisals, information and advice for eventual treatment should be part of a human resources policy that is easily available for all members of the orchestra. The stigma that Kampouris suffered after decades of service casts a shadow on his former employer. Until the real issues concerning the painful side of performance and the well-being of employees is central within the orchestral organization, defining issues in *Kampouris* remain unresolved.

9.10 PRINCIPAL PLAYERS STRIKE BACK: THE PHOENIX SYMPHONY CASES

The next phase of this inquiry takes us to the Phoenix Symphony (PS) during a dark period in the orchestra's labor history in which eight full-time symphony members filed age discrimination complaints with the EEOC and several cases led to litigation at the National Labor Relations Board (NLRB). The only full-scale orchestra in the state of Arizona, the PS had established an enviable reputation for innovative programming and performance since its inception in 1947. During the mid-1970s, the up-and-coming conductor Eduardo Mata stood at its helm and like his Atlanta-based contemporary Robert Shaw was a strong proponent of orchestral professionalization. While Shaw's plans affected the careers of some older players as the *Hendrickson* case illustrated, there are no records of employment contraventions during Mata's musical reign.

The Phoenix litigation reveals a particularly noxious trio of legal and management matters: discriminatory practices, poor board/management-orchestral relations and last but certainly not least, the impact of a young, ambitious music director whose agenda clashed with some of the best musicians in the orchestra as well as the strongest personalities in the orchestra.[1200] Granted, each music director is entitled to establish and set forth his/her blueprint for his/her orchestra. However, as the Phoenix story and the *Wetherill* case in Indianapolis illustrate, personal vendetta at the expense of experienced players who do not fit within the maestro's blueprint can lead to discriminatory practices.

The PS employment crisis began 30 years after the symphony's glorious Mata days when another young rising star, Michael Christie, was appointed MD. While the great conductors of the 19th and 20th century were more often than not mature musicians who had learned their craft after years of instrumental study, the appointment of a young, flamboyant character with a penchant for piloting planes and the gift of gab seemed to fit with a pattern established during the Mata years. Unfortunately, another side of Christie's personality soon came to the fore. His disdain toward a number of principal players, vociferous section leaders who had never hesitated to make their opinions heard on behalf of their colleagues, was palpable from the onset of his tenure. "Facial expressions at the onset, the frown, the sneer, the obvious dislike that is how it started ... by the time it ended there were dismissals, lawsuits and an

---

1200. Comprehensive reporting *Phoenix New Times* blog https://www.phoenixnewtimes.com/topic/feathered-bastard-6498369.

orchestra with a broken spirit."[1201] Veteran cellist Delaine Salt who had been a member of the PS for 41 seasons opted out of extending her contract citing unbearable stress levels and an increasingly hostile work situation as her primary reasons for departure.[1202]

A recapitulation of the dismissals at the PS shows a distinct pattern in which highly proficient, well-respected players were replaced by inexperienced newcomers. Taking on the role of devil's advocate for a moment, readers are asked to put themselves into the position of a young conductor taking on the challenges of a music director's position. Would you (as conductor) prefer to stand in front of musicians who look up to you or deal with musicians who might question your authority? Interviews with PS musicians point to a clash between the newly appointed music director's insecurity and the established musicians' know-how and power.

Richard Bock, principal cellist from 1984 to 2007, an internationally recognized cellist whose level of playing was irreproachable according to expert witnesses, was fired on January 14, 2008. Principal violist Peter Rosato, a particularly outspoken individual whose musical prowess was undisputed was demoted, and eventually fired in 2008. Both players were not only celebrated within the local classical music circuit but also enjoyed significant national and international musical careers.

The news of irregularities at the PS reached the ears of colleagues at the internationally renowned US summer festival, the Grand Teton Music Festival (GTMF), in July 2008, where Rosato had performed. In an act of solidarity, orchestral musicians from leading US symphonies registered their outrage at the Phoenix situation.[1203] As the consolidated case that Messrs. Bock and Rosato brought before the NLRB revealed, the GTMF letter was considered to be a concerted activity for the purpose of mutual aid protected under the National Labor Relations Act (NLRA).[1204] Rosato was directly threatened by the PS, if he continued to engage in concerted activities, he would not receive the payments due to him.[1205]

The reluctance of the orchestra's board and management to perceive that what might look good for the community is not good for the musicians is a crucial factor not only in the PS case but also in other orchestral employment-related disputes. Not a

1201. Interview section player not involved in the dismissal threat, anonymity assured.

1202. Stephen Lemons reporting *Phoenix New Times*, March 23, 2009 https://www.phoenixnewtimes.com/news/michael-christie-and-the-ongoing-rumble-in-the-phoenix-symphony-6503427.

1203. *See Epilogue: Appendix* 9 for a copy of the signed Grand Teton Music Festival musicians protest.

1204. Quoting from the NLRA website: Section 7 National Labor Relations Act (the Act) guarantees employees "the right to self-organization, to form, join, or assist labor organizations, to bargain collectively through representatives of their own choosing, and to engage in other concerted activities for the purpose of collective bargaining or other mutual aid or protection," and the right "to refrain from any or all such activities." Section 8(a)(1) of the Act makes it an unfair labor practice for an employer "to interfere with, restrain, or coerce employees in the exercise of the rights guaranteed in Section 7" of the Act. *See* https://www.nlrb.gov/rights-we-protect/whats-law/employers/interfering-employee-rights-section-7-8a1.

1205. *Phoenix Symphony Association d/b/a The Phoenix Symphony and Richard C. Bock, Peter Rosato and Local 585 American Federation of Musicians* before the National Labor Relations Board Region 28 (Consolidated case) Case 28-CA-22325, https://www.nlrb.gov/case/28-CA-022325 §5(c).

clash of the titans, but certainly a clash in which the music director attempted to go after principals who not only held tenure but also were perceived as influencers. The power of the music director discussed at length in an earlier *movement* reinforced by the powers held by the Board and management held the orchestra members at bay and served to augment the music director's command.

Those experienced in the lore of US orchestras might remember that Christie's tenure with the PS coincided with tenure as MD at New York's Brooklyn Philharmonic (2005-2010). Praised by music critics for innovative programming, Christie's tenure brought criticism from the AFM Local 802:

> Crippled by lack of money, the orchestra had cancelled its entire previous season. The painful question remains: did anyone notice? Once an important group, especially for modern music, under the distinguished batons of Lukas Foss, Dennis Russell Davies, and Robert Spano, the orchestra saw its overall quality fall off drastically under music director Michael Christie. Christie developed stylish concert programs but put less care into rehearsing and developing the ensemble--the music director's primary responsibility.[1206]

As of 2018, Christie's career declined from directing distinguished ensembles such as the Phoenix and Brooklyn orchestras to serving as Music Director of the New West Symphony Orchestra, a regional orchestra in the Los Angeles metropolitan area. "Maybe, just maybe there is such thing as musical if not poetic justice."[1207]

Bock filed several discrimination charges against the Phoenix Symphony Association (PSA), the governing body of the PS with the EEOC, claiming age discrimination and retaliation. According to reports inside the PS, a member of the orchestra's board of directors carped to members of the orchestra about the "musicians who had filed age discrimination claims and indicated that the filing of those claims was underhanded and out of order, that it must stop, and that punishment and termination of the musicians would be considered." Reacting to Bock's suit, Edwin Wolf, a PSA Board member, warned the cellist that there would be repercussions if the case were to continue. Bock fought his suspension and dismissal and together with Peter Rosato filed a case at the National Labor Relations Board (NLRB) on January 22, 2009, to continue their struggle against retaliation on the part of the orchestra.[1208] Bock proceeded to sue for wrongful termination, and Rosato sued for both wrongful termination and unpaid wages. Bock's suit centered on "unfair and inconsistent treatment in comparison to other employees" and eventual job termination "replacement by a much younger person." The Phoenix NLRB office issued a formal complaint charging the Phoenix Symphony's CEO, MD, and Board with discrimination, unlawful termination and fostering a hostile work environment engendered by the Symphony's leadership.[1209]

1206. George Grella. "Alan Pierson: Making Brooklyn's Orchestra," *The Brooklyn Rail*, September 9, 2011, https://brooklynrail.org/2011/09/music/alan-pierson-making-brooklyns-orchestra.
1207. Former bass player Brooklyn Philharmonic echoing the sentiments of a Phoenix Symphony Orchestra string player, anonymity assured.
1208. Consolidated case, *supra*.
1209. Stephen Lemons. "Ongoing Angst at the Phoenix Symphony." *Musical America Worldwide*, March 25, 2009.

The PSA responded that Bock's firing had nothing to do with discrimination. In a legally questionable move, CEO Maryellen Gleason publicly stated that Bock was fired for breaching Arizona law referencing Title 12 of the Arizona Revised Statute, A.R.S. 12-2238, a piece of legislation that concerns mediation process privilege. Essentially, this procedural rule serves as a checklist as to how courts should consider the admissibility of information gleaned during mediation. The question arises as to how this statute could possibly lead to an accusation of breaking the law in *Bock*. According to the PSA powers-that-be, Bock purportedly breached by discussing the extent of the PSA's discriminatory practices with local journalists. In the logic or rather illogic of the PSA, legitimate information-sharing was tantamount to a criminal act. In a memo released to the orchestra, management stated that "even if this issue is not covered in the master agreement, you can't break the law and work for the Phoenix Symphony. Gleason went on to give the example of someone who shoots someone not being able to keep their job even though shooting someone is not covered in the master agreement."[1210]

In May 2009, the PSA issued a press release proclaiming "Phoenix Symphony Musicians and Symphony Board Reach Landmark Accord." Yet, in terms of employment, the agreement was disastrous as musicians were pressured into accepting a whopping 17% pay cut effective immediately. According to the CEO, the persistent financial fallout from the recession exacerbated by the 2007-2008 financial crisis led to a decrease in donors and a decline in endowments compounding the orchestra's financial woes. However, her story did not accord with speeches made by PSA executives who had raved to donors as well as orchestral musicians about balanced budgets and sell-out concerts.[1211]

A Phoenix-based arts blogger reported that Gleason wanted to reduce the size of the orchestra to around 50 players (from 79) and to perform only 28 nonconsecutive weeks, as opposed to nine months with rehearsals to take place in the evenings and on weekends. In short, the orchestra would be forced to revert to its nonprofessional status prior to the 1960s, when it achieved a coveted major rating from the American Symphony Orchestra League. Certainly, cutbacks in arts organizations are nothing new, even in the best of financial times. The difference that lies beneath the surface in the Phoenix story is how these cutbacks were managed and sold to the musicians and the greater community. With all those glowing reports, why was it necessary for the musicians to take a 17 % pay cut, especially when their base pay ranked next to the very bottom of comparative salaries, weighing in at $35,000 per year? And what sort of ethical compass leads a CEO to blame the cuts on lawsuits from musicians who were forced to leave their jobs for reasons that had little to do with their musicianship or leadership, the essentials of their job descriptions? Reports from the *Phoenix News* present a disturbing pattern of lies and whispers. An outsider to the music profession would assume that such actions on the part of a general manager would lead to professional discredit. Yet, promoting herself as a leader in high-velocity turnarounds

1210. An insider writing under the pen name appalled music lover on Wednesday June 11, 2009, https://adaptistration.com/2009/06/10/reeling-from-a-one-two.
1211. *See* Lemons, *supra*.

in the performing arts, Gleason moved from Phoenix to take over a top position at the Milwaukee Symphony in 2010. Within two years, that orchestra and its board took the dramatic decision to hire a musician to replace Gleason. Phoenix orchestral insiders speculated that perhaps her alacrity to cut them without heed had come home to roost.[1212]

Prior to the NLRB hearing, the PSA Board capitulated and reached a settlement with Messrs Bock and Rosato. The musicians were required to withdraw all formal complaints and were presented with the option to return to the PS with full restitution of back pay or drop all claims against the PSA in exchange for a financial settlement. Referring to a poisoned atmosphere as a result of how serious claims were trivialized, the musicians elected to leave the orchestra. Bock revealed that the amount he received was "certainly well-deserved and substantial. I never asked for this treatment, nor did I deserve it in any way. It's sad to say that part of the reason that musicians are compelled to sue the very orchestras they once called home is to prove to the greater music world out there that we can never ever accept such treatment. Such wrongs deserve remedies no matter how tough and long the fight is. Sadly, most musicians do not have the wherewithal to stand up against an unfair employer."[1213] Nowadays, Bock pursues his two vocational loves with great success: he is a sought-after cellist on the chamber music circuit and carries forward his love of Italian food at the prize-winning restaurant he owns, where culinary art is "music to the palate."[1214]

Ultimately, the PSA was required to post a list of prohibited activities, *inter alia*, noninterference with the employees' rights to engage in protected activities, those very activities that the wronged musicians had engaged in such as filing age-discrimination cases at the EEOC and protecting themselves through such actions as the GTMF letter.[1215] The question making the rounds post-litigation was whether the symphony was insured for such settlements or whether the musicians' pay cuts subsidized managements' actions.[1216] It is impossible to fathom the loss that occurred as a result of the Phoenix imbroglio.

9.11 PHOENIX SYMPHONY REVISITED: *JOHN WETHERILL V INDIANAPOLIS SYMPHONY ORCHESTRA*

Almost a decade post *Bock*, the Indianapolis Symphony Orchestra's (ISO's) principal bassoonist John Wetherill was pitted in a losing battle against a new music director who sought to replace him. Mr. Wetherill joined the ISO's bassoon section in 1989 winning the principal bassoon audition 11 years thereafter. As a principal player, his contract authorized extra compensation and additional remuneration for seniority. His employment troubles began after the young (31-year-old) Polish maestro, Krzysztof

1212. Conversations with Phoenix Symphony musicians, anonymity assured.
1213. Conversations with Richard Bock.
1214. Bock's restaurant Giuseppe's on 28th is a five-time winner of the Diners' Choice Award.
1215. Corroborated by David Kelley, Deputy Assistant General Counsel at the NLRB, Deputy Regional Attorney NLRB.
1216. Dmitri Drobatschewsky, "About That 'Landmark Accord' in Phoenix," MusicalAmerica.com https://conductingmasterclass.wordpress.com/2009/06/14/more-bad-press-for-christie/.

discrimination case. Brushing aside the central question, SCOTUS chose to analyze if the burden of persuasion shifts to the employer in a mixed-motive discrimination claim. The majority found that under the ADEA a plaintiff has to present persuasive evidence that age was the "but for" cause of the employer's decision to take adverse action. But for? Taking a markedly black letter approach, SCOTUS made a distinction between the language of Title VII and the ADEA. To recall, under the ADEA, "[i]t shall be unlawful for an employer ... to fail or refuse to hire or to discharge any individual with respect to his compensation, terms, conditions, or privileges of employment, because of such individual's age." Thus, age had to be the reason for the adverse action, "but for" age the action would have never taken place.

The close-call 5-4 decision was considered to be an overwhelming victory for employers: even if a plaintiff like Gross introduced evidence to show that age was an important motivating factor in an ADEA age discrimination claim, the burden of persuasion would not shift to the employer to prove that it would have taken the action regardless of the plaintiff's age. SCOTUS imposed a higher burden of proof on workers who asserted specifically age discrimination claims against their employers under the ADEA as opposed to a lower burden of proof for claims asserting other forms of discrimination such as gender, racial or religious discrimination.

Cogent criticism points to mixed-motive age discrimination cases that wallow in ambiguity. To bring back memories inspired by *Henrickson* and *Karella*, how should a lower court react to a case in which a plaintiff who is a member of a protected age group is not performing up to par? If a plaintiff in the protected age group underperforms, and the employer terminated the employee due to a combination of age and sub-par performance (a mixed-motive justification), has the employee met the "but for" test? Neither age nor performance deficiencies on their own could result in termination. If the two are combined, has the "but for" test been satisfied?

The *Gross* decision begs the question as to if and when Congress will step in to correct the rigid ADEA standard imposed by SCOTUS. The court made no reference to the lopsided legal standard in which the ADEA remains unchanged. In a response to Senator Grassley's plea for congressional action, the Executive Vice President of the American Association for the Advancement of Retired People asserted that "too many older workers have been victims of unfair age discrimination and are denied a fair shake in our justice system. The time for Congress to act is now."[1227] Her words resonate with opinions expressed by the orchestral musicians who attempted to mount age discrimination cases but were often thwarted by the system and its handmaidens: EEOC requirements and the judicial penchant for screening cases "to preclude judgment as a matter of law" that has all but closed the doors to summary judgment. From the front lines of orchestral musician's age discrimination, the disproportionality between a musician's resources to litigate and the employer's resources should not be underestimated: many who would and should stand up for their rights, cannot.[1228]

1227. Nancy LeaMond, AARP Executive Vice President and Chief Advocacy & Engagement Officer, quote cited on Senator Grassley's website, *supra*.
1228. Conversations with Richard Bock.

IV Closing Chords

10 The Curtain Falls? Orchestras in Times of Pandemic

> "And now, in this solemn and deeply stirring moment, when the confusion and distractions of everyday life are lifted like a hood from our eyes, a voice of awe-inspiring solemnity chills our heart, a voice that, blinded by the mirage of everyday life, we usually ignore: 'What next?' it says. "And we must answer this question if we are to go on living."[1229]

> The uncertain fear is of the future. Government subsidies may be reduced significantly, sponsors may dramatically cut donations, families may be reluctant to send their kids to music lessons if their own financial situations have significantly deteriorated; there could be fewer jobs and fewer concerts for musicians, there are so many live streams and videos online for free, what will musicians' lives post COVID-19 be like?[1230]

10.1 COVID-19 PANDEMIC

Of all the challenges that orchestral musicians and their organizations have been forced to confront, none came close to the havoc wreaked by COVID-19. Regardless of geographic location, size and/or reputation, orchestras and their employees landed in the precarious position of not knowing if, how, and when they would be able to re-engage in live concerts. "The very essence of an orchestra's raison d'être depends on audience proximity and building a community of listener-participants, first through concerts and then broadcasts-recordings. When that disappears, the centrality of the concert experience is compromised. Those adversely affected by economic downturns during the pandemic are reticent to part with their savings and government grants

1229. Gustav Mahler, Symphony No. 2 Resurrection Symphony, https://archive.org/stream/gustavmahlermemo00mahl/gustavmahlermemo00mahl_djvu.txt.
1230. Kyoko Hashimoto, piano professor McGill University, placed the text on her Facebook page.

earmarked for culture are reserved for the major players in the field."[1231] In terms of the orchestral labor force, two other major issues emerged after concert halls worldwide closed in mid-March 2020: the sustainability of ongoing compensation for salaried orchestral musicians, and the loss of revenue sources for freelance musicians.

Culture vultures not to speak of the general public were jolted by the news that one of the Netherlands' premier venues for large-scale performances (capacity of just under 16,500) could not welcome Europe's glitzy blockbuster, the 2020 Eurovision Song Contest in May 2020. European Broadcasting Union organizers were forced to cancel due to growing concerns related to the rapid spread of the virus. More sobering news followed in mid-April 2020 when the Dutch government announced that the massive venue was to be transformed into an emergency hospital in order to accommodate the rising numbers of pandemic victims. In the US, many orchestras announced 2020-2021 season closures, a steady stream of orchestras furloughed their employees in 2020, and the percentage of freelance musicians relegated to collect unemployment rose sharply. The largest performing arts organization in the US, the mighty Metropolitan Opera (MET), announced layoffs that impacted musicians and stage-related employees in mid-March.[1232] While heavily endowed top-tier orchestras hope to weather the pandemic storm and top-ticket maestros exemplified by Gustavo Dudamel and Jaap van Zweden[1233] renounced portions of their salaries to contribute to the greater good, smaller orchestras were acutely threatened as a wave of restructuring loomed large.[1234]

10.2 BACKTRACK TO A PREVIOUS PANDEMIC

From virology to the differences in local and international reactions to a killer virus, parallels between the Spanish flu epidemic 1918-1919 and the COVID-19 pandemic 2020 more than a century later are startling. First reported in March 1918 as US troops returned home from European battlefields, the 20th-century scourge spread rapidly cross-country. A quick look back to reports from 1918 reveals a perplexing narrative of chaos and denial. Newspaper clippings recount tales of enraged entrepreneurs who threatened to sue the government for temporarily closing their businesses, as economic turmoil turned the tides from "patriotic acceptance to exasperated defiance."[1235] A treasure trove of articles reported on the 1918 pandemic's negative effects on the burgeoning film industry. "Because of the deplorable epidemic of influenza ... the

1231. Conversations with impresario Marco Riaskoff, forced to close down his world-renowned Meesterpianisten Concertgebouw Concert Series 2021-2022 after 33 successful years.
1232. US statistics on orchestral employment compare April 2020 to August 2020, https://adaptistration.com/2020/08/31/state-of-employment-poll-review-aug-31-sep-6/.
1233. https://www.broadwayworld.com/article/Music-Director-Jaap-van-Zweden-Donates-500000-to-NY-Phil-Plays-On-Emergency-Fund-20200616?fbclid=IwAR2Stm-5FICrxUpxMci2m0miYqMfrkJmcHguhGIy3AYcxDWkXb3DW__K6Vs.
1234. https://adaptistration.com/2020/05/01/streamlining-the-employment-status-reporting-process/#more-49951.
1235. Richard Koszarski. "Flu Season: 'Moving Picture World' Reports on Pandemic Influenza 1918-19," 2005, 466-485.

clock of the motion picture industry has been stopped."[1236] The great unknown, the question as to how to evaluate and proceed toward an eventual return to normalcy was as troubling then as it is now. "Some towns which closed theaters allowed churches to remain open, while Louisville, for example, closed theaters and churches but allowed saloons to operate. New York City never closed at all. When theaters did reopen, business was not always as good as expected, especially if a resurgence of the epidemic kept frightened audiences away."[1237]

The same fears resounded over a century later. Discrepancies between countries in which culture is (partially) subsidized and countries in which cultural support depends on the market were magnified as a leading opera director reported: "when your art form is a hundred people on stage, a hundred in the pit, and 2,700 in the audience, when your financial model means you break even when you sell 95% of your tickets, when public subsidy accounts for only 20% of your income ... it is obvious that you are going to hit the buffers."[1238] The very image of frightened audiences avoiding theater entrances back in 1918 depicted in cartoons is every bit as pertinent in the 21st century as it influences decisions on how to open halls and reach out to audiences in a brave new world of distanced seating and masked musicians.[1239] The question as to when to open was based on compliance with national health and safety requirements. Yet in both countries studied, there was no clear consensus with regard to opening dates; no recipe for post-pandemic success.

10.3 ORCHESTRAL MUSICIANS IN DIRE STRAITS

As the *movement* centered on freelance orchestral musicians emphasized, the musicians who work as freelance substitute players in orchestras earn incomes that offer little room to create financial buffers to compensate for a lack of social security benefits. To exemplify, the number of Dutch-based self-employed workers who relied on government assistance by late May 2020 was a staggering 240,000 of the 933,000 registered self-employed workers in the Netherlands, and freelance performing artists lost an average of €20,000 per person in income in 2020.[1240] Those who were not officially registered as self-employed workers were not entitled to the aid packages, and thousands of self-employed orchestral musicians do not receive any form of aid. "Within the orchestral sector, safe but sorry to report that all of the self-employed musicians are hard hit and many of them cannot even apply for aid as their situations do not tick all the boxes required to receive funds."[1241]

1236. *Moving Picture World* October 26, 1918.
1237. *Ibid.*
1238. Alex Beard, Royal Opera House (London) Chief Executive "We could go to the wall in 12 weeks': are we just going to let classical music die?" The Guardian June 9, 2020.
1239. *See* Koszarski, *supra*.
1240. Centraal Bureau voor de Statistiek. COVID-19-related statistics https://www.cbs.nl/.
1241. Conversations with Caroline Cartens, cofounder of the Platform voor Freelance Musici (PvFM).

Taking a look at the impact of the pandemic on the venues that offer musical performances sheds light on the effects of the crisis on those who perform in those halls. Statistics provide stark evidence of the crisis in the cultural sector starting with the March 12, 2020 shutdown of all halls, theaters, and public spaces in the Netherlands. A task force of accountants and cultural advisors who studied the economic consequences of the pandemic on over one hundred Dutch cultural venues reported losses of close to €1 billion by late May 2020.[1242] Ton van Capelle, an accountant in the cultural sector, noted: "[t]he smaller halls are transferring the financial 'pain' to the artists, technicians and suppliers."[1243] Answering the call for a major infusion of funding, the Dutch government announced €300 million in extra support for the cultural sector in May 2020 with funds earmarked for the national treasures, the most prominent major venues including museums and major concert halls. "Although the Minister alluded to a trickle-down effect for smaller venues, and last on the list those who work in those venues, there is no trickle down to the freelancers. Once a hall goes dark, that's it, no performances."[1244]

One small step from bad news at the venue level preceded a debacle at the personnel level. Unlike the situation in the US where even top-tier orchestras shut down and furloughed musicians and staff members, the subsidized Dutch BIS orchestras[1245] continued to pay musician salaries. Subsidized Dutch orchestras availed themselves of regulated short-time-work options, in which a percentage of the employee's salary was covered by unemployment insurance. "Normally, our orchestra [the world-renowned Rotterdam Philharmonic] plays with a full complement and employs many freelancers. At the beginning of the 2020-21 season, a high percentage of colleagues were forced to stay home because they could not risk working alongside a full complement of musicians. Yet, how long can you pay workers to stay home?"[1246] Dutch subsidized orchestras initially promised to pay out contracted freelancers for canceled performances scheduled during the lockdown (March 12, 2020) until the end of the season (for most orchestras, late June-early July, with some variance). Although these orchestras were legally obligated to compensate contracted players, the payout only had an effect on the top echelon of freelancers who had been contracted long in advance. "With an agenda that has gone from full of diverse concerts and festival performances, I now have absolutely nothing. Blank. What will happen to all the freelancers whose concerts do not exist anymore? We are skirting the edge of insolvency."[1247]

1242. Henk Vlaming "De klap in de cultuursector komt volgend jaar." *NBA-platform voor accountants en financials* 25 juni 2020.
1243. *Ibid.*
1244. Remark made by Dorine Schoon, cofounder PvFM.
1245. *See FAQs*, BIS = Basic Infrastructure Subsidy allotted to nine Dutch state-subsidized orchestras as of 2020.
1246. Conversations with Quirine Scheffers, associate concertmaster Rotterdam Philharmonic Orchestra.
1247. Conversations with a Dutch freelance cellist, anonymity assured.

10.4 OTHER THREATS I: LIVESTREAMS AND ZOOMS REPLACE LIVE CONCERTS

As concert halls and opera houses closed their doors and music festivals the world over announced cancelations, a record number of individual musicians, ensembles, and orchestras answered silence with live streams from empty halls and homes. The New York Philharmonic's 2020 Mahler Festival redeployed from diverse New York venues to a two-week digital gala jamboree replete with symphonic performance, and for those who sought to combine lockdown listening with culinary arts, Viennese recipes. Sinfonia Rotterdam, one of the first Dutch orchestras to rethink reopening in a creative way, opted for a live stream concert in the cavernous magnificence of a large church with 30 audience members in attendance.[1248] Reactions were overwhelmingly positive, and tens of thousands of listeners followed on social media platforms. The what's next factor became apparent as participants and audience members shared the view that this launch could lead to "start the ball rolling to do more than get through the crisis, but to actually to bring something new and exciting into being."[1249]

High-profile artists filled Facebook, Instagram, Spotify, Twitter, and YouTube with resourceful solutions to fill the vacuum left by silenced live performances. Individual artists and orchestras with lucrative record label representation can earn well from streaming as data journalist David McCandless first revealed in his groundbreaking studies in 2010.[1250] A caveat: until earnings models based on massive downloads espoused by Instagram, Spotify and the rest of the popularly streamed platforms change, it is obvious that only the superstars will benefit financially from putting their performances out, while the vast majority will receive next-to-nothing. To Jennifer Koh, a successful violin soloist with an international career, streaming classical music is problematic. "We don't really have the ability to monetize as much as other fields of music, because the place where we are able to make income is the live performance space. We're in an incredibly fragile position, all of us freelancers."[1251] In a 2020 BBC Radio 4 interview, star British violinist Tasmin Little divulged that her earnings from over five million Spotify streams netted her the trivial sum of £12.34.[1252]

10.5 OTHER THREATS II: CONSERVATORIES REACT TO THE CORONAVIRUS

While the pandemic raged in China, much of the Western world downplayed the possibility of a pandemic spreading until Italy reported its first cases on January 30,

1248. Relive the Sinfonia Rotterdam experience, https://www.youtube.com/watch?v=mIgSV9jQ4K4.
1249. Conversations with Sinfonia Rotterdam's Music Director, Conrad van Alphen.
1250. https://informationisbeautiful.net/2010/how-much-do-music-artists-earn-online/ updates available online.
1251. Jennifer Koh, National Public Radio broadcast March 18, 2020.
1252. Tasmin Little's tweet, https://twitter.com/tasminlittle/status/1262323181228036097 Reference to BBC4 interview, https://www.classicfm.com/music-news/87p-streams-musicians-hit-out-spotify-earnings-mp-inquiry/.

2020. The very next day, the prestigious Santa Cecilia Conservatory (Rome) canceled lessons for its "oriental" students alluding to their purported direct link to COVID-19. Despite outpourings of outrage in mainstream and social media, the illustrious institution defended its choice, stating that it was duty bound to protect its students and faculty even at the cost of discriminating against a specific group of students. Fearing an upsurge in backlash measures on the part of other institutions and the general public, a solidarity movement #JeNeSuisPasUnVirus gained momentum with millions voicing their abhorrence. Although other institutions did not follow the questionable tactics of Santa Cecilia, most conservatories closed down by the second week in March taking "the unprecedented step of going to remote learning."[1253] Reports on the ups and downs of online lessons filled the pages of social media with grave concerns about the viability of long-distance learning for a hands-on craft.

10.6 DOLLARS AND SENSE

By early April 2020, the financial losses to nonprofit cultural organizations resulting from canceled events, forced staff reductions, and closures in the US were estimated at $4.5 billion.[1254] Yet, like the crisis measures adopted in the Netherlands, the trickle-down effect on those at the bottom of the receiving line, freelance musicians, was minimal. "Business as usual, those with the loudest voices and most influential lobbies will receive aid, by the time freelancers or formerly much-in-demand ensembles will receive anything, it will be too late."[1255] On March 27, 2020, Congress passed the CARES Act, a $2.3 trillion aid package to offer financial support to small businesses and independent contractors as a result of their losses during the COVID-19 pandemic, and one week later, the Department of Labor provided guidelines for a Pandemic Unemployment Assistance (PUA) program to provide benefits for individuals who did not qualify for regular unemployment compensation.[1256] In addition, musicians' unions provided regular updates on extra resources for musicians in dire straits. The AFM Musicians' Relief Fund offered up to $300 to freelance members adversely affected by the crisis, and the AFM James Petrillo Fund granted additional funds for musicians diagnosed with COVID-19.[1257]

10.7 DUTCH VERSUS US FINANCIAL COMPENSATION

Dutch government programs intended to benefit the self-employed as well as employers who have suffered a loss of income transitioned through several stages of development within the first COVID-19 six-month timespan. General loans to cover the

1253. https://www.juilliard.edu/campus-life/covid-19-response.
1254. The survey started March 13, 2020, received thousands of responses, https://www.americansforthearts.org/by-topic/disaster-preparedness/coronavirus-covid-19-resource-and-response-center?qt-view__content_fed_quick_tab__block_1=2#survey.
1255. Formerly active New York-based freelance musician, anonymity assured.
1256. Unemployment Insurance Program Letter Directive No. 16-20, https://wdr.doleta.gov/directives/corr_doc.cfm?DOCN=4628.
1257. https://afm47.org/covid19.

costs of employee salaries were granted to employers whose businesses suffered a minimum of 20% pandemic-related income loss.[1258] Orchestras and smaller music ensembles soon discovered that the checklists for these loans were not designed for performing arts organizations. The Platform voor Freelance Musici (PvFM) website was replete with posts on the vicissitudes of receiving aid under relief programs in a sector that operates quite differently from other freelance sectors. "Some of our work is really seasonal, with highs in December and April and lows in the summer months. This influences how income is calculated … something else that set us apart from other freelancers is that you need to have a separate studio or workspace to qualify for relief. Most musicians practice at home and couldn't even dream of being able to afford a private studio!!"[1259]

10.8 VIABLE OPTIONS FOR GENERAL BENEFIT, ORCHESTRAL SURVIVAL

Two weeks after his orchestra furloughed its 79 musicians, a Nashville Symphony cellist related:

> So as of today, the Nashville Symphony, my employers for the last 36 years, ceases to exist in the form many of you know and love. And it won't be back … for a long time, if ever. So gone is the orchestra that recorded Grammy winning recordings on a regular basis. History has taught management and musicians, but perhaps not the ones in charge (our board). During the last shutdown, we lost a significant number of our players and nearly all of our management.[1260]

To achieve grassroots and solid financial support for not only famed concert halls but also the musicians that bring life to those halls, national and international recovery funds in which musicians join forces with policymakers and the general public are crucial to ensure the survival of the sector. During the COVID-19 years, fear and silence heightened the perception of a bleak future. Yet, as the COVID-19 weeks turned to months and years, the perception that cultural events could contribute to healing the isolation caused by social distancing and play a part in unifying communities took hold in both countries studied. Perhaps, music could serve as a panacea for the alienation, isolation, and malaise that magnified pandemic woes. "COVID-19 could give us a chance to break with a somewhat broken past and call out to all who believe in the viability of musical arts to rethink along the lines of Kate Raworth's doughnut model that integrates social justice and circular economy with other sectors."[1261]

1258. Temporary Emergency Measure Bridging Employment, English translation of the (NOW), https://www.uwv.nl/werkgevers/overige-onderwerpen/now/eerste-aanvraagperiode-now/index.aspx.
1259. Conversations with Caroline Cartens.
1260. Steven Drake's report, https://slippedisc.com/2020/07/a-us-cellist-writes-my-orchestra-has-just-ceased-to-exist/.
1261. Conversations with Ariane Todes, former editor of *The Strad* magazine and music blogger. For more on the doughnut model and economic circularity, *see* https://www.kateraworth.com/doughnut/.

In place of an endgame, the door eventually opened for many orchestras in both countries studied. Yet, the post-COVID-19 return to normalcy for orchestras has been fraught with significant challenges. Two years following Steven Drake's plea, the Nashville Symphony announced an ambitious 2023-2024 concert season.[1262] Yet beneath the surface of its diverse offerings, a closer look at the orchestra's post-COVID-19 personnel list shows that within the first and second violin sections, one-third of the personnel listed are replacement/extra players.[1263] Does this reflect personnel loss, the orchestra's financial inability to offer contracted positions or a bit of both? Post-pandemic, orchestras on both sides of the Atlantic report that to compensate for lagging subscription and ticket sales, fewer concerts are planned per season, a move that has a great impact on the most vulnerable, the freelance musicians.[1264]

1262. https://tntribune.com/nashville-symphony-announces-2023-24-season/.
1263. https://www.nashvillesymphony.org/about/orchestra-conductors/.
1264. https://www.nytimes.com/2022/08/21/arts/performing-arts-pandemic-attendance.html.

11
Coda: New Vistas on Orchestral Employment Post-COVID-19

The word "coda" entails a musical conclusion that is intended to leave the listener with a sense of balance, as it reiterates tonal material from previous *movements*. This coda reflects on vulnerabilities examined in past pages and offers readers insights into the future. While *Haydn rewrites history* paid homage to a great composer/conductor and his striking musicians in the 18th century, there is a lesser-known letter H composer whose *Symphonic Metamorphosis of Themes by Carl Maria von Weber* is the true musical godfather of this project. Paul Hindemith's conscious reflection and transformation of four forgotten musical themes that lead to an expansive coda is the source for more than a title for this inquiry; not only the music but also the man and his actions were meritorious. The wide range of subject matter inspired by musicians' input led to the choice of a symphonic metamorphosis, a tone poem that evolves as it moves through different jurisdictions and encounters with vulnerability.

11.1 VULNERABILITIES IN CONTEXT

Paul Hindemith chose to leave Germany for several reasons. First, the National Socialists banned performances of his "decadent" music in 1936. Second and exceptionally considering the actions of the vast majority of his colleagues, he refused to disassociate himself from the plight of Jewish musicians. Hindemith followed the courage of his convictions to leave his beloved homeland at the height of his career, exposing himself to what he referred to as the ultimate precarity, the unknown.[1265] He took to the road and sought refuge in several countries before settling in the US, grateful to accept a professorship at Yale in 1940.

1265. The Paul Hindemith Collection, Yale University Repository. Series V: Correspondence and Journals, 1934-1960, https://archives.yale.edu/repositories/6/archival_objects/2654175.

The first composition completed in his newly adopted homeland paid respect to the father of German romantic music, Carl Maria von Weber. Normally a strict stickler for form, Hindemith departed from traditional symphonic classical sonata form in his *Symphonic Metamorphosis*. "While model and original essentially agree on matters of melody, harmony, rhythm, and form, closer scrutiny reveals the process of metamorphosis to extend beyond surface modifications ... which ultimately affect every level and component of the composition's structure."[1266] In addition to his compositional contributions to the canon of 20th-century music, Hindemith was a preeminent scholar of music theory and composition. His dedication to adapting the old to pave the way for the new resonates with research objectives revisited here.

From Frances Henrickson's tremulous pleas to Elizabeth Rowe's clarion call, from Haydn's "Farewell" Symphony to the trials and tribulations of US orchestras in lockdown, from the silenced RKF to the eerie hush at Lincoln Center during the COVID-19 pandemic in 2020, different variations on the theme of orchestral musicians' vulnerabilities and reactions to those vulnerabilities have filled these pages.

I embarked on this journey to provide musicians and jurists with a description and analysis of diverse employment-related vulnerabilities faced by a category of workers overlooked by mainstream studies. With its aims to describe musicians' vulnerabilities in terms of internal and external factors shared by orchestral players the world over, this book hopes to lay the groundwork for future research to inspire and motivate a rethink in terms of musician empowerment. Although the scope of the inquiry was large, there are many lines of reasoning and areas of research left untouched. One area conspicuously missing from these pages is new ways and means to engage unions in cooperative efforts with grassroots collaboratives such as the PvFM. Another area worthy of future examination with an eye to redressing vulnerable employment in the sector is the realm of public policy, as the *Requiem movement* intimates. Circling back to solutions within a legal framework, far more research on the impact of workplace regulation with regard to discrimination is essential, as discussed in *Dissonance: Orchestral Workplace Discrimination*. In light of recent Fair Practice initiatives in the Netherlands, research concerning the coverage and resilience of these regimes is also of the essence.

11.2 A COMMUNITY OF MUSICIANS

> A re-imagined freedom of association with broad application to all workers, including the self-employed.[1267]

1266. Gene Anderson. "Musical Metamorphoses in Hindemith's "March" from *the Symphonic Metamorphosis of Themes by Carl Maria von Weber*," 3.
1267. Ruth Dukes and Wolfgang Streeck. "Labour Constitutions and Occupational Communities: Social Norms and Legal Norms at Work." *Journal of Law and Society* 2020, 22 DOI: 10.1111/jols.12254.

In 1987, Ernest Fleischmann, the revered former executive director of the London Symphony and the Los Angeles Philharmonic, opened the floodgates of a debate on the position of orchestral musicians in an address to conservatory graduates:

> As you prepare to enter this demanding perplexing, enticing ... profession that is part craft, part art, part sport, part magic, as you contemplate your musical future, I really need to ask you to commit a crime. I want you to become arsonists, yes arsonists, to join me and lots of musicians, administrators, and trustees in setting the symphony orchestra ablaze. If the music we care about so deeply is to survive, we must accept that the orchestra is burnt out, but from its ashes something infinitely richer, more varied, more satisfying can arise if we all work together to create it—the symphony orchestra is dead, long live the Community of Musicians.[1268]

Five years later, his successor in Los Angeles[1269] responded to predictions of impending disaster with more fighting words: "if we accept these dire future forecasts, it is clear that something has to change. There are two ways change can occur: one is by taking the drive over the cliff, and the other is the tough work of building real partnerships where all parties are enfranchised in the results."[1270] It could be argued that the Fleischmann-Borda gauntlet has been taken up far from Los Angeles. In the Netherlands, the aforementioned PvFM, a collective of orchestral freelancers, has formed a strong protective front to represent the rights of the most vulnerable orchestral musicians. Small steps forward exemplify how musician solidarity can mitigate financial vulnerability.

11.3 COUNTERVAILING REACTIONS TO VULNERABILITY

> Organizing freelancers is like organizing cats, or maybe, more like giving a cat a bath.[1271]

The quote above with its reference to real cats as opposed to gigging musician-cats bears further investigation. As several *movements* have highlighted, employers, judges, legislators, and politicians in jurisdictions far and wide have applied their expertise to the ins and outs of categories of workers, the problems inherent to misclassification, and the differences between the false self-employed and their entrepreneurial self-employed colleagues. As noted in *En Route to the FNV*, the ECJ's ruling in *FNV* established a "pattern of understanding and acceptance" of the concept of the false self-employed status of orchestral freelance musicians. Yet, quo vadis? Union organizers have attempted valiantly to pave the way to collective bargaining for cultural workers regardless of classification, and leading academics ponder ways to transmute hybrid employee-worker categories into positive legislation.

1268. Ernest Fleischmann, Commencement Address Cleveland Institute of Music 1987.
1269. Deborah Borda, since 2017 CEO New York Philharmonic.
1270. *The Wolf Report*. June 1992, 69.
1271. Speech Thérèse Boutin, former CEO Orchestre Symphonique du Québec, FIM International Conference, Montreal, Canada, May 2017.

11.4 COUNTERVAILING OR CONTROVERSIAL? THE FAIR PRACTICE CODE

In the Netherlands, the boots on the musical ground are increasingly concerned about continuing austerity in terms of cultural financing and new vulnerabilities in the wake of fair practice legislation. In 2017, a joint report published by the Dutch Social and Economic Council (SER) and the Council for Culture (RvC) on the consequences of the 2007-2008 economic crisis and subsequent government cutbacks on the cultural sector drew disturbing conclusions.[1272] According to their analysis, the culture cuts impacted the sector to the tune of a loss of 20,000 jobs, five times higher than the national average.[1273] Hard figures led to a soft solution: a Labor Market Agenda with its centerpiece, the Fair Practice Code (Code), presented in 2017. Ingrid van Engelshoven, Minister of Education, Culture and Science, mandated that cultural organizations would not be eligible to receive government subsidies if they did not comply with the Code by 2021. Hopes ran high that cultural institutions would raise employee remuneration, equalize the pay scales for freelance and part-time staff, and of special significance within the orchestral sector, pay for structural overtime not previously compensated. Ongoing criticism of the Code underscores three main issues: the astronomical costs of implementation, its limited scope, and the lack of an enforcement mechanism to guarantee that employers are adhering to fair pay under fair play principles.[1274] The Minister opted for soft but firm encouragement by stating that "institutions must provide insight into how the core values underlying the Code in the period 2021-2024 are translated into concrete policy."[1275] Musicians begged to differ: the government, as the commissioning authority, should take responsibility for Fair Practice implementation and enforcement. In a report submitted by the Dutch Broadcasting Foundation (SOM) to the RvC in 2023, the SOM explicitly referred to the need for total government subsidy support to cover the cost of Fair Practice payments to freelance substitute musicians. As compliance with the Code moves beyond the suggested behavior stage to the requirement for subsidy stage, the real fear is that orchestras will opt to make changes in their programming in order to downsize the number of players required to perform. The issue of the complement discussed in the *FAQs* at some length returns in a new and distressing guise.

An additional vexing question for vulnerable orchestral musicians on the effects of the Fair Practice Code discussed in *A long and winding road* is: can fair pay initiatives actually accelerate a decrease in employment for freelancers? A case in point:

1272. Advies 17/07 Passie gewaardeerd Versterking van de arbeidsmarkt in de culturele en creatieve sector. April 2017, https://www.ser.nl/-/media/ser/downloads/adviezen/2017/passie-gewaardeerd.pdf.

1273. *Ibid.*

1274. Additional personnel costs estimated at €20.1 per annum. The Fair Practice Code applies only to institutions and festivals that receive multiyear government subsidies. Kamerbrief Fair Practice Code, 19 februari 2020, https://www.kunsten92.nl/wp-content/uploads/2020/02/Kamerbrief-Fair-Practice-Code.pdf?utm_source=MailingLijst&utm_medium=email&utm_campaign=19-02-2020.

1275. *Ibid.*, "Instellingen moeten inzichtelijk maken hoe de kernwaarden die ten grondslag liggen aan de Fair Practice Code in 2021-2024 (stapsgewijs) vertaald worden in concreet beleid."

orchestral employers in the Netherlands link a freelance substitute player's number of years of professional experience to pay scales in a system similar to the pay scale determinations for the regularly employed. What could be seen as a resounding success for fair pay has created a great deal of concern among older players about their employability. The PvFM website resounds with questions such as, "should I tell the employer the truth about my years of experience or lower the magic number to make myself more competitive in terms of remuneration?" with the implicit fear that older players will be less desirable as hires simply because they are more expensive than younger freelance colleagues. Issues brought forward in *Greener Pastures* resound in a somber timbre.

A close reading of *Follow the money* correlated with the information detailed in *Requiem for an orchestra* shows that political will is of paramount importance to win the cultural subsidy sweepstakes. All too often, the voices of those who perform, the voices of the most vulnerable, did not reverberate in the halls of policymaking. They do, however, thanks to recent lawsuits in the Netherlands, resound at the courts.

11.5 THE SWEET SOUNDS OF SUCCESS: EMPLOYMENT *PUR SANG*

The sweet sound of success in cases brought by freelance substitute players against Het Ballet Orkest (HBO) has given a renewed sense of empowerment to musicians whose false self-employment has taken on its true colors: employment with no falsification attached. The PvFM's cofounder Dorine Schoon worked regularly as a substitute oboist at HBO until the summer of 2020. Following years of regular work, she was informed that her services were no longer necessary in the orchestra she had considered her home base. Speculation ran high: her vociferous actions on the part of the PvFM made her a target for the employer. "After all, who wants to hire someone who will stand up for the rights of others especially if those others are vulnerable?"[1276] Supported by the Kunstenbond union, Schoon opted for a test case. How would her years of freelance work with one employer be assessed? Unlike Pintus, Schoon did not seek permanent employment at HBO, but rather, amends for unexpected work loss. On February 10, 2021, the Amsterdam subdistrict court confirmed that regardless of the terms used in a contract ("gastspeler"—guest player was HBO's term of art) substitute musicians were employees under Dutch law. The intention of the parties with regard to the contract was not the overriding factor: an employment relationship arises when the manner in which work is performed meets the criteria of an employment contract and Schoon was entitled to recompense for work loss.

Fast forward to 2023. Each passing day records new challenges: as policymakers in the Netherlands navigate a course on how to align Fair Practice with the rising expenses of orchestral institutions,[1277] news from New York informs that the union (Local 802, AFM) plans to bring charges against the producers of an upcoming Broadway show, "Here Lies Love," who plan to stage the production with recorded

1276. Helmke Jansen at a PvFM meeting, Amsterdam 2019.
1277. In May 2023, State Secretary Gunay Uslu pledged €34,1 million to explore concretization and enforcement mechanisms in relation to the Fair Practice Code.

tracks, circumventing the services of live musicians. The AFM website banner tells all: *A Direct Attack on Broadway and Live Music.*[1278] Plus ça change, plus c'est la même chose.

Martha Nussbaum, the grand dame in the field of legal philosophy, explained the study of law to those starting out on their educational paths: "Law is [to be] understood as not simply a set of technical maneuvers, but as a way of being active and influential in public life that has a definite normative ethical dimension."[1279] Recasting her words into the orchestral sphere uncovers the true reason for spending years treading along a research path that has led to more questions and fewer answers.[1280] The technical maneuvers found in analyses of jurisprudence and legislation recount but a small part of orchestral musicians' employment sagas. By describing, evaluating, and reconsidering internal and external factors that influence orchestral musicians' vulnerability, it is possible to re-connect with the underlying values inherent to the musician's predispositions: the love of music for music's sake and the push to communicate and make music against all odds, to some noteworthy degree a musical ethical dimension. Perhaps a symphonic metamorphosis is an apotheosis, a chimera of harmonic resolution in a dissonant epoch, or just maybe, as countless examples cited in these pages suggest, metamorphosis lies within reach.

1278. Tino Gagliardi, President Local 802 AFM https://www.local802afm.org/2022/04/presidents-report/.

1279. Martha C. Nussbaum. "Cultivating Humanity in Legal Education" *University of Chicago Law Review* 70(1) 2003, 271 DOI: 10.2307/1600558.

1280. Irresistible not to share a reference to Charles Ives' masterpiece *The Unanswered Question*.

Epilogue: Appendices

North Netherlands Orchestra (NNO): One of the few Dutch orchestras where members have 100% contracts. There have been no official cuts or reorganization process; however, an increase in the number of part-time jobs since 2015 has been observed.

Netherlands Philharmonic Orchestra (NedPhO): The complement works 100%; however, the number of part-time contracts offered in the past several years has increased. Musicians complain of heightened work stress following the introduction of personal portfolios in which musicians must fulfill a set number of "employment hours" above and beyond the traditional rehearsal-concert-recording duties to fulfill the requirements of the job.

Het Ballet Orkest (Dutch Ballet Orchestra (HBO)): A substantial reduction in the size of the workforce post-crisis and a heavy dependence on substitutes and freelancers to perform the standard ballet repertoire. The reduced complement of musicians under contract since the 2013 reorganization are employed under 70% contracts.

The Dutch Broadcasting Foundation Musical Entities: Stichting Omroep Muziek (SOM):

The Netherlands Radio Symphony Orchestra and the Netherlands Radio Chamber Orchestra, both renowned worldwide, were merged into a single entity during the first major round of orchestral cuts in the new millennium, 2005-2006. The second wave of cuts occurred in 2012-2013.

The Radio Philharmonic Orchestra is the sole post-reorganization Dutch radio orchestra. Many musician members had to accept part-time positions ranging from 50% to 80%.

Metropole Orchestra (MO): The pop and jazz orchestra formerly funded by the Dutch Broadcasting Foundation became an independent orchestral entity after the 2012-2013 cuts. As of 2017, the MO was granted coveted state-subsidized status. All positions are 50% (half-time) positions.

The Royal Concertgebouw Orchestra (RCO): 100% employment contracts under a special RCO collective bargaining agreement.

APPENDIX 2

Overview of US Lockouts/Strikes Post-2007-2008 Financial Crisis

- 2010 Detroit Symphony Orchestra strike, six months in duration. After the musicians' three-year contract expired, management proposed a 20% pay cut; new members contracted would receive 40% below that level. Musicians accepted a 25% first-year cut, a complement reduction from 96 to 81 musicians with an increase to 85 in the 2013-2014 season. The total number of weeks dropped from full time (52 weeks) to 40 weeks.
- September 2012: Atlanta Symphony Orchestra lockout. Musicians complement reduced; musicians conceded to a shorter season and pay cuts.
- September 2012: Indianapolis Symphony Orchestra lockout one month in duration, pay cuts.
- September 2012: Chicago Symphony Orchestra strikes for higher wages and health care, ending up with a slight raise and higher health insurance costs.
- October 2012: Minnesota Symphony Orchestra locked out for a record 16 months, the longest lockout in US orchestral history. Radical changes in board composition and the departure of Michael Henson, President and CEO announced in August 2014. The complement of 96 musicians was initially reduced to 77 with an increase to 77 musicians in 2017. Wages increased to the 2012 pre-lockout level in 2020.
- 2013: San Francisco Symphony musicians on strike.
- 2014: Atlanta Symphony Orchestra, second lockout in two years. Health care costs increase, small salary increase to repair 2012 cuts.
- September 2016: Fort Worth Symphony Orchestra strike, three months duration. Musicians' vacation period shortened.
- October 2016: Pittsburgh Symphony Orchestra strike. Considerable concessions: 7% pay cut for several consecutive years. Defined-benefit pension plan discontinued.

- 2018: Lyric Opera of Chicago strike. The season was cut by several weeks, complement decreased, residual members received a 5.6% salary increase.
- 2019: Chicago Symphony Orchestra musicians' strike. Main issues: higher pay and the preservation of the defined pension plan. Pay increases are linked to the CSO's competitive level as international top orchestra. If salaries fall below other top orchestras, the status of the orchestra is lessened and its ability to attract top players is diminished. It is interesting to reiterate that this same argument was presented by Jan Raes, former Managing Director of the Royal Concertgebouw Orchestra.

APPENDIX 3

Geloofsbrief (Statement of Intent) Frans Brüggen

Amsterdam,25 febr.1992

Geloofsbrief, aangeboden aan het Radio Kamer Orkest

Mijn voorstel is om in drie jaren te geraken tot een volledige technische en retorische beheersing van cliché's in de periode 1720 - 1 850.

Dat geeft inzicht,houdt netjes en ,hand in hand met talloze onregelmatigheden, resulteert in een vanzelfsprekende, ongeaffecteerde schoonheid,in zoiets als een Senegalese vrouw met een kruik op haar hoofd.

Een simpele greep uit een eenvoudig geneel:
hoog - laag
lang - kort
luid- zacht
moeilijk - makkelijk
samen - ieder voor zich
zuur - zoet - zout - bitter

Het retorische restaurant is dan uiteindelijk instaat om zonder mankeren zoutzachte,bittermoeilijke of zuurlage gerechten te serveren, en godzijdank niemand die nog over "interpretatie" spreekt.

Vrienden, Eet Smakelijk!

FR.

Amsterdam, 25 Feb. 1992

Recommendations (letter of credentials) presented to the Radio Chamber Orchestra

My proposal is to achieve full technical and rhetorical control of clichés in the period 1720-1850 within three years. That provides insight, keeps it neat and tidy and hand-in-hand with countless irregularities results in a self-evident unaffected beauty, something like a Senegalese woman with a jug on her head.

A simple selection from a simple whole:

high - low
long - short
loud - soft
difficult- easy
together- each for himself
sour- sweet- salty- bitter

The rhetorical restaurant is ultimately capable of serving salty-soft, bitter-difficult or sour-dishes without fail, and thank goodness, no one will keep harping on 'interpretation.'

Friends, Enjoy your meal!

APPENDIX 4

"Kaasschaaf en Cultuur: Culture on the Cutting Board"

KAASSCHAAF EN CULTUUR

As musicians, we are more comfortable picking up violin bows than pens and are more accustomed to let our music speak for us than to resort to raised voices or harsh polemic. But now, early in the 21st century, a crisis in terms of cultural consciousness translating directly into the allocation of Dutch government subsidies for the arts and public media threatens not only our future but more importantly, the roots of the culture which binds us all.

The latest in a line of Dutch musical institutions to reach the firing line Het Radio Kamerorkest, is a group 40 members strong, internationally commended for its commitment to refreshing interpretations of old music and cutting-edge performance of contemporary music.

There are many politicians and polemicists who pay lip service to the tenet that orchestras are dinosaurs, aging artifacts with the questionable task of recreating the music of long dead, politically incorrect white men. A quick glance at the repertoire of the RKO and fellow radio orchestras points to other truths. (Mention variety of cd's/Edisons/special repertoire concerts). The very week crucial decisions concerning the survival of this leading Dutch ensemble will be made, the RKO will travel to Budapest to premiere works by the Dutch composer Michel van der Aa and the Hungarian, Peter Eotvos.

At a time when the Dutch government seeks means to integrate ever-increasing minorities into the mainstream, it is time for all of us to consider what that mainstream should advocate, both socially and culturally.

The spontaneous reaction from cultural icons, famed musicians at home and abroad can open the door to constructive political debate. The South African born, Italian-based conductor Gerard Korsten queries: "I can only hope that the Dutch Government will not make the same mistake as what has happened here in Italy. Is "Big brother",or all the other rubbish we see here on Television,and hear on the radio, the future of our world. Does the young generation not deserve better? This is not a privilege,it is a right,for all to make a better world! I can only hope for a better world,for the Netherlands to be an example to the rest of Europe and the world!" And Sir Peter Maxwell Davies eloquently notes, " until now the cultural riches of the Dutch Broadcasting System have been an example to us all, and the envy of the world. It seems to me that Holland is beginning to cut out its own living heart here – to tamper with such institutions is to damage the very soul of the country."

A consciousness raising commentary is not the place to indulge in a detailed history of the Dutch Broadcasting Service, its 4 orchestras, chorus and other services. It is also not the place to point the finger at an ever-widening array of broadcasting bobos, politicians and advisory boards who might or might not be responsible for the breakdown of our music, our culture with a well-deserved capital letter C. After all, historians might look back to Minister Brinkman's Mediawet (1987)which created the free fall Dutch broadcast media suffers from. The legacy of those media laws has left us with discussions concerning quality soap operas instead of attention paid to developing real quality opera let alone documentary films. Perhaps a look across the English Channel to the BBC model of a streamlined broadcasting system should inspire us lowlanders to use our cultural resources more wisely. Quality, originality and forward-thinking ensembles should be rewarded rather than given the kaasschaaf treatment.

Heather Kurzbauer

APPENDIX 5

Dienstverband (Employment Letter) June 19, 2012 (in Dutch)

BEZOEKADRES
Heuvellaan 33
NL 1217 JL Hilversum

POSTADRES
Postbus 125
NL 1200 AC Hilversum

T +31 (0)35 671 41 00
F +31 (0)35 671 41 71
I www.mco.nl

MUZIEK centrum van de OMROEP

[redacted]

referentie	datum	telefoon
PZ 2012324	19 juni 2012	+31(0)35 - 6714119

betreft	e-mail
Dienstverband	f.blessing@mco.nl

Geachte mevrouw [redacted],

In 2011 heeft het kabinet besloten om de subsidie aan het MCO vanaf seizoen 2013-2014 terug te brengen tot 14 miljoen euro. De afgelopen maanden heeft het MCO zich gebogen over de ingrijpende gevolgen die dit heeft voor het personeel.
Om deze personele gevolgen op te vangen heeft de Minister van OC&W het MCO verzocht een Sociaal Plan op te stellen.

Het MCO heeft met de vakbonden FNV Kiem, NTB en de ondernemingsraad een principe akkoord bereikt over het Sociaal Plan. Het Plan is beschikbaar gesteld via intranet. Samen met deze brief ontvangt u een kopie van het Plan.

Het principe akkoord dat wij hebben bereikt is onder het voorbehoud dat wij een schriftelijke en onherroepelijke toezegging van het Ministerie hebben dat de kosten die voortvloeien uit dit Sociaal Plan volledig zullen worden gedragen door de Rijksoverheid, al dan niet gefinancierd vanuit het mediabudget.

Op 26 april 2012 heeft de directie een adviesaanvraag over de voorgenomen reorganisatie van Klassiek (RFO en RKF) en GOK bij de Ondernemingsraad (OR) ingediend. Op 11 juni jongstleden heeft de OR ons laten weten niet direct positief in te stemmen met alle besluitvoornemens, maar wel akkoord te gaan met het voeren van gesprekken om medewerkers te informeren over hun voorziene individuele situatie per 1 augustus 2013.

Aanbod vrijwillig vertrek
Zoals op maandag 25 juni 2012 mondeling aan u is medegedeeld doen wij u een aanbod tot vrijwillig vertrek. Wanneer u hiermee akkoord gaat, wordt uw arbeidsovereenkomst per 1 augustus 2013 beëindigd. Met u is afgesproken dat u vóór 20 augustus 2012 een besluit zal nemen over het al dan niet akkoord gaan met dit aanbod over het beëindigen van uw dienstverband bij het MCO per 1 augustus 2013. Wij verzoeken u uiterlijk 20 augustus 2012 aan de manager HR met bijgaand formulier te laten weten of u dit aanbod zult accepteren.

STICHTING MUZIEKCENTRUM VAN DE OMROEP
Fortis Bank 637976088 IBAN NL84FTSB0637976088 BIC FTSBNL2R KvK Hilversum 41194669 BTW NL 80 34 27 967 B01
GROOT OMROEPKOOR · METROPOLE ORKEST · RADIO FILHARMONISCH ORKEST · RADIO KAMER FILHARMONIE · MUZIEKBIBLIOTHEEK

BEZOEKADRES
Heuvellaan 33
NL 1217 JL Hilversum

POSTADRES
Postbus 125
NL 1200 AC Hilversum

T +31 (0)35 671 41 00
F +31 (0)35 671 41 71
I www.mco.nl

MUZIEK centrum OMROEP

Vervolg brief mevrouw [redacted]

Ontvangen wij voor die datum geen reactie, dan gaan wij er van uit dat u het aanbod niet accepteert en zullen wij overgaan tot een alternatieve formatiereductie.

Vaststellingsovereenkomst
Uw arbeidsovereenkomst met het MCO zal door middel van een vaststellingsovereenkomst per 1 augustus 2013 worden beëindigd. De gemaakte afspraken bij beëindiging van het dienstverband worden in het kader van deze reorganisatie gemaakt en worden in de overeenkomst op een dusdanige wijze verwoord dat duidelijk wordt dat het ontslag u niet verwijtbaar is. U treft een concept vaststellingsovereenkomst bij deze brief aan.

Financieel advies
In de financiële bijlage bij deze brief treft u de berekening aan van de ontslagvergoeding die voor u voortvloeit uit het Sociaal Plan. U kunt een afspraak inplannen bij een onafhankelijk financieel adviseur om uw persoonlijke situatie te bespreken. Na afloop van dat gesprek ontvangt u een schriftelijke vertrouwelijke rapportage met daarin een op maat geschreven financieel advies. De onafhankelijk financieel adviseur houdt spreekuur in het MCO gebouw. U kunt via de afdeling HR een afspraak in laten plannen.

Juridisch advies
Eventuele kosten die u maakt bij het raadplegen van een jurist worden tot een maximum bedrag van € 650,= vergoed. In de bijlage treft u drie namen aan van juristen die u kunt benaderen. Het staat u vanzelfsprekend vrij om een andere jurist in te schakelen. De jurist dient de manager HR van het MCO rechtstreeks te factureren.

Mobiliteitsbureau
Daarnaast kunt u vanaf nu gebruik maken van de diensten van het mobiliteitsbureau. Dit mobiliteitsbureau is in het MCO gebouw ingericht. Desgewenst kunt u ook kiezen voor een locatie in Utrecht. U kunt via de afdeling HR een afspraak in laten plannen.

Vragen
Omdat wij op dit moment, vanwege alle ingeplande gesprekken met musici, niet direct in de gelegenheid zullen zijn om inhoudelijke vragen over deze brief of de bijlagen persoonlijk te beantwoorden, verzoeken wij u eventuele vragen per mail te richten aan reorganisatie@mco.nl. Uw vragen worden zo spoedig mogelijk en uiterlijk binnen 1 werkweek beantwoord. U kunt in het bericht ook vragen om een tweede gesprek indien u daar behoefte aan heeft.

STICHTING MUZIEKCENTRUM VAN DE OMROEP
Fortis Bank 637976088 IBAN NL84FTSB0637976088 BIC FTSBNL2R KvK Hilversum 41194669 BTW NL 80 34 27 967 B01
GROOT OMROEPKOOR · METROPOLE ORKEST · RADIO FILHARMONISCH ORKEST · RADIO KAMER FILHARMONIE · MUZIEKBIBLIOTHEEK

APPENDIX 6

Save the Symphony: A Call for Solidarity, Netherlands Radio Chamber Orchestra, 2004

CONCEPT BRIEF AAN DIRIGENTEN/COMPONISTEN/SOLISTEN

Esteemed colleague,

While a New Year should be associated with optimism and bold creative plans, 2004 purports to be a somber year for musical life in The Netherlands. Recently, the Dutch Parliamentary Under-Secretary for Culture announced draconian cut-backs that would directly impact the conglomerate of renowned Dutch broadcast orchestras: Radio Philharmonic Orchestra Holland; The Netherlands Radio Symphony Orchestra; The Netherlands Radio Chamber Orchestra and the Metropole Orchestra. The proposed funding reductions would eliminate at least one ensemble and impair the remaining ensembles irreparably.

Throughout the last half-century, the orchestras of the Dutch Broadcast System have earned worldwide acclaim not only for the admirable quality of their performances but for their commitment to provide notable renditions of contemporary music and masterpieces by oft-neglected composers. Tours throughout Europe, the international distribution of radio and television broadcasts, and a plethora of cd releases have brought the musical message of these respected ensembles to audiences throughout the world.

We, the musicians of the Dutch Broadcast orchestras call out to you, leading conductors and performers, to join us in registering our condemnation of the proposed budget cuts. We hope that your signature(s) added to this [email/letter] and personal comments related to your experiences working with our musicians will persuade politicians far-removed from the music world, our incredible cosmos of creativity and communication, to reconsider this far-reaching measure.

[Kindly add your signature in the space below. If the spirit moves, you are welcome to write your own text or make amendments to the text above].

Hoping for the opportunity to make music together in the near future, we wish you an inspired 2004.

Respectfully,

The musicians:

Radio Philharmonic Orchestra Holland
The Netherlands Radio Symphony Orchestra
The Netherlands Radio Chamber Orchestra
Metropole Orchestra

Appendix 7

RCO Urgent Letter (Brandbrief) to Minister Wouter Koolmees October 18, 2019

CONCERTGEBOUWORKEST

Aan de Minister van Sociale Zaken en Werkgelegenheid
Zijne Excellentie W. Koolmees
Parnassusplein 5
2511 CV DEN HAAG

Amsterdam
18 oktober 2019

Met cc aan de Minister van OCW, mw. I van Engelshoven

Brandbrief

Excellentie,

Het Koninklijk Concertgebouworkest (het "Concertgebouworkest") wendt zich, mede namens de Vereniging voor Nederlandse Orkesten ("VvNO") en de Vereniging van Stichtingen Remplaçanten Nederlandse Orkesten, met deze brandbrief tot U in verband met een aantal dringende vragen over de mogelijke gevolgen die de Wet arbeidsmarkt in balans ("Wab") zal hebben voor de positie van de remplaçanten die het Concertgebouworkest inhuurt ten behoeve van zijn orkest.

Het Concertgebouworkest vraagt u om hem zo spoedig mogelijk, maar (in verband met de budgetbehandeling van Kunstenplan 2021-2024 in de Tweede Kamer) **uiterlijk voor 8 november a.s.**, schriftelijke duidelijkheid te verschaffen over de volgende drie vragen:

1. Kwalificeert de inzet door het Concertgebouworkest van remplaçanten als payrolling als bedoeld in artikel 1 Waadi na wijziging daarvan door de Wab?
2. Indien uw antwoord op vraag 1 bevestigend luidt, heeft de kwalificatie van payrolling tot gevolg dat deze remplaçanten aanspraak maken op tenminste dezelfde arbeidsvoorwaarden zoals die zijn overeengekomen met de vaste orkestleden van het Concertgebouworkest?
3. Indien uw antwoord op vraag 1 bevestigend luidt: kunt u bevestigen dat de kwalificatie van payrolling geen gevolgen heeft voor de bepaling uit de CAO Remplaçanten ter zake de uitsluiting van de ketenbepaling als bedoeld in artikel 7:668a BW?

Het Concertgebouworkest licht deze vragen en de achtergrond daarvan toe. Uit deze toelichting zal ook duidelijk worden dat uw schriftelijke antwoord op deze vragen niet alleen voor het Concertgebouworkest **van levensbelang** is, maar ook voor de overige symfonieorkesten binnen de basisinfrastructuur, die zijn verenigd in de VvNO en de Vereniging van Stichtingen van Remplaçanten Nederlandse Orkesten. Deze brief is daarom ook mede door hen ondertekend.

Koninklijk Concertgebouworkest | *Beschermvrouwe* | info@concertgebouworkest.nl
Postbus 78098 | Hare Majesteit | +31 20 305 10 10
1070 LP Amsterdam | de Koningin | www.concertgebouworkest.nl

RCO

Toelichting

Vraag 1
Sinds jaar en dag vangt het Concertgebouworkest gaten in zijn bezetting op door middel van remplaçanten. Met de inzet van remplaçanten wordt onder andere voorzien de opvang van (aan het begin van het concertseizoen) voorzienbare (bijvoorbeeld wegens reeds gepland verlof) en niet-voorzienbare afwezigheid (zoals ziekte) van de vaste orkestleden van het Concertgebouworkest. Verder wordt van remplaçanten gebruik gemaakt voor het spelen van instrumenten die niet tot het standaardinstrumentarium behoren (bijvoorbeeld een bijzonder instrument als een mandoline in de Zevende symfonie van Mahler), als ook ten behoeve van het spelen van werken die wat bezetting betreft de beschikbare vaste capaciteit van het orkest te boven gaan. Het betreft voor het Concertgebouworkest gemiddeld ongeveer 5.500 zgn. podiumdiensten (concerten en repetities) per jaar. De loonkosten per dienst zijn ongeveer EUR 160 (inclusief werkgevers-lasten), zodat met de inzet van remplaçanten per jaar een kleine EUR 9 ton aan loonkosten gemoeid is. In aantallen betreft het tussen de 100 en 150 individuele remplaçanten per seizoen. Vertaald in FTE zijn dat er ongeveer 20 (op een totaal van 120 FTE in dienst van het Concert-gebouworkest). Zonder de inzet van deze remplaçanten kan het Concertgebouworkest zijn exploitatiemodel niet realiseren, noch de met hem in het kader van aan hem verleende subsidies gemaakte prestatie-afspraken nakomen. Deze situatie geldt evenzeer voor de overige symfonieorkesten.

De remplaçanten worden ingehuurd via de Stichting Remplaçanten van het Koninklijk Concertgebouworkest (de "Stichting Remplaçanten"). Die sluit daartoe jaarlijks (per seizoen) met deze remplaçanten raamovereenkomsten af, op basis waarvan telkens - per inhuur - arbeidsovereenkomsten ontstaan. Die arbeidsovereenkomsten zijn telkens van zeer korte duur, namelijk de duur van de programma's (doorgaans ongeveer een week) die door de remplaçant gespeeld worden. Op deze arbeidsovereenkomsten is de CAO Remplaçanten Nederlandse Orkesten van toepassing (de "CAO Remplaçanten"). In deze CAO Remplaçanten is bepaald dat artikel 7:668a BW op de arbeidsovereenkomsten niet van toepassing is, zodat in geen enkel geval een arbeidsovereenkomst voor onbepaalde tijd ontstaat. Deze bepaling is gebaseerd op een daartoe strekkende ministeriele regeling d.d. 24 juni 2015 (Stct. 2015, 17972). Kopie van dat besluit is **bijgevoegd**.

Over het algemeen geldt bij de inzet van remplaçanten door het Concertgebouworkest dat werving en selectie door het Concertgebouworkest zelf wordt gedaan. Voor zover het de betreffende arbeidsovereenkomst betreft (die zoals gezegd telkens van zeer korte duur is), wordt de remplaçant exclusief door de Stichting Remplaçanten aan het Concertgebouworkest ter beschikking gesteld. Maar buiten die arbeidsovereenkomst(en) om werkt de remplaçant ook voor andere symfonieorkesten, of - buiten de orkestensector - als zzp-er voor andere muziekgezelschappen of -opdrachtgevers.

Gelet op het feit dat de remplaçant daarmee - buiten de zeer korte arbeidsovereenkomsten die worden gesloten ten behoeve van het spelen van een specifiek programma bij het Concertgebouworkest - niet exclusief aan het Concertgebouworkest ter beschikking wordt gesteld, is de eerste vraag of deze vorm van terbeschikkingstelling valt onder de definitie van payrolling als bedoeld in artikel 1 Waadi na wijziging daarvan door de Wab.

Vraag 2
Als Uw Minister die vraag bevestigend beantwoordt, rijst vervolgens de vraag of dat betekent dat de remplaçanten aanspraak maken op tenminste dezelfde arbeidsvoorwaarden als de vaste orkestleden van het Concertgebouworkest.

De Wab bepaalt, dat als sprake is van payrolling, de arbeidskracht die ter beschikking wordt gesteld, recht heeft op tenminste dezelfde arbeidsvoorwaarden als die gelden voor werknemers werkzaam zijn in gelijke of gelijkwaardige functies in dienst van de onderneming waar de terbeschikkingstelling plaatsvindt. Heeft de onderneming waar de terbeschikkingstelling plaatsvindt geen werknemers in dienst in gelijke of gelijkwaardige functies, dan heeft de payroll-werknemer recht op tenminste dezelfde arbeidsvoorwaarden als die gelden voor werknemers werkzaam zijn in gelijke of gelijkwaardige functies in de sector van het beroeps- of bedrijfsleven waarin die onderneming werkzaam is.

Toegepast op de situatie van de remplaçanten betekent dit, dat - als zou moeten worden aangenomen dat een remplaçant werkzaam is in functies die als "gelijk of gelijkwaardig" kunnen worden aangemerkt als die van orkestleden die in dienst zijn van het Concertgebouworkest - de Stichting Remplaçanten verplicht zal worden aan de remplaçanten tenminste dezelfde arbeidsvoorwaarden te bieden als die van de orkestleden van het Concertgebouworkest die in die gelijke of gelijkwaardige functies werkzaam zijn.

De vraag is gerechtvaardigd of dat het geval is. Er zijn krachtige argumenten die wijzen op het tegendeel, omdat de groep remplaçanten een zo specifieke en van de vaste orkestleden afwijkende groep werknemers is, dat niet kan worden geconcludeerd dat zij hun werkzaamheden ten behoeve van het orkest uitvoeren in functies die "gelijk of gelijkwaardig" zijn aan die van de vaste orkestleden. Anders gezegd: zij hebben binnen het Concertgebouworkest geen "evenknie". Voor het bijzondere, van vaste orkestleden afwijkende, karakter van deze groep kan onder andere bevestiging worden gezocht in de volgende omstandigheden:

(1) De functie-inhoud van remplaçanten is slechts dezelfde als die van vaste orkestleden, voor zover het gaat om het spelen van concerten (en het meedoen aan de daarbij behorende repetities). Anders dan voor vaste orkestleden het geval is, hoeven remplaçanten daarvoor overigens niet voorafgaand met goed gevolg een proefspel af te leggen. Belangrijke andere taken, die wel tot het takenpakket van vaste orkestleden behoren, worden echter niet door remplaçanten uitgevoerd. Dit betreft onder meer een hele reeks werkzaamheden die noodzakelijk zijn voor een adequate productie-voorbereiding zoals het maken van groepsindelingen en roulatieschema's, het in overleg met de orkestbibliotheek aanbrengen van (technische) speelinstructies in het muziekmateriaal, het opstellen van paklijsten van instrumentarium dat mee gaat op reis en het zorgdragen voor het goede onderhoud aan muziekinstrumenten in bezit van de werkgever. Daarnaast maken remplaçanten - anders dan vaste orkestleden - geen deel uit van (bijvoorbeeld) de Artistieke Commissie, of andere (beleidsadviserende) orkestcommissies of een Ondernemingsraad, die alle wezenlijke taken ten behoeve van de interne organisatie uitvoeren. Vaste orkestleden hebben een verantwoordelijkheid in de beoordeling van de te contracteren dirigenten en solisten, remplaçanten hebben deze verantwoordelijkheid niet. Remplaçanten dragen geen verantwoordelijkheid voor

de werving en selectie van nieuwe orkestleden, zoals vaste orkestleden dat wèl doen via hun rol in vastgelegde procedures via selectie- en proefspelcommissies etcetera. Ook worden remplaçanten, opnieuw anders dan de vaste orkestleden, niet ingezet voor educatieve en/of representatieve taken ten behoeve van het orkest buiten de podiumdiensten, noch worden zij ingezet voor activiteiten ten behoeve van fondsenwerving en dergelijke. Het takenpakket/de functie van de remplaçant beperkt zich daardoor tot het puur uitvoerend-muzikale deel van de activiteiten en is aldus aanzienlijk beperkter dan dat van het vaste orkestlid.

(2) Ook de omstandigheid dat deze werknemers, anders dan de vaste orkestleden, **uitsluitend incidenteel** worden ingezet, maakt dat kan worden betoogd dat zij niet werkzaam zijn in "gelijke of gelijkwaardige" functies als in de Wab bedoeld, nu dat voor vaste orkestleden immers niet geldt. In die zin zijn remplaçanten veel meer te vergelijken met uitzendkrachten, die met de Wab nu juist uitdrukkelijk zijn afgebakend van de payroll-werknemer. De inzet bij het orkest geschiedt bij de remplaçant ook meer op grond van diens bereidheid om het werk te accepteren dan bij de vaste musicus aan wie uit hoofde van zijn aanstelling meer dwingend zijn taken kunnen worden opgelegd.

(3) Reeds sinds jaar en dag wordt (dan ook) voor remplaçanten een **eigen cao** gesloten, die voor alle bij die cao aangesloten Stichtingen Remplaçanten van toepassing is en die de bijzondere arbeidspositie van de remplaçanten regelt.

(4) Reeds sinds jaar en dag bestaat bovendien de bijzondere **ministeriële regeling** op grond waarvan de remplaçanten, gelet op hun bijzondere positie/functie, zijn uitgezonderd van de wettelijke ketenbepaling van artikel 7:668a BW (zie daarover ook hierna onder de toelichting op vraag 3).

Betoogd zou in dit verband kunnen worden dat de wetgever met het gelijke behandelings-voorschrift de situatie op het oog heeft waarin een werkgever gebruik maakt van payrollkrachten die in niets te onderscheiden zijn van zijn vaste werknemers, behalve dan dat de ter beschikking stellende payrollonderneming er als een soort salarisadministratiekantoor "tussen" geschoven is. Van zo'n situatie is bij de remplaçanten geen sprake.

Als dit betoog (dat er bij het Concertgebouworkest geen "gelijke of gelijkwaardige" werknemers zijn met wie de remplaçant kan worden vergeleken) als juist wordt aanvaard, dan geldt dat de arbeidsvoorwaarden waarop de remplaçanten recht hebben tenminste dezelfde moeten zijn *als die van andere remplaçanten* – lees: als die zoals bepaald in de CAO Remplaçanten.

Als de hiervoor aangedragen argumenten echter niet als juist zouden worden aanvaard, en in plaats daarvan zou gelden dat de remplaçanten aanspraak hebben op tenminste de arbeidsvoorwaarden van vaste orkestleden, dan betekent dat voor onze organisatie een bijkomende kostenpost van krap EUR 1 MIO aan primaire en secundaire arbeidsvoorwaarden.

Deze bijkomende kostenpost zal door de Stichting Remplaçanten voor rekening worden gebracht van het Concertgebouworkest. Voor de goede orde: het Concertgebouworkest, dat voor zijn financiële middelen voor het overgrote deel (thans 48%; voor de andere symfonieorkesten varieert dat zelfs tussen 60 en 80%) afhankelijk is van overheidssubsidie, beschikt niet over de financiële middelen om deze bijkomende kostenpost te kunnen betalen. Hij zal daarom die bijkomende middelen alsnog van overheidswege moeten zien te verkrijgen om op het huidige topniveau te kunnen blijven presteren (wegen tot verdere verhoging van de eigen inkomsten zijn er niet of nauwelijks). Tijdige helderheid over het antwoord op deze vraag is daarom voor het Concertgebouworkest (en voor zijn collega-orkesten) van **levensbelang**.

Vraag 3

In de Wab is bepaald dat ten aanzien van payrollwerknemers afwijkingen van driekwartdwingend recht (zoals de ketenbepaling) alleen mogelijk zijn als dat voor werknemers in gelijke of gelijkwaardige functies bij de inlenende werkgever op grond van diens cao ook mogelijk is. Afwijkingen in de 'eigen' cao van de payrollwerkgever prevaleren slechts boven die in de cao van de inlener, wanneer die ten voordele strekken van de werknemer. Blijkens de toelichting op deze wetsbepaling is daarmee bedoeld dat de payrollwerknemer wel beter, maar niet slechter mag worden behandeld dan zijn 'evenknie' bij de inlener.

Daarmee rijst de vraag of de Stichting Remplaçanten na invoering van de Wab nog gebruik zal kunnen maken van de uitsluiting van de ketenbepaling. Naar de beoordeling van het Concertgebouworkest c.q. de Stichting Remplaçanten is dat het geval, nu immers de uitsluiting van de ketenbepaling in de CAO Remplaçanten is gebaseerd op artikel 7:668a lid 8 BW. Die wetsbepaling maakt het mogelijk dat de gehele wettelijke ketenregeling bij cao buiten toepassing wordt verklaard op grond van een daartoe strekkende ministeriële regeling. Daarvan is, zoals hiervoor al aangegeven, in het geval van remplaçanten sprake.

In de betreffende regeling heeft de minister de functie van remplaçanten aangewezen als een functie die het *noodzakelijk* maakt arbeid uitsluitend te verrichten op grond van arbeidsovereenkomsten voor bepaalde tijd. Deze specifiek op de remplaçanten gerichte regeling (in feite een 'lex specialis') verliest naar de beoordeling van het Concertgebouworkest c.q. de Stichting Remplaçanten zijn gelding niet door de introductie van de Wab. Daar komt nog bij, dat de CAO Remplaçanten blijkens artikel 2.1 een standaardkarakter heeft, waardoor afwijkingen van de cao niet zijn toegestaan, tenzij de mogelijkheid tot een (uitsluitend positieve) afwijking in de cao zelf is vermeld. Die afwijkingsmogelijkheid is niet opgenomen bij de uitsluiting van de ketenbepaling. Dat betekent dat op grond van het standaardkarakter van deze cao-bepaling het de Stichting Remplaçanten niet is toegestaan ten positieve van deze bepaling af te wijken.

Ook op dit punt is duidelijkheid voor het Concertgebouworkest (en de Stichting Remplaçanten) van **levensbelang**. Het Concertgebouworkest vraagt u daarom de juistheid van zijn standpunt op dit onderwerp te bevestigen. Zou immers op basis van de telkens zeer korte

arbeidsovereenkomsten met remplaçanten tussen hen en de Stichting Remplaçanten bij de vierde inzet een arbeidsovereenkomst voor onbepaalde tijd ontstaan, dan wordt daarmee de inzet van remplaçanten door het Concertgebouworkest onmogelijk als daarvoor geen extra inkomsten kunnen worden verworven. Immers, noch de Stichting Remplaçanten noch het Concertgebouworkest beschikt over de financiële middelen om de daaruit voortvloeiende financiële- en overige werkgeverslasten te kunnen dragen.

***

RCO

Het Concertgebouworkest verzoekt u zoals gezegd om hem schriftelijke duidelijkheid te verschaffen op de in deze brandbrief aan U voorgelegde vragen. Het belang van tijdige duidelijkheid op die vragen voor het Concertgebouworkest en zijn collega-symfonieorkesten kan niet genoeg worden onderstreept.

Als zou komen vast te staan dat de bepalingen in de Wab zonder meer van toepassing zijn op de inzet van remplaçanten, maar niet tevens de financiële middelen beschikbaar komen om de financiële gevolgen daarvan te dragen, zou dat tot gevolg hebben dat orkesten eenvoudigweg geen gebruik meer zullen kunnen maken van remplaçanten. Dat zou betekenen dat niet alleen voor een aanzienlijke groep van musici in Nederland een belangrijk deel van hun werkgelegenheid verdwijnt, maar ook dat het uitzonderlijk hoge artistieke niveau van het unieke Nederlandse orkestlandschap onder ernstige druk zou komen te staan.

Gelet op de mogelijke financiële gevolgen van uw beantwoording op deze vragen voor de financiële positie van het Concertgebouworkest en van onze collega-symfonieorkesten, zenden wij een kopie van deze brief aan een van onze belangrijkste subsidieverschaffers, te weten de Minister van Onderwijs, Cultuur en Wetenschap, mevrouw I. van Engelshoven.

Wij zien uw spoedige beantwoording van de in deze brandbrief gestelde vragen met belangstelling tegemoet.

Hoogachtend,

Koninklijk Concertgebouworkest

De heer J. Raes
Algemeen Directeur

Vereniging van Nederlandse Orkesten

De heer C. Wiegel
Voorzitter, tevens Algemeen directeur
Rotterdams Philharmonisch Orkest

Vereniging van Stichtingen Remplaçanten Nederlandse Orkesten,

De heer D. Bazen
Voorzitter, Tevens Zakelijk directeur
Koninklijk Concertgebouworkest,
Bestuurslid Vereniging van Nederlandse Orkesten

Bijlage: Ministeriele regeling d.d. 24 juni 2015 (Stct. 2015, 17972).

APPENDIX 8

Minister Koolmees' Response to the RCO Urgent Letter (Brandbrief) December 11, 2019

Ministerie van Sociale Zaken en Werkgelegenheid

> Retouradres Postbus 90801 2509 LV Den Haag

Directie Arbeidsverhoudingen
Afdeling Arbeidsrecht en Diversiteit

Postbus 90801
2509 LV Den Haag
Parnassusplein 5
T 070 333 44 44
www.rijksoverheid.nl

2019-0000174073

Datum 11 DEC 2019
Betreft Brandbrief stichting remplaçanten

Geachte

In uw brief van 18 oktober jl. heeft u zich tot mij gewend met vragen over de mogelijke gevolgen die de Wet arbeidsmarkt in balans (hierna: de Wab) zal hebben voor de positie van de remplaçanten die het Concertgebouworkest inhuurt ten behoeve van zijn orkest.

Middels deze brief kom ik graag tegemoet aan uw verzoek waarbij ik nader in ga op de vragen in uw brief.

1. Allereerst vraagt u zich af of de inhuur van remplaçanten via de Stichting Remplaçanten van het Koninklijk Concertgebouworkest (de "Stichting Remplaçanten") gekwalificeerd moet worden als payrolling zoals voorzien met de inwerkingtreding van de Wet arbeidsmarkt in balans per 1 januari 2020.

Voor de vraag of er sprake is van payrolling zijn twee voorwaarden bepalend.

Ten eerste is het een vereiste bij payrolling dat de formele werkgever geen allocatiefunctie heeft vervuld. Hiervan is sprake als de werving en selectie door de inlener is gedaan. U geeft in uw brief aan dat voor remplaçanten de werving en selectie door het Concertgebouworkest (de inlener) wordt gedaan.

Het tweede vereiste bij payrolling is dat er sprake van exclusieve terbeschikkingstelling van de werknemer door de formele werkgever aan de inlener. Hierbij wordt gekeken naar de relatie tussen de formele werkgever (in casu: de Stichting), de werknemer en de inlener (in casu: het Concertgebouworkest).

U geeft in uw brief aan dat de Stichting werknemers exclusief aan het Concertgebouworkest ter beschikking stelt.

Pagina 1 van 3

Hierbij wordt opgemerkt dat voor de beoordeling van de exclusieve terbeschikkingstelling de omstandigheid dat een werknemer naast zijn terbeschikkingstelling ook ander werk heeft, dus los van de formele werkgever (in casu: de Stichting) en de inlener (in casu: het Concertgebouworkest), niet relevant is. Van belang is of de Stichting de werknemer exclusief ter beschikking stelt aan het Concertgebouworkest of dat de werknemer door de Stichting ook aan andere inleners ter beschikking wordt gesteld om daar onder toezicht en leiding te werken.

Directie Arbeidsverhoudingen
Afdeling Arbeidsrecht en Overleg
2018/0…

11 DEC 2018

Als aan beide voorwaarden zoals hierboven genoemd wordt voldaan, dan is er sprake van payrolling.

Bij een geschil hierover tussen partijen is het uiteindelijk aan de rechter om uitsluitsel te geven.

2. Verder vraagt u of de kwalificatie van payrolling tot gevolg heeft dat deze remplaçanten aanspraak maken op tenminste dezelfde arbeidsvoorwaarden zoals die gelden voor de vaste orkestleden van het Concertgebouworkest.

Als er sprake is van payrolling, dan zijn daar door de wetgever gevolgen aan verbonden. Met de Wab krijgt een werknemer recht op dezelfde rechtspositie en arbeidsvoorwaarden als werknemers in gelijke of gelijkwaardige functies direct in dienst bij de inlener. Voor het antwoord op uw vraag gaat het erom of de functie van remplaçant valt te beschouwen als een gelijke of gelijkwaardige functie als die van 'vast orkestlid' van het Concertgebouworkest.

U geeft in uw brief aan dat u betwijfelt of dit het geval is. Het gaat hier inderdaad om een beoordeling van de verschillende functietaken en rollen, die ook hierna

3. Tot slot wilt u weten of de kwalificatie van payrolling geen gevolgen heeft voor de bepaling in de huidige CAO Remplaçanten waar de uitsluiting van de ketenbepaling als bedoeld in artikel 7:668a van het Burgerlijk Wetboek van toepassing is.

Als er sprake is van payrolling geldt voor payrollwerknemers dat afwijkingen van driekwartdwingend recht (zoals de ketenbepaling) inderdaad en alleen mogelijk zijn als die voor werknemers in gelijke of gelijkwaardige functies bij de inlenende werkgever op grond van diens cao ook mogelijk zijn. Om te bepalen of afwijking bij cao mogelijk is, geldt dat eerst vraag 2 beantwoord moeten worden, namelijk of remplaçanten een gelijkwaardige functie vervullen ten opzichte van de vaste orkestleden. Als er sprake is van een gelijkwaardige functie als een vast orkestlid, dan is de afwijking bij cao voor remplaçanten niet toegestaan.

Als er sprake is van payrolling kunt u in overleg nagaan in hoeverre er sprake is van een gelijkwaardige functie als die van een vast orkestlid. Daarbij kunt u betrekken dat in 2015 cao-partijen bij het verzoek om remplaçanten uit te zonderen van de ketenbepaling aannemelijk hebben gemaakt dat er sprake is van een aparte functie. Het verzoek om de functie van remplaçanten uit te zonderen van de ketenbepaling is toen gehonoreerd[1].

Als de functie van remplaçant inderdaad gezien moet worden als een aparte functie en dus niet gelijkwaardig is aan die van vaste orkestleden van het Concertgebouworkest dan is afwijking bij cao voor remplaçanten toegestaan en kan besloten worden die cao voort te

[1] Staatscourant 2015, 17971

Pagina 3 van 5

zetten. Om gebruik te kunnen maken van de huidige uitzondering van de ketenbepaling moet er wel sprake zijn van een geldige cao.[1]

Directie Arbeidsverhoudingen
[illegible]

11 DEC 2019

De functie waarvoor de ketenbepaling buiten toepassing is verklaard is beperkt tot de functie van remplaçant in dienst bij de door de Nederlandse orkesten opgerichte Stichtingen Remplaçanten of het Muziekcentrum van de Omroep is. Dit betekent dat een remplaçant die rechtstreeks in dienst is bij het Concertgebouworkest niet onder de huidige uitzondering valt. Uiteraard kunnen cao-partijen hiertoe -indien wenselijk- gezamenlijk een nieuw verzoek aan mij richten.

Ik zal de vakorganisaties eveneens voorzien van deze informatie.

Ik vertrouw erop u hiermee voldoende te hebben geïnformeerd.

Met vriendelijke groet,
de Minister van Sociale Zaken
en Werkgelegenheid,

W. Koolmees

[1] [illegible]

Pagina 2 van 2

APPENDIX 9

Grand Teton Music Festival Musicians' Protest Letter on Behalf of Phoenix Symphony Colleagues

Recapitulation: Sources

Abbing, H. *Why Are Artists Poor? The Exceptional Economy of the Arts.* Amsterdam University Press 2004.

Abeles, H. and S. Porter. "The Sex-Stereotyping of Musical Instruments." *Journal of Research in Music Education 26* 1978.

Adiv, N. "Goodbye to the NEA?" *Arts Journal* February 7, 2018.

Aldrich, R. "Permanent Orchestra Season a Bad One." *New York Times* May 3, 1903.

Algemene, R. *Bezuiniging op cultuur; Realisatie en effect* 2015, http://www.rekenkamer.nl/Publicaties/Onderzoeksrapporten/Introducties/2015/02/Bezuiniging_op_cultuur.

Allen, W.D. "An Overview of Black Concert Music and Musicians in Northern California from the 1940s to the 1980s" *Black Music Research* 9(1) Spring 1989.

Allmendinger, J., J. Richard Hackman and E.V. Lehman. "Life and Work in Symphony Orchestras." *Musical Quarterly* 1986.

American Symphony Orchestra League. *Americanizing the American Orchestra: A Task Force Report.* American Symphony Orchestra League 1993.

American Symphony Orchestra League. *Americans for the Arts, Arts & Economic Prosperity IV: The Economic Impact of Nonprofit Arts and Culture Organizations and Their Audiences* 2012 http://www.americansforthearts.org/information_services/research/services/economic_impact/default.asp

Ammer, C. *Unsung: A History of Women in American Music.* Amadeus 2001.

Anderson, G. "Musical Metamorphoses in Hindemith's 'March' from the *Symphonic Metamorphosis of Themes by Carl Maria von Weber.*" *Journal of Band Research* 20(1) Fall 1994.

Andersson, T, M. Engelkes and B. Schouten. *Opgegraven historie en vertelde geschiedenis 50 jaar Radio Kamerorkest.* Hilversum 1996.

Arian, E. *Bach, Beethoven, and Bureaucracy: The Case of the Philadelphia Orchestra.* University of Alabama Press 1971.

Archives of the New York Philharmonic. *Black Musicians Human Rights Commission Hearings 1969,* https://archives.nyphil.org/index.php/artifact/abb6b2d1-5a2e-4a0d-888d-6ba897f038e6-0.1/fullview#page/1/mode/2up.

Attali, J. *Noise: The Political Economy of Music* (translation Brian Massumi) Manchester University Press, 1985.

Avery, P. "The Diluted Equal Pay Act: How Was It Broken? How Can It Be Fixed?" *Rutgers Law Review* 56 2004.

Ayer, J. *More Than Meets the Ear: How Symphony Musicians Made Labor History*. Syren Book Co., 2005.

Bakeart, X, G. Jonk and J. Raes. *Toonaangevend: Wat Topbedrijven kunnen leren van Het Concertgebouworkest, en Top Restaurant en een Rugbyploeg*. Lannoo Meulenhoff 2006.

Barenberg, M. "The Political Economy of the Wagner Act: Power, Symbol, and Workplace Cooperation." *Harvard Law Review* 106 1992-1993.

Barnard, C. "The Charter in Time of Crisis: A Case Study of Dismissal" in *Resocialising Europe in a Time of Crisis*. N. Countouris & M. Freedland (eds.) Cambridge University Press 2013.

Barthes, R. "From Word to Text" in *Image, Music, Text*. S. Heath (ed.) Hill and Wang 1977.

Baumol, W.J. "Symphony Orchestra Economics: The Fundamental Challenge." *Harmony* 2006.

Baumol, W.J. "The Arts in the 'New Economy'" in *Handbook of the Economics of Art and Culture*. V. Ginsburgh and C.D. Throsby (eds.) Vol. 1. Elsevier 2006.

Baumol, W.J. *The Cost Disease: Why Computers Get Cheaper and Health Care Doesn't*. Yale University Press 2012.

Baumol, W.J. and W.G. Bowen. *Performing Arts: The Economic Dilemma*. Twentieth Century Fund 1966.

Boumans, T. *Een Schitterend Vergeten Leven: de Eeuw van Frieda Belinfante*. Balans 2015.

Beecham, Sir T. *Beecham Stories: Anecdotes, Sayings and Impressions of Sir Thomas Beecham*. Warner 1993.

Bekker, S. "Flexicurity in the European Semester: Still a Relevant Concept?" *Journal of European Public Policy* 25(2) 2018.

Bennett, M. "Essay: From the 'No Spittin,' No Cussin' and No Summary Judgment Days of Employment Discrimination Litigation to the Defendant's Summary Judgment Affirmed Without Commend Days" *New York Law School Review* 2012-2013.

Berg van den, S. "Minister stuurt rekening fair practice naar initiatiefnemers." *Theaterkrant* 18 juni 2019.

Berlioz, H. *Mémoires De Hector Berlioz: Comprenant Ses Voyages En Italie, En Allemagne, En Russie Et En Angleterre, 1803-1865*. Gregg 1969.

Blanning, T.C.W. *The Triumph of Music: The Rise of Composers, Musicians and Their Art*. Harvard University Press 2008.

Blaug, M. *The Economics of the Arts*. Westview Press 1976.

Boekman, E. *Overheid en kunst in Nederland*. Boekmanstichting/Van Gennep 1989 (published dissertation 1939).

Boekmanstichting (Lahaut, D. & K van Aart). *Staat van cultuur 2: Cultuurindex Nederland 2005-2013*, 2004, http://www.cultuurindex.nl.

Boulez, P. "Where Are We Now?" in *Orientations: Collected Writing* (translation Martin Cooper) J.-J. Nattiez (ed.) Harvard University Press 1967.
Bouma, H, "Concertgebouw wil lonen verhogen." *Financieele Dagblad* 25 februari 2019.
Bourdieu, P. *Distinction: A Social Critique of the Judgement of Taste.* Routledge 1984.
Bourdieu, P. "The Scholastic Point of View". *Cultural Anthropology* 5 1990.
Bowers, J.M. and J. Tick. *Women Making Music: The Western Art Tradition, 1150-1950.* University of Illinois Press 1987.
Brandl, B. and F. Traxler. "Labour Relations, Economic Governance and the Crisis: Turning the Tide Again?" *Labor History* 2011.
Brodsky, W. "In the Wings of British Orchestras: A Multiple-Episode Interview Study among Symphony Players." *Journal of Occupational and Organisational Psychology* 79 2006.
Broer, T. and T. Niemantsverdriet. "Niet Raad voor Cultuur maar publiek moet bepalen wat goede kunst is." *Vrij Nederland* 12 januari 2011.
Broughton, A. "Collective Bargaining in the Arts and Culture Sector: An Examination of Symphony Orchestras in Germany and the U.K." *European Journal of Industrial Relations* 7 2001.
Brunet, E. "The Efficiency of Summary Judgment." *Loyola University Chicago Law Journal* 43 2012.
Burney, C. *Dr. Burney's Musical Tours in Europe: Being Dr. Charles Burney's Account of His Musical Experiences.* P.A. Scholes (ed.). Oxford University Press 1959.
Carse, A. *The Orchestra in the XVIIIth Century.* W. Heffer & Sons, 1940.
Case, K. "The Commoditization of Symphony Orchestra Musicians." *Case Arts Law* 2012, http://www.caseartslaw.com/perch/resources/article-re-commoditization.pdf.
Castel, R. "Die Wiederkehr der sozialen Unsicherheit." *Prekarität, Abstieg, Ausgrenzung.* Campus Verlag 2009.
Charry, M. *George Szell: A Life of Music.* University of Illinois Press 2011.
Chin, D. "Summary Judgment in Employment Discrimination Cases: A Judge's Perspective." *New York Law Review* 57 2012-2013.
Clark, C.E. "The Federal Rules of Civil Procedure: 1938-1958." *Columbia Law Review* 58 1958.
Clark, C.E. and C. Samenow. "The Summary Judgment." *Yale Law Journal* 38 1929.
CNO et al., *We gaan het verdienen, we zijn het waard! De visie van sociale partners op modernisering van arbeidsverhoudingen binnen de symfonieorkesten*, 2008.
Colker, R. "The Americans with Disabilities Act: A Windfall for Defendant." *Harvard Civil Rights-Civil Liberties Law Review* 34 1999.
Commissie Hierck. *Met het oog op de toekomst. Rapport van de adviescommissie Muziek.* S.I. 2011.
Commissie Nederlandse beroepsorkesten. *Orkesten van nu van waarde voor de toekomst. De gezamenlijke Nederlandse Symfonieorkesten over het huidige orkestenlandschap in de toekomst*, 2014.
Conant, A. "The Status of Women in German Orchestras: A Report Based on Practical Experience." *Viva Voce* 48 December 1998.

Connolly, K. "European Arts Cuts: 'Simple Maths' Forces German Orchestras to Merge." *Theguardian.com. Guardian News and Media* August 3, 2012.
Cooper, M. "Roll over Mahler: U.S. Orchestras Are Shrinking." *New York Times* November 22, 2014.
Cooper, M. "Cleveland Orchestra Suspends a Star after Allegations of Assault." *New York Times* July 27, 2018.
Coppock, B. "Radical Revenue: A New Business Model Challenges Industry Thinking." *Symphony* January-February 2008.
Countouris, N. *The Changing Law of the Employment Relationship: Comparative Analyses in the European Context.* Routledge 2016.
Countouris, N. and M. Freedland. *Resocialising Europe in a Time of Crisis.* Cambridge University Press 2013.
Countryman, V. "The Organized Musicians (Part I)." Faculty Scholarship Series 1948, http://digitalcommons.law.yale.edu/fss_papers/4778.
Cowan, T. "Why I Do Not Believe in the Cost Disease." *Journal of Cultural Economics* 20(3) 1996, 207-214.
Cowan, T. *In Praise of Commercial Culture.* Harvard University Press 2000.
Cowling. M. *The Cello* (2d ed.). Batsford Press 1983.
Coyle, D. *The Talent Code: Unlocking the Secret of Skill in Maths, Art, Music, Sport, and Just about Everything Else.* Arrow Press 2010.
Crawford, R. "A Historian's Introduction to American Music." Speech revised 1979, http://www.americanantiquarian.org/proceedings/44539323.pdf.
Cray, D. and L. Inglis. "Strategic Decision Making in Arts Organizations." *Journal of Arts Management, Law and Society* 7 2011.
Cultuur-Ondernemen et al. *Sectorplan Cultuur voor een duurzame arbeidsmarkt.* 2014a.
Cultuur-Ondernemen et al. Governance Code Cultuur. *Goed bestuur en toezicht in de cultuursector.* 2014b.
Danni, E. "NLRA Values, Labor Values, American Values." *Berkeley Journal of Employment and Labor Law* 26 2005.
Davies, A. "Regulating Atypical Work: Beyond Equality" in *Resocialising Europe in a Time of Crisis.* N. Countouris and M. Freedland (eds.) Cambridge University Press 2013.
Day, E. "Why Are Our Orchestras So White?" *The Guardian* September 14, 2008.
Deakin, S. "What Directors Do (and Fail to Do): Some Comparative Notes on Board Structure and Corporate Governance." *New York Law School Review* 55 2010.
de Beaujour, L.A.F. *Aperçu Des États-Unis … Depuis 1800 Jusqu'en 1810 Cahiers 3.* Republished by Nabu Press 2010.
de Beer, P. and E. Verhulp. *Dertig vragen en antwoorden over flexibel werk.* University of Amsterdam, Amsterdam Institute for Advanced Labour Studies 2017, http://www.uva-aias.net/nl/research-projects/flexibel-werk.
de Boer, J. *Omroep en publiek in Nederland tot 1940.* Leiden 1946.
de Brabandere, A., et al. *De kunstenaar, een ondernemer?* Lannoo 2011.
de Brosses, C. *Lettres familières écrites d'Italie en 1739 et 1740.* E. Perrin 1885.

Dekker, E. "The Economic Legitimation and De-legitimation of Arts Subsidies." *Economic Rationalities: Economic Reasoning as Knowledge and Practice Authority* 2017, http://hdl.handle.net/1765/102082.

Dent, E.J. "Italian Opera in London." in Proceedings of the Royal Musical Association 71st Session 1944-1945.

De Stefano, V. "The Rise of the 'Just-in-Time Workforce': On-Demand Work, Crowd Work and Labour Protection in the 'Gig-Economy.'" *Comparative Labor Law & Policy Journal* October 28, 2015.

de Tocqueville, A. *Democracy in America*, Vol. 2 Chapter XI "In What Spirits Americans Cultivate the Arts." http://www.gutenberg.org/ebooks/815.

Dickson, H.E. *Beating Time: A Musicians Memoir.* Northeastern Press 1995.

DiMaggio, P. and B. Pettit. "Public Opinion and Political Vulnerability: Why Has the National Endowment for the Arts Been Such an Attractive Target?" *Princeton University Center for the Arts and Cultural Policy Studies* 1999.

Dixon, L. "Is It Artistic Judgment or Is It Discrimination?" *New York Times* August 1, 1971.

Defoe, D. *Augusta Triumphans: Way to Make London the Most Flourishing City in the universe—A Proposal to Prevent the Expensive Importation of Foreign Musicians* J. Roberts 1728.

Dohman, J. "Bij ons in Hilversum." *NRC Handelsblad Weekblad* 13-19 juni 2009.

Downey, C.T. "BSO Bids Reluctant Farewell." *Washington Post* June 9, 2019.

Drenth, B., et al., *Naar nieuwe prestatiemodellen voor orkesten.* Berenschot 29 april 2011.

Drenth, B., et al., *Toekomstscenario's voor het Muziekcentrum van de omroep.* Berenschot 13 mei 2011.

Dreyfus, L. "Hermann Levi's Shame and Parsifal's Guilt: A Critique of Essentialism in Biography and Criticism." *Cambridge Opera Journal* 6(2) 1994.

Drobatschewsky, D. "About That 'Landmark Accord' in Phoenix." MusicalAmerica.com https://conductingmasterclass.wordpress.com/2009/06/14/more-bad-press-for-christie/.

Dubois & Co., *Er zit muziek in de Nederlandse symfonieorkesten. Visie op het businessmodel van symfonieorkesten.* Dubois & Co., 2010.

Duchen, J. "Why the Male Domination of Classical Music Might Be Coming to an End." *The Guardian* February 28, 2015.

Dukes, R. and W. Streeck. "Labour Constitutions and Occupational Communities: Social Norms and Legal Norms at Work." *Journal of Law and Society* 47(4) 2020.

Dunlop, A. "Forgotten Musicians: Documenting Musical Life at the Viennese Imperial Court in the Eighteenth Century." *Musicologica Brunensia* 47(1) 2012.

Dworkin, R. "Pragmatism, Right Answers and True Banality" in *Pragmatism and Law* M. Brint and W. Weaver (eds.) Westview Press 1991.

Edgers, G. "A Star Flutist Has Sued the Boston Symphony Orchestra." *Washington Post* December 11, 2018.

Eindrapport van de Commissie Regulering van Werk. *In wat voor land willen wij werken? Naar een nieuw ontwerp voor de regulering van werk.* 23 januari 2020, https://reguleringvanwerk.archiefweb.eu/#archive.

Elias, G. *Labor of Love: A Primer in Symphony Orchestra Musician/Management Relations* posted 13 May 2013, http://www.reichelrecommends.com/labor-of-love-a-primer-in-symphony-orchestra-musicianmanagement-relations/.

Elwell, H. "Women Score in First Debut Concert." *Cleveland Plain Dealer* November 18, 1936.

Faine, H. "Cooperative Bargaining in Nonprofit Arts Organizations." *The Journal of Arts, Management and Law* 1985.

Falckenberg, H. "The Art World We Deserve?" *Financial Times* April 11, 2014.

Faster, K. "Taste Inequalities in the Art Consumption of Prince Nicolaus I Esterházy 'the Magnificent'" in *A Taste for Luxury in Early Modern Europe: Display, Acquisition and Boundaries*. J. Ilmakunnas and J. Stobart (eds.) Bloomsbury 2017.

Faulkner, R. "Orchestral Interaction: Some Features of Communication and Authority in an Artistic Organization." *Sociological Quarterly* 14(2) Spring 1973.

Flanagan, R.J. "Symphony Musicians and Symphony Orchestras." Stanford University Graduate School of Business Research Paper No. 1989 revised 2008.

Flanagan, R.J. "The Economic Environment of American Symphony Orchestras." *GIA Reader* 19(2) 2008.

Flanagan, R.J. *The Perilous Life of Symphony Orchestras: Artistic Triumphs and Economic Challenges*. Yale University Press 2012.

Flothuis, M. and J. Giskes (eds.). *Waar bemoei je je mee: 75 jaar belangenstrijd van de Vereniging "Het Concertgebouworchest."* 1989.

Flury, D. *Revolutionär war im Wiener Vormärz die Idee einer demokratischen Künstlervereinigung, die später die noch heute gültige Rechtsform eines Vereines bekam.* 2017, https://blog.lucernefestival.ch/blog/2017/09/09/im-gespraech-mit-dem-schweizer-solofloetist-der-wiener-philharmoniker-di/

Flynn, J. "A Quiet Revolution at the Labor Board: The Transformation of the NLRB 1935-2000." *Ohio State Law Journal* 61 2000, 1361.

Fogel, H. "Are Three Legs Appropriate? Or Even Sufficient?" *Harmony* 10 2000.

Freedland, M. and N. Countouris. *The Legal Construction of Personal Work Relations*. Oxford University Press 2011.

Freedland, M. and N. Kountouris. "Some Reflections on the 'Personal Scope' of Collective Labour Law." *Industrial Law Journal* 46(1) March 1, 2017.

Freeman, R. *The Crisis of Classical Music in America*. Rowman & Littlefield 2014.

Frucht, S. "Embouchure Dystonia: A Video Guide to Diagnosis and Evaluation." *Journal of Clinical Movement Disorders* 3 June 18, 2016.

Fudge, J., S. McCrystal and K. Sankaran. *Challenging the Legal Boundaries of Work Regulation*. Hart 2012.

Fullerton, D. "On Justifications for Public Support of the Arts." *Journal of Cultural Economics* 15(2) 1992.

Gapinski, J. "The Production of Culture." *Review of Economics and Statistics* 62(4) 1980.

Gay, M. "BSO Flutist Settles Equal-Pay Lawsuit with Orchestra." *Boston Globe* February 14, 2019.

Geiringer, K. *Haydn: A Creative Life in Music*. University of California 1982.

Gembris, H., et al. "Health Problems of Orchestral Musicians from a Life-Span Perspective: Results of a Large-Scale Study." *Music & Science* 1 January 2018.

Getman, J.G. *The Supreme Court on Unions: Why Labor Law Is Failing American Workers*. Cornell University Press 2016.

Getman, J.G. "The NLRB: What went Wrong, and Should We Try to Fix It?" *Emory Law Journal* 64 2015, 1495.

Ghilarducci, T. *When I'm 64: The Plot Against Pensions and the Plan to Save Them*. Princeton University Press 2008.

Glesen, P. "Daniele Gatti werd haastig geofferd op het altaar van het reputatiemanagement." *Volkskrant* 27 Februari 2019.

Glynn, M.A. "When Cymbals Become Symbols: Conflict over Organizational Identity Within a Symphony Orchestra." *Organization Science* 2000.

Goldfield, M. *The Decline of Organized Labor in the United States*. University of Chicago Press 1992.

Goldin, C. and C. Rouse. "'Orchestrating Impartiality: The Impact of Blind' Auditions on Female Musicians." *The American Economic Review* 2000.

Goldstein, D.H. "Sex-Based Wage Discrimination: Recovery under the Equal Pay Act, Title VII, or Both." *Alabama Law Review* 56 1995, 294.

Gompes, L. and M. Ligtelijn. *Spiegel Van Amsterdam: Geschiedenis Van Felix Meritis*. Stichting Felix Meritis en Rozenberg Publishers 2007.

Grella, G. "Alan Pierson: Making Brooklyn's Orchestra." *Brooklyn Rail* September 9, 2011.

Griesinger, G.A. *Joseph Haydn: Eighteenth-century Gentleman and Genius: A Translation with Introduction and Notes by Vernon Gotwals of the Biographische Notizen über Joseph Haydn by G.A. Griesinger and the Biographische Nachrichten von Joseph Haydn by A.C. Dies*. University of Wisconsin Press 1963.

Grosheide, E. and M. Barenberg. "Minimum Fees for the Self-Employed: A European Response to the Uber-ized Economy." *Columbia Journal of European Law* 22 2015-2016, 193.

Grosheide, E. and B.T. Haar. "Employee-Like Worker: Competitive Entrepreneur or Submissive Employee? Reflections on ECJ, C-413/13, FNV Kunsten Informatie." In *Law and Social Rights in Europe: The Jurisprudence of International Courts. Selected Judgements*. University of Gdansk Press 90(4) 2018.

Grout, D.J. and C.V. Palisca. *A History of Western Music*. Norton 1980.

Guyer, I.D. *History of Chicago: Its Commercial and Manufacturing Interests and Industry*. Church, Goodman & Cushing Book 1862.

Harich, J. "Das Haydn–Orchester im Jahr 1780." *Haydn Jahrbuch* 8 1971.

Hart, P. *Orpheus in the New World: The Symphony Orchestra as an American Cultural Institution*. W.W. Norton 1973.

Heilbrun, J. and C.M. Gray. *The Economics of Art and Culture*. Cambridge University Press 2001.

Hermann, C. "Crisis, Structural Reform and the Dismantling of the European Social Model(s)." *Economic and Industrial Democracy, Economic and Industrial Democracy* 38(1) 2014.

Hewett, I. "America's Musicians Are Greedy and Overpaid." *Telegraph* October 2, 2013.

Heyes, J. "Flexicurity in Crisis: European Labour Market Policies in a Time of Austerity." *European Journal of Industrial Relations* 19(1) 2013.

Hinley, M.B. "The Uphill Climb of Women in American Music: Conductors and Composers." *Music Educators Journal* 70(8) 1984.

Holden, J. *Capturing Cultural Value: How Culture Has Become a Tool of Government Policy*. Demos 2004.

Horvath, J. "Cara Mia's Story," in *Playing Less Hurt*. Hal Leonard Books 2010.

Hunt, J. "A State-by-State Examination of Nondiscrimination Laws and Policies." *Center for American Progress* June 2012.

International Labor Organization (ILO). *The Scope of the Employment Relationship*. ILO 2003.

International Labor Organization (ILO). "Non-standard Forms of Employment." Governing Body, Conclusion of the Meeting of Experts 323rd Session March 23-27, 2015 Geneva 2015.

Jaeger, T. "Danielle Gatti en Concertgebouworkest bereiken 'overeenkomst.'" *NRC Handelsblad* 23 april 2019.

Jakes, F. "All White on the Night: Why Does the World-Famous Vienna Philharmonic Feature So Few Women and Ethnic Minorities?" *Independent* March 4, 2010.

Jarvis, A. "German Musicians in London, c. 1750-c. 1850." In *Migration and Transfer from Germany to Britain, 1660 to 1914*. S. Manz (ed.) Saur 2007.

Johnson, L. "CSO Musicians, Management Need to End Strike Now: For the Good of Chicago and Themselves." *Chicago Classical Review* April 19, 2019.

Jones, D.W. *The Life of Haydn*. Cambridge University Press 2009.

Judy, P.R. "The Uniqueness and Commonality of American Symphony Orchestra Organizations." *Harmony* October 1, 1995.

Kaiser, M.M. *Curtains? The Future of the Arts in America*. Brandeis University Press 2015.

Kanbur, R. "*Pareto's Revenge.*" 2005 http://www.arts.cornell.edu/poverty/ *kanbur*/ ParRev.pdf.

Khuner, F. *A Violinist's Journey from Vienna's Kolisch Quartet to the San Francisco Symphony and Opera Orchestras: An Oral History Transcript/1996*. Available at https://archive.org/details/violinistsjourn00khunrich.

Klamer, A. *The Value of Culture: On the Relationship Between Economics and Arts*. Amsterdam University Press 1997.

Kneeland, T. *Today's Social Issues: Democrats and Republicans*. ABC-Clio 2016.

Koch, P. "The Contest for American Culture: A Leadership Case Study on The NEA and NEH Funding Crisis." http://www.upenn.edu/pnc/ptkoch.html.

Kok, L.M. *Musculoskeletal Health in Musicians: Epidemiology & Biomedics* (dissertation, Leiden University Medical Center) 2018.

Komesar, N.K. *Law's Limits: The Rule of Law and the Supply and Demand of Rights*. Cambridge University Press 2001.

Kooke, S. "Spanning stijgt voor bedreigde orkesten" *Trouw* 2 februari 2001.

Kooke, S. "Omroeporkesten slachtoffer van weeffout" *Trouw* 27 juni 2003.

Kooke, S. "Musici zijn het zat om voor nop te komen spelen" *Trouw* 10 mei 2019.

Koszarski, R. "Flu Season: 'Moving Picture World' Reports on Pandemic Influenza, 1918-19." *Film History* 17(4) 2005.

Kraft, J.P. "Artists as Workers: Musicians and Trade Unionism in America, 1880-1917." *Musical Quarterly* 7(3) 1995.

Kulenkampff, H,-W. *Musiker im Orchester*. C.F. Peters 1980.

Kurzbauer, H. "Help Wanted." *The Strad* December 11, 2011, http://www.thestrad.com/help-wanted.

Kurzbauer, H. "United We Stand." *Blogpost* May 30, 2017, https://www.violinist.com/blog/hkurzbauer/20175/21191/

Kurzbauer, H. "Singing the #metoo Classical Music Blues." *Blogpost*. August 3, 2018, https://www.violinist.com/blog/hkurzbauer/20188/27393/

Landon, H.C.R. *Haydn Chronicle and Works*. Indiana University Press 1976.

League of American Orchestras (formerly, American Symphony Orchestra League) www.symphony.org Orchestral Statistical Reports (OSRs) New York: League of Symphony Orchestras, 1963-2000.

League of American Orchestras (formerly, American Symphony Orchestra League). *Orchestra Facts 2006-2014: A Study of Orchestra Finances and Operations*. 2016, http://www.culturaldata.org/learn/data-at-work/2016/league-of-american-orchestras-releases-orchestra-facts-2006-2014/.

Lebrecht, N. *The Maestro Myth: Great Conductors in Pursuit of Power*. Carol Publishing Group 1991.

Lebrecht, N. *Who Killed Classical Music? Maestros, Managers and Corporate Politics*. Carol Publishing Group 1997.

Le Goff, J. "Métiers licites et illicites dans l'occident medieval" in *Pour un autre moyen âge. Temps, travail et culture en Occident: 18 essais*. Gallimard 1978.

Leibowitz, L, "The Myth of the Structural Deficit." 802 *Legal Corner* Volume CIV, No. December 12, 2004.

Lemons, S. "Ongoing Angst at the Phoenix Symphony." *Musical America Worldwide* March 25, 2009.

Leiter, R.D. "Supervisory Employees and the Taft-Hartley Law." *Southern Economic Journal* 15(3) January 1949.

Levine, S. and R. Levine. "Why They're Not Smiling: Stress and Discontent in the Orchestra Workplace." http://esm.rochester.edu/iml/prjc/poly//wp-content/uploads/2012/02/Stress_Discontent_Levine.pdf.

Lewis, Z. "Cleveland Orchestra Economic Impact Report Details Large Financial Footprint." *The Cleveland Plain Dealer* September 26, 2019.

Locke, R. and C. Barr. *Cultivating Music in America: Women Patrons and Activists since 1860*. University of California Press 1997.

Lorey, I., A. Derieg and J. Butler. *State of Insecurity: Government of the Precarious*. Verso 2015.

Maitland, P. *Directeuren willen meer*. Uitgave Maitland Search & Advies 2016.

McArdel, M. "No Country for Young Men." *The Atlantic* January/February 2008.

McCloskey, D. "Battles to Be Won." *Windy City Times* September 17, 2014.

McGeary, T. *The Politics of Opera in Handel's Britain*. Cambridge University Press 2013.

McKnight, S. "Impasse Implementation of Final Offers Reviewed by Unionists and Academics." *Collective Bargaining Bulletin* 2, January 16, 1997.

McVeigh, S. "Italian Violinists in Eighteenth-Century London" in *The Eighteenth-Century Diaspora of Italian Music and Musicians*. R. Strohm (ed.) Brepols 2001.

Meiser, R. "Sour Notes." *Cleveland Scene* February 14, 2007, https://www.clevescene.com/cleveland/sour-notes/Content?oid = 1497679.

Mengelberg, R. *50 Jaar Concertgebouw 1888-1938* [50-year anniversary publication]. 1938.

Menger, P.-M. "Artistic Labor Markets and Careers." *Annual Review of Sociology* 25 1999.

Mertens, G. *Symphony and Chamber Orchestras*, http://www.miz.org/musical-life-in-germany/download/06_Symphony_and_Chamber_Orchestras.pdf.

Micheels, P. *Muziek in de schaduw van het Derde Rijk: de Nederlandse symfonieorkesten 1933-1945*. Walburg Pers 1993.

Midgette, A. and P. McGlone. "Assaults in Dressing Rooms: Groping During Lessons—Classical Musicians Reveal a Profession Rife with Harassment." *Washington Post* July 25, 2018.

Milhous, J. and R.D. Hume. "Opera Salaries in Eighteenth-Century London." *Journal of the American Musicological Society* 46(1) 1993.

Ministerie van Onderwijs, Cultuur en Wetenschap, *Cultuur als confrontatie — Uitgangspunten voor het cultuurbeleid 2001-2004*. Zoetermeer 2005.

Ministerie van Onderwijs, Cultuur en Wetenschap. *Brief uitgangspunten cultuurbeleid*. Halbe Zijlstra 6 december 2010.

Ministerie van Onderwijs, Cultuur en Wetenschap. *Meer dan kwaliteit. Een nieuwe visie op cultuurbeleid* Den Haag 2011b.

Ministerie van Onderwijs, Cultuur en Wetenschap. *De betekenis van cultuur in een veranderende samenleving* Den Haag 2013a.

Ministerie van Onderwijs, Cultuur en Wetenschap. *Handboek verantwoording cultuursubsidies instellingen 2009-2017*

Ministerie van Onderwijs, Cultuur en Wetenschap. Cultuur in beeld (Culture at a glance 2014-2017). Den Haag.

Ministerie van Onderwijs, Cultuur en Wetenschap. *Ruimte voor talent in cultuurbeleid* Den Haag 2014a.

Ministerie van Onderwijs, Cultuur en Wetenschap. *Cultuur verbindt. Een ruime blik op cultuurbeleid* Den Haag 2014c.

Ministerie van Onderwijs, Cultuur en Wetenschap. *Cultuur in een Open Samenleving*. March 12, 2018.

Mnookin, R. *Bargaining with the Devil: When to Negotiate, When to Fight*. Simon & Schuster 2010.

Mnookin, R. with Gary Friedman and Joel Cutcher-Gershenfeld. "A New Direction: Transforming Relations Within the San Francisco Symphony." *Harmony* 13 2001.

Mozart, W.A. *Briefe und Aufzeichnungen* Vol. III, Kassel 1963.

Mozart, W.A. *The Letters of Mozart and His Family*. Macmillan Reference 1997.

Mueller, J.H. *The American Symphony Orchestra: A Social History of Musical Taste.* Indiana University Press 1951.

Mulder, C.P. "The London Symphony Orchestra: Still Afloat" in *Transcending Capitalism Through Cooperative Practices.* Palgrave Macmillan 2015.

"The Musicians' Company." *Musical Times* 60 1919.

M. van de Omroep. *Meerjaren Beleidsplan 2011-2015*, internal sources.

Nardo, M. and F. Rossetti. *Final Report on Flexicurity in Europe.* European Commission 2013.

Neus-Bates, C. *Women in Music: An Anthology of Source Readings from the Middle Ages to the Present.* Harper & Row 1982.

New Grove Dictionary of Music and Musicians 1980.

Nösselt, H.-J. *Das Gewandhausorchester* 52-57 Koehler und Amelang 1943.

Noteboom, L.J. *Good Governance for Challenging Times.* Harmony 2003.

Nussbaum, M.C. "Cultivating Humanity in Legal Education." *University of Chicago Law Review* 70(1) 2003.

Nwankoku, Chi-chi. "Classical Music Is Overwhelmingly White and Male." *The Guardian* July 26, 2019.

O'Brien, D. *Measuring the Value of Culture.* DCMS 2010.

OECS StatExtracts Trade Union Density 2012, http://stats.oecd.org/Index.aspx?QueryId=20167.

Oestrich, J.R. "Even Legends Adjust To Time and Trend, Even the Vienna Philharmonic." New York Times February 28, 1998.

Offenbach, J. *Offenbach en Amérique: Notes d'un musicien en voyage* (1877) Facsimile Publisher 2013.

O'Hagan, J.W. *The State and the Arts: An Analysis of Key Economic Policy Issues in Europe and the United States.* Edward Elgar 1998.

O'Leary, L. *Employment and Labour Relations Law in the Premier League, NBA and International Rugby Union.* TMC Asser Press 2017.

Orchestrate Excellence. "A Tale of Two Orchestras." October 17, 2013, http://www.orchestrateexcellence.org/a-tale-of-two-orchestras/.

Osborne, W. "Art Is Just an Excuse." *International Alliance of Women in Music Journal* October 1996.

Peacock, A.T. "Economics, Cultural Values and Cultural Policies." *Journal of Cultural Economics* 1992.

Piketty, T. (translation Arthur Goldhammer). *Capital in the Twenty-First Century.* Belknap Publishers 2014.

Pilzer, P.Z. *Other People's Money: The Inside Story of the S&L Mess.* Simon and Schuster 1989.

Piperek, M. *Stress and Music: Medical, Psychological, Sociological., and Legal Strain Factors in a Symphony Orchestra Musician's Profession—A Study Commissioned by the Vienna Symphony.* Braumüller 1981.

Pohl, C.F. *Joseph Haydn*, vol. 1. Verlag von Sacco Nachfolger, 1875.

Polanyi, K. *The Great Transformation.* Beacon 1957.

Posner, R.A. "The Problematics of Moral and Legal Theory." *Harvard Law Review* 111 1997.

Potuček, M. *Theory and Practice of the Welfare State in Europe in 20th Century*. Z. Zudová-Lešková and E. Voráček (eds.) 2014.

Price, A. "Pit of Despair." *The Guardian* February 2, 2006.

R. voor Cultuur. *Advies bezuinigingen cultuur 2013-2016: Noodgedwongen keuzen* 2012, https://www.cultuur.nl/upload/documents/adviezen/RvC_adviesnoodgedwongen-keuzen.pdf.

R. voor Cultuur. *Advies Agenda Cultuur: 2017 –2020 en verder* april 2015.

R. voor Cultuur. *Passie gewaardeerd: advies over versterking arbeidsmarkt culturele sector* 21 april 2017.

Rabban, D. "Can American Labor Law Accommodate Collective Bargaining by Professional Employees?" *The Yale Law Journal* 99 1990.

Reich, N. "Women as Musicians: A Question of Class" in *Musicology and Difference: Gender and Sexuality in Music Scholarship*. University of California Press 1993.

Risak, M. and T. Dullinger. "The Concept of 'Worker' in EU Law: Status Quo and Potential for Change." ETUI Research Paper-Report 140 2018.

Rohr, D. *The Careers of British Musicians 1750-1850: A Profession of Artisans*. Cambridge University Press 2004.

Rohter, L. "In Europe, Where Art Is Life, Ax Falls on Public Financing." *New York Times* March 24, 2012.

Rosen, C. *The Classical Style: Haydn, Mozart and Beethoven*. W.W. Norton 1971.

Rousseau, J.-J. *A Complete Dictionary of Music* (translation William Waring) 1779.

Rubinstein, M.N. "Employees, Employers, and Quasi-Employers: An Analysis of Employees and Employers Who Operate in the Borderland Between an Employer-and-Employee Relationship." *University of Pennsylvania Journal of Business Law* Spring 2012.

Rutherglen, G. *Civil Rights in the Shadow of Slavery: The Constitutions, Common Law, and the Civil Rights Act of 1866*. Oxford University Press 2013.

Sachs, H. *Toscanini: Musician of Conscience*. Liveright 2017.

Salmen, W. *Der fahrende Musiker im europaäischen Mittelalter*. Kassel 1960.

Sanders, A. "The Changing Face of 'Flexicurity' in Times of Austerity?" in *Resocialising Europe in a Time of Crisis*. N. Countouris and M. Freedland (eds.) Cambridge University Press 2013.

Sandgruber, R. "Wirtschaftsentwicklung Einkommensverteilung und Alltagsleben zur Zeit Haydns." In Katalog: *Joseph Haydn in seiner Zeit*. Eisenstadt 72 (1982).

Scharpf, F.W. "The Asymmetry of European Integration, or Why the EU Cannot Be a 'Social Market Economy'." *Socio-Economic Review* 8(2) April 2010.

Schonberg, H. *The Great Conductors*. Simon & Schuster 1967.

Schuller, G. *Musings: The Musical Worlds of Gunther Schuller*. Oxford University Press 1989.

Schumann, C. *The Letters of Clara Schumann, and Johannes Brahms* 1853-1896 (B. Litzmann (ed.). Vienna House 1971.

Schumpeter, J.A. *Capitalism, Socialism, and Democracy*. Harper 1947.

Scott, A.O. "The Squeeze on the Middle Brow." *New York Times* August 3, 2014.

Scutari, M. "From Mahler to the Masses." *Inside Philanthropy* May 5, 2017.

Selmi, M. "Why Are Employment Discrimination Cases So Hard to Win?" *Los Angeles Law Review* 61 2001.

Seltzer, G.A. *The Professional Symphony Orchestra in the United States: An Anthology*. Scarecrow 1975.

Service, T. "Why Are Salaries So Markedly Different Between British and U.S. Orchestras?" *The Guardian* June 26, 2014.

Shaw, G.B. *London Music in 1888-89 as Heard by Corno di Bassetto (Later Known as Bernard Shaw) with Some Further Autobiographical Particulars*. Constable and Company Limited, 1950.

Shaw, H. "You've Come a Long Way, Baby." *Senza Sordino* Volume XVIII February 1980.

Skolnick, R.G. "Control, Collaboration or Coverage: The NLRA and the St. Paul Chamber Orchestra Dilemma." *Washington University Journal of Law & Policy* 20 2006.

Slocum, K. "'Confrérie, Bruderschaft' and Guild: The Formation of Musicians' Fraternal Organisations in Thirteenth- and Fourteenth Century Europe." *Early Music History* 14 1995.

Smith, D. "The Great Symphony Orchestra: A Relatively Good Place to Grow Old." *The International Journal of Aging and Human Development* 27(4) December 1988.

Somfai, L. "Haydn at the Esterházy Court" in *The Classical Era: Man & Music*. N. Zaslaw (ed.). Palgrave Macmillan London 1989.

Spel, M. "De Radio Kamer Filharmonie verdwijnt." *NRC Handelsblad* March 5, 2012.

Spitzer, J. and N. Zaslaw. *The Birth of the Orchestra: History of an Institution, 1650-1815*. Oxford University Press 2004.

Staehelin, M. "Orchester" in *Handwörterbuch der musikalischen Terminologie*. H.H. Eggebrecht (ed.). Steiner Verlag 1972.

Standing, G. *The Precariat: The New Dangerous Class*. Bloomsbury Academic 2011.

Strasser, O. *Und dafür wird man noch bezahlt. Mein Leben mit den Wiener Philharmonikern*. DTV Deutscher Taschenbuch 1990.

Strauss, G.H. and T.H. Hammer. *Worker's Participation in the United States*. UC Berkeley Press 1987.

Supiot, A. "Revisiter les droits d'action collective." *Droit Social* 2001.

Swafford, J. *Beethoven: Anguish and Triumph—A Biography*. Faber & Faber 2015.

Swindler, W.F. *Court and Constitution in the Twentieth Century*. Bobbs-Merrill 1969.

Szigeti, J. *Szigeti on the Violin* 1970 https://archive.org/details/szigetionviolin0000szig_h2g4.

Taruskin, R. "In Theory" in *Text and Act: Essays on Music and Performance*. Oxford University Press 1995.

Throsby, D. *The Economics of Cultural Policy*. Cambridge University Press 2010.

Towse, R. *A Handbook of Cultural Economics* 2d ed. Edward Elgar 2013.

Tsioulcas, A. "Cleveland Orchestra Fires 2 Leading Musicians after Sexual Misconduct Investigation." NPR (National Public Radio) October 24, 2018.

UNESCO. "Recommendations Concerning the Status of the Artist." Adopted by the General Conference at its Twenty-First Session, Belgrade October 27, 1980.

UNESCO 2009. *Measuring the Economic Contribution of Cultural Industries: A Review and Assessment of Current Methodological Approaches*, http://www.uis.unesco.org/culture/Documents/FCS-handbook-1-economic-contribution-culture-en-web.pdf.

van de Keuken, T. "De flexibele schil is het smerigste begrip uit het bedrijfsleven." *Volkskrant* 14 juni 2020.

van der Ploeg, R. "The Making of Cultural Policy: A European Perspective" in *Handbook of the Economics of Art and Culture*. V.A. Ginsburgh and D. Throsby (eds.). Elsevier 2006.

van der Waa, F. "Andrew Manze." *Volkskrant* 13 juli 2012.

van Klink, P. "Dirigenten kosten ons te veel geld." *Volkskrant* July 15, 2008.

Vinogradov, A. *The Condemnation of Paganini* (translation) Stephen Garry. Hutchinson & Co 1946.

Vlaming, H. "De klap in de cultuursector komt volgend jaar." *NBA-platform voor accountants en financials* 25 juni 2020.

Webster, J. *Haydn's "Farewell" Symphony and the Idea of Classical Style: Through-Composition and Cyclic Integration in His Instrumental Music*. Cambridge University Press 2004.

Wilkens, N. *Music in the Age of Chaucer*. D.S. Brewer 1979.

Wolf Report. *The Financial Condition of Symphony Orchestras: Part I—The Orchestra Industry*. American Symphony Orchestra League 1992.

Wolfe, Z. "Baton Inflation: American Conductor Salaries Hit a New High." *New York Times* July 27, 2018.

Woodruff, B. "Unprotected Until Forty: The Limited Scope of the Age Discrimination in Employment Act of 1967." *Indiana Law Journal* 73 1998.

Yamamoto, E.K., et al., "Summary Judgment at the Crossroads: The Impact of the Celotex Trilogy." *University of Hawaii Law Review* 12 1990.

I.

Recitative: The interviewed

Face-to-face interviews took place with the following musicians, board members, conductors, management team members, and additional experts in the orchestral field.

With a few exceptions, interviews were transcribed within two days of the interview. In some cases, notes were translated (French-English; Dutch-English) to maximize conformity and ensure comprehension. Focus group interviews took place throughout the years of inquiry to continue the dialogue on orchestral employment challenges in times of crisis.

Special thanks to the musicians of the Netherlands Radio Chamber Orchestra/Radio Chamber Philharmonic; Netherlands Radio Philharmonic Orchestra; Sinfonia Rotterdam and the Grand Teton Music Festival

I.I CONDUCTORS

Marin Alsop
Conrad van Alphen
Paavo Berglund
Herbert Blomstedt
Pierre Boulez
Frans Brüggen
Amaury du Closel
Sergiu Comissiona
Stéphane Denève
Mark Elder
Peter Eötvös
Libia Hernandez
Jean-Jacques Kantorow
Bernard Klee
Yakov Kreizberg

Christopher Keene
Roland Kieft
Eri Klas
Reinbert de Leeuw
David Lockington
John Mauceri
James MacMillan
Meir Minsky
Kenneth Montgomery
Otto-Werner Mueller
Yannick Nézet-Séguin
John Nelson
Giuseppe Patanè
Donald Runnicles
Hyman Schandler
Michael Schønwandt
David Shallon
Joseph Silverstein
Etienne Siebens
Jeannette Sorrell
Jan Stulen
Ling Tung
Hans Vonk
Edo de Waart
Jaap van Zweden
Nikolaj Szeps-Znaider

I.II Orchestral Musicians (U.S.)

I.II.I Concertmasters/principal players/section leaders

Bill Bennett	San Francisco Symphony
Richard Bock	Phoenix Symphony
Julia Bogorad	St. Paul Chamber Orchestra
Max Bonecutter	Minnesota Orchestra; Metropolitan Opera Orchestra
Steve Braunstein	San Francisco Symphony
Sara Cutler	New York City Ballet Orchestra
Michael Davis	Louisville Orchestra
Robert Davidovici	Vancouver Symphony
Angela Fuller Heyde	Dallas Symphony
Valerie Heywood	Buffalo Philharmonic
William Hill	Colorado Symphony

Rebekah Johnson	New Jersey Symphony
Holly Mulcahy	Chattanooga Symphony; Wichita Symphony
Daniel Majeske	Cleveland Orchestra
Ralph Matson	Utah Symphony
Roger Oyster	Kansas City Symphony
Charles Pikler	Chicago Symphony
Brian Prechtl	Baltimore Symphony
Joseph Silverstein	Boston Symphony
Gregory Raden	Dallas Symphony
Joseph Robinson	New York Philharmonic
Peter Rosado	Phoenix Symphony
Jennifer Ross	Pittsburgh Symphony
Roger Ruggieri	Milwaukee Symphony
Jonathan Sherwin	Cleveland Orchestra
Zachariah Spellman	San Francisco Opera Orchestra
Rachel van Voorhees	Louisiana Philharmonic
Larry Zalkind	Utah Symphony
Roberta Zalkind	Utah Symphony

I.II.II Section Players (additional members from the Grand Teton Music Festival (GTMF))

Lucina Horner	Alabama Symphony
Judith Cox	Atlanta Symphony
Karen Freer	Atlanta Symphony
Raymond Leung	Atlanta Symphony
Brian Prechtl	Baltimore Symphony
Max Raimi	Chicago Symphony
Kathleen Collins	Cleveland Orchestra
Paul Kushious	Cleveland Orchestra
Gino V. Raffaelli	Cleveland Orchestra
Leonard Samuels	Cleveland Orchestra
Isabel Trautwein	Cleveland Orchestra
Carolyn Gadiel Warner	Cleveland Orchestra
Stephen Warner	Cleveland Orchestra
Maurice Wolfson	Cleveland Orchestra
Doris Allen	Metropolitan Opera Orchestra
Browning Cramer	Metropolitan Opera Orchestra
Marcia Peck	Minnesota Orchestra

David Williamson	Minnesota Orchestra
Martin Andersen	New Jersey Symphony
Susan Gellert	New Jersey Symphony
Rebekah Johnson	New Jersey Symphony
Dawn Hannay	New York Philharmonic
Ken Merkin	New York Philharmonic
Judy Nelson	New York Philharmonic
Barbara Scowcroft	Utah Symphony

I.III Orchestral (Europe and NL)

I.III.I Concertmasters/Leaders:

Thanos Adamopoulos	Orchestre de la Monnaie, Brussels
Noah Bendix-Balgley	Pittsburgh Symphony, Berlin Philharmonic
Julia Bogorad	Saint Paul Chamber Orchestra
Kam-Lung Cheng	North Netherlands Philharmonic
Vesko Eshkenazy	Royal Concertgebouw Orchestra
Jorja Fleezanis	Minnesota Orchestra (1989-2009)
Karen Freer	Atlanta Symphony
Sarah Kapustin	North Netherlands Philharmonic
William Hill	Colorado Symphony
Alex Kerr	Royal Concertgebouw Orchestra; Dallas Symphony
John Kinzie	Colorado Symphony
Vera Laporeva	Metropole Orchestra
Danny Laufer	Atlanta Symphony
Carla Leurs	Orkest van het Oosten (Het Orkest; Phion)
Daniel Majeske	Cleveland Orchestra
Olga Martinova	Netherlands Philharmonic Orchestra
Emi Ohi Resnick	North Netherlands Philharmonic
René Pagan	Hague Philharmonic and Saint Paul Chamber Orchestra
Cordelia Paw	Sinfonia Rotterdam
Evelien Prakke	Het Balletorkest (Netherlands Ballet Orchestra)
Sarah Oates	Associate Leader, Philharmonia Orchestra
Quirine Scheffers	Rotterdam Philharmonic Orchestra
Michel Schwalbé	Berlin Philharmonic Orchestra
Jan Spronk	Royal Concertgebouw Orchestra
Radoslav Szulc	Bavarian Radio Orchestra

Dimiter Tchernookov	Netherlands Radio Philharmonic (formerly, RKF)
Quirijn van Regteren Altena Hague Philharmonic	

I.III.II Section Players (selection)[1282]

Orsze Adam	Holland Symfonia
Andrew Faughnan	Holland Symfonia
Nitzan Laster	Netherlands Philharmonic Orchestra
Carol Harte	Royal Concertgebouw Orchestra
Julia Tom	Royal Concertgebouw Orchestra
Rachel Browne	Rotterdam Philharmonic Orchestra
Itamar Shimeon	Rotterdam Philharmonic Orchestra

With special thanks to Sinfonia Rotterdam musicians and members of the Dutch radio orchestras, pre-2012-2013 reorganization

I.IV Musician members of the PvFM Orkest remplaçanten

Platform for orchestral freelancers: Caroline Cartens, Dorine Schoon, and Casper Donker, Helmke Jansen, Tinneke de Jong, Daan Kortekaas, Saskia Rekké

Special inspiration from conversations with:

Eve Adamopoulos
Martin Bungeroth
Leendert Booyens
Norma Brooks
Vanessa Damanet
Susanne Degerfors
Katja Dirven Didychenko
Anne van Eck
Rafaella Engelsberg
Marta Ephrat-Lemanska
Ephraim Feves
Frank van Kooten
John van Lierop
Kristen Linfante
Ewoud Mahler
Annemieke Marinkovic
Paul Medeiros
Florin Negreanu

1282. Anonymity assured to others.

Matthias Naegele
Gideon Nelissen
Ingrid Nissen
James Oesi
Steuart Pincombe
Ivana Poparic
Wendy Rijken
Magrita Rondeel
Naomi Rubenstein
Stefano Sancassan
Cyril Scheepmaker
Stamatis Sachas
Ikuko Takahashi
Samuel Tamarit Otero
Maximiano Vera
Bernadette Verhagen
Inger van Vliet
Coleman Willis
Katya Woloshyn

I.V Freelance musicians USA

Special thanks from the ranks of musicians at the Grand Teton Music Festival (GTMF); New York freelance musicians, members AFM local 802, Graduating seniors, the Juilliard School of Music 2017

I.VI Management team/ Board members

David Bazen	Commercial director, Royal Concertgebouw Orchestra (RCO)
Peter Benoliel	Board chairman emeritus, The Philadelphia Orchestra, Life board member Grand Teton Music Festival
Ella Broekstra	HRM Director, Dutch Broadcasting Music Center (MCO)
Bruce Coppock	Managing director, St. Paul Chamber Orchestra (1999-2008 and 2013-2015), former Executive director, St. Louis Symphony (1992-1997)
Chris Dingjan	Secretary General, Vereniging van Nederlandse Orkesten (VvNO) Association of Dutch Orchestras
Kees Dijk	former Manager, Netherlands Radio Philharmonic Orchestra, Netherlands Radio Chamber Philharmonic (2208-2013)

Arthur van Dijk	former Manager, Brabant Symphony Orchestra (2009-2013)
Joel Fried	former director, Artistic Administration, Royal Concertgebouw Orchestra (1999-2020)
Angela Garland	Artistic affairs coordinator, Netherlands Philharmonic Orchestra
Piet van Gennip	Director, Het Balletorkest
Hein Glaubitz	former Manager, Radio Philharmonic, Radio Chamber Philharmonic (2006-2008)
Maurits Haenen	Interim director, Dutch Broadcasting Music Center (MCO Hilversum)
Ben Janssen	Director, MCO (1995-2004)
Wim van Loon	Personnel manager (former) Netherlands Chamber Orchestra
Jan Willem Loot	Director, Amsterdam Philharmonic Orchestra; Netherlands Philharmonic Orchestra; Royal Concertgebouw Orchestra (1998-2008)
Roland Kieft	Artistic director, The Hague Philharmonic
Anton Kok	Director, Dutch Broadcasting Music Center (2005-2013)
Jonathan Martin	CEO Dallas Symphony (2012-2017)
Robert Massey	President & CEO, Jacksonville Symphony, USA
Stan Paardekooper	Former director, Brabants Orchestra; Holland Symfonia; Netherlands Broadcasting Music Center
Stefan Rosu	Intendant, South Netherlands Philharmonic
Senator Alan K. Simpson	Lifetime board member, Grand Teton Music Festival
Henk Swinnen	former General manager, L'orchestre de la Suisse Romande, Artistic Director De Filharmonie
Rob Streevelaar	General manager, Netherlands Philharmonic Orchestra
Jean-Marc Vogt	German Orchestra Foundation (DOV) Executive Board and Frankfurt Opera Orchestra Board; professional violist
Margot Walk	Founder and past President, Grand Teton Music Festival
Simon Woods	CEO League of American Orchestras; former CEO Los Angeles Philharmonic; former CEO Seattle Symphony

Jeff Woodruff	General manager, Harrisburg Symphony, former Executive Director, Houston Symphony

I.VII Additional experts (lawyers, mediators, publicists, union advisors)

Allison Beck	Deputy Director Federal Mediation and Conciliation Service, Washington D.C. appointed in 2015
Jan Bastiani	Trombone; Legal and policy advisor, Metropole Orchestra
Naomi Bensdorf Frisch	Regional Orchestra Players Association (ROPA) American Federation of Musicians Delegate-at-Large
Cathrien van Bunningen	Senior advisor Dutch Ministry of Education, Culture and Science (OCW) performance division; violist
Max Bonecutter	Attorney; former bass trombonist, Metropolitan Orchestra; the Minnesota Orchestra
Mark Bruwel	President, Symphony Orchestra Musicians' Association Australia
Iain Burnside	BBC London music commentator, music publicist, professional pianist
Kevin Case	Musicians employment lawyer, founder, Case Arts Law LLC
Sara Cutler	Executive Board, Associated Musicians of New York, AFM local 802, professional harpist
Charles Daval	Trumpet, lawyer, and expert on orchestral relations
Harrald Eggebrecht	Senior music critic, publicist Süddeutschen Zeitung, Munich, Germany
Deborah Cheyne	former vice-president FIM; VP SindMusi Rio de Janeiro musicians union; violist
Rick Finlay	Executive Committee The Musicians' Union U.K., drummer and percussionist
Tino Gagliardi	President, Associated Musicians of New York, AFM Local 802.
Mark Gerrits	Executive, Kunstenbond (Netherlands)
Monica Germino	Performance artist; violinist
Lord John Hendy KC	Trade union rights expert

Eileen Barkas Hoffman	Commissioner ADR and International Services, Federal Mediation & Conciliation Service, Washington D.C.
Miles Hoffman	Violist; founder American Chamber Players, National Public Radio (NPR) commentator *Morning Edition*
Todd Jelen	Negotiator, AFM, New York
Catharina Kat	Lawyer, Catlaw Amsterdam
Soye Kim	Attorney, National Relations Labor Board (NLRB)
Martin Kothman	Senior Director, FNV Media Culture/orchestral division
Boris Kuschnir	International violin pedagogue; member Koppelman Quartet
Glen Kwok	Executive Director, International Violin Competition of Indianapolis; President, World Federation of International Music Competitions (2009-2015)
Janine Jansen	Concert violinist
Vanessa Lann	Composer
Anders Laursen	Vice-President FIM; President Dansk Musiker Forbund, Denmark
Benoît Machuel	Secretary General, International Federation of Musicians (FIM)
Sylvia Marcovici	Concert violinist
Harvey Mars	Legal consul, AFM Local 802
Gerald Mertens	Managing Director, German Musicians Union (DOV)
Michel-Etienne Van Neste	Secretary-General, Queen Elisabeth Competition
Garrick Ohlsson	Concert pianist
Karan O'Loughlin	Services, Industrial, Professional and Technical Union (SIPTU) Sectoral organizer, Arts and Culture
Tara Persaud	Associate director, Solea Concert Management
Maciej Pacula	ZZ PAMO Polish Orchestral Musicians trade union
Leonard Paduret	FAIR-Media Sind Romanian trade union
Javier Ramirez	Director, Field Programs & Innovation, Federal Mediation and Conciliation Service, USA
Marco Riaskoff	Founder and CEO, Riaskoff Concert Management

Bruce Ridge	Chair, International Conference Symphony and Opera Musicians (ICSOM)
Loris Rossi	Slc-CGIL, Italy
Yves Sapir	President, SNAM, France
Ab Sengupta	Director Artistic Planning Carnegie Hall; former Artistic Director, Baltimore Symphony; professional violist
Pauline Sick	Labor and employment lawyer, Boontje Advocaten Amsterdam
Morris Shanker	Professor of Law, Case Western Reserve School of Law
Holly Slocum	Community activist, Minnesota Orchestra
Nadja Salerno-Sonnenberg Concert violinist	
Meredith Snow	Chair, ICSOM; violist Los Angeles Philharmonic
Karlheinz Stockhausen	Composer
Ariane Todes	Editor (former) *The Strad*, **London; Elbow Music**
Jean-Marc Vogt	President, German Musicians Union (DOV); violist Frankfurt Opera orchestra
Bart de Vroe	Labor and employment lawyer, Vestius Advocaten Amsterdam
Krzysztof Wegrzyn	Professor emeritus, Hochshule fur Musik, Hannover; former director Joseph Joachim International Competition
Eric Wen	Senior lecturer, Juilliard School of Music; the Curtis Institute, Editor (former) The Strad
Randy Whatley	President, Cypress Media Group
Ronald Wilford	President, Columbia Arts Management Inc. (CAMI)
Nikolaj Szeps-Znaider	Concert violinist; Music director Orchestre national de Lyon

I.IX With special thanks to these exceptional colleagues, the musician members of the Players Committee, Grand Teton Music Festival

Kristin Linfante, Chair
Martin Andersen
Juan de Gomar
Jennifer Marotta
Gabby Mulcahy
Mick Mulcahy
Greg Raden
Kristen Sonnenborn

BCLR - BULLETIN OF COMPARATIVE LABOUR RELATIONS

Vol. Author/Title/Year/ISBN

1. Roger Blanpain, *Individual Employment Contracts: Collective Agreements*, 1970.
2. Roger Blanpain, *Social Planning*, 1971 (ISBN 90-312-0018-2).
3. Roger Blanpain, *Guaranteed Income Funds*, 1972 (ISBN 90-312-0019-0).
4. Roger Blanpain, *Employee Participation at the Level of the Enterprise*, 1973 (ISBN 90-312-0020-4).
5. Roger Blanpain, *Vastheid van Betrekking: Staking en Bezetting*, 1974.
6. Roger Blanpain, *Labour Law and Industrial Relations (International Bibliography)*, 1975 (ISBN 90-312-0023-9).
7. Roger Blanpain, *Multinational Enterprises*, 1976 (ISBN 90-312-0024-7).
8. Roger Blanpain, *Worker's Participation in the European Company*, 1977 (ISBN 90-312-0044-1).
9. Roger Blanpain, *Women and Labour*, 1978 (ISBN 90-312-0077-8).
10. Roger Blanpain, *European Conference on Labour Law and Industrial Relations: Multinational Enterprises*, 1979 (ISBN 90-312-0091-3).
11. Roger Blanpain, *Job Security and Industrial Relations*, 1980 (ISBN 90-312-0147-2).
12. Roger Blanpain, Greg Bamber & Russell Lansbury, *Technological Change and Industrial Relations: An International Symposium*, 1983 (ISBN 90-312-0205-3).
13. Roger Blanpain, James Janssen van Raay & A. Moulty, *Worker's Participation in the European Community: The Fifth Directive*, 1984 (ISBN 90-654-4187-5).
14. Roger Blanpain, *Equality and Prohibition of Discrimination in Employment*, 1985 (ISBN 90-654-4215-4).
15. Roger Blanpain, *Restructuring Labour in the Enterprise: Law and Practice in France, F.R. of Germany, Italy, Sweden and the United Kingdom*, 1986 (ISBN 90-654-4283-9).
16. Roger Blanpain & E. Kassalow, *Unions and Industrial Relations: Recent Trends and Prospect: A Comparative Treatment*, 1987 (ISBN 90-654-4294-4).
17. Roger Blanpain & Marco Biagi, *Trade Union Democracy and Industrial Relations*, 1988 (ISBN 90-654-4394-0).
18. Roger Blanpain & Jelle Visser, *In Search of Inclusive Unionism*, 1990 (ISBN 90-654-4439-4).
19. Roger Blanpain, *Flexibility and Wages: A Comparative Treatment*, 1990 (ISBN 90-654-4461-0).

20. Roger Blanpain, Stephen Frenkel & Oliver Clarke, *Economic Restructuring and Industrial Relations in Industrialised Countries*, 1990 (ISBN 90-654-4488-2).
21. Roger Blanpain & Friedrich Fürstenberg, *Structure and Strategy in Industrial Relations*, 1991 (ISBN 90-654-4559-5).
22. Roger Blanpain, Amira Galin & Ozer Carmi, *Flexible Work Patterns and Their Impact on Industrial Relations*, 1991 (ISBN 90-654-4572-2).
23. Roger Blanpain, *Workers' Participation: Influence on Management Decision-Making by Labour in the Private Sector*, 1992 (ISBN 90-654-4600-1).
24. Roger Blanpain, Brian Brooks & Chris Engels, *Employed or Self-Employed*, 1992 (ISBN 90-654-4613-3).
25. Roger Blanpain & Tiziano Treu, *Industrial Relations Developments in the Telecommunications Industry*, 1993 (ISBN 90-654-4642-7).
26. Roger Blanpain & Marco Biagi, *Industrial Relations in Small and Medium Sized Enterprises*, 1993 (ISBN 90-654-4696-6).
27. Roger Blanpain & Marco Biagi, *Participative Management and Industrial Relations in a Worldwide Perspective*, 1993 (ISBN 90-654-4769-5).
28. Roger Blanpain, Jacques Rojot & Hoyt N. Wheeler, *Employee Rights and Industrial Justice*, 1994 (ISBN 90-654-4804-7).
29. Roger Blanpain & Ruth Ben-Israel, *Strikes and Lock-Outs in Industrialized Market Economies*, 1994 (ISBN 90-654-4841-1).
30. Roger Blanpain, Kazuo Sugeno & Yasuo Suwa, *The Harmonization of Working Life and Family Life*, 1995 (ISBN 90-411-0064-4).
31. Roger Blanpain & Laszio Nagy, *Labour Law and Industrial Relations in Central and Eastern Europe*, 1996 (ISBN 90-411-0298-1).
32. Roger Blanpain, *Labour Law and Industrial Relations in the European Union*, 1997 (ISBN 90-411-0527-1).
33. Taco Van Peijpe, *Employment Protection under Strain*, 1998 (ISBN 90-411-0528-8).
34. Roger Blanpain, Takashi Araki & Ryuichi Yamakawa, *The Process of Industrialization and the Role of Labour Law in Asia*, 1999 (ISBN 9-041-1104-7-X).
35. Roger Blanpain & Marco Biagi, *Non-standard Work and Industrial Relations*, 1999 (ISBN 90-411-1117-4).
36. Roger Blanpain, *Private Employment Agencies: The Impact of ILO Convention 181 (1997) and the Judgment of the European Court of Justice of 11 December 1997*, 1999 (ISBN 90-411-1118-2).
37. Roger Blanpain, *Multinational Enterprises and the Social Challenges of the XXIst Century: The ILO Declaration on Fundamental* Principles *at Work, Public and Private Corporate Codes of Conduct*, 2000 (ISBN 90-411-1280-4).
38. Roger Blanpain, Ryuichi Yamakawa & Takashi Araki, *Deregulation and Labour Law: In Search of a Labour Concept for the 21st Century*, 2000 (ISBN 90-411-1370-3).
39. Roger Blanpain, *The Council of Europe and the Social Challenges of the XXIst Century*, 2001 (ISBN 90-411-1543-9).

40. Roger Blanpain, *On-Line Rights for Employees in the Information Society, Use & Monitoring of E-Mail & Internet at Work*, 2002 (ISBN 90-411-1626-5).
41. Roger Blanpain, *The Evolving Employment Relationship and the New Economy: The Role of Labour Law & Industrial Relations*, 2001 (ISBN 90-411-1691-5).
42. Roger Blanpain, *Involvement of Employees in the European Union, Works Councils, Company Statute, Information and Consultation Rights*, 2002 (ISBN 90-411-1760-1).
43. Michele Colucci, *The Impact of the Internet and New Technologies on the Workplace: A Legal Analysis from a Comparative Point of View*, 2002 (ISBN 90-411-1824-1).
44. Roger Blanpain, *White Paper on the Labour Market in Italy: The Quality of European Industrial Relations and Changing Industrial Relations*, 2002 (ISBN 90-411-1841-1).
45. Roger Blanpain, Russell D. Lansbury & Young-Bum Park, *Impact of Globalisation on Employment Relations: A Comparison of the Automobile and Banking Industries in Australia and Korea*, 2002 (ISBN 90-411-1850-0).
46. Roger Blanpain & Antoine Jacobs, *Employee Rights in Bankruptcy: A Comparative-Law Assessment*, 2002 (ISBN 90-411-1942-6).
47. Roger Blanpain, Takashi Araki & Shinya Ouchi, *Corporate Restructuring and the Role of Labour Law*, 2003 (ISBN 90-411-1949-3).
48. Roger Blanpain, *Collective Bargaining, Discrimination, Social Security and European Integration*, 2003 (ISBN 90-411-2010-6).
49. Roger Blanpain & Luis Aparicio-Valdez, *Labour Relations in the Asia- Pacific Countries*, 2004 (ISBN 90-411-2239-7).
50. Roger Blanpain & Ronnie Graham, *Temporary Agency Work and the Information Society*, 2004 (ISBN 90-411-2252-4).
51. Roger Blanpain, *The Actors of Collective Bargaining: A World Report*, 2004 (ISBN 90-411-2253-2).
52. Roger Blanpain & Michele Colucci, *The Globalisation of Labour Standards: The Soft Law Track*, 2004 (ISBN 90-411-2303-2).
53. Roger Blanpain, Takashi Araki & Shinya Ouchi, *Labour Law in Motion: Diversification of the Labour Force & Terms and Conditions of Employment*, 2005 (ISBN 90-411-2315-6).
54. Roger Blanpain, *Smoking and the Workplace*, 2005 (ISBN 90-411-2325-3).
55. Roger Blanpain, *Confronting Globalization: The Quest for a Social Agenda*, 2005 (ISBN 90-411-2381-4).
56. Roger Blanpain, Thomas Blanke & Edgar Rose, *Collective Bargaining Wages in Comparative Perspective: Germany, France, the Netherlands, Sweden and the United Kingdom*, 2005 (ISBN 90-411-2388-1).
57. Roger Blanpain & Anne Numhauser-Henning, *Women in Academia & Equality Law: Aiming High - Falling Short?*, 2006 (ISBN 978-90-411-2427-6).
58. Roger Blanpain, *Freedom of Services in the European Union: Labour and Social Security Law: The Bolkestein Initiative*, 2006 (ISBN 978-90-411-2453-5).
59. Roger Blanpain, Frans Pennings & Nurhan Sural, *Flexibilisation and Modernisation of the Turkish Labour Market*, 2006 (ISBN 978-90-411-2490-X).

60. Roger Blanpain & Boel Flodgren, *Corporate and Employment Perspectives in a Global Business Environment*, 2006 (ISBN 978-90-411-2537-X).
61. Roger Blanpain, Shinya Ouchi & Takashi Araki, *Decentralizing Industrial Relations and The Role of Labor Unions and Employee Representatives*, 2007 (ISBN 978-90-411-2583-3).
62. Roger Blanpain, *European Framework Agreements and Telework: Law and Practice: A European and Comparative Study*, 2007 (ISBN 978-90-411-2560-4).
63. Roger Blanpain, Jim Kitay, Leanne Cutcher & Nick Wailes, *Globalization and Employment Relations in Retail Banking*, 2007 (ISBN 978-90-411-2620-1).
64. Roger Blanpain, Russell Lansbury, Jim Kitay, Nick Wailes & Anja Kirsch, *Globalization and Employment Relations in the Auto Assembly Industry:* A *Study of Seven Countries*, 2008 (ISBN 978-90-411-2698-6).
65. Roger Blanpain & Michele Tiraboschi, *The Global Labour Market: From Globalization to Flexicurity*, 2008 (ISBN 978-90-411-2722-8).
66. Roger Blanpain, Michele Colucci & Frank Hendrickx, *The Future of Sport in the European Union: Beyond the EU Reform Treaty and the White Paper*, 2008 (ISBN 978-90-411-2761-7).
67. Roger Blanpain, Linda Dickens, *Challenges in European Employment Relations: Employment Regulation, Trade Union Organization, Equality, Flexicurity, Training and New Approaches to Pay*, 2008 (ISBN 978-90-411-2771-6).
68. Roger Blanpain, Hiroya Nakakubo & Takashi Araki, *New Developments in Employment Discrimination Law, 2008* (ISBN 978-90-411-2782-2).
69. Roger Blanpain, Andrzej Marian wiątkowski, *The Laval and Viking Cases: Freedom of Services and Establishment v. Industrial Conflict in the European Economic Area and Russia*, 2009 (ISBN 978-90-411-2850-8).
70. Roger Blanpain, William Bromwich, Olga Rymkevich, Silvia Spattini, *The Modernization of Labour Law and Industrial Relations in a Comparative Perspective*, 2009 (ISBN 978-90-411-2865-2).
71. Roger Blanpain, Juan Pablo Landa & Brian Langille, *Employment Policies and Multilevel Governance*, 2009 (ISBN 978-90-411-2866-9).
72. Roger Blanpain, European Works Councils; *The European Directive 2009/ 38/EC of 6 May 2009, 2009* (ISBN 978-90-411-3208-6).
73. Roger Blanpain, William Bromwich, Olga Rymkevich & Silvia Spattini, *Labour Productivity, Investment in Human Capital and Youth Employment: Comparative Developments and Global Responses*, 2010 (ISBN 978-90-411-3249-9).
74. Greg J. Bamber & Philippe Pochet, *Regulating Employment Relations, Work and Labour Laws: International Comparisons between Key Countries*, 2010 (ISBN 978-90-411-3199-7). General Editor: Roger Blanpain.
75. Roger Blanpain, Desislava Nikolaeva Dimitrova, *Seafarers' Rights in the Globalized Maritime Industry*, 2010 (ISBN 978-90-411-3349-6).
76. Roger Blanpain, Hiroya Nakakubo & Takashi Araki, *Regulation of Fixed- Term Employment Contracts*, 2010 (ISBN 978-90-411-3356-4).

77. Roger Blanpain, William Bromwich, Olga Rymkevich & Iacopo Senatori, *Rethinking Corporate Governance*, 2011 (ISBN 978-90-411-3450-9).
78. Roger Blanpain & Frank Hendrickx, *Labour Law between Change and Tradition: Liber Amicorum Antoine Jacobs*, 2011 (ISBN 978-90-411-3424-0).
79. Roger Blanpain, Thomas Klebe, Marlene Schmidt & Bernd Waas, *Trade Union Rights at the Workplace*, 2012 (ISBN 978-90-411-3460-8).
80. Roger Blanpain, William Bromwich, Olga Rymkevich & Iacopo Senatori, *Labour Markets, Industrial Relations and Human Resources Management: From Recession to Recovery*, 2012 (ISBN 978-90-411-4004-3).
81. Roger Blanpain, Hiroya Nakakubo & Takashi Araki, *Systems of Employee Representation at the Enterprise: A Comparative Study*, 2012 (ISBN 978-90-411-4080-7).
82. Roger Blanpain & Frank Hendrickx, *Temporary Agency Work in the European Union and the United States*, 2013 (ISBN 978-90-411-4769-1).
83. Roger Blanpain, Toker Dereli, Y. Pınar Soykut-Sarıca & Aslı en-Tabaı, *Emerging Patterns of Work and Turkish Labour Market Challenges under Globalization: Readings on Labour and Employment Relations*, 2014 (ISBN 978-90-411-4983-1).
84. Roger Blanpain, Pablo Arellano Ortiz, Marius Olivier & Gijsbert Vonk, *Social Security and Migrant Workers: Selected Studies of Cross-border Social Security Mechanisms*, 2014 (ISBN 978-90-411-4770-7).
85. Roger Blanpain & Nikita Lyutov, *Workers' Representation in Central and Eastern Europe: Challenges and Opportunities for the Works Councils' System*, 2014 (ISBN 978-90-411-4746-2).
86. Roger Blanpain, Ulla Liukkunen & Chen Yifeng, *China and ILO Fundamental Principles and Rights at Works*, 2014 (ISBN 978-90-411-4984-8).
87. Roger Blanpain, *The Use of Languages and Employment Relations*, 2014 (ISBN 978-90-411-5606-8).
88. Roger Blanpain, Hiroya Nakakubo & Takashi Araki, *Protection of Employees' Personal Information and Privacy*, 2014 (ISBN 978-90-411-5608-2).
89. Roger Blanpain, Jan Wouters, Glenn Rayp, Laura Beke & Axel Marx, *Protecting Labour Rights in a Multi-polar Supply Chain and Mobile Global Economy*, 2015 (ISBN 978-90-411-5662-4).
90. Roger Blanpain & Stefania Marassi, *Globalization and Transnational Collective Labour Relations: International and European Framework Agreements at Company Level*, 2015 (ISBN 978-90-411-4748-6).
91. Roger Blanpain, Frank Hendrickx & Petra Herzfeld Olsson, *National Effects of the Implementation of EU Directives on Labour Migration from Third Countries*, 2016 (ISBN 978-90-411-6257-1).
92. Roger Blanpain, Frank Hendrickx & D'Arcy du Toit, *Labour Law and Social Progress: Holding the Line or Shifting the Boundaries?* 2016 (ISBN 978-90-411-6747-7).

93. Roger Blanpain & Frank Hendrickx, *Reasonable Accommodation in the Modern Workplace: Potential and Limits of the Integrative Logics of Labour Law*, 2016 (ISBN 978-90-411-6258-8).
94. Roger Blanpain, Frank Hendrickx & Bernd Waas, *New Forms of Employment in Europe*, 2016 (ISBN 978-90-411-6239-7).
95. Roger Blanpain, Frank Hendrickx, Hiroya Nakakubo & Takashi Araki, *The Notion of Employer in the Era of the Fissured Workplace: Should Labour Law Responsibilities Exceed the Boundary of the Legal Entity?*, 2017 (ISBN 978-90-411-8470-2).
96. Elena Sychenko, *Individual Labour Rights as Human Rights: The Contributions of the European Court of Human Rights to Worker's Rights Protection*, 2017 (ISBN 978-90-411-8629-4).
97. William Bromwich & Olga Rymkevich, *Improving Workplace Quality: New Perspectives and Challenges for Worker Well-Being*, 2017 (ISBN 978-90-411-8628-7).
98. Sarah De Groof, *Work-Life Balance in the Modern Workplace: Interdisciplinary Perspectives from Work-Family Research, Law and Policy*, 2017 (ISBN 978-90-411-8630-0).
99. Sylvaine Laulom, *Collective Bargaining Developments in Times of Crisis*, 2018 (ISBN 978-90-411-8999-8).
100. Frank Hendrickx & Valerio De Stefano, *Game Changers in Labour Law: Shaping the Future of Work*, 2018 (ISBN 978-90-411-9953-9).
101. Ivana Palinkaš, *The Legal and Institutional Framing of Collective Bargaining in CEE Countries: Between Europeanisation and Decentralisation*, 2018 (ISBN 978-90-411-9199-1).
102. Jeremy Waddington, *European Board-Level Employee Representation: National Variations in Influence and Power*, 2018 (ISBN 978-90-411-9202-8).
103. Jan Pichrt & Kristina Koldinská, *Labour Law and Social Protection in a Globalized World: Changing Realities in Selected Areas of Law and Policy*, 2018 (ISBN 978-94-035-0093-5).
104. Matthew W. Finkin, *American Labor and the Law: Dormant, Resurgent, and Emergent Problems*, 2019 (ISBN 978-94-035-0654-8).
105. Giuseppe Casale & Tiziano Treu, *Transformations of Work: Challenges for the Institutions and Social Actors*, 2019 (ISBN 978-94-035-0891-7).
106. Miguel De la Corte-Rodríguez, *EU Law on Maternity and Other Child-Related Leaves: Impact on Gender Equality*, 2019 (ISBN 978-94-035-1452-9).
107. Valeria Pulignano & Frank Hendrickx, *Employment Relations in the 21st Century: Challenges for Theory and Research in a Changing World of Work*, 2020 (ISBN 978-94-035-1764-3).
108. Matteo Bottero, *Posting of Workers in EU Law: Challenges of Equality, Solidarity and Fair Competition*, 2021 (ISBN 978-94-035-2860-1).
109. Bernd Waas & Christina Hießl, *Collective Bargaining for Self-Employed Workers in Europe: Approaches to Reconcile Competition Law and Labour Rights*, 2021 (ISBN 978-94-035-2373-6).

110. Mathias Wouters, *International Labour Standards and Platform Work: An Analysis of Digital Labour Platforms Based on the Instruments on Private Employment Agencies, Home Work and Domestic Work*, 2022 (ISBN 978-94-035-4024-5).
111. Luca Ratti, *In-Work Poverty in Europe: Vulnerable and Under-Represented Persons in a Comparative Perspective*, 2022 (ISBN 978-94-035-4996-5).
112. Silvia Rainone, *The Role of the Court of Justice in EU Labour Law: A Case Study on the Transfer of Undertakings Directive*, 2023 (ISBN 978-94-035-2896-0).
113. Frank Hendrickx, Elena Gramano & David Mangan, *Privacy@work: A European and Comparative Perspective*, 2023 (ISBN 978-94-035-3106-9).
114. Elena Sychenko & Adalberto Perulli, *Employment Law and the European Convention on Human Rights: The Research of the Recent Jurisprudence of the ECtHR Related to Employment Law (2017-2021)*, 2023 (ISBN 978-94-035-3556-2).
115. Ilda Durri, *Casual Work Arrangements and Platform-Based Work: The Casual Work Agenda as a Way to Enhance the Labour Protection of Platform Workers*, 2023 (ISBN 978-94-035-3107-6).
116. Charalampos Stylogiannis, *Collective Labour Rights for Self-Employed Workers: A Human Rights-Based Approach of Platform Work*, 2023 (ISBN 978-94-035-0667-8).
117. Heather Kurzbauer, *Employment Vulnerabilities in the World of Orchestral Musicians: Symphonic Metamorphoses*, 2023 (ISBN 978-94-035-2737-6).

Made in United States
North Haven, CT
10 November 2026

22096535R00233